A Companion to Shakespeare

Blackwell Companions to Literature and Culture

This new series offers comprehensive, newly written surveys of key periods and movements, and certain major authors, in English literary culture and history. Extensive volumes provide new perspectives and positions on contexts and on canonical and post-canonical texts, orientating the beginning student in new fields of study and providing the experienced undergraduate and new graduate with current and new directions, as pioneered and developed by leading scholars in the field.

1 A Companion to Romanticism   *Edited by Duncan Wu*
2 A Companion to Victorian Literature and Culture   *Edited by Herbert F. Tucker*
3 A Companion to Shakespeare   *Edited by David Scott Kastan*

A COMPANION TO
SHAKESPEARE

EDITED BY **DAVID SCOTT KASTAN**

Copyright © Blackwell Publishers Ltd, 1999
Introduction, selection, and arrangement copyright © David Scott Kastan 1999

First published 1999

2 4 6 8 10 9 7 5 3 1

Blackwell Publishers Ltd
108 Cowley Road
Oxford OX4 1JF
UK

Blackwell Publishers Inc.
350 Main Street
Malden, Massachusetts 02148
USA

Library of Congress Cataloging-in-Publication Data has been applied for.

ISBN 0–631–20665–5

British Library Cataloguing in Publication Data

A CIP catalogue record for this book is available from the British Library.

Typeset in 11/13 pt Garamond 3
by
Pure Tech India Ltd, Pondicherry
http://www.puretech.com
Printed in Great Britain by T.J. International, Padstow, Cornwall
This book is printed on acid-free paper

Contents

Illustrations   viii
Notes on Contributors   ix

Part One Introduction

1 Shakespeare and the "Element" he Lived in   3
   David Scott Kastan

Part Two Shakespeare I

2 Shakespeare the Man   9
   David Bevington

Part Three Living

3 Shakespeare's England   25
   Norman Jones
4 Shakespeare's London   43
   Ian W. Archer
5 Religious Identities in Shakespeare's England   57
   Peter Lake
6 The Family and the Household   85
   Susan Dwyer Amussen
7 Shakespeare and Political Thought   100
   Martin Dzelzainis
8 Political Culture   117
   David Harris Sacks

Part Four Reading

9 "The Great Variety of Readers" and Early Modern Reading Practices 139
   Heidi Brayman Hackel

10 Reading the Bible   158
    David Daniell
11 Reading the Classics   172
    Robert S. Miola
12 The Shapes of History   186
    D. R. Woolf
13 Reading Vernacular Literature   206
    Diana E. Henderson and James Siemon

Part Five Writing

14 Professional Playwrighting   225
    Scott McMillin
15 Shakespeare's 'Natiue English'   239
    Jonathan Hope
16 Hearing Shakespeare's Dramatic Verse   256
    George T. Wright
17 Shakespeare and Rhetorical Culture   277
    Peter G. Platt
18 Shakespeare and Genre   297
    Jean E. Howard

Part Six Playing

19 The Economics of Playing   313
    William Ingram
20 The Chamberlain's–King's Men   328
    S. P. Cerasano
21 Shakespeare's Repertory   346
    Roslyn L. Knutson
22 Shakespeare's Playhouses   362
    Andrew Gurr
23 Licensing and Censorship   377
    Richard Dutton

Part Seven Printing

24 Shakespeare in Print, 1593–1640   395
    Thomas L. Berger and Jesse M. Lander
25 "Precious Few": English Manuscript Playbooks   414
    William B. Long
26 The Craft of Printing (1600)   434
    Laurie E. Maguire
27 The London Book-Trade in 1600   450
    Mark Bland

28 Liberty, License, and Authority: Press Censorship and Shakespeare   464
    Cyndia Susan Clegg

Part Eight Shakespeare II

29 Shakespeare: The Myth   489
    Michael D. Bristol

Index   503

Illustrations

Page showing "Principall Actors" (first folio, 1623)   329
Portrait of the actor John Lowin (1640)   337
A plan of the Rose's remains, as identified in 1989 by English Heritage   364
Detail from the Utrecht 'View of London from the North', showing the
    Theatre on the left and the Curtain with its flag on the right   366
A plan by Pentagram of the new Globe in Southwark at ground level   370
The Merchant of Venice, Q1 (1600)   399
Catalogue of plays from the Shakespeare folio (1623)   407
Imposition for a quarto sheet   441

Notes on Contributors

Susan Dwyer Amussen is on the faculty of the College of Graduate Studies of the Union Institute. She is the author of *An Ordered Society: Gender and Class in Early Modern England* (1988) and of a forthcoming study on violence, power and identity in the early modern English world.

Ian W. Archer is Tutor and University Lecturer in Modern History at Keble College, Oxford. Specializing in early modern British history, he is the author of *The Pursuit of Stability: Social Relations in Elizabethan London* (1991).

Thomas L. Berger teaches English at St Lawrence University. He has edited *2 Henry IV* (Q1) and *A Midsummer Night's Dream* (Q1) in facsimile for the Malone Society, as well as (with Suzanne Gossett) a collection of seventeenth-century academic plays. Currently he is co-editing *Henry V* for the New Variorum Shakespeare.

David Bevington is the Phyllis Fay Horton Professor of Humanities at the University of Chicago. Among his publications are *From 'Mankind' to Marlowe* (1962), *Tudor Drama and Politics* (1968), and *Action is Eloquence: Shakespeare's Language of Gesture* (1984). He has edited *The Complete Works of Shakespeare* in paperback for Bantam (1988) and for Longman (4th edn, 1997), and also edited *Medieval Drama* (1975) and *The Macro Plays* (1972). Most recently he has edited *Troilus and Cressida* (1998) for the Arden Shakespeare.

Mark Bland has written extensively on early modern printing practices and is the consulting Textual Editor to the forthcoming Cambridge edition of Ben Jonson.

Michael D. Bristol is Professor of English at McGill University in Montreal, Quebec. His most recent book is *Big-Time Shakespeare* (1996).

S. P. Cerasano, Professor of English at Colgate University, is the author of many articles on Renaissance theatre history. Presently she is completing a biography of the Renaissance actor-entrepreneur Edward Alleyn.

Cyndia Susan Clegg is Professor of English at Pepperdine University. She has written widely on Renaissance literature and culture and most recently is the author of *Press Censorship in Elizabethan England* (1997).

David Daniell is Emeritus Professor of English in the University of London. Among his many publications are books on *The Tempest* (1989) and *Coriolanus* (1980), editions of the Tyndale Bibles, and *William Tyndale: A Biography* (1994).

Richard Dutton is Professor of English at Lancaster University. His publications include *Mastering the Revels: The Regulation and Censorship of English Renaissance Drama* (1991) and *Ben Jonson: Authority: Criticism* (1996). An edition of *Four Plays by Thomas Middleton* is in press for Oxford World's Classics, and he is currently completing a book provisionally entitled *Buggeswords: Licensing and Authorship in Early Modern England*.

Martin Dzelzainis is Senior Lecturer in English at Royal Holloway, University of London. He has edited *John Milton: Political Writings* (1991) for Cambridge Texts in the History of Political Thought, and (with Warren Cherniak) *Marvell and Liberty*, forthcoming from Macmillan.

Andrew Gurr is Professor of English at the University of Reading and Director of Research at the Globe Theatre in London. Among his many publications are editions of five Elizabethan plays and four books on Renaissance theatre, most recently *The Shakespearian Playing Companies* (1996).

Heidi Brayman Hackel is an Assistant Professor of English at Oregon State University and is completing a book on early modern reading and reading practices, entitled *Impressions from a 'Scribbling Age'*.

Diana E. Henderson is Associate Professor of Literature at the Massachusetts Institute of Technology. She is the author of *Passion made Public: Elizabethan Lyric, Gender, and Performance* (1995) and is presently completing a book entitled *Uneasy Collaborations: Rewriting Early Modern Drama across Time and Media*.

Jonathan Hope teachers linguistics and literature at Middlesex University in London and is the Linguistics Advisor to the Arden Shakespeare. His *The Authorship of Shakespeare's Plays* appeared in 1994.

Jean E. Howard is Professor of English and Comparative Literature at Columbia University, where she also directs the Institute for Research on Women and Gender.

Her most recent books are *The Stage and Social Struggle in Early Modern England* (1994) and most recently (with Phyllis Rackin) *Engendering a Nation: A Feminist Account of Shakespeare's English Histories*) (1997). She is presently at work on a new book, *Theater of a City*, on the non-Shakespearean drama of the first decades of the seventeenth century.

William Ingram teachers at the University of Michigan in Ann Arbor and has written on various topics in theatre history. His most recent book is *The Business of Playing: The Beginnings of the Adult Public Theater in Elizabethan London* (1992).

Norman Jones is Professor and Chair of History at Utah State University. He is the author of many studies of early modern English history, including *Faith by Statute: Parliament and the Settlement of Religion, 1559* (1982), *God and the Moneylenders: Usury and Law in Early-Modern England* (1989), and *The Birth of the Elizabethan Age: England in the 1560s* (1993).

David Scott Kastan is Professor of English and Comparative Literature at Columbia University. He serves as one of the General Editors of the Arden Shakespeare and is presently editing *1 Henry IV* for that series.

Roslyn L. Knutson, Professor of English at the University of Arkansas at Little Rock, is the author of *The Repertory of Shakespeare's Company, 1594–1613* (1991). She is currently working on the economic issues of company repertories, some of which material has been published in *Shakespeare Quarterly, English Literary Renaissance, Shakespeare Survey*, and *A New History of Early English Drama*.

Peter Lake is Professor of History at Princeton University. The author of a number of studies on politics and religion under Elizabeth I and the early Stuarts, he is currently completing a study of English Conformist thought from Hooker to Laud.

Jesse M. Lander is Assistant Professor of English at Texas Christian University. He is completing a book on print, Protestantism, and polemic in Early Modern England.

William B. Long has taught English Renaissance drama at Washington University, St Louis, and at the City of College of New York and currently is an independent scholar in New York City. He has written extensively on the surviving English Renaissance manuscript playbooks, the textual transmission of play texts, and on other facets of theatre history.

Laurie E. Maguire is Associate Professor of English at the University of Ottawa. She is the author of *Shakespearean Suspect Texts* (1996), the co-editor with Thomas L. Berger of *Textual Formations and Reformations* (1998), and has published several articles on Renaissance drama.

Scott McMillin, Professor of English at Cornell University, is the author of *The Elizabethan Theatre and "the Book of Sir Thomas More"* (1987), *Shakespeare in Performance: 1 Henry IV* (1998), and (with Sally-Beth MacLean) *The Queen's Men and their Plays* (1998). He has also edited the *Norton Critical Edition of Restoration and Eighteenth-century Comedy* (1997). He is currently writing a book on the American musical theatre.

Robert S. Miola is the Gerard Manley Hopkins Professor of English at Loyola College in Maryland. He has written on classical backgrounds to Renaissance Literature and is presently editing Jonson's *Every Man in his Humour* for the Revels series.

Peter G. Platt is an Assistant Professor of English at Barnard College. He is the author of *Reason Diminished: Shakespeare and the Marvelous* (1997) and is editing a forthcoming book of essays on wonders, marvels, and monsters.

David Harris Sacks, Professor of History and Humanities at Reed College, is the author of *The Widening Gate: Bristol and the Atlantic Economy, 1450–1700* (1991) and co-editor with Donald R. Kelley of *The Historical Imagination in Early Modern Britain: History, Rhetoric, and Fiction, 1500–1800* (1997). He is completing a book on the political and economic culture of late sixteenth- and early seventeenth-century England.

James Siemon is Professor of English at Boston University. He is the author of *Shakespearean Iconoclasm* (1985) and the forthcoming *Word against Word: 'Richard II' as Bakhtinian Utterance*. He is currently editing *Richard III* for the Arden Shakespeare.

D. R. Woolf is Professor of History and Associate Dean of the Faculty of Graduate Studies at Dalhousie University, Halifax, Canada. Among his publications are a number of essays on early modern historical thought and a book *The Idea of History in Early Stuart England* (1990).

George T. Wright, Regents' Professor of English Emeritus at the University of Minnesota, is the author of *Shakespeare's Metrical Art* (1988) and of "Hendiadys and Hamlet" (1981). He has also published books on modern poetry and many articles, reviews, and poems. He lives in Tucson, Arizona.

PART ONE
Introduction

1

Shakespeare and the "Element" he Lived in

David Scott Kastan

No doubt the most familiar of the clichés of Shakespeare studies is that he is our contemporary. Certainly there is some sense in which the claim is true and worth reiterating. If it is no longer quite the case (if indeed it ever was) that, as Edmund says in *Mansfield Park*, "we all talk Shakespeare," Shakespeare, along with Jane Austen, has at the very least recently emerged as our favorite middle-brow screenwriter, and, quill in hand, he serves us, via advertising, as a readily identifiable icon of both taste and value. And, of course, Shakespeare stands at the still point of the ever-changing English curriculum in both secondary schools and universities. Nonetheless, we often forget that Shakespeare's currency flows only one way. He may conceivably be our contemporary; but we are not his. Like every age that does what is necessary to stay in contact with him, we drag him forward into our present, ignoring how much he is a stranger in it.

This is not, of course, to suggest that the proper goal of our engagement with Shakespeare is to sequester him safely back in his own time, to confront him only as a matter of a pious antiquarianism. It couldn't in fact be done. Shakespeare is now one of our playwrights, exactly as in the eighteenth and nineteenth centuries he was one of theirs. Any search of the theatrical repertory would prove this point. But there is a danger in too quickly and too easily collapsing the distance between us. Not to respect that distance is to risk Shakespeare becoming of merely notional significance, an expensive mirror reflecting our own values, anxieties, and dreams. Too often, we eagerly appropriate his cultural prestige but ignore the authority of his own voice – though it should be noted at once that if one major objective of this book is to allow that voice to be heard, it is to do so by insisting on how fractured "his own voice" is; "Shakespeare," as a proper noun, not only names the playwright from Stratford but is a convenient synecdoche for the multiple collaborations necessary to produce his voice.

Yet, as both historical agent and trope, Shakespeare existed in circumstances markedly different from those of our own world, and, though continuities can be sensed between our ages (there is something to be said for the currently fashionable period marker, "early modern"), the differences must be insisted upon. Indeed, any intrinsic value that Shakespeare may have for us – that is, any value accruing before we register the "value added" of his massive cultural authority – must at least begin with the recognition of his distance from us rather than with an assumption of his essential contemporaneity. When we disregard that distance, the static of our desire to claim him as our contemporary disrupts his voice, as we listen less to his concerns than to his anticipations of our own. It is one thing to "talk Shakespeare," quite another to hear him talk.

We can, however, attend to the distinctiveness of his voice and still marvel at its enduring appeal. Shakespeare is no doubt the closest thing we have to an "EVER-LIVING POET," as the title page of the 1609 edition of the sonnets terms him. Though clearly he does live in ways that his contemporaries do not, thriving in a rich history of determined engagement and appropriation by later ages, it is not, I think, because he is in any meaningful sense "timeless," speaking some otherwise unknown, universal idiom. He is ever-living, paradoxically, because he is so intensely of his own time and place. As Jonson recognized in his commendatory poem in the 1623 folio, Shakespeare is the "Soule of the Age" both before, and as the condition of, his being "for all time."

Unwittingly forced to serve as our contemporary, however, he not infrequently becomes something of an embarrassment; too much needs to be ignored or explained away. (Think of eighteenth-century efforts to render him contemporary by "improving" the supposed infelicities of his art.) But as a voice from the past he is irresistible. His engagement with his own world is the most vital record we have of that world's struggle for meaning and value, allowing each age that reaches out to him to see what it has been and also, in measuring its distance from that world, what it has become. To read Shakespeare historically, then, is not least to discover the possibility of change, or, put differently, to discover ourselves as historical beings; and that discovery is not the least of our debts to him.

It is, therefore, our distance from Shakespeare that this book attempts to survey and bridge. It seeks to provide an authoritative account of the historical world in which Shakespeare worked, of the imaginative and institutional conditions that enabled and, in some cases, inhibited his art, insisting that we see his artistry in its own, originating terms without prematurely filtering it through our own. (The emphasis here, I should note, is on "prematurely"; I assume that such filtering will, and indeed should, take place in both scholarship and performance.) The riches of his extraordinary artistic achievement, like Antony's "delights," may well raise themselves "dolphin-like . . . above / The element they lived in" (*Antony and Cleopatra*, V. ii. 89–90), but they can never fully escape it; even the acrobatic dolphin is dependent upon its natural element for life and can never safely be removed from it for any length of time.

To see Shakespeare working within the historical circumstances that stimulated and challenged his imagination, then, is not to evade or diminish his remarkable artistry; rather, to see him thus is crucial if we are properly to understand or even adequately to admire his achievement. Art is not, of course, reducible to its historical determinants, but it is neither useful nor realistic to pretend that it erupts into being independent of them. However seductive is a romantic notion of artistic genius, solitary and sovereign, untouched by the world, all artists work within a web of engagements with the world, work always and only within the set of imaginative, material, and institutional possibilities that are available to them. Great artists may transcend these, but they cannot ignore them. Their own talents and temperaments individualize their work, insist that they are not simply products of the historical moment; but if they are always more than their history, they are still always of that history. There is no pure art uncontaminated by contingency. Thus, to see art whole, as humanist critics have long urged, must be to see it clearly as it has emerged from the generative conditions of its making, rather than envisioning it as some radical epiphany with no plausible principle of realization.

This is, as I have indicated, a principal goal of this collection of essays: to see Shakespeare's art as it develops in response to the particular imaginative challenges and provocations that existed for him, as well as to the specific institutional contexts of his playmaking. In other words, this book explores the networks of dependency that are indispensably part of what we have come to call "Shakespeare." With regard to a dramatist, of course, such a commitment should not be controversial (and for virtually any dramatist other than Shakespeare it would not be). Drama is self-evidently a collaborative activity, depending not merely on the dramatist's access to a treasury of linguistic and cultural resources, but, more materially, on the interactions of the playwright with those other theater artists and technicians needed to put a play onstage, as well as with the various practitioners of the book trade, necessary to get a playbook into a reader's hands.

Indeed, all intellectual and artistic activity is dependent in similarly imaginative and material ways; it is necessarily social. None takes place in isolation or is self-contained. In this regard, Shakespeare's is certainly not the exception, though the enormous cultural investment in the idea of his unique genius (a concept virtually invented for him) has often made us reluctant to acknowledge the multiple agencies necessary for his plays to be produced. This *Companion*, by contrast, seeks to make visible the sustaining collaborations of his art. The twenty-eight essays that follow – two on the figure of Shakespeare, first as man and then as myth, bracketing five sections that attempt to define the conditions of possibility in which he wrote – represent the best of modern scholarship. Individually, each stands as a definitive account of its subject; collectively, they form a detailed and arresting mosaic of Shakespeare's artistic environment, of the cultural and material mediations that permitted the plays to be written, performed, printed, and read.

It should go without saying that to focus on the enabling conditions of Shakespeare's art is not to detract from the plays they enable, nor is it to elevate the circumstances of playmaking above the intelligence, intentions, or, should we merely say, *will* of the playwright; though it is perhaps worth remarking that this will becomes manifest only in the context of other wills, other intelligences and intentions that are necessary to produce the plays onstage or as playbooks. Even so, recovery of the matrix of indebtedness in which Shakespeare worked obviously cannot substitute for a full engagement with the plays themselves. It is at best a necessary precondition for such an engagement. The essays in this volume are what (or at least some of what) we ideally should know as we read or see Shakespeare. The plays themselves, however, demand to be encountered with as much alertness, intelligence, and imaginative sympathy as we can bring to bear upon them. Nonetheless, this *Companion to Shakespeare* should make it easier to understand what it is that we encounter, reinstating the plays in their own dynamic, complicating history, if only so that they may live vitally in our own.

PART TWO
Shakespeare I

2

Shakespeare the Man

David Bevington

"He was indeed honest, and of an open and free nature," noted Ben Jonson of Shakespeare in his *Timber, or Discoveries*, written some time after Shakespeare had died. He "had an excellent phantasy, brave notions, and gentle expressions." By *phantasy* Jonson meant imagination, the ability of the mind to form mental representations of things not actually present; and by *brave notions* he meant bold and wonderful concepts, ideas. These jottings are grouped under the rubric, *De Shakespeare nostrati*, "concerning our Shakespeare, the Shakespeare who belongs to us and to our country."[1] From Ben Jonson to Jan Kott, author of *Shakespeare Our Contemporary*,[2] the world has been eager to claim Shakespeare as one of us.

Jonson's outpouring of affection for a man of decency, brilliance, and especially of gentleness is all the more persuasive in that it occurs in a passage that is also sharply critical. "I remember, the players have often mentioned it as an honor to Shakespeare that in his writing, whatsoever he penned, he never blotted out line," writes Jonson. "My answer hath been, would he had blotted a thousand." The attack continues. Protesting that "I loved the man, and do honor his memory (on this side idolatry) as much as any," Jonson deplores a facility so fecund "that sometime it was necessary he should be stopped. . . . His wit was in his own power; would the rule of it had been so too." Jonson goes on to particularize some carelessnesses that "could not escape laughter" and are in fact "ridiculous." Jonson refuses to fall into idolatry, as though anticipating already the sentimentalizing and commercializing of Shakespeare that would lead to the Stratford Great Shakespeare Jubilee of 1769 and all that has happened since in the Shakespeare industry; yet the burden of Jonson's candid remarks is both admiring and affectionate. Shakespeare "redeemed his vices with his virtues. There was ever more in him to be praised than to be pardoned."[3]

No contemporary portrait, I think, gives us a more rounded sense of Shakespeare the man and artist. Jonson's criticisms are of a piece with his loving praise. Elsewhere, he inveighs against dramatists who

> make a child, now swaddled, to proceed
> Man, and then shoot up, in one beard, and weed,
> Past threescore years

or who

> with three rusty swords,
> And help of some few foot-and-half-foot words,
> Fight over York and Lancaster's long jars,
> And in the tiring-house bring wounds to scars.[4]

The chief targets of these satirical barbs are Shakespeare's romances like *The Winter's Tale*, in which Perdita ripens from birth to a marriageable age (Christopher Marlowe's *Doctor Faustus* is also an apt candidate), and the *Henry VI* plays and *Richard III*, with their chronicling of England's great civil wars of the fifteenth century over a period of some sixty years (roughly from the 1420s to 1485).

In 1614, in his Induction to *Bartholomew Fair* (printed in 1631), Jonson inveighs against "those that beget *Tales, Tempests*, and suchlike *Drolleries*," with obvious reference to Shakespeare's *The Tempest* (ca. 1611).[5] He complains to William Drummond of Hawthornden (1619) that Shakespeare "wanted art" and that in a play (i.e., *The Winter's Tale*) he had "brought in a number of men saying they had suffered shipwreck in Bohemia, where there is no sea near by some 100 miles."[6] Even in his commemorative poem written for the great Shakespeare folio of 1623, celebrating the "soul of the age" and the "delight" and "wonder of our stage," the "Sweet swan of Avon," Jonson cannot refrain from chiding his author for having had only "small Latin and less Greek."[7]

We owe Jonson a great debt of gratitude for giving us a believable Shakespeare, a complex human being, one who in Jonson's view was erring and frail even though he was an unbelievably great writer. His "faults" in Jonson's estimate are qualities we are much more inclined to forgive, or rather to judge by more inclusive standards: a blithe disregard for classical "rules" against mixing comedy and tragedy, a willingness to stretch the neoclassically desired "unities" of time and place out of all recognizable proportion, and the like. Shakespeare is, as Jonson saw, a poet of the imagination, one with an astonishing gift for giving to "airy nothing" a "local habitation and a name."[8] He does indeed people his plays with "drolleries," with harpies, fairies, gods, and goddesses, and makes them theatrically convincing. His style is most emphatically not Jonson's neoclassical style of satirical social comedy and "correct" five-act tragedy, which again is what makes Jonson's praise of him so remarkable. At the same time, Jonson is surely right that Shakespeare is capable of lapses, perhaps the result of writing so fast; my own candidates would include the brief scene in *Othello* in which Cassio brings forward a group of clownish musicians to serenade Othello and thus help to restore Cassio to favor (III. i. 1–30), or the wailing of the Capulets for a Juliet who is not actually dead (*Romeo and Juliet*, IV. v. 14–64), or some of the pedantic and arch wordplay in *Love's Labor's Lost* (e.g., IV.

ii). Shakespeare was also apparently capable, as we shall see, of being irritable, vengeful, and uncharitable. The point is that Shakespeare was not perfect. Nobody's perfect.

Jonson's judicious estimate, spoken as a friend and a professional rival, helps to explain what many have seen as a mystery: how a boy from a country town who never attended a university could have written all those amazing plays and poems. Jonson is amazed, too. After all, Jonson did go to a university, and was as learned as anyone in his day. Why could not his superior knowledge of the ancients enable him to be top man? Jonson is acutely aware that Shakespeare is a "player," a professional actor belonging to London's premier acting company – indeed, the company that performed a number of Jonson's plays. Jonson is undoubtedly talking about William Shakespeare of Stratford-upon-Avon, for he calls him "Sweet swan of Avon." Jonson even laughs at the funny name of one who in his writings "seems to shake a lance" – shake-spear. And yet this very ordinary Englishman, "my gentle Shakespeare," has become "the star of poets."[9]

When in classical fashion Jonson finds himself obliged to measure Shakespeare's achievement against those of both moderns and ancients, his conclusion is that Shakespeare has no peer. He is not to be lodged by Chaucer, Spenser, or Beaumont. As a dramatist he did "our Lyly outshine," along with "sporting Kyd" and "Marlowe's mighty line." Instead, one must proceed backward in time to those ancient writers in Latin and Greek who serve as the ultimate standard, and here, as a tragedian, Shakespeare ranks equal with "thundering Aeschylus, Euripides, and Sophocles." High praise, indeed. Yet greater praise is reserved for Shakespeare as a comic writer. When it comes to comedy, Jonson apostrophizes Shakespeare:

> Leave thee alone for the comparison
> Of all that insolent Greece or haughty Rome
> Sent forth, or since did from their ashes come.

Truly, Shakespeare is "not of an age, but for all time," one whose achievement creates for him "a monument without a tomb."[10]

How is it possible that a Stratford citizen could have done all this? The first attempt at an answer is to ask another question: how is it possible for any human being to have written so well? The second answer, as Jonson reminds us, is that "a good poet's made, as well as born."[11] We need to know, then, how Shakespeare the man was able to make himself into the poet he became. We should leave open the very real possibility at the start that the making of such a poet and dramatist was (and is) as fully realizable for a person of Shakespeare's social background as for a member of England's ruling class. To believe otherwise is snobbery.

Jonson's swipe at Shakespeare for having "small Latin and less Greek" is, para-doxically, a clue. William Shakespeare was born into a prosperous family, and had the advantage of excellent schooling. His father, John Shakespeare, though he appears to have suffered financial and legal difficulties around 1577 or 1578 when William (born in 1564) was thirteen or fourteen, was a person of consequence in Stratford-upon-

Avon. His wife, Mary Arden, came from a family that owned a good deal of property. John served at various times as a kind of inspector, petty constable, assessor of fines, glove manufacturer and salesman, city treasurer, alderman, and high bailiff – the highest municipal office, essentially equivalent to that of mayor. The Shakespeares owned a fine house.

Fire and other ravages of time have destroyed a great many documents, of course, and so we do not have an actual record of William Shakespeare's attendance at school. Nevertheless, the King's New School was one of Stratford's most prized institutions. We cannot doubt the reliability of a tradition reported by Nicholas Rowe, Shakespeare's first extensive biographer (1709), that Shakespeare studied "for sometime at a Free-School."[12] As eldest son of such an important citizen as John Shakespeare, he would have been entitled; and indeed the school served any well-to-do family intent on educating its children.

Shakespeare would have been admitted to this school at the age of seven or thereabouts, after having gained proficiency in the reading and writing of English. His school day would have extended pretty much from dawn until dark. The curriculum emphasized Latin – years and years of it, with perhaps some Greek toward the end. Schoolmasters tended to be authoritarian; a charming scene between a pedagogue and a young pupil in *The Merry Wives of Windsor* (IV. i) may give us some flavor of what Shakespeare's schooling was like (a lot of rote recitation of conjugations and declensions, motivated by the fear of being whipped for mistakes) and what the author later thought of his classroom experience.

In any event, what we know of school curricula in Shakespeare's day fits perfectly with what we find in his early plays: familiar quotations from Ovid, Juvenal, Virgil, Horace, and the like, combined with a wide but amateur familiarity with classical myth: the labors of Hercules, Jupiter's rapes of Leda and Europa and Danaë, the story of Atalanta and Meleager, and so on. The author of the early plays is acquainted with the best-known dramas of Plautus and Seneca and understands how neoclassical dramaturgy can bring them up to date in the world of the Renaissance. The learning on display in Shakespeare's early career, including the poems of *Venus and Adonis* and *The Rape of Lucrece* that were to be the first and only publications that he personally saw through the press (1593–4), consistently reflects the kind of education that Shakespeare must have received.

University training, on the other hand, was rather specialized and technical. It prepared its students mainly for the Church or for governmental service. The curriculum was not only in Latin and Greek but dealt extensively with theology. Undergraduates could and did, of course, find a good deal of intellectual excitement, partly in talking and reading on their own; Christopher Marlowe clearly found Cambridge galvanizing. Others who were to become writers also attended the universities: Jonson, Thomas Nashe, Robert Greene, Thomas Kyd, and others. Yet so many of them found themselves unfitted for employment in the Church or in the government, owing to disinclination or lack of social qualifications, that they gravitated to London and earned for themselves the sobriquet of "the University Wits," educated beyond their social expectations and so thrown on their cleverness as a means of survival. Some of them wrote for the burgeoning acting companies, which were always hungry for new plays. The courses of instruction they encountered at the universities had little to teach them about the rough-and-tumble of daily life; this they found out about in the city of London itself, in their reading of new translations from continental languages (not being taught at the universities), and in their comradeship and writing.

Some who came to London to be professional writers had not attended a university – some of the best, in fact, like Thomas Dekker and John Webster. Shakespeare was one of these. His social background resembles that of his fellow writers in important ways. He needed to make his way in the world; his father was not yet a gentleman, though Shakespeare, once he had begun to be prosperous and famous, made a real effort to gain for his father the right to bear arms. (The petition was granted by the Herald's Office in 1596 and confirmed in 1599.[13]) Most great writers in the early modern period came from unpretentious social backgrounds and were in need of income from their writings. Jonson was the son of a clergyman and stepson (after his father's death) of a bricklayer. Marlowe, coming from a family of shoemakers in Canterbury, went to Cambridge on a scholarship. Edmund Spenser began his life in a sail-maker's family; he served as a personal secretary to a lord for a time and continued to need aristocratic patronage in order to publish his poetry. Shakespeare came from just that kind of background. Aristocrats like Henry VIII, the seventeenth earl of Oxford, and Sir Thomas Sackville wrote elegantly on occasion; the Tudor monarchs encouraged this kind of amateur grace and skill, along with the ability to compose a song or sing part music. Sir Philip Sidney, born to the purple, became a major writer, and George Herbert chose to turn his back on the wealth and privilege to which he was born; but most members of the ruling class were too occupied with ruling or whatever it was they did. Shakespeare had to work in order to succeed.

We do not know why Shakespeare did not attend a university. Perhaps his father's financial difficulties came at a bad time. Perhaps Shakespeare's precipitous marriage may have made further study impossible, even if he had wished to go on. He married, at eighteen, a woman (Anne Hathaway) who was eight years older than himself and already pregnant at the time of the marriage; an official waiver had to be obtained from the bishop of Worcester for a marriage without preliminary reading of the banns, and the child (Susanna) was born six months later, in May of 1583.

We can only speculate on the success or lack of success of this union. Shakespeare remained loyal to his family and supported them very well as he became rich. His daughter Susanna married handsomely. Shakespeare lived apart from his family, in London, much of the year. He returned home on occasion, owned real estate in Stratford, clearly took pride in being one of the city's first citizens, and was buried beneath the altar of the parish church when he died in 1616. Shakespeare's last will and testament, executed and signed when he was evidently in poor health, is laconic and perhaps even ungenerous in its lack of attention to his wife Anne (she is left his "second-best bed"), but she was well provided for. So were his two married daughters, although Shakespeare's relationship with his second son-in-law, Thomas Quiney, married to Judith in early 1616, was not good. By the time of his death, Shakespeare had lost his only son, Hamnet, in 1596, at the age of eleven. He had no male heirs. The writings (the *Sonnets* and *Macbeth*, for example) suggest that this loss was an unsupportable burden for him, as it would have been for any caring father and for any male in an essentially patriarchal society. The family line died out after a time. Shakespeare has no living descendants, for all his urgent advice in the *Sonnets* to "get a son" (7. 14).

What was Shakespeare like as a young man, in London, living apart from his family, striving to find a suitable career? He seems to have made few enemies; even the famous attack on him in 1592 by Robert Greene as "the only Shake-scene in a country," the "upstart crow" who is "beautified with our feathers"[14] – that is, decked out in inventions he has plagiarized from other writers like Greene himself – was so self-evidently motivated by envy that Greene's literary executor found himself compelled to issue an apology.

Henry Chettle's statement provides early evidence of Shakespeare's reputation as a decent, wonderful human being. "Myself have seen his demeanor no less civil than he excellent in the quality he professes," Chettle wrote. "Besides, divers of worship have reported his uprightness of dealing, which argues his honesty and his facetious grace in writing that approves his art."[15] By "the quality he professes" Chettle means Shakespeare's achievement as an actor and man of the theater, thus testifying to an early success that is also evident in Shakespeare's triumph during those same years with his *Henry VI* plays and *Richard III* (ca. 1589–94). No less significantly, Chettle gives Shakespeare the accolade of being upright, honest, and fecund as a writer. This portrait at the beginning of Shakespeare's career is of a piece with what Jonson says of him in 1623. "Gentle" Shakespeare – the adjective never seems to have deserted him.

We can only guess what Shakespeare may have done between the time of his marriage in 1582 and his arrival in London, perhaps at the end of the 1580s. Twins were born to him and Anne in 1585, Hamnet and Judith, but we do not know how Shakespeare was then employed. Uncertain tradition offers us the options of his having taught for a while, or having served some kind of apprenticeship in Stratford, or having joined a company of traveling players, or perhaps making his way to London, where he might have picked up work in a theater as some kind of extra or floor-sweeper. We do know that he was eager to capitalize on his acquaintance with a Stratford neighbor, Richard Field, who was now a successful printer in London, and that from this association came Shakespeare's first two serious publications, *Venus and Adonis* and *The Rape of Lucrece* (published in 1593 and 1594).

The data collected about Shakespeare's twenty-two or so years in London chiefly concern his professional life. We know some of the addresses at which he lived; we hear of an occasional lawsuit in which he was a witness (since legal records are especially apt to have been preserved). We know that he joined a premier acting company, the Lord Chamberlain's Men, in 1594; prior to that date, we cannot be sure where his plays were staged or by whom. The Lord Chamberlain's Men included in its ranks at various times Richard Burbage, William Kempe, Thomas Pope, John

Heminges, Henry Condell, Augustine Phillips, Robert Armin, John Lowin, Alexander Cooke, and George Brian; they, along with Shakespeare, were actor-sharers who owned the company, sharing its risks and eventually its enormous profits. The company roster changed from time to time, though it was generally stable; some of these men were Shakespeare's lifelong colleagues. The company became the King's Men when James I came to the English throne in 1603, in recognition of their excellence. They acquired an interest in an indoor "private" theater, the Blackfriars, and made increasing use of it in their later years. More usually, Shakespeare and his colleagues acted in large public theaters: at the Theatre from 1594 to about 1599, and then, after a hiatus required for moving, at the newly erected Globe Theatre from 1599 until it burned down in 1613 during a performance of one of Shakespeare's last plays, *Henry VIII*.

We also learn about Shakespeare's success in his career from an extensive array of testimonials and from publication of his plays in quarto single volumes. Francis Meres, writing in 1598, praises Shakespeare as worthy of comparison with Ovid, Plautus, and Seneca, and usefully gives us an impressively accurate list of Shakespeare's plays and poems up to that time: *Venus and Adonis, Lucrece*, the *Sonnets, The Two Gentlemen of Verona, The Comedy of Errors, Love's Labor's Lost, Love's Labor's Won, A Midsummer Night's Dream, The Merchant of Venice, Richard II, Richard III, Henry IV, King John, Titus Andronicus*, and *Romeo and Juliet*.[16] Except for the titillating reference to *Love's Labor's Won*, and the lack of any mention of *Much Ado* and *The Taming of the Shrew* (could one of these be the "lost" *Love's Labor's Won*?) and the *Henry VI* plays, this list confirms what more than three centuries of scholarship have been able to discover. The roster of other contemporaries who spoke praisingly of Shakespeare – John Weever, Gabriel Harvey, William Camden, Anthony Scoloker – is a long one.

His plays started appearing in quarto, in rapid succession, in the late 1590s: *Titus Andronicus* (1594), *Richard II* (1597), *Richard III* (1597), *Love's Labor's Lost* (1598), *1 Henry IV* (1598), *2 Henry IV* (1600), *A Midsummer Night's Dream* (1600), *The Merchant of Venice* (1600), and *Much Ado About Nothing* (1600), with more to follow. Shakespeare's name began appearing on the title page of these volumes with *Love's Labor's Lost* in 1598, a sure sign of his commercial viability. Unauthorized quartos of *The First Part of the Contention . . . of York and Lancaster* (a version of *2 Henry VI*) in 1594, *The True Tragedy of Richard Duke of York* (a version of *3 Henry VI*) in 1595, *Romeo and Juliet* in 1597, *Henry V* in 1600, *The Merry Wives of Windsor* in 1602, and *Hamlet* in 1603 offer eloquent evidence of popular demand for Shakespeare's plays. A number of these unauthorized texts were then quickly "newly corrected and augmented" by authorized publication; and the title page of *Love's Labor's Lost* suggests, by its use of this phrase, that a surreptitious copy of that play too had made its way to the bookstalls prior to 1598. "Falstaff" became a household word almost immediately after the performance of *1 Henry IV* in about 1597.

Even though Shakespeare was his company's chief playwright once his fame had been established, he continued to act in his own plays and those of other dramatists throughout much of his career. He was a professional through and through; his plays constantly reveal the presence of a theatrical intelligence. He presumably was on hand in the theater to coach his fellow players in rehearsal, though acting companies at that time did not have the luxury of long rehearsal periods under an official "director." Shakespeare's own roles may have been relatively unglamorous and self-effacing. Tradition has it that he performed the old servant Adam in *As You Like It* and the Ghost in *Hamlet*. He is listed as one of the "principal comedians" in Jonson's *Every Man in His Humor* in 1598, though without specification of his role; and his name appears in other such lists. His lifelong friend and colleague Richard Burbage normally took the major roles in Shakespeare's plays.

These are the records of accomplishment of the official man, the successful playwright and actor. What do they tell us about the person? First, importantly, they point uniformly to a single identity: Shakespeare of Stratford, Shakespeare the actor, and Shakespeare the famous playwright. Any theory that the actor from Stratford was a front man for some great aristocrat (such as the seventeenth earl of Oxford) who actually wrote the plays but wished to hide his identity (because professional play writing was beneath his social dignity) must do battle with the impressive number of testimonials to Shakespeare as man and writer. The theory must also struggle with the irrefutable fact that Oxford died in 1604, before the performance of many of Shakespeare's greatest plays: *King Lear* (1605–6), *Macbeth* (ca. 1606–7), *Timon of Athens* (ca. 1605–8), *Antony and Cleopatra* (1606–7), *Coriolanus* (ca. 1608), *Pericles*, (1606–8), *Cymbeline* (ca. 1608–10), *The Winter's Tale* (ca. 1609–11), *The Tempest* (ca. 1611), *Henry VIII* (1613), and (in collaboration with John Fletcher) *The Two Noble Kinsmen* (1613–14). Some of those who praised Shakespeare with loving warmth, like Jonson, knew him as a lifelong friend and acquaintance and had every good reason to know that the "swan of Avon" was indeed the author of the plays and poems.

More tellingly, perhaps, the accomplishments of Shakespeare's amazing career as a writer do give us a portrait of the man who wrote. Autobiographical reading of the corpus is full of hazards, of course. We must not assume that Shakespeare's portrayal of the murder of a wife in *Othello* came to him through personal experience, or that Shakespeare had to murder a king (or anyone else, for that matter) in order to be able to depict the agony of Macbeth's soul struggle, or that Shakespeare knew at first hand what it was like to be thrown out of the house by his own daughters (as in *King Lear*). By the same token, we must approach the *Sonnets* with caution and not assume that they relate autobiographically a tortured account of deep and jealous infatuation with a young male friend.

What we can say about Shakespeare the man, as revealed in his writing, is that he chose to celebrate and explore the great emotional rites of passage that mark the stages of any person's life, especially that of a male growing up in Elizabethan society. His great topics are love, friendship, personal ambition, jealousy, loyalty, desertion, betrayal, revenge, fear of abandonment, anxiety about aging, concern about immortality, pride and humility about artistic accomplishment – all the great emotions that reflect what it is to be fully human and vulnerable. The uglier and more destructive of these emotions are portrayed with the same intensity and persuasiveness as the nobler and more attractive emotions, suggesting what we must assume to be true: that Shakespeare knew what it was to hate and experience jealousy and thirst for revenge just as surely as he knew what it was to aspire to heroism or fall in love.

The comedies of the 1590s are not just about falling in love; they are astonishingly insightful as regards the hazards that young people encounter in attempting to negotiate the painful transition from adolescent friendship to heterosexual companionship and consummation. The history plays of the same period, especially the so-called Henriad about the coming of age of Prince Hal as once and future king, thoughtfully explore what it is for a young man to admire and fear the father to whose place he will eventually succeed. These plays are historical chronicles of England's great civil wars, but they are also about fathers and sons to an extraordinary degree, and about domineering women (Queen Margaret in the *Henry VI* plays and *Richard III*) or women as victims of war. The plays of the 1590s thus seem strikingly relevant to the life cycle of the author himself, still young and vigorous, gaining in reputation with every passing year, and making a successful move to earn for his father the right to bear arms. About Shakespeare's love life in the 1590s we know nothing other than what we read and see in his marvelous comedies, which offer us unparalleled portraits of young men and young women in love – the men generally unsure of themselves and all too prone to mistrust the chastity of the women they adore (Claudio in *Much Ado*, for example), the women constant, yet repeatedly suspected of being men's worst enemy. We do not need to posit any particulars of autobiography to imagine into this creative act a deeply emotional involvement and fascination. The plays and poems are the record of a young man needing to understand, and to communicate understanding about, an infinitely complex, necessary, and nearly universal human experience.

Read in the same way, Shakespeare's plays around 1600 reveal an intense portraiture of new turmoil and conflict, as the maturing Shakespeare addresses painful issues as yet skirted or unresolved. The Dark Lady in the *Sonnets* turns out to be unfaithful in fact, confirming the paranoia experienced earlier by fearful men like Claudio (in *Much Ado*) or Bassanio (in the "ring" episode of *The Merchant of Venice*). Similarly, Shakespeare's heretofore nourishing and unthreatening young heroines – Hermia, Juliet, Rosalind, Viola, and others – give way to Cressida in *Troilus and Cressida* (1601–2), who, however sympathetically portrayed, comes to her role with an infamous history as the type of betraying woman. *Measure for Measure* (1603–4) and *All's Well That Ends Well* (ca. 1601–5), absorbed with the breakdown of human relationships, subvert and complicate the happy celebration of marriage with which the early comedies had conventionally ended.[17] The transition from *Henry V* to *Julius Caesar* (both 1599) moves from the patriotic reassurances of English history to the secular ironies of ancient Rome, and from the political success story of Prince Hal (however ironically anatomized) to a saga of assassination of a political leader and father-figure. The motif of father-murder continues into *Macbeth* (ca. 1606–7), where the mother or wife is no less foreboding – a notable example of what Janet Adelman calls the "suffocating mother" in Shakespeare's later plays.[18] *Hamlet* (ca. 1599–1601) broods darkly on misogyny – "Frailty, thy name is woman" – as well as the killing of a king.

As Shakespeare investigates new and experimental genres during this transitional period around the turn of the century, then, he moves imaginatively and creatively into a more troubled phase of the human life cycle. Courtship and success give way to impasse, disillusionment, melancholy, bitterness, self-destructive behavior, self-hatred, and tragic failure. This is not to argue, as romantic critics like Edward Dowden used to insist,[19] that Shakespeare himself necessarily entered into a period of gloom, perhaps in response to the death of his son Hamnet in 1596 or of his father in 1601, or, more broadly, to anxieties about the end of Elizabeth's reign, or simply to *fin de siècle* ennui. We know far too little to make such a claim, and must remember that great composers, for example, did not choose to write in a minor key simply because things were not going well for them. We can sense, nonetheless, that as Shakespeare matured in his art, he saw the necessity of opening Pandora's box, of anatomizing the hard and painful issues of adult life that he had tended to relegate to an important but still subsidiary position in his earlier work.

His portrait of marriage in *Othello* (ca. 1603–4) gives us a moment of rich happiness dissolving into an unparalleled nightmare of sexual jealousy, all the more painful in that Desdemona as victimized wife is innocent, like her prototypes in the earlier comedies. Whatever experiences Shakespeare may have had of jealousy in his own life, we can perceive that he now felt he knew enough about it, and cared enough about it, to give it intense dramatic treatment. The jealousy reminds us of the *Sonnets*; Shakespeare had been there, too, whether in personal experience or in the life of the mind. All of us experience jealousy at some point, of course; the universality is what makes our interest in the dramatic presentation so compelling. Still, that universality also argues against any necessary particularity in Shakespeare's own life. We are safe in saying only that a play like *Othello* must reveal his own intense feelings about jealousy and his humane view of it: the emotional devastation, the self-blindness, the sorrow experienced for failing in this way, the self-accusation, the willingness finally to acknowledge with generosity of spirit that the fault was the man's alone, the need for remorse, and the unwillingness to forgive oneself.

The same can be argued about his portrayal of what we today would call midlife crisis in *Antony and Cleopatra*. A significant proportion of the medical profession today holds the view that midlife crisis is predictable and unavoidable.[20] In males, it strikes when a man finds himself overwhelmed by fears of aging, loss of sexual potency, loss of political influence and power, loss of physical attractiveness. *Antony and Cleopatra* (1606–7), read or seen in this way, is overpoweringly persuasive in its portrayal of the experience. It was written at a time when one might expect Shakespeare to have been going through midlife crisis. To assume this is not to say much about the man biographically, since it implies a universal experience; as a result, we have no idea as to whether Shakespeare is commemorating some glorious and ruinous *folie à deux*. After all, North's Plutarch gave Shakespeare the material he needed to dramatize such a story.[21] Yet we wonder. Could a man have written that incredible play without having known deeply what it is to throw away one's best shot at a career in pursuit of a maddeningly attractive and possibly duplicitous woman? We will never know; we need not know. We have the play, and that is everything. Once again, too, it reveals values and idealisms that give us, I think, a glimpse of Shakespeare the man: the deep generosity of Antony toward Enobarbus and indeed everybody, the incomparably greater stature of both Antony and Cleopatra as compared with the self-denying and anal Octavius Caesar, the fascination with daring and dreaming. And, I suspect, the self-hatred is no less personally revealing.

King Lear has three daughters; Shakespeare had two, and a son who died. Edgar's perfidious brother is named Edmund; Shakespeare's brother Edmund died in 1607. Shakespeare's daughter Susanna married Dr John Hall in Stratford in that same year. Judith did not marry Thomas Quiney until early 1616, the year in which Shakespeare died. This last marriage was not a happy one, and Shakespeare seems to have been bitterly opposed to it.[22] He wrote *King Lear* in about 1605–6, long before the unhappy struggle with Thomas Quiney as a son-in-law took place. What can we make of all this? The most compelling biographical thesis is that Shakespeare had deeply personal reasons for choosing to dramatize a story about ungrateful daughters and their husbands at this time in his life. Shortly before, in *Othello*, he had touched on the seeming disobedience of daughters to their fathers when they marry, and he was to pursue the topic in his late romances as well. The painful subject bespeaks an absorption in the agony of aging and of seeking desperately for philosophical calm in the face of approaching death. Shakespeare must have known these emotions at first hand, however much he may also have realized that there was a lot to be grateful for. We have every reason to think that he was proud of Susanna's marriage and happy for her seemingly secure future; Hall's Croft, where she and her husband lived in Stratford, is still there with its reassuringly beautiful gardens to encourage our hope that Shakespeare was blessed in this daughter's marriage. But we have the plays as well to assure us that he was deeply aware of the potential consequences of conflict.

The late plays are about many of these same compelling human topics and also about lost, sometimes recovered wives. In *Pericles* (1606–8), the hero is obliged to cast his apparently dead wife overboard in a storm; she is washed ashore, miraculously restored to life by a kind of magician-figure who recurs in these late plays, and is given back to the grieving husband after long absence. *The Winter's Tale* (ca. 1609–11) narrates a tale of a husband who, like Othello and Troilus and many another fearful male, suspects that his partner is unfaithful; years later, the wife whom he believes he has killed is restored to him as though by a miracle. *Cymbeline* (ca. 1608–10) portrays the agony of Posthumus Leonatus as he suspects his wife and arranges for her a death that is unexpectedly aborted, so that she too may be restored to him.

It cannot be merely coincidence that Shakespeare himself, after an early and probably unsatisfactory marriage, and after years of living in London apart from his family other than on infrequent visits home, chose to give up his lodgings in London some time around 1611–12 and retire to Stratford. He seems then to have come out of retirement fitfully, to work on *Henry VIII* and *The Two Noble Kinsmen*. Was he bored in retirement, as many persons are? Did he find continuous cohabitation with Anne to be not quite the blissful, tearful, forgiving reunion that he had fantasized in his plays? We will never know, probably, but we do have the incredible dramatic record of that emotional roller-coaster ride.

We have in *The Tempest* (ca. 1611) the saga of a father who is left alone on a desert island, having been betrayed by his brother, having no company other than that of his dearest daughter, whom he manages to give away in marriage with all the grace and dignity that he can muster. There is no mother for Miranda; she is mentioned once, but Prospero is left alone to work out his highly wrought emotional feelings toward aging, death, the marriage of a daughter, and the end of a career in art. Prospero is impatient, patriarchal, bossy, and inclined to vengeance until he manages to get his feelings under some control. He reminds us of the writer of whom we catch glimpses in Shakespeare's last years, quarreling angrily with his son-in-law Thomas Quiney, redrafting his will in such a way as to snub his brother-in-law William Hart, unforgiving, seeing to it that his widow would not be able to interfere with the terms of his last will and testament.[23] Yet Prospero struggles to rise above his occasionally mean-spirited self: he is managerial but solicitous, harsh and yet striving to learn the hard lesson of forgiveness of those who have done him wrong, petty at moments but also deeply moral in his compassionate view of human weakness and even guardedly hopeful for a future that can never be his. In today's critical stance toward *The Tempest*, Prospero's stock has diminished considerably; yet I cannot but imagine that I see in Prospero the deep conflict between pride and humility in the artist as he considers his creation and reflects on what it will be to lay aside not only art but life itself.

NOTES

1   Repr. in E. K. Chambers, *William Shakespeare: A Study of Facts and Problems*, 2 vols (Oxford: Clarendon Press, 1930), vol. 2, p. 210.

2   Jan Kott, *Shakespeare Our Contemporary*, trans. Boleslaw Taborski (Garden City, N.Y.: Doubleday Anchor, 1966).

3   Repr. in Chambers, *Shakespeare*, vol. 2, p. 210.

4   Prologue to *Every Man in His Humor*, folio text, 1616, in *Ben Jonson*, ed. C. H. Herford and Percy and Evelyn Simpson, 11 vols (Oxford, Clarendon Press, 1925–52), vol. 3.

5   Induction to *Bartholomew Fair*, produced in 1614; from the 1631 text, in *Jonson*, ed. Herford and Simpson, vol. 6, p. 16.

6   Repr. in Chambers, *Shakespeare*, vol. 2, p. 207.

7   Jonson, "To the memory of my beloved, the author Mr. William Shakespeare, and what

he hath left us," in *Mr. William Shakespeare's Comedies, Histories, & Tragedies* (London: printed by Isaac Jaggard and Ed. Blount, 1623); repr. in *The Norton Folio of Shakespeare*, prepared by Charlton Hinman (New York: Norton, 1968), pp. 9–10.

8   *A Midsummer Night's Dream*, V. i. 16–17. Citations are from *The Complete Works of Shakespeare*, ed. David Bevington, 4th edn updated (New York: Longman, 1997).

9   "To the memory," *Norton Folio*, p. 10.

10   Ibid., pp. 9–10.

11   Ibid., p. 10.

12   Nicholas Rowe (ed.), *The Works of Mr William Shakespear*, 6 vols (London, 1709), vol. 1.

13   For this and other life records discussed in this essay, see S. Schoenbaum, *William*

Shakespeare: A Documentary Life (Oxford and New York: Oxford University Press, 1975), and *idem, William Shakespeare: Records and Images* (Oxford and New York: Oxford University Press, 1981).

14 Robert Greene, *A Groats-Worth of Wit Bought with a Million of Repentance* (1592), in *The Life and Complete Works of Robert Greene*, ed. Alexander B. Grosart, 15 vols (London, for private circulation, 1881–3), vol. 12, p. 144.

15 Henry Chettle, Epistle "To the Gentlemen Readers," in *Kind-Heart's Dream* (London: for Wm Wright, 1592).

16 Francis Meres, *Palladis Tamia* (London, 1598).

17 Richard P. Wheeler, *Shakespeare's Development and the Problem Comedies: Turn and Counter-Turn* (Berkeley: University of California Press, 1981).

18 Janet Adelman, *Suffocating Mothers: Fantasies of Maternal Origin in Shakespeare's Plays,* *"Hamlet" to "The Tempest"* (London and New York: Routledge, 1992).

19 Edward Dowden, *Shakespeare: A Critical Study of His Mind and Art* (London: Routledge & Kegan Paul, 1875; 3rd edn, 1905).

20 On midlife crisis, see Daniel J. Levinson, *The Seasons of a Man's Life* (New York: Knopf, 1978).

21 Thomas North (trans.), *Plutarch's Lives of the Noble Grecians and Romans* (London, 1579).

22 E. A. J. Honigmann, "The second-best bed," *New York Review of Books*, 7 Nov. 1991, pp. 27–30. The matter is ably discussed in Stanley Wells, "Shakespeare's lives: 1991–1994," in *Elizabethan Theater: Essays in Honor of S. Schoenbaum*, ed. R. B. Parker and S. P. Zitner (Newark, Del.: University of Delaware Press; London: Associated University Presses, 1996), pp. 15–29.

23 Ibid.

PART THREE
Living

3

Shakespeare's England

Norman Jones

William Shakespeare was born into a dying culture. In 1564 England was still reeling from the massive social dislocation called the Reformation. The religious and social world his parents knew as children had been destroyed by new ideas and government actions. Churches that had embodied much of the identity of villages, guilds, and grieving families had been cleansed of their "superstitions" or dissolved altogether, along with the monasteries that had anchored the medieval system of salvation. Purgatory was officially gone, too, and with it much of the reason for social philanthropy. John Shakespeare, William's father, belonged to a generation caught between pre-Reformation culture and the culture that would emerge by the end of the century. Had he been asked what the future held for his son, he might well have shaken his head and said it was anyone's guess. He and his fellows had seen the world change with unimaginable rapidity. What would William see?

The children of the 1560s were handed the job of building a new, Protestant culture on the ruins of the old religion. The first English generation to inherit the Reformation, they invented a new intellectual culture, revamped their nation's political ideology, were forced to discover a new place for the individual in their society, reinvent their national identity, and build a new economy. By the time Shakespeare died in 1616, he and his contemporaries – Francis Bacon, Philip Sidney, Christopher Marlowe, Francis Drake, Walter Ralegh, Ben Jonson, Robert Smythson, William Perkins, Robert Cecil, James I, and many others – had witnessed and prompted the remodeling of the English.

The net result of all these changes was the emergence of a new conception of the place of the individual in English society. The origins of this conception are diverse and debatable, but on the level of culture they stem primarily from the slow imposition of Protestantism on a culture that had been profoundly Catholic. The first shock was felt in the 1530s. Henry VIII's divorce from Catherine of Aragon in 1532 was made possible by the rejection of papal authority in England. Henry, declaring himself Supreme Head of the Church in England, was by no means a Protestant; but his anti-papal position created a breathing space for those like William Tyndale and Thomas Cranmer who were, giving them a chance to introduce changes favorable to their theology. Most important, the English Bible emerged from Tyndale's pen and was printed, with Cranmer's help, in 1535. Most notable was the wave of monastic dissolutions in the late 1530s, which put an end to ascetic Christianity in the lands ruled by Henry VIII. Although he had dissolved the monasteries, Henry VIII quickly sought to stem the spread of Protestant ideas, and his Act of Six Articles of 1540, known to Protestants as the "whip with six strings," sent some Protestants to execution and others into exile.

The next round of religious change came in 1549. Young King Edward VI's regency council, led by the duke of Somerset, began a thorough Protestantization of the nation. Purgatory was abolished, and the chantries that had remembered the souls of the dead consigned there for purification were seized as Crown property. Officially this ended the "cult of the dead" that had marked late medieval religion, but, as Hamlet's father's ghost testifies, knowledge of, and perhaps belief in, Purgatory was not so easily abolished.

Along with the end of Purgatory came true Protestantism, embodied in the English Prayer Book of 1549, revised in 1552 and revived by Elizabeth I in 1559. With its imposition on the Church, Latin masses ceased, along with veneration of the saints. Bishops who resisted the changes were removed and replaced with Protestants. Although the Book of Common Prayer was only mildly Protestant in its first form, the introduction of an English liturgy sparked a revolt in the West Country that had to be put down with bloody ruthlessness.

Almost before people had taken in the changes in worship, it changed again. Edward died on 6 July 1553, and his sister, Mary Tudor, succeeded to the throne, despite the attempt of the earl of Northumberland to install a Protestant queen in the form of Lady Jane Grey. Mary, daughter of Catherine of Aragon and Henry VIII, was the victim of Henry's divorce of her mother. Naturally she brought England back to Catholicism and obedience to the Pope. Leading Protestants fled abroad or were captured, tried, and burned for heresy. Monasteries were refounded, mass began to be said again, altars were reinstalled in the churches, statues of the saints were restored, and a few chantries were begun anew. Bishops removed by Edward VI were reinstated, and Protestant bishops were deposed and, like Hugh Latimer and Thomas Cranmer, were often executed for heresy.

Mary married Philip II of Spain. This marriage, more than the restoration of Catholicism, created intense resistance in the nation. Thomas Wyatt led an armed uprising against Mary in 1554, but was defeated.

Mary died on 17 November 1558. Had she lived longer, England might have remained Catholic and kept its traditional alliance with Spain; but her successor, Elizabeth I, had every reason to break with Rome. Her mother, Anne Boleyn, had prompted Henry VIII to declare himself Supreme Head of the Church. Elizabeth's legitimacy depended on the belief that the king in Parliament was supreme over the Church. So her first Parliament returned the nation to the religious settlement in place in late 1552. The queen was declared to be "Supreme Governor of the Church in England," the English Prayer Book of 1552 was reimposed, the new monasteries and chantries were closed, masses were stopped once again, altars were again removed from the churches, and saints, roods, and stained glass windows depicting superstitions were again destroyed, and Catholic bishops replaced by Protestant bishops – but not killed.

England remained Protestant after 1559, but for people of John Shakespeare's generation there was no religious certainty. The great lesson of the period between 1532 and 1559 was that religion was undependable. It was a toy of the state, a game played by religious fanatics and crafty politicians. Many of them still sought a middle ground in ideology, as did William Cecil and Queen Elizabeth, neither of whom was inclined to launch a hunt for heretics or Catholics. The famous Anglican *via media* was a product of their attempt to be politic about religion. They knew its power to destroy.

The children of John's generation grew up in a different religious world. It was a world in which the official religion of the state was triumphant, though lacking in definition. It was also a world in which there was acute awareness of the possibility of individual choice in matters of religion. By the middle of the 1570s there were a number of possible religious allegiances from which English people might choose. First, one could conform to the Established Church. This was the avenue of least resistance, and by about 1580 it is possible to speak of "Prayer Book religion" in England. After twenty years the cadences of the Prayer Book had become comfortable and sacred to many people. For many of this ilk, the community aspect of worship was very important. In the parish church the body of the community was present and participating, pleasing God while making local government work. Churchwardens not only looked after the church fabric; they policed the moral conduct of the parish, giving it considerable local autonomy.

But not everyone was willing to be part of a mixed community. To some Protestants, and especially young people in the 1570s and 1580s, the religious moderation of the Elizabethan Settlement was only a halfway house. They wanted the Reformation to be completed on a model provided by Jean Calvin's Geneva. Loosely known as Puritans, they wanted the Church "purified" of all "popish rags," until there was nothing left that reminded people of the old faith. In its presbyterian form this meant that bishops should be abolished and replaced by presbyteries of elders within the congregations. Throughout the 1580s they sought to enact this in Parliament, along with further reform of the Prayer Book, but the queen and much of the nation were hostile to their efforts.

They had better luck with what is known as the "Reformation of Manners." As the famines, wars, and economic troubles of the age bit harder, those who saw the world through Puritan eyes knew that God was punishing the nation for its lewd living. Seeking to create purified communities of worship, and believing that God elected some to salvation and others to damnation, they sought to control the reprobate in the interest of the godly, in order to take away the punishment. All his life Shakespeare was exposed to their demands that swearing, drunkenness, fornication, bastardy, sabbath breaking, maypole dancing, ill-rule, gambling, and a host of others crimes be ended. The theater was one of their targets, and in 1605 they succeeded in getting legislation through Parliament that forbade blaspheming onstage. On the stage Shakespeare got his revenge by portraying Puritans as pompous hypocrites; but this did not stem the tide of their zeal. In towns in which they had control they created things like Colchester's tribunal on fornication to ferret out sinners. By the beginning of the seventeenth century their efforts focused more on social reform, even as they lost faith in government's ability to bring it about.

When James VI of Scotland inherited the throne of England in 1603, he was met in Northamptonshire by delegates bearing a petition said to be signed by more than 1,000 ministers. The Millenary Petition begged him to further reform the clergy, ceremonies, and doctrine of the Church of England. He responded by conferring at the Hampton Court Conference with his bishops and representatives of the petitioners. He was willing to hear both sides, but in the end he was unwilling to make the changes they sought. "No bishop, no king," he opined. But he did order one thing they wanted: a new edition of the Bible. In 1611 the King James Bible appeared.

For the people disillusioned by the king's support of his bishops, it was a short step to withdrawing into their own religious communities and separating from the body of the parish. Soon some were separating completely and moving to Calvinist Holland and on to New England.

Whether tending toward Lutheran or Calvinist versions of Protestantism, English Protestants accepted a model of salvation that cut out the middlemen of the Church. Protestants took it as a given that people are saved by faith alone, not by any works they have done, and that they are to be guided by Scripture alone, not by tradition or authority *qua* authority. Whether one believed that one was predestined to salvation or damnation, as Calvinists did, or simply that one is saved if one accepts God's gracious offer of faith, the onus of salvation falls on the individual, not on the community. People have a duty to God to monitor their states of grace, inspecting their motives and emotions for signs of either dutiful obedience or sinful obstinacy. Salvation was no longer a matter of doing the right thing. It was a matter of proper intentions. The results of this belief system were political, and social realignment as ideological orientation became more important than social groupings like the parish or the county.

Although most of the English population had, by 1600, left the confusion of the middle century behind and become at least conforming Anglicans, there remained an important minority of Catholics in the country. They, even more than their Protestant brothers and sisters (and parents and children in many cases), lived in a world of religious choice. From the early 1570s onward they were under increasing pressure to conform to the state religion and abandon Catholicism.

When Shakespeare was young, most of the Catholics around him – and there were many, including many of his relatives and possibly his father and mother – were "old" Catholics. That is, they had been raised in a world that practiced pre-Reformation

Catholicism. Deprived of most of the infrastructures of that worship, they clung to the mass and the other sacraments of the Catholic Church, while remembering the old days and hoping for their return. As late as the year in which William Shakespeare died, old Roger "The Recusant" Martin composed a nostalgic memoir about how worship was performed in his village of Long Melford before the Reformation.

These "old" Catholics tended either to die off or to conform, and it is known that many people in the Anglican pews were crypto-Catholics. These were folk who conformed to avoid fines for not attending church, but who, in their hearts and their private prayers, were Catholics.

In addition to this wavering and shrinking group were the "new" Catholics, whose faith was shaped and supported by the missionary priests of the Catholic underground. When the 1569 revolt of the northern earls failed to remove Elizabeth and restore Catholicism, it became obvious that England would not soon revert to the old religion. Then English exiles began training seminary priests to work underground in England to keep the faith alive until Elizabeth might be deposed.

The same revolt, which provoked a papal bull, *Regnans in excelsis*, declaring Elizabeth a heretic and absolving her subjects from obedience, convinced Elizabeth that Catholics were potential enemies of the state. The activities of the seminary priests proved that there was an international Catholic conspiracy against her throne, and when, in 1579, an Irish revolt was blessed by the Pope and partially led by Nicholas Sanders, a papal representative, official paranoia was shown to be reasonable.

Elizabeth began executing Catholic priests for treason in 1581. As they were caught, they were examined, often under torture, to discover if they recognized Elizabeth as the true and lawful queen of England. This "bloody question," devised by Lord Burghley, was designed to elicit proof that they were traitors and deserved to be hanged, drawn, and quartered. Note that they were never accused of false religious belief, only of false political allegiance.

When John Gerard was asked this question in 1594, he answered: "I am a loyal Catholic and I am a loyal subject of the Queen." It was, for many Catholics a true answer, but one that worked only as long as they were not put to the test of having to choose. Luckily for them, Elizabeth had little desire to make them choose so long as they behaved loyally, and her refusal to persecute lay Catholics with more than fines often undermined their will to resist. Gerard, who was a Jesuit missionary to England, noted that many would have remained or become Catholics, but they could not afford the fines, so they conformed to the Anglican Church.

The net effect of these religious choices and the queen's toleration of religious ambiguity was that people of William Shakespeare's generation became used to religious tension and confusion at a very personal level. Whatever William himself was, members of his family spanned the entire spectrum of choice, as did his neighbors. Even eminent men in government and religion had ideological variations in their home circles. Francis Alford, a leading member of Elizabeth's parliaments for almost the entire reign, returned each night to a wife who invited illegal priests to celebrate mass in his own home. People who live with this sort of religious ambiguity learn to deal circumspectly with their neighbors if any business is to be done. As Shakespeare put it in *All's Well That Ends Well*, philosophizing on cuckoldry, "for young Charbon the puritan and old Poysam the papist, how-some'er their hearts are severed in religion, their heads are both one" (I. iii.). Folk of this ilk conformed to the state's variety of Protestantism and got on with their lives.

By the 1580s royal policy had become explicitly anti-Catholic. In part this was natural, and in part it was linked to international politics. The 1579 revolt in Ireland, though it had been blessed by the Pope, was supported by Spanish troops and Spanish money. Philip II became involved because of English intervention in the Spanish Netherlands, where Protestant Dutch rebels had been fighting the Spanish since the early 1560s. Elizabeth had been reluctant to do more than send money for years, but conflict with Spain seemed inevitable after 1579. In the summer of 1585 she committed an expeditionary force, commanded by the earl of Leicester, to support the Protestant rebels against the Catholic Spanish in the Dutch War.

Taking up arms against Catholic enemies intensified the fear of Catholics at home, and made the situation of Mary Stuart, queen of Scotland, even more strategic. In 1568 Mary, heir presumptive to the throne of England, sought political asylum in England. Once there, the Scottish queen became part of a chess match with Elizabeth. On Elizabeth's side were the Protestants; on Mary's were those who hoped for a Catholic successor and pinned their aspirations on her. In 1569 the northern earls revolted, hoping that she would marry the duke of Norfolk and displace Elizabeth. The revolt failed, and Norfolk was executed in 1572; but Mary lived on, and the game continued. It was an elaborate, complicated game, but in 1585 letters to Mary from a young Catholic, Anthony Babington, were discovered hidden in a beer barrel. Babington offered to assassinate Elizabeth, and Mary accepted the offer. Tried by special commission and then condemned by Parliament, Mary was sentenced to die. Elizabeth, however, procrastinated about signing the death warrant until February 1586, and afterward at least pretended not to have wanted Mary executed. We now know that she preferred secret murder to public execution to get rid of Mary, but her chosen instrument refused to oblige.

Mary's execution and the dispatch of an army to the Spanish Netherlands prompted the next move in the international game. Philip II of Spain determined to crush England: to wipe out his political enemies and gain credit with God for once again restoring Catholicism to England. He began to prepare an armada for an invasion. In England the House of Commons was asked for money to defend England from "the Catholics abroad, the Pope, the King of Spain, the . . . papists at home and their ministers." In 1587 the English attacked Lisbon to disrupt the construction of the great fleet, but their attack failed.

The defeat of the Spanish Armada in July 1588 is perhaps the best-known episode in Elizabethan history. Francis Drake and his little navy attacked the Spanish galleons with superior English gunnery, and God, according to Protestant preachers, sent a storm to prevent the Spanish from linking up with the invasion army poised in the Low Countries. It was a defeat that surprised Europe and left the English more than a little proud of themselves. Protestantism and nationalism became fused in 1588, and the 1590s would see the wild popularity of nationalist history. New histories and reprinted histories poured from the presses, and from Shakespeare's pen. As one historian has remarked, Shakespeare rode this wave of nationalistic historicism with nine history plays between 1589 and 1599, working on the principle "You've read the book; now see the play."[1]

The anti-papal diatribe of *King John* and the sentiments of Henry V's St Crispin's Day speech fit the moment, for the 1590s were fraught with wars and rumors of wars. The fighting with Spain continued until 1604, with punch and counter-punch. In 1596 the English fleet surprised and sacked the city of Cadiz in Spain, provoking the Spanish to plan another invasion of England. Fighting continued in the Netherlands, too, until the Treaty of London of 1604 ended England's conflict with Spain and settled the division of the Netherlands.

Elizabethan Ireland was a source of constant trouble and expense to the Crown. Irish lords were frequently in rebellion against Tudor rule, and the Reformation gave the Irish a religious reason to resist. In 1594 Hugh O'Neill, earl of Tyrone, launched a rebellion that lasted until 1603. O'Neill's aim in the Nine Years' War was to use Catholicism to unite Ireland against the English, earning both papal and Spanish support for his plan. It was a war against foreign domination and alien religion, but as such, it did not have much appeal to the Irish. The harshness of the English response, however, convinced many Irish people to resist. Moreover, Spain intervened in Ireland in 1601, making it part of the international conflict already raging in northwest Europe. The impact of this intervention on England was enormous, draining taxes and militia levies into a morass that the peace in 1603 did little to stabilize. At times military operations in Ireland were costing Elizabeth's government as much as 20 percent of its annual revenue.

The Irish conflict provided the background for the Essex Rebellion. The earl of Essex was Elizabeth's last favorite. A reckless, self-satisfied young man, he had been given important commands at an early age. In 1599 he was sent to Ireland, bragging that he would "beat Tyrone in the field"; but he not only failed to vanquish the Irish, he fell under suspicion of selling out when he met Tyrone alone in a field without witnesses. Great things had been expected of Essex, as the original version of *Henry V* reflects when it speaks of "the general of our gracious empress, – As in good time he may, – from Ireland coming, Bringing rebellion broached on his sword" (V, v, 30–2). He not only failed to deliver great things; he disobeyed the queen's explicit orders and returned from Dublin to London. Dishonored and discredited, he began plotting revenge against his enemies and begging the queen for money. She refused to give him any.

Essex plotted with dissatisfied courtiers, men who believed the parsimonious queen had not rewarded them sufficiently, to seize the throne. The plotters used a performance of Shakespeare's *Richard II*, with its deposition scene in which Henry IV removes the corrupt Richard and his sycophants, to harden their resolve. However, they were discovered and forced to choose between submission and rebellion. They chose rebellion, but no one else did, and Essex paid with his life. Elizabeth shortly afterward observed to William Lambarde, "I am Richard II, know ye not that?"

Meanwhile England had other internal enemies, English Catholics whose desire to restore their religion made them obvious participants in plots against the Crown. Luckily for Elizabeth, they were so internally divided that they could not rouse themselves to concerted action. In the 1590s Catholic priests imprisoned at Wisbeach had begun a "stir" about who had proper authority over missionaries working in England, the Jesuits or others. This debate divided the community and led to the "Archpriest Controversy" that began in 1598, in which it was disputed whether the English should have bishops appointed for them (the Jesuit position) or be governed by an archpriest and twelve assistants. Fought out in the papal court, this led to an unlikely proposal from Pope Clement VIII to Elizabeth. For a brief moment it was hoped that Elizabeth would grant toleration to Catholics. Elizabeth refused, but Catholic gentry petitioned James in 1604 for toleration, promising in exchange to expel the Catholic priests among them. He played with them, but, as he did with their Puritan enemies, gave them no satisfaction, reimposing the recusancy laws as soon as he had a peace with Spain.

Another uncompromising faction among the Catholics wanted action against the heretics in power. They were unwilling to beg for toleration at the expense of their True Church. A tiny group hatched the Gunpowder Plot, intending to blow up Parliament, and the king with it, when he came to open it on 5 November, 1605. But unfortunately for them, there were several Catholic peers of the realm who would have been blown up too, and when Lord Mounteagle was warned to stay away, he reported the plot to the Privy Council. Searchers found Guy Fawkes, an English exile with a reputation for reckless bravery, in the cellar beneath the Parliament chamber surrounded by barrels of gunpowder. Naturally, Fawkes was executed for treason, and the English nation began the celebration of God's providence in saving his nation from the plots of Antichrist that is still held every 5 November. Once again Catholics were proved to be England's greatest enemy, and God was seen to be English.

The accession of James I changed the political circumstances in which the English lived, creating new opportunities and new challenges. Although James brought the war with Spain to a close and ushered in a long period of peace, his very presence created new political problems. A royal court geared to the cult of Elizabeth the virgin queen, in which courtiers danced attendance on their queen bee, hoping for – but seldom receiving – her largesse, was replaced by a male establishment full of Scots, in which the king and his family spent liberally. Unlike Elizabeth, James was aloof and uninterested in the details of government. She had kept her servants on a short chain; he allowed his so much latitude that corruption was soon rampant. She had played heavily on her Englishness; James was a foreigner and could not have been expected to understand fully the finer points of English law and politics, though he kept Elizabeth's English counselors, including Robert Cecil. Elizabeth had been a gifted natural politician; James wrote *The True Law of Free Monarchies* on the divine right of kings and *Basilikon Doron* on the obligations of kingship, but his political style was less attractive than Elizabeth's – as was his life-style. He seems to have doted on his wife, Anne of Denmark, but he was also attracted to handsome boys – which did not impress his many puritanical subjects.

For his less puritanical subjects, James's reign brought new opportunity and hope. In May 1603 James appointed the King's Men, including William Shakespeare, to play in his name, and the theater entered a prosperous time. Perhaps *Macbeth*, on a Scottish history theme that celebrated James's ancestor Banquo and played to James's well-known interest in witches, is the greatest monument to the king's patronage. Presented to the king at Hampton Court, *Macbeth's* Act IV scene i, allowed the witches to show Macbeth the line of the Scots kings descended from Banquo down to James himself.

Whatever James's good qualities, he was bound to have difficulties in England because he was also king of the Scots, and because England was in dire financial shape. He came from an impoverished nation with few cities and little trade, a nation still dominated by powerful clans. His Scots subjects saw England as their traditional enemy, and as a fat sheep to be fleeced. James himself must have believed himself to be unimaginably rich after he inherited England. The English deeply distrusted their old enemy, the Scots, and they were not rich. The nation was in the midst of an economic crisis of pan-European proportions.

The financial problems did not impress themselves on the new king, and he spent lavishly, turned a blind eye to his courtiers' corruption, and failed to mind the store, with the result that the war debt he had inherited from Elizabeth grew and grew into the greatest deficit in English history. Not all of this was James's fault. The structure of taxation in England was antique, depending on occasional subsidies voted by occasional parliaments. And even if Parliament approved a tax, the real property values on which taxes were based were as much as ten times greater than their assessed values, which often had not changed for half a century, despite rapid inflation. Otherwise, the king had revenue from customs taxes and his own lands. Robert Cecil, earl of Salisbury and effectively Prime Minister, did what he could to raise more money by raising excise taxes, selling Crown lands, and asking Parliament for more money, but still James spent about £75,000 more a year than he took in. Desperate, Salisbury offered Parliament the "Great Contract," a request for a single grant of £600,000 to pay the king's debts. Parliament refused to grant it, and Salisbury was forced to resort to things like more efficient collection of fees and selling titles. Men whose incomes made them worthy were expected to buy knighthoods, at a good price, resulting in the so-called inflation of honors. Under the circumstances, tax increases were necessary – the yield of taxation in real terms kept declining because of inflation – but Parliament was not desirous of paying more for government. It believed in governmental austerity, with the result that many things were undone or ill-done that needed to be done.

The English economy began to fall apart in the early 1590s, victim of inflation, war taxation, war disruption, harvest failure, and the general European slump. By the late

1590s the English were suffering the troubling social dislocations that went with war, unemployment, and lack of markets.

William Hext, a justice of the peace in Somerset, wrote to Lord Burghley in 1596, explaining the dire straits of his county and expatiating on their origins. In his eyes the authors of the burdens daily laid on his countrymen, and of the high prices and shortages of food, were "wicked, wandering, idle people" whose thefts were at the heart of all the trouble. Because of a justice system afraid to hang as many as it ought, Hext believed, these vagrants had lost all respect for their betters, fear of the law, or fear of God. Worse, the cost of imprisoning them all meant there was no money left over to relieve the truly needy poor. His answer to these problems was straightforward: harsher laws and sharper law enforcement to stop the mouths of these people who "laugh in their sleeves at the lenity of the law and the timorousness of the executioners of it."[2] Contemporaries added other criminals to the list of causes – notably usurers, whose demands for interest robbed and impoverished good citizens.

Parliament's responses to these hard times were two new, important laws. The first was the 1597 Act for the Relief of the Poor. It could be called an "act for the punishment of the poor," but it did address the problem squarely, creating a national system of parish workhouses in which the able-bodied poor could be made to spin and card wool and perform other useful work to defray the cost of their keep. Their children would be put out to service by the overseers of the poor. These same poor people were forbidden to travel in search of work, since such travel would have been defined as vagrancy and would have come under the other new statute, the Act for the Punishment of Rogues, Vagabonds, and Sturdy Beggars. Under this act, every parish was to have a "house of correction" in which vagrants could be imprisoned. As was traditional, vagrants born outside the parish could be "stripped naked from the middle upwards and . . . be openly whipped until his or her body be bloody" in every parish between the point of arrest and the home parish. If that failed to keep them from wandering, beggars might be banished from the realm and, if they returned, condemned as felons and hung.

Modern historians looking at the same troubles see larger causes. The root of the problem was demographic expansion. The population of England had increased by roughly 35 percent in Elizabeth's reign, growing about 1 percent every year. The implications of this increase were ominous. Elizabeth's reign had begun with bad harvests and famine, and it would end the same way. The nation could not always feed itself, and the major cities often imported grain from the Baltic in order to cushion the sharp price increases and shortages that went with a bad harvest. Beginning in 1594 there were four bad harvests in a row, with 1596 and 1597 seeing crop failures in some parts of the country. By 1596 the price of grain was almost quadruple its 1592 level. Hext's vagabonds were often people desperately seeking food and work.

The same population increase that drove up the price of food drove down the price of labor. In the course of the sixteenth century the price of food rose about 600 percent, while real wages fell. In the building trades a day's real wage for a laborer in 1615 was only a half or a third of what it had been in 1500. And that was if people could get work. In the 1590s, war gave jobs to many men, but when they were discharged, there was little or no work for them, creating the dangerous phenomenon of armed beggars. The 1597 poor law singled them out as special objects of charity as they attempted to get home from the ports in which they were discharged. Of course there were no national provisions to help maimed soldiers, either.

Real food prices rose, real wages fell, and the gap between the poor and the rest widened. In country districts the demand for land rose as the population increased, not only because more people were looking for places to live and work, but also because as the price of food and the demand for raw materials increased, the profit that could be derived from the land rose, too. Landowners found themselves with larger and larger profits as demand for their produce rose and their labor costs decreased.

For this lucky group life was good. Across England there was a massive redistribution of income in favor of the landed classes between 1580 and 1620. Much of this was at the expense of the agricultural laborers, rather than the tenant farmers, who benefited, albeit to a lesser extent, from the same forces that made the landowners better off. Great landowners and lesser gentry alike expressed their new wealth in architecture. Late Elizabethans built lavishly – so lavishly that houses built between 1580 and 1620 are a hallmark of the English countryside. In this process, dubbed "the great rebuilding," new architectural concepts came into play as men and women sought to express their rank and importance. At the upper end of the scale, Elizabeth, countess of Shrewsbury, known as Bess of Hardwick, stands as an example of both a social climber and a great builder. After four advantageous marriages, the last to the earl of Shrewsbury (she and the earl detested one another), she inherited his vast wealth and invested it in her home, Hardwick Hall.

The countess had already rebuilt her parents' home of Hardwick Hall in the 1580s, but she began building a new home beside the old one right after the death of her husband in November 1590. Possibly working to a design by the great architect Robert Smythson, her craftsmen produced a house walled in glass that played with light and perspective as well as with romantic Flemish and Palladian elements, making it one of England's outstanding pieces of architecture. Bess moved in, to the sound of musicians playing, in October 1597, as the country suffered its second year of dearth.

Among the gentry it was becoming fashionable to build in stone or brick because the price of timber was rising quickly, driven by glass and iron smelting and the demand for domestic fuel. But the scale of the buildings proves that economy was not the only consideration. The new houses had many more rooms, with extra parlors and butteries, milk cellars, brew houses, and kitchens incorporated into the plans.

There is no doubt that John and William Shakespeare benefited from this rising tide. Large new houses and substantial investments in agricultural land, as well as the acquisition of a coat of arms, marked the family's rise. When, in 1601, William bought 100 acres of arable land in Old Stratford, he was simply acting as any prudent investor of the time would. Land was a sure thing.

In 1598 a survey of the borough of Stratford found William Shakespeare to be hoarding eighty bushels of malt, an offense against the market regulations that aimed to keep food available to the poor at reasonable prices. In this he also proves himself to be a gentleman, standing on the higher side of the class divisions. The prosperity of the landowners was being matched by the misery of the laborers, who had a hard time feeding themselves and blamed the rich. There was much seditious talk (for which many were hanged), and in Kent alone there were eleven riots connected with the shortage of grain between 1585 and 1603. In Oxfordshire in 1596 four men attempted to launch a rebellion to put down enclosures that robbed the poor of the common lands, thereby increasing hunger and unemployment, and to protest the high price of grain. They intended to march on London, making common cause with the apprentices there. The ringleaders gave a rebellion, but no one came. Nonetheless, they badly frightened the Privy Council, which was all too aware of the social discontent in the country.

In 1597 England and Scotland suffered a "crisis of subsistence," when famine combined with plague to ravage cities all over the island. The food shortages made the plague more virulent than usual, but plague was something all Europeans knew well. When it struck, it brought business to a standstill, disrupted trade, and killed large numbers of people in the poorer parts of the insanitary towns. London saw it more often than other towns, and it was often most deadly there because of the living conditions, especially in the crowded eastern parishes. In 1582, 1592–3, 1597, 1603, and 1606–10 bubonic plague and other diseases doubled the death rate and disturbed the city. Immediately after the King's Men was created in 1603, it was forbidden to perform lest it draw crowds and spread the contagion.

By the first decade of the seventeenth century, social, ideological, and political tensions were being felt throughout the country. All this was aggravated by economic changes that added to the tension, even as they provided cures for some of the problems. When William Shakespeare was a child, he lived in a nation that produced mostly raw materials and imported finished goods. Located on the periphery of Europe, it was not very important to Europe's economy. Known for its wool, it was not known for fine cloth, and it depended on the export of wool to pay for its appetite for manufactured goods. In the 1560s this picture began to change, as civil wars on the Continent disrupted traditional markets, and entrepreneurs, often with the help of government monopolies, found it profitable to make in England what had previously been purchased abroad. Moreover, Shakespeare's contemporaries actively sought new markets for English goods in the Levant, Muscovy, India, Africa, and the Americas.

A new economy was emerging that had a different attitude to risk, to social aggrandizement, and to money. In the middle years of the sixteenth century people had talked about the "commonwealth" as a social and political ideal. Inherent in this idea was a *noblesse oblige* that expected people to keep to their places and play their assigned parts on all social levels. Anything which encouraged people to neglect their roles or change their social positions was considered unhealthy for the commonwealth.

Understood in religious terms, the desire to get ahead, to make more money, to advance socially, was evidence of greed, a cousin of theft and oppression, proof of one's sinful nature. God did not like social climbers or those whose actions undermined the social hierarchy.

In Elizabeth's reign the old commonwealth ideal began to break down, replaced by a much greater tolerance of individual advancement. One driving force of this change was the emergence of new opportunities that had no place within the fixed boundaries of traditional social relationships. All sorts of new manufacturing ventures were encouraged and launched in Elizabeth's reign. Some were for strategic goods, such as gunpowder, armor, and bronze. Many others sought to make at home luxuries previously made abroad. Felt hats, playing cards, pins, leather goods, white rag paper, starch, soap, all sorts of fine cloth, and many other items became the object of "projects" that sought to displace imports. Along the way these industries, and others already established, used more and more raw material produced in England, providing more opportunities. The growing of woad for dying cloth, for instance, was a booming business in the second half of the sixteenth century.

All these new industries helped provide work for England's plentiful, cheap labor, but they were risky, and every home manufacture that found a market decreased the Crown's revenue from import duties. In order to insure manufacturers against risk, and to replace some of the lost customs revenue, Elizabeth's government began issuing patents of monopoly in 1560. In their pure form they protected new manufacturing processes from theft by competitors, but they quickly turned into a tool for lining the pockets of unscrupulous businessmen and courtiers. By the 1590s there was a national outcry against the monopolies. Parliaments took up the issue and tried to curb their use, so Elizabeth revoked some of them, on things like vinegar, salt, brushes, bottles, and fish oil. James revoked all of them in 1603, unless they were held by companies and corporations. His proclamation protected trading monopolies like the Levant Company and the East India Company, but it also prompted the creation of new groups like the Starchmakers' Company and the Pinmakers' Company. Since the companies were generally nothing more than associations of former monopolists, abuses of the system did not stop.

The fact that the government was so willing to meddle in the economy with patents, statutes, monopolies, licenses, and other tools also meant that it could be invoked to hinder the growth of new industries and competition. Frequently men and industries of influence used their power to get new manufactures banned or heavy taxes imposed on their competitors. The makers of woolen caps, for instance, got a law made that required everyone to wear a woolen cap on Sunday, rather than the fashionable felt hats. Starch-makers, whose product went to stiffen the ruffs worn by all classes, were frequently the victims of changing policies and social necessities. Their trade might be banned or curtailed by puritanical zeal against fancy clothes or by concern about the amount of grain consumed by starch making in times of dearth.

All this economic activity provoked a growing concern over the proper use of money. Just as starch-manufacturers were condemned for using grain for fashion rather than for food, many believed that money, unlike food, was static and could be hoarded at the expense of others. It was sterile and could not reproduce itself, so lending it at interest was a form of theft. This had been the official view of lending with the intent of making for a guaranteed rate of return – usury – throughout the Middle Ages. In Elizabeth's time, however, people began to think about money differently, and by the end of James I's reign the science of economics was in its first generation.

In 1571 Parliament had discussed liberalizing the law against usury, concluding instead that it was not fine-tuned enough to be effective. It therefore created two offenses: "petty usury," when the loan bore an interest rate of 10 percent or less, and "usury," when it bore a rate of more than 10 percent. Without intending to, Parliament had created a ceiling for interest rates that also acted as a floor, so that 10 percent (a very low return in 1571) came to be the standard rate. Nonetheless, usury remained a technically illegal activity, because it was forbidden by the law of God. When Christ said "Lend freely expecting nothing in return," he meant it. Besides, was not the love of money the root of all evil? The specific evil encouraged by usury was social decay, as the truly needy and the naïve sons of men of wealth were trapped by the usurers and sucked dry. Good Christians and proper citizens did not commit usury.

It was a position well understood by William Shakespeare, whose Shylock embodies popular myths about Jews and usurers. Jews were, for his contemporaries, stereotypical usurers, but his portrayal of Shylock conforms to a much larger understanding of how the illegal market in loans actually worked. (In fact, Shakespeare clearly understood the legal nuances of lending, since Shylock's bargain with his victim turns on a penal bond, not a usurious transaction, as the offended Jew makes clear when he says "he was wont to call me usurer; let him look to his bond." Mistress Overdone in *Measure for Measure* was a genuine usurer, practicing fraud to obtain illegal interest from Master Rash: "he's in for a commodity of brown paper and old ginger, ninescore and seventeen pounds; of which he made five marks, ready money.") Although Shakespeare espoused a very conservative position, portraying the usurer in very traditional, very negative terms, he ought to have known better, since his own father practiced usury (or at least he was informed against for practicing it), and William himself, as a businessman, certainly participated in the lucrative money market. Men of his generation in London were often of two minds about moneylending. They condemned it with their lips, but in their hearts they knew it was proper and necessary to borrow and lend at interest if the borrower and the lender mutually agreed to the terms, and the loan produced a profit for both parties. So they did it, but in a highly charged moral atmosphere.

Beginning with the 1604 session, Parliament debated changing the usury laws, essentially in order to lower interest rates. The economic crises had depressed money markets, so that the Dutch were lending at 8 percent while the English were still allowed 10 percent.

This sparked a heated debate in commercial and religious circles. Conservatives wanted the penalties stiffened and saw lending at interest as a primary cause of their woes, a sin which threatened to impoverish living people and damn the souls of dead lenders. The progressives wanted credit loosened for the good of the nation, finding nothing in the Bible that strictly prohibited friendly loans.

Those who wished to redefine usury as a sin only when committed with guilty intent carried the day, thanks to powerful theological forces that allied themselves with the argument that the intent of the lender was known only to God. Traditionally, God had condemned the act without regard to the intent, but casuists across Europe, faced with the confusion brought about by the Reformation and the obvious need to set God's law higher than men's laws when religious conviction conflicted with state religion, argued for the primacy of conscience. In England Puritans, separatists, and Catholics all made a scruple of their conscience in dealing with the officially imposed state Church. Defenders of lending at interest drew on the same arguments to insist that, properly used, capital could be borrowed and interest paid without spiritual consequences. As Walter Howse put it in 1605, a creditor may lend, binding the borrower with bills and bonds, so long as the creditor adds "a proviso written in the book of his conscience" that he will not invoke the penalties if the lender defaults through no fault of his own. If, however, the debtor does not meet the terms of the contract for other reasons, God requires the creditor to enforce the law against him. For Howse the ultimate test was the lender's intent. If he lent with a modest desire for gain, never charged excessive interest, bore the conditions of the borrower in mind, took no interest unless it was compatible with the common good, and thanked God for his blessings, he could lend as he wished.[3] When the 1571 usury statute was replaced in 1624, Parliament saw fit to remove all mention of God from the law, specifying that although the state could regulate usury, only the law of God in conscience could determine the propriety of a loan.

This test of intention permitted good Christians to be good capitalists, which in turn blessed the social climbing of men like William Shakespeare. Certain in their own minds that they were doing right, and that God's blessing was moving them up the social ladder, they were sure that faith and capitalism were compatible.

This argument for the importance of conscience as an arbiter of human behavior was expressed in other areas by Shakespeare's generation. The younger generation of Elizabethans had come of age with a heightened sense of personal choice. The religious change, the social shifts, the changing economy, all confirmed the possibilities from which they might choose. But this was not entirely a pretty picture. One had to make the right choices. God still ran the world, demanding obedience. But obedience to which theology? Which Church? Which economic order? Which master? Where could a person turn for intellectual certainty in a world of choice and confusion? It is hardly surprising that this generation produced both creative theologians and great skeptics.

All educated English people of the period were educated as both Christians and Aristotelians, believing in the primacy of Scripture and in some version of natural law.

The ways in which they combined these beliefs led to powerful justifications of conflicting versions of Truth. This education led many to garden-variety, traditional views of social hierarchy and religious duty of the kind seen in the anti-usury arguments, and to the belief in the divine right of kings so important to James I. Others went in more novel directions. The place that produced the most interesting new theories was Cambridge University. There, men like Lawrence Chaderton, William Perkins, and William Ames, the leading minds of the Puritan movement, took the logical tools of Peter Ramus, a French Protestant critic of Aristotle, and developed an applied theology. Identifiable by its use of "cases of conscience," this theology sought to teach the believer how to make rational choices in line with God's will. Their method depended upon the identification of true axioms, deduced, in the first instance, from Scripture, in accordance with which singular problems could be resolved. From the axioms, the schematics of salvation could be elaborated in a system known as "technometria," which showed the relationship of all things to God's intent.

Needless to say, the followers of Ramus, asserting the truth of their system, were often at odds with those following other systems for discovery of universal truths. Their arguments, and the doubt introduced by the religious debate in general, blended to produce another French movement with implications for England: skepticism.

Of course, there was nothing new about skepticism. It was an ancient philosophy, known to most Elizabethans from the works of Sextus Empiricus, published in Latin in 1569. Taken up by, among others, Erasmus of Rotterdam to challenge Luther's belief in free will, it was popularized by Michel de Montaigne and other French thinkers in the late sixteenth century. They used it to challenge claims of knowledge in philosophy, science, and, most important, theology, by focusing on the unreliability of human reason as a tool to discover Truth. Skeptical philosophy was used by enemies of Protestantism to undermine any certainty about the meaning of the Bible or one's sense of election. But it was a two-edged sword. To argue, as Pierre Charron did in the 1590s, that there is no adequate evidence that either atheism or Protestantism is more true than Catholicism, is not a strong defense of any religion. At best it led to resigned fideism.

Martin Luther had replied to Erasmus's skepticism by pointing out that the Holy Spirit is not a skeptic, but the damage was done, and agnosticism looked attractive. Students in English universities were aware of skepticism, with its devastating critique of human reason as a tool in religious disputes. One mainstream Anglican theological response was to argue that though certainty beyond doubt is impossible, one can accept things which are highly probable. Another was to attempt, as Francis Bacon did, to find new grounds for certainty. If no preconceived or received notion about the natural world could be proved correct, a new epistemology was needed. Arguing for naturalistic and materialist bases for the acquisition of knowledge, he published, in 1605, his *Advancement of Learning*. In 1620 it was followed by his formal treatise on method, *The New Organon*. With a nod to Aristotle's *Organon*, Bacon built his epistemology on Aristotelian induction, with its insistence on reason from observation and on experimental verification of sense-data. Missing from the system was God. Bacon argued that atheism is more conducive to human progress than faith; and, more importantly, he relegated belief to the realm of personal opinion. What faith is was a mystery that could not be resolved by science, since the experience of faith could not be verified experiment-ally. This meant that because all faiths are essentially matters of personal testimony, none of them can be demonstrably more true than the others. Only conscience can tell you what to believe; no human agency can have sure knowledge about God and faith.

The learned debate about the certainty of knowledge and the reality of faith echoes in, and is echoed by, Hamlet's madness. Inhabiting a world where perception is everything and nothing is sure, Hamlet's madness is or is not real. For Shakespeare and his contemporaries, this was the ultimate question. How were people to live in a world full of competing, often contradictory truths?

And that is the irony of the English Renaissance. For most people alive at the time it had its glorious moments, but it was also a time of great discomfort. Religious tension was a fact of daily life. Theological disagreements turned constantly into political and social tensions, splitting families and communities. Disagreements about economic behavior and the genuine misery of adaptation to a changing economic world did the same thing. Religious disagreement and economic disputes became intertwined, since they are in practice all part of the same moral universe. Politically England was generally stable, though contemporaries noticed food riots and Catholic plots much more than historians do, but it was a very uncertain time on the world stage. War was a constant element of the later Elizabethan world, and, though James I brought peace, he did not bring concord. He brought union to two kingdoms that neither liked nor trusted one another, prompting questions about political identity and allegiance that added one more brick to the load of confusion already toted by Elizabethans. All this made attempts to puzzle out the organization of reality very important to the age in which even those most certain about God's plans were uncertain about today's necessities.

Confusion made Shakespeare's age one of the most culturally productive in English history. Crisis and confusion gave point to the nation's dialogue with itself about what it was and how it ought to live.

When William Shakespeare died in 1616, he was part of a new English culture. Indeed, he became so much a part of the bedrock of that culture that he is an inextricable element of the curriculum in English-speaking schools. But when he retired to Stratford to live off his revenues as a landed gentleman, he could not have known the fame in store for him. His experience was of a world that was still trying its wings, attempting to make sense of demographic change, economic difficulty, moral confusion, theological gridlock, political tension, and social displacement. When a consensus was reached, much later, his words came to embody the new world view that emerged from that confusion.

NOTES

1 James H. Forse, *Art Imitates Business: Commercial and Political Influences in Elizabethan Theatre* (Bowling Green, Oh: Bowling Green State University Popular Press, 1993), pp. 34–8.

2 R. H. Tawney and Eileen Power, *Tudor Economic Documents* (London: Longmans, 1963), vol. 2, pp. 339–42.

3 Norman Jones, *God and the Moneylenders: Usury and Law in Early Modern England* (Oxford: Blackwell, 1989), 156.

4

Shakespeare's London

Ian W. Archer

'Thou art the goodliest of thy neighbors, but the prowdest; the welthiest, but the most wanton. Thou hast all things in thee to make thee fairest, and all things in thee to make thee foulest; for thou art attir'de like a Bride, drawing all that looke upon thee, to be in love with thee, but there is much harlot in thine eyes.' These words, addressed to the city of London by the pamphleteer and playwright Thomas Dekker, encapsulate the ambivalence of attitudes to the nation's capital in the later sixteenth and early seventeenth centuries. It was the Bible which provided its citizens with the antithetical images of the city as the 'holy city, new Jerusalem' and 'Babylon the Great, the mother of harlots and abominations of the earth'. London was 'the very ark of the presence of God, above all other places of this land'; but it was also one of those 'Greater Cities' which 'for theyr contempte . . . hathe more plentifull tast of hys plags before other places'. From the open-air pulpit at St Paul's Cross, 'the chiefest watch-tower' and 'the very stage of this land', the preachers explored the relationship between God and the Londoners, who, although extraordinarily blessed with the benefits of the true religion, nevertheless provoked the providential chastisings of the Lord by their addiction to covetousness and prodigality.[1] The preachers and moralists were articulating a truth that London's remarkable growth was achieved at considerable social and moral cost. What this chapter will do is to explore the nature of London's growth, the anxieties it generated, the social tensions it brought in its wake, and the degree to which those tensions and anxieties were resolved.

Growth

The most salient feature of London's history during Shakespeare's lifetime was its extraordinary growth in population from about 80,000 in 1564 when he was born to over 200,000 when he died in 1616. This growth had commenced in the 1520s, and was fuelled by an extraordinary surge of immigrants to the capital from all parts of the kingdom. London could not sustain its population without regular injections of new blood from the provinces, because high levels of infant and child mortality cancelled out the effects of relatively high fertility. It has been estimated that London required about 6,000 immigrants each year to sustain the levels of growth that it experienced during the later sixteenth century. Probably only about 20 per cent of the adult inhabitants of London had been born there.

What brought these immigrants to the capital? It was not, as the older accounts tell us, a movement of an oppressed peasantry expropriated from the land by a greedy gentry class, but was rather sustained by a migration of offspring of moderately prosperous rural folk who came to the capital to learn a trade. Between 4,000 and 5,000 young men (usually in their late teens or early twenties) arrived in London each year around 1600 to begin apprenticeships, undertaking to train under the supervision of a master for a minimum of seven years. Doubtless some were encouraged by the myth of metropolitan opportunity, for it was at this time that the story of Dick Whittington, the boy of humble parentage catapulted to the position of lord mayor of London, achieved popularity. There were indeed London aldermen who rose from the ranks of the yeomanry or provincial tradesmen to dizzying fortunes. Thus William Craven (*c.*1545–1618), second son of a Yorkshire yeoman, rose to run one of the largest domestic cloth-dealing businesses in the capital, serving as lord mayor in 1610–11, living in a splendidly decorated house of sixty-two rooms in Leadenhall Street, and leaving a personal fortune at his death conservatively estimated at £125,000. Craven's success was probably due to his partnership with his former master and to an advantageous marriage to the daughter of a wealthy merchant-adventurer. Whatever their ambitions, many other apprentices left the capital after only a few years' training, doubtless to ply their trades in the provinces. This fact enhances London's importance in the cultural life of the nation. The 'revolving door' of London migration meant that probably one in eight people in England had experience of living in London at some point in their lives.

London's prominence derived from two features of its urban role: that it was a port and that it was a capital. As a port, London developed as a satellite of the continental entrepôt of Antwerp, exchanging broadcloths and kerseys for the luxury goods which were widely available there, and sucking up much of the trade of the provincial outports. As a spokesman for the provincial ports put it in 1604, 'merchants of London have all trades . . . [they] go around the world'.[2] The expansion in the export of cloth from London in the early sixteenth century had been a major factor in the capital's growth, with up to 40 per cent of the work-force enjoying membership in one of the cloth-related guilds. Although the growth in cloth exports faltered in the later sixteenth century with the increasing difficulties of the Antwerp mart, London entered a new phase of 'import-led' growth in trade. By Shakespeare's death the major growth points were the Levant, whence England drew silk, currants, cotton, wool and mixed fabrics, and the East Indies, where, in spite of ferocious Dutch competition, Londoners drove an increasingly profitable trade in silks and spices. Across the Atlantic other Londoners, often of a godly persuasion in religion, were about to embark on the development of the tobacco trade. The expansion of trade encouraged industrial development. In the ten years after 1607 no less than 15,000 tons of shipping was built in the East India Company dockyards at Blackwall and Deptford, representing a capital investment of £100,000. New industries such as sugar refining and silk weaving were among the spin-offs of the expansion in overseas trade.

As a capital, London was a beneficiary of Tudor centralization and the cultural shifts which turned it into a theatre of aristocratic display. The presence of the royal household in the vicinity of the capital was a factor of such importance in sustaining demand that, whenever Elizabeth was absent from Westminster, we are told, 'the poor people forthwith complain of penury and want, of a hard and miserable world'.[3] The royal court also attracted hordes of patronage-seekers, and their increasing settlement in the western suburbs encouraged the development of a London season. Many preferred residence in the capital to the countryside, holding that it was one of the advantages of metropolitan life that one could choose one's own dinner guests, 'men of more civilitie, wisdome and worth, then your rude Countrey Gentlemen or rusticall Neighboures'.[4] By the 1610s the country's social élite were preferring to buy rather than rent houses in the capital, reflecting the development of an aristocratic culture that was civic in nature. Another key development was the increasing recourse to the law courts, a function both of the increase in commercial transactions and of the success of the Tudors in persuading their subjects to wage law rather than war. Whereas in 1560 there were about 5,000 cases at an advanced stage in the central common law courts of King's Bench and Common Pleas, by the beginning of the reign of James I the figure was over 23,000. The effect of this on levels of consumer demand in the capital can be judged by the fact that during term time when the courts were sitting the city consumed 13 per cent more grain than during the vacation. When Bess of Hardwick, countess of Shrewsbury, arrived in London on legal business in 1519–20 for a stay of seven months, her retinue numbered forty. It was to nourish this kind of aristocratic demand that the imports of luxury goods like wines and silks swelled.

Anxiety

For many, the commercial wealth of London, a 'store house of all terrestrial blessings under the sun', was an object both of wonderment and celebration. The historian William Camden marvelled at the shipping in the River Thames, 'a very wood of trees disbranched to make glades and let in light, so shaded it is with masts and sails'. Edmund Howes, the continuator of John Stow, described the capital as a 'city filled more abundantly with all sorts of silks, fine linens, oils, wines, and spices, perfection of arts, and all costly ornaments and curious workmanship, than any other province, so as London well deserves to bear the name of the choicest storehouse in the world'. Even foreign visitors were impressed by the shops in Cheapside. The pageants which accompanied the lord mayor's inauguration included increasingly frank acknowledgements of the contribution of the élite to commercial prosperity. In 1614, for example, Anthony Munday's pageant *The Triumphs of Old Drapery* included a representation of English cities whose 'best advantage ever ensued by making of woollen cloths for the continuance of England's drapery'.[5]

But in other quarters and other contexts the city's prosperity occasioned much greater anxiety. The acquisitive drive on which its wealth rested sat uneasily with the dictates of Christian morality. Preachers did not pull their punches in fulminating against the covetousness identified by silver-tongued Henry Smith, lecturer at St Clement Dane's, as the Londoners' sin. Smith could hardly have been more pointed when he warned that 'the riches and lands of aldermen and merchants and others in London do not last so long nor endure so well as the riches and lands of others in the country', and found the explanation in the providential chastising of the élite for their usury. To the claims that usurers 'do good service in the city, are very profitable members, and might be ill spared', William Fisher replied that 'if you take him [a usurer] and look in his mouth, you shall see his teeth all gore blood with eating and devouring of his needy debtors'.[6] There was, then, something schizophrenic about the attitudes of contemporaries to the wealth of the London business élite. Thomas Middleton, author of several city pageants which celebrated the benefits of the city's wealth, also wrote comedies which ruthlessly exposed the money-grubbing charlatans operating within the capital. The city's indefatigable chronicler John Stow admired the charitable endeavours of earlier generations of London merchants, but felt uneasy about the social mobility released by the production of wealth, recording with grim satisfaction the fate of alderman Sir John Champeneys, whose presumption in building a brick tower in his house to overlook his neighbours was punished with blindness, and commenting of Thomas Cromwell's arbitrary seizure of surrounding properties to extend his garden that 'the suddaine rising of some men causeth them to forget themselves'.[7]

Other anxieties focused on the challenge to conventional social ordering entailed by the culture of consumption. A stream of largely ineffective proclamations instructed the gentry to return to their rural estates and maintain hospitality in the interests of neighbourliness and good order. As James I put it in a speech of 1616, 'as every fish lives in his own place, some in the fresh, some in the salt, some in the mud: so let everyone live in his own place, some at Court, some in the Citie, some in the Countrey'.[8] It was not only the stability of the countryside that was undermined, however, for the emulative habits of consumption fostered by the metropolitan environment threatened to erode conventional social boundaries of age and gender. 'Of late tyme servauntes and apprenteces within this cytty ar by indulgence and lack of convenient severytie growne to grete disorder in excess of Apparrell and fasshions therof uncomly for ther caulinges,' declared the mayor's proclamation of 1572, which formed the basis for later regulative drives. Foreigners like Frederick of Württemberg, visiting London at the turn of the century, were impressed by the 'exceedingly fine clothes' of London women of relatively meagre means, for 'they give all their attention to their ruffs and stuffs to such an extent indeed that . . . many a one does not hesitate to wear velvet in the streets, which is common with them, whilst perhaps at home they have not a piece of dry bread'.[9] As Karen Newman has observed, consumption was seen as a predominantly female activity, James I attributing the flocking of the gentry to London to the pressure of their wives, 'because the new fashion is to be had nowhere but in London'. The desire for goods was linked in the minds of the moralists with the desire for sex, and it was often through promises of rich clothing that brothel-keepers lured women into prostitution: 'yf thou wille be ruled by me I will get thee a cote and thou shalte not lacke any thing that I can do thee', 'it will be as good as a new petiecote that the gentlemen wolde give her', 'she shold have a ryoll for her labor and she shold be mayteyned fynely like a gentlewoman'.[10]

London confused moral categories and blurred social boundaries, but it also threatened to destabilize the culture of deference on which political stability was supposedly based. As the proclamation of 1580 which attempted to restrain building in the capital bluntly put it, 'such multitudes could hardly be governed by ordinary justice to serve God and obey her Majesty'.[11] The metropolitan environment with its plethora of pulpits, its exposure to the printed word, its high levels of literacy and its highly developed entertainment industry fostered a vibrant political culture. The worlds of the city and the court were so intertwined that the Crown could not easily control the outflow of information. Paul's Walk and the Royal Exchange, 'the ear's brothel', buzzed with political gossip, which fed off the printed word, and among the commons of the city, habits of political comment and speculation formed, which could be threatening to the wielders of power. Sir Anthony Benn, recorder of the city, observed that 'as into the ark of the highest mysteries every Tinker will in these days be peeping, and not satisfied will also be prating, so there are in government and state affairs certain Eavesdroppers and wise fellows that will not only let and hinder this chariot . . . but other there are that will be ever reforming the reins'.[12] His remarks are confirmed by the popular hostility in the capital to Elizabeth's projected marriage to the duke of Anjou in 1579, the mobilization of a popular following for the earl of Essex by the preachers in the later 1590s, and the littering of the streets with libels against unpopular ministers like Robert Cecil.

In the eyes of moralists London became the cynosure of the sins of the nation. 'Thou dost overflow with sin,' fulminated Thomas White from the open-air pulpit of St Paul's Cross in 1578. 'Even as a Cundite spouteth out water, and the sea foameth with myre and gravell: so thou dost discover thine owne shame. Prodigalitie, and pride, deceit and fraud, and all the rest, it was first begun in thee. Thou hast infected both Court and Countrey.'[13]

Tensions

The growth of the capital brought a plethora of social problems in its wake. London was perhaps not as sharply polarized as some other pre-industrial cities. A high proportion (possibly as high as 75 per cent) of its adult male householders enjoyed citizenship through their membership in one of the guilds (or livery companies). Most were self-employed, owning small workshops or retail outlets with no more than two apprentices and perhaps a journeyman. James Dalton, author of the *Apology of the City of London*, which was appended to John Stow's survey, claimed that 'they of middle place' were the most numerous in sixteenth-century London.[14] However, conditions in the poorer suburbs where most of the population growth was located were much less favourable. Among the most miserable were those in St Botolph's, Aldgate, an eastern extramural parish. Its population had grown from probably 2,500 in 1550 to 5,500 by 1600. Stow is eloquent on the disfiguring of the urban fabric by the phenomenon of suburban growth: Hog Lane, which ran along the eastern boundary of St Botolph's, had within his lifetime been flanked by pleasant fields in which the citizens could recreate themselves, but within a few years it had been made 'a continuall building throughout of garden houses, and small cottages; and the fields on either side be turned into garden plottes, teynter yards, bowling allyes, and such like'. It was in areas of this kind that the city's reserve army of casual labour mustered. In 1618 the vestry of St Botolph's reported that the parish's inhabitants consisted of many poor, 'most having nether trades nor meanes to live on but by their handy labour, as porters, carmen, waterbearers, chimney sweepers, servants in silk mylls, brewers' servants, the rest carpenters, bricklaiers, plaisterers, coopers, smiths, butchers, chandlers, keepers of sylk mills, priests, schoolmasters, vitulers, and brokers'.[15] This was a population which was extremely vulnerable to downswings in the economy or dearth conditions. In 1595 some 44 per cent of the householders in St Botolph's were reported to be in need of poor relief. The suburbs were also prone to the depredations of plague. Whereas the wealthier inhabitants of the inner city, whether because of precautions against the disease or flight from the capital, were less prone to plague as the period progressed, the poorer parishes which ringed the city bore the brunt of a disease which sent mortality levels in St Botolph's spiralling to over six times their normal level in 1593. As Thomas Dekker tells us of the plague of 1603, death was like a 'Spanish leaguer or rather like a stalking Tamberlain', who pitched his tents 'in the sinfully polluted suburbs'.[16]

Contemporaries saw the connection between poverty and crime. William Fleetwood, recorder of the city (its chief legal officer), complained in 1582 that 'here are fortie brables and pickeries done abowt this towne more in any one daye than when I first came to serve was done in a moneth. The reason is these multitude of buildings being stuffed with poore, needie and of the worst sort of people.' The problems were most serious in those suburban districts often outside the jurisdiction of the city fathers. 'What are thy suburbs but licensed stews?', Nashe asked the embarrassed aldermen, and his judgement is confirmed by the concentration of bawdy-houses in St John Street, Clerkenwell, Whitechapel and Shoreditch. It was also in these areas that the problems of vagrancy were most acute: nearly one-quarter of the vagrants and night-walkers arrested in Jacobean London were picked up in the parish of St Sepulchre without Newgate in the north-western suburbs. The anxieties of the magistrates were often exaggerated, but they had reason to be worried by some of the distinctive features of their problems. The scale of individual thefts was greater than in the provinces, and cash rather than goods was more likely to be the thief's target, reflecting the higher levels of wealth and commercialization in the London economy. Although much crime remained opportunistic, it was sometimes more organized. Criminals were able to draw on a network of safe houses and receivers. In July 1585 Fleetwood was able to name forty-four 'maisterless men and cutpurses whose practice is to rob gentlemen's chambers and artificers' shops in and about London' and eighteen notorious 'harbouring houses for maisterless men'. Gangs, admittedly often rather ephemeral, organized horse stealing, highway robbery and some of the more spectacular burglaries. Prostitution was co-ordinated by pimps enjoying connections with numerous bawdy-houses, men like Melcher Pelse 'who is every day upon the Exchange and brings strangers to lewd women'.[17]

Fleetwood's correspondence testifies to the vigour with which city magistrates approached the task of disciplining criminals. Although the recorder complained regularly about the traffic in reprieves of criminals centring on the royal court ('when the court is furthest from London then is the best justice done in England'), the near-monthly sessions of gaol delivery offered regular spectacles of exemplary punishment. 'There is condemned at one sessions 30, 40, 50, yea sometymes 60 parsons', remarked William Smith in 1588, 'of which parsons so condemned there is executed in one day 20 or 30 & I have known 36 at a tyme to suffer, and within a moneth after peradventure as many more.'[18] Petty delinquents, fornicators and prostitutes were likely to find themselves hauled up before the governors of Bridewell Hospital, whose discretionary jurisdiction gave them the power to sentence offenders to whipping or hard labour. Moreover, the harsh conditions at the turn of the century resulted in a series of initiatives whereby the magistrates set a sterner face against the misdemeanours of the poor. Serious rioting in 1595 led to the appointment of two provost marshals who patrolled the streets accompanied by mounted attendants, rounded up petty criminals, and mobilized to 'prevent any distemperature of youth'.[19] Several parish vestries in the suburbs appointed new officials, 'surveyors of inmates', whose job it was to check up on newcomers and remove suspicious characters from the parish. The vagrancy legislation of 1598 devolved to parish officials the power to whip vagrants, and the freshly painted whipping posts which sprang up all over the city suggest that it was a power they eagerly embraced.

But it would be naïve to suggest that London was simply divided between rich and poor. As we have seen, many of the anxieties of the moralists centred on the position of women and the young, categories which cut across the lines of wealth division. The position of both women and the young in early modern London was at odds with elements of the prevailing patriarchal ideology, and the inevitable result was a flurry of regulative concern. London was remarkable for the extraordinary number of young males in its population, apprentices accounting for at least 10 per cent of London's population in the mid-sixteenth century. That such a high proportion of the population should have been subject to the kind of constraints which apprenticeship placed upon accumulation, sexual expression and the free use of leisure time was a major source of friction in metropolitan society. The moral entrepreneurs continually stressed that their ideals were in tension with the youthful milieu. The young had a conception of work that was task- rather than time-orientated, and their leisure preferences were at odds with the discipline articulated by the authorities. Another source of friction between the young and the world of adult authority lay in the stringent limitations placed on their sexual activity. Moralists were intensely concerned that fornication was regarded as 'but a trick of youth';[20] the sexual energies of the young found an outlet in sex between servants and in the recourse that apprentices seem to have had to brothels.

Women probably enjoyed more independence in the capital because of the nature of their work: participating at the front of the shop, running an alehouse, buying provisions in the market. But certain demographic peculiarities of the metropolitan scene help to account for the intensity of anxieties about women. High mortality in London meant that many households, no fewer than 16 per cent in Southwark in the 1620s, were headed by women. It also meant that remarriage in the capital was common; no fewer than 25 per cent of the marriages of London tradesmen were to widows, running counter to the recommendations of the moralists that the husband should always be older, and thereby giving women greater leverage within the household. Women engaged in litigation on their own account in the capital to a far greater extent than elsewhere in the kingdom. Their lack of confinement impressed foreign visitors, who commented on their serving in shops, drinking in taverns and engaging in unsupervised sports in the fields outside the city with members of the opposite sex. Through their own networks of sociability, women acquired an informal authority over their neighbours, gossip serving to define reputations and acting as a sanction on deviant behaviour. Although these sanctions were most often applied to women who had transgressed the boundaries of sexual propriety, they might also police male behaviour in so far as men who failed to maintain their authority over their wives were humiliated by being labelled as cuckolds. It is clear that this authority was exercised over relations within the household, and that women normally lacked a public voice. But, as Bernard Capp has remarked, 'women's respect for authority in the public sphere was by no means total or automatic'.[21] The popular Puritan preacher of the Blackfriars, William Gouge, was criticized by the women of his congregation for his very restrictive interpretation of their property rights within marriage. Still more remarkably, Edmund Grindal, as bishop of London, had his palace invaded by crowds of women when he attempted to discipline Nonconformist ministers in 1566.

Another source of tension within the metropolis was the presence of large numbers of gentry. In the course of one week in June 1584 Fleetwood reported three serious brawls between gentlemen and apprentices and a fray between two gentlemen. Although the violence of the gentry was gradually being subdued by new honour codes influenced by humanist and Protestant discourses stressing moderation, sobriety and self-restraint, elements of the traditional honour culture of lineage persisted, and the feuds of the gentry often spilled out on to the streets of the capital. The gentlemen of the Inns of Court represented a particularly disruptive force, their patronage of both the theatres and the brothels a thorn in the flesh of the city fathers. Their regular clashes with the apprentices indicate the status uncertainties endured by many apprentices in the superior trades, who had themselves been recruited from gentle backgrounds. Thus a gentleman sneered at an apprentice he encountered outside the Curtain Theatre in 1584: 'the apprentice was but a rascal, and some there were little better than rogues which took upon themselves the name of gentlemen, and . . . the prentices were but the scum of the world'.[22] The gentle origins of many apprentices (about one-third of those in the Grocers' Company were recruited from gentle backgrounds in the early seventeenth century) reminds us that the problem of youth was not simply another manifestation of the problem of the poor. The apprentices who gathered at the Bell Tavern in Distaff Lane and whose antics of banqueting, dicing and whoring so shocked the governors of Bridewell in 1576 were merchants' apprentices who had supported their debauchery by embezzling monies from their masters. For men from these backgrounds the restrictions of the apprentice indentures must have been all the more irksome.

Solidarities

For all the anxieties expressed by contemporaries, most recent commentators have been impressed by the fundamental orderliness of the capital. The force of disorder was defused both because Londoners tended to seek scapegoats for misfortunes in the alien population in their midst and because they personalized their animus by directing their criticism at individual magistrates rather than seeing themselves as the victims of a class conspiracy. There is no doubt that the threat of a repetition of Evil May Day of 1517, when apprentices had rioted against aliens, caused the magistrates serious anxieties in 1586–7 and again in 1592–3. It was the background of simmering anti-alien feeling which explains the intervention of the government censor, the Master of the Revels, Sir Edmund Tilney, in the performance of the *Sir Thomas More* play (which dramatized the events of Evil May Day and the grievances of the apprentices) in 1593: 'Leave out ye insurrection wholy wt ye Cause ther off.'[23] But anti-alien feeling served to earth more serious discontents, and it proved possible for the guilds to channel much of the hostility into legalistic channels, as alien craftsmen became the victims of litigation and campaigns in Parliament. There were more serious problems in 1595, when the traditional sanctions failed to defuse a series of food riots (in themselves extraordinary events in the capital) as apprentices rescued their imprisoned fellows, threatened the lord mayor personally, and rioted in the Tower liberty, a politically and militarily sensitive area. But the virulence of the rioters was directed at the unpopular lord mayor, Sir John Spencer, rather than at the élite as a whole: thus Spencer was compared unfavourably with the godly alderman and promoter of poor relief schemes, Sir Richard Martin. The tendency to personalize grievances and so to defuse them was fostered by the rotation of the key magisterial offices which saw a new mayor in office each year.

The government of the city was formally oligarchic. The twenty-six aldermen were responsible for routine administration, initiated legislation in the common council, and wielded considerable judicial authority. Controlling recruitment to their own ranks, they represented the city's wholesaling élite. But power was more widely diffused, because of the impossibility of implementing policies without the co-operation of subordinate groups. Thus parishes, wards and guilds offered opportunities for broader political participation. Holding office as a churchwarden, constable or guild master was not only a mark of status within the local community, but also gave the incumbent real power over others. Churchwardens administered the church stock, and made presentments of moral offenders to the church courts; constables were important in local policing; and guild masters maintained standards of craft production, regulated the supply of labour to the workshop, and controlled access to guild resources. All might be involved in the arbitration of local disputes and the distribution of poor relief. Membership of guilds and parishes fostered a sense of belonging through the services that they provided for participating groups. If we can rely at all on the statistics of Easter communion attendance drawn from early seventeenth-century Southwark or on levels of compliance with the broadly based parish rates, then the parochial framework in late Elizabethan and Jacobean London provided a point of contact for the majority of the inhabitants. Identity with guilds was perhaps rather more emphemeral, as they were often large, geographically dispersed associations with an already diverse occupational composition; but for an active core they remained vital institutions in representing craft interests, and for the majority they were a defining element of citizenship and the political and economic privileges that it entailed. These communities were of course subject to relationships of power which makes it difficult to know whether the impression of consensus of the 'official transcript' reflects the social realities; but the rhetoric of community was a powerful one, which could be manipulated by the lower orders in ways not always pleasing to their superiors.

The role of parishes and guilds in integrating Londoners underlines the fact that the city was not always the anonymous, alienating force it is sometimes made out to have been. Although apprenticeship was, as we have seen, an often fraught relationship, the care that parents took in finding masters, mobilizing their kin contacts in the capital, and their continued interest in their sons, intervening in cases of abuse, suggests that efforts were often made to ensure that the apprentice received proper training and appropriate sponsors in the city. Likewise, the young women who came to work in domestic service in the city were not entirely bereft of support networks. Over a third of the migrant women who sought marriage licences in early seventeenth-century London had kin in the capital, and a fifth resided with them. Others drew on the support of friends who had also migrated to the capital; most were able to make new friends among their fellow servants. The restrictions on leisure among servants were never so great as to prevent association between servants in different households. The aldermen and common council complained regularly and ineffectively of apprentices playing games like 'trap and cat' and football in the streets. Although London parishes had high levels of population turnover, with half the heads of household typically disappearing over a ten-year period, this was perfectly compatible with an intense sense of neighbourhood, where reputations were constantly being evaluated, and privacy was vulnerable. Life was lived very much in the street. Foreigners commented on apprentices standing in front of their masters' shops and accosting passers-by; defamation cases suggest that 'the doorstep was a crucial vantage point for the exchange of insult';[24] and most Londoners seem to have eaten in alehouses or inns or bought take-aways from cook-shops.

Charity played a crucial role in blunting the tensions produced by periods of difficulty like the 1590s or the 1620s. The haemorrhaging of charitable resources at the Reformation, with the dissolution of religious houses and fraternities, had alarmed the city fathers, who had successfully petitioned the Crown for the grant of former religious properties to support an integrated scheme of poor relief, which was established between 1547 and 1552. St Bartholomew's and St Thomas's catered to the sick, Bethlem to the insane, Christ's to the orphans, and Bridewell set the idle to work. Decayed householders were supported by a poor rate levied through the parishes. It was by no means an ideal system. It was more successful in dealing with the needs of the impotent poor (that is, the old, orphans and the very sick), much less so in dealing with the conjunctural poverty occasioned by severe winters, industrial crisis or harvest failure. Parishioners proved sluggish in increasing rates to meet the burgeoning numbers of poor. The decentralization of fund raising meant that resources were not concentrated on areas of most need. The hospitals (especially Bridewell) were under-funded; and there were disastrous errors of judgement, such as the mingling of children on industrial training schemes with delinquents in Bridewell Hospital. But the system gave the city's common councillors and vestrymen considerable discretionary power over the lives of the poorer inhabitants, which might be used to encourage compliance. It was also supplemented by a great outpouring of private charity. Over the Elizabethan decades the contribution of private charity to the support of the poor was rather more impressive than the static poor rates: from £2,218 per annum given in the 1570s, the money left in charity by Londoners in their wills increased to £5,853 per annum in the 1590s, compared with a poor rate which yielded only about £2,250 per annum until the doubling of the rates in the wake of the reorganization of 1598.

Ideological forces worked to reinforce loyalties to a greater degree than is often realized. Some historians of the English Reformation have suggested that Protestantism widened the divide between the élites and the commons by reinforcing economic divisions with cultural ones, as a logocentric and intellectually demanding religion alienated the majority by its attack on the traditional festive culture. But Protestantism had a much greater popular potential in the capital because of its saturation by preachers and its higher levels of literacy. Although few (and not even, it seems, Lord Treasurer Burghley, who had less excuse) internalized the new theology, most probably came to think of themselves as in some sense Protestant, if only because they knew

what they were against: the Pope and all his works. In 1586 the news of the arrest of
the Babington conspirators, who had plotted the death of the queen, was greeted in the
capital with an extraordinary civic communion. Sixty bonfires were set up between
Ludgate and Charing Cross, and neighbours joined in street parties, sometimes singing psalms together. So great was the harmony that 'manie a privat reconciliation was
procured by this mutuall meeting of neighbours'.[25] It was not always so easy to control
the anti-popery of the crowd. In 1622 Londoners fell violently upon the victims of a
disaster when the floor of a garret in the Blackfriars gave way under the weight of
Catholic worshippers, the so-called fatall vesper celebrated in sermons, engravings and
ballads as an example of the providential intervention of the Lord against his enemies.
The strength of providential understandings of the world among the populace reminds
us of ways in which the godly were able to tap powerful veins of popular sentiment.
When the lord mayor wrote to Burghley in 1582 after the death of spectators at a bearbaiting at Paris Garden as a scaffold collapsed, suggesting that this disaster 'giveth
great occasion to acknowledge the hande of God for suche abuse of the sabbath daie', he
was reflecting a mental framework which was probably shared by most of those over
whom he ruled. It was a value system invoked by Joan Alleyn, wife of the theatre
proprietor (and therefore prime target of the preachers' providential thunderings!)
Edward Alleyn, when, during the plague of 1593, she prayed 'unto the Lord to cease
his punishing us with his cross'.[26] As individuals sought to walk in the paths of
righteousness, these providential understandings encouraged self-discipline and
restraint, reinforcing the culture of order drummed home through repeated catechizing in parish churches and households.

All forms of community rely on some form of exclusion to maintain themselves.
Guilds sought to prevent non-freemen (at least one-third of the male householders)
from practising their trades; parishes tried to restrict immigration, and adopted
discriminatory residence qualifications for poor relief; and the Protestant culture
was defined by hostility to Catholics. Shakespeare's own career forcibly reminds us
that not everyone was an insider in Elizabethan and Jacobean London. Shakespeare was
never a member of a guild; he was associated with a trade which in the eyes of the
magistrates and moralists provoked God's wrath and was therefore confined to the
suburbs; he never held office in his parish in spite of his wealth; he does not seem to
have taken communion in Southwark; his religious sympathies (like his father's) may
well have been Catholic. Unlike his fellow dramatists Ben Jonson and Thomas
Middleton, he was never employed by the city to write pageants for the lord mayor's
inauguration; he never took contemporary London as a setting for his plays; nor did he
choose to produce plays of implausibly heroic apprentices so popular at the turn of the
century with certain sections of his audience. Echoes of contemporary London can of
course be found in his plays. Falstaff and his companions are examples of precisely the
kind of gentry disorder which challenged the authority of the aldermen. *The Taming of
the Shrew* gives expression to contemporary anxieties about the independent woman.
Measure for Measure includes an analysis of metropolitan corruption which would have
resonated powerfully in London, given the memories of the collapse of the last major

drive against prostitution in the later 1570s amidst charges that the Bridewell establishment was corrupt. Through the merchant Antonio, the gentleman Bassanio and the Jew Shylock, *The Merchant of Venice* offers a variety of perspectives on belonging to the city community. The crowds who mill around threateningly in *Coriolanus* give vent to sentiments of class division which were as relevant to the experience of sections of the audience as they were to classical Rome. But the genius of Shakespeare in the constantly shifting perspectives of his plays probably owes something to his very lack of rootedness in the metropolitan milieu.

NOTES

1 T. Dekker, *The Seven Deadly Sinnes of London* (London, 1606); T. Jackson, *The Converts Happiness* (London, 1609); J. Stockwood, *A Sermon Preached at Paules Crosse on Bartholomew Day* (London, 1578).

2 *Journals of the House of Commons, 1547–1628* (London: House of Commons, 1852), p. 987.

3 J. Norden, *Speculum Britanniae: The First Parte. An Historicall and Chorographicall Discription of Middlesex* (London, 1593), p. 47.

4 *Cyvile and Uncyvile Lyfe: A Discourse Very Profitable, Pleasant and Fit to be Read of all Nobilitie and Gentlemen* (London, 1579).

5 W. Camden, *Britannia* (1586), trans. Philelmon Holland (London, 1610), p. 421; J. Stow, *Abridgement of the Chronicles of England* (London, 1611); A. Munday, *Himatia-Poleos. The Triumphs of Old Drapery* (London, 1614).

6 H. Smith, *Sermons* (London, 1591); W. Fisher, *A Sermon Preached at Paules Crosse the Firste Sunday After New Yeeres Day Beeing the Thirde Day of Ianuary 1580* (London, 1580).

7 J. Stow, *A Survey of London*, ed. C. L. Kingsford, 2 vols (Oxford: Oxford University Press, 1908), vol. 1, pp. 133, 179.

8 C. H. McIlwain (ed.), *The Political Woks of James I* (New York: Russell and Russell, 1965), p. 344.

9 Corporation of London Records Office, Journal of Common Council, 20, fo. 13; W. B. Rye, *England as Seen by Foreigners in the Days of Elizabeth and James the First* (London: John Russell Smith, 1865), pp. 7–8; McIlwain (ed.), *Political Woks of James I*, pp. 343–4.

10 K. Newman, City Talk: Women and Commodification, in D. S. Kastan and P. Stallybrass (eds), *Staging the Renaissance: Reinterpretations of Elizabethan and Jacobean Drama* (London: Routledge, 1991), pp. 181–95; Bridewell Court Books, III, fos 19ᵛ 156ᵛ 194ᵛ (microfilm at Guildhall Library).

11 P. L. Hughes and J. F. Larkin (eds), *Tudor Royal Proclamations*, 3 vols (New Haven and London: Yale University Press, 1964–9), vol. 2, pp. 466–7.

12 Bedfordshire Record Office, L28/46, fos 44ᵛ-5.

13 T. White, *A Sermon Preached at Powles Crosse 3 Nov 1577* (London, 1578).

14 Stow, *Survey of London*, vol. 2, p. 208.

15 Ibid. vol. 1, p. 127; Bodleian Library, Rawlinson MS D796B, fo. 86.

16 T. Dekker, *The Wonderfull Yeare* (London, 1603).

17 T. Wright, *Queen Elizabeth and her Times*, 2 vols (1838), vol. 2, pp. 171, 248–50; T. Nashe, *Christs Teares Over Jerusalem* (London, 1593); Bridewell Court Books, III, fo. 22ᵛ.

18 Wright, *Queen Elizabeth and her Times*, vol. 2, pp. 21, 170, 243, 245, 247; British Library, Harleian MS 6363.

19 J. Stow, *The Annales or Generall Chronicle of England* (London, 1615), pp. 768–9.

20 A. Dent, *A Plaine Mans Path-Way to Heaven* (London, 1601), p. 63.

21 B. Capp, Separate Domains? Women and Authority in Early Modern England, in P. Griffiths, A. Fox, and S. Hindle (eds), *The Experience of Authority in Early Modern England* (Basingstoke: Macmillan, 1996), p. 139.

22 Wright, *Queen Elizabeth and Her Times*, vol. 2, pp. 227–9.

23 *Sir Thomas More: A Play by Anthony Munday and Others*, ed. V. Gabrieli and G. Melchiori (Manchester: Manchester University Press, 1990), p. 17.

24 L. Gowing, *Domestic Dangers: Women, Words, and Sex in Early Modern London* (Oxford: Oxford University Press, 1996), p. 98.

25 *Holinshed's Chronicles of England, Scotland and Ireland*, 6 vols (London: J. Johnson et al., 1808), vol. 4, p. 900.

26 Corporation of London Records Office, Remembrancia, I, no. 456; W. W. Greg (ed.), *Henslowe Papers* (London: A. H. Bullen, 1907), pp. 34–41.

BIBLIOGRAPHY

Archer, I. W., *The Pursuit of Stability: Social Relations in Elizabethan London*. Cambridge: Cambridge University Press, 1991.

Barron, C., Coleman, C. and Gobbi, C. (eds), The London journal of Alessandro Magno. *London Journal*, 9 (1983), pp. 136–52.

Barry, J. and Brooks, C. (eds), *The Middling Sort of People: Culture, Society and Politics in England, 1550–1800*. London: Macmillan, 1994.

Beier, A. L. and Finlay, R. (eds), *London 1500–1700: The Making of the Metropolis*. London: Longman, 1986.

Boulton, J. P., *Neighbourhood and Society: A London Suburb in the Seventeenth Century*. Cambridge: Cambridge University Press, 1987.

Brigden, S., *London and the Reformation*. Oxford: Oxford University Press, 1989.

Capp, B., *The World of John Taylor the Water Poet, 1578–1653*. Oxford: Oxford University Press, 1994.

Colvin, H. and Foister, S. (eds), *The Panorama of London Circa 1544 by Anthonis van den Wyngaerde*. London: London Topographical Society, 1996.

Fisher, F. J., *London and the English Economy, 1500–1700*. London: Hambledon Press, 1990.

Foster, F. F., *The Politics of Stability: A Portrait of the Rulers of Elizabethan London*. London: Royal Historical Society, 1976.

Gowing, L., *Domestic Dangers: Women, Words, and Sex in Early Modern London*. Oxford: Oxford University Press, 1996.

Griffiths, P., *Youth and Authority: Formative Experiences in England, 1560–1640*. Oxford: Oxford University Press, 1996.

Gurr, A., *Playgoing in Shakespeare's London*. Cambridge: Cambridge University Press, 1987.

Manley, L., *Literature and Culture in Early Modern London*. Cambridge: Cambridge University Press, 1995.

Manley, L. (ed.), *London in the Age of Shakespeare: An Anthology*. London: Croom Helm, 1986.

Newman, K., City talk: women and commodification, In D. S. Kastan and P. Stallybrass (eds), *Staging the Renaissance: Reinterpretations of Elizabethan and Jacobean Drama* (London: Routledge, 1991), pp. 181–95.

Paster, G. K., *The Idea of the City in the Age of Shakespeare*. Athens, Ga.: University of Georgia Press, 1985.

Pearl, V., Change and stability in seventeenth-century London, *London Journal*, 5 (1979), pp. 3–34.

Prockter, A. and Taylor, R., *The A to Z of Elizabethan London*. London: London Topographical Society, 1979.

Ramsay, G. D., *The City of London in International Politics at the Accession of Elizabeth Tudor*. Manchester: Manchester University Press, 1975.

Rappaport, S., *Worlds within Worlds: Structures of Life in Sixteenth-Century London*. Cambridge: Cambridge University Press, 1989.

Slack, P., *The Impact of Plague in Tudor and Stuart England*. London: Routledge, 1985.

Smith, D. L., Strier, R. and Bevington, D. (eds), *The Theatrical City: Culture, Theatre and Politics in London, 1576–1649*. Cambridge: Cambridge University Press, 1995.

Stow, J., *The Survey of London*, 2 vols. Oxford: Oxford University Press, 1908.

Unwin, G., *Industrial Organization in the Sixteenth and Seventeenth Centuries*. Oxford: Oxford University Press, 1904.

Walsham, A., 'The fatall vesper': providentialism and anti-popery in late Jacobean London, *Past and Present*, 144 (1995), pp. 36–87.

5

Religious Identities in Shakespeare's England

Peter Lake

I want to start with two quotes. The first describes, from a mid-Elizabethan perspective, the recent course of English religious history, the second the effects of that history on the religious condition of Elizabethan England.

> In one man's memory... we have had to our prince, a man, who abolished the pope's authority by his laws and yet in other points kept the faith of his fathers; we have had a child, who by his like laws abolished together with the papacy the whole ancient religion; we have had a woman who restored both again and sharply punished protestants; and lastly her majesty that now is, who by the like laws hath long since abolished both again and now severely punisheth catholics as the other did protestants; and all these strange differences within the compass of about thirty years.[1]

Moreover, our author might have added, there was no reason to suppose that the chaotic succession of (either religiously motivated or at least religiously charged) *coup* and counter *coup* that had started, if not with the fall of Wolsey, then certainly with the fall of Ann Boleyn, was over yet. The eccentric marital history and distinctive personal political style of Henry VIII had from the early 1530s established a potentially destabilizing link between religious division and the intermittently cutthroat factional and personal politics of the court. Since Henry's death the effects of that connection had been compounded by the existence of a series of reversionary interests of precisely the opposite religious complexion from that of the current occupant of the throne. And that was a source of tension and instability that had certainly not been removed by the accession of the still childless Elizabeth. After all, in the event of her death the obvious – even natural – heir to the throne was the Catholic Mary Stuart.

But, of course, all this chopping and changing had religious and cultural as well as political effects. On the one hand, it produced a level of *de facto* religious pluralism unprecedented in English history; on the other, it sparked off a process of ideological polarization between what became, as the century wore on, increasingly coherent and adversarily defined confessional identities. This combination of increasingly stringent and polarized ideological self-definition together with a proliferation of a very wide variety of religious styles and commitments could not help but be potentially explosive. Thus, by 1580, another contemporary commentator could inform the queen that "there are in this your majesty's realm four known religions, and the professors thereof, distinct both in name, spirit and doctrine, that is to say the catholics, the protestants, the puritans and the householders of love. Besides all other petty sects, newly born and yet grovelling on the ground.[2] Yet, as Conrad Russell, amongst others, has so forcibly reminded us, it remained axiomatic for the majority of contemporaries that unity in religion was a *sine qua non* for political and social order (as well as being an essential prerequisite for the continued favor towards any Christian commonwealth of a variously constructed but uniformly jealous God).[3]

How did contemporaries respond to the disturbing, yet incontrovertible, facts of religious change? How did they handle the contradictions between their own experience of change, cacophonous disagreement, and instability and their equally powerful commitments to unity and uniformity as both normal and normative states, without which no political society or social entity could long subsist? Well, clearly, depending on their initially contingent but increasingly structural relationships with events, different ideological factions, groups, and individuals told themselves and others different stories about where they were and how they got there, producing in the process most of the vocabulary, the categories of religious affiliation and classification – Puritan, Papist, Protestant, Catholic, Familist, Separatist, Conformist, Church Papist – that modern historians habitually use to analyze, describe, or evoke the religious scene of Elizabethan England.

Now, this is a point of some significance, since it would scarcely be an exaggeration to say that many of the most controversial questions which anyone wanting to dilate upon the religious condition of Shakespeare's England must address – when, if ever, did England become a Protestant nation? what was the relationship between Protestantism, Puritanism, and "the people"? is the fate of English Catholicism during this period best described in terms of continuity? – all turn on the definition and application of terms – Catholic, Protestant, Puritan, Papist, and Church Papist – many of which were and are deeply embedded in contemporary narratives and discourses about and from the period. But terms and categories generated by contemporaries, as part of the struggle to interpret and control, to their own advantage, their own necessarily partial and fractured experiences of the inherently political and polemical processes of religious identity formation and confessional and factional conflict, might seem to provide a somewhat shaky basis for the "objective" analyses of the modern historian.

Historians have long been aware of this. Thus, one of the more persistent objections to the use of the appellation "Puritan" as a term of art has always been that it was a contemporary term of abuse and therefore ill suited to the analytic purposes of the historian.[4] Of late we have been confronted with a rush of revisionist writing which has claimed to be especialy sensitive to the implications of modern analysis in terms and assumptions produced in and by the period itself. Indeed, it would not be too much to say that a central legitimating strand of recent "revisionist" reinterpretations of the Reformation has been the expunging of all such inherently Whiggish *ex post facto* terms and assumptions. Thus it has become something of an axiom amongst revisionist scholars that, in reacting against received narratives of the period, they are in fact reacting against an inherently teleological, and in fact intensely Protestant, vision of the English Reformation, the origins of which stretch back at least as far as John Foxe.[5]

But given the imbrication of our whole range of analytic terms, up to and including the master categories Protestant and Catholic, in the debates, the claims and counter-claims of the period under study, it may not be as easy to escape the compromising embrace of contemporary narratives and assumptions as revisionist scholars appear to think. We have, more or less, and with some definitional tweaking and creative word shuffling here and there, to make do with the range of terms that both the period itself and subsequent scholarly usage and tradition have bequeathed to us. But that, I want to argue, is not only inevitable, a necessary evil to be resisted and struggled against at all costs, but a positively good thing, which, exploited properly, can provide us with perhaps our most promising way into the concerns of contemporaries. The point here is, even as we use the terms themselves, to be as self-conscious as possible about their contemporary derivations, often convoluted polemical histories, and sometimes complex, and contradictory, meanings and connotations. Historians who do not do this seem doomed to slip quite unselfconsciously from one set of con-temporary assumptions and narrative tropes into another as, in their enthusiasm, in typical revisionist fashion, to turn received opinion almost symmetrically on its head, they run the risk of lurching, with Christopher Haigh, from, say, Jesuit to appellant versions of the course and fate of the Catholic mission, and from accounts of the progress of Protestantism tinged with Foxean triumphalism to others just as colored by an anxiety and pessimism typical of Puritan complaint literature and hot Prot-estant clerical navel gazing.

To further explain what I mean, I want to return to the two quotes with which I started, the authors of which were respectively William Allen and Robert Parsons, two of the leading English Catholic controversialists and ecclesiastical statesmen and Machiavels of the period. What difference does the identity of the two authors make to the evaluation of the passages quoted? On the face of it, not much. After all, Allen seems merely to be stating the obvious; there had indeed been (depending on how you count the various tergiversations of policy under Henry VIII)[6] at least four changes of religion in England over the preceding fifty or so years. As for Parsons, while his claims seem more extreme, they have in fact been, if anything, confirmed by recent research. By 1580 few would deny that there were significant divisions between forward or perfect Protestants or Puritans who wanted to crack on with the multiple processes of institutional, liturgical, and spiritual reform and renewal which they assumed had been unleashed by the recently reopened breach with Rome and other, more staidly conformist Protestants who were prepared to accept and defend, if not quite yet to celebrate, the English Church as the settlement of 1559 had established it.[7] Revisionist historians would be only too glad to accede to Parsons's claim that even as late as 1580 "Catholics" represented a major, perhaps even, in terms of numbers, the predominant body of religious opinion in an England that, as both modern revisionists and contemporary Puritan complaint literature agree, had been only partially or formally Protestantized.[8] And here the overall project of Parsons's book, which was to insist that if they wanted to be really Catholic, partially conforming persons of Catholic mind had to become full-scale recusants, adverted to a whole series of gradations of, and debates about, the nature and possible terms of existence of 'Catholicism' under a heretical regime. As for Parsons's insistence on the prevalence and free-standing status as a separate religion of the Family of Love, that, too, has been confirmed by the brilliant researches of Dr Marsh, who has established solid connections between the known areas of most intense Familist activity in rural East Anglia and the centre of the royal court itself, where in the very same year in which Parsons's book was published, a Puritan-inspired investigation had unearthed Familists amongst the yeomen of the guard.[9]

Yet the passage from Parsons was part of a larger polemical/political agenda that seriously affected the way in which he deployed his key terms. His claim that Protestants and Puritans represented different "religions" was of a piece with his emphasis on the Family of Love as a free-standing sectarian entity or religion, which claims spoke to his larger contention that under the impact of heretical rule, religious unity and uniformity had suffered a *de facto* collapse in Elizabethan England, a fact that the government implicitly recognized by the lenience of its treatment both of Puritan nonconformity and Familist heresy. Only Catholics, who were, on Parsons's account, the largest, oldest, and most benign of the contending religious groups, were made to pay a material and physical price for the singularity of their religious beliefs and practices. According to Parsons's argument, that was a situation that fitted neither the demands of natural equity nor those of political prudence or self-interest.

However, confronted with what was recognizably the same situation, perfect Protestants and Puritans produced an altogether different analysis. It was an analysis that used many of the same key terms as Parsons, but construed and applied them in very different ways. Thus, for hot Protestants the great religious divide was that which separated anti-Christian popery from true religion. Familism, too, featured in their analysis as a distinct religion. For them, Familism represented a particularly sinister form of sectarian heresy, which had nothing to do with the mainstream of Reformed orthodoxy which they espoused. Indeed, in doctrinal terms, Protestants argued that, what with its notions of free will and human perfectibility, Familism had far more in common with popery than with Protestantism. Between these two extremes of sectarian heresy and popery was to be found the mainstream of true orthodox, catholic Christianity to which the Church of Rome falsely laid claim, but which was, in fact, to be found in the international community of Reformed churches.

Thus stressing the unity of the English Church with its sister Reformed churches in the struggle for orthodoxy against sectarian heretical excess, Bishop John Jewel could refer quite unselfconsciously to the time when "we" burnt Servetus. "We" here referred not to the particular ecclesiastical and secular authorities in Geneva who dispatched the unfortunate heretic, but to the international Reformed community or church in whose name Jewel clearly thought Servetus had been rightly condemned.[10]

Within the Reformed mainstream thus defined, no matter how bitter their disagreements and how extreme their mutually condemnatory rhetoric might become, no Elizabethan Protestant would have accepted Parsons's claims that Protestants (in Parsons's terms, enthusiastically conforming members of the national Church) and Puritans constituted separate or different "religions." At the height of the Admonition Controversy (the great debate of the 1570s about the polity of the English Church), even as committed a defender of the ecclesiastical *status quo* as John Whitgift could accept, without question, that in terms of doctrine, there were no significant differences separating Puritans and Conformists. Their disagreements concerned the mere externals of church government and outward worship, which, for Whitgift, were in themselves indifferent – i.e., not subject to direct scriptural authority or prescription, and therefore free to be decided and regulated by the relevant human authorities, which, in Elizabethan England, was the Christian prince. On one level, of course, this meant that the Puritans' fault could be presented as all the more heinous. After all, they were disturbing the peace of the realm and defying the magistrate, all because of things which were none of them central to either the being or the purposes of a true church. But if this rendered Puritans peculiarly worthy of sharp reproof and punishment, it also meant that the grounds of their basic disagreement with the likes of Whitgift remained located safely under the sign of adiaphora.

The more moderate Puritans agreed with Whitgift that the ceremonies and institutions in question were indeed indifferent, but denied that, in their present form, it was fit or convenient that they should be enforced or even retained in the Church. Crudely, they were too reminiscent of popery, and thus likely to mislead the unwary into an unwarranted and potentially damning assumption that very little had changed in 1559. On the other hand, they were just as likely egregiously to offend the self-consciously godly, who were deathly afraid that not enough had yet been done to expel the remnants of popish superstition from the national Church. More radical Puritans and Presbyterians went further than this, arguing that both the ceremonies and the liturgy of the Church were subject to direct divine injunction and scriptural authority, and that they knew what God wanted done in these matters, and that the ecclesiastical authorities did not. However, even relative extremists like these did not altogether follow the logic of their own arguments and elevate issues of church government or ceremony to the status of saving necessities, things so crucial that they could provide grounds to unchurch the national Church. In short, in Parsons's terms, they refused to claim that their position constituted a separate "religion" from that adopted by the national Church. On the contrary, they too continued to insist on the doctrinal unity that bound them and even their most bitter Conformist opponents together as part of one international Reformed cause or religion. Indeed, they went on to deploy that claim in their own denunciations of the small groups of Separatists who argued that the corruptions and faults in the ceremonies and government of the national Church did indeed constitute reason sufficient to declare the Church of England a false Church and hence justified formal withdrawal or separation. In taking this step, Separatists claimed merely to be being true to principles and arguments espoused by advocates of Presbyterian reform, principles which the Presbyterians themselves were too weak-kneed to follow to their logical conclusions. In the mainstream, Puritan response to such Separatist claims, the doctrinal soundness of the national Church was regarded as something of a clinching argument. Again, the meta-struggle against Rome could also be mobilized to play down the seriousness of the divisions of opinion that separated Puritans from Conformists. Thus, in the face of what we have seen was a persistent popish harping on the internal divisions that plagued the Elizabethan Church, William Whitaker could tell William Rainolds that "our religion is not like yours, consisting in outward show of gestures, garments and behaviour; so that our external ornaments may be changed without any alteration or change in our doctrine."[11]

"Puritan" was first developed as a term of abuse by Catholic writers in the late 1560s. When it and various synonyms came to figure in Conformist discourse also as a term of abuse, centred on issues of external obedience to the properly constituted authority of the Christian prince in Church and State, most of those so labeled replied by repudiating the term itself. True Puritans, they argued, were those who separated themselves from their fellow Christians as somehow purer, more perfect, or godly than the rest of fallen humanity. If that was the case, then only the familists or perhaps the Separatists deserved the title "puritan." For, at least according to mainstream Puritans, both groups did indeed think of themselves as ethically or spiritually pure, and thus withdrew from the national Church into their own societies or gathered churches.

Some people reacted to the use of the term "Puritan" against themselves and their friends by going a step further in their analysis of this particular linguistic usage. On this view, the epithet "Puritan" or its synonyms became a label used by the ungodly, the Papists and sometimes even by careerist Conformists (who should have known better) to discredit the best – indeed, in their own eyes, perhaps the only real – Protestants in England. We are dealing here with self-selecting groups of perfect Protestants who tended to identify themselves with increasing self-consciousness as "the godly." These were people who had internalized the saving message of the Gospel and sought to give external shape to the inner workings of God's grace in their outward works, social relations (particularly with one another), and indeed in their public activities as ministers, magistrates, and active members of the commonwealth. Thus, intended as a term of abuse, the appellation "Puritan" became a badge of honor, for those ("the godly") against whom it was habitually mobilized, and a badge of shame for those ("the ungodly") who had recourse to it as a term of dismissal and contempt for the godly. In their own eyes, at least, this latter group were a saving remnant, "the leaven that leavened the whole lump" of the surrounding society. For their sake, God continued to protect Protestant England against its internal and external (mostly popish) enemies. Their godliness, their fasts, their tears and prayers, tipped the scales of divine justice against all the atheistical indifference, the sin, corruption, and residual popish superstition that characterized the lives of so many of their country-persons. It was to this group, serving as lay elders, magistrates, and ministers that a Presbyterian reformation of the English Church would have handed and, indeed, was intended to hand, *de facto* power. In the event of the queen's death or of a Catholic putsch in favor of Mary Stuart, it was people like this who would stand in the gap and protect and perpetuate the Protestant regime of Elizabethan England. For when the chips were down and God's judgements were being visited on the English (either in the form of external threats, wars and rumors of war, internal insurrections, or natural disasters like plagues or earthquakes or bad harvests), ordinary conforming members of the Church of England, mere Conformists, statute Protestants, would be of use to neither God nor man.[12]

Such ordinary members of the national Church caused almost as much terminological discomfort for contemporary observers as they have subsequently for modern historians (although contemporaries did enjoy the singular advantage of never having heard of "Anglicanism"). What one called and therefore made of them depended, of course, on the ideological and subject position from which one viewed them. Seen from, say, the perspective adopted by conformist Protestants like Whitgift (and even more like Whitgift's successor in the anti-Presbyterian struggle, Richard Hooker), everyone who was not an overt recusant – everyone, that is, who went, on something like a regular basis, to church – had to be accepted as a member of the national Church, and since that Church had been, since 1559, formally Protestant, as some sort of protestant.[13]

This rendered the national Church a very broad Church indeed; one which, given the laxity with which conformity was, in practice, enforced under Elizabeth, included everyone who was not a Protestant sectary or Separatist or an avowedly popish recusant. Indeed, given the insistence placed in, say, Whitgift's account of church membership, on external conformity or obedience, even the more enthusiastically churchly Church Papists and certainly Familists (who were, after all, punctilious in their external conformity) were more secure and welcome members of the national Protestant Church than even moderately non conformist Puritans, since the former at least did what the magistrate told them to do, which was more than could be said for the latter. Nor was this mere theory. Thanks to the brilliant research of Dr Marsh, we now know that that austere anti-Puritan conformist Andrew Perne was far nicer, far more tolerantly complaisant, in the face of the outward compliance of what he must have known was a nest of Familists in his rural Cambridgeshire parish than he was when confronted by even the appearance of Puritan scruple or solidarity in Cambridge University.[14]

Here the experience of Familists, along, as we shall see below, with that of Church Papists, stood for a far wider, by Elizabeth's reign, almost structural, aspect of the

English Reformation. Started by the erratic, stop-go course of the Henrician Reformation and compounded by the equally erratic switchback course of religious policy
under Edward, Mary, and Elizabeth, this amounted to a bizarre combination of the
extreme politicization of some of the outward forms of "religion" with a form of *de
facto* religious pluralism. Thus while, on the one hand, the profession of certain
religious opinions and the performance of nonperformance of certain "religious"
actions became synonymous certainly with political disloyalty and sometimes even
formally with treason, the range of available, self-consciously adversarial or mutually
exclusive religious positions at large in the land greatly increased. Under Elizabeth
this produced, on the part of the regime, a renewed insistence on external conformity
and obedience. Francis Bacon's famous dictum about the queen – that she did not
wish to make windows into men's souls – here acquired a particular political edge;
allegiance was not to be rendered dependent on religious opinion, inward conviction,
or the spiritual commitments of individuals, but on outward (religious or rather
ecclesiastical) behavior. From the outset a Protestant queen, Elizabeth – her instincts
here confirming the interpretations of later revisionist historians – was not going to
be marginalized as only a queen of Protestants, in effect shrinking her support base to
a minority of religiously defined *engagés*, rendering her claims to legitimacy and
obedience dependent on a religiously defined and hence inherently febrile and contested category or status. This, at least potentially, opened up a gap between the
inward and the outward, the real inner convictions of a person and his or her outward
behavior, a space which, it seemed to many contemporaries, could be exploited for all
sorts of dissimulation and pretence by the faithless and the unscrupulous. Here, rather
than in some nebulous practice called "Renaissance self-fashioning," may be a major
source of the contemporary obsession with dissimulation and the *de facto* atheism of
the Machiavel. It certainly explains the continued presence of all those Familists at
court. For Familists, with their acknowledged combination of obscure yet entirely
heterodox inner convictions with a perfect display of outward religious, social, and
political conformity, were located slap bang on top of this, surely the single most
threatening of the fault-lines running through Elizabethan religion, culture, and
politics. Yet, if the current analysis is right, the queen's priorities, which saw outward
obedience, conformity, and compliance as the highest political (if not religious)
virtues, could scarcely have been signaled more clearly than by the continued protection of what appeared, to her hot Protestant subjects, to be this nest of heretical vipers
at the very centre of the court.[15]

   All this also goes some way to explaining the polemical fury directed by the godly
at Familism, and indeed Parsons's insistence on Familism as the fourth religion of
Elizabethan England. For the situation, as I have just described it, while it might have
met the queen's or Andrew Perne's or even, to an extent, John Whitgift's objectives
and priorities, drove both Catholic and Puritan activists and *engagés* to distraction.
Viewed from, say, parsons's perspective when he wrote his *Brief Discourse* of 1580, such
a capacious view of the membership of the national Church threatened to suck in large
numbers of cursorily conforming "Catholics," leaving only formal recusants as real

Catholics. The Puritans' beef was related, but very different. They were forced to watch as what they regarded as some of the leading preaching ministers of the day, the most forward Protestants and enthusiastic campaigners against popish darkness, were suspended and even removed from the ministry because of their refusal to use vestments and ceremonies which even the authorities conceded were in themselves indifferent. At the same time, all sorts of ignorant, unpreaching, sinful, and crypto-Catholic non-entities got off scot-free, just because they used the ceremonies. Meanwhile, the Church over which this riffraff presided continued to foster all sorts of popular ignorance, irreligion, and popish superstition.[16]

The evangelical radicals on both sides of the confessional divide reacted in broadly similar ways to the regime's *de facto* distinction, even disjunction, between the outward and the inward, between the mechanics of outward conformity and compliance and the inner workings of the spirit and the heartfelt beliefs of the individual Christian. First, both groups insisted that the two realms must remain linked, no matter how inconvenient the consequences. On their view, the regime ought not to need to make windows into its subject's souls in order to see where they stood on the great religious issues of the day. After all, both Puritan nonconformity and Catholic recusancy were external expressions of religious profession and identity, gestures of dissent directed against outward forms pushed by the regime which both Catholics and Puritans, albeit for different reasons, regarded as unlawful, potentially polluting, or offensive. Secondly, having provided rites of separation whereby true Christians must pronounce their apartness from the encompassing popish or heretical mass, both Puritans and Catholic *engagés* set about recategorizing the conformist residuum, in order, semantically and then practically, to recapture it from the outwardly Protestant national Church of Queen Elizabeth and John Whitgift.

It was in order to perform this task that both sides – Catholic and Puritan – developed another key term, another imagined religious identity, that has proved to be of much interest to recent commentators – that of the Church Papist. As Dr Walsham has shown, the term became current around 1580 in both hot Protestant or Puritan and Catholic circles. In the mouths of both groups it seemed to denote or refer to a roughly similar area of the contemporary religious scene. And indeed, as we shall see, there was some overlap in the opinions and activities to which hot Protestants and Catholics intended to advert when they employed the term; but the fit or congruence between their usages was anything but exact. Indeed, in practice, the two groups used the term for very different purposes and to refer to ultimately very different things.

For Catholics, the meaning of the term was relatively constricted; it denoted persons who in their own minds were Catholics, that is, would-be devotees of the old religion, would-be loyal sons and daughters of the Church of Rome, who, because of the legal, social, and financial consequences of recusancy, continued to attend, in some often fairly nugatory capacity, the services of the national Church. Catholics sometimes referred to such people as schismatics, to distinguish them from out-and-out heretics; to denote, in other words, persons of Catholic opinion and intention who were too weak to pay the price of full recusancy. Such people did not so much need to be converted from full-fig Protestantism or even weaned away from Protestantizing error. Rather, they had to be persuaded of the sinfulness of any continued contact with the heretical national Church and then reconciled in full to the Church of Rome. As Father McCoog has pointed out, even for its most seemingly insistent and unbending clerical proponents, recusancy was always a counsel of perfection, and, in practice, as the casuistical manuals written by those same clerical ideologists of recusancy assumed, priests were expected to be able to tell genuinely Catholic Church Papists from real heretics. While offering confession and the sacraments to the former, they were to treat the latter with all due caution.

For hot Protestants or Puritans, on the other hand, the term had altogether broader connotations. They very often used it alongside a whole slew of other derisive, slighting terms, like "atheist," "statute Protestant," "conformitan," to refer to all those Christians who did not conform to their notion of a proper profession of true religion but who continued nonetheless to conduct and regard themselves as members of the English Church – indeed, as Christian professors in good standing with God and man. These people "conformed," that is, they went to church, they had their children baptized, they received communion at Easter, they had their dead buried and their wives churched – in short, they did what they took to be their religious and social duty, but they neither understood the central saving truths of Protestant religion, nor had they fully repudiated the Pelagian, merit-mongering and idolatrous mental habits and assumptions that characterized the religion of real Papists. "Although they be not rank papists," remarked George Gifford, that astute observer of what he termed the "country divinity" of the people, "yet have they in them still a smack and savour of popish principles." These were not Church Papists of the sort condemned with such contempt by Parsons, self-conscious Catholics who remained in semi-detached connection with the national Church only in order to avoid the penalties of the law. In the words of Dr Walsham, "such individuals betrayed their adherence to the Romish Antichrist not so much in a positive, voiced endorsement of its untenable theology, as in their reactionary resistance to" and resentment of "the saving message of the gospel" as it was brought to them by the godly clergy and through their "vague nostalgia for a golden age" of social cheer and plenty before the religious upheavals of the Reformation and the unreasonable and divisive demands and habits of the godly preachers and their lay acolytes had arrived to mess everything up.

On occasion, indeed often, but in some areas more than others, and decreasingly so everywhere as the reign wore on, there was indeed a positive correlation between Church popery, as, say, Parsons described it, and the mental habits and social reactions lambasted as Church Papist by the Puritan ministry. And yet there is no reason to suppose that that was always and everywhere the case. As Walsham has argued, just as the godly came to see the use of the word "Puritan" as an insult as typical of the "ungodly," so they themselves came to use the appellation "Papist" or "Church Papist" as a coded response, a counter insult, to fling back in the faces of their enemies amongst the profane multitude. But there was more than invective, mere name calling, at stake in these exchanges. For in using the word "popery" in this context, the Puritans were labeling or naming a number of central features of their experience in ways that rendered them explicable in terms of the basic structuring assumptions of their world view. Thus central elements in their experience of the world, which might otherwise have caused them severe cognitive dissonance and self-doubt, perhaps even despair, were rendered explicable in ways that, in fact, served to confirm their view of the world and sense of themselves.[17]

For, from the outset, it had been axiomatic for Protestants that once the word had been freed from the corrupting penumbra of false, human interpretation, ecclesiastical tradition, and idolatrous flimflam, with which the Church of Rome had sought to conceal it, and been loosed in its pristine, unmediated state upon the people, it would work wondrous, transforming effects. Indeed, as both Catharine Davies and Patrick Collinson have pointed out, during the Edwardian and early Elizabethan periods there had been a markedly populist strand in Protestant discourse. In this rendition of the current situation, the people were pictured not as the Gospel's recalcitrant enemies, but as its actual or, at least, its potential friends. Subjected to what had amounted to a clerical confidence trick, their spiritual liberties trampled under foot, their property wheedled and extorted from them by a corrupt popish clergy selling utterly worthless religious services and outward works, the people were prime subjects for spiritual liberation by the unvarnished Word, purveyed to them through the endeavors of increasing numbers of painful Protestant preachers. Moreover, as Professor Collinson has pointed out, this transformation was to be worked not only through the pulpit. During this relatively early, optimistically populist phase of Protestant thought, it was considered perfectly legitimate – indeed, rather a good idea – to appeal to them through a whole range of popular cultural forms and genres – ballads, music, plays, interludes, and pictures – forms and genres which by the second half of Elizabeth's reign would all come to be seen as suspiciously popular, carnal, and popish by many of the hot Protestants and Puritans who had before been perfectly willing to use them in order to make their pitch to the people that much more vivid and effective.[18]

Now the results of this evangelizing process were expected by hot Protestants to be spectacular, nothing short of a complete spiritual and moral renewal of people, Church, and commonwealth; in Dr Haigh's formulation, not so much a Protestant nation as a nation of Protestants indeed. There was, of course, something eschatologically utopian in such expectations. But then, for these people, the Reformation was an event of world-historical significance, a crucial stage in the divine plan whereby Antichrist was to be brought down and, in the process, the terms of human existence, at least within the True Church, transformed, in this, the last age before Christ returned in glory at the end of the world. When things did not pan out like this, and the mass of the people remained frustratingly unconverted, the social world recalcitrantly untransformed, complaint and disappointment were the inevitable result, rendered so as much by the very exalted nature of the initial expectations as by any events in the world.

There remained, however, ideological resources available to the godly with which such an outcome could not only be rendered explicable but even enlisted as part of the hortatory rhetoric of further reformation. As Walsham and others have shown, the godly came to analyze their world in terms of a rigidly bipolar, dichotomous vision of reality. For them the world was divided between the forces of Christian light, on the one hand, and of Antichristian darkness, on the other. Accordingly, their self-image was always that of an oppressed minority, struggling in the face of a corrupt, godless, potentially idolatrous, hence popish world. Applying such heuristic models to their own experience, the godly found it relatively easy to assimilate incomprehension of, resistance and hostility to, some of the key doctrines of the Reformed faith, boredom, inattention or distaste in the face of the word preached, an addiction to popular sports and pastimes, and nostalgia for an ill-defined golden age before Puritan spoilsports had assumed many of the levers of local power, to the viscerally residual popery of the populace. To hot Protestants such an attachment seemed all too natural, since they conceived of popery itself as a religion of external idolatrous show, of seemingly commonsensical "will worship" perfectly designed to appeal to the corruption and self-love of a fallen and fleshly human nature. Collinson argues that it was precisely such attitudes that, around 1580, led perfect Protestants to repudiate many of the popular cultural forms they had been quite happy to employ as profane and even popish. In the process they were redefining the boundaries between pukka, perfect Protestantantism and a populace increasingly conceived as recalcitrantly, indeed popishly, hostile to the demands of the Gospel.

Moreover, if Protestant expectations were tinged with eschatological excitement, they were not simply millenarian. These may well have been the last days, but the last days could last a long time and were themselves a time of stress and struggle. Antichrist would fall and Christ triumph, but there was many a slip betwixt cup and lip. The True Church in general would triumph, but not necessarily the True Church in England. As Protestant zealots never tired of remarking, God had allowed churches as eminent as those of Asia to disappear forever beneath the waves of Islam. No one individual national Church had a certain grip on divine protection. For all the triumphalism and flattery about the achievements of the Elizabethan regime and the inevitable victory of the light of the Gospel over the Antichristian darkness of popery that suffused hot Protestant discourse, there was a persistent undertone of panic and pessimism running through much Protestant comment on the contemporary world.[19]

As, of course, there well might have been. Well within living memory, what had become by 1553 a remarkably successful, secure, and indeed, as Diarmaid MacCulloch has recently shown, still dynamically open-ended Reformed regime, had collapsed like a house of cards with the death of that godly imp, the young Josias, Edward VI.[20] (Catholics, of course, had experienced the equally traumatic, because precisely parallel, collapse of an almost equally well-established Catholic regime in 1558.) As Collinson has repeatedly pointed out, as long as Mary Stuart remained alive, Elizabeth remained childless, and the succession remained unsettled, that same fate continued to stare English Protestants in the face.[21] There was, therefore, in fact as well as in providential and eschatological theory, no reason to suppose that the Gospel in England was any safer now than it had proved to be under Edward VI. Almost before that reign had ended, Protestants had been working on a properly providential and edifying explanation for the debacle. Under Edward, they argued, the cupidity and self-interest of the elite and the indifference of the people had led God to remove the Gospel, plunge the nation back into Antichristian darkness, and generally to visit upon the English the sufferings of Mary's reign (war, persecution, foreign rule, plague or at least a virulent and extremely deadly flu epidemic). Now, the horrors and martyrdoms of Mary's reign had elicited a second chance from an ever merciful, as well as ever just, God. (Again the sufferings, the tears, the prayers, and sacrifices of the godly, this time in exile and at the stake, had bailed out the nation at large.) But the English, a nation in a covenant relation with God, were still living on borrowed time. Unless they got their act together, what had happened before could happen again.[22]

And yet, as we have seen, the hot Protestant vision of a nation discharging its obligations to God remained impossibly utopian. The godly's definition of what constituted true religion – a genuine, transformative understanding and internalization of the central truths of the Reformed faith, leading to an equally reformed outward conversation or pattern of conduct – was always going to be the religion of a self-conscious minority of zealots (the godly). Applying such criteria to the religious attitudes and performances of their country persons, the godly could only ever be disappointed, and the effect of the Gospel on the people could only ever be counted as some sort of failure.

The effects of this, as it were, conceptual or discursive double bind were compounded by certain, what one might term, external – political, institutional, cultural, and social – circumstances and constraints within which perfect Protestants had to operate during much of Elizabeth's reign. Few can doubt, following the recent writings of Christopher Haigh, J. J. Scarisbrick, and most notably Eamonn Duffy, that at the outset of the reign the majority of the English population remained wedded, with various degrees of enthusiasm, to some version or other of "the old religion."[23] Given the brevity of the Protestant Reformation under Edward and the paucity of the proselytizing resources available both to the Edwardian and Elizabethan churches, this was almost inevitably the case, since great chunks of the population had never really been exposed to Protestantism. As Duffy, Hutton, and Whiting have all shown, however, nearly everyone had experienced the negative, destructive effects of the reformations unleashed by the reigns of Henry VIII, Edward VI, and Elizabeth. In particular, the researches of Hutton into the surviving churchwardens' accounts have shown how remarkably effective each successive Tudor regime was in gaining local compliance to a variety of often directly contradictory instructions and demands. But, as both hot Protestant and Catholic *engagés* and evangelicals realized, compliance in externals was not conversion. And the Elizabethan regime in Church and State lacked the resources of trained, committed clerical manpower, the centralized control over ecclesiastical patronage, and the fine-grained spiritual discipline (not to mention the sort of centralized control over the personnel and course of local secular government) which would have enabled it to effect, or rather enforce, the conversion of England on anything like a scale or a schedule sufficiently rapid to meet hot Protestant expectations.[24]

It was this situation that produced Puritanism, defined in its classic primary sense, as a series of proposals and agitations for the further reformation of the liturgical and institutional structures of the Elizabethan Church, all of which schemes were designed, in their different ways, to make that Church a more efficient and less compromised Protestant proselytizing machine. It was also here that the hot or perfect Protestant tendency to attribute the failure of the Gospel to work a full reformation, even twenty or thirty years after its restoration, to the residual popery of the people came into its own. First, this was a move that explained the failure of perfect Protestants' own entirely unrealistic expectations of almost immediate cultural and spiritual transformation without calling into question any of the basic presuppositions of their own world view. Rather, the recalcitrance of the people was explained as a function of the more than human (because ultimately satanic) capacity of popery to both appeal and give expression to the fleshly corruption of a fallen human nature. Such a diagnosis served to tie together the otherwise arguably distinct issues of evangelical conversion, social discipline, and political security and to attach them, thus conjoined, to the Puritans' own schemes to rid the liturgy and government of the English Church of their last vestiges of popery. If, at a whole number of levels – political, cultural, doctrinal, institutional – popery was indeed the problem, then the godly and their plans for further reformation could plausibly be presented as the answer. Thus, an analysis of short- or medium-term "failure" could be presented as a necessary part of inevitable long-term success, since Antichrist must fall and the Gospel ultimately triumph, and both events would happen sooner rather than later if the English commonwealth actually started to do what God wanted and reform itself.[25]

As Walsham has argued, in the process, the godly organized, under the sign of popery, a number of attitudes and activities that had no necessary connection to any religious system that contemporary Catholic *engagés* (either clerical or lay) would have recognized as Catholic. Even the most cursory examination of the burgeoning literature on the impact of the Counter-Reformation on rural society on the Continent proves conclusively that lay impatience with the protracted performances of the clergy, inattentive, apparently disrespectful behavior in church, and popular ignorance of what to evangelicals seemed to be the crucial, saving truths of Christianity, were neither peculiar to post-Reformation England nor telltale signs of enthusiasm for anything that contemporary arbiters of Catholic propriety would have recognized as distinctively Roman Catholic.[26] In accepting that there was such a correlation between popular hostility or resistance to the rigors of perfect Protestant or Puritan religion, as the godly purveyed it, and "Catholicism" or even "Church popery," we run the risk of seeing the world through the eyes of the most rabidly anti-Catholic elements in Elizabethan England; of accepting as value-free social reportage what were deeply ideological, polemically structured acts of interpretation, textual interventions produced from within, conditioned by and designed to further, a radical Protestant – indeed, Puritan – vision of the world and agenda for further reformation.

Even if we suppose that initial hostility to the austerities and demands of perfect Protestantism was always and everywhere based on a nostalgia for, or attachment to, the "old religion" that amounted to a species of Church popery, recognizable to Parsons as schism not heresy, it is by no means clear that this situation persisted indefinitely. For, as the reign wore on, as Maltby has argued, it became clear that for parishioners lumbered with a perfect Protestant or Puritan minister they hated, the easiest way to get back at him was by prosecuting him in the Church courts for failure to observe the formularies and procedures of the national, Protestant Church. Here we might see the beginning of popular implication in, and attachment to, the protocols and procedures of the national Protestant Church in the almost subterranean world of personal friction, antipathy, and local dispute between the godly and their enemies, as alienated or alarmed (in Puritan parlance, and perhaps at first, in reality, "popish" or "Church Papist") parishioners or exasperated fellow clergy cited personally obnoxious, self-righteous, or aggressively divisive godly Puritan ministers before the Church courts for various types of nonconformist or socially divisive behavior. And all this at the same time that Catholic *engagés* and evangelicals like Parsons and Campion were developing the concept of the Church Papist as a way to tighten the dominant definition of what being a Catholic in England meant and thus force as many Church Papists into overt recusancy as possible. On this view, the godly may have been the leading agents of Protestantization in more senses than the one they so proudly claimed for themselves, and popular "Anglicanism" (Maltby's "Prayer Book Protestantism"), in part, at least, the unintended consequence of both Catholic and Protestant evangelical rigorism, a *via media* indeed.[27]

Nor was this an entirely attritional, unselfconsciously gradualist process. As the reign wore on, and the claim to represent the only version of Protestantism worthy of the name was used to legitimate and push increasingly divisive, disobedient, and controversial purposes by the godly (otherwise known as the Puritans), the area of overlap between the self-identified godly and the self-consciously non-popish – indeed, anti-popish – politically loyal, participant membership of the national Protestant Church grew ever smaller. This process of conformist peel-back or differentiation can be traced most clearly, at the level of self-conscious theory and formal argument, in the anti-Puritan and anti-Presbyterian works of conformist polemicists like Whitgift or Bridges, Bancroft or Hooker, all of whom took themselves to be, and, of course, were, aggressively Protestant – indeed, in many cases, reformed in their attitudes both to the Church of Rome and to many of the central theological issues of the day.[28]

Walsham, of course, knows all this well enough, and on one level her book represents a wonderful study of the complexities of category formation, as both hot Protestant and Catholic evangelicals came simultaneously to invent seemingly the same category – Church Papist – but then proceeded to use it for very different polemical purposes. Yet, having noted that fact, she then proceeds to advance the term as a precise analytical category with which to address some of the most vexed questions in the religious history of the period. This surely will not do. But if it is a mistake, it is one that Walsham is far from alone in making. For it has been a central feature of much revisionist writing on the religious history of the period that, while it has repudiated the narrative forms of "the Reformation process" that owe most to the manifest destiny providentialism of the Protestant and Whig traditions, it has, in its definition of basic terms and categories, replicated almost perfectly the core assumptions and terms of reference of the jeremiads and complaint literature produced by the perfect Protestant or Puritan commentators of the day. It has done so for quite explicit historiographical purposes, expanding the term "Catholic" to its maximum, paranoid, perfect Protestant extent, whilst simultaneously shrinking the term "Protestant" until it can be used legitimately only to refer to the sorts of exclusivist, self-selectingly elitist notions of godliness that the godly themselves invoked to both legitimate and glamorize their own self-identities and situation. On this basis, but only really on this basis, can the simple continuity of something called Catholicism through the English Reformation be vindicated and the failure – indeed, the status as non-event – of the Reformation itself be asserted. But, as we have seen, the period during which the master categories in terms of which the continuity argument is framed were being developed and contested, continually being shaped and reshaped by a whole host of ideological fractions and social groups, was precisely the same period during which their "continuity," their "success" or "failure," are being notionally tested or gauged by modern historians. And if this is most obviously the case for Protestantism, on closer inspection it turns out to be just as true for the opposite term in the equation – "Catholicism."[29]

And here we come up against perhaps the greatest single obstacle in the way of the continuity of Catholicism thesis, the revisionists' own – or rather, to be more precise, Eamonn Duffy's – brilliant analysis of the social context and affective content of Catholic piety before the Reformation. Using material, architectural, and liturgical evidence, Duffy has reconstructed a form of piety to which sacred places, times, objects, and performances were crucial. He pictures a world in which there was no real divide between individual religious affect or interiority and outward communal practice. On Duffy's view, both individual and communal belief and observance fed off the same Christian – indeed, Christocentric – body of texts, images, and symbols; the one fed into and confirmed and strengthened the other.

Duffy presents his analysis as a refutation of the sort of dichotomized, developmental hierarchy or progression posited by Keith Thomas and others, on the one side of which we would place religion defined as a body of internalized belief and doctrine (i.e., Counter-Reformation Catholicism and Protestantism and perhaps the religion of some of the literate elite before the Reformation) and, on the other, religion conceived of as a ritualized way of life, a series of collective and individual performances and practices (pre-Reformation Catholicism *tout court* and central aspects of post-Reformation popular religion, on both sides of the confessional divide). Indeed, Duffy has pointedly rejected the binary opposition between (Christian) religion, on the one hand, and superstition or magic, on the other, that Thomas, for one, has drawn out of such a hierarchy of ideal types. Duffy has been insistent that his subject is an organic unity called late medieval Christianity, traditional not popular religion. He has been still more insistent that there is no useful distinction to be drawn between a penumbra of sub- or, indeed, essentially un-Christian superstitions, beliefs, and practices that both accreted to and developed out of the central tenets and beliefs, liturgical texts and rituals, of the medieval Church and traditional Christian religion. What is superstition to Thomas is religion to Duffy, and vice versa.

But without having recourse to the rhetoric of superstition or to Thomas's essentially secularizing, developmental hierarchy of religious forms, we can see in Duffy's picture of late medieval Christianity a religious system absolutely centred on holy objects, spaces, and times and on corporate and communal acts of worship. And in the second half of the book we are shown the extent of the damage wreaked on those places, objects, times, and performances by the English Reformation in its various guises and phases. An analysis of late medieval Catholicism predicated on the Protestant polemic that pictured it as a religion of mere externals and instrumentally superstitious observances, as say those of Dickens and Thomas arguably did, might expect that religion to have collapsed under such an onslaught, as indeed Dickens more or less claimed that it did. But, whatever the over-optimistic hopes of certain zealously iconoclastic contemporary Protestants, given Duffy's analysis of the religious system at stake here, such an expectation is and was absurd. But, by the same token, anyone who takes Duffy's analysis seriously cannot suppose that the destruction described in the second half of his book would or could be altogether without effect.[30]

Of course, Haigh is quite right to assert the relatively uneven geographical and temporal impact of Protestant deconstruction at the start of Elizabeth's reign. Some parishes like Weaverham in Cheshire or Ardingly in Sussex did indeed manage to retain many of the outward forms of Catholic worship into the late 1570s or 1580s. In some areas Haigh may well be right to argue that "a family, a group, even a hamlet or village may gradually change the form of its catholicism, moving in stages from conservative practices within the parish church to total withdrawal, so that catholicism may remain the social norm and individuals may move into recusancy by conformity to community standards." But we should probably resist the impulse to rewrite the history of Elizabethan England in terms of places like Weaverham in 1578, if only because, as Haigh himself has pointed out elsewhere, the diocese of Chester was scarcely the English Church writ small, and anyway the reign did not end in the late 1570s.[31]

Moreover, if we take Duffy seriously, the remodeling of the parish church, and still more the move out of the building itself, when they came, as, given the queen's longevity, come they must, surely involved a radical change in what it meant or felt like to be a Catholic. Battling against the image of Catholicism as "a secretive, persecuted sect," Haigh cites two examples from the early seventeenth century, both from Lancashire. One involves the activities of a Jesuit named John Layton who was preaching and holding masses in an enlarged, decorated barn, on occasion attracting large crowds not only of avowed recusant Catholics but of Church Papists and seeming conformists. The other concerns the standing of Ambrose Barlow in the parish of Leigh, where Barlow fulfilled many of the functions and enjoyed a public reputation rivaling that of the parish minister. In Leigh, at least (and, it seems certain, in other parts of a Lancashire that by the early seventeenth century, if not before, was notorious – one is tempted to say uniquely so – for the levels and intensity of its popular Catholicism) Haigh is surely quite justified in concluding that the Catholics were operating not as a persecuted sect but as "an open denomination."[32]

Now whatever this is, it is not clear that it is best described as continuity. Clearly the move from church to barn, which did happen, even in Lancashire, mattered. Indeed, it serves as a nice symbol for far wider shifts and changes in the lives of Catholics that were directly, if not immediately, consequent upon the settlement of 1559 and Queen Elizabeth's refusal to die. It stands, in fact, for the shift from possession of all the central symbols of social solidarity and communal unity, from sole control of the rites of passage, from being the utterly unchallenged arbiters and celebrants of the fixed points in the liturgical year, of all the festivals, performances, symbols, and texts in terms of which both communal and corporate identities and solidarities were created and affirmed and individual affective religious life was lived, to being, even in Lancashire in the 1620s and 1630s (i.e., in the most favorable of available circumstances), merely an "open denomination" and, in less favorable locales and more stressful times, something much more like a "secretive and persecuted sect."

Now all the sources that Haigh uses to document the activities of Layton and Barlow are Catholic ones. In employing them to gain a view of illicit Catholic activity and piety, as it were, from the inside, a view that other judicial sources simply cannot provide, he is, of course, following on from a distinguished line of historians of Puritanism who have used similar godly lives and hagiographies to illuminate the norms and forms of what Collinson has famously termed Puritan "voluntary religion." If we compare the view of Catholic voluntary religion that emerges from the Catholic sources with the view of Puritan voluntary religion that emerges from, say, Samuel Clarke's *Lives*, we find some remarkable parallels and similarities. Thus, the relationship between, say, Layton or Barlow and the local Protestant parish minister is highly reminiscent of that enjoyed by popular and (at least, according to Clarke) often persecuted nonconformist, Puritan lecturers or ministers and their (again, according to Clarke) far less godly, assiduous, and popular conformist colleagues and neighbors. They, too, drew an audience from other men's congregations, if not quite emptying, then certainly depleting the attendance at neighboring churches. Their audiences, too, were presumably mixed, comprising a hard core of self-identified godly (the equivalents of the recusant, papalist Catholics in Layton's audience), but including other sorts of conforming Protestants of various degrees of personal zeal or overt godliness (the Church Papists and occasional or regular conformists who also turned up to hear Layton at times). If the godly gadded to sermons, so too did various sorts of Catholics and anti-Puritans, sometimes, as Haigh has pointed out, seeking in other parishes not only sermons but sacraments administered with the full panoply of ceremonies prescribed by the national Church, rather than the pared-down, Reformed versions offered by many Puritan ministers.[33]

Again, if we compare, say, Robert Parsons's accounts of certain Catholic gatherings in the 1580s with several priests meeting together with large numbers of laypersons for the celebration of a whole series of masses and the preaching of multiple sermons, we are reminded of nothing so much as the day-long fasts and exercises or perhaps the lectures by combination which drew the godly together in similar outbreaks of voluntary religion and sermon-based piety. And finally, as Bossy first pointed out years ago, there is the centrality, both in the rhythms of everyday religious life and in the logistics of edification by which both groups sustained themselves, of household worship and the crucial links of mutual respect and support between Puritan/Catholic gentry and their allies amongst the religiously zealous and committed clergy. For, if under certain circumstances, Catholicism became a seigneurial religion, so too did Puritanism. Just as the Catholic gentry created enclaves in an otherwise hostile environment in which Catholic priests could operate, so too did Puritan gentry protect their clerical clients from the hostile attentions of conformist episcopal authority, allowing overt and inveterate nonconformists like John Dod or William Bradshaw to exercise their calling as preachers over long stretches of time. And here we might ponder again the testimony of witnesses like Parsons, Thomas Bell, and others (as well as, on the Puritan side, Samuel Clarke) to the large popular attendances at day-long religious exercises, featuring, amongst the Catholics, at least, both the celebration of multiple masses and the preaching of the word. Might not such evidence suggest that the either/or choice between a popular and a seigneurial or gentry-based religion, accepted as unproblematically self-evident by both Haigh and Bossy, does not quite do justice to the realities of Catholic voluntary religion under a hostile, heretical regime?[34]

For on this basis, we might, then, want to conclude that we are dealing here with two different but parallel types or versions of what Professor Collinson has termed "voluntary religion." Are we in fact returning to Parsons's vision, with which we started, of an England with four religions? Adding the Family of Love to the equation, as Marsh quite rightly insists that we should, perhaps. But before we get carried away with the comparison, we need to remember that, certainly until the rise of Laudianism in the next century, the form of voluntary religion we might want to label Puritan enjoyed very close, if intermittently troubled, relations with the dominant Protestant ideology in Church and State. At certain times more than others, and in some places more than others, to quote Collinson, the "mainstream of the protestant reformation was . . . a puritan maintream."[35] For much of Elizabeth's reign, even the more radical proponents of Puritan notions of reformation and religion like that English Knox, John Field, enjoyed close links of patronage with central figures in the regime like the earl of Leicester, Sir Francis Walsingham, and even Burghley.[36]

The same connections often served to give the godly (both clerical and lay, minister and magistrate) the initiative in the localities where the political imperative to have local power in reliably, indeed zealously, Protestant (and hence *faute de mieux* often

Puritan) hands ceded control, even over narrowly ecclesiastical affairs, to groups which even the most enthusiastically conformist of bishops could not always control. In counties like the Suffolk described by MacCulloch the locally dominant, "official" face of Elizabethan Protestantism was a Puritan face, and Catholicism was reduced to a faith centred on the households of a number of recusant or Church Papist gentry who were largely excluded from the formal exercise of local power. As the remarkable example of the remote island enclave of Lothingland shows, even in Suffolk popular Catholicism was not altogether dead. The enclave in Lothingland nestled for years under the protection and patronage of the Jerninghham family but, as the connections with Lord Burghley himself enjoyed by that other leading Suffolk Catholic gentle-man, Sir Thomas Cornwallis, show, even overtly Catholic gentry were not altogether without friends and protectors in high places.[37] At times of crisis, in the late 1560s and perhaps again during the brief period when the Anjou match looked like a done deal, the continuing social power and potential political influence of prominent Catholics looked as though it might seriously alter the balance of the government's religious stance. But for the most part, and increasingly so after the revolt of the northern earls, the levers of power, both at the centre and in the localities, rested in Protestant and even Puritan hands.[38]

Political predominance had other than merely political consequences. While the likes of Layton and his flock met in barns and private households, the godly inherited the public space of the parish church. And where the altars had been effectively stripped, that was now a public space that proclaimed, at a number of levels, the alteration of religion. The prominently displayed royal coat of arms aside, wall paintings had been whitewashed over, the Ten Commandments and the odd scriptural verses replacing them. The altar was now a communion table; the rood loft with its doom images as well as the images of the saints had been removed. The liturgy was in English, not Latin; the mass had been replaced with a communion service. No trace of the cult of the saints or the notion of Purgatory – such central features of the religious system described by Eamon Duffy – was left in either the service book or the outward ceremonial face of the Church. Again, whatever else this was, it was not continuity. As Haigh and others have observed, Marian priests and conservatives could try to make the communion service look as much like the mass as possible, and certainly the notional revolution in the appearance of church interiors described above did not arrive everywhere overnight.[39] And, as ever, the godly were anything but satisfied, wanting further to alter the liturgy and the vestments of the clergy, in order to efface entirely what they took to be the deceiving, even damning, remnants of popery.

Yet it is hard not to see here an unequivocal message that things had changed and that "Catholicism" had been expelled from the public spaces and settings from which it had taken at least some of its power as a public or communal religion. This was an expulsion registered in some of the earliest gestures of Catholic dissent (or "continu-ity") chronicled by Haigh, as some Marian priests, who retained their livings in the national Church, proffered their flocks Prayer Book services in the parish church while providing the mass in private.[40] Similar considerations applied, too, to the more public of the forms of voluntary religion adopted by the godly. Catholics might meet in barns and gentry households, but, while household religion did indeed hold a central place in their overall economy of observance, the godly were also able to organize a good deal of their voluntary religious life around the public space of the parish church and pulpit, holding lectures by combination on market days in centrally placed towns and using the parish church as the setting for their stipendiary lectures and public fasts. In some instances, this occupation of a variety of public spaces was dramatized by acts of iconoclasm, both in churches and outside, as in the assault on the market cross in Banbury. Very often such actions were controversial and divisive in their immediate impact (as powerful dramatizations of difference and change that, after all, were what they were for). But even where such, often officially sponsored outbreaks of religiously motivated vandalism ran directly counter to what one might term local majority opinion, they still represented powerful seizures of public space and the symbols of communal unity and authority by and for the values of perfect Protestantism.[41]

And this in turn raises a hitherto unlooked-for aspect of Protestant religion. It has become something of a commonplace amongst modern historians to juxtapose an ideal type of hot Protestant or Puritan religion against a very different ideal type of popular Catholicism. Protestantism was word-centered, not merely iconoclastic but iconophobic, individualizing, centered more on the household than on the parish, and in its most effective and affective forms on the individual soul confronting the internal workings of divine grace. Here, in short, was a religion for the literate, indeed for pointy-headed intellectuals. Traditional Catholicism was, on the other hand, a religion of ritual practice, communal observance, centered on the sacraments and particularly on the mass rather than the word, either read or preached. Clearly, there is some truth to such a contrast, but just as Eamonn Duffy has called our attention to the intense personal piety and affectivity implicit in many of the forms of late medieval Catholicism, so we should probably be more attuned to the corporate, communal, representational, and even ritual aspects of post-Reformation English Protestantism, even in its more Puritan, ostensibly word-centered forms. For many ordinary Christians the "word" was experienced not so much as a text, words on a page, but as both object and performance.[42] The often huge royal coats of arms in Elizabethan and early Stuart parish churches; the massive presence, in the middle of the church, of the pulpit, with its sounding board looming over the pews beneath; the ubiquity of vernacular Scripture; the often dominating presence of the funeral monuments of the godly gentry and clergy, their austere, often kneeling images clutching Prayer Books or Bibles; the rhythms of a sabbath observance enforced by both local lay and ecclesiastical courts and authorities;[43] the ebb and flow of the word preached, as it was dispensed with calming regularity both on the Lord's day and at weekday lectures; the presence of often hot Protestant preachers at assize meetings, executions, and market days, at the royal court and Paul's Cross, in other words at some of the most politically and ideologically charged occasions, when the majesty of the law and the sheer crushing ubiquity of order and authority, as they were personified by the powers that were in Church and State, were asserted and celebrated[44] – all these outward forms and ritual practices served to integrate Protestantism, often of an austerely Puritan sort, into the very structures of reality and everyday experience. As David Cressy has shown, even the liturgical year came to incorporate new royal, Protestant, and national days of celebration. The result was a species of secularized, or rather Protestantized, holy days which staged very effectively the congruences between Englishness, non-popishness, loyalty to legitimate monarchical authority, and the providential preservation of the national community, thus defined, from foreign popish threat, upon which the claims to legitimacy of the post-Reformation English monarchical state came to rest.[45]

Thus, if there is some value, certainly by the second half of the reign (although sooner in some places and later in others) in seeing certain styles of Catholicism and Puritanism as two competing versions of voluntary religion, we also need to register that the two styles enjoyed entirely asymmetrical relations with the structures and symbols of legitimacy and power. And that is a conclusion we have reached without so much as a mention of the increasingly stringent laws that penalized recusancy and labeled acts crucial to the continued maintenance of Catholicism in England as treasonable. Every now and again during Elizabeth's reign the most recalcitrant of Puritan nonconformist ministers got into trouble with the law; sometimes they were suspended from the ministry, and sometimes they were even deprived of their livings. More often than not, however, they were protected by the often ideologically motiv-ated neglect or complaisance of sympathetic perfect Protestant bishops or by the support of lay friends in high places. Occasionally the author of a really intemperate Puritan tract might end up in gaol or be forced into exile. Even then, this did not usually mean a definitive banishment from the country or even from an active exercise of the ministry. Both those two Presbyterian firebrands, John Field and Thomas Cartwright, were able to return, sheltered under the wing of the earl of Leicester.[46] By contrast, a full quarter of the foreign-trained Catholic priests who entered the country under Elizabeth were executed, their deaths carefully staged dramatizations of the equation between treason and Catholicism that both the regime and the free-lancing godly tried so hard, through a number of media, to establish in the public mind. And that is not to mention the many other priests who were captured, imprisoned, or exiled. Under these circumstances it would surely be unwise, to have recourse, with Haigh, to "the social exclusiveness" and martyr complex of the clergy and the "selfishness of the gentry" to explain the outcome of what had surely become, as the reign entered its second and third decades, an entirely unequal contest between the forces of Protestant and Catholic evangelism and renewal.[47]

And that, ultimately, is probably the best way to envision the religious scene during this period. The tergiversations of the previous decades had left a cultural terrain strewn with the wreckage of partially disrupted belief systems, sets of assump-tions about how the world worked and where the holy was to be found and how it might be approached, invoked, and manipulated. Much, indeed most, of this cultural stuff might be said, in some loose sense, to have been "Christian." By that I mean, on the one hand, that, like witchcraft, the beliefs and practices involved, whatever their origins, were assimilable and indeed frequently assimilated to a variety of explicitly Christian views of the world. On the other hand, I mean that however heterodox their current use may have become, however far removed they may have been from their liturgical or paraliturgical sources, they were, in origin, offshoots from or appropriations of recognizably Christian texts, beliefs, or practices in Bossy's memorable formulation, overspills of the divine power generated by the central social miracle of the mass. In bestowing the epithet "Christian" upon them, I do not, of course, mean to suggest that they were accepted by either Catholic or Protestant rigorists as, in any sense, "orthodox."[48]

This variegated Christian and sub-Christian *bric-à-brac* was to be found all over the social, conceptual, and representational landscape of the period. To the consternation of the godly, some of it could still be found in the liturgy and practices of the national Church; it could be found in the fabric of the very churches themselves, in a vast compendium of popular and proverbial sayings which, like the notion that "murder will out" contained or implied an essentially providential sense of the workings of divine justice and its relationship to often near-miraculous events in the world. Popular witchcraft beliefs at least contained the germs of a construal of the world as the scene of a struggle between satanic evil and divine good. And in that struggle, as it was dramatized in a variety of witchcraft accusations, prosecutions, and pamphlets, the divinely sanctioned forces of good were identified with notions of good neighborhood, remaining in charity with one's neighbors, and the maintenance of social unity. The crucial stages in the life cycle, and particularly the necessity of a good death, retained a glow of religious significance.[49]

Now it would probably not be sensible to view this assemblage of beliefs, assumptions, and practices as either Catholic or Protestant, certainly as those terms were coming to be defined by *engagés* on both sides by the mid to late sixteenth century. Nor would it be entirely sensible, with Haigh, to view the relations between various sorts of Protestant and anti-Catholic discourse and the stuff of contemporary Christian religion as simply or only adversarial. Rather, the available cultural materials were intensely glossable, subject to different interpretations and appropriations, and the religious scene of Elizabeth's reign is best seen as a number of attempts, conducted at very different levels of theoretical self-consciousness and coherence, at creative bricolage, mixing and matching, as a variety of cases or pitches were made for popular support in terms of many of the central religious attitudes and values sketched above. In those struggles, perfect Protestants were active, competitive participants with powerful ideological and discursive weapons at their disposal. Their natural recourse to notions of providence and of direct divine intervention in the human world described under that rubric; their tendency to see the world in Manichaean, antipapal terms; the highly dramatized images of evangelical conversion imposed on more traditional notions of the good death – all these were likely to resonate with a popular audience.[50] As Ian Green has demonstrated, vast amounts of print and presumably also of clerical and parental breath were expended in an attempt to catechize the stuff of Christian culture, as the Reformation had left it, into forms of profession recognizable to the better sort and clergy as orthodox (i.e., non-popish) Christianity. Martin Ingram and Laura Gowing have both shown that the church courts continued to attract the business of the laity. Here was order being defined and redefined, personal reputations being vindicated, and social peace of a sort being established or reestablished all through the institutional and judicial mechanisms of a now Protestant national Church.[51]

Now the outcome of all these interactions between the stuff of post-Reformation Christian culture, the religion of the godly, and the claims to obedience and sacrality of the Tudor monarchy was not (in Haigh's parlance) a nation of Protestants or even a Protestant nation as the godly would have conceived of either of those ideal types. On the contrary, we have page upon page of Puritan and hot Protestant complaint literature to assure us that this was not the case. But it is not necessary to argue that the more assertively godly aspects of all these cultural transactions and practices were either wildly popular or even often evangelically effective (in terms recognizable as success to the godly) in order to conclude that they were important in shifting dominant notions of national identity, political loyalty, and social order in distinctly Protestant directions. The more likely end result was the sort of anti-Catholic, post-Reformation Christianity identified by Tessa Watt in much of the cheapish religious print of the period.[52] And that was never enough to satisfy the godly, although as Green's massive study of catechisms, many of them written by hot Protestant and Puritan divines, shows, it did provide them with a basis from which to build. But if this was not reformation as the godly understood it, neither was it "Catholic continuity." When the godly viewed the resultant mixture, the commonsensical merit-mongering, the rote conformity, even to ostensibly non-Catholic or Protestant outward forms and observances, they tended to express their disgust by calling it popish or Church Papist. There is, however, no good reason why we should simply agree with them.

NOTES

1 W. Allen, *An Apology and True Declaration of the Institution and Endeavours of the Two English Colleges* (1581), pp. 34–34a.

2 R. Parsons, *A Brief Discourse* (1580), p. 34a.

3 C. Russell, "Arguments for religious unity," in *Unrevolutionary England* (London: Hambledon Press, 1992).

4 On this issue see P. Collinson, "Concerning the name Puritan, a comment," *Journal of Ecclesiastical History*, 31 (1980), pp. 463–88; also see P. Lake, "Defining puritanism – again?," in *Puritanism* ed. F. Bremer (Boston: Massachusetts Historical Society, 1993), pp. 3–29.

5 C. Haigh, *English Reformations* (Oxford: Oxford University Press, 1993). Dr Haigh has been no less proud of his achievement in seeing through the (in his phrase) "fairy story" spread by the seminary priests and Jesuits that it was they, rather than their Marian predecessors, who, in fact, saved (and in the process effectively re-created) an English Catholicism threatened, on the one hand, by the depredations of a heretical regime and, on the other, by the laxity and indecision of a moribund indigenous Catholic clergy and laity. On this see Haigh's "From monopoly to minority,"

Transactions of the Royal Historical Society, 5th ser., vol. 31 (1981), pp. 129–47.

6   Compare on this point the different accounts given in D. MacCulloch, *Thomas Cranmer* (New Haven and London: Yale University Press, 1996); Haigh, *English Reformations*, and E. Duffy, *The Stripping of the Altars* (New Haven and London: Yale University Press, 1992).

7   P. Collinson, *The Elizabethan Puritan Movement* (London: Cape, 1967), and P. Lake, *Anglicans and Puritans* (London: Allen and Unwin, 1988).

8   C. Haigh, "The continuity of catholicism in the English reformation," *Past and Present*, 93 (1981), repr. in ed. C. Haigh *The English Reformation Revised*, (Cambridge: Cambridge University Press, 1987).

9   C. Marsh, *The Family of Love in English Society, 1550–1630* (Cambridge: Cambridge University Press, 1994).

10 As quoted in P. Collinson, "Calvinism with an Anglican face," in *Godly People* (London: Hambledon Press, 1983), p. 214.

11 Lake, *Anglicans and Puritans*; P. Lake, *Moderate Puritans and the Elizabethan Church* (Cambridge: Cambridge University Press, 1982), chs 4 and 5. For the quote from Whitaker, see ibid., p. 114. The key term here, of course, is "religion"; all Elizabethan Protestants (save Separatists) conceived of themselves as devotees of the same religion and members of the same Church, a Church defined at base by its possession of right doctrine and properly administered sacraments. On the same basis many of them, with Jewel, conceived of themselves as members of an international Reformed Church. In this thought world, the notion of an "elect nation" was a nonsense. However, formal agreement on these issues did not of course mean that they "agreed" about everything else, or even that they shared the same styles of piety or views of the world. On this point see P. Lake, "The significance of the Elizabethan identification of the pope as Antichrist," *Journal of Ecclesiastical History*, 31 (1980), pp. 161–78; and idem, *Anglicans and Puritans*, esp. ch. 1 and 3.

12 Lake, *Moderate Puritans*, p. 132, and C. Dent, *Protestant Reformers in Elizabethan Oxford* (Oxford: Oxford University Press, 1983), pp. 195, 205; also more generally, see Lake, "Defining Puritanism – again?"

13 Lake, *Anglicans and Puritans*, ch. 1.

14 C. Marsh, "Piety and persuasion in Elizabethan England: the Church of England meets the Family of Love," in *England's Long Reformation, 1500–1800* ed. Nicholas Tyacke (London: University College, London, Press, 1997), pp. 141–65; for Perne's anti-Puritanism see Lake, *Moderate Puritans*, pp. 62–3, and more generally, P. Collinson, "Perne the turncoat; an Elizabethan reputation," in *Elizabethan Essays* (London: Hambledon Press, 1994), pp. 179–217.

15 Marsh, *Family of Love*, ch. 5. For a potentially ground-breaking but, in fact, sadly confused and confusing attempt to open up what is admittedly a central issue in the period, see R. Targoff, "The performance of prayer: sincerity and theatricality in early modern England," *Representations*, 60 (1998), pp. 44–69.

16 Lake, *Anglicans and Puritans*. To make the point, the Puritans produced their famous surveys of the ministry to demonstrate just how dreadful the run-of-the-mill conforming ministers of the national Church were compared to their godly but often persecuted brethren.

17 A. Walsham, *Church Papists* (Woodbridge: Boydell Press, 1993), esp. chs 4 and 5; quotations at p. 103. For McCoog's comment, see his *The Society of Jesus in Ireland, Scotland and England, 1541–1588* (Leiden: Brill, 1996), p. 145, n. 56.

18 C. Davies, "Towards a godly commonwealth" (Ph.D. Thesis, University of London, 1988); P. Collinson, *The Birthpangs of Protestant England* (London: Macmillan, 1988), ch. 5.

19 R. Bauckham, *Tudor Apocalypse* (Abingdon: Sutton Courtenay Press, 1978); C. Davies, "'Poor persecuted little flock' or 'commonwealth of Christians': Edwardian protestant concepts of the church," in *Protestantism and the National Church*, ed. P. Lake and M. Dowling (London, 1987), pp. 78–102; Lake, "Significance of the Elizabethan identification"; P. Lake, "Anti-popery: the structure of a prejudice," in *Conflict in Early Stuart England*, ed. R. Cust and A. Hughes (London: Longman, 1989),

pp. 72–106; Collinson, *Birthpangs*, chs 1 and 4; Walsham, *Church Papists*.

20 MacCulloch, *Thomas Cranmer*.

21 P. Collinson, "The monarchical republic of Elizabeth I," in *Elizabethan Essays*, pp. 31–57; *idem* "The Elizabethan exclusion crisis," *Proceedings of the British Academy*, 84 (1994), pp. 51–92.

22 Davies, "'Poor persecuted little flock'"; J. Shakespeare, "Plague and punishment," and J. Facey, "John Foxe and the defence of the English church," in *Protestantism and the National Church*, ed. Lake and Dowling, pp. 103–23, 162–92, respectively; Collinson, *Birthpangs*, ch. 1.

23 Haigh, *English Reformations*; J. J. Scarisbrick, *The Reformation and English People* (Oxford: Blackwell, 1984); Duffy, *Stripping of the Altars*.

24 Duffy, *Stripping of the Altars*, pt II; R. Hutton, "The local impact of the Tudor reformations," in *English Reformation Revised*, ed. C. Haigh; R. Whiting, *The Blind Devotion of the People* (Cambridge: Cambridge University Press, 1989), pp. 114–38. For the practical, institutional obstacles to Protestant proselytizing, see, e.g., F. Heal and R. O'Day, eds, *Continuity and Change: Personnel and Administration in the Church of England, 1500–1642* (Leicester: Leicester University Press, 1976), esp. chs 2, 6, and 7.

25 The classic narrative account is, of course, Collinson, *Elizabethan Puritan Movement*. On the ideological impact of the movement see Lake, *Anglicans and Puritans*, and for the complexities of Puritan engagement with the Elizabethan establishment, see Lake, *Moderate Puritans*.

26 Out of a vast and growing literature see e.g. R. Briggs, *Communities of Belief* (Oxford: Oxford University Press, 1989), chs 7 and 9; W. A. Christian, *Local Religion in Sixteenth-century Spain* (Princeton: Princeton University Press, 1989); Sara T. Nalle, *God in La Mancha: Religious Reform and the People of Cuenca, 1500–1650* (Baltimore: Johns Hopkins University Press, 1992).

27 J. Maltby, *Prayer Book and People in Elizabethan and Early Stuart England* (Cambridge: Cambridge University Press, 1998).

28 Lake, *Anglicans and Puritans*.

29 I refer here most particularly to the work of Christopher Haigh, which is suffused with these interpretational assumptions and commitments. See e.g. his articles, "Puritan evangelism in the reign of Elizabeth I," *English Historical Review*, 92 (1977), pp. 30–58, and "The church of England, the catholics, and the people," in *The Reign of Elizabeth I*, ed. Haigh (London: Cambridge University Press, 1984), pp. 195–219; and most recently his *English Reformations*. By now, it should be obvious that, from the perspective adopted in this essay, the debates about the continuity or otherwise of "Catholicism," about the "failure" or otherwise of "the Reformation," are best regarded as the result of *questions mal posés*. They are inappropriate for the Elizabethan period precisely because they owe their interest and analytic purchase to debates about the origins and course of the early Reformation. One can quite see why it might be important for someone with Haigh's revisionist interpretative stake in the earlier Reformation to inflect his account of the later period in this way. His (entirely justified) sense of the strength of a popular Catholicism that was neither moribund nor superstitiously corrupt (in Dickens's priceless phrase a "mere peasant conservatism") and his equally justified emphasis on the actual and potential achievements of the Marian regime both lead him to view the Elizabethan period from a certain early to mid-sixteenth-century "Reformation" perspective. For others, interested in the Elizabethan or post-Reformation period for its own sake, more concerned with what actually did happen, rather than with what might or could have happened; who want, with Bossy, to see the period as the starting point for a variety of post-Reformation problematics rather than as the fag end of a debate about the Henrician Reformation, such an approach cannot but seem both limiting and, in the end, distorting. The crucial insight into the coexistence of multiple Catholicisms during this period is to be found in M. C. Questier, *Conversion, Politics and Religion in England, 1580–1625* (Cambridge: Cambridge University Press, 1996). I should

like to thank Dr Questier for many discussions of this and other central themes pursued in this essay.

30 Duffy, *Stripping of the Altars*, pt I; for the critique of Thomas see pp. 1–8 and *passim*. For Thomas's own position see his *Religion and the Decline of Magic* (London: Weidenfeld and Nicolson, 1970). Also see A. G. Dickens, *The English Reformation* (London: B. T. Batsford, 1964).

31 Haigh, "Continuity of catholicism," pp. 43–4. The use of the historic present in that passage may be taken to denote a necessarily hypothetical mode of argument; for, as Haigh observes later on the same page, "the process by which a small group or community retained catholic norms during a movement from conformist conservatism will, in the nature of things, be largely unrecorded, since official documentation means outside interference and the disruption of the process we are trying to trace."

32 Ibid. pp. 45–6.

33 For the notion of voluntary religion, see P. Collinson, *The Religion of Protestants* (Oxford: Oxford University Press, 1982), ch. 6; also see his "The English conventicle," in *Voluntary Religion*, ed. D. Wood and W. Sheils. Studies in Church History, 23 (Oxford: Blackwell, 1986), pp. 223–59. For the use of Clarke's *Lives* as a historical source, see Collinson, "A 'magazine of religious patterns'; an Erasmian topic transposed in English protestantism," in his *Godly People*, pp. 499–526. For sacrament gadding, see Haigh, "The Church of England."

34 J. Bossy, *The English Catholic Community, 1570–1850* (London: Oxford University Press, 1975). For meetings of up to 120 people at mass and sermons at Lady Montagu's house, see A. C. Southern, ed., *An Elizabethan Recusant House* (London and Glasgow: Sands and Co., 1954), p. 43, or see Thomas Bell's account of meetings of ten or twelve priests for multiple masses and sermons in Lancashire, Archiepiscopal Archives Westminster, series A, vol. 14, no. 38. For Parsons, see L. J. Hicks, ed., *Letters and Memorials of Robert Parsons, S. J.*, Catholic Record Society, 39 (London, 1942), p. 86. I

owe these references to the kindness of Michael Questier and Margaret Sena.

35 P. Collinson, in M. Spufford, ed., *The World of Rural Dissenters, 1520–1725* (Cambridge: Cambridge University Press, 1995), p. 394. More generally on the same theme see his article "Towards a broader understanding of the dissenting tradition," in *Godly People*, pp. 527–62.

36 P. Collinson, "John Field and Elizabethan puritanism," in *Godly People*, pp. 335–70.

37 D. MacCulloch, *Suffolk and the Tudors* (Oxford: Oxford University Press, 1986). Also see his "Catholic and puritan in Elizabethan Suffolk: a county community divides," *Archiv für Reformationsgeschichte*, 72 (1981), pp. 232–89.

38 J. Bossy, "English catholics and the French marriage, 1577–81," in *Recusant History*, vol. 5, pp. 1959–60. For officially sponsored Puritan rule in the North see C. Cross, *The Puritan Earl* (London: MacMillan, 1966), and M. C. Questier, "Practical antipapistry during the reign of Elizabeth I", *Journal of British Studies*, 36 (1997), pp. 371–96.

39 For the assault on the more traditional aspects of church fabric and ornament, see M. Aston, *England's Iconoclasts* (Oxford: Oxford University Press, 1988); Haigh, "Continuity of catholicism", pp. 40–1.

40 Haigh, "Continuity of catholicism," pp. 40–1.

41 Collinson, *Birthpangs*, pp. 137–9.

42 Arnold Hunt is currently working on the performative aspects of preaching in this period.

43 K. Parker, *The English Sabbath* (Cambridge: Cambridge University Press, 1988).

44 P. Collinson, "Lectures by combination," in his *Godly People*, pp. 467–98, and *idem, Birthpangs*, ch. 2. On court preaching, now see P. McCullough, *Sermons at Court: Politics and Religion in Elizabethan and Jacobean Preaching* (Cambridge: Cambridge University Press, 1998).

45 D. Cressy, *Bonfires and Bells* (London: Weidenfeld and Nicolson, 1989).

46 Collinson, *Elizabethan Puritan Movement*, pp. 291–6.

47   Haigh, "From monopoly to minority," and see his subsequent exchange with McGrath: P. McGrath, "Elizabethan Catholicism: a reconsideration," *Journal of Ecclesiastical History*, 35 (1984), pp. 414–28 and C. Haigh, "Revision, Reformation, and the history of English Catholicism," same journal, 36 (1985), pp. 394–406.

48   This is to attempt to synthesize the claims and counter-claims of Duffy and Thomas (for which see n. 30) by viewing their altercation through the lens supplied by T. Watt, *Cheap Print and Popular Piety, 1550–1640* (Cambridge: Cambridge University Press, 1991). Given the present paper's concern with the multivarious and problematic ways in which the terms within which we more or less have to conduct our modern analyses of early modern religion are implicated in – indeed, often replicate or reinscribe – the structures of thought, polemical commitments, and underlying assumptions of contemporaries, the exchange between Duffy and Thomas is very instructive. For in many ways their debate replays sixteenth-century debates between Catholics and Protestants. Here Thomas is in the role of the Protestant critic of popish superstition, citing as he does – and perhaps more than he should – the testimony of later, even Elizabethan, Protestant writers to fuel his analysis of late medieval popular religion. Duffy, of course, assumes the role of the Catholic apologist, indignantly pointing out the highly respectable, thoroughly orthodox, learned, patristic, and scriptural origins of many of the practices and beliefs being fingered by Thomas and his often Protestant sources and witnesses as crypto-pagan, magically instrumental, mechanistically materialist, spiritually empty, or simply superstitious.

49   D. Cressy, *Birth, Marriage and Death* (Oxford: Oxford University Press, 1997).

50   I summarize here the general argument of P. Lake, "Deeds against nature: cheap print, protestantism and murder in early seventeenth-century England," in *Culture and Politics in Early Stuart England*, ed. K. Sharpe and P. Lake (Basingstoke: Macmillan, 1994), pp. 257–84; and P. Lake and M. C. Questier, "Agency, appropriation and rhetoric at the foot of the gallows: puritans, Romanists and the state in early modern England" *Past and Present*, 153 (1996), pp. 64–107, and *idem*, "Priests, prisons and people," in *England's Long Reformation*, ed. N. Tyacke., pp. 195–233. The basic claims advanced in these articles are in many ways confirmed with massive bibliographic learning by A. Walsham, "Aspects of Providentialism in Early Modern England" (Ph.D. thesis, University of Cambridge, 1995), a reworked version of which is forthcoming from Oxford University Press.

51   I. Green, *The Christians ABC* (Oxford: Oxford University Press, 1996); M. J. Ingram, *Church Courts, Sex and Marriage in England, 1570–1640* (Cambridge: Cambridge University Press, 1987); L. Gowing, *Domestic Dangers: Women, Words and Sex in Early Modern London* (Oxford: Oxford University Press, 1996). Also see M. K. McKintosh, *Controlling Misbehaviour in England, 1370–1600* (Cambridge: Cambridge University Press, 1998), and the forthcoming special number of the *Journal of British Studies* discussing the wider implications of McKintosh's book.

52   Watt, *Cheap Print and Popular Piety*.

6

The Family and the Household

Susan Dwyer Amussen

It is easy for readers of Shakespeare's plays to grasp the importance of family in Shakespeare's England. From the ubiquitous struggles between parents and children over marriage, to the eagerness of those who have been lost to reconnect with their families, the plays repeatedly make "family" a central theme. Yet the families described in the plays bear only a partial relation to the families of Shakespeare's England. As a result, one can almost imagine Shakespeare's audiences evaluating the families onstage against their own experience. To understand the import of Shakespeare's use of the family in his plays, it is helpful to examine the nature of family experience in his time.

The term "family," as it was used at the end of the sixteenth century, included not only the married couple at its head and their children, but also any servants or apprentices who worked with the family. Families at this time were usually small, averaging just under five people. Family size varied, as one might expect, with wealth: the richer members of society – yeomen, gentlemen, and nobles, as well as wealthy merchants in the towns – had larger households, while poor families were usually smaller, consisting of only three or four people.

The family was not just a residential unit: it was the place where much of the economic production of the sixteenth and early seventeenth centuries took place. In the countryside families farmed the land; other families worked together to weave cloth or to knit. In the towns, families worked together in the shops of bakers, butchers, tailors, and grocers; they worked as printers and turners, merchants and innkeepers. Most such enterprises required several workers, and many had separate roles for women and men. While some businesses were much larger and used additional laborers and workers, most of those working in a business lived on the premises. The economic role of the family meant that many families not only lived together, but worked together all day long.

The small size of households indicates also that most of them were nuclear – that is, they included only parents and children; there were relatively few extended households in England. The average age at first marriage between 1600 and 1650 was twenty-six for women, twenty-eight for men. As a result, by the time they married, most adults had experienced the death of at least one parent. Once they married, most couples set up their own household. Women usually bore between five and six children, of whom about four survived to adulthood.

Such structural information, however, is only a small part of the meaning of the family in Shakespeare's England. The family was not only the cornerstone of the economic order, it was at the center of the political order as well. The Puritan writer William Gouge called the family "a little commonwealth . . . a school wherein the first principles and grounds of government and subjection are learned." Well-ordered families, all contemporary commentators agreed, were essential to a well-ordered state. So what made for good order in the family?

Husbands and Wives

The true entry into adulthood in Shakespeare's England was marked not by age but by marriage. It was with marriage, and the establishment of an independent household, that men and women came to be seen as adults. As we have seen, this was usually relatively late by modern standards. The Elizabethan ambassador Sir Thomas Smith made the importance of marriage clear when he sought to define the yeoman, the prosperous and independent farmer of the English countryside: "commonly we do not call any a yeoman, till he be married, and have children, and as it were have some authority among his neighbours."[1]

The family was patriarchal. That is, power resided primarily in the male head, who was expected both to represent his family to the outside world and to govern all those in it so that it was orderly and peaceful. In this he was to be assisted by his wife. While the wife was certainly subordinate to the husband, she was also his helpmeet and shared much of the responsibility for the household. Thus John Dod and Robert Cleaver wrote: "the Governors of families . . . are first the *chief governor*, which is the *Husband*, secondly a *fellow-helper*, which is the Wife."[2] Dorothy Leigh framed it more starkly: "If she be thy wife, she is always too good to be thy servant, and worthy to be thy fellow."[3] The husband's role, all the contemporaries agreed, was to govern his household and run the enterprise; the wife was responsible for feeding and maintaining the household, supervising servants, and for any particular tasks that emerged from the family business. A wife's tasks also frequently included selling some of the products of her work – eggs, butter, or cheese, or wool that had been spun – at the market.

In towns wives occasionally had independent employment, usually in businesses based on household skills – spinning, laundry, provisioning, and the like. Such employment served to supplement the household income of laborers; it was rarely adequate to support a household. Unmarried adult women might continue to work in their parents' household or work as servants; more rarely, they lived and worked independently – though this was frowned on. Indeed, after 1563 it was illegal for unmarried women or men between the ages of fifteen and forty-five to live out of service: they were expected to be part of someone's household. Widows had somewhat more freedom to practice trades and often continued their husband's business – either independently or with the assistance of a journeyman or an apprentice. In Oxford during the sixteenth and seventeenth centuries, widows ran businesses (and took apprentices) as mercers, ironmongers, vintners, and tailors, as well as in more conventional trades.

The patriarchal order sounds simple: all a wife had to do was to be "chaste, silent and obedient," and everything would be all right. But the tasks allotted to the wife were neither trivial nor simple. When Sir John Oglander reflected on his prosperity, he wrote: "I could never have done it without a most careful, thriving wife, who was up before me every day, and oversaw all the outhouses, one that would not trust her maid with directions, she would wet her show to see it all herself acted."[4] The expectation of silence was virtually impossible to meet. A woman could not manage a household, especially one with several servants who had to be taught, without talking herself. The market, where women sold their own goods and bought provisions for the family, was not a silent place; nor did one succeed in the market if one were too meek or obedient. Bargaining was central, and as those who have tried it know, it is not for the faint of heart. Women might be silent or obedient in their husbands' presence, but they certainly could not do their jobs if they took that into the outside world. Many contemporary observers noted the *de facto* independence of women in England. Sir Thomas Smith wrote that "they be not kept so strait as in mew and with a guard as they be in Italy and Spain, but have almost as much liberty as in France." This independence was needed, Smith added, because women had "for the most part all the charge of the house and household."[5] Thomas Platter recorded the contemporary proverb that England was a woman's paradise, a servant's prison, and a horse's hell, and added that women "have far more liberty than in other lands."[6] If anything, however, such relative independence increased anxiety about women's behavior.

We can see in English society in Shakespeare's time two consequences of the concern with women's obedience. From the perspective of men, there was great anxiety about women who might *not* be chaste and silent. Thus there are numerous attacks on scolding women, and shaming rituals directed at women who beat their husbands. While this anxiety is not new and is certainly not unique, it appears to be more common and widespread in this period than other periods. In addition to Shakespeare's *Taming of the Shrew*, the period saw numerous attacks on women who stepped out of their roles. In 1615 Joseph Swetnam published *The Arraignment of Lewd, Idle, Froward, and Unconstant Women*, which alleged that women were repositories of all the vices – disobedient to their husbands, extravagant, unfaithful, and manipulative; five years later an anonymous writer published an attack on women that focused on dress, *Hic Mulier; or The Man Woman*. Both pamphlets obviously hit a nerve, and generated a lively debate; Swetnam went through ten editions in twenty years, *Hic Mulier* two editions in one year. Both generated a number of (far less popular) defenses of women as well. Anxiety about unruly women extended not only to those who were married, but perhaps even more to those who were not – single women and widows who were not controlled by any man. The Southampton authorities worried frequently in this period about charwomen – those who lived independently in the borough and worked in other women's houses; in Norwich the authorities were also particularly concerned about young women "living at their own hand."

While some men responded to the impossible expectations of women by criticizing those who did not meet them, women appear to have taken another approach. Married women were deeply concerned about their reputations. But the reputations they defended – at least in the courts – were for sexual chastity. They responded to charges that they were whores or that their husbands were cuckolds. Thus one servant said of her mistress, "My dame is a whore and an arrant whore and that which she hath gotten she hath by turning up her tail on the wool packs" – that is to say, her mistress had become pregnant through adultery. The accusations directed at women by way of their husbands were more indirect, but more than comprehensible at the time. Everyone understood the implications when Joanne Lane said to Mary Frary that her "husband's head was so big that it could scarce come forth of the door, and bade her the said Mary graft on fewer horns upon her husband's head, and that if the said Mary had had her right she should have been in the stewes." Such accusations of cuckoldry – often made, as in this case, using the symbol of the cuckold, the horns – could be responded to by a husband and wife jointly or by the wife alone: both reputations were damaged by the charge. The cuckold was a target of both mockery and humor; but, as in *The Merry Wives of Windsor*, some of the humor reflected anxieties about the consequences of women's unfaithfulness.

All marriages, happy and unhappy, were carefully watched by neighbors. In both town and countryside, people expected to know what others were doing: our idea that family life is "private" was not part of sixteenth-century thinking. Such observation was easiest in towns and villages, where proximity made observation simple. People knew who went to whose house and at what time: thus in 1596, neighbors suspected Henry Keymer's wife of adultery because she had been seen "many and sundry times as well in winter as in summer time late in the evening go to and come from Chosell his chamber... when it had been more meet or fit for her to have been at home in her own house in her husband's company." Similar observation was used in cases of domestic violence; in 1639 it was reported that William Markall of Mileham in Norfolk had been so drunk that "he beat his wife about the street so as the neighbours could not rest in their beds he kept such a disorder." Even when the beating was less public, neighbors intervened: Edward Dowding of Cerne Abbas, Dorset, beat his wife inside his house, but the commotion drew a crowd, including the constable, who used his authority to make peace.

Divorce was rare in Shakespeare's England, but marriages did break down and separations occur. The church courts gave legal separations – from "bed and board" –

but such separations did not give the right to remarry. In any case, the process was lengthy and relatively expensive. More often, couples agreed to separate, often after negotiations by families or friends, and went their separate ways. Thus when the inhabitants of Cley, Norfolk, heard that Gawen Brown had a previous wife living in the North, some local seamen went to find her and his children when they were in Berwick; still, they did nothing to disrupt his "marriage" in Cley to another woman. This case is remarkable for the countenancing of a bigamous marriage. More often, a separation was agreed, and property divided. The conflict between Anne and Thomas Felmingham first came to public attention with a violent incident in 1589; although a reconciliation was attempted, they separated soon after, and Thomas walked off with all the household goods, leaving her destitute. She then lived in the household of her daughter and son-in-law; it was not until 1596 that the separation case came before the court. At that point it served to legitimate an existing situation, not create a new one.

Those who quarreled within their families might create other problems. Simon Keeper of Norfolk not only beat his mother and locked her in the house, he caused strife between neighbors, and encouraged fights between minister and parish, landlord and tenant. In 1624 neighbors complained that Richard Sheepheard beat his wife and her children and also brought lawsuits without cause, only to drop them when neighbors had begun their defense. When he was asked to pay the rent on his town-owned house, he abused and cursed the churchwardens and other residents so much that they were afraid he would set the town on fire – a serious threat. Even worse were households where husbands and wives co-operated in creating disorder. In 1600 neighbors alleged that Hugh Ithell, Gent., "doth consort himself with many such bad and lewd persons being his servants and retainers as are ready at his or his wife's request to commit any enormity." When Richard Cutter and his wife Frances were found cutting other people's wood, Frances would allege that she had been raped to undermine the accusation of theft. When disorder spread outside the household, it undermined the role of the family as center of government. The attention paid to such behavior by neighbors underlines the important role of the family in society.

Of course, it is easiest to find out about families when things went wrong. There is little reason for us to learn of compatible or happy marriages. Within the structure of patriarchy, there were marriages where husband and wife found a way to work and live together with respect and affection. Not only do happy marriages not turn up in court; they are not a particularly interesting topic for humor, drama, or popular literature. But they certainly existed; we know of a few from the diaries and letters of people at the time. These are mostly of the upper ranks of society, as such documents survive only from those ranks. Men frequently reflected on the virtues of their wives and the comfort their wives brought them. After his wife's death in 1649, Sir Anthony Ashley Cooper wrote

> She was a lovely beautiful fair woman, a religious devout Christian; of admirable wit
> and wisdom beyond any I ever knew; yet the most sweet, affectionate, and observant

wife in the world. Chaste without suspicion of the most envious to the highest assurance of her husband; of a most noble and bountiful mind, yet very provident in the least things, exceeding all in anything she undertook.[7]

Ashley Cooper reflects both on her conventional virtues – thrift and chastity – as well as on the quality of her mind. His affection is evident, though it would be interesting to have her view of him as well.

Many women were deeply attached to their husbands. Lady Anne Clifford, in the midst of a very public argument with her husband (as well as her uncle and cousin, and eventually the king) about a claim to property, wrote in 1616 that she "came to [her] lodgings with a heavy heart considering how many things stood between my Lord and I." A year later she reported that because of the conflict, he did not spend the night with her.[8] And, Lady Fanshawe's grief when her husband died in 1666 was profound, though she focuses on his public, rather than private, demeanor:

> O all powerful Lord God, look down from heaven upon me, the most distressed wretch upon earth. See me with my soul divided, my glory and my guide taken from me, and in him all my comfort in this life. See me staggering in my path, which made me expect a temporal blessing for a reward of the great integrity, innocence, and uprightness of his whole life, and his patience in suffering the innocencies of wicked men.[9]

Husbands and wives negotiated a complex set of demands on them as they sought to build a family that was orderly, loving, and prosperous. These demands were met under the watchful eyes of families and neighbors. While the precise nature of households varied – between rural and urban, farmers and laborers – the household was still the "little commonwealth." And families were judged on the basis of how well they supported that model.

Children

If the relationship between husbands and wives was founded on contradiction, the relation of parents and children was far simpler. Children were to obey their parents, who raised them, introduced them to work and the world, and would ultimately (so, at least, the theory went) help their children choose a spouse so that they could become householders themselves. The experience of children differed sharply, depending on the wealth of their parents. While the turning points in childhood came at roughly the same ages for all children, other aspects of experience were far more varied. For instance, children of the gentry and aristocracy were frequently wet-nursed, since nursing was supposed to make women less sexually desirable to their husbands. Urban women also frequently employed rural wet-nurses – in this case in order to free up their time to work in the family business. However, the vast majority of women nursed their own children, usually for about two years.

For the purposes of this discussion, I will focus primarily on the vast majority of children – those who, though they did not live in abject poverty, were not members of the gentry or the aristocracy. Until the age of six or seven, girls and boys were raised together, usually wearing similar clothes (children's versions of women's clothes) and engaging in similar activities. There might be some introduction to work, but there would have been no expectation of an economic contribution from children this young. At the age of five or six, many children, both girls and boys, might be sent for a year or two to a local dame school, where they would be taught the basics of reading. (Writing was not usually taught until children were seven or eight.) In the early 1640s, Oliver Sanson "was put to school to a woman, to learn to read." He was so good that within four months he could read a chapter in the Bible "pretty readily."[10] Those who were sent to school were usually reading fluently by the age of seven; they began to learn to write after that. Such education, which often also included the catechism, not only gave children some exposure to the written word but occupied their time. Somewhere about the age of six or seven, boys moved into a different world from girls: they started wearing breaches, and their education and training took a different turn.

Most commentators seemed to think that it was at about the age of seven that children could begin to make an economic contribution. It was at this age that distinctions not only of gender became salient, but also of wealth. Few girls continued in school beyond this point – though in wealthier families they might continue to be taught at home. Among boys, those who would continue in school did so. They usually moved out of the village dame schools to free schools or the lower forms of grammar schools in a nearby town, taught not by a woman but by a man, frequently one with some university education. Such schools taught not just writing, but also arithmetic and the classics in Latin and Greek. This education was required for merchants, who needed to be able to deal with long-distance trade; it was also helpful for many of the wealthier farmers, who helped run their villages as well as their own farms. A few of those who went to grammar schools would continue to university.

Those who did not go to school went to work; between the ages of seven and about fourteen, children usually worked in the context of the family, though they might work for others. Thomas Tryon was put to work spinning and carding at the age of about six, a bit earlier than usual because of his family's poverty, and boasted that by the age of eight, he was earning two shillings a week.[11] The children of laborers would work with their parents and earn some money; children in families which had their own businesses or land would work with their parents. While their strength and skills were limited, there were many tasks they were able to undertake. While working with their parents, they would begin to learn the more specialized skills they would need as adults.

During this time, most children lived at home with their parents, though a few were sent to live with other families. This was particularly true of poor children, who might be sent to relatives who were more prosperous or who had no children of their own. Also, children were often sent to other households for a time after a parent's death. Finally, some children attended schools that were too far from their homes to go daily, so they would lodge in the town where their school was. Even when children were living away from home, parents monitored their progress as best they might; in a letter in 1595 John Hill told his brother-in-law George Sawer that "Alice your daughter is in health and more grown in height...and frameth to her business reasonably well." Still, until their early teens, most English children were at home.

The next major transition in the life of children came in their early to mid-teens. Sometime between the ages of thirteen and sixteen most children left home for more formal training. Such training could take many forms. The one that is most familiar to us – continuing attendance at educational institutions – affected a relatively small number of boys. This could be at either the universities (Oxford and Cambridge) or the Inns of Court in London, where lawyers were trained. While the numbers were small, the period between 1560 and 1640 saw a vast expansion of educational opportunity; in the 1630s about 2.5 percent of young men between the ages of sixteen and twenty engaged in higher education, a higher proportion of the age group than would be in higher education until the mid-twentieth century.

Attendance at university or the Inns of Court prepared young men for the professions – the Church, law, and medicine. The training for other employments was experiential. That is, young women and men worked as servants or apprentices to people in a particular trade and in so doing learned the skills that were necessary for adult work. The nature of that training differed between town and countryside. In the country, as we have seen, children often went into service in early adolescence. As farm servants hired out by the year or the task, they continued to develop their skills as workers. Girls learned to do all the tasks of running a household, from cooking and cleaning to dairying; they also frequently learned to spin if they had not already. Boys learned the basics of the husbandry appropriate to their region – keeping sheep or cattle, plowing, harvesting. By the age of fifteen, boys employed on the Stiffkey estate in Norfolk earned close to adult wages. Poor children who were sent away to families to be taught were described as being apprenticed in "huswifery" and "husbandry." Both these categories actually included a wide range of activities and skills. Scattered evidence suggests that by sometime in their late teens, young people had acquired both the skills and the strength expected of adult workers. Other children were apprenticed in rural trades, from weaving to lace-making, blacksmithing to cooping. They would be bound for a period of years to a master or mistress who was obliged to feed and house them and teach them the trade. These arrangements were more formal than the ordinary forms of service and were agreed by the parents and the master or mistress, in consultation with the young person. In the 1630s Richard Davies's parents, who had a small farm in North Wales, decided to apprentice him to a shopkeeper; when that did not work out, Davies eventually found a felt-maker willing to take him as an apprentice, and the arrangement was worked out between him, his parents, and his master.

Such rural apprenticeships, usually in small market towns, were similar to arrangements in larger towns and cities. However, in the towns and cities with formal structures of self-government, apprenticeship not only provided training, its success-ful completion was usually a way to obtain the rights and privileges of a freeman of the town – to trade freely, to vote for town officers, and (ultimately) even to serve as one. Such privileges could also be passed from father to son. Some evidence suggests that young people in towns stayed at home, being trained by their parents, more often than did rural children. Still, the model of apprenticeship was substantially the same.

Apprenticeships cost some money, though for most trades the sums were relatively modest, given that they covered both board and training. In Bristol between 1615 and 1630, 85 percent of apprenticeships cost less than £10. This covered the cost of boarding a young person until he or she knew enough to make a contribution to the enterprise. Unlike servants, apprentices were paid no wages, but the skills they obtained were expected to provide access to a secure trade. The parents of apprentices to the most lucrative trades paid enormous sums; in London in the seventeenth century between 20 and 30 percent of apprentices in the grocery, drapery, and haberdashery trades, which dominated both the export and the carriage trades, were sons of knights, esquires, and gentlemen.

Apprenticeship offered occupational training in a familial context. This context, it was expected, would ease the transition into the working world for young people. It also ensured that there was someone who was responsible for adolescents and their behavior; it helped to maintain order. It meant that while there were many young people in large towns and cities, they could to a great extent be controlled. They were still under authority – though young people frequently tried to escape from it!

Education at a university was also available to a relatively broad social range. It was made more affordable by the scholarships and endowments that were given to many Oxford and Cambridge colleges to educate future clergy. In many cases the colleges had relationships with a number of grammar schools, whose brightest boys would be sent on. The Church was a profitable employment for young men, and a university education was increasingly necessary for employment in it. Attendance at university was, for the sons of yeomen, an increasingly important avenue for social mobility.

Of course, not all those who attended university or the Inns of Court were there for purposes of social mobility. Increasingly, attendance at university or the Inns of Court provided part of the training of the sons of the upper gentry and aristocracy. These boys would not necessarily complete their studies, but their attendance and the learning they received provided a necessary grounding for their role as members of the English governing elite. At university they would supplement the traditional syllabus – logic and philosophy, physics, theology and geometry – with more liberal studies in Latin literature and history. There were also diversions, respectable (dancing and hunting) or not (drinking). The legal training provided by the Inns of Court was particularly useful for landowners in defending their property, serving as justices of the peace, and, if they served as Members of Parliament, in drafting legislation. In the early seven-teenth century Sir William Wentworth advised his son: "have some insight in the laws, for it will be a great contentment, comfort and credit and quiet for you."[12] Edward Waterhouse, writing later in the century, was more specific: noblemen and gentlemen "have great estates, and great trusts in government; in which ignorance of the laws will not well set them off."[13] The libraries of the elite always had large collections of legal books, and the political debates of the seventeenth century were saturated with legal knowledge. Finally, whether at a university or an inn of court, education provided an opportunity to build a circle of friends with similar knowledge and experience. At Oxford, Sir Nicholas Le Strange wrote to his son, "you might have a new acquaintance wholly to choose, and I hope you have contracted it with such sober and discreet young persons, with whom you may spend some hours of business with advantage, and your Times of Leisure with Innocence."[14] Education, for the sons of the elite, marked a path into the wider social world in which they would function.

The educational opportunities for girls were more limited than those for boys. Few girls attended school after the age of about seven, though girls from gentry families might be educated at home. Because education was expected to prepare children for their adult lives, the education of girls was largely domestic. The skills of the housewife were clearly skills, but they were not specialized ones; beyond that, the expectation was that they would work with their husband in whatever trade he followed. Therefore, girls' education sought to give them a range of skills which could be adapted to whatever activity, commercial or agrarian, their husbands might pursue.

The training that English youth received in the late sixteenth and early seventeenth centuries meant that by late adolescence most young people were living away from home. Although most of them were still living in the context of a household, in which their status was akin to, but somewhat distinct from, that of children, they had considerable independence. In towns and villages across England, young people who were apprentices or servants gathered at church, at fairs, and other events. There was an extensive and, to a great extent, unregulated social life, though it was never completely independent of adults, and earnest efforts were often made to suppress it. Young people in Noke, Oxfordshire, played a game of stoolball in the churchyard on a Sunday in 1596, while at Keevil in Wiltshire in 1624 young men alleged that "there is usually dancing in Keevil upon the Sabbath days . . . after evening prayer."[15] In Dorchester, young people frequently gathered at alehouses in groups that combined the sons of respectable citizens and less respectable apprentices – not just in the evening, but during the day as well. It was in this informal social life that most men and women met their spouses. Andrew Fooke and Katherine Goodfellow of Dorchester missed church on a summer Sunday, going into the country with friends "to eat milk and cream";[16] they were later married.

Decisions about marriage were ones that young people were expected to make in conjunction with their parents or "friends." Surviving evidence indicates, however, that preliminary decisions were made by the young people; the parents were usually brought into the discussion only later. This was largely a logistical decision: if young people were together in service, they might be some distance from the homes of their parents. While most young people were in service within about ten miles of their native village, this was still far enough to make contact infrequent. Although the preliminary decisions were made independently, most often agreements were premised on the agreement of parents or "friends" – a nebulous term that referred to more distant family who had the interests of a young person at heart. Thus in 1563 Anne Spooner of Walberswick, Suffolk, told Stephen Gurney that "she would make him promise if he could get the good will of most of her friends," while some ten years later Robert Pernell of Rollesby, Norfolk, told Clara Bateman that he thought of her as his wife, but pulled out of a marriage because of his father's opposition.

It was only in the upper ranks of society that arranged marriages were the norm. Even so, most parents consulted their children before completing the arrangements for a marriage. There might be an extended negotiation between parents and children on the subject of marriage. Mary Boyle turned down one extremely eligible suitor chosen by her father, and though she promised never to marry without her father's consent, she also told him that she would only marry Charles Rich, a younger son; Boyle's father eventually relented. Marriage for love – which was assumed to be infatuation – was frowned on, but it was common knowledge that marriage without affection was a source of disaster. Sir Edward Turnor spoke for many when he told his daughter in the late seventeenth century that he sought "to dispose of our brother and yourself in marriage as might make you both and myself most pleased and happy therein."[17] The idea that both parents and children should be pleased – that worldly considerations and personal ones should be balanced – was common. Modern readers are apt to consider arranged marriages and marriages by inclination as entirely different. But it is more useful to think of a continuum, from the completely free choice of a spouse to completely arranged marriages. Very few marriages in Shakespeare's time were at either end of the scale; most fell somewhere in the middle, with a balance between the viewpoints of the potential partners and their parents. Marriage for all young people was considered an important matter – too important to be left entirely to them.

Property was in some way a central consideration in most marriages. That property consisted of whatever the young people themselves had saved, as well as whatever their "portion" from their parents might be. Among those with land, the bulk of the land – whether a 30-acre farm or an enormous estate – usually went to the oldest son. However, most fathers tried to give their younger children some portion with which to establish themselves: it might be the value of an apprenticeship and the purchase of a shop, or a smaller landholding, or the money with which to purchase a "living." Daughters too received portions, almost always in cash. Sons who inherited land from their fathers were frequently responsible for paying their siblings' portions from the profits of the land. As a result, conflict between parents and children and between siblings about portions and inheritance were frequent: they had important consequences for all those involved.

Sexuality

Officially, sexual relations were condoned only within marriage. Readers will not be surprised to learn that this official expectation was not the whole story of sexual activity. While we can say little about the subjective experience of sexuality, we can understand some of the contexts and meanings associated with various kinds of illicit sexual activity.

One form of illicit sexual activity depended on the definition of marriage. According to the Church, a properly worded promise between two people to marry was binding: if the promise was made in the future tense, it would become an official marriage at some point in the future (or when sexual relations took place); when the words were spoken in the present tense, they constituted a full marriage. The importance of even a promise to marry in the future – which made it impossible to marry anyone else – meant that allegations of promises were powerful tools in local negotiations; in some cases at least, witnesses were alleged to have been suborned to give false testimony of a promise. The complications of the legal system led to increasing pressure to ensure that promises were made before witnesses and that the wedding took place in church. Still, many women agreed to sexual relations on the promise of marriage; as far as they were concerned, they were married. It is not surprising that, given this custom, between 10 percent and 30 percent of all brides in Shakespeare's time were already pregnant.

The laws of marriage which made it common for brides to be pregnant at marriage also provided an excellent cover for sexual exploitation. Under the promise of marriage, men would persuade women to sleep with them, and then fail to fulfill their promise. In these cases, the privacy of the promise – or even cleverly phrased conditional language – made it virtually impossible to enforce. However, as with couples who were already married, neighborhood observation provided some protection for young women. In 1623 Helen Hathwayt of York complained that she had been contracted to George Hunter, who disappeared, leaving Helen pregnant, shortly before the wedding; the clothes had been bought and guests invited, but Hunter had since married another woman and was living in Essex. Sometimes, of course, it was pressure from the man's family that blocked a marriage: at Christmas 1581 Edward Planders and Francys Brooke contracted themselves in marriage, and Francys became pregnant; but Edward pulled out of the match from fear of his father's displeasure.

If the complexity of the law of marriage created opportunities for sexual exploitation, the household arrangements of the period created another. Servants were frequently propositioned, harassed, and ultimately raped by their masters or their masters' sons. With the sons there might be a vague promise of marriage, but such promises were not generally possible for masters. While occasionally these relationships might reflect romance, they were more often coercive: the women involved had little power and few resources against their masters. William Dey, the rector of Cranwich, Norfolk, in the 1590s had sexual relationships with two of his servants, one of whom bore him a child. In 1622, Henry Eaton, having made his servant Marie Hobbert pregnant, first sought to have her accuse others of paternity, then gave her savine as an abortifacient, "affirming that it was no sin so to do ... and that it was a common thing in London, for such women, to use such practices in such cases." When Marie publicly accused him of paternity, he threatened to beat her brains out. One could scarcely describe either of these as romantic or loving relationships: the men simply took advantage of women in their power for their own pleasure.

The exchange of sex for favors – money, food, or clothing – was undoubtedly a common occurrence; in these instances sexual activity might supplement inadequate wages for poor women, especially those whose income was limited because they had borne illegitimate children. A more formal trade in prostitution was present primarily in London, though it probably also existed in other cities. In London there were both brothels, where women were employed by pimps to provide sexual services, and inns, which rented rooms to women who entertained men. In the 1570s there was an attempt to crack down on the brothels – an attempt that included prosecution of patrons as well as prostitutes – but it was not successful: there is evidence of at least 100 bawdy-houses operating in the later 1570s. And by the early seventeenth century, it was "customary" for London apprentices to attack the brothels on Shrove Tuesday. Whether these attacks represented a preparation for the abstinence of Lent or the open expression of resentment because the apprentices could not afford the prostitutes' services is not clear.

There was also run-of-the-mill adultery. Both men and women sometimes tired of their spouse and sought sexual satisfaction elsewhere. The implications of adultery for women and men were very different, however. While a man who committed adultery betrayed his wife, the "worst" that contemporaries thought could happen was that he would father an illegitimate child that would become a burden to the parish. A woman who committed adultery, on the other hand, disrupted the order of the household and might bear a child that was not her husband's but would then have inheritance rights. The birth of sons and daughters, of course, meant different things: in a 1635 court case, a witness said of a child born to a married woman, "if it had been a boy it should have been Mr Harman's man's, but being a girl, Nathaniel Stallworthy [her husband] was fain to father it." The prospect of raising (and providing for) another man's child provided the name for a man whose wife was unfaithful: cuckold, after the cuckoo who lays her eggs in another bird's nest. Adultery by a woman was sufficiently serious to be a legitimate cause of separation in the church courts; a man's adultery on its own was not.

Finally, there is scattered evidence of male homosexual practices in the period, but little detailed information. While moralists frequently condemned homosexual behavior (which they assumed was centered in London), their condemnations are conventional and offer little detail. Francis Bacon was widely rumored to have sexual relations with his male servants and was prodigiously generous with them; in 1631 England was scandalized by the case of the earl of Castlehaven, accused of sodomy with his servants and of assisting one of them in the rape of his wife. Prosecutions for homosexuality were quite rare and were most common when there was violence or other aggravating circumstances. Records are silent about sexual relations between women.

It is not the existence of these forms of illicit sexual activity that is important as much as the response to them. All forms of illicit sexual activity – that is, all such activity outside marriage – were considered dangerous. They threatened the social order by creating bonds between people that had not been sanctioned publicly and that might undermine existing legitimate relationships. Even when both partners were unmarried, the lack of responsibility entailed in the relationship made it troubling to neighbors and friends, who wanted to know who was responsible for what. As long as marriage was the cornerstone of the social order, sexual relations outside marriage had implications far beyond the mere fact of them.

It sounds simple to say that household and family were at the center of the social order in early modern England. That apparently simple idea, however, obscures a more complex reality. The inhabitants of Shakespeare's England knew both the expectations of them and the difficulties many people had in meeting them. They knew how many people failed to meet the expectations that were articulated in sermons, advice books, and catechisms; they knew how they themselves failed to meet them. Some of the failures were accepted, if not welcomed; others were deeply troubling to those who observed them. It was this complex reality that was part of the framework not just for Shakespeare, but for his audiences too.

NOTES

1   Sir Thomas Smith, *De Republica Anglorum: A Discourse on the Commonwealth of England*, ed. L. Alston (Cambridge, 1906), p. 45.

2   Cited in Susan D. Amussen, *An Ordered Society: Gender and Class in Early Modern England* (Oxford and New York, Blackwell, 1988), p. 41.

3   Ibid.

4   Quoted in Ralph Houlbrooke, *English Family Life 1576–1716* (Oxford and New York: Blackwell, 1988), p. 65.

5   Quoted in Amussen, *Ordered Society*, p. 49.

6   Ibid.

7   Cited in Houlbrooke, *English Family Life*, pp. 69–70.

8   *The Diaries of Lady Anne Clifford*, ed. D. J. H. Clifford (Stroud, Glos.: Alan Sutton, 1990), pp. 30, 54.

9   *The Memoirs of Anne, Lady Halkett, and Ann, Lady Fanshawe*, ed. with an introduction by John Loftis (Oxford: Clarendon Press, 1979), p. 185.

10 Quoted by Margaret Spufford, *Small Books and Pleasant Histories: Popular Fiction and its Readership in Seventeenth-Century England* (Cambridge and New York: Cambridge University Press, 1981), p. 24.

11 Ibid., p. 28.

12 Quoted by Felicity Heal and Clive Holmes, *The Gentry in England and Wales 1500–1700* (Stanford, Calif.: Stanford University Press, 1994), p. 272.

13 Quoted by Lawrence Stone, *The Crisis of Aristocracy 1558–1641* (Oxford: Clarendon Press, 1965), p. 691.

14 Quoted by Heal and Holmes, *Gentry in England*, pp. 268–9.

15 Martin Ingram, *Church Courts, Sex, and Marriage in England, 1570–1640* (Cambridge and New York: Cambridge University Press, 1987), p. 117.

16 David Underdown, *Fire from Heaven: Life in an English Town in the Seventeenth Century* (London: HarperCollins, 1992), p. 81.

17 Heal and Holmes, *Gentry in England*, p. 62.

Suggestions for Further Reading

Adair, Richard, *Courtship, Illegitimacy and Marriage in Early Modern England*. Manchester and New York: Manchester University Press, 1996.

Amussen, Susan D., *An Ordered Society: Gender and Class in Early Modern England*. Oxford and New York: Basil Blackwell, 1988.

——"Being stirred to much unquietnesse": violence and domestic violence in early modern England. *Journal of Women's History*. 6 (1994), pp. 70–89.

Archer, Ian W., *The Pursuit of Stability: Social Relations in Elizabethan London*. Cambridge and New York: Cambridge University Press, 1991.

Ben-Amos, Ilana Krausman, *Adolescence and Youth in Early Modern England*. New Haven and London: Yale University Press, 1994.

Bray, Alan, *Homosexuality in Renaissance England*. London: Gay Men's Press, 1982.

Cressy, David, *Birth, Marriage, and Death: Ritual, Religion, and the Life-Cycle in Tudor and Stuart England*. Oxford and New York: Oxford University Press, 1997.

Gowing, Laura, *Domestic Dangers: Women, Words, and Sex in Early Modern London*. Oxford: Clarendon Press, 1996.

Griffiths, Paul, *Youth and Authority: Formative Experiences in England, 1560–1640*. Oxford: Clarendon Press, 1996.

Heal, Felicity and Holmes, Clive *The Gentry in England and Wales 1500–1700*. Stanford, Calif.: Stanford University Press, 1994.

Henderson, Katherine Usher and McManus, Barbara F., *Half Humankind: Contexts and Texts of the Controversy about Women in England, 1540–1640*. Urbana and Chicago: University of Illinois Press, 1985.

Herrup, Cynthia, The patriarch at home: the trial of the 2nd earl of Castlehaven for rape and sodomy. *History Workshop Journal*, 41 (1996), pp. 1–18.

Houlbrooke, Ralph, *English Family Life 1576–1716*. Oxford and New York: Basil Blackwell, 1988.

Ingram, Martin, *Church Courts, Sex, and Marriage in England, 1570–1640*. Cambridge and New York: Cambridge University Press, 1987.

Jones, Jeanne, *Family Life in Shakespeare's England: Stratford-upon-Avon, 1570–1630*. Thrupp, Glouc.: Sutton Publishing, for the Shakespeare Birthplace Trust, 1996.

Laurence, Anne, *Women in England, 1500–1760: A Social History*. London: Weidenfeld and Nicolson, 1994.

Mayhew, Graham, Ben-Amos, Ilana Krausman, and Sharpe, Pamela, Service and apprenticeship in pre-industrial England, *Continuity and Change*, 6 (1991), pp. 201–70.

Pollock, Linda, *Forgotten Children: Parent–child Relations from 1500 to 1900*. Cambridge and New York: Cambridge University Press, 1983.

Prior, Mary, *Women in English Society, 1500–1800*. London and New York: Methuen, 1985.

Sharpe, J. A. *Early Modern England: A Social History 1550–1760*. London: Edward Arnold, 1987.

Spufford, Margaret, *Small Books and Pleasant Histories: Popular Fiction and its Readership in Seventeenth-Century England*. Cambridge and New York: Cambridge University Press, 1981.

Stone, Lawrence, *The Family, Sex and Marriage in England 1500–1800*. London: Weidenfeld and Nicolson, 1977.

Underdown, David *Fire from Heaven: Life in an English Town in the Seventeenth Century*. London: HarperCollins, 1992.

—— The taming of the scold: the enforcement of patriarchal authority in early modern England. In Anthony Fletcher and John Stevenson (eds), *Order and Disorder in Early Modern England*, Cambridge: Cambridge University Press, 1985.

Wiltenburg, Joy, *Disorderly Women and Female Power in the Street Literature of Early Modern England and Germany*. Charlottesville: University Press of Virginia, 1992.

7

Shakespeare and Political Thought

Martin Dzelzainis

I

When Sir Philip Sidney surveyed the literary landscape, to his dismay, in *A Defence of Poetry*, it was at the start of the last decade – the 1580s – in which this could be done without being confronted by the imposing figure of Shakespeare. From the 1590s onwards, poets and critics had to labour, often to *their* dismay, in the shadow of his presence. But while it is now difficult to imagine a literary history of the period from which Shakespeare is absent, as far as the history of political thought is concerned, he seems to be literally a nonentity. Thus in a recent 350-page volume of essays on *The Varieties of British Political Thought, 1500–1800*, his name appears only three times. The explanation is that

> Shakespeare was perhaps the last great English poet unaffected by the constant production of political controversy in print; all his canonical successors – Milton, Marvell, Dryden, Defoe, Swift, Pope, Johnson, Blake, Wordsworth, Coleridge, Byron, Scott – not only wrote their poems and other literary works surrounded by this component of a print culture, but contributed to it, very often in the prose genres peculiar to it. (Pocock 1993: 3)

Since Shakespeare produced almost no non-dramatic prose (and in this was unlike not only his canonical successors but also contemporaries such as Spenser, Ralegh, and Donne), his exclusion from a history based on 'the broadsheet, the pamphlet, the newsletter, the journal, and the essay, treatise or learned folio seen as interacting with all these' follows as a matter of course (ibid.).

Nor is there much prospect of the embargo being lifted, given that there is

> a division of labour between those who study genres which make them 'historians of political thought' and those whose studies make them 'historians of literature', and to

some extent the two groups produce, for both good and ill, non-identical understandings of what 'politics' and even 'history' are. (Ibid.)

It might well be objected that such purism flouts the trend in favour of dissolving boundaries between adjacent disciplines. But any protest to this effect is bound to remain muted so long as literary historians themselves remain doubtful whether there actually is any such thing as a Shakespearian 'variety' of political thought. For if they are not convinced that Shakespeare demands to be considered in these terms, then it is far from clear why others should be. It is necessary, therefore, to begin by assessing the nature of these doubts.

Scepticism about Shakespeare's credentials as a political thinker has chiefly taken two forms. The first is the long-standing view that he has nothing new or significant to offer in terms of political thought, but is content merely to rehearse a familiar repertoire of doctrines and figures (the Tudor myth, the great chain of being, degree, obedience, the many-headed multitude, the Machiavel, the king's two bodies), drawn from a familiar range of sources (the Bible, the Homilies, Tudor treatises like Sir Thomas Elyot's *The Boke Named the Governour* (1531), other plays). For some, this disposition to subscribe to, rather than challenge, existing beliefs makes him the very model of a traditionalist; for others, it is what transfixes him in the posture of a reactionary.

Before pinning these labels on too firmly, it should be recognized that Shakespeare's practices were rooted in the rhetorical culture of which he was a product. Two of its features in particular need to be grasped if we are to understand why these claims about Shakespeare appear plausible. The first is that the classical rhetoricians and their Renaissance followers agreed that a vital stage in composition was *inventio*, or the seeking out of the most appropriate and persuasive arguments in *loci communes*; that is, in the most likely or common places (see Skinner 1996: 111–19). The aim was to promote facility in argument so that, as Francis Bacon (thinking of lawyers) put it, 'pleaders should have all Places whereof they have most continual use ready handled in all the variety that may be' (Bacon 1996: 223). More generally, the term 'commonplaces' applied not only to these forms of argument but also to the stock of proverbs, maxims and aphorisms which lent weight to any speech. Thus Erasmus supplied guidance on methods of composition in his *De copia* (a text widely used in grammar schools), and ready-made collections of commonplaces in his *Adagia* and *Apophthegmata* (see Jones 1977: 11–13, 21). While warning that 'the use of common-place books' might result in 'a retardation of reading' and a 'relaxation of memory', Bacon still thought of the practice as one which 'assureth copie of invention, and contracteth judgement to a strength'. He himself appended a treatise *Of the Colours of Good and Evil*, consisting of several 'places of persuasion and dissuasion', to the 1597 edition of his *Essays*, so that wits could be sharpened on these 'colours' (or 'popularities' and 'appearances', as he also termed them), to discover 'in what cases they hold, and in what they deceive' (Bacon 1996: 97, 229).

Shakespeare's rhetorical training helps to explain his copiousness in turning out on average two plays a year. At times, however, he self-consciously dramatizes the process of invention itself, as characters (to use Bacon's terms) seek 'colours' or 'places of persuasion' to justify courses of action. In *2 Henry VI*, for example, once the king has abandoned the protector, Duke Humphrey of Gloucester, the nobles set about plotting – or inventing – his murder. Winchester declares

> That he should die is worthy policy,
> But yet we want a color for his death.
> 'Tis meet he be condemn'd by course of law.
>   (III. i. 235–7)

To Suffolk, this 'were no policy' at all, since 'yet we have but trivial argument / More than mistrust, that shows him worthy death' (III. i. 238, 241–2). The debate about how best to do away with Gloucester proceeds in the coded form of Ovidian commonplaces about eagles and chickens and foxes and lambs until Suffolk aphoristically concludes that

> 'tis no matter how,
> So he be dead; for that is good deceit
> Which mates him first that first intends deceit.
>   (III. i. 263–5)

Suffolk thus becomes one of Shakespeare's earliest exponents of the view that policy can override law and justice and license deceit.

Similarly, the conspiracy scene in *Julius Caesar* opens with Brutus soliloquizing that 'It must be by his death'. While admitting that Caesar has always been ruled by 'his reason' rather than 'his affections', he observes that ''tis a common proof / That lowliness is young ambition's ladder', leading inexorably to 'the upmost round' (II. i. 10, 20–1, 24). Taking this commonplace as a guide to how Caesar may act, he continues;

> Then lest he may, prevent. And since the quarrel
> Will bear no color for the thing he is,
> Fashion it thus: that what he is, augmented,
> Would run to these and these extremities.
>   (II. i. 28–31)

Since the facts in the case ('quarrel') will not sustain a probable argument or even the appearance of one ('color'), he must change ('fashion') the facts by augmenting them. It could thus be said that the reasons Brutus arrives at for assassinating Caesar are, at least in the technical sense, the purest invention.

The other aspect of rhetorical culture we need to consider is the method of arguing *in utramque partem* (on either side of the question). The ability to speak with equal plausibility for and against any given proposition was the one most prized by Roman and Tudor rhetoricians alike (see Skinner 1996: 27–30, 97–9). Thus when Bacon wrote *A Letter to Sir Henry Savile, touching helps for the intellectual powers*, among the exercises he urged upon him was the 'ancient habit of the philosophers; "Si quis quaerat in utramque partem de omni scibili" ("If only people would debate all things knowable from both sides")' (Bacon 1996: 118, 574). This is not to suggest that the habit was the preserve of a philosophical élite; on the contrary, pupils at grammar schools were expected to acquire proficiency in arguing *in utramque partem*, and routinely honed their dialectical skills by composing orations on controversial themes like the one suggested by Erasmus in *De copia*: 'Was Brutus right or wrong in murdering Caesar?' (Jones 1977: 16).

As Emrys Jones remarks, Shakespeare 'profited more from this method than any one else in his time' (ibid. 14). His unrivalled ability to stage situations requiring the expression of opposed views is displayed to full effect in the competing funeral orations, in prose and verse, of Brutus and Mark Antony (*Julius Caesar*, III. ii). However, as the sequence of confrontations – amounting virtually to an anatomy of the commonwealth – in Act IV of *2 Henry VI* shows, he was adept at composing in this vein from the outset. Thus the exchange between Lord Say and Jack Cade takes the form of a pair of declamations, *pro* and *contra*, in verse and prose, on the theme of education. Cade's indictment of Say attacks the very foundations of English human-ism: he 'has most traiterously corrupted the youth of the realm in erecting a grammar school'; 'caus'd printing to be us'd' and 'built a paper-mill'; put the poor 'in prison, and because they could not read . . . hang'd them' (IV. vii. 32–4, 36–7, 43–4). Say opens his defence with a commonplace from Caesar's *Commentaries*. In the circum-stances, however, this proves a fatal lapse in decorum, for the more eloquent he is in defending learning, the more he succeeds in piling up evidence against himself. Although moved by Say's speech, Cade pushes his case to its logical conclusion: 'He shall die, and it be but for pleading so well for his life' (IV. vii. 106–7: see Patterson 1989: 49–50; Leggatt 1988: 18–19).

Cade's power is broken in the scene where he competes with Clifford for the loyalty of the rebels (a precursor of the Forum scene in *Julius Caesar*, with Cade as Brutus and Clifford as Antony). His appeal to the principle of 'ancient freedom', and scorn for those who 'delight to live in slavery to the nobility', proves less winning than Clifford's appeal to national pride, in which he calls to mind first the heroic figure of Henry V and then an image of the old enemy, the French, 'lording it in London streets' (IV. viii. 27–8, 45). Cade's disruptive energies lead finally – and symbolically – to a walled garden in Sussex where he is put to the sword by its owner, Alexander Iden. Forced by hunger 'to see if I can eat grass' (IV. x. 7–8), Cade resembles Nebuchadnezzar, who 'was driven from men, and did eat grass as oxen' (Dan. 4: 33: see Leggatt 1988: 17); indeed, he speaks as one who is barely human, a 'stray' animal about to be impounded by the 'lord of the soil' (IV. x. 24–5). Iden, by contrast, speaks in the accents of the landed gentry, issuing a stream of commonplaces on the virtues of rural self-sufficiency:

> Lord, who would live turmoiled in the court
> And may enjoy such quiet walks as these?
> This small inheritance my father left me
> Contenteth me, and worth a monarchy.
> I seek not to wax great by others' [waning],
> Or gather wealth, I care not with what envy.
> Sufficeth that I have maintains my state
> And sends the poor well pleased from my gate.
>   (VI. x. 16–23)

Notwithstanding these Senecan incentives to the retired life, the next time we see Iden, he is in fact waxing great at court.

Shakespeare's grounding in rhetoric thus provided both the stimulus and the means to amplify the political content of his plays. At the same time, however, his use of these techniques makes it harder to see where he stands politically. An Erasmian fondness for commonplaces thickens the texture of his speeches, but renders him less visible. It also makes him appear, by our lights, uninventive. Bacon did concede that the 'invention of speech or argument is not properly an invention', if what was meant by that was 'to discover that we know not'. In the context of rhetoric, however, invention meant the opposite; the recovery of 'the knowledge whereof our mind is already possessed' (Bacon 1996: 222–3). Moreover, as Bacon's allusion to 'popularities' suggests, the most inventive speech was the one which accommodated itself most adroitly to the knowledge or beliefs whereof its audience was already possessed (see Skinner 1996: 117). From here it is but a short step to the conclusion that to investigate Shakespeare's thought can amount to little more than inspecting the accepted thinking of the time.

His constant practice of putting both sides of the case introduces a further complication. Any attempt to abstract a coherent set of political beliefs from the plays will be thwarted by his 'willingness to lend a voice of the utmost eloquence to every point of view' (Jones 1977: 15). As a result, there is in principle nothing to choose between, for example, Cade and Iden (though as a matter of fact critics have tended to opt for the latter as the play's 'symbol of degree' (Tillyard 1966: 181)). Once again, it is only a short step to the conclusion that Shakespeare's position was in effect one of having no position at all, and thus that the plays are best thought of as 'a place of improvisation where all the beliefs of the culture are trotted out, tried on, but where none is ultimately adopted' (Goldberg 1989: 230–1).

The other form of scepticism about Shakespeare's credentials as a political thinker is the more thoroughgoing kind associated with the New Historicists. What this school bids us accept is that, even if some or other political belief could be ascribed to Shakespeare with certainty, this would be of no compelling significance, since what matters is not such facts but the 'powerful logic' which 'governs the relation between orthodoxy and subversion'. Institutional power, we are told, 'defines itself in relation to . . . threats or simply to that which is not identical with it'. Hence it will always be in the interests of power to encourage simulacra of opposition, in triumphing over which it can reinvigorate itself; invariably, 'actions that should have the effect of radically undermining authority turn out to be the props of that authority'. The most compelling fact about Shakespeare is not that he was a progressive or a reactionary, as the case may be, but that he was a New Historicist *avant la lattre*, since he 'seems to have understood very early in his career' that this was how power achieves its purposes, and set about exploiting the theatrical potential of this discovery in plays that 'are centrally, repeatedly concerned with the production and containment of subversion and disorder' (Greenblatt 1988: 23, 37, 40).

For an example of this kind of analysis, we can turn to Phyllis Rackin's account of the confrontation between Cade and Iden. Although Cade may address 'real social ills', we should not be distracted by this from discerning his real function as 'a mechanism for ideological containment'. This is achieved by virtue of his being composed of

> the stereotypes of murdering thief and comic villain, the first to project and the second to defuse the anxieties of privileged property owners who could find a flattering portrait of themselves in Alexander Iden, the virtuous country gentleman. (Rackin 1990: 216–17)

Iden's role in this exercise in subversion and containment is to mystify matters. Anxious that Iden should not be identified as the agent of 'a harsh new ideology of private property', Shakespeare allows him to redescribe his action 'in the old feudal terms as service to his king' (ibid. 215–16). Rhetorically opposed though Cade and Iden are, they work towards a common ideological end.

It should be stressed that in all this the *political* disposition of the individual playwright is hardly relevant. Christopher Marlowe, as it happens, rebelled against orthodoxy; but, as Stephen Greenblatt assures us, his protagonists' 'acts of negation not only conjure up the order they would destroy but seem at times to be themselves conjured up by that very order'. William Shakespeare, as it happens, was 'a dutiful servant' of his culture, 'content to improvise a part of his own within its orthodoxy'. In his case, however, such 'intimations' as there are in the plays of 'liberation from the massive power structures which determine social and psychic reality' take the form of hyperbolical conformity, 'a peculiarly intense *submission* whose downright violence undermines everything it was meant to shore up' (Greenblatt 1984: 210, 253–4). Even those inclined to dissent from this Foucauldian thesis can do little more than invert its main contention. Faced with the claim that Shakespeare could not but help buttress the powers that be, they respond that he could not but help destabilize them. This was because the act of representing the monarch on the stage was inherently subversive, even revolutionary. As David Kastan puts it, irrespective of 'their overt ideological content, history plays inevitably, if unconsciously, weakened the structure of authority' (1986: 461). But this of course was true of any playwright, not just Shakespeare.

The outcome of these approaches is to deny Shakespeare a meaningful political identity, either by rendering his utterances indistinguishable from those of the prevailing discourse, or by leaving him inescapably compliant with (or subversive of) the powers that be. This being so, the historians of political thought may appear vindicated in deciding to exclude him from their proceedings. But rather than persist in analysing these positions, I shall turn to the historical record to open up an alternative perspective on Shakespeare and political thought, though one already – and perhaps surprisingly – gestured at in the book which has done most to entrench the notion of his orthodoxy: E. M. W. Tillyard's *Shakespeare's History Plays* (1966).

Since much is often made of the work's patriotic wartime origins, it is worth recalling that, when first published in 1944, it addressed an already war-weary public. For these readers, the repeated invocations of Shakespeare's 'official self' must also have conjured up thoughts of his non-official, demobilized alter ego. Tillyard himself finds as much respite in the 'timeless lyricism' of *Love's Labour's Lost* as he imagines Shakespeare did when 'disregarding the external pressure of contemporary ideas on politics'. Disenchanted with the idea of Shakespeare as a mere apologist for the Tudor regime, he is at pains to distance him from 'less inquiring spirits' who expressed a 'simple detestation of rebellion and civil war', and who saw in Elizabeth 'a symbol of the good state of affairs' which marked England off from Europe. Shakespeare, he insists, was not a 'tinker of others' matter, but an original poet', while his ideas, far from being platitudes, were 'the property of a select and educated class, that ally [him] with Chapman and Daniel and Sir John Hayward', and display 'the academic side of himself that was so prominent in his early years'. What Tillyard actually wishes to promote is the image of 'a poet more rather than less like Dante and Milton in massiveness of intellect and powers of reflection' (Tillyard 1966: 147, 148, 152, 163, 325). What, we may ask in turn, was the political thinking to which *this* Shakespeare was likely to have been drawn?

II

The best place to begin in trying to answer this question is not with a play but with a narrative poem, *The Rape of Lucrece* (1594). This was the 'graver labour' promised by Shakespeare in the dedication to *Venus and Adonis* (1593), and it could hardly have dealt with weightier matters: namely, the sexual scandal which led to the expulsion from Rome of the Tarquins by Lucius Junius Brutus, who, according to the prose argument prefixed to the poem,

> acquainted the people with the doer and vile manner of the deed; with a bitter invective against the tyranny of the King, wherewith the people were so moved, that with one consent and a general acclamation the Tarquins were all exiled, and the state government changed from kings to consuls. (41–5)

While the poem may have originated in an academic exercise of the kind found in one edition of *De copia*, requiring students to compare the history of Lucretia in Ovid's

Fasti with that in Livy's history of Rome, its political intent seems obvious (though this is frequently denied: see Patterson 1993: 297–312). Like its companion piece, Lucrece was dedicated to the earl of Southampton. Some doubt whether Shakespeare would have presumed to offer the earl lessons in statecraft, and argue that to identify his patron implicitly with the rapist, Tarquin, would have been the height of folly. But the more obvious identification, and one to which Southampton would have been receptive, is with Brutus rather than Tarquin. In 1601, Southampton was imprisoned for his part in the Essex Rebellion, but his republican interests actually dated from the early 1590s, when Essex sent his secretary, Henry Cuffe, to Paris to expound Aristotle's *Politics* to him (see Jardine and Grafton 1990: 33; Heinemann 1991: 68). In choosing the foundational event of the Roman republic as his topic, Shakespeare in fact showed a remarkably shrewd sense of what was likely to appeal to his patron's political tastes.

To print *Lucrece*, Shakespeare turned to Richard Field, a Stratford contemporary who had made good in London. Nearly a third of Field's output consisted of theological and devotional works, but he was also highly active in channelling the flood of propaganda materials generated by the French Wars of Religion. In addition, he produced an impressive sequence of texts on politics and statecraft, including Justus Lipsius, *Six Bookes of Politickes or Civil Doctrine* (1594); works by Petruccio Ubaldini such as *Lo stato delle tre corti* (1594) and *Militia de gran duca di Thoscana* (1597); Francesco Guicciardini, *The Historie of Guicciardini* (1599); William Fulbecke, *An Historicall Collection of the Continuall Factions, of the Romans and Italians* (1601); and John Hayward, *An Answer to the First Part of a Certaine Conference, Concerning Succession* (1603). Of these books, possibly the Lipsius alone was known to Shakespeare, but what the connection with Field suggests is just how difficult it would have been for him to isolate himself from this aspect of print culture.

Given the milieu from which *Lucrece* emerged, Shakespeare may have been closer than we think to the so-called new humanism of the 1590s. Most accounts of the political morality of the *fin de siècle* revolve around Machiavelli (1469–1527), author of *The Prince* and the *Discourses* on Livy, whose name was constantly invoked by writers discussing *ragion di stato* (reason of state, though until the 1620s the favoured term was 'policy': see Burke 1991: 480). Reason of state allowed conventional morality to be overridden when the preservation of the commonwealth was at stake, and interest in the doctrine was greatest in France and the Netherlands, where the wars of religion had been most destructive (see Skinner 1978: i. 248–54). Thus the Flemish scholar Lipsius (1547–1606) protested in his *Six Bookes* (first published in Latin in 1589) that some 'rage too much against Machiauell' for maintaining that '*there is a certaine honest and laudable deceipt*'. His own view was that the prince should 'be able to intermingle that which is profitable, with that which is honest', and 'in desperat matters, should alwaies follow that which were most necessarie to be effected, not that which is honest in speech'. In matters of 'publike profit', the prince '*hauing to deale with a foxe*' should '*play the foxe*' (Lipsius 1594: 113, 114, 123). Likewise, the French essayist Montaigne (1533–92) avowed in 'Of the useful and the honourable' that there are times when 'public interest requires men to betray, to tell lies and to massacre'. These actions might be thought to form a special category of 'vices' which are 'legal', but it would be more correct to say that a prince obliged by 'urgent necessity' to behave in this way is not acting viciously at all: 'vice it is not, for he has abandoned his own right-reason for a more powerful universal one' (Montaigne 1991: 892, 898, 902).

Recently, however, the rise of reason of state theory has been seen as predicated upon a decisive break with earlier forms of humanism. This occurred when 'scepticism, Stoicism and Tacitism came together to make a mixture as powerful and soon as all-pervasive as the Ciceronian humanism of the Quattrocento had been' (Tuck 1993: 63; see Burke 1991). The histories in which Tacitus laid bare the treachery and corruption of imperial Rome spoke powerfully to the court culture of the late sixteenth century (see Smuts 1994). Tacitus initiated his readers into secrets of state (*arcana imperii*), especially in his portrait of the emperor Tiberius as an arch-exponent of political manipulation. While the histories could be taken as a republican critique of the principate, the dominant reading, following Guicciardini's lead, was that they taught subjects how to survive under a tyranny, and the tyrant how to set one up. These lessons chimed with those offered by Stoicism and scepticism, both philosophies which encouraged an attitude of detachment from the world and constancy in the face of its trials. The Stoics held that the way to achieve this was by controlling the passions, while sceptics maintained that the path to tranquillity lay in suspending judgement about all questions of truth and morality. But in the absence of a way to determine the correct view to take of any proposition, there was no real reason not to conform to, and every reason in terms of personal survival why one should fall in with, the religious and political norms of the community in which one happened to live.

Montaigne and Lipsius also dominate the revised account (see Tuck 1993: 45–64). However, the emphasis now falls on Lipsius the classical scholar, who, in 1574, published a major edition of Tacitus and, in 1604, an edition of Seneca, the Stoic philosopher. The latter appeared in the wake of a hugely successful exposition of Stoic values, De Constantia (1584; translated into English as *Two Bookes of Constancie* in 1595), in which Lipsius warned against religious and political involvements. Even the *Sixe Bookes* took the form of a patchwork of classical citations, with no fewer than 547 from Tacitus (see Burke 1991: 485). This account also throws into relief Montaigne's interest in Tacitus, a writer of the utmost relevance to 'a sickly and troubled nation like our own is at present'. However, the *Essays*, which began to appear in 1580, were mostly devoted to the exploration of sceptic and Stoic themes in which Seneca was one of the most frequently cited authors. Montaigne's retirement from the duties and dangers of public life in 1570 was testimony in itself to the value which, like Lipsius, he placed on inner freedom: 'it is his soul that a wise man should withdraw from the crowd, maintaining its power and freedom freely to make judgements, whilst externally accepting all received forms and fashions' (Montaigne 1991: 133, 1066).

One reason why this brand of humanism established itself as quickly as it did in late Elizabethan England is that the regime was in the throes of what can aptly be called a crisis; primarily a medical term, 'crisis' was beginning to acquire its political overtones from experts on *ragion di stato* who cast themselves as physicians to the body politic (see Burke 1991: 482–3). A combination of debilitating factors – the war with Spain, military intervention on the side of the Huguenots in France and the Dutch rebels in the Low Countries, rebellion in Ireland, the struggle at court between the Essex and Cecil factions, and, above all, the unresolved matter of the succession – meant that the English body politic too looked in dire need of alternative therapies. Another reason for this success is that one function of the secretariat in households like Essex's was precisely that of assimilating such materials (see Jardine and Grafton 1990: 33–5), and an interest in the new humanism was to prove a distinguishing feature of the Essex circle (see Tuck 1993: 105–8). A key text was the 1591 translation of Tacitus by Sir Henry Savile, a protégé of Essex (see Smuts 1994: 25–30). In 1597, Francis Bacon, one of Essex's advisers, published his *Essays* as a 'politic' guide to public life, though the full extent of his familiarity with Tacitus, Machiavelli, Guicciardini and Lipsius is evident only in later works like *The Advancement of Learning* (1605) and the 1625 essay 'Of simulation and dissimulation'. But by far the most notorious work in this vein was John Hayward's *The First Part of the Life and Reign of Henry IIII* (1599). Dedicated to Essex and drawing extensively on Savile's work, it led directly to Hayward's imprisonment in 1600 following the earl's disgrace (see Smuts 1994: 22).

This makes it all the more intriguing that Shakespeare's one undoubted reference to a contemporary event should be the forward glance to Essex's return from Ireland in the Chorus to Act V of *Henry V* (22–34). Much attention has been devoted to this passage, as well as to the fact that on the eve of the attempted *coup* some supporters of Essex commissioned a special performance of a play about Richard II, assumed to be Shakespeare's (see Patterson 1989: 71–92; Norbrook 1996). But illuminating though these readings are, they relate to the turn of the century, by which time Shakespeare had written well over half his plays. The crucial question which needs to be addressed, therefore, is the extent to which – if at all – his earlier work exhibits traits which can be aligned with the political and intellectual agenda of the Essex circle.

There is in fact no evidence that Shakespeare read Tacitus for himself, while the claim that Savile's translation was a source for *3 Henry VI* is unconvincing (see Womersley 1985). Several of the plays are, clearly informed, however, by Stoic and sceptical attitudes. While Iden in his praise of the retired life rehearses the familiar Senecan topos of country versus court (though only to ironize it by his prompt defection), *Julius Caesar* subjects the central Stoic value of constancy to a sustained critique which, according to Geoffrey Miles, shows that Shakespeare 'must have been aware of the contemporary debate'. Thus when Caesar denies that he can be moved because he is 'constant as the northern star' III. i. 60), he is laying claim to what Lipsius in the English translation of *De Constantia* called 'that great title, the neerest that man can have to God, To be immooveable' (Miles 1996: 63, 134). It is Montaigne's 'deeply sceptical critique of constancy', however, which is said to offer 'the most illuminating parallel with Shakespeare's treatment'. The difficulty here is that such evidence as there is that he knew Montaigne relates to John Florio's translation, published in 1603. Miles does canvass the view that Shakespeare had access to Florio's text in manuscript, but fails to pronounce on the issue, insisting nevertheless that 'it was Montaigne who focused and shaped his interest in the theme of constancy' (ibid. 82–4).

While the sceptical themes of the fallibility of the senses and the power of opinion which dominate *Julius Caesar* also fascinated Montaigne, there seems no real need to bring him in. Academic scepticism was widely known through the writings of Cicero, and it is in precisely this guise (rather than that of the orator) that he features in *Julius Caesar*. When Casca feverishly interprets the storm as a dire portent, Cicero imperturbably observes that 'men may construe things after their fashion / Clean from the purpose of the things themselves' (I. iii. 34–5), an insight which is borne out several times over in the course of the play. But Shakespeare is no less concerned with a form of scepticism which originated not in philosophy but in rhetoric. As we have seen, the materials with which orators dealt were the received opinions of their audience. And since the status of these opinions was no higher than that of 'probabilities', they were always capable of being debated *in utramque partem*. The outcome of such debates might be to sway opinion one way or the other, but what they could never achieve was to establish the truth of the matter, as is illustrated by the Forum scene and, perhaps even more graphically, by the inconclusive councils in *Troilus and Cressida*. The phenomenon which some have labelled 'improvisation' is actually more a matter of rhetorical scepticism.

Another key feature of the new humanism is encapsulated in Suffolk's Lipsian phrase 'good deceit' (a phrase which so troubles some editors that they emend it to 'good conceit'). Although Shakespeare provides two full-scale representations of a Renaissance court, the Elsinore of *Hamlet* and the Whitehall of *Henry VIII*, politics as practised there is not categorically different from what we find in the nominally late medieval history plays or, for that matter, the works set in the classical past. This is true, for example, of the soliloquy in which Richard of Gloucester itemizes the abilities which will enable him to 'catch the English crown' (*3 Henry VI*, III. ii. 179):

> I'll play the orator as well as Nestor,
> Deceive more slily than Ulysses could,
> And like a Sinon, take another Troy.
> I can add colors to the chameleon,
> Change shapes with Proteus for advantages,
> And set the murtherous Machevil to school.
>   (III. ii. 188–93)

Sinon, the Greek who persuaded the Trojans to accept the gift-horse, and Ulysses, who was a notorious liar, are commonplace figures of deceit. Nestor is less obviously so, but the implication of placing him in this company is that his famed eloquence was just an aptitude for rhetorical deceit writ large, an implication underscored in the play on 'colors' – each of the first three lines in the passage having its counterpart in the second trio. The allusions to the chameleon/Nestor and to Proteus/Ulysses recapitulate the theme, which reaches its anachronistic climax in the invocation of the Machevil as the supreme embodiment of political violence and fraud.

Richard invents himself as Machevil/Sinon in the course of a single speech; by comparison, *Lucrece* offers an anthology of deceit. Having threatened his victim with death and shame if she does not yield, Tarquin switches to extenuating the harm if she does:

> A little harm done to a great good end
> For lawful policy remains enacted.
> The poisonous simple sometime is compacted
>   In a pure compound; being so applied,
>   His venom in effect is purified.
>
> (528–32)

This proposition actually consists of two strands of argument. One is that wrongdoing as such is sometimes countenanced by the law under the heading of 'lawful policy'. The other is that wrongdoing sometimes loses its quality of wrongfulness altogether, just as poisons can be medicinal when mixed with other ingredients, and thereby cease to be poisonous.

Arguments of this type, not to mention medical metaphors, were a standard feature of the discourse of *ragion di stato*, but Tarquin's proposition appears to combine material drawn specifically from two passages in Lipsius's *Sixe Bookes*. In the first, when discussing '*mixed prudence*', Lipsius argues that this virtue will be unchanged by an admixture of deceit:

> Wine, although it be somewhat tempered with water, continueth to be wine: so doth prudence not change her name, albeit a fewe drops of deceipt bee mingled therewith: For I always meane but a small deale, and to a good end. (Lipsius 1594: 114)

In the second, discussing the category of what he calls '*middle deceipt*', he argues that this vice will sometimes lose its viciousness:

> the profit of the common wealth . . . easilie draweth and draineth to itselfe, all the venime of vice that is therein. And as in the application of medicines, they do with approbation mingle venimous drugs for the good of the patient, so *these things* do seeme *profitable as it were a medecine*. (Ibid. 119)

We should note that Lipsius (unlike Tarquin) is not claiming that any end will justify the means; his view is emphatically that to practise deceit other than for the public good is to commit 'not onely an offence, but a great sinne' (ibid. 120).

The doctrine abused by Tarquin is none the less recognizably Lipsian. The suggestion is thus that, even if Shakespeare did not read Tacitus, he read the nearest thing to him, either in the original Latin or in the translation printed by Field. *Lucrece* was registered on 9 May 1594, while William Jones's dedication of the *Sixe Bookes* is dated 1 January 1594 (sig. Aiiᵛ). It is true that Jones's date may be old style, and so may refer to January 1595, but a translation was first registered in November 1589, while Shakespeare's known contacts with Field began in April 1593 with the registration of *Venus and Adonis*. But this is as far as we can go in ushering Shakespeare towards one of the mainsprings of the new humanism, especially given the variety of ways in which materials were then disseminated. After all, Tarquin's lines on policy themselves achieved the status of a commonplace when anthologized in *England's Parnassus* (1600).

The difference between the other deceivers in the poem, Brutus and Sinon, is best captured by the distinction embodied in a pair of Latin verbs: *Simulare* (to pretend) and *dissimulare* (to disguise). This pairing eventually formed the core of Bacon's essay 'Of simulation and dissimulation', where simulation is defined as 'when a man industriously and expressly feigns and pretends to be that he is not', and dissimulation as 'when a man lets fall signs and arguments, that he is not that he is' (Bacon 1996: 350). That is to say, the terms register the difference between actively putting on an appearance at odds with the true state of affairs, and more or less passively concealing the true state of affairs. Obviously, there is a tendency for these notions to collapse into each other, and an effort is required to keep them conceptually distinct. But Shakespeare, like Bacon, thought the distinction an important one to uphold, and for the same reason: that it was politically indispensable.

Sinon enters the poem in circumstances calculated to raise our awareness of these subtleties. After the rape, the distraught Lucrece is drawn to a painting which depicts the fall of Troy. Yet we are constantly reminded that the painting itself, like the narrator's verbal re-creation of it, is, so to speak, an exercise in simulation: 'For much imaginary work was there: / Conceit deceitful' (1422–3). The traitorous Sinon, the last figure viewed by Lucrece, also poses the most severe challenge to the artist: to simulate dissimulation:

> In him the painter laboured with his skill
> To hide deceit, and give the harmless show
> An humble gait, calm eyes.
>
> (1506–8)

Lucrece is almost persuaded by these 'signs of truth' (1532) into believing that Sinon is not that he is; a traitor. Drawing on her bitter experience with Tarquin, however, she finally proves able to discriminate between 'outward honesty' and 'inward vice' (1545, 1546).

Brutus, by contrast, is a simulator. In representing him as such, Shakespeare was guided by the phraseology in one of his main sources, Livy's *Ab urbe condita* (see Livy 1961: 194, 'simulationem' (1. 56. 7); 206, 'simulatum' (1. 59. 8)). According to Livy, Brutus embarked on his career as a simulator when his family fell victim to the tyranny of Tarquin's father, King Tarquinius Superbus, and to save himself, he 'deliberately assumed the appearance of stupidity' (*ex industria factus ad imitationem stultitiae*: Livy 1961: 194 (1. 56. 8)). This phrase furnishes the key to his character in *Lucrece*, as well as the form of words which Bacon later pressed into service when defining simulation. Livy also relates that Lucius Junius completed the pretence by adopting a surname – Brutus – which meant 'imbecile'. That this was something he was not is made abundantly clear by Shakespeare. While Lucrece's husband and father are preoccupied with lamenting her suicide, Brutus

> Began to clothe his wit in state and pride,
> Burying in Lucrece' wound his folly's show.
> He with the Romans was esteemed so
>> As seely jeering idiots are with kings,
>> For sportive words, and utt'ring foolish things.
>
> But now he throws that shallow habit by,
> Wherein deep policy did him disguise,
> And arm'd his long-hid wits advisedly.
>
> (1809–16)

Although regarded by the Romans much as monarchs regard their jesters, Brutus is no licensed fool, but an exponent of 'deep policy', who in fact seizes the occasion to overthrow monarchy itself. Whereas Tarquin cynically treated 'policy' as a mere *façon de parler*, Brutus treats it as a programme for political action.

Ulysses features only briefly, in the preview of the painting conducted by the narrator for the reader's benefit. He is not one of the figures scrutinized by Lucrece, leaving the narrator free to comment that the 'mild glance that sly Ulysses lent / Showed deep regard and smiling government' (1399–1400). Not only is he 'sly', but the adjective 'mild' associates him with Sinon (see 1505, 1520). In *Lucrece*, as throughout Shakespeare's works, Ulysses dissimulates.

It is therefore all the more surprising that his great speech on 'Degree' in *Troilus and Cressida* (I. iii. 75–137) has so often been taken at face value and assumed to constitute the philosophical bedrock of the play (see Skinner 1978: i. 239–40). This is just about as plausible as allowing the whole weight of *2 Henry VI* to rest on Iden's speech in praise of country ways. There is, however, one occasion when Ulysses perhaps discloses more of himself than is required for the purposes of manipulation. By way of preparing Achilles for the news that his letters have been intercepted, Ulysses delivers an overwhelming invocation – and evocation – of state power:

> The providence that's in a watchful state
> Knows almost every [grain of Pluto's gold],
> Finds bottom in th' uncomprehensive depth,
> Keeps place with thought and almost, like the gods,
> Do thoughts unveil in their dumb cradles.
> There is a mystery (with whom relation

> Durst never meddle) in the soul of state,
> Which hath an operation more divine
> Than breath or pen can give expressure to.
>   (III. iii. 196–204)

The *topos* of ineffability, usually devoted to a mistress's charms, is here lavished on the *arcana imperii*. Otherwise detached from the febrile eroticism of the play, Ulysses for once speaks with genuine ardour. And while he tells Achilles that 'I as your lover speak' (III. iii. 214), it would appear that the true object of his affections is *region di stato*.

III

The conclusion to be drawn from this survey is that Shakespeare was working to the agenda of the new humanism in the 1590s. This would remain the case even on the assumption that he never read Tacitus, Savile, Lipsius, Montaigne, Bacon or Hayward, or that he was never recruited into the Essex circle. The point is that he wrote about deceit as subtly as Lipsius, read Livy with as keen an eye as Bacon, was as given to rhetorical scepticism as Montaigne, and contrived to be as elusive in his religious commitments as any of them. However, this may not be sufficient of itself to extricate him from the web of conformity and complicity in which critics have sought to entangle him. It could be claimed that, even if the pack of commonplaces has been shuffled, nothing else has changed. Alternatively, it might be pointed out that an engagement with the new humanism, given its emphasis on conformity with local custom, would tend to leave Shakespeare in the same posture as before of submissiveness to the powers that be. Or it could even be argued that to delve into the *arcana imperii* was in effect only to discover new and more devious forms of subversion and containment.

However, it would be a mistake to suppose that the new humanism can be accommodated seamlessly within the usual understandings. On the contrary, it shows up their shortcomings. While it is perfectly true that the combination of Stoicism, scepticism and reason of state was deployed in mainland Europe for 'the purpose of state-building on a proto-absolutist model', what it promoted in England was 'an ideology of critical detachment from the increasingly overbearing late Elizabethan and Jacobean state' (Collinson 1993: 79). This critical ideology was, moreover, distinctly republican in tone, a claim which is less dramatic than it sounds to the extent that monarchy and republic were not necessarily seen as antithetical terms. For example, when describing English institutions, Sir Thomas Smith (who served as ambassador to France under Elizabeth) unequivocally placed 'royal and kingly majesty' at the apex; notwithstanding this, the work appeared in 1583 under the title *De Republica Anglorum* – the commonwealth of England. Such 'quasi-republican modes of political reflection and action' were in fact present at all levels of Elizabethan society, from the Privy Council to village communities (Collinson 1990: 22–3). As Markku Peltonen has recently demonstrated, the assumption that these ideas and values simply disappeared after flourishing briefly in the early part of the sixteenth century, to reappear only in the 1650s, is untenable. Nor is it quite the case that Ciceronian humanism was entirely eclipsed by the new Tacitean version. Rather the two coexisted, so that 'many of the English authors who developed Tacitean themes were ready to endorse the central convictions of classical Ciceronian humanism' (Peltonen 1995: 135). One example of this is Bacon, who combined a mastery of the vocabulary of reason of state with a commitment, both in his life and in his writings, to serving the public good. Another is Shakespeare, who, after all, portrayed Ulysses and Brutus with equal conviction.

We should, finally, consider the implications of Collinson's resonant phrase that, in late Elizabethan England, 'citizens were concealed within subjects' (Collinson 1990: 24), since it appears to have been an idea of which the Elizabethans themselves were well aware. In 1596, Bacon advised Essex that dissimulation was the only way of dealing with his dangerous reputation for 'popularity':

> And therefore take all occasions, to the Queen, to speak against popularity and popular courses vehemently; and to tax it in all others: but nevertheless to go on in your honourable commonwealth courses as you do. (Peltonen 1996: 297)

Did Shakespeare's Brutus, the archetype of those who simulate in the republican interest, convey the same advice to Southampton, who, according to a later account, was one of 'the gallant spirits that aimed at the public liberty' and 'carried his business closely and slyly' (Heinemann 1991: 63)?

REFERENCES

Bacon, Francis 1996: *Francis Bacon*, ed. Brian Vickers. Oxford: Oxford University Press.

Burke, Peter 1991: Tacitism, scepticism and reason of state. In J. H. Burns with the assistance of Mark Goldie (eds), *The Cambridge History of Political Thought 1450–1700*, Cambridge: Cambridge University Press, 479–98.

Collinson, Patrick 1990: *De Republica Anglorum Or, History with the Politics Put Back: Inaugural Lecture delivered 9 November 1989*. Cambridge: Cambridge University Press.

—— 1993: The Elizabethan exclusion crisis and the Elizabethan polity. *Proceedings of the British Academy*, 84, 51–92.

Goldberg, Jonathan 1989: *James I and the Politics of Literature: Jonson, Shakespeare, Donne and their Contemporaries*. Stanford, Calif.: Stanford University Press.

Greenblatt, Stephen 1984: *Renaissance Self-fashioning: From More to Shakespeare*. Chicago and London: University of Chicago Press.

—— 1988: *Shakespearean Negotiations: The Circulation of Social Energy in Renaissance England*. Berkeley: University of California Press.

Heinemann, Margot 1991: Rebel lords, popular playwrights, and political culture: notes on the Jacobean patronage of the Earl of Southampton. *Yearbook of English Studies*, 21, 63–86.

Jardine, Lisa and Grafton, Anthony 1990: 'Studied for Achon': how Gabriel Harvey read his Livy. *Past and Present*, 129, 30–78.

Jones, Emrys 1977: *The Origins of Shakespeare*. Oxford: Clarendon Press.

Kastan, David 1986: Proud majesty made a subject: Shakespeare and the spectacle of rule. *Shakespeare Quarterly*, 37, 459–75.

Leggatt, Alexander 1988: *Shakespeare's Political Drama: The History Plays and the Roman Plays*. London and New York: Routledge.

Lipsius, Justus 1594: *Sixe Bookes of Politickes or Civil Doctrine*, trans. William Jones, London: William Ponsonby.

Livy 1961: *Livy {Ab urbe condita, I–II}*, ed. B. O. Foster. London and Cambridge, Mass.: Heinemann.

Miles, Geoffrey 1966: *Shakespeare and the Constant Romans*. Oxford: Clarendon Press.

Montaigne, Michel de 1991: *The Complete Essays*, trans. M. A. Soreech. Harmondsworth: Penguin.

Norbrook, David 1996: 'A liberal tongue': language and rebellion in *Richard II*. In John M. Mucciolo with the assistance of Steven J. Doloff and Edward A. Rauchut (eds), *Shakespeare's Universe: Renaissance Ideas and Conventions. Essays in Honour of W. R. Elton*, Aldershot: Scolar Press, 37–51.

Patterson, Annabel 1989: *Shakespeare and the Popular Voice*. Oxford: Blackwell.

——1993: *Reading between the Lines*. London: Routledge.

Peltonen, Markku 1995: *Classical Humanism and Republicanism in English Political Thought 1570–1640*. Cambridge: Cambridge University Press.

——1996: Bacon's political philosophy. In Markku Peltonen (ed.), *The Cambridge Companion to Bacon*, Cambridge: Cambridge University Press, 383–410.

Pocock, J. G. A., with the assistance of Gordon J Schochet and Lois G. Schwoerer (eds) 1993: *The Varieties of British Political Thought, 1500–1800*. Cambridge: Cambridge University Press.

Rackin, Phyllis 1990: *Stages of History: Shakespeare's English Chronicles*. London: Routledge.

Skinner, Quentin 1978: *The Foundations of Modern Political Thought*, 2 vols. Cambridge: Cambridge University Press.

——1996: *Reason and Rhetoric in the Philosophy of Hobbes*. Cambridge: Cambridge University Press.

Smuts, Malcolm 1994: Court-centred politics and the uses of Roman historians, *c.*1590–1630. In Kevin Sharpe and Peter Lake (eds), *Culture and Politics in Early Stuart England*, Basingstoke: Macmillan, 21–43, 325–31.

Tillyard, E. M. W. 1966: *Shakespeare's History Plays*. Harmondsworth: Penguin.

Tuck, Richard 1993: *Philosophy and Government 1572–1651*. Cambridge: Cambridge University Press.

Womersley, D. J. 1985: *3 Henry VI*: Shakespeare, Tacitus, and parricide. *Notes and Queries*, 230, 468–73.

8

Political Culture

David Harris Sacks

Introduction: "Culture" and "Politics"

Our subject is "political culture," a phrase that combines two of the most conceptually complicated words we can encounter in English. The roots of the first word are Greek; they take us back to the ancient city-state, the *polis*, and its distinctive forms of public and collective life. The roots of the second are Latin, from *cultura*, referring to the tilling of land or the care bestowed in growing plants. Yoking these two ideas together as adjective and noun, therefore, asks us to think about those modes – those rules and norms, habits of mind, manners of speaking, and common practices – employed in ruling, running, maintaining, and advancing, or possibly resisting, the polity. However, the meaning of this combination of ideas is far from straightforward when applied to Shakespeare's world.

Culture and the cultural

The word "culture" was never employed by Shakespeare in any of his surviving works. It was not a word in widespread usage in his time, and when it was adopted, it most often carried meanings connecting it narrowly and exclusively to agricultural activities. But these simple etymological facts belie the already complex heritage the word carried to people whose education had introduced them to Latin, even the "small Latin" attributed to Shakespeare himself. In Latin, *cultura* can mean the cultivation of farm land, but primarily refers to living or inhabiting a place such as a town. But its meaning also extended to cover the cultivation of one's person or appearance or way of life, and especially the worship or veneration of the divine or the performance of religious or social obligations. In English, the cognate word carries a similar range of meanings; it can just as easily refer to the tilling of fields, the development of personal character, the formation of social mores, or the training of the human mind.[1]

From this complex set of meanings, one line of development stresses the idea of refinement. Sir Francis Bacon, for example, speaks of "the culture and manurance of Mindes," by which we might bring forth the richest harvest from each educated individual.[2] Following this route, culture became identified with imaginative literature and the fine arts, those hallmarks of the cultivated and civilized. But there has also been a second, more recent line of etymological development, one that connects culture with "a particular way of life."[3] When first employed in the later eighteenth and early nineteenth centuries, the broader usage of "culture" defended the common traditions and folk practices of particular communities and peoples against the material forces and activities of the bureaucratic state and market capitalism that were seen as eroding them away in the name of progress. But in the hands of twentieth-century anthropologists this second line of development has been used primarily to carve out an area of inquiry peculiarly concerned with the conventions, mentalities, customs, and values of a people, period, or group.

It is this second, anthropological sense that normally is intended in the phrase "political culture." Nevertheless, this anthropological meaning has never been completely disentangled from what we might call the aesthetic one, and there remains an open question whether we shall find the best examples of the culture we wish to study in its learned discourse and imaginative literature or in everyday behavior and common practices.[4]

Politics and the political

In the present day the word "political" commonly refers to the business of government, especially the allocation of public goods and the formation and enforcement of law and public policy. This modern usage assumes the existence of the modern concept of the state, built upon foundations of man-made law and administrative regulation, authorized and enforced by specialized institutions of government decision making and administrative bureaucracy. Accordingly, the modern state is best understood, in Quentin Skinner's definition, as "a form of public power separate from both the ruler and the ruled, and constituting the supreme political authority within a certain defined territory." It is an "independent political apparatus" which the ruler has "a duty to maintain" and the subjects or citizens have an obligation to finance, support, and obey; it is therefore distinct from those who operate it and from the particular individuals whom it governs.[5]

However, this modern conception of the state itself has a history – one that was only just beginning in Shakespeare's day. Before then, the word "state" carried much the same meaning as "status," also originating in Latin and signifying "condition." However, in *The Maxims of State*, an early seventeenth-century work attributed to Sir Walter Ralegh, "state" is defined as "the frame or set order of a Commonwealth, or of the Governours that rule the same, specially of the chiefe and Soveraigne Governour that commands the rest." Here, the "sovereignty of state," consisting solely in governmental powers, is understood to be a feature of a commonwealth, not the commonwealth as a whole. But when the newer, political meaning of "state" first developed, it rarely differentiated the state apparatus from the totality of society. This ambiguous usage left open whether it was only the governing authorities or all subjects in the realm who shared responsibility for the welfare of the state.[6]

Without a firmly established concept of the state in its modern form, the definition of the word "political" also remained in transition. In earlier Christian thinking – for example, in St Augustine's *The City of God* – government was deemed a divinely ordained instrument for overcoming the evil humans do in consequence of original sin, not as a human creation and pursuit intrinsically valuable in its own right. But, as Skinner has stressed, Aristotle in his *Politics*, one of the most widely familiar works among the educated in Shakespeare's England, had treated "the sphere of politics . . . as a distinct branch of moral philosophy," and the recovery of his writings in the Middle Ages had made it possible for political thinkers once again to consider politics a fit subject for Christians to study and comment upon.[7]

Nevertheless, in the absence of a modern conception of the state, Aristotle's conception of the "political" complicates our task. According to the opening sentences of the *Politics*, every community, from the household to the village to the *polis* itself, has the good as its aim. But the *polis*, as the "highest of all" communities, embracing "all the rest, . . . aims at good in a greater degree than any other, and at the highest good."[8] Since this "highest good" incorporates the full range of activities necessary for human flourishing, not just those connected to government, politics in the Aristotelian "state" necessarily encompasses the entire realm of social relations, and every morally valuable activity is "political," subject to "political" judgment. It does so, moreover, without canceling the contributions to the good made by lesser communities. Early modern authors writing in the "commonwealth" tradition, treat the family or the town in this fashion, each a little commonwealth of its own embedded within the larger commonwealth of England, and each possessing inevitably its own form of politics understood in the same broad terms. On this view, the study of "political culture" is indistinguishable from the study of culture as a whole, not an independent realm of inquiry of its own.

To avoid taking on so broad a mandate, we shall confine our definition of the "political" to activities connected with early modern England's system of governance and institutions of rule. During Shakespeare's days, politics on this definition had not yet fully emerged as an autonomous arena, incontrovertibly operating within a national framework of ruling bodies exercising a sovereign monopoly of authoritative power and coercive force. On the one hand, it remained subject to religious and ethical claims that transcended considerations of time, place, and immediate circumstance – claims retaining the Aristotelian linkage between politics and the "highest good." On the other, it depended on the indistinct boundaries between local, provincial, and central structures of governance and administration, which permitted the continued blurring of the relationship between the commonwealth and the state. These characteristics depended on widespread participation by the English in their own rule at every level, from the parish and the village to the town and the county to the

Parliament and the royal court. They created the framework within which England's political culture was formed. It was, to adopt one formulation, "self-government at the king's command," or, to employ another, the politics of a "monarchical republic" – a "commonwealth" in which yeomen, husbandmen, and town burgesses as well as noblemen and gentry shared with the monarch and the royal officials in ruling themselves.[9]

What follows illustrates a few of the distinctive features of this participatory political culture – some representative conventions, norms, practices, and language focusing on three concrete instances that bracket Shakespeare's life as a playwright. The first two, from the late 1570s, are devoted to some characteristics of politics in Parliament and at court and are quite well known; the third, from 1615, explores some related features in local politics and is much less so.

Consent and Counsel: Peter Wentworth at St Stephen's Chapel, 1576

In the Parliament of 1576, Peter Wentworth, an outspoken advocate of parliamentary privilege, offered a powerful, though half-delivered, defense of freedom of speech in the House of Commons. Why he was prevented from completing his remarks need not detain us. For our purposes, the important features of the speech concern his analysis of the "the commodityes that grow to the prince and the whole state by free speech used" in the House of Commons.[10]

Parliament's main function, according to Wentworth, is the making of laws for the honor and glory of God, the preservation of the monarch, and the "surety, safekeeping, and inrichment of this noble realme of Englande."[11] Members of Parliament, he said, "are chosen of the whole realme of a special trust and confidence" to perform this task,[12] and

> if we will discharge our consciences and be true to God, our prince, and state, we must have due consideration of the place and the occasion of our coming together, and especially have regard unto the matter, wherein we shall both serve God and our prince and state faithfully and not dissembling as eye pleasers, and so justly avoyd all displeasures both to God and our prince.[13]

For Wentworth, the Commons is a place for truth-telling – even to the point of insisting that the queen herself "hath committed great faultes ... dangerous ... to her selfe and the state," which it is his duty – a duty to her as well as the realm – to help her remedy and avoid.[14] Each member is to draw on his conscience for his motive to speak and to take the advancement of the general welfare of the realm as his goal. "For free speech and conscience in this place are granted by a speciall law as that without which the prince and the state cannot be preserved or mayntayned."[15] This use of the word "state" approaches the modern meaning; it represents the realm as a collective political society whose members shared a common duty to assure its welfare.

Free speech in the Commons, Wentworth insists, could never do any harm to the prince and the state, since its use would expose evil persons and their wicked designs, even as it advanced the true and the good. He is confident that the Parliament itself could correct any dangers or shortcomings in the speeches or measures laid before it. "[I]f the envious doe offer anything hurtfull or perilous to the prince or state in this place," he asks,

> what incommodity doth grow thereby? Verily I think none; nay will you have me say my simple opinion therein? Much good cometh thereof. How forsooth? For by the darkness of the night the brightness of the sunn sheweth more excellent and cleare, and how can the truth appeare and conquer untill falsehood and all subtillties that should shadow and darken it be found out? For it is offered in this place as a piece of fine needle worke unto them that are most skillful therein, for there cannot be a false stiche (God ayding us) but wilbe found out.[16]

In thus equating discussion and lawmaking in Parliament with the collective making of a piece of fine needlework, Wentworth calls upon the division of labor to reinforce his view of the duties of MPs. Just as craftsmen ought to share their God-given skills for the good of the finished work, so too MPs should use their capacities to reason and persuade to advance the general good.

Wentworth's confidence in the power of parliamentary free speech has antecedents in ancient rhetoric. The Renaissance was a great age of rhetoric, marked by the publication of numerous editions, translations, and paraphrases of the major rhetorical writings of Aristotle, Isocrates, Cicero, Quintilian, etc., which also formed the basis for most Renaissance treatises.[17] What drove this market were the demands of grammar school education, not only for potential members of the clergy and lawyers, but also for those, like Wentworth himself, who as propertied men might be expected to perform public duties in their localities or in the kingdom at large. Their educations were directed to preparing them for a life devoted to public service and the profit of mankind, on the model of the *vita activa* that Cicero had outlined in *De Officiis*, another of the most widely know ancient works in Shakespeare's England.[18]

Behind this emphasis on rhetoric was a social theory ultimately dependent on the famous passage in Aristotle's *Politics*, where he writes of a human beings as "political animals." "[W]hereas," the philosopher says,

> mere voice is but an indication of pleasure and pain, and is therefore found in other animals ... the power of speech is intended to set forth the expedient and inexpedient, and therefore likewise the just and the unjust. And it is a characteristic of man that he alone has any sense of good and evil, of just and unjust, and the like, and the association of living beings who have this sense makes a family and a state.[19]

Directed to its highest and best use, speech transformed distinct households and divided interests into a united community.

Cicero held very similar views. On his theory, the power of persuasion not only first brought human beings, living scattered in the fields, together for common benefit in civil society, but in society especially "renders life safe, honourable, glorious and even agreeable."[20] For Cicero and his Renaissance adherents, it is the duty of all men "to contribute to the general good by an interchange of acts of kindness, by giving and receiving, and thus by our skill, our industry, and our talents to cement human society more closely together, man to man."[21] In this context, the making of a speech, especially a speech of advice, was the equivalent of the giving of a gift – a preeminently moral and political act – and those who possessed the skill were under a particular obligation to use it for the advantage of the common-wealth.[22]

Seneca, another ancient moral thinker widely known in the Renaissance, in his moral letter "On the value of advice," also argues that the provision of counsel based on accumulated wisdom was itself one of the principle gifts a person could bestow on those for whose welfare he had responsibility or concern.[23] Wentworth's *persona* as the voice of parliamentary conscience, his repeated use of proverbial sentences in his 1576 speech, as well as a number of his arguments in that speech closely parallel this Senecan discussion. For him the possession of freedom of speech by MPs imposed a moral duty on those who held it. "Mr Speaker," he said,

> I find written in a little volume words in effect, "Sweet indeed is the name of libertye and the thing itself a value beyond all inestimable treasure": soe much the more it behooveth us to take heed least we, contenting our selves with the sweetnes of the name onely, doe not loose and forget the value of the thing; and the greatest value that come unto this noble realme by the inestimable treasure is the use of it.[24]

Here Wentworth treats liberty as the equivalent of riches and then relies on a conventional moral precept to explain the consequence: "for what availeth it to have riches, if we do not have the use thereof?"[25]

The "little volume" from which Wentworth was quoting is Thomas Norton's exhortation against the northern rebels of 1569, published in four editions in that year. Norton was the co-author of *Gorboduc* and, like Wentworth, one of those "froward" men-of-business in the parliaments of the 1560s and 1570s who sought to protect England against perceived threats from Catholicism, foreign and domestic, and to advance the cause of the true Protestant religion at home and abroad. Very probably he was sitting in the Commons in 1576, as Wentworth quoted from his book. Norton had especially distinguished between the rebellious earls of North-umberland and Westmoreland, those "licentious bosters of libertie, that will bring you in deed nothing but bondage," and "her maiestie her selfe, and her nobility, clergie, and other good subiectes," who were the defenders of true liberty.[26] "The common weale," he said, is the ship we sayle in, no one can be safe if the whole do perish. To God, & then to the realme, to the croun, to the law and gouernement, youre leaders and you and we all do owe our selues and all that we haue, in highest degree of duetie: All other inferior dueties are but meanes that these may be better performed.[27]

Wentworth's words in 1576 echo these same Ciceronian sentiments in connecting liberty to duty.

Wentworth's speech is grounded in the firm conviction that one of the functions of the House Commons, supported by the exercise of free speech there, is the giving of "sound counsel" to the monarch, which the monarch in turn has the duty to receive, duly distinguishing "faithfull advice from trayterous . . . speeches." "[F]or noe estate," he says, "can stand where the prince is not governed by counsel."[28] "Free speech" in the Commons was requested on behalf of the members at the opening of each Parliament by the Speaker of the House. The privilege took its full form only in Henry VIII's reign, when requests were made by the Speaker of the House to allow the members to speak their minds on the matters before them without fear of punishment for the words or arguments they had used.[29] However, by early in Elizabeth's reign, the Speaker's petition had already become a ritualized litany requesting, as in 1563, that "the assembly may have franck and free liberty of speech to speak their mindes without any controllment, blame, grudge, menaces or displeasures according to the old ancient order."[30]

In exercising this freedom of speech, was the Commons able to offer counsel to the monarch on high policy such as her potential marriage, the succession, relations between England and foreign princes, the reform of religion, and other great matters? The answer was by no means certain. In 1563 Elizabeth's *pro forma* reply to the Speaker granted his petition for free speech, "so that it be reverently used," eschewing any direct reference to the receiving of such counsel from the members, but hinting that it would be unwelcome.[31] About the same time, Sir Thomas Smith was carefully delineating the functions and powers of Parliament in his *De Republica Anglorum*. He held that "[t]he most high and absolute power of the realme of Englande, consisteth in the Parliament," which "representeth and hath the power of the whole realme both the head and the bodie," which, therefore, had the capacity to assent on behalf of the realm to the laws and taxes imposed on it. What is done "by this consent . . . is taken for lawe," Smith stressed, "[f]or everie Englishman is entended to bee there present, either in person or by procuration and attornies, of what preheminence, state, dignitie, or qualitie soever he be, from the Prince (be he King or Queene) to the lowest person of Englande. And the consent of the Parliament is taken to be everie mans consent," since it is "the Princes and the whole realmes deede: whereupon justlie no man can complaine, but must accommodate himselfe to finde it good and obey it."[32]

But was the granting of consent also the giving of counsel? Sir Thomas More, as Speaker of the House in 1523, treated it in this manner in his request for the privilege of free speech. "[C]onsidering that in [the] high of Parliament is nothing entreated but matter of weight and importance concerning [the] realm and...royal estate," about which the members are to offer "their advice and counsel," he petitioned the king "to give all your Commons...your most gracious license and pardon, without doubt of your dreadful displeasure, every man to discharge his conscience, and boldly in every thing incident among they to declare his advice."[33] However, More's remarks refer only to the freedom to speak on the business laid before the Commons; he leaves open whether members, or the Commons as a whole, can independently provide counsel on matters of high policy where the monarch had not asked for any action. In 1571 Elizabeth, reacting to earlier efforts of the Commons to press her to marry, made it clear that in her judgment they could not. In answering the Speaker's petition for free speech in 1571, she had the lord keeper declare that in light of the disorder and offenses in the last Parliament, "they should do well to meddle with no matters of State, but such as should be propounded unto them, and to occupy themselves in other matters, concerning the Common-Wealth."[34] The queen, in effect, declared that on the everyday business of legislation, the Commons could freely offer their advice in the form of bills presented for her approval or veto. But on the great matters of state – matters falling within her royal prerogative – they had no right to give counsel, only to grant or withhold their consent to what was presented to them. The responsibility to maintain the "state" was solely hers. Anything less, she implied, would threaten the peace, order, and safety of the realm.

It is a central feature of early modern England's political culture that the English conceived of themselves as living under a regime of consent – a regime governed politically as well as royally as Sir John Fortescue had put it in dialogue in his *In Praise of the Laws of England*. In that widely known work, Fortescue attributed the prosperity and military prowess of the English to their regime of consent, which prevented the monarch from making laws or imposing taxes without consulting them and receiving their assent to his actions. "Ruled by laws they themselves desire," he said, "they freely enjoy their goods, and are despoiled neither by their own king or any other."[35] Was the distinction drawn by Elizabeth in 1571 adequate to assure this outcome?

In contrast to his queen, Wentworth was certain it could not. For him, consent required counsel – required, that is, the full airing of everything affecting the commonwealth, especially those great matters of state most vital to the welfare of the realm as a whole which the queen sought to preserve to her own initiative and discretion. "[T]here is nothing soe necessary for the preservacion of the prince and state" as this sort of unencumbered "free speech," he said in 1576, "and without it it is a scorne and mockery to call it a parliament house for in truth it is none, but a very school of flattery and dissimulation and soe a fitt place to serve the Devill... and not to glorifye God and benefitt the comonwealth."[36] In the absence of a free right in Parliament to give counsel to the monarch on all vital matters, an MP would become nothing but a dissembling courtier whose well-being and advancement depended solely upon the royal will. He would cease to be "a councellor to the whole state," as Wentworth insisted he was.[37]

Although in the Parliament of 1576 Wentworth had no large body of followers rising to insist he be allowed to finish his speech when he was silenced by the Speaker, he nonetheless had made a significant point on behalf of his fellow MPs about the character of England as a "monarchical republic" on Fortescue's model. The ideal of counsel carries with it the same focus on the "highest good" that characterizes the active life of statesmen and citizens in city-states and republics invoked by Aristotle and Cicero. As Sir Francis Bacon said, "[t]he greatest trust between man and man is the trust of giving counsel," because "to such as they make their counsellors, they commit the whole" of their lives. Even "God himself" was not without counsel, since he had "made . . . one of the great names of his blessed Son; *The Counsellor.*"[38] Still, for Bacon, the giving of this sort of counsel belonged to duly appointed counsellors selected by the ruler for this purpose, or to peers and courtiers, not to the elected representatives of the people. For Wentworth, however, to a be a free subject in a free monarchy, it was insufficient merely to consent to laws and taxation; it was also necessary to share in the activity of politics itself in advancing "the glory of God," in providing for "the prince's safetye," and in upholding "the libertie of the parliament house whereby the state is maintayned."[39]

Honor and Liberty: Philip Sidney at the Greenwich Tennis Court, 1579

Our next story, involving the young Philip Sidney, also began as a matter of counsel. Sidney, the twenty-five-year-old nephew of the earl of Leicester, was no sworn counsellor to the queen when in 1579 he nonetheless undertook openly and vigorously to support his uncle in advising against her possible marriage with the Catholic duke of Anjou, then under negotiation with the French. Sidney was a courtier on the model developed in Castiglione's *Book of the Courtier*, favored with the humanist education and the careful cultivation and refinement of his person advocated in that work. His family connections enabled him to enjoy ready access to the court, to be regularly in the presence of the queen, and to engage actively in the political discussions and maneuverings undertaken in that setting. It is Sidney the courtier that is of interest for present purposes.[40]

Early modern courts were both arenas and theaters of power. As arenas of power, they were places where contests for the advancement of personal and political interests occurred, where policies were promoted, and were offices or favors were pursued for oneself or for kin and clients. They were also points of contact with the larger polity – places where those on the inside communicated to the prince the needs or desires of his subjects and informed the subjects of their prince's wishes and will. In these respects, they were instruments for the making and administering of governmental and political decisions across the whole range of activities that fell within the authority and responsibility of the emerging princely states. Their functioning depended on the striving of each member for proper recognition and reward of his merits and achievements, and the consequent clashes of views.

Theaters of power, however, are places of social harmony and hierarchical order. A theater of power represents the world of the court as a microcosm of the balanced, ordered universe created and ruled by God, and it treats the prince as a kind of god on earth – the possessor of perfect wisdom, the exemplar of supreme majesty, and the fount of ultimate justice. If in the court as an arena of power the give-and-take of discussion, conversation, and debate is the paradigmatic cultural form, in the court as a theater of power it is ceremony – the rhythms and regularities of ritual processions, state celebrations, royal entries and entertainments, and similar events – which brings the courtiers into an ordered relation not only to one another but to the prince. What is paramount is respect for honor – that is, due recognition of those intrinsic qualities of worth that mark each person's proper station in the court hierarchy.

How was it possible to reconcile the requirements of life in an arena of power with the characteristics of a theater state? In the former, competition was not just an unfortunate fact of life, but a guiding principle, necessary for the formulation of wise policy and the making of good appointments. But in the latter, it represents not just a source of instability and disorder, but a violation of its leading idea. By transforming the prince and his courtiers into political instruments engaged in the exercise of government and allocation of resources, it distances them from their capacities to serve as living images of legitimate authority, virtue, and order.

Castiglione's *Book of the Courtier*, first translated into English in 1561, offers an insight.[41] A courtier, Castiglione says, should "steer away from affectation at all cost, as if it were a rough and dangerous reef, and (to use perhaps a novel word for it), to practice in all things a certain nonchalance which conceals all artistry and makes whatever one says or does seem uncontrived and effortless." The novel word in Italian is *sprezzatura*. The passage goes on:

> I am sure that grace springs especially from this, since everyone knows how difficult it is to accomplish some unusual feat perfectly, and so facility in such things excites the greatest wonder, whereas in contrast to labour at what one is doing and, as we say, to make bones over it, shows an extreme lack of grace and causes everything, whatever its worth, to be discounted. So we can truthfully say that true art is what does not seem to be art; and the most important thing is to conceal it, because if it is revealed this discredits a man completely and ruins his reputation.

If people know of your skills, Castiglione explains, they will be "frightened of being deceived" and resist your attempts to win them to your favor or your point of view.[42]

In order to distinguish himself as uniquely worthy and especially deserving of praise and reward, the courtier engaged in willful acts of self-fashioning, modeling his public image in light of the expectations of his audience and adapting his persona to his surroundings, performing a tightrope act of self-discipline as he constantly monitored the results of his actions on his fellows – in effect making himself a member of his own audience. Accordingly, the character of the courtier was the result not only of his education and experience, but also of his own decisions and actions. Even as he adjusted his behavior to the requirements of the occasion and the expectations of his audience, he became the agent of his own virtue.

For all the contradictions apparent in this complex form of public behavior, it was well-suited for reconciling the competitiveness of court life, which turned on the recognition of individual achievement, with its hierarchical form of organization, which depended on accepting as just and natural the unequal distribution of honor among the courtiers. *Sprezzatura* represents carefully honed achievements as the natural consequences of virtues and treats the resulting structure of honor as the inevitable expression of the proper order of things. Success in the competition can be redescribed, therefore, as confirming the triumph of noble qualities and public good over baser instincts and private evil. When successful, this approach defused the explosive mixture of honor and competition at court. It restrained the courtier in his behavior towards his fellows in maintaining civil discourse with them, in keeping his anger under control, and in taking their outlooks and likely reactions into account in framing his own presentation of himself before them.

But such sociable interaction and the maintenance of balanced harmony was not always possible, especially when a great matter like Elizabeth's possible marriage to a foreign and Catholic prince was under discussion. However, with so much at stake for the future of the kingdom, there was no decision that could satisfy all interests or viewpoints. It is no surprise, therefore, that the Anjou match generated faction at court. In these circumstances, personal honor readily became the coinage with which power and policy were negotiated, and the court could move from a vigorous exchange of views to open violence between adversaries. Among the supporters of the Anjou match, opposing Leicester and his allies, was Edward de Vere, earl of Oxford. His clash with Sidney illustrates how the defense of honor might also entail the upholding of moral autonomy and personal liberty, and how along with being an arena and theater of power the court might also become a tribunal for the testing of character.

According to Fulke Greville, Sidney's friend and contemporary biographer, Sidney's "worth, truth, favour, and sincerety of heart" were the "privileges" that allowed him "to oppose himself against his sovereign's pleasure" regarding the Anjou match and to offer his views "by a due address of his humble reasons to the Queen herself." Sidney may have expected a just reward for the prudence of his advice, but instead of entry into office, he was allowed "the freedom of his thoughts, with all recreation worthy of them," as Greville puts it. Indeed, although Sidney was on the winning side, from the viewpoint of his personal advancement, his aggressive giving of counsel to the queen, "being neither magistrate nor counsellor," was a major miscalculation. It is probably one reason why Sidney never received the offices or honors from the queen he clearly expected and Greville thought he plainly deserved.[43]

The next move in the tale came in the aftermath of Sidney's intervention, but before the question of the marriage had been finally disposed of. With the French ambassadors still at Greenwich, one day Sidney was enjoying his tolerated and enforced freedom from affairs by playing a match of tennis at the palace, when the earl of Oxford, "born great," Greville says, "and greater by alliance, and superlative in the prince's favour, came abruptly into the tennis-court, and speaking out of these three paramount authorities he forgot to entreat that which he could not command."[44] Oxford demanded that Sidney yield the tennis court to him. The very demand was a symbolic challenge for primacy, not merely to Sidney's person, but to his party.

According to Greville, Sidney, knowing what was due to himself and what to others, met these "mists of my lord's passion swollen with the winds of his faction" with an implacability that demonstrated his virtue above Oxford's birth. But "the less amazement or confusion of thoughts [Oxford] stirred up in Sir Philip, the more shadows this great lord's own mind was possessed with, til at last with rage ... he commands them to depart the court." To Oxford's demand, Greville says, Sidney answered "that if his lordship had been pleased to express desire in milder character ... he might have led out those that he should now find would not be driven out with any scourge of fury. This answer – like a bellows blowing up the sparks of excess already kindled – made my lord scornfully call Sir Philip by the name of puppy." The French ambassadors, in audience in the private galleries overlooking the tennis court, "instantly drew all to this tumult," creating a large audience for what followed. Sidney,

> rising with an inward strength by the prospect of a mighty faction against him, asked my lord with a loud voice that which he heard clearly enough before, who like an echo that still multiplies by reflections, repeats this epithet of puppy the second time. Sir Philip resolved in one answer to conclude both the attentive hearers and passionate actor, gave my lord a lie impossible (as he averred) to retort: in respect all the world knows puppies are gotten by dogs and children by men.[45]

Sidney, in a nearly paradigmatic *sprezzatura* performance, had offer his challenger a brutal insult.

Giving Oxford the lie was itself a serious matter, since a gentleman's honor inhered in the veracity of his words. Sidney, therefore, had rejected the very foundations of respect on which rested Oxford's own claim to deference. But the matter went deeper. Oxford, who was known not to be living with his wife at the time, had been notoriously unsuccessful in fathering an heir. Sidney was saying in words, and demonstrating in his calm command of himself as the incident seemingly raged out of control on Oxford's side, that while he himself was a man, his opponent was not. There could be no other outcome but a duel, which might lead to the deaths of one or other or both of the antagonists.

Greville says that after Sidney uttered his response, he and Oxford "both stood silent a while like a dumb show in a tragedy" until Sidney departed.[46] Some days later Oxford issued a formal challenge, but whether he planned to go through with it is not clear – Sidney was so much his inferior in rank that even agreeing to the fight would have risked diminishing Oxford's honor yet further. In the face of this dilemma, Oxford contemplated avenging himself by preemptive attack, using armed retainers to kill Sidney in his bed, rather than fight him openly on the field of honor.[47]

Had the matter come to actual blows, there is no doubt that it would have produced an irreparable tear in the fabric of Elizabethan court life. The queen could not permit it. Here too is a lesson about the world of the courtier. Using her authority over both these men, she intervened to restore the court to its proper order, persuading each of the parties to refrain from their intended actions while acknowledging their rights to them. This yields one moral of the tale: in restoring Oxford and Sidney to their places at her court, she was also restoring her own command over it as an enclosed, harmonious, ordered community of cultivated and loyal servants. But, from Sidney's perspective, there was a second, more fundamental lesson.

According to Greville, Elizabeth sought to persuade Sidney to give over his duel by evoking the values of hierarchy and harmony of the court, laying

> before him the differences in degree between earls and gentlemen; the respect inferiors ought to their superiors; the necessity in princes to maintain their own creations, as degrees descending between the people's licentiousness and the anointed sovereignty of crowns; how the gentleman's neglect of the nobility taught the peasant to insult upon both.[48]

For the queen, good order in the kingdom depended on a great chain of being, maintained by her majesty and power; any breach threatened chaos. The same vision is manifested in the Church of England's "Homily on Obedience," and in Ulysses' oft-quoted speech on order in Shakespeare's *Troilus and Cressida*.[49]

A court *society* had indeed emerged in Elizabethan England, centered on the queen and peopled by courtiers dependent in considerable measure upon her goodwill. However, for Sidney and gentlemen reared like him in the traditions of humanist learning and of good service to the commonwealth, the life of the courtier could never be one of complete dependency on the monarch. They understood their honor to belong intrinsically to them as their birthright, protected by the same guarantees of liberty as belonged to all Englishmen. Howsoever sovereign she was, Greville reports Sidney saying, "yet was she content to cast her own affections into the same moulds her subjects did; and govern all rights by their laws." He therefore asked her "to consider that although [Oxford] were a great lord ... yet he was no lord over him."[50] Sidney rested his case not on any claim to respect as a gentleman, but on the protection owed him as a freeborn Englishman under the law, thereby linking his own honor with rights and protections enjoyed by the very peasantry about whom the queen had raised her doubts. Sidney owes Oxford, he says, no more than the respect due his rank – not the obedience of an underling to a master. In effect, he tells the queen the same thing. Against her demand for obedience and good order, he insists on her obligation to protect him against the loss of his just rights, in the process emphasizing that her own capacity to rein in her over-mighty subjects – the "grandees" as Greville calls them – depends precisely on her support of her free subjects against their pretensions and predations.

Greville wrote his *Dedication to Sir Philip Sidney* early in the second decade of the seventeenth century, ten years into the reign of James I, whose published writings, speeches to Parliament, and troubled relations with the political nation over taxation and prerogative power had raised their own questions about the proper relationship between monarch and subject in a kingdom ruled politically as well as royally.[51] In this context, Greville transformed Sidney into the exemplar of right action for a freeborn Englishman and true patriot, someone who could defer to the queen without abandoning his dignity or his principles. The "constant tenor of truth," Greville says, that Sidney

> took upon him, which, as a chief duty in all creatures – both to themselves and the
> sovereignty above them – protected this gentleman (though he obeyed not) from the
> displeasure of his sovereign; wherein he left an authentical precedent to after ages that
> howsoever tyrants allow of no scope, stamp, or standard but their own will, yet with
> princes there is a latitude for subjects to reserve native and legal freedom by paying
> humble tribute in manner, though not in matter, to them.[52]

The distinction between "tyrant" and "prince," and the stress on the "native and legal freedom" of the English – their ancient constitution – calls up once again the image of the monarchical republic, of the realm ruled politically as well as royally, which Wentworth too had invoked.[53]

Authority and Justice: Nicholas Wilkins, Jeffrey Wherrat, and Henry Cater at the Warwick Alehouse, 1615

Our final story, which in its own way also depends on ideas of honor, concerns persons as obscure as Peter Wentworth and Philip Sidney are well known. They are the local magistrates and some of the more boisterous citizens of the town of Warwick. In the late sixteenth and early seventeenth centuries, the central point of tension in the town's politics turned on the desire of the local officials to impose a sober respect for authority and a strict social discipline upon Warwick, and on the equally strong desire of a portion of its citizenry for the restoration of communal spirit among the magistracy in the conduct of the town's business. In 1615 this strain erupted in a topsy-turvy mock trial criticizing the town fathers for their allegedly arbitrary actions in suppressing an unlicensed alehouse and in convicting and punishing various townsmen for what the magistrates identified as "abuses and disorders" committed in the borough.[54]

According to the complaint presented in Star Chamber by John Townsend and the other members of the town corporation, Nicholas Wilkins, recently convicted for keeping an unlicensed alehouse, joined with a large number of fellow townsmen to

bring the magistrates "into hatred, derision, and detestation among all the inhabitants."[55] "In scorn and contempt...of the meetings of the Bailiff and Principal
Burgesses," the complaint says, Wilkins and the others set themselves up, in yet
another unlicensed alehouse, after the fashion of a town court. Jeffrey Wherrat became
the judge of this body, and Henry Cater was appointed to act as crier, whereupon the
two began to summon a jury, which all agreed would consist only of "whoremasters."
Cater, calling out the "Oyez" and willing all to be silent in mimicry of the procedures
of an ordinary law court, then summoned John Townsend, one of the principal
burgesses and twice the town's bailiff, to be the first juror. Wherrat, when asked his
judgment of the worthiness of this individual for the service, replied that he indeed
was "an old gouty whoremaster, and that he owed more than he was worth." After the
loud and rude laughter had died down, Cater repeated this procedure for Richard Lee,
another principal burgess of Warwick, who was quickly judged a "greedy Cormorant,"
also worthy of service. A third magistrate was identified as bankrupt, one who "would
bee a beggar within these two years." In like manner, every member of the Warwick
Corporation was called, and each in turn was judged sufficiently debauched and
corrupt for this upside-down jury.

We know only the barest facts about the perpetrators of this outrage, and almost
nothing of the disruptive acts for which they previously had been punished; probably
they concerned their operation of unlicensed alehouses. Wilkins was a freeholder with
property to rent to others. His fellow defendants were independent men, witnesses to
the sealing of the lease between him and one William Clemens, another unlicensed
alehouse-keeper, which was the occasion for this topsy-turvy trial. While hardly
among the town's wealthiest individuals, their position in the town was of sufficient
weight to attract a considerable throng to witness their mockery of constituted
authority. These men and the members of their large alehouse audience had come to
judge their governors as undeserving of respect. They viewed the suppression of
Wilkins's alehouse as an act of injustice, worthy only of whoremasters and self-serving
hypocrites, and they used their wit to subject them to "derision and disgrace" before
the rest of the town, creatively appropriating the language of justice, where honor and
rectitude were preeminent, and the conventions of the market, where honor and
credit-worthiness were all important, to condemn the very men who normally
employed the law to discipline them and who dominated them in the marketplace.

In this way Jeffrey Wherrat and Henry Cater, judge and crier of the alehouse
courtroom, performing the roles of actor-playwrights, represented in their little drama
the problem of authority in their community. By repeatedly calling in doubt the
magistrates' honor and credit-worthiness, doubts which in the early modern era might
threaten their very livelihoods as tradesmen, this exercise in alehouse justice inflicted
not only personal ridicule but social harm. The magistrates were well aware of the
possible damage. They saw themselves as "grave, discreet and honest" men of good
conversation and reputation, whose civil positions, personal honor, and credit granted
them high station in the town. They were charged to "preserve the liberties, privileges, order and good government" of Warwick, "and for the execution of Justice

... uppon ye Malefactors and offenders within the jurisdiction of the ... borough." In their view, as Townsend said, the actions of the alehouse judiciary not only brought the principal burgesses of Warwick "into hatred & disgrace amongst all the Inhabitants of the said Town and of the Countrey thereabouts, but as much allsoe as in them laye to bringe the very Magistracy itt selfe into Contempt and scorne and vtterly to subvert all manner of order and government within the said Towne." Hence the magistrates too sought retribution, using the court of Star Chamber to punish their enemies by requiring them to bear the costs and suffer the fear of answering for themselves to that terrifying body.

Townsend and the principal burgesses and Wilkins and his alehouse brethren participated in a common arena of politics in Warwick, operating with common codes of honor, justice, and authority. To answer the magistrates' claim to authority, there was the citizens' demand that it be exercised justly and fairly according to the standards of the community. However, when the magistrates' earnest efforts to suppress unlicensed alehouses confronted the customary practices of sociability and traditions of good fellowship observed by some of the citizens, the simple rules of reciprocity broke down, and disorder ensued. When it did, the differences of approach employed by the members of the Warwick Corporation and the supporters of Wilkins revealed a gap between the magistrates and the ordinary citizens of the town. The magistrates, backed by the power of the emerging English state, symbolized in this instance by the court of Star Chamber, looked upon themselves as participating in the widening world of affairs linking local government with the Crown, the Privy Council, and the court. The citizens, who as a practical matter could employ only the weapon of community scorn to avenge the wrongs done to them, saw themselves as participating with their magistrates in upholding the spirit of commonality within their local community. For them, the very honor claimed by the magistrates and their demands for deference from the citizenry became weapons with which their opponents could criticize and punish them.

Conclusion: Political Culture

For modern sensibilities it is easier, perhaps, to think of a kingdom or a community as possessing a structure of power through which particular individuals and groups exercise dominion over others, than to think of it as possessing a structure of authority. Power can be maintained by force; authority requires inferiors to accept the legitimacy of their superiors' rule over them. It depends, at a minimum, upon reciprocity in relations between the governors and the governed. This means, in turn, that every structure of authority necessarily contains within itself a standard of justice against which the validity of claims to power can be measured. In Warwick those in the self-perpetuating civic body looked upon themselves as in command of their town, free to exercise their judgments as royal lieutenants unrestrained by their social inferiors. In this they shared much with the outlook of Elizabeth herself and of

James I, her successor, and of many of their sworn counsellors. Those who opposed the Warwick magistrates, however, looked upon their governors as servants of the community who were to put personal interests aside to devote themselves to the maintenance of the commonweal. In this they joined in the claims to liberty and counsel expressed by Peter Wentworth and Philip Sidney – claims not simply to freedom from interference with their desires, but to the freedom of the community of which they were members and the freedom to participate in its public life.[56]

NOTES

1 See Raymond Williams, *Keywords: A Vocabulary of Culture and Society*, rev. edn (New York: Oxford University Press, 1983), pp. 57–60, 87–93; see also David Harris Sacks, "Searching for 'culture' in the English Renaissance," *Shakespeare Quarterly*, 39–4 (Winter 1988), pp. 466–7. I am grateful to the *Shakespeare Quarterly* for permission to use materials from this article here and elsewhere, as noted, in this essay.

2 Francis Bacon, *Of the Proficience and Aduancement of Learning* (London, 1629; STC 1165), sig. Ff 4ᵛ.

3 Williams, *Keywords*, p. 90.

4 Ibid., p. 91.

5 Quentin Skinner, *The Foundations of Modern Political Thought*, 2 vols (Cambridge: Cambridge University Press, 1978), ii. 353; see also Quentin Skinner, "The state," in *Political Innovation and Conceptual Change*, ed. Terence Ball, James Farr, and Russell L. Hanson, (Cambridge: Cambridge University Press, 1989), pp. 90–131.

6 David Harris Sacks, "The paradox of taxation: fiscal crises, Parliament, and liberty, 1450–1640," in *Fiscal Crises, Liberty, and Representative Government, 1450–1789*, ed. Philip T. Hoffman and Kathryn Norberg, (Stanford, Calif.: Stanford University Press, 1994), pp. 31–3; the work attributed to Ralegh first appeared as *The Prince, or Maxims of State, written by Sir Walter Rawley, and presented to Prince Henry* (London, 1642; Wing, STC R179), and the passage quoted appears on p. 1 of this edition. It was probably not written by him and perhaps was not yet in being during his lifetime. For discussion of this text's place in the canon of Ralegh's writing, see Pierre Lefranc, *Sir Walter Ralegh, écrivain: l'oeuvre et les idées* ([Paris]: Librairie Armand Colin, Les Presses de l'Université Laval, 1968), pp. 67–70.

7 Skinner, *Foundations*, i. 50–1; ii. 349–50; on the significance of Aristotle's *Politics* in Renaissance England, see Gabriel Harvey to Edmund Spencer (1579), in *Letter-Book of Gabriel Harvey, A.D. 1573–1580*, ed. Edward J. I. Scott, Camden Society, n.s. 33 (1884), p. 79.

8 *Politics* 1. 1. 1252a1–6, in Aristotle, *Politics*, trans. B. Jowett, in *The Complete Works of Aristotle: The Revised Oxford Translation*, ed. Jonathan Barnes, 2 vols (Princeton: Princeton University Press, 1994), vol. 2, p. 1986.

9 Patrick Collinson, "The monarchical republic of Queen Elizabeth I," in *Elizabethan Essays* (London: Hambledon Press, 1994), pp. 31–56, esp. pp. 32–4; see also Patrick Collinson, "*De Republica Anglorum*: or: history with the politics put back," in *Elizabethan Essays*, pp. 1-29; Sir Thomas Smith, *De Republica Anglorum: A Discourse of the Commonwealth of England*, ed. L. Alston (Cambridge: Cambridge University Press, 1906), see esp. pp. 29–47. *De Republica Anglorum* was first published in 1583, but was written ca. 1563.

10 T. E. Hartley (ed.) *Proceedings in the Parliaments of Elizabeth I*, vol. 1: *1558–1581* (Leicester: Leicester University Press, 1981), p. 425. For the context and some analysis see J. E. Neale, *Elizabeth I and her Parliaments, 1559–1581* (London: Jonathan Cape, 1953), pp. 318–32; *idem*, "Peter Wentworth," *English Historical Review*, 39 (1924), pp. 36–54,

175–205; T. E. Hartley, *Elizabeth's Parliaments: Queen, Lords and Commons, 1559–1601* (Manchester and New York: Manchester University Press, 1992), pp. 125–43, esp. pp. 127–34; P. W. Hasler (ed.), *The House of Commons, 1558–1603*, 3 vols (Cambridge: Cambridge University Press, 1981), vol. 3, pp. 597–601.

11 Hartley (ed.) *Proceedings*, p. 425.

12 Ibid., p. 428.

13 Ibid., p. 427.

14 Ibid., p. 430.

15 Ibid., p. 429.

16 Ibid., p. 426.

17 Brian Vickers, *The Defence of Rhetoric* (Oxford: Clarendon Press, 1988), p. 256. On the significance of rhetoric and rhetorical education in sixteenth-century England, see Quentin Skinner, *Reason and Rhetoric in the Philosophy of Thomas Hobbes* (Cambridge: Cambridge University Press, 1996), Part 1: "Classical Eloquence in Renaissance England," pp. 19–211.

18 *De Officiis*, I. xxi. 70, in Cicero, *De Officiis*, ed. and trans. Walter Miller (Cambridge, Mass.: Harvard University Press, 1975), pp. 70–2; see also Cicero, *On Duties*, ed. and trans. M. T. Griffin and E. M. Atkins (Cambridge: Cambridge University Press, 1991), p. 28. For the place of *De Officiis* in grammar school education see T. W. Baldwin, *William Shakespeare's Small Latine & Lesse Greeke*, 2 vols (Urbana: University of Illinois Press, 1944), vol. 2, pp. 578–616. The text was widely available in Latin. Between 1574 and Shakespeare's death in 1616, there were eleven individual editions; in addition, *De Officiis* also appeared as the lead item in six editions of Cicero's works in Latin designed for school use. Finally, an English translation by Nicholas Grimalde, first published in 1556 (STC 5281), saw seven further editions by 1600.

19 *Politics*, 1. 2. 1253a10–18, in Aristotle, *Complete Works*, vol. 2, p. 1988.

20 *De Inventione*, I. ii. 2–3, I. iv. 5, in Cicero, *De Inventione. De Optimo Genere Oratorum. Topica*, ed. and trans. H. M. Hubbell (Cambridge, Mass., and London: Harvard University Press, 1949), pp. 4–7, 12–13.

21 *De Officiis*, I. vii. 22, in Cicero, *De Officiis*, pp. 22–5; see also Cicero, *On Duties*, pp. 9–10.

22 See *De Officiis*, I. xvi. 50, I. xvii. 58, in Cicero, *De Officiis*, pp. 52–5, 60–1; see also Cicero, *On Duties*, pp. 21, 24.

23 Seneca, *Moral Epistle*, XCIV: "On the giving of advice," in Seneca, *Ad Lucilium Epistolae Morales*, ed. and trans. Richard A. Gummere 3 vols. (Cambridge, Mass.: Harvard University Press, 1971), pp. 10–58.

24 Hartley (ed.), *Proceedings*, p. 425.

25 Reginald Scot, *The discoverie of witchcraft* (London, 1584; STC 21864), epistle to Sir Thomas Scot, Sig. A4[g]; see David Harris Sacks, "Parliament, liberty, and the commonweal," in *Parliament and Liberty from the Reign of Elizabeth to the English Civil War*, ed. (Stanford, Calif.: Stanford University Press, 1992), pp. 94, 293 n. 34. Both Wentworth and Scot appear to be paraphrasing Seneca's "On the giving of Advice," *Moral Epistle*, XCIV. 72, in Seneca, *Epistolae Morales*, vol. 3, pp. 56–7: "When men praise great incomes, he should praise the person who can be rich with a slender estate and measures his wealth by the use he makes of it." Seneca's point in turn is grounded on Aristotle's distinction between use-value and exchange-value: *Politics*, I. 8–10. 1256a1–1258b8, in Aristotle, *Complete Works*, vol. 2, pp. 1992–7.

26 [Thomas Norton], *To the Queens Maiesties' poore deceiued Subjects of the Northe countreye drawen into the rebellion of the Earles of Northumberland and Westmerland* (London, 1569; STC 18679.5), Sig. F1ᵛ. On Norton see Neale, *Elizabeth I and her Parliaments*, pp. 91–240, *passim*; Hasler (ed.), *House of Commons*, vol. 3, pp. 145–9; Michael A. R. Graves, *Thomas Norton: The Parliament Man* (Oxford: Blackwell, 1994); *idem*, "Thomas Norton the Parliament man: an Elizabethan MP. 1559–1581," *Historical Journal*, 23 (1998) pp. 17–35; *idem*, "The management of the Elizabethan House of Commons: the Council's "Men-of-Business," *Parliamentary History*, 2 (1983), pp. 11–38, Patrick Collinson, "Puritans, men of business and Elizabethan Parliaments," in Collinson, *Elizabethan Essays*, pp. 72–7.

27 [Norton], *To the Queens Maiesties poore deceiued Subjectes*, Sig. 92ᵛ.

28 Hartley (ed.), *Proceedings*, p. 431.

29 See J. E. Neale, "The Commons' privilege of free speech in Parliament," in *Tudor Studies Presented... to Albert Frederick Pollard*, ed. R. W. Seton-Watson (London: Longmans, Green & Co., 1924), pp. 257–86; G. R. Elton, *The Parliament of England, 1559–1581* (Cambridge: Cambridge University Press, 1986), pp. 330–1, 341–7.

30 Hartley (ed.), *Proceedings*, p. 77.

31 Ibid., p. 78.

32 Smith, *De Republica Anglorum*, pp. 48–9.

33 William Roper, *The Life of Sir Thomas More*, in Richard S. Sylvester and Davis P. Harding (eds), *Two Early Tudor Lives* (New Haven and London: Yale University Press, 1962), pp. 204–5.

34 Hartley (ed.), *Proceedings*, p. 199.

35 Sir John Fortescue, *On the Laws and Governance of England*, ed. Shelley Lockwood (Cambridge: Cambridge University Press, 1997), p. 17; see also *idem, De Laudibus Legum Anglie*, ed. and trans. S. B. Chrimes (Cambridge: Cambridge University Press, 1949), pp. 24–7. This work of Fortescue's was first published in Latin in 1543 (STC 11193), and then with an English translation by Richard Mulcaster in 1567 (STC 11194). The Mulcaster edition and translation had three subsequent editions in 1573 (STC 11195), 1599 (STC 11196), and 1616 (STC 11197). It entered the English stock of the Company of Stationers in 1620.

36 Hartley (ed.), *Proceedings*, p. 426.

37 Ibid., p. 435.

38 Sir Francis Bacon, "Of counsel," in *Essays*, ed. Michael J. Hawkins (London: J. M. Dent, 1994), p. 53; for similar ideas see Ben Jonson, "Of statecraft," in *Ben Jonson's Timber or Discoveries*, ed. Ralph S. Walker (Syracuse, NY: Syracuse University Press, 1953), pp. 74–82.

39 Hartley (ed.), *Proceedings*, p. 437.

40 For Sidney's views on the Anjou match see "A letter written by Sir Philip Sidney to Queen Elizabeth touching her marriage with monsieur," in *Miscellaneous Prose of Sir Philip Sidney*, ed. Katherine Duncan-Jones and Jan Van Dorsten (Oxford: Clarendon Press, 1973), pp. 46–57; for background see Wallace MacCaffrey, *Queen Elizabeth and the Making of Policy, 1572–1588* (Princeton: Princeton University Press, 1981), pp. 243–66; *idem, Elizabeth I* (London: Edward Arnold, 1993), pp. 198–217; Blair Worden, *The Sound of Virtue: Philip Sidney's Arcadia and Elizabethan Politics* (New Haven and London: Yale University Press, 1996), pp. 89–114; Susan Duran, *Monarchy and Matrimony: The Courtships of Elizabeth I* (London and New York: Routledge, 1996), pp. 154–94.

41 The translator was Sir Thomas Hoby, who earlier in his career had supplied Sir Henry Sidney, Philip's father, with an Italian grammar: Peter Burke, *The Fortunes of the Courtier: The European Reception of Castiglione's Cortegiano* (University Park, Pa.: Pennsylvania State University Press, 1995), pp. 56, 66–77. Many of Castiglione's ideas on the role of counsel in princely courts were made available in English soon after the appearance of Castiglione's *Il Cortegiano* (1528), by Sir Thomas Elyot's *The Boke Named the Governour*, first published in 1531; see F. W. Conrad, "The problem of counsel reconsidered: the case of Sir Thomas Elyot," in *Political Thought and the Tudor Commonwealth: Deep Structure, Discourse and Disguise*, ed. Paul A. Fideler and T. F. Mayer (London and New York: Routledge, 1992), pp. 91 and 75–107 *passim*.

42 Baldassare Castiglione, *The Book of the Courtier*, trans. George Bull (Harmondsworth: Penguin, 1967), p. 67.

43 Fulke Greville, *A Dedication to Sir Philip Sidney*, in *The Prose Works of Fulke Greville, Lord Brooke*, ed. John Gouws (Oxford: Clarendon Press, 1986), p. 37. Although in describing this incident Greville repeatedly refers to Sidney as "Sir Philip," Sidney was not knighted until 1583.

44 Ibid., p. 38.

45 Ibid., pp. 38–9.

46 Ibid., p. 39.

47 Katherine Duncan-Jones, *Sir Philip Sidney, Courtier Poet* (New Haven and London: Yale University Press, 1991), p. 166. I am grateful to Alan Nelson for sharing materials with me and for these points.

48   Greville, *Dedication*, p. 40.

49   "An exhortacion concernyng good ordre and obedience to rulers and magistrates," in *Certain Sermons or Homilies (1547)* and *A Homily against Disobedience and Wilful Rebellion (1570): A Critical Edition*, ed. Ronald A. Bond (Toronto: University of Toronto Press, 1987), pp. 161–73; Shakespeare, *Troilus and Cressida*, I. iii. 78–124.

50   Greville, *Dedication*, p. 41.

51   Ibid., pp. xxi–xxiv; Ronald A. Rebholz, *The Life of Fulke Greville, First Lord Brooke* (Oxford: Clarendon Press, 1971), pp. 205–15, 328–37.

52   Greville, *Dedication*, p. 41.

53   CF. Debora Shuger, "Castigating Livy: The Rape of Lucretia and *The Old Arcadia*," *Renaissance Quarterly*, 51 (1998), pp. 526–45. Shuger argues in favor of Sidney's "aristocratic" outlook and against his "republicanism," at least as his views are manifested in *The Old Arcadia*. Greville, however, connects Sidney's aristocratic values and commitments with ideals of mixed government, the protections of the law and the possession of rights. The theory of mixed government granted a special place and privileges to the aristocracy in bringing balance and order to the regime; see Michael Mendle, *Dangerous Positions: Mixed Government, the Estates of the Realm, and the Answer to the xix propositions* (University, Ala.: University of Alabama Press, 1985), pp. 21–96; see also James M. Blythe, *Ideal Government and the Mixed Constitution in the Middle Ages* (Princeton: Princeton University Press, 1992).

54   This section derives from Sacks, "Searching for 'Culture'," pp. 484–6.

55   PRO, STAC 8/282/29, *Townsend et al. v Wilkins et al.* Subsequent quotations are from this Star Chamber bill.

56   This paragraph derives from Sacks, "Searching for 'Culture'," p. 487.

PART FOUR
Reading

9

The "Great Variety" of Readers and Early Modern Reading Practices

Heidi Brayman Hackel

John Heminge and Henry Condell address their prefatory letter to Shakespeare's first folio "To the great Variety of Readers," defining this "variety" as encompassing readers "From the most able, to him that can but spell."[1] Like the playhouses, the folio ushers in a diverse audience of readers, whose numbers and practices are the subject of this essay. By juxtaposing representations of literacy in Shakespeare's plays with the habits of actual readers, this essay explores the "great variety" of readings performed in early modern England.

Early Modern Literacies

Once largely the domain of social and intellectual elites, reading and book ownership had become available by 1600 to a broad range of English men and, to a lesser extent, English women (Clark 1976). Seizing upon this new audience, many authors and publishers advertised books as suitable for socially heterogeneous audiences, addressing "all degrees of men," "al estates," and the "young or olde / Ritche, poore, of high or low degree."[2] However, some authors and publishers reacted defensively to the growing market for their wares and intervened between book and buyer. In striking contrast to Heminge and Condell's invitation to various readers, Ben Jonson diverts potential buyers from *his* first folio, instructing the bookseller not to attract the attention of "some clerk-like serving-man, / who scarce can spell the hard names" ("To my Bookseller," lines 9–10). Published one year later in 1617, the "Post-script" to *Satyres and Satyrical Epigrams* directs the stationer in even greater detail to keep the book away from many customers:

> Let not each *Pesant*, each *Mecannick Asse*,
> That neer knew further then his *Horn-booke* crosse.
> Each rauin *Rusticke*: each illiterate *Gull*:
> Buy of my *Poesie*, by pocket full.
>
> .   .   .   .
>
> Others I wish the *Stationer* fore-warne,
> With a *Hand's off: It is not for your turne.*
> (Fitzgeffreys G4^v, G6^v)

Henry Fitzgeffrey's address to the bookseller exaggerates the goal of many early modern preliminaries: to define the audience of a book by drawing in desirable readers and sending others away. Unlike Jonson and Fitzgeffrey, Heminge and Condell include in the prospective audience of Shakespeare's first folio the *"Mecannick Asse"* who has not made it past his hornbook, the starting point for reading instruction in seventeenth-century England. For Heminge and Condell, basic literacy, rather than social rank or learned sophistication, is the criterion for inclusion. In welcoming all readers, Heminge and Condell privilege commercial interests over contemporary anxieties about the spread of literacy. Urging the reader to "buy...what euer you do, Buy," Heminge and Condell show little of the concern expressed in contemporary prefaces about the worthiness of prospective readers.

The readers about whom Jonson and Heminge and Condell disagree are those who "can but spell" – that is, those on the cusp of literacy who read letter by letter.[3] While such readers may seem unlikely to have had the means or the inclination to purchase Jonson's *Works* or Shakespeare's first folio, they were clearly envisaged as part of the potential audience for both of these sophisticated and expensive folios. These least skilled readers – who alternately prompted scorn and solicitude in the book trade – are precisely those most elusive for modern historians.

Contemporaneous assessments place literacy rates anywhere between 1 percent and 60 percent of the population (Bennett 1969: 27–9), and surviving records offer clues deeply at odds with one another.[4] Throughout the period, writers express alarm that "readers too common, and plentifull be" (Speght 1621), yet a contemporary proclamation suggests a culture still largely illiterate:

> considering the multitude of our good people are unlearned, and thereby not able by reading hereof to conceive our mind...we will that, beside the ordinary publication hereof...all curates in their parish churches shall...read this admonition to their parishioners. (Quoted in Thomas 1986: 106)

Attempts to quantify the unlearned "multitude" have produced problematic statistics. In *Literacy and the Social Order*, the standard study in the field despite its limitations, David Cressy calculates the percentage of English men and women who made marks rather than writing their signatures on legal documents, ecclesiastical records, and loyalty oaths between 1510 and 1730; he then equates these figures to rates of illiteracy. The loyalty oaths of the 1640s supply Cressy with a sample of over

40,000 male subscribers, a full 70 percent of whom used a mark rather than a signature to affirm their declarations. This figure, Cressy suggests, probably captures the level of illiteracy in rural England, but this average obscures the variations between parishes. Literacy rates in the early 1640s vary from 6 percent in a parish in northern Westmorland to 93 percent in one parish in Huntingdonshire (Cressy 1980: 191–201, 72–3). Suddenly, the range of 1–60 percent in contemporary estimates of literacy seems understandable.

Scholars have criticized Cressy's equation of signature and literacy rate, although all agree that the English population became increasingly, if not steadily, literate between 1500 and 1700.[5] A historically invisible skill, reading survives in the historical record only when accompanied by writing. Yet in early modern England the skills of reading and writing were acquired separately; consequently, many people, especially women, were probably able to read but not write.[6] While Elizabethan actors' wills testify to their "bookishness" (Honigmann and Brock 1993: 4), a sixteenth-century document preserves the marks, rather than signatures, of several players who presumably would have been able to read (Ford 1993: 33). Because of such problems with partial literacy, Keith Thomas suggests that Cressy's literacy figures may be a "spectacular underestimate" (1986: 103), while Margaret Spufford urges that they be taken as a bare minimum (1981: 22).

In the 1620s, when Heminge and Condell wrote their preface, 70 percent of London tradesmen, 50 percent of northern tradesmen, 34 percent of Essex husbandmen, 33 percent of rural weavers, 21 percent of northern yeomen, and a mere 10 percent of female Londoners qualified as literate by Cressy's count.[7] Even by the 1640s, less than one-third of all men and one-tenth of women demonstrated their literacy by signing their names on documents (Cressy 1980: 2). Of course, these figures were much higher within certain groups; gentlemen and clergy, except in northeastern England, were almost wholly literate by the standards of signatures (ibid. 118–24).

Literacy rates based on signatures fail to capture the degree of a reader's skill and sophistication; they do not, that is, locate the signer along the spectrum of readers "from the most able, to him that can but spell." A professional scholar like Gabriel Harvey, therefore, appears indistinguishable from someone like the country fellow to whom Nicholas Breton gives voice in *The Court and the Country* (1618). This country fellow describes for his courtier cousin the limited uses of learning for rural folk:

> this is all we goe to schoole for: to read common Prayers at Church, and set downe common prises at Markets, write a Letter, and make a Bond, set downe the day of our Births, our Marriage day, and make our Wills when we are sicke, for the disposing of our goods when we are dead: these are the chiefe matters that we meddle with. (C2ᵛ)

To register the difference between this country fellow's literacy and Gabriel Harvey's, one must speak of "literacies" in early modern England. In a period with a profusion of scripts and typefaces, proficiency in one does not guarantee proficiency in another. For instance, someone with rudimentary skills may have been able to "spell" black letter but not roman typeface; a more able reader, print but not secretary hand (Thomas 1986: 99–101).

Heminge and Condell's preface, for all its egalitarian gestures, nevertheless does differentiate between prospective readers of the folio.[8] Throughout the preface, Heminge and Condell acknowledge that it is the reader's "priuiledge" and "prouince" to censure or to praise the work. And yet their preface and the other preliminaries carefully circumscribe this province. Heminge and Condell assert that to understand Shakespeare is to like him, and in their final gesture, they direct readers towards the other preliminaries, the commendatory poems, which further influence the reader's "priuiledge":

> And so we leaue you to other of his Friends, whom if you need, can bee your guides: if you neede them not, you can leade your selues, and others. And such Readers we wish him.

What will a reader find who turns to the commendatory poems as "guides"? Rather than providing any specific tips for reading the folio, these "Friends" – Ben Jonson, Hugh Holland, L. Digges, and I. M. – memorialize Shakespeare's "lines and life" (A5[r]). A reader looking for guidance might glean several points from all four poems: the identification of the man and the work, the strong connection between these pages and the stage, and the promise of eternal fame for these plays. Not only do these four friends praise Shakespeare, but the preliminaries attest to the high regard in which his plays were held by Queen Elizabeth, King James, the earl of Pembroke, and the earl of Montgomery (A4[v], A2[r]). Ultimately, therefore, these preliminaries are guides not to the process of reading but rather to its conclusion – the formation of an opinion – and they make clear that the proper response to the first folio is praise, not censure.

In addition to consulting the commendatory poems, readers who need guidance in understanding may get it from another source: more able readers. Like many contemporary preface-writers, Heminge and Condell give some readers – presumably "the most able" – license to skip the other preliminary materials and "leade your selues, and others."[9] Further, it is these readers, who do not need guidance and who can influence other readers, that the publishers most desire to purchase and read their volume. While marketing the folio to all readers, Heminge and Condell, by the end of the preface, have established a hierarchy of readers of varying skills.

Staging Illiteracy

Throughout Shakespeare's plays, we witness the commonplace nature of illiteracy. For instance, when an uneducated character (usually a servant or a rural person) needs a letter read aloud, illiteracy is a mild inconvenience, which often jogs the plot along (e.g., *Love's Labor's Lost*, IV. ii). Such a scene in *Romeo and Juliet* suggests the fluidity of illiteracy across social lines. In preparation for the feast, Capulet sends a servant to invite "those persons out / Whose names are written there" (I. ii. 34–5), without realizing that his illiterate servant cannot make sense of the names. Turning to "the learned" for help, the servant approaches Romeo and mistakes his witty understatement for an honest confession:

SERVANT.   But / I pray, can you read anything you see?
ROMEO.   Ay, if I know the letters and the language.
SERVANT.   Ye say honestly. Rest you merry.
ROMEO.   Stay, fellow. I can read.

(I. ii. 59–63)

Capulet's and his servant's misapprehensions suggest that rank did not always dictate a level of learnedness: Capulet assumes his servant can read; the servant accepts that a young gentleman cannot. In early modern England, if not Verona, although most nobles were literate, gentility was not "impugned" or "revoked by illiteracy" (Cressy 1980: 124).

The play in which illiteracy figures most prominently is *2 Henry VI*, where literacy becomes, for Jack Cade and his followers, one of the primary markers of the elite and hence grounds for death. It is in reading this play, rather than in the comic moments of illiteracy elsewhere, that one becomes convinced of Margaret Ferguson's claim that literacy "constituted a major site of social conflict in the early modern period" (1988: 115). Cade identifies enemies of the rebellion by their literacy, and he defines the injustice of the current legal system partly in terms of literacy. Intent on upsetting an order in which men who cannot read are hanged (IV. vii. 38–41), Cade inverts the benefit of clergy, ordering death for a clerk who can write his name: "Away with him, I say. Hang him with his pen and inkhorn about his neck" (IV. ii. 97–8). Lord Say is similarly denounced when he quotes a bit of Latin: "Away with him, away with him! He speaks Latin" (IV. vii. 52). (For all his learning, Lord Say clearly – and fatally – does not know his audience: he responds to this indictment by glossing his statement with a reference to Caesar's *Commentaries*.) Certainly, Say's fluency in Latin marks him generally as a learned, rather than specifically a literate, man, but among his other crimes in Cade's eyes are the advocacy of printing and the building of a grammar school:

Thou hast most traitorously corrupted the youth of the realm in erecting a grammar school; and whereas, before, our forefathers had no other books but the score and the tally, thou hast caused printing to be used, and, contrary to the king his crown and dignity, thou hast built a paper mill. (IV. vii. 28–33)

Cade grounds his hostility towards literacy and learning in the material details of book production, which are all the more striking for their anachronism. In condemning Lord Say, Cade rails against printing presses and paper mills, though in 1450 neither had been established in England.[10] This enmity towards literacy is wholly absent from Shakespeare's main sources, Raphael Holinshed's (1587) and Edward Hall's (1548) accounts; in fact, Holinshed's rebels use written documents, and Hall's Cade is encouraged in the rebellion by "pryvye scholemasters" (Kiefer 1996: 80; Sousa 1996: 185). Anti-literacy sentiments did drive an earlier rebellion, the Peasants' Revolt, but in 1381, it was even further removed from print concerns (Sousa 1996).

Violent imagery associated with the printing press was current in the 1590s when this play was first performed: in his preface to *The Wonderfull Yeare* (1603), Thomas Dekker fears "a pressing to death" (A2^v), and other contemporary prefaces link "pressing" to sexual violence (Wall 1993: 181–8). But Cade does not confine the criminality of literacy to the technology of printing; he also vilifies the tools of manuscript production. Cade orders the clerk hanged "with his pen and inkhorn about his neck," and he describes the production of parchment as an act of brutality:

> Is not this a lamentable thing, that of the skin of an innocent lamb should be made parchment? that parchment, being scribbled o'er, should undo a man? (IV. ii. 71–4)

Cade's unrealized (and unrealizable) fantasy is, appropriately, a return to an exclusively oral culture. Ironically, the composite account of Cade's rebellion in *2 Henry VI* survives because of the convergence of oral and print culture in the Elizabethan theaters – first as a manuscript that drew on printed chronicles, then as a promptbook transformed into an oral performance (in which the actors' trick is to do without the book), and finally as a succession of printed texts that continue to be read and performed.

Playhouses and Playbooks

As Heminge and Condell invite prospective buyers and readers to judge the First Folio, they suggest a hierarchy of opinion:

> Then, how odde soeuer your braines be, or your wisedomes, make your license the same, and spare not. Iudge your sixe-pen' orth, your shillings worth, your fiue shillings worth at a time, or higher, so you rise to the iust rates, and welcome. But, what euer you do, Buy. (A3^r)

Having first urged the reader to judge according to his wit, Heminge and Condell then propose a sliding scale of prices, which seem to refer to the book. Yet the price of the folio volume would not have been so variable; nor is it likely that someone would have bought a share of the volume.[11] Perhaps Heminge and Condell are recommending that a buyer judge the folio in bits – play by play, say – allotting a portion of the total cost (and right to censure) each time. The instructions, however, evoke the language of the playhouse, where admission prices did, in fact, operate on a sliding scale. The Induction to Ben Jonson's *Bartholomew Fair* plays on this heterogeneity of expenses when the Scrivener presents the "Articles of Agreement" to the "spectators or hearers" at the Hope Theater. These articles grant members of the audience the right to judge the play according to their investments:

> it shall be lawful for any man to judge his six pen'orth, his twelve pen'orth, so to his eighteen pence, two shillings, half a crown to the value of his place: provided always his place get not above his wit. . . . marry, if he drop but sixpence at the door, and will censure a crown's worth, it is thought there is no conscience in that.[12]

In much the same language that Heminge and Condell use, Jonson's Scrivener, however sardonically, ties judgment of the play to both the spectator's wit and his expenditure.

This blurring of the language of booksellers and playhouses suggests the close, often fraught relationship between performances and playbooks. Publishers emphasized the connection of a text to a performance by advertising the name of a playhouse on the title page.[13] Prefaces, too, frequently stress the priority of stage to page. John Marston bemoans that "scenes invented merely to be spoken should be enforcively published to be read," and Ben Jonson and John Webster similarly stress the aural aspect of plays (Kiefer 1996: 13). To ward off potential critics, Heminge and Condell insist upon the theatrical success of the plays, which "haue had their triall alreadie" on the stage.

Some authors and publishers, however, distance their commodities from the stage. The 1609 reissued quarto of *Troilus and Cressida* announces itself immediately as a text for readers rather than spectators. A title page that makes no mention of the stage replaces the first-issue title page, which advertised the play's history as a public performance ("As it was acted by the Kings Maiesties seruants at the Globe"). And, unlike the other Shakespeare quartos published before the first folio, it opens with a sustained letter to the reader, which promises a play "neuer stal'd with the Stage, neuer clapper-clawd with the palmes of the vulger" (A2^r).[14] Similarly associating vulgarity with the stage, critics of the theater often attacked playbooks as corrupted by their association with the public theaters.[15]

As Heminge and Condell's dedicatory epistle makes clear, many readers nevertheless delighted in the "trifles" of the playhouse (A2^r). The typography of playbooks suggests that publishers considered educated readers among the potential buyers of their books, and records of contemporary book ownership confirm that they succeeded in marketing playbooks to a broad range of readers.[16]

Scenes of Reading

Reading matter proliferates on the stage in Shakespeare's plays: proclamations, indictments, guest lists, inventories, notebooks, broadsides, funerary monuments. Letters, in particular, figure prominently in the action of many plays, but books also appear frequently as objects on the stage and as topics of conversation.[17]

Characters search for books, send servants to fetch them, swear oaths on them, speak of lending them, mark their places in them, plan to destroy them, renounce them, and, on occasion, read them onstage. Described in an unusually full stage direction, King Henry VIII cuts a sad and solitary figure as he reads: "the King draws the curtain and sits reading pensively" (II. ii. 60. s.d.); Suffolk comes upon him and observes, "How sad he looks; sure he is much afflicted." Hamlet's mother similarly marks the approach of her bookish son: "But look where sadly the poor wretch comes reading" (II. ii. 168). Both readers are quickly interrupted, and most other scenes of reading are narrated rather than enacted onstage.

Asked by Polonius what he is reading, Hamlet replies, "Words, words, words" (II. ii. 191). For all its sarcasm, Hamlet's response typifies the role of books as props in the plays. Certainly, some books are named – Ovid's *Metamorphoses*, a "Book of Songs and Sonnets" (perhaps Tottel's *Miscellany*), the "Book of Riddles" – but most books are identified generically, if at all. Books of prayer, books of love, books in Greek and Latin: such books serve as shorthand to identify their possessors as variously devout, amorous, or learned. Onstage, books evoke a range of possible associations, due largely to the "legacy of the mixed, even antithetical, attitudes" towards print in the early modern period (Kiefer. 1996: 296). This versatile, generic quality of books applies at the level of the stage property as well. As Kiefer suggests, a single printed book "could serve in dozens of plays," the implication being that a godly book might serve as a book of love in the following production (p. 286). This interchangeability of books seems to have carried further than genre; cheap printed books, rather than historically accurate manuscript scrolls, were probably used in plays set in classical times.[18] A few accounts of reading move beyond this generic shorthand and provide detailed scenes of reading: on the evening she is betrayed, Imogen reads in bed by candlelight between the hours of 9:00 and midnight, losing track of time, tiring her eyes, and finally bidding her servant to turn down the page to mark her spot – portentously, in the story of Tereus and Philomela (II. ii. 1–7, 44–6).

For all its internal drama, reading as an activity is treated much like sleep or prayer onstage: we hear of it or witness it at the moment of its interruption. Solitary, silent reading, which was becoming increasingly common in the period, is usually a physically uneventful activity, marked more by stillness than by theatrics. Those readers who do read books onstage often bring extraordinary qualities to the scene: Prospero uses books to make storms, and Lavinia overcomes unspeakable horrors when she reads and writes onstage. Newly bereft of both hands and tongue, Lavinia seizes upon books as the way to reveal the nature and the perpetrators of her violation. Having pursued her nephew until he throws down his books in understandable terror, Lavinia "cull [s]" from the heap of scattered books a copy of Ovid's *Metamorphoses*, "tosseth" it about, "busily... turns the leaves" until she reaches the passage she "quotes" (*Titus*, IV. i. 41–50). The aggressive, violent nature of her reading in this scene begins to suggest, by contrast, the visual dullness of a more ordinary scene of reading.

Despite the absence of sustained staged scenes of reading, books emerge as vital, valued objects in Shakespeare's plays. Even when books are not visible on the stage, characters report the private spaces that books occupy: pillows, pockets, bedchambers, and beds. Characters place a high value on books: Prospero "prize[s]" his books above his dukedom (*Tempest*, I. ii. 167–8), and Slender prefers his "Book of Songs and Sonnets" to forty shillings – a sum that might otherwise buy him eighty quarto playbooks or two large folios bound in calf.[19] Although Prospero is the most obvious example, other characters also acknowledge the transformative power of reading. Titus hopes that Lavinia can "beguile" her sorrow in his library (*Titus*, IV. i. 34–6), and the crowd listening to the singing of a printed ballad is so transfixed that Autolycus easily steals most of their "festival purses" (*Winter's Tale*, IV. iv. 597–609).

While we surely should not take as normative the powerful reading of Prospero or the pathetic "quoting" of Lavinia, the scenes of reading in Shakespeare's plays often do provide glimpses of contemporary reading practices. As Lena Cowen Orlin argues, "fiction, too, can be an archive" (1994: 10): Shakespeare's scenes of reading do suggest contemporary habits, expectations, and transgressions. Material evidence in early modern books demonstrates that many qualities of these staged readings were common practice among those in the audience.

Habits of Reading

As the varied sites of reading in the plays suggest, early modern readers were not always seated at a desk when they read. Contemporary accounts reveal readers in diverse spaces: gardens, beds, churches, studies, taverns, coaches, ships, court, play-houses, battlefields, and coffee houses.[20] This variety indicates the growing presence of books and the multiple habits of reading in early modern England.

Like Hamlet, Ophelia, and Celia, who read while walking, Samuel Pepys records his perambulatory reading in his journal entries of 1666.[21] The inwardness that Roger Chartier attributes to Pepys's mobile reading is more usually seen in enclosed domestic spaces, especially the bedchamber and the book closet. Imogen reads in bed, finally bringing on sleep (*Cymbeline*, II. ii); and Brutus picks up a book, it seems, in order to lull himself to sleep (*Julius Caesar*, IV. iii). Although beds were generally only semi-private spaces in the early modern period (Orlin 1994: 185), they never-theless seem to have provided havens for book-lovers. Doctor William Denton, for instance, when sick in bed in 1653, describes himself as "an old, old, old man, with a bed-full of books" (Verney 1894: 202). Potentially the most private space in an early modern household, the book closet became an increasingly common feature of aristo-cratic households. Credited by scholars with the development of notions of privacy and of selfhood, these small interior chambers housed books and offered unpre-cedented opportunities for privacy for both men and women.[22]

The private reading allowed by the book closet and epitomized in the scene of Henry VIII's devotional reading has been called "one of the major cultural develop-ments of the early modern era" (Chartier 1989a: 125). Perhaps even more important than the architectural developments that fostered domestic privacy, the spread of silent reading (yet another of the many "literacies" of the period) encouraged a new relationship between reader and book that was characterized by greater immediacy and intimacy.[23] The cognitive shift to silent reading had begun in the eleventh century in cathedral schools and was widespread among the nobility and professions by the fifteenth century; members of more recently literate groups, of course, may have taken longer to acquire the skill.[24]

Except for those "that can but spell," most readers in sixteenth-century England would have been able to read silently. Yet many still read aloud. For some, oral reading was a way to expand the circle of literacy and share the written or printed word with nonreaders. Literate laborers read broadsides to their friends in taverns; merchants, by royal decree, could read the vernacular Bible aloud to their families. One Elizabethan preacher counselled people who could not read to "repayre to those places where they may haue the Scriptures read vnto them" and, further, to "get the Bibles into their houses" so that the family could hear the Bible read aloud should someone literate pay a visit.[25] Despite the spread of silent reading, many early modern people – most, if we accept Cressy's (1980) literacy figures – experienced reading primarily aurally rather than visually. Such nonreaders would nevertheless still see a lot of print and might even post broadside ballads in their homes (Watt 1990: 62–3; Thomas 1986: 112).

For others, communal reading was a social practice with a long history among the educated. Joyce Coleman (1996) has demonstrated the vitality of group reading until the end of the fifteenth century, well after the acquisition of silent reading among the elite, and indeed this practice continued throughout the early modern period. Scholars have documented the lively coterie circulation of manuscripts in seventeenth-century England; we might expand these notions to include coterie reading as well. Holinshed chronicles the prevalence of this practice at Queen Elizabeth's court, noting its seeming strangeness to someone from abroad:

> the stranger that entereth into the court of England upon the sudden, shall rather imagine himselfe to come into some publike schoole of the universities, where manie give eare to one that readeth, than into a princes palace, if you conferre the same with those of other nations. (Holinshed 1587:. 197; quoted by Kiefer 1996: 12)

Although Holinshed distinguishes Queen Elizabeth's court for its bookishness, communal reading was an "essential ingredient of social life, even among the elite" from 1500 to 1800 on the Continent as well (Chartier 1989a: 147).

Just as town squares, taverns, and the court were sites of communal reading, so was the aristocratic household. Sir Edward Dering (1598–1644), for instance, may have arranged private performances at home in the 1620s; his purchases of multiple copies of books and of "heades of haire and beardes" suggest an elaborate version of communal reading that verged on theater (Krivatsy and Yeandle 1992: 139). Far more typical of domestic reading is a scene from *Titus Andronicus*. Lavinia, Titus, and young Lucius retire to Lavinia's book closet to pass the time reading "sad stories" together (III. ii.

81–5). Both onstage and in households, early modern readers retreated to book closets for communal, as well as solitary, reading. Even this archetypal space of privacy and selfhood, therefore, was not always a cloistered, hushed space.

In their book closets and in larger spaces, noblewomen especially seem to have frequently listened as others read. In her diary of 1616–19, Anne Clifford (1924) refers twenty-three times to a scene of reading; nineteen of these record an experience in which Clifford "spent [the day] in *hearing* of reading" (my emphasis). An anonymous seventeenth-century inscription in a copy of *Barclay his Argenis* also records this practice:

> I began to reade this booke to your Ladiship the xvj[th] day of January: 1625: and ended it the xxv[th] of the same moneth:/ (Huntington Library, RB 97024)

The *Argenis* consists of five books and about 400 pages, so this pair – a reader and a noblewoman – read the romance at the fast clip of forty folio pages a day. Significantly, it is the reader of the book, not the female listener, who has recorded its reading history. Ben Jonson refers in *Bartholomew Fair* to the "spectators or hearers" at a playhouse, a category that we might too quickly contrast to the readers of a playbook. But clearly, many early modern people were "spectators or hearers" of playbooks as well.

The voracity of the readers of the *Argenis* typifies "extensive" reading, a term used by Rolf Engelsing to describe the wide-ranging habits of most modern readers in contrast to an earlier, more meditative "intensive" mode of reading based upon repeated encounters with a text.[26] Sir Edward Dering's acquisition of playbooks similarly suggests a wide-ranging appetite for books: in the winter of 1623, he bought 156 playbooks in London, plus two copies of Shakespeare's first folio and a copy of Jonson's *Works* (Krivatsy and Yeandle 1992: 141). Yet, in the preface to the first folio, Dering would have been instructed to read it "and againe, and againe" (A3[r]) – quite a task for a man with 159 new playbooks on his shelves. In urging readers to turn again and again to the folio, Heminge and Condell distance the volume from ephemeral trifles, situating it instead as a volume, like Scripture or a scholarly text, that demands and rewards rereading.

Among the most common strategies for digesting a book and preparing it for future readings or readers, handwritten marginalia provide intimate glimpses into the practices and habits of reading. "From the most able, to him that can but spell," early modern readers filled the margins and other blank spaces of their books with a full range of handwritten marks: asterisks, pointing hands, private symbols, summaries, cross-references, assessments, signatures, even doodles and drawings. Scholars have analyzed the marginalia of some of the "most able" early modern readers – Gabriel Harvey, John Dee, Ben Jonson – and begun to examine their contemporaries' often anonymous marks.[27] The elaborate, multilingual marginalia of Harvey reveal a professional scholar deeply engaged in his reading, forging paths through texts, linking disparate texts, and returning again and again to the same books (Jardine and Grafton 1990). At the other end of the spectrum are the semi-literate readers of

Edmund Coote's *English Schoole-Maister* (1596), whom he instructs to "make a marke with a pen or pin" next to any "hard" words; readers should then ask their ministers about these points in the text (A3^r).

Readers' marks in Bibles, polemical tracts, and law books are especially common, but no genre or format seems to have eluded the scribbling hands of readers entirely. Annotations appear in herbals, romances, dictionaries, sonnet sequences, jestbooks, duodecimos, even on broadsides. Despite their reputation as "trifles" and their connection to oral performance, playbooks, too, bear the material traces of early owners and readers. Nearly all the Folger first folios, which represent perhaps a tenth of the original press run, contain some marks left by readers or owners.[28] Over one-third of these marks can be dated with certainty to the seventeenth century, and fully one-third of these (or ten folios) have been inscribed by women.[29] Many more copies, of course, may have been annotated by seventeenth-century readers, but faded and obliterated signatures and nonverbal markings do not allow precise dating.

As one of the most fetishized books printed in English, the first folio has an unusual history of ownership and conservation. Made-up copies, bleaching, and trimming have limited the survival of readers' marks in these valuable volumes, but as a group the Folger first folios nevertheless contain many examples of the most common forms of marginalia. Underlining in the text and pointing hands in the margins suggest the passages that most struck a reader (Folger no. 15); other readers took these nonverbal marks a step further and copied lines in the margins or other blank spaces. At the end of *Titus Andronicus* a seventeenth-century reader has loosely transcribed two lines from Act III, scene i: "for fiue and twenty valiant sonnes I never wept / Because they died in hono*r*s lofty bed" (Folger no. 38, 2e2^v). Another contemporary reader also attended closely to *Titus Andronicus*, emending, for example, "Ad manus fratrem" to "Ad manes fratrum" (Folger no. 51, 2c4^v). Imperfections in this copy, so typical of the folios, prevent us from knowing more about this reader learned enough to spot an error in a Latin line and careful enough to correct it. The preliminaries are mutilated and patched, so some ownership information may have been lost, and forty-nine leaves are supplied from other copies. The textual emendations that survive in *Hamlet* and *Titus*, therefore, may have extended to other plays as well in the original volume. Summaries of action suggest someone reading for the plot, as the annotator who scribbled "[D]emetrus awakd" in the margins of *A Midsummer Night's Dream* (Folger no. 71, N5^v); while a Restoration reader of another copy seems to have had theatrical interests, jotting down lists of *dramatis personae* and noting at the end of *The Taming of the Shrew*, "something prety might be made of this in pastarole."[30]

While a reader's marks often inform us of reactions at the most local level of a single line, some readers scribbled down their assessments of the whole work, as did this reader of *The Taming of the Shrew*. Another reader deemed the *Tempest* "a very good one" (Folger no. 54, B4^r), while a reader of the second folio singled out *Titus* for special praise: "Will Shakespeare that more then Excellent Drammatiq*ue* poet by this Dolefull tragedy has merited immortal fame immortal fame [sic]: so says Sam: Danvers" (second folio, Folger no. 47, 2g1^v). Such comments remind us both of the eccentricity of individual readers and of the historical contingencies of reading, for few modern readers, I suspect, would imagine *The Taming of the Shrew* as a pretty pastoral, and Shakespeare's "immortal fame" has not rested upon *Titus*, though it may well have begun with it (Bate 1995: 1). Samuel Danvers's marginal praise of *Titus*, along with other contemporary readers' attentiveness to this play, suggests the early modern popularity of *Titus* as a text as well as a performance.

Sometimes, the margins and flyleaves did not offer enough space, and readers turned to separate manuscript volumes in which they transcribed passages from many texts. Comenius presents the compilation of a commonplace book as an alternative to marginalia:

> a *Student* ... whilst he readeth *Books*, which being within his reach, he layeth open upon a *Desk* and picketh all the best things out of them into his own *Manual*, or marketh them in them with a dash, or *a little star*, in the *Margent*. (*Orbis sensualium pictus*, 200–1; quoted in Love 1993: 222)

Like a pointing hand in the margin, the presence of a passage in a commonplace book signals its significance to the reader. The "quintessentially humanist method of reading and storing information" (Blair 1992: 541), the commonplace book allowed a reader to collect and organize bits of texts for later use in speaking or writing. Despite its associations with humanist pedagogy and classical learning, the commonplace book shows up as a tool for readers of varying sophistication. Nicholas Breton's country fellow, who sees little use for learning in rural life, nevertheless remembers his father's notes in a manuscript volume that sounds much like a commonplace book (1618: 202). And, if we are to trust Shakespeare's pedlar Autolycus, this country fellow might have bought such a notebook from a traveling pedlar who, like Autolycus, may have sold "table-books" along with his ballads (*Winter's Tale*, IV. iv. 590–2).

As this range of readers suggests, commonplace books were not exclusively repositories for *sententiae* from Cicero. Like printed pages of classical texts, the typography of vernacular works often called readers' attention to weighty or witty passages. G. K. Hunter has documented the use of numerous pointing devices in Elizabethan plays, poems, and romances. Certainly, those works with "academic pretensions" are more heavily and systematically marked (Hunter 1951: 174–5), but the presence of gnomic pointing in English plays suggests that readers who did transcribe bits from plays were not acting entirely eccentrically. While Henry Oxinden (1608–70) recorded in his commonplace book merely the titles of 123 plays that he seems to have owned (Dawson 1935), Gunnar Sorelius has identified fragments of a massive commonplace book that included quotations from thirty-six Shakespeare plays and many other dramas. Compiled *c.*1660, this volume organized passages in the style of a humanist commonplace book under headings such as "Abasement," "Abilities," "Vsurpation & Vsurping" (1973: 296–7). Of the estimated 13,700 original quotations, 749 survive, all but a handful of which come from Shakespeare's plays.[31] While this compiler seems to have copied passages from printed texts, other compilers transcribed bits from both playbooks and performances. The manuscript notebooks of Edward Pudsey (1573–1613), for example, include extracts from several quarto editions of Shakespeare's plays and from a performance of *Othello*, which was not printed until after Pudsey's death (Honigmann and Brock 1993: 94).

In the Prologue to *The Woman Hater*, Beaumont and Fletcher (1607) chase away any theatergoers with plans like Pudsey's:

> if there bee any lurking amongst you in corners, with Table bookes, who have some hope to find fit matter to feede his——mallice on, let them claspe them up, and slinke away, or stay and be converted.[32]

This warning to lurking scribblers at the playhouse recalls Jonson's agreement with the "spectators or hearers" at the Hope Theater performance of *Bartholomew Fair*. Just as we must include "spectators or hearers" in the realm of reading in early modern England, so should we remember that writers and readers mingled with the spectators and hearers at the playhouse. On the stage and in the historical record, we glimpse reading both vocal and silent, public and private, shared and solitary, eccentric and representative. Both the fictions and the archives testify to the "great variety" of readers and reading practices acknowledged in the preliminaries of the first folio.

NOTES

1   A3[r]. Quotations from the first folio preliminaries come from the facsimiles in Hinman's (1968) edition; all quotations from Shakespeare's plays are taken from Harbage's edition (Shakespeare 1984). In writing this essay, I have benefited from the suggestions and help of David Scott Kastan, Richmond Barbour, and Robert Schwartz.

2   Hoby 1561: A3[v]; Edwards 1585: title page; H. C. 1579: Aii[r].

3   Unlike the modern usage of "spell," which links reading to writing ability, "spell" in 1600 was associated with rudimentary or oral reading (*OED*). For a discussion of reading instruction beyond "spelling," see Kintgen 1996: 18–57.

4   For clear, concise summaries of literacy scholarship, see Ford 1993, Thomas 1986, and Kiefer 1996: Appendix 1. Jonathan Barry (1995) usefully discusses literacy in the context of popular culture.

5   While Cressy (1980) recognizes many of the limitations of signature rates (pp. 55–9), he defends signatures as the only type of literacy that is "directly measurable" (p. 53). Although he remains vulnerable to charges that signature rates underestimate literacy, Cressy ably defends his approach against suggestions that signing one's name might be an isolated skill (pp. 55–7).

6   Spufford (1981) provides the fullest statement of this position. Cressy (1980) describes the "massive illiteracy" of Englishwomen until the late seventeenth century in London (p. 128); women were "almost universally unable to write their own names" for most of the period (p. 145). Not only were women more likely to be partially literate than men, as Spufford (1981) argues, but women may have chosen not to write in public because of cultural associations between such public display and promiscuity.

7   Cressy 1980: 144–52. The figures for northern tradesmen come from the diocese of Durham; those for Essex include husbandmen in

Hertfordshire. The figures for the 1620s are far less comprehensive than those for the 1640s, but the percentages from the 1620s fit the overall trends of the surrounding decades.

8 Leah Marcus argues, on the contrary, that the preface "lumps all potential readers of the First Folio together" (1988: 22). See the first chapters of her *Puzzling Shakespeare* and of Margreta de Grazia's *Shakespeare Verbatim* (1991) for unusually attentive discussions of these preliminaries.

9 The most powerful and highly skilled readers are addressed, if at all, in dedicatory epistles; they are then frequently exempted from all other preliminary guides. Sometimes, a patron's interpretive skills are described as so finely honed that he or she need not even read the entire book. Mulcaster, for example, in the dedicatory epistle to Queen Elizabeth in his *Positions* (1581), proposes that the queen might read one heading, and from it, judge the whole book as one might judge a lion by its paw.

10 Michael Hattaway (1991) points out these anachronisms in his notes to this speech: Holinshed (1587) dates the first printing press in England to 1477, and English mills began producing paper in 1495. Frederick Kiefer (1996) notes a similar anachronism in *Cymbeline*: Imogen tells her servant to "fold down the leaf" of a book, suggesting it is a book with paper leaves, rather than a more historically accurate manuscript scroll (p. 276). Brutus, too, seems to be reading a paper book when he looks for "the leaf turned down / Where I left reading" (*Julius Caesar*, IV. iii. 273–4).

11 As Peter Blayney explains, one must think of "a range rather than a price" for the first folio: 15 shillings unbound or 16 shillings to one pound bound, depending on the quality of the binding (1991: 32).

12 Jonson Induction, 1976: ll. 91–103. Ann Jennalie Cook determines that these prices are "in line with many other references," as she argues that most theater patrons spent far more than the penny for standing room (1997: 317).

13 The playhouse is named on the title pages of 150 of the roughly 500 extant plays published during the reign of Charles I (Gurr 1987: 76).

14 The 1622 quarto of *Othello* opens with a short formulaic preliminary address to the reader, in which the stationer stresses the conventional nature of prefaces: "To set forth a booke without an Epistle, were like to the old English prouerbe, A blew coat without a badge" (A2^r).

15 For a fuller discussion, see Hackel 1997.

16 After 1593, few playbooks were printed in black letter, a typeface associated with lower levels of literacy and education than roman type (Blayney 1997: 414–15). For examples of ownership of playbooks among the elite, see Birrell 1991 and Hackel 1997: esp. 122–7.

17 In a study of "bits of paper" onstage, Jonas Barish (1991) counts sixty-seven cases of documents and letters read aloud onstage and another eighty instances of documents brought onstage for show or summary. Only *Two Noble Kinsmen* has none (pp. 32–5). Literate women in Shakespeare read letters far more often than books (Teague 1996: 361). For further discussions of books and letters as stage properties, see Bergeron 1996a, and Kiefer 1996: esp. Appendices 2 and 3, which provide a catalog of examples. Dessen and Thomson's forthcoming *Dictionary of Stage Properties* promises to be an invaluable source for further work.

18 Kiefer 1996: 276. One cannot be certain because books and paper do not show up in the property inventories of the Admiral's Men in 1598, an omission Kiefer attributes to the low value of these properties (p. 286).

19 *Merry Wives of Windsor*, I. i. 176–7). On the prices of books, see Johnson 1950, along with Blayney's corrections (1997: 410–11). For the price of folios in different bindings, see Blayney 1991: 25–32. Six pence was a typical, though not standard, price for play quartos (1997: 411).

20 Harold Love discusses four main sites of reading in seventeenth-century England: country houses, coffee houses, the court, and the Inns of Court and universities (1993: 195–230).

21 Chartier cites Pepys's entries as examples of the potential mobility of solitary reading (1989a: 141–3). Harold Love wonders if plays mislead us by associating reading and walking, but he then notes cases of historical readers strolling (1993: 196–7).

22 Ranum traces the development of the closely related study, *studiolo*, cabinet, and closet in Italy, France, and England (1989: 225–9). For the implications for privacy, see Chartier 1989a: 134–7 and Stewart, who sees the retreat to the closet as "a very public sign of privacy" (1997: 168). Orlin argues that the study "not only inaugurated the experience of a private behavior but also nourished the apprehension of individual selfhood" (1994: 188). For examples of women's book closets, see Hackel 1997: 118–19 and Stewart 1997: 163–70. In Shakespeare's plays, Lavinia, Lady Macbeth, Ophelia, and Gertrude spend time in their closets (*Titus*, III. ii. 81–5; *Macbeth*, V. i. 7: *Hamlet*, II. i. 77–84, III. iv).

23 Saenger (1982) and Chartier both explore the psychological and intellectual implications of the shift from vocalized to silent reading, which Chartier argues constitutes the "other revolution" to the more noted "printing revolution" (1989a: 125–7).

24 Darnton argues that silent reading may have begun as early as the seventh century in monasteries (1986: 23), but Saenger makes the compelling case that "true silent reading" – as opposed to merely quiet mumbling – was possible only with the development of the convention of word division (1982: 384). University libraries began requiring silence in the early fourteenth century, and later in the century vernacular authors imagined their audiences as silent readers (Saenger 1982: 397, 411).

25 Bownde 1595: 202. For the reading of broadsides, see Watt 1990. A Henrician act of 1543 governed the reading of the Bible (Bennett 1969: 27).

26 William Sherman (1997) finds evidence in marginalia that early modern readers engaged in "extensive" reading well before the eighteenth century. See Chartier for several examples of "intensive" reading in early America (1989a: 133–4).

27 See Jardin and Grafton 1990, Sherman 1995, and Riddell and Stewart 1995 for studies of individual annotators.

28 Peter Blayney supposes "a relatively small edition [of the first folio] – probably no more than 750 copies, and perhaps fewer," and he counts the Folger Shakespeare Library's holdings at eighty-two folios, including substantial fragments (1991: 2, 45–6).

29 Bound into an eleventh volume (Folger no. 33) is a second folio title leaf inscribed "Anne Lady Crewe," and one of the Folger first folio fragments bears the inscription of "Elizabeth C[ountess of] Hamilton," to which Peter Blayney directed me (Box 83). Elizabeth Hageman and Sara Jayne Steen come up with a slightly higher proportion ("almost a fifth") of Folger first folios inscribed with the names of seventeenth-century women (1996: v). My figures are based upon my examination of the folios in consultation with the catalogue notes of Donald Farren, cataloguer of the Folger Shakespeare folios under grants from the US Department of Education, Title II-C, and the Carl and Lily Pforzheimer Foundation. I am grateful to the staff of the Folger Library for their assistance in my study of the folios and to Donald Farren and Peter Blayney, who shared their extensive notes with me and answered many questions.

30 Peter Blayney discusses these inscriptions in Folger no. 73, dating them to the 1670s or earlier (1991: 34).

31 Sorelius 1973: 297. This odd sample results from the preservation of Shakespeariana by various collectors; the known fragments of the original volume survive in the Halliwell–Phillips scrapbooks in Stratford-upon-Avon and in three manuscript volumes at the Folger Library.

32 A2[r]. Ann Jennalie Cook refers to this prologue as evidence of spectators writing down the good bits of plays (1997: 311).

REFERENCES

Barish, Jonas 1991: "Soft, here follows prose": Shakespeare's stage documents. In Murray Biggs et al. (eds), *The Arts of Performance in Elizabethan and Early Stuart Drama:*

Essays for G. K. Hunter, Edinburgh: Edinburgh University Press, 32–49.

Barry, Jonathan 1995: Literacy and literature in popular culture: reading and writing in historical perspective. In Tim Harris. (ed.), *Popular Culture in England, c.1500–1850*, New York: St Martin's Press, 69–94.

Bate, Jonathan 1995: Introduction to *Titus Andronicus*, by William Shakespeare, in The Arden Shakespeare, London: Routledge, 1–121.

Beaumont, Francis and Fletcher, John 1966: *The Woman Hater*. In Fredson Bowers (ed.), *The Dramatic Works*, vol. 1, Cambridge: Cambridge University Press.

Bennett, H. S. 1969: *English Books and Readers, 1475 to 1557*, 2nd edn. Cambridge: Cambridge University Press.

Bergeron, David M. 1996a: Treacherous reading and writing in Shakespeare's romances. In Bergeron 1996b: 160–77.

Bergeron, David M. (ed.) 1996b: *Reading and Writing in Shakespeare*. Newark, Del: University of Delaware Press; London: Associated University Presses.

Birrell, T. A. 1991: Reading as pastime: the place of light literature in some gentlemen's libraries of the 17th century. In Robin Myers and Michael Harris (eds), *Property of a Gentleman: The Formation, Organisation and Dispersal of the Private Library 1620–1920*. Winchester: St Paul's Bibliographies, 113–31.

Blair, Ann 1992: Humanist methods in natural philosophy: the commonplace book. *Journal of the History of Ideas*, 53, 541–51.

Blayney, Peter W. M. 1991: *The First Folio of Shakespeare*. Washington, D.C.: Folger Library Publications.

——1997: The publication of playbooks. In Cox and Kastan 1997: 383–422.

Bownde, Nicholas 1595: *The Doctrine of the Sabbath*. London.

Breton, Nicholas 1618: *The Court and Country, or A Briefe Discourse Dialogue-wise set downe betweene a Courtier and a Country-man*. London.

C. H. 1579: *The Forest of Fancy*. London.

Chartier, Roger 1989a: The practical impact of writing. In Chartier 1989b: 111–59.

Chartier, Roger (ed.) 1989b: *A History of Private Life*, vol. 3: *Passions of the Renaissance*, trans. Arthur Goldhammer. Cambridge, Mass.: Belknap Press, Harvard University Press.

Clark, Peter 1976: The ownership of books in England, 1560–1640: the example of some Kentish townsfolk. In Lawrence Stone (ed.), *Schooling and Society: Studies in the History of Education*, Baltimore: Johns Hopkins University Press, 95–111.

Clifford, Lady Anne 1924: *The Diary of the Lady Anne Clifford*, ed. V[ita] Sackville-West. London: Heinemann.

Coleman, Joyce 1996: *Public Reading and the Reading Public in Late Medieval England and France*. Cambridge: Cambridge University Press.

Cook, Ann Jennalie 1997: Audiences: investigation, interpretation, invention. In Cox and Kastan 1997: 305–20.

Cox, John D. and Kastan, David Scott (eds) 1997: *A New History of Early English Drama*. New York: Columbia University Press.

Cressy, David 1980: *Literacy and the Social Order: Reading and Writing in Tudor and Stuart England*. Cambridge: Cambridge University Press.

Darnton, Robert 1986: First steps toward a history of reading. *Australian Journal of French Studies*, 23, 5–30.

Dawson, Giles E. 1935: An early list of Elizabethan plays. *Library*, 15, 445–56.

de Grazia, Margreta 1991: *Shakespeare Verbatim: The Reproduction of Authenticity and the 1790 Apparatus*. Oxford: Clarendon Press.

Dekker, Thomas 1603: *The wonderfull yeare*. London.

Dessen, Alan C. and Thomson, Leslie forthcoming: *A Dictionary of Stage Properties in English Drama, 1581–1642*. Cambridge: Cambridge University Press.

Edwards, Richard 1585: *The paradyse of daynly deuises*. London.

Ferguson, Margaret W. 1988: A room not their own: Renaissance women as readers and writers. In Clayton Koelb and Susan Noakes (eds), *The Comparative Perspective on Literature*, Ithaca, NY: Cornell University Press, 93–116.

Fitzgeffrey, Henry 1617: *Satyres and satyricall epigrams with certaine observations at Blach-Fryers*. London.

Ford, Wyn 1993: The problem of literacy in early modern England. *History*, 78, 22–37.

Gurr, Andrew 1987: *Playgoing in Shakespeare's London*. Cambridge: Cambridge University Press.

Hackel, Heidi Brayman 1997: "Rowme" of its own: printed drama in early libraries. In Cox and Kastan 1997: 113–30.

Hageman, Elizabeth H. and Steen, Sara Jayne 1996: From the editors. *Shakespeare Quarterly*, 47, v–viii.

Hall, Edward 1548: *The vnion of the two noble and illustre famelies of Lancastre & Yorke*. London.

Hattaway, Michael (ed.) 1991: *The Second Part of King Henry VI*, by William Shakespeare. Cambridge: Cambridge University Press.

Hinman, Charlton (ed.) 1968: *The Norton Facsimile: The First Folio of Shakespeare*. New York: Norton.

Hoby, Sir Thomas (trans.) 1561: *The Courtier*, by Baldassare Castiglione. London.

Holinshed 1587: *The First and Second Volumes of Chronicles*. London.

Honigmann, E. A. J. and Brock, Susan (eds) 1993: *Playhouse Wills, 1558–1642: An Edition of Wills by Shakespeare and his Contemporaries in the London Theatre*. Manchester: Manchester University Press.

Hunter, G. K. 1951: The marking of *sententiae* in Elizabethan printed plays, poems, and romances. *Library*, 6, 171–88.

Jardine, Lisa and Grafton, Anthony 1990: "Studied for action": how Gabriel Harvey read his Livy. *Past and Present*, 129, 30–78.

Johnson, Francis R. 1950: Notes on English retail book-prices, 1550–1640. *Library*, 5, 83–112.

Jonson, Ben 1975: *The Complete Poems*, ed. George Parfitt. New Haven: Yale University Press.

—— 1976: *Bartholomew Fair*. In Russell A. Fraser and Norman Rabkin (eds), *Drama of the English Renaissance*, vol. 2: The Stuart Period, New York: Macmillan, 193–239.

Kiefer, Frederick 1996: *Writing on the Renaissance Stage: Written Words, Printed Pages, Metaphoric Books*. Newark, Del.: University of Delaware Press; London: Associated University Presses, 1996.

Kintgen, Eugene R. 1996: *Reading in Tudor England*, Pittsburgh Series in Composition, Literacy, and Culture. Pittsburgh: University of Pittsburgh Press, 1996.

Krivatsy, Nati H. and Yeandle, Laetitia 1992: Sir Edward Dering. In R. J. Fehrenbach and E. S.

Leedham-Green (eds), *Private Libraries in Renaissance England: A Collection and Catalogue of Tudor and Early Stuart Book-Lists*, vol. 1, Binghamton, NY: Medieval and Renaissance Texts and Studies, 137–269.

Love, Harold 1993: *Scribal Publication in Seventeenth-Century England*. Oxford: Clarendon Press.

Marcus, Leah S. 1988: *Puzzling Shakespeare: Local Reading and Its Discontents*. Berkeley: University of California Press.

Orlin, Lena Cowen 1994: *Private Matters and Public Culture in Post-Reformation England*. Ithaca, NY: Cornell University Press.

Ranum, Orest 1989: The refuges of intimacy. In Chartier, 1989b: 207–63.

Riddell, James A. and Stewart, Stanley 1995: *Jonson's Spenser: Evidence and Historical Criticism*. Pittsburgh: Duquesne University Press.

Saenger, Paul 1982: Silent reading: its impact on late medieval script and society. *Viator: Medieval and Renaissance Studies*, 13, 367–414.

Shakespeare, William 1984: *The Complete Works*, ed. Alfred Harbage. New York: Viking.

Sherman, William H. 1995: *John Dee: The Politics of Reading and Writing in the English Renaissance*. Amherst: University of Massachusetts Press.

—— 1997: Marking readers, circa 1590. Paper read at the Modern Language Association Convention, Toronto, 28 Dec. 1997.

Sorelius, Gunnar 1973: An unknown Shakespearian commonplace book. *Library*, 28, 294–308.

Sousa, Geraldo U. de 1996: The Peasants' Revolt and the writing of history in *2 Henry VI*. In Bergeron 1996b: 178–93.

Speght, Rachel 1621: To the reader. In *Mortalities Memorandum*, London.

Spufford, Margaret 1981: *Small Books and Pleasant Histories: Popular Fiction and its Readership in Seventeenth-century England*. Cambridge: Cambridge University Press.

Stewart, Alan 1997: *Close Readers: Humanism and Sodomy in Early Modern England*. Princeton: Princeton University Press.

Teague, Frances 1996: Judith Shakespeare reading. *Shakespeare Quarterly*, 47, 361–73.

Thomas, Keith 1986: The meaning of literacy in early modern England. In Gerd Baumann (ed.), *The Written Word: Literacy in Transition*, Oxford: Clarendon Press, 97–131.

Verney, Margaret M. 1894: *Memoirs of the Verney Family*, vol. 3: *During the Commonwealth, 1650 to 1660*. London: Longmans, Green and Co.

Wall, Wendy 1993: *The Imprint of Gender: Authorship and Publication in the English Renaissance*. Ithaca, NY: Cornell University Press.

Watt, Tessa 1990: Publisher, pedlar, pot-poet: the changing character of the broadside trade, 1550–1640. In Robin Myers and Michael Harris (ed.), *Spreading the Word: The Distribution Networks of Print, 1550–1850*, Winchester: St Paul's Bibliographies, 61–81.

10

Reading the Bible

David Daniell

Shakespeare knew the Bible with an understanding that is in most ways strange to us. So did his first audiences and readers. His knowledge can be seen most obviously as he quotes, often from unfamiliar places. In *The Merchant of Venice*, I. iii, he makes Shylock, in his first scene, recount an incident in the story of Laban from Genesis 30. To tell a story from the Hebrew Scriptures (to Christians, the Old Testament) is a natural thing for a Jew to do: yet Shakespeare has the confidence that his hearers and readers (quite unlike modern audiences and readers) will not only know the strange tale, but ask themselves why Shylock is telling it here.

Shakespeare makes other, less open references. Isabella in *Measure for Measure*, II. ii, retorts to the deputy's Draconian 'Your brother is a forfeit of the law' with

> Alas! alas!
> Why, all the souls that were were forfeit once:
> And He that might the vantage best have took
> Found out the remedy.

Her evocation of the biblical account of the blameless life of Christ, and his work of the redemption of the world in his death, as Christians believe, is at that moment in the play subtly resonant. Isabella takes her theology further:

> How would you be
> If He, which is the top of judgement, should
> But judge you as you are? O, think on that;
> And mercy then will breathe within your lips
> Like man new made.

Her main nouns and verbs are biblical words, especially 'souls', 'judge', 'judgement' and 'mercy'. The deputy, Angelo, is being brought up against the Bible in a new way, even though the city of Vienna that he is supposed to be governing is also supposed to be Christian. He has a programme for reform which is rigid with denials that are both impossible and cruel. Isabella gives him a possibility of release – of being in a different drama, as we might put it, under an even higher authority. The title of the play, *Measure for Measure*, is an echo of a remark of Christ's in Matthew 7:

> Judge not, that ye be not judged. For with what judgement ye judge, ye shall be judged, and with what measure ye mete [i.e., measure], it shall be measured to you again.

Those sentences echo an Old Testament idea: just retribution, or moderation as a virtue, or both. Their biblical significance for that theatrical moment, in the second scene of the second act of the play, is both explicit and multiple, being about God judging Angelo, Angelo judging Isabella's brother Claudio, and the very experience of people relating to people – particularly men to women and women to men, matters essential to this play. Though it is wrong to make *Measure for Measure* into a Christian allegory, as some have tried to do, or even into a Christian play, its five acts reflect an undulating presence of theological thought that expects a quite sophisticated knowledge of the Bible.

Shakespeare quotes and refers extensively and with freedom, sometimes movingly, as in Richard II's reference to Judas's 'All hail' to Christ in IV. i; quite often comically, as when in *Much Ado About Noting*, II. i, Benedick says he would not marry Beatrice, 'though she were endowed with all that Adam had left him before he transgressed'; and even indirectly, as when Bottom, waking up from his 'dream' in *A Midsummer Night's Dream*, IV. i, misquotes Paul ('The eye of man hath not heard...'). More interestingly, however, Shakespeare makes large assumptions about the biblical understanding of his ordinary hearers and readers: such assumptions have for a long time now been in another world from the modern. They allow him, for example, to follow New Testament thought into one of its sixteenth-century developments, that encapsulation of New Testament theology, particularly that of Paul, that became known as Calvinism, so that both *Julius Caesar*, to some extent, and *Hamlet*, certainly, written close together in 1599 and 1600, are in part Calvinist plays. That is a colouring that is invisible without the spectacles of ready familiarity with the Bible. How Shakespeare's hearers and readers came to have that familiarity is the subject of this essay.

The King James Bible, 1611

Almost at the end of Shakespeare's writing life, the year in which he wrote *The Tempest*, his last play as sole author, a London publisher issued the heavy, handsome black letter folio which announced itself as:

> The Holy Bible, containing the Old Testament and the New: newly translated out of the original tongues: & with the former translations diligently compared and revised, by

his Majesty's special commandment. Appointed to be read in Churches . . . Anno Dom.
1611.

This became known in Britain as the 'Authorized' version (though it was never
'authorized' at all). It is now more commonly known outside the United Kingdom
as the 'King James Bible' (though His Majesty had very little to do with it, apart from
giving one or two regrettable commands at the start of the enterprise, like insisting
that the work be based on the least accurate of the earlier translations, the Bishops'
Bible). The 'AV' or 'KJB' has been the most widely read book in the world. As the
British spread their empire round the globe, so they took their Authorized Versions
with them, and planted them among the conquered people. As the Union Jack flew in
the village square, wherever in the world that might have been, so the 'AV' was used
for worship daily and, especially, on Sundays. It was every English-speaking person's
Bible, from China to Peru. In the West, among the ignorant and the impressionable,
superstitious claims began to be made about its supposed 'inspiration', which
strengthened its hold. It was – and still is – loved for its message and for the beauty
of its language.

Sometimes schoolteachers, noting the coincidence of the dates of the 'greatest poet
that ever lived' and the 'greatest story ever told', have taught their classes that 'King
James brought Shakespeare in to add the poetry to his Bible'. Shakespeare had
nothing whatsoever to do with the 1611 Bible (though Rudyard Kipling made a
fine short story out of the notion, 'Proofs of Holy Writ'). What was in King James's
Bible did, however, have a great deal to do with Shakespeare, though not in that 1611
version. Everyone rightly admires certain biblical phrases: 'Let there be light', 'With
God all things are possible', 'In him we live and move and have our being', 'the signs
of the times', 'the powers that be', 'Ask, and it shall be given you; seek, and ye shall
find; knock, and it shall be opened unto you'. It seems right that such simple biblical
English, as well as long passages of great and intense beauty, should have come at the
end of the very decade when Shakespeare was at his greatest with *Hamlet, Othello, King
Lear, Macbeth, Antony and Cleopatra, The Winter's Tale* and *The Tempest*, to name but half
the plays he wrote between 1600 and 1613. After all, the English language had by
then come to a wonderful fruition. Shakespeare's century had opened with English as a
poor language, an uncertain mixture of Middle English, court French and the
barbarous Latin of the professions (law, the Church, medicine). True, high Middle
English had produced poets of genius in Chaucer and Langland, but that had been 150
years before, in the 1380s. From 1500 until around 1530, over two decades into the
reign of Henry VIII, no one would have dreamed that English could carry any
worthwhile freight at all. It had become a shabby, uncouth cousin, unknown on the
continent of Europe. The English chancellor Sir Thomas More wrote his famous
Utopia in 1516 in Latin, and refused to consider any translation into English lest it
should be marred by the common people (the first published English translation was
in 1551, long after his death). The only language for anything serious was Latin. So
the growth of English in stature, range and flexibility through the decades of the

sixteenth century is a marvel to watch. By the time of Shakespeare's apprenticeship to playwriting, round about 1590, there seems to be nothing that English cannot do. So by the time of King James, the power of English was a triumph, and those biblical phrases quoted above seem to belong there. Yet every one of them, and almost all those long passages of great and intense beauty (the thirteenth chapter of 1 Corinthians, for example) were created not in 1611, when Shakespeare was at his height and the language had grown so wonderfully, but around 1530, when the language was almost nothing. What had happened?

The answer is a mixture of two elements, one frequently forgotten and one absolutely lost to sight. Generally forgotten is the story of the successive translations into English of the Bible. Lost to our modern sight are the sixteenth-century readers.

Translations

The Bible was originally written in two languages: the old Testament, which is the Jewish Scriptures, in Hebrew (with a small part in the late dialect of Aramaic); the New Testament in Greek. The Hebrew of the Old Testament was unique to the Scriptures, and was written nowhere else. The Greek of the New Testament was the common working language of the eastern Mediterranean, and was known throughout half the Roman Empire. The Hebrew Scriptures were written in the thousand years before Christ. The New Testament was written in the second half of the first century. The Hebrew Scriptures circulated widely throughout the Roman world in a Greek version, the Septuagint. Latin versions of both Testaments and of the whole Bible also circulated. In the fourth century AD, the scholar Jerome made a Latin version, which became the Bible of the spreading Church. It remained 'the Bible' for nearly 1200 years. It is still known as the 'common version', in Latin the 'Vulgate'.

In England in 1500, only the professionally trained knew any Latin. The ordinary people of all the villages and small towns which made up the nation – the workers in the fields and at the looms, the carpenters, the blacksmiths and makers of wheels, and their wives and children – were almost totally cut off from the Bible. The mass was in Latin. All church services, including christenings, weddings and funerals, were in Latin. Though priests could, and did, translate the biblical texts on which they based their sermons into the English in which they preached; though the people could sometimes see stained-glass windows telling a Bible story, or at the right season, a play, of Cain and Abel or the women at the tomb on Easter Day, almost all the Bible was hidden from them in Latin. The poetry and prophecy which make up so much of the Old Testament, for example, or all twenty-three books of the New Testament that are not the Gospels, remained almost completely unknown. It is difficult to write a play about Paul's Epistle to the Romans, one of the central documents of the New Testament, and thus of Christian theology. Moreover, the Church made increasingly popular expansions of the Gospels which gave fanciful accounts of things nowhere to be found in the Bible at all – like Mary's long meditations while feeding the infant

Jesus at her breast; excellent piety, no doubt, but not the milk of the true New Testament Word.

In the 1380s, contemporary with Chaucer, John Wyclif, Master of Balliol College, Oxford, was instrumental in making Bibles in English. His translators worked from the Latin Vulgate, and at first produced an English version so close to the Latin in vocabulary and word order that it is often unreadable. Revision produced a version of considerable value. This 'Wyclif B' sometimes reads easily: a verse from Matthew 5, for example, known to us in the King James version and many others since in the words 'Blessed are they that mourn, for they shall be comforted' is in Wyclif B 'Blessed ben thei that mornen, for thei schulen be confortid'. Wyclif B's previous verse, however, for the King James 'Blessed are the meek, for they shall inherit the earth' has 'Blessed ben mylde men, for thei schulen welde the erthe'. Sometimes one can find in Wyclif B an almost exact familiar phrase. More often, however, that version is so far away from later speech as to seem to be from another planet, as in 'And the halidai of therf looues, that is seid pask, neiyede' or 'Prohetis tweine or thre seie, and othere wiseli deme' (the first is Luke 22: 1, the second 1 Corinthians 14: 29).

The Wyclif translations were made long before printing: yet many hundreds of handwritten copies of the whole Bible, or of the New Testament, were made (about 240 have survived). They were expensive, and owned, sometimes beautifully decorated, by the wealthy. Plain copies were brought to poorer people by travellers, and possibly copied again locally: they were much in demand, and eagerly read. Wide circulation of these manuscripts, entire or in parts (or even in bits), to give the people of England the Bible, was one of the tenets of that anticlerical pastoral and preaching movement whose preachers and groups of Bible students were called Lollards: the word was rude, and deliberately vague in its application. After 1400, Lollardy was strong enough in England to cause the officials of the Church great alarm. The Wyclif translations had in no way been sanctioned by them. To give ordinary people the entire Bible in English would lead to serious abuses; without the guidance of priests, common men and women could not possibly understand it: besides, such people might discover that many of the doctrines and practices of the fifteenth-century Church were not in the Bible at all. (An example would be the practice of mortuaries, where at a death the priest could, and frequently did, take for himself the most valuable object in the deceased's household.) In 1408 the archbishop of Canterbury, at a special assembly in Oxford, forbade translating or reading an English Bible on pain of punishment, including death by being burned alive. Uniquely in Europe, the English were officially denied their Bibles. During the hundred years, and more, after those constitutions of Oxford, many Lollards were martyred, including the Herefordshire squire Sir John Oldcastle, whose name long after, by a devious route, and largely transformed, became the 'original' of Shakespeare's Sir John Falstaff.

In the 1490s, in the county of Gloucestershire, which adjoins Herefordshire, lived a well-connected family called Tyndale. A son, William Tyndale, went to Magdalen Hall, Oxford, and learned there good 'humanist' Latin, and Greek, which was just beginning to be taught at Oxford and Cambridge – indeed, the greatest scholar in

Europe, Desiderius Erasmus, was at Cambridge teaching Greek for a year or two while Tyndale was at Oxford. After taking his BA and MA, Tyndale was at last allowed by the regulations to read some theology (he was in Oxford for about ten years). To his disgust, theology meant the logic of Aristotle and obscure Church Fathers. No Scripture of any kind was studied.

In 1516, while Tyndale was at Magdalen Hall, Erasmus, back on the continent of Europe, published his own new Latin translation of the New Testament. He had the stature to challenge the strongly defensive line the Church took with regard to its own Latin Vulgate, which from Jerome's time had never been free from errors, some serious. The Vulgate had become an embarrassment to 'humanist' scholars. Erasmus's Latin version was strikingly new, and he was attacked by the Church for it. But it was not his Latin which – it is no exaggeration – changed the course of history in England and across Europe, but the fact that to show the accuracy of his version he printed alongside it, in a parallel column, his source: the original Greek New Testament (not even mentioned on his long title page). For the first time, the fundamental documents of the Christian faith, as they were written, were freely available. Greek was newly being taught at universities throughout Europe, so for the first time translations of the New Testament could be made into vernacular languages directly from the Greek, bypassing the Latin. In 1522, Martin Luther printed his ground-breaking New Testament, translated from the Greek into a German which gave the divided states of Germany a common, and excellent, language. The same quickly happened throughout Europe.

In England, William Tyndale, after possibly a short time at Cambridge (no records of this have survived), took up a quiet position in Gloucestershire, which allowed him to work with Erasmus's Greek New Testament. He began to translate it into English. The very rapid spread of the radical reforms, strongly based on the New Testament, known as 'Lutheranism' (on the back of the rapid dissemination of printed texts) was again alarming the English Church, and even in Gloucestershire Tyndale was outspoken. When an ignorant cleric argued that 'we were better without God's law than the Pope's', Tyndale replied:

> I defy the Pope and all his laws . . . if God spare my life, ere many years I will cause a boy that driveth the plough shall know more of the scripture than thou dost.

Tyndale took his plans for an English New Testament translated from the Greek to the scholarly Bishop of London, Cuthbert Tunstall. The latter was a friend of Erasmus who had found for him some necessary Greek manuscripts of parts of the New Testament. Since 1408, anyone wanting to translate more than a few words of the Bible into English had to have the permission of a bishop: Tunstall was an obvious choice. But he snubbed Tyndale, who, sadly recognizing that 'there was no place in all England' where an English Bible could be made, went with money from London merchants to Germany, first to Cologne and then to Worms, before settling in Antwerp. His first English New Testament, printed in Worms in 1526, is a landmark of English cultural history. It is a small, well-printed book for the ploughboy's pocket – all Tyndale's books were pocket-books, for reading wherever you happened to be. Copies were smuggled down the Rhine and across the North Sea in bales of cloth, and eagerly bought and read. Out of probably 6,000 printed, only three have survived, one seriously defective and only one perfect. The bishop of London arranged for the confiscation of great numbers, and burned them at a special ceremony at St Paul's Cathedral, where he preached a sermon denouncing Tyndale's thousands of 'errors' – that is, where he had translated the original Greek, not the Church's Latin.

The impact on English people of the words of all the New Testament in a clear, modern English is hard for us to grasp. For the first time one could *read* 'And there were in the same region shepherds abiding in the field . . . , in Luke's Christmas story in chapter 2; or 'Let not your hearts be troubled, believe in God and believe in me' of John 14; or 'Why seek ye the living among the dead? He is not here, but is risen' of Luke 23. The whole of Paul, the mainspring of Reformation – indeed, Christian – theology, was immediately available, in all the developments of 'we are justified by faith' in Romans 5. Yet Tyndale not only gave the English people the Greek New Testament accurately in English. He gave the nation, and eventually the world, a Bible language of simple beauty that speaks directly to the heart – the end of Luke 15: 'for this thy brother was dead, and is alive again: and was lost, and is found'; Ephesians 6: 10: 'Finally, my brethren, be strong in the Lord, and in the power of his might.'

Tyndale, in Worms, was appalled that the bishop of London had burned the Word of God. A lesser man would have given up. But Tyndale learned Hebrew; where, we do not know. No one in England knew that language (apart from two Cambridge scholars, quite uninterested in translation), but there were centres of Hebrew learning in Germany. The result was that, in 1530, little books began to be smuggled into England entitled *The first book of Moses called Genesis*, which introduced the Penta-teuch, the first five books of the Hebrew Scriptures. This was the first time that Hebrew had been translated into English and printed. Once again, it is hard to grasp the effect of finding, on the opening page of a book that is easily held in the hand, God's word not as *Fiat lux, et lux erat*, nor even Wyclif's first 'Be made light, and made is light', revised as 'Light be made, and light was made'.

In Antwerp, Tyndale revised his New Testament in 1534. (Queen Anne Boleyn had her own copy, now in the British Library, and is said to have held it at her execution in 1536.) He then translated the next section of the Old Testament, the historical books, Joshua to 2 Chronicles. The plots of his enemies in the Church were succeeding, however, and with his work unfinished, and after sixteen months in a prison cell outside Brussels, during which he had been condemned as a heretic, on the morning of 6 October 1536, at a public ceremony, he was taken out, strangled and burned.

Tyndale's work was immediately taken into complete Bibles, which from 1537, with one or two checks, could freely circulate in the British Isles throughout the rest of the sixteenth century, and ever after. The missing second half of Tyndale's Old Testament was supplied from the complete English Bible that Miles Coverdale printed (in Antwerp, as we now know) in 1535. Coverdale was gifted and accomplished, and used all the aids he could, but he lacked Hebrew and much Greek. Coverdale worked presently on the only fully 'authorized' Bible in English history, the 'Great' Bible of 1539, a copy of which was to be placed in every church, openly accessible. Queen Mary, who reigned from 1553 to 1558, tried with the tools of terror to reverse her father, Henry VIII's, Reformation. Many Reformed Church leaders and scholars fled to Europe. Those in Geneva took advantage of the new Bible scholarship there under Theodore Beza, and in 1557 printed, outstandingly well, a new English New Testament. In 1560 they were able to present to Queen Elizabeth, now at the start of her long reign, their complete 'Geneva Bible'. This remarkable volume is a monument to Renaissance and Reformation scholarship. Its new readings, from better understanding of the Hebrew, and its expanded marginal notes, better pictures, maps, summaries, lists, concordances and essays, usually with the Book of Common Prayer bound in, and metrical psalms, made it a Bible for use, for study at home or with congregations. It very rapidly became the Bible of the English people, going through many editions in a hundred years. Conservative English bishops, distressed that the Church's Latin was no longer the source-text, produced their own retaliation in 1568: this 'Bishops' Bible' was also widely used, though both the scholarship and the English phrasing are frequently unhappy. (The same is true of the official Roman Catholic retort, the Rheims New Testament, of 1582.) The notes to the 1560 Geneva New Testament were revised in 1576 by the Oxford scholar Laurence Tomson. In 1599 editions of 'Geneva' first carried the copious notes by 'Junius' to the book of Revelation, and 'Geneva–Tomson–Junius' became a standard Bible until well into the seventeenth century, and was still reprinted in the eighteenth.

The point here is threefold. First, from 1526, the English people were reading the Bible in great numbers: we know that in the second half of the century, with an English population of six million, half a million copies of an English Bible were bought. Secondly, the English people were reading the Bible in a clear plain style, the gift to the nation of William Tyndale. Every sixteenth-century Bible is Tyndale only a little revised in wording, and almost invariably it is Tyndale in sentence structure and rhythm. This is often true even for those makers of Bibles who knew Tyndale only as a heretic, the translators of the Bishops' and Rheims versions. Thirdly, Shakespeare's household Bible was one or more of the English Geneva versions. Some of his biblical echoes have been traced to the Bishops' version: but he was a Geneva reader. Europe's first vernacular Bibles were from Wittenberg, and Lutheran. The next wave came from Geneva, and were Calvinist. (The Calvinism should not frighten us: it is only in later times that this Augustinian, and ultimately New Testament, dogma became a general stigma. Most of Elizabeth's courtiers were Calvinist: the Anglican Book of Common Prayer itself is Calvinist.) The third and lasting wave was peculiarly English, and came from London.

The churchmen and scholars who created King James's Bible for publication in 1611 used Tyndale a great deal, which is one reason why that version endured. Though His Majesty had presented each member of the three panels with a large Bishops' Bible with which to work, hoping to ensure that the Geneva version was ignored (he had his own reasons for trying to pretend that the Geneva Bible did not exist), the translators followed Geneva and in particular Tyndale. Latinity from the Bishops' Bible comes through the 1611 version; yet phrase after phrase, sentence after sentence, is Tyndale unaltered. Recent computer calculations show that the total amount of unaltered Tyndale in the 1611 New Testament is 83 per cent. In the story of Gethsemane in Matthew 26, for example, in Tyndale Jesus says:

> O my father, if it be possible, let this cup pass from me: nevertheless, not as I will, but as thou wilt. And he came unto the disciples, and found them asleep, and said to Peter: what, could ye not watch with me one hour? Watch and pray, that ye fall not into temptation. The spirit is willing, but the flesh is weak.

The changes in the 1611 version are few, and away from directness: there, Jesus 'cometh', 'findeth' and 'saith unto' them, giving a touch of archaism, and distance. Adding an unnecessary 'indeed' to 'the spirit' in the last sentence has the same effect. The last sentence of Matthew 6 in the 1611 version is the well-known 'Sufficient unto the day is the evil thereof', directly from the Vulgate's *Sufficit diei malitia sua*. But Tyndale had 'for the day present hath ever enough of his own trouble'.

Shakespeare's Bible, the Geneva versions and those before them, spoke memorably. That is important. Most of the Bible was originally written to be remembered, and Tyndale used his scholarship, his linguistic skills (he is convincingly credited with eight languages) and his craft of rhetoric to make his translation easy to reproduce from memory. That is also one of the skills of the dramatist, to make memorable words that the actor wants to speak at that point. One of several reasons for the rise of the theatres and so much dramatic writing from the early 1580s in England could be that playwrights and audiences had had in their bones for more than a generation past a memorable, direct plain English style, from the English Bible, known in large parts by heart.

> And when Ahab saw Eliah, he said unto him: art thou he that troubleth Israel? And he said: it is not I that trouble Israel, but thou and thy father's house, in that ye have forsaken the commandments of the Lord and hast followed Baal. (1 Ks 18, Tyndale)

That is already high dramatic speech, rich when spoken.

In the first decade of the sixteenth century, Erasmus brought a revolution to English education with his new instruction in the art of rhetoric. One of his beguiling demonstrations was writing 'Your letter has given me much pleasure' 150 ways. By Shakespeare's time, two generations of boys at English grammar schools had become skilled in the art of putting words together for precise effect. No wonder there was such an outpouring of fine English poetry and prose from the 1580s, with Shakespeare on the crest of the flood. That cannot be the whole story. Erasmus's textbook of rhetoric for schoolboys, *De copia*, was in Latin: the school exercises were in Latin. Yet an effect to watch as the century progresses is that everyone, all men and women, whether they have Latin or not, can now communicate clearly and well in English. Not only the courtly have something to say and can say it.

A Common English Plain Style

The story of the development of the English Plain Style through the sixteenth century has been told a number of times, with rival claims about its most likely models. The prose of Sir Thomas More has been offered, though his English works were not published until 1557, and had a limited readership. Let us be clear about what happened, lest we take it for granted. By 1530 English was beginning to be used instead of Latin for local and domestic matters like churchwardens' accounts and wills. For anything of any weight, however, English was struggling against Latin. Latin dominated English, with French forms also getting in the way. This is Lord Berners in 1523 introducing his translation into English of Froissart's *Chronicle*:

> Thus, when I advertised and remembered the manifold commodities of history, how beneficial it is mortal folk, and else how laudable and meritorious a deed it is to write histories ... [he turned to Froissart] which I judged commodious, necessary, and profitable to be had in English.

Such writing is not easy to commit to memory. Seventy years later, Shakespeare mocked it in *Love's Labour's Lost*, where his schoolmaster Holofernes says 'in the posterior of the day', and his curate Nathaniel requests the players to 'abrogate scurrility'. In the 1540s, Archbishop Thomas Cranmer wrote

> My chief study be to speak so plainly that all men may understand ... my words be so plain, that the least child in the town may understand them.

English could well not have gone down that path. It could have continued to wander, half Middle English and half French in vocabulary, and more than half Latin in vocabulary and syntax. But here is Cranmer again, in 1547:

> And as drink is pleasant to them that be dry, and meat to them that be hungry: so is the reading, hearing, searching, and studying of holy scripture, to them that be desirous to know God or themselves, and to do his will.

That simplicity remained available – its use increased – until the death of Shakespeare in 1616, and far beyond. Can we suggest a model?
    Indeed, we can.

> And Eliah came unto all the people and said: why halt ye between two opinions? If the Lord be very God, follow him: or if Baal be he follow him. And the people answered him not one word.

That is Tyndale translating 1 Kings 18 in 1535. No one else was writing like that in the 1530s. The plain words and direct rhythms are magnificent for the occasion, and memorable. (King James's men spoiled the last three splendid thumps, 'not one word', by substituting 'not a word', less satisfactory because lighter.) Moreover, no one in the 1530s could match Tyndale in any way at all for his sheer range of writing in English. The sixty-six books of the Bible demonstrate many more than sixty-six verbal styles. A good translator transmits the differences. There are many contrasts in the book of Genesis alone. The tragi-comic rawness of the Fall story in Genesis 2 is very different in the Hebrew from the strange, spare starkness of Abraham going to sacrifice Isaac in Genesis 22. Tyndale gets the differences across in English, allowing a touch of dark comedy in Genesis 2 with the serpent's 'Ah, sir,' and 'Tush ye shall not die'. When he comes to the long Joseph story which ends Genesis, he translates, accurately, a different way again – for example, in Genesis 43:

> When Joseph came home, they brought the present into the house to him, which they had in their hands, and fell flat on the ground before him. And he welcomed them courteously saying: is your father that old man that ye told me of, in good health? and is he yet alive?

This is not what is thought of as 'biblical' English: it belongs to the later drama, or the social novel, and could even be Defoe. Right through the first half of the Old Testament, and in all the New Testament, Tyndale's gift to the English people was a skill with dozens of different registers and tones, yet usually clear. In other words, what, after the 1530s, the English people were reading so hungrily was, of course, the Word of God at last printed in English, but as well, models of English Plain Style, in extraordinary variety. Tyndale, we may say, contributed to the availability of English registers for Shakespeare. Polysyllabic Latin is useful to him: Macbeth in II. ii looks at his bloody hand and says it will 'the multitudinous seas incarnadine'; but then he suddenly switches to Saxon words with 'making the green one red'. Falstaff is capable of elaborate syntactical structures and Latinist forms, especially when he wants to slip out of responsibility: 'Thou shalt find me tractable to any honest reason. Thou seest I am pacified still.' But when he wants suddenly to turn our hearts over, Shakespeare does not make Falstaff say before the Battle of Shrewsbury, in *1 Henry IV*, V. i as would befit a Latin-educated knight, 'The advent of the imminent confrontation elevates my apprehensions', but 'I would 'twere bed-time, Hal, and all well'.

Bible Reading

The one book that everyone read, or heard read, in that century after the 1530s, was the English Bible. Over forty editions of the Bible were published in the short six-year reign of Edward VI. While national events like royal births and deaths were fully recorded, the meeting of a few people in a room to read the English Bible, or a solitary man reading at a field's edge, could not be registered. Secondary evidence, and some primary, suggests that it was a widespread phenomenon in the British Isles, from Henry VIII's time. In the reign of Edward VI, local gatherings began (later known as 'prophesyings') which spent whole days each week, from early morning to late at night, reading and studying the Bible. In such assemblies women had equal status with men, and there were apprentices and schoolboys. One group in London was so powerful that even in Queen Mary's reign it was left alone to continue its weekly all-day Bible readings. Literacy was high. Sir Thomas More, writing in 1533 against the English Bible, noted that only four out of every ten in the population, even in country districts, could not read – and reading at this time, we should always remember, meant reading aloud. These experiences make a hidden history of the kingdom, and go a long way to explain why in mid-century, in her reactionary five-year reign, Queen Mary did not succeed in reattaching the country to Rome. The scale on which men and women were reading the Scriptures was invisible to her. Her archbishop, Pole, had not been in the country for thirty-four years, and the mood of the land had greatly changed. The Bible, the Word, was now central, not the drama of the mass in a language not understood.

Personal records have survived of how a life was changed, for example, by reading a Testament in a barn. John Foxe's massive *Acts and Monuments* of 1563, 1570, 1570 and 1574 (expanding greatly in size in successive editions) is reliable in its records; he prints similar accounts. From the opposite end, we can deduce the hunger in Britain for the Bible in English by simply computing the print-runs. Adding the runs of the subsequent Antwerp piracies to the original print-run even of Tyndale's first, 1526 New Testament gives a total of 22,000 copies. Printers are not fools: they print for profit, and must have known the eagerness to purchase. Moreover, John Foxe prints accounts of men and women, brought before the Church commissioners for investigation, who startle their interrogators with their detailed and wide-ranging knowledge of the Scriptures – even though they could not read: this bespeaks a level of attention almost beyond our comprehension.

How did the English read the Bible? First, of course, as the Word of God, the primary source of his revelation, the standard against which individuals, and the Church, are judged: even more, the spring of salvation in the believer's heart. But there was far more. Old Testament history, for example, was being re-experienced in Tudor England. Courtiers of the young Edward VI wrote and spoke of their monarch as Josiah. His story is told in 2 Kings 22–3 and 2 Chronicles 34–5. Josiah was crowned king of Judah at the age of eight. When he was eighteen, he was told that in the course of the necessary repairs to the Temple which he had ordered, an old book had been found. This was 'the book of the law' (preserved for us in Deuteronomy) which set out God's will for the people and his laws which had been neglected. Josiah, after national mourning for the neglect, instituted complete (and long-lasting) reforms of the religious, social and moral life of the nation. King Edward came to the English throne at nine years old, and in his short life carried forward strongly the English Reformation, based on a newly found book, the Bible. It is now clear that

King Edward's political mentors thought, first, biblically. The English Bible was in the very blood and bones and nerves of court political life. Thirteen years after Edward's accession, the Geneva Bible margin at 2 Kings 22: 5 noted, about the royal command to repair the Temple, 'This declareth, that they that have a charge, & execute it not, ought to have it taken from them' – a reference to the state of the Church before the Reformation. Geneva marginal notes at 2 Chronicles 34 commented, on this king who 'destroyed the altars and . . . the images',

> This great zeal of this godly king the holy Ghost setteth forth as an example and pattern to other kings and rulers, to teach them what God requireth of them

and 'he thought it his duty to see that all should make profession to receive the word of God'. This re-enacting of the Old Testament is in a different realm from, say, the idea of King Arthur or the Faerie Queen, pretty games played at court in Queen Elizabeth's later life. The Bible for the Tudors was not, as it can be in modern times, a file to be called up: it was the life-blood, the daily, even hourly, nourishment of the nation and of ordinary men and women. It was known with a thoroughness that is, simply, astonishing. To read the Tudor Reformation writers on the monarchy, on religion in the nation, or on practical politics, is to have to follow a system of thinking and a kaleidoscope of reference that are today quite beyond most of us. Polemicists like George Joye or John Bale, as well as established men like Cranmer, refer pointedly to Jehoshaphat or Hezekiah, and more obscure figures, knowing that readers will immediately take the point. That is biblical typology, a theological method as old as the words of Jesus, and something more. Josiah is the type of reforming king, true: but Edward visibly *is* Josiah, as well.

John Bale may take the modern reader into the new Tudor thinking about the last book in the Bible, Revelation. The Church had always been uneasy about this book, and even European Reformation scholars like Erasmus and Tyndale avoided commenting on it. Bale, ultimately following Augustine and some European thought of the previous 150 years, propounded from it two churches, those of the spirit (the model being Jesus in his humble poverty) and the flesh (the Pope in his enormous wealth). Moreover, Bale found English history in detail in Revelation, suddenly giving the nation great stature in God's plan. Bale's understandings were taken further in 1592 by a French Protestant theologian, François du Jon, whose *Brief and Learned Commentary* (on Revelation) is both sane and clear, and rich with amazing imagery: du Jon, or Junius as he was known throughout Europe, expounded from Revelation, and from history, the end of Christian time. The shorter version of his commentary is printed in Geneva Bibles of 1599. There can be no doubt that Shakespeare knew it. Hold *King Lear* close to Junius's Revelation, and the play glows with sudden response. The Fool quotes Revelation, of course, and even adds to it. The play's imagery of cracking thunder, catastrophic earthquakes, eclipse of sun and moon, wheel of fire, lake of darkness, sulphurous pit, wrathful dragon, prince of darkness, black angel, monsters of the deep and much else is steeped in that book of the Bible, and would be additionally pointed for that reason. Further, Junius's commentary points in a new way to the end of Christian time, to a consummation, which is also deep within *King Lear, Macbeth and Antony and Cleopatra* – deep, indeed, within Shakespeare's tragic understanding.

11

Reading the Classics

Robert S. Miola

He remembered perhaps enough of his schoolboy learning to put the hig, hog, hag, into the mouth of Sir Hugh Evans {Wives, IV. i. 42}, and might pick up in the writers of the time or the course of his conversation a familiar phrase or two of French or Italian, but his studies were most demonstratively confined to nature and his own language.

(Richard Farmer, *An Essay on the Learning of Shakespeare*)

Revealing Shakespeare's reliance on translations instead of original texts, Richard Farmer wielded wit, learning, and scorn against advocates of the poet's classical learning. Thanks largely to Farmer, Ben Jonson's notorious notice of Shakespeare's "small Latin and less Greek" came in the eighteenth century and later to characterize the poet as a natural rather than learned genius. In 1944 T. W. Baldwin took up the question again, demonstrating that the Elizabethan grammar school curriculum, inspired by the humanist rediscovery of antiquity, offered substantial classical training. Students memorized hundreds of passages and practiced reading, writing and speaking the ancient languages. Recommended authors and texts included (in Greek) Isocrates, the New Testament, Homer, Demosthenes, Hesiod, Aesop, Euripides, catechisms, Psalms, Basil's Epistles, Dionysius of Halicarnassus, Heliodorus, Lucian, Pindar, Plutarch, the *Tabula Cebetis*, Theocritus, and Xenophon; (in Latin) Cato's *Disticha*, Terence, Plautus, Cicero, Quintilian, *Ad Herennium*, Ovid, Virgil, Horace, Juvenal, Lucan, Sallust, Catullus, and such later writers as Susenbrotus, Erasmus, Palingenius, and Mantuanus. Baldwin found no solid evidence of Shakespeare's learning in Greek but noted everywhere in the canon the impress of his grammar school training in Latin. Kenneth Muir (1977: 5) observed additionally that Shakespeare's fluency in Latin manifested itself as well in his coinages, which "compare favourably with those of Marston and Chapman." In 1968 John W. Velz compiled a comprehensive annotated bibliography (2,487 entries), *Shakespeare and the Classical Tradition: A Critical Guide to Commentary*, 1660–1960. Cognizant of sources as traditions, attentive to the synthetic processes of poetic imagination, and attuned to the pervasive classicism in Elizabethan culture, this work (now being updated with thousands of additional entries) portrayed a poet deeply, though not always directly, immersed in classical thought and literature.

But who or what constituted classical thought and literature for Shakespeare and his time? Certainly not the figures and texts we moderns might expect, accustomed to the tidy order and amplitude of well-published editions and series – Oxford Classical Texts, Teubner, and Loeb – not to mention electronic data bases like *Thesaurus Linguae Graecae*, featuring in its 1990 version 3,165 authors and over 9,400 pieces of text. Only a fraction of these authors was available to Shakespeare, and even fewer attained currency. Plato was known largely through Ficino and Neoplatonist commentary, only one dialogue being available in English, the *Axiochus* (1592), translated by E. Spenser. The Aristophanes play most often produced and translated was not *Birds, Lysistrata,* or *Clouds,* but the pseudo-allegorical *Plutus,* or *Wealth.* In Europe and in the East Aeschylus's reputation rested on the Byzantine triad – *Prometheus, Seven against Thebes,* and *Persae* – not on the *Oresteia.* The sole English imprint of Sophocles in the *Short-Title Catalogue* is Thomas Watson's Latin translation of *Antigone,* replete with *thema* and *pompae* (processions) to point the moral and adorn the tale. On the matter of ancient Troy, Dares and Dictys, perpetuated in the medieval retellings of Benoît de Saint-Maure and Guido delle Colonne, still held sway over Homer, though Chapman's translation was on the horizon of the early seventeenth century. Geoffrey of Monmouth's myth of New Troy, the founding of Albion by Aeneas's great grandson Brute, similarly dominated chronicle and fiction until the disputations of such historians as William Camden and John Selden. Latin everywhere predominated over Greek. An abiding emphasis on rhetoric elevated to prominence Cicero and Quintilian. Seneca served as a model for tragedy, as Plautus and Terence did for comedy, the latter also winning admiration for his Latin style. Virgil, revered throughout the Middle Ages, appeared in a number of unfamiliar forms: two satires of Juvenal accompanied an edition of the *Eclogues* (1634); Gavin Douglas (1553) and Thomas Twyne (1573) both published translations of the *Aeneid* with Mapheus Vegius's thirteenth book, which completed the hero's allegorical journey to heaven.

Prominent in the early modern period are other surprising entries. Diogenes Laertius's *Dictes* and Valerius Maximus's *Factorum et dictorum memorabilium libri* enjoyed wide circulation. Dionysius Periegetes, author of a popular medical text, and Horapollo, author of a work on Egyptian hieroglyphs, attained wide popularity, as did Greek romances – fanciful, episodic works like Chariton's *Chaereas and Callirohoe* and Heliodorus's *Aethiopica.* The *Tabula Cebetis,* a moral allegory ascribed to Cebes of Thebes, Socrates' companion, though actually a first-century composition, frequently appeared with the *Enchiridion* of Epictetus and with Erasmus; in Europe it attracted fourteen vernacular translations and five commentaries. Cato's *Disticha* affords a Latin parallel: a collection of various moral sayings by various authors, this book appeared sometimes with Erasmus's collection of proverbs from the seven Greek sages or his *Christiani hominis institutum,* with precepts from Ausonius or the *Mimi Publiani,* or with Isocrates' exhortation to Demonicus. Enjoying numerous editions, the *Disticha* was a virtually inescapable Latin primer, dispensing such admonitions as the following:

> Nolo putes pravos homines peccata lucrari:
> Temporibus peccata latent et tempore parent.
>
> (1540, sig. Biii^v)

> (Do not think that wicked men gain profit from their sins:
> In time sins lie hidden and in time they will be revealed.)

Informed by such precepts, dramatists like Chapman, Marston, and Shakespeare (one thinks of *Macbeth*) created complex and powerful tragedies.

As even so brief a sampling shows, early modern editors sometimes published different authors in one volume. The Roman satirists Juvenal and Persius also appear together in early modern editions, just as they had in the earliest medieval manuscripts. Reading practices of the day encouraged analogical thinking and cross-referencing. (There is even evidence of a "reading wheel," which stacked books on a rotating device to make possible the simultaneous reading of many texts.) The humanist project of recovery, sometimes brilliantly prophetic of modern editorial practice, more often urgent in application and unsystematic in method, applied most of its energies to exhumation and dissemination, not to the establishment of authoritative texts or individual authorial canons. Consequently, it fostered fragmentation: authors and readers collected excerpts from ancients for commonplace books, arranged rhetorically or thematically, and for florilegia like Octavianus Mirandula's *Flores poetarum*. Sometimes a single author furnished a collection, Terence, for example, supplying Nicholas Udall's *Flowers for Latin Speaking*. Everyone, it seems, took occasional shortcuts to Parnassus via handbooks like Boccaccio's *De genealogia deorum*, Thomas Cooper's *Thesaurus linguae*, complete with the appended *Dictionarium*, Lilius Giraldus's *De deis gentium*, the lexicons of Charles and Robert Stephanus, Natalis Comes' *Mythologiae*, Vincenzo Cartari's *Le imagine*. Emblem books like Andreas Alciatus's *Emblemata* supplied popular and picturesque routes to ancient *sententiae*, figures, and themes. Lord Berner, William Baldwin, Thomas North, William Painter, and George Pettie served up in English collections hundreds of classical anecdotes and stories, replete with sententious commentary. There were also Erasmus's proverb collections, various epitomes, commonplace books, and, of course, translations.

Translations figure largely in the story of Elizabethan, specifically Shakespearian, classicism. Then, as now, translation enabled the ancient writers to speak to states unborn in accents yet unknown. Often, however, the original text lay several removes from its English equivalent, having been mediated by continental versions or redactions. Jane Lumley's translation of Euripides' *Iphigeneia in Aulis* (1555?) probably stems from a Latin version; George Gascoigne and Francis Kinwelmershe's *Jocasta* (1566), advertised on the title page as a translation, actually derives from Dolce's Italian version, which is, itself, based on a Latin translation. These plays, the only surviving versions of Euripides in English, are not unusual in their geneaology. Homer's fiery breath directly inspired George Chapman's *Iliad*, or so he claimed, but it reached him through the sometimes unfortunate intermediaries of Spondanus's bilingual edition, Divus's Latin translation, Stephanus's redactions, and Scapula's lexicon. Thomas North read Plutarch in Amyot's French version, itself indebted to a Latin translation. William Caxton's *Eneydos* (1490) rendered in English LeRoy's French translation of an Italian text that paraphrased the *Aeneid* and Boccaccio's *Fall of Princes*. Such intermediation did not prevent editors and translators from applying ancient wisdom to contemporary problems and political events. Thomas Wilson's translation of Demosthenes (1570) directed its warning against Philip of Spain ("in these dangerous days"), not Philip of Macedon. C. Watson annexed to his Polybius (1568) an account of the life of Henry V, because an oration from that English history inspired him to review classical orations. Spenser added to his *Axiochus*, based on a Latin text, incidentally, a speech spoken at a triumph at Whitehall. Philemon Holland's translation of Xenophon's *Cyropedia* (1632) concludes with Abraham Holland's account of the Battle of Lepanto (1571).

Though not as explicitly political as some translations, editions of classical authors were frequently polemical. Throughout the period they manifested contradictory impulses: the desire to understand classical authors historically and scientifically on their own terms and in their own contexts and the desire to appropriate them for the rhetorical, civic, and moral improvement of the reader. Expressing this second impulse, some prefatory material, notes, and commentary aggressively managed reading, directly and indirectly conforming classical text to Christian revelation. Fulgentius, Landino, and Pontanus reread Virgil allegorically, glossing the text with influential interpretive commentary; Alexander Ross, like Maphaeus Vegius mentioned earlier, actually rewrote him. *Vergilius evangelisans* (1634) adapts Virgil's verses to the life of Christ: the opening lines sing of the acts (*acta*), not the arms, of the man who came from the shores of heaven (*caeli*), not Troy, buffeted on land and sea by the strength of the Pharisees and the wrath of savage Herod (*vis pharisaeorum, saevique Herodis ob iram*), not by the gods and Juno, because of our sin (*fraus nostra*), not the judgment of Paris. The traditions of *Ovide moralisé* furnish other examples of accommodation. Berchorius read Pyramus as a figure of Christ, separated from Thisbe, the human soul, by the wall of sin, but reunited through death on the cross (the mulberry tree). More secularly, George Sandys (156–7), in his important summary of moralizing traditions, observed that the lovers' deaths "upbraid those parents, who measure their children's by their own outworn and deaded affections"; lest any young readers get the wrong idea, Sandys wagged a finger at them too, saying that the tale "exemplifies the sad success of clandestine loves and neglected parents."

Drama too, as Sir Philip Sidney and others explained, furnished examples of virtues for imitation and vices for avoidance. The various editions, translations, and adaptations of classical tragedy and comedy amply illustrate this interpretive strategys featuring prefatory lectures and edifying marginalia. Terence's bright and lively *Andria*, a standard school text, for example, appeared in the Lyons edition, as tiny islands of text amidst a sea of commentary, grammatical, lexical, and moral. The preface to the first scene (20), for example, directs the reader to five salutary lessons, *ethices praecipua capitua*: Sosia illustrates the duties of a servant, Pamphilus the manners and pursuits of the adolescent, Glycerium the loving duty of a sister, and so on. Actions are moralized analytically and microscopically according to different types of character. The first English book on Seneca, William Cornwallis's *Discourses upon Seneca the Tragedian* (1601) consists of meditative commentaries on eleven sentences drawn from the tragedies.

  Early modern readers, particularly dramatists, did not need to go directly to editions or translations to have access to antiquity. Greek and Latin writers lived everywhere around them in contemporary literature and drama. The ancients were the models for various kinds of writing: Virgil for epics and for pastorals, Juvenal and Horace for satire, Plautus and Terence for comedy, Seneca for tragedy. Nashe (ed. Smith. 1. 312), in fact, complained of Seneca's "being let blood line by line and page by page" on the stage. Thomas Kyd's popular *The Spanish Tragedy* brought Seneca to abundant and fecund life in Elizabethan London; Heywood, Shakespeare, and Jonson did the same for Plautus and Terence. Classical rhetoric, allusion, design, and character lived abundantly in contemporary Italian and English literature and drama, exerting a pervasive, often indirect, influence. Plautus's *Captivi* and Terence's *Eunuchus*, for example, inspire the disguises and identity switches in Ariosto's *I suppositi*, which Gascoigne translates as *Supposes*, which in turn inspires the Lucentio–Bianca plot in *The Taming of the Shrew*. Boccaccio, Giraldi Cinthio, and Guarini, as well as Marlowe, Greene, Lyly, and Chapman, all steeped themselves in classical writers and passed them on to new readers in new forms. The humanist emphasis on antiquity and the prevailing poetics of *imitatio* created a richly complex hermeneutic of intertextual writing and reading. Reading literature, learned and popular, in Elizabethan England almost always meant listening to the voices, sometimes faint and sometimes loud, of ancient authors.

  The peculiar shape and form of the classics in early modern Europe defined in important ways Shakespeare's reading of ancient texts and authors. First and most obviously, the humanist interest in antiquity bore fruit in Shakespeare's repeated efforts to imagine the ancient world in his poems and plays: *Venus and Adonis, The Comedy of Errors, The Rape of Lucrece, Titus Andronicus, A Midsummer Night's Dream, Julius Caesar, Troilus and Cressida, Antony and Cleopatra, Coriolanus, Timon of Athens, Pericles, Cymbeline*, and (with John Fletcher) *The Two Noble Kinsmen*. Second, in these and other works throughout his career, Shakespeare used classical authors as direct sources, as books on the desk that he plundered for plots, characters, and language. Scholars generally agree that Ovid's *Fasti* is a source for *Lucrece*, his *Metamorphoses*, usually but not always in Golding's translation, for *Venus and Adonis*, the sonnets, *Dream, Wives*, and *Tempest*. Plutarch's *Lives* in North's feisty translation directly provides material for *Titus, Dream, Julius Caesar, Antony and Cleopatra, Coriolanus, Timon of Athens*, and possibly *Lear*. Seneca *tragicus* inspires *Titus Andronicus, Richard III, Hamlet, Othello, Macbeth*, and *King Lear*. Plautus directly supplies *The Comedy of*

Errors. Elsewhere readers have detected also Adlington's Apuleius, Livy (possibly in Painter's translation), Grenewey's Tacitus, Chapman's Homer, Holland's Pliny, and possibly Lucian and Appian in translation.

Shakespeare's favorite tutelary shade, Ovid, lives deep in his work, evident both as a glint in the surface of the text – in image, turn of phrase, movement of metaphor – and, deeper still, in structural pattern and motif, especially in the motif of metamorphosis. Medea's speech (*Metamorphoses*, 7. 197ff.), for example, directly inspires Prospero's climactic celebration of his magical power. Medea invokes elements in nature: *auraeque et venti montesque amnesque lacusque / dique omnes nemorum dique omnes noctis adeste* (7. 197–8); in Golding's translation, "Ye airs and winds, ye elves of hills, of brooks, of woods alone / Of standing lakes, and of the night, approach ye everyone!" Compare Prospero:

> Ye elves of hills, brooks, standing lakes, and groves,
> And ye that on the sands with printless foot
> Do chase the ebbing Neptune, and do fly him
> When he comes back.
>
> *(Tempest*, V. i. 33–6)

Shakespeare follows Golding in phrasing the invocation (though substituting elves for the natural forces themselves and for the gods); as the speech goes on, he may borrow details directly from the Latin ("oaks" from *robora*, e.g.). But Shakespeare expands the invocation to imitate the swelling and ebbing of the sea personified as Neptune in the rhythmically enjambed lines (lines 35–6); he also adds the enchantment of native fairy lore by invoking the "demi-puppets that / By moonshine do the green sour ringlets make," as well as those who make "midnight mushrumps" (lines 36–9). Medea goes on to recount her magical achievements: she has returned amazed rivers to their sources, shaken the seas, called forth the winds, moved rocks and trees, made mountains tremble, called the moon down, and darkened the sun. So Prospero:

> I have bedimm'd
> The noontide sun, call'd forth the mutinous winds,
> And 'twixt the green sea and the azur'd vault
> Set roaring war; to the dread rattling thunder
> Have I given fire, and rifted Jove's stout oak
> With his own bolt; the strong-bas'd promontory
> Have I made shake, and by the spurs pluck'd up
> The pine and cedar. Graves at my command
> Have wak'd their sleepers, op'd, and let 'em forth
> By my so potent art.
>
> *(Tempest*, V. i. 41–50)

The adjective–noun combinations (e.g., "azur'd vault," "strong-bas'd promontory") read like epithets and bestow grandeur. Vivid verbs ("bedimm'd," "rifted," "pluck'd up"), strong participles ("roaring," "rattling"), and striking images empower the verse. The superb command of sound, rhythm, enjambment, and caesura recall the fluidity and mastery of Ovidian verse rather than Golding's end-stopped fourteeners. At the end of the speech, Prospero's voice changes register, the verse becomes simpler and quieter, the lines moves with the rhythm of regret and resignation. "But this rough magic / I here abjure" (lines 50–1). Medea's prefatory celebration of her power becomes Prospero's renunciation of magic at the end of the play.

The dialogue between Ovid and Shakespeare here is revealing: the tribute of *imitatio* exhibits throughout the subtler dynamic of competition and transformation. This is entirely characteristic of Shakespeare's use of Ovid (and of classical authors in general), as *A Midsummer Night's Dream* brilliantly illustrates. Ovid's *Metamorphoses* provides a subtext for the various transformations wrought by love and the imagination. Shakespeare may derive the name Titania from Ovid, who uses it five times in the *Metamorphoses*, once for Diana in the narrative of Actaeon. Bottom's transformation into an ass comically replays the tragic tale of Diana and Actaeon, as well as borrowing from the tale of Midas and Apuleius's *The Golden Ass* in Adlington's translation (1566). Shakespeare domesticates the terror and strangeness of Ovid's story and dallies playfully with its erotic potentialities. Later, Theseus rejects several other tragic Ovidian subjects – the battle of the Centaurs and Lapiths and the dismemberment of Orpheus – before selecting Ovid's story of Pyramus and Thisbe for his wedding entertainment. Ovid's witty, complex, and poignant narrative becomes a humorous parody of Elizabethan Seneca – replete with formal apostrophe, an invocation to Night, anguished soliloquizing, and melodramatic imperatives. The hilariously inept players onstage reflect at odd angles the reasonable Athenian lovers in the audience, who previously also met in the forest against parental opposition, swore, protested, swaggered, mistook, suffered, and loved passionately and rhetorically. Love makes metamorphoses wondrous and strange. The story of the mulberry, parti-colored from the Ovidian lovers' blood, becomes in the play the story of the pansy, love-in-idleness (II. i. 148ff), magically empowered by Cupid's errant arrow. Leonard Barkan (1986) astutely observes that the transference of the flower from Ovid's conclusion to the beginning of the drama shows Shakespeare's interest in transformation as cause rather than effect.

Shakespeare's use of North's Plutarch in *Julius Caesar* also illustrates Shakespeare's competitive transformation of a classical text, though earlier commentators – Nicholas Rowe, Samuel Johnson, G. G. Gervinus, and Paul Stapfer, for example – criticized the play for excessive reliance on the source. Recent observers, however, at least since M. W. MacCallum (1910), have admired Shakespeare's creative adaptation of his source, particularly his additions and expansions (the character of Lucius, the mob, Casca, the quarrel scene), omissions (most of Caesar's early career), compressions (the events of the civil war), and transferences (the duplicate revelation of Portia's death to the quarrel scene). At times Shakespeare contradicts Plutarch outright: Caesar suspects those "lean and whitely faced fellows" Brutus and Cassius, not just Cassius; Octavius and Antony's conflict about leading the right wing of the army actually occurs between Brutus and Cassius; Plutarch's Casca cries out in Greek at the assassination, but Shakespeare's cannot understand that language; Caesar tries to read Artemidorus's bill of warning, but cannot because of the crowd; Shakespeare's, in a significant gesture, refuses to consider it: "What touches us ourself shall be last serv'd" (III. i. 8).

Despite its extensive indebtedness in action and language and character to North's rendering of Plutarch's lives of Caesar, Brutus, and Antony, the play is Shakespeare's own creation. Furthermore, *Julius Caesar* well illustrates Shakespeare's style in reading the classics. Passages that do not have verbal echoes in the play nevertheless have deep resonance in its conception and articulation. Witness Cassius's discussion of Epicureanism, for example:

> In our sect, Brutus, we have an opinion that we do not always feel or see that which we suppose we do both see and feel; but that our senses being credulous, and therefore easily abused (when they are idle and unoccupied in their own objects) are induced to imagine they see and conjecture that which in truth they do not. For our mind is quick and cunning to work without either cause or matter anything in the imagination whatsoever. And therefore the imagination is resembled to clay and the mind to the potter, who, without any other cause than his fancy or pleasure, changeth it into what fashion and form he will. (1579: 1072)

This passage strikes the note of skepticism that resounds through the play, notably in Cicero's calm response to the portents: "But men may construe things after their fashion, / Clean from the purpose of the things themselves" (I. iii. 34–5). Throughout, the play demonstrates the delusory nature of the senses, the instability of judgment, the difficulty – nay, impossibility – of knowing rightly and judging truly. The imagination construes and fashions, sees through a glass darkly. Is Caesar a tyrant or a just king? Is Brutus a hero or a fool? Shakespeare could find some of this ambivalence in North's Plutarch, but that account was much more didactic and repeatedly moralized Roman history *sub specie aeternitatis*. There the gods ordain Caesar's death and punish Pompey's murderers through Brutus. Shakespeare gives us no such reassuring clarities. The main difference between play and source resides in what one commentator has called "the undular structure" of *Julius Caesar*, the inevitable rhythm of rise and fall – Pompey, Caesar, Brutus, Antony, Octavius – driven as much by human ambition, weakness, and virtue as by providential design. Portraying this rhythm, Shakespeare suppresses many of Caesar's imperial provocations (the arrogant dismissal of the Senate, for example), leaving Brutus and Cassius to strike down the foremost man in Rome out of personal pique and a fear of what might chance; thus Antony becomes a conspirator and revenger in turn, displaying his rhetorical trickery and cynicism in the Forum, his cruelty in the Proscription. Plutarch supplies the raw materials for this play, but Shakespeare assembles them into a distinctly modern vision of history – cynical and knowing, fully attuned to *Realpolitik*, devoid of illusion.

In addition to encouraging choice of subject and source, Shakespeare's classical training also instilled certain habits of reading. The emphasis on memorization and the impulse to topical collection encouraged analogical thinking, or the assembling of various authors and texts under single rubrics. Menenius's belly fable (*Coriolanus*, I. i. 96ff), for example, may derive from five separate accounts – those of Plutarch, Livy in Holland's translation, Sidney, Camden, and Averell. On a larger scale, a play like Titus Andronicus fluently blends classical sources throughout, particularly North's Plutarch, Virgil, Seneca, Ovid's *Metamorphoses* and *Fasti*, and Livy. Plutarch's "Lives" of Scipio and Coriolanus contributed several proper names and enhanced Shakespeare's portrait of Titus as representative of antique Roman *virtus* as well as Lucius's march against city. Like Virgil's Aeneas, Titus is *pius*, an exemplar of heroic virtue portrayed also as a suffering human being; Aaron and Tamora's lustful tryst in the cave replays parodically the similar encounter of Aeneas and Dido; Demetrius and Chiron's rape of Lavinia parody her Virgilian namesake's courtship and marriage by Aeneas. Ovid supplies pattern and precedent for much of the action. The *Metamorphoses* literally appears onstage as a prop (IV. i); Titus quotes a line in Latin, "Terras Astraea reliquit" (IV. iii. 4), and Ovidian stories, notably the myth of the world's four ages and the Philomel–Procne–Tereus myth organize much of the action. According to the latter myth, Demetrius and Chiron play the role Tereus, barbarian rapist and murderer; Lavinia plays Philomel, ravished innocent; Titus plays Pandion, injured father, then Procne, the revenger. As he says, "For worse than Philomel you us'd my daughter, / And worse than Progne I will be reveng'd" (V. ii. 194–5). Titus makes good his promise here, carving up and cooking two corpses to Procne's one, then presenting the meal to their mother Tamora. Here as elsewhere in the Renaissance, competition with the classical prototype often takes the form of sheer multiplication.

Thinking analogically, Shakespeare turns also to Seneca for inspiration, imitating the elaborate preparations for the killing, the conflation of cook and killer, and the public ceremony of the feast in *Thyestes*, which supplied as well a model of revenge action for the Renaissance. Elsewhere in the play characters quote from Seneca's *Phaedra* (II. i. 135 and IV. i. 81–2), which also inspires the horrific depiction of *scelus* (crime) onstage. Finally, Shakespeare grafts Ovidian myth, combined with Senecan action and rhetoric, onto what Jonathan Bate has called "the Lucrece pattern from classical history (available to him in both Livy's *History of Rome* and Ovid's *Fasti*)" (92). There are explicit comparisons of Lavinia, Saturninus, and Tamora to Lucrece, Tarquin, and his queen (II. i. 108–9; III. i. 298–9; III. iv. 164); and Bate well notes the parallel in action: the historical Lucius Junius Brutus and Shakespeare's Lucius (cf. IV. i. 89–93) both experience exile, and both return to expel the wicked tyrant and establish a new republican order.

This habit of analogical thinking leads naturally to the mixing of classical and nonclassical texts. The Bible, English history, Italian story, earlier and contemporary drama, popular reading, and ballads – all join unpredictably with classical works. Falstaff, for example, plays the Lord of Misrule, the Vice from the morality plays, that wittily irreverent misleader of youth, and several stock characters from New Comedy: the clever servant tricking his betters, the cowardly but swaggering soldier, the sponging parasite obsessed with his belly. Shylock too incorporates numerous other familiar figures: usurer, New Comic miser, *senex iratus*, Italian pantaloon, and stage Jew. In both cases the whole, of course, is greater than the sum of the parts. Falstaff's wit draws his various selves into coherence and pointedly opposes the heroic myths enacted elsewhere in the play. Shylock was once a lover himself, we note, as he laments the loss of Leah's ring, and he has suffered bigotry and persecution from the Christians, so-called, in Venice.

Classical and nonclassical elements compose on a broad scale the language, character, and design of *Macbeth*. Macbeth's "Things bad begun make strong themselves by ill" (III. ii. 55; cf. III. iv. 135–7) recasts a well-known Senecan sentence, "per scelera semper sceleribus tutum est iter" (*Agamemnon*, 115). Throughout the play he speaks the rhetoric of willful Senecan protagonists, echoing their invocations to night (I. iv. 50–1; III. ii. 46–7), hyperbolic catalogues (III. iv. 99ff), and mesmerized, tormented urgings of self to *scelus* (crime) (I. iii. 128ff; IV. i. 146ff). Similarly, Lady Macbeth sounds like Seneca's Medea in her repudiation of female affection and in her fascination with infanticide (I. v. 40ff). *Hercules Furens*, a play Shakespeare seems to have used here and in other tragedies, may inspire the powerful imagery of bloody hands that runs throughout the play, including Macbeth's anguished question:

> Will all great Neptune's ocean wash this blood
> Clean from my hand? No; this my hand will rather
> The multitudinous seas incarnadine,
> Making the green one red.
>
> (II. ii. 57–60)

> quis Tanais aut quis Nilus aut quis Persica
> uiolentus unda Tigris aut Rhenus ferox
> Tagusue Hibera turbidus gaza fluens
> abluere dextram poterit? Arctoum licet
> Maeotis in me gelida transfundat mare
> et tota Tethys per meas currat manus
> haerebit altum facinus.
>
> (*Hercules Furens*, 1323–9)

(What Tanais, what Nile, what Tigris, violent with Persian wave, what fierce Rhine, or flowing Tagus, thick with Hibernian treasure, will wash clean this hand? Though frigid Maeotis should pour over me its northern sea, though all Tethys' ocean should flow through my hands, the deep stain will cling, indelible.)

Direct influence is probable, though by no means certain (the passage has a parallel in the *Phaedra* (715–18) and Shakespeare might have come across an adaptation). But the anguished questioning, registering specifically the incapacity of the ocean to wash hands clean of blood, bespeaks in both texts a similar shock of recognition and moral repugnance at what the hero has become.

Nonclassical texts and traditions everywhere in *Macbeth* engage classical ones. Holinshed supplies most of the plot and the characters. The gigantic shadow of Herod from the medieval mystery play further shapes the action of the play. Commentators note the parallel confrontations with prophecies of displacement and both tyrants' desperate reaction – the slaughter of children. The appearance of Banquo's ghost recalls the appearance of Death at Herod's feast in the *Ludus Coventriae* cycle. Classical and native tyrants coalesce. Other Christian traditions, suffused in the rhetoric of the play, redefine its action. Like no Senecan tyrant, Macbeth imagines the "angels, trumpet-tongu'd" pleading against "the deep damnation" of his deed (I. vii. 19–20). He worries about "the common enemy of man," Satan, who strives for possession of that "eternal jewel," an immortal soul (III. i. 67–8). Immediately after Duncan's murder, he reflects wistfully, "Had I but died an hour before this chance, / I had liv'd a blessed time" (II. iii. 91–2). Before his end, Macbeth confesses to Macduff: "But get thee back, my soul is too much charg'd, / With blood of thine already" (V. viii. 5–6). Such assertions, introducing post-classical ideas of sin and damnation, reshape the universe of the play and profoundly transform its classical elements. Scottish warrior, Senecan tyrant, and sinful murderer coexist in one complicated figure, whose vaunts mingle dissonantly with the sad elegiac music of his regrets; the compelling dissonance thereby resulting signals to Macbeth and the rest of us just what he has lost.

The humanists' didactic, Christianizing appropriation of antiquity bears here and throughout Shakespeare much fruit. But there are no easily defined conflicts and victories over antiquity; the dramatist generally refuses to stage the simple dichotomies and peremptory theses of the moralists. As in Prospero's renunciation of Medean magic for mortality, and in Macbeth's struggle with heroic self-assertion and sinful pride, classical and Christian values continually engage each other in complex harmonies and counterpoints. By fits and starts, for another example, Hamlet, more antique Roman than Dane, plays Senecan avenger, Plautine *adulescens*, epical hero, Stoic wise man, human sinner, and faithful witness to a Providence that cares for the sparrow and shapes our ends. Shakespeare builds his play on the archetypal curve of revenge action – initial atrocity, theatrical self-creation, concluding atrocity – that shapes Senecan tragedy and its numerous descendants, including any number of contemporary action films. Yet Shakespeare complicates the formula at every point: he presents a problematic ghost and confused history, plunges the protagonist into ethical uncertainties and dilemmas, inverts the final scenario so that the revenger is also victim. Hamlet executes Polonius, Rosencrantz and Guildenstern, Laertes, and, finally in bitter fury, Claudius the king; but Horatio still bids farewell to a virtuous Christian prince: "Now cracks a noble heart. Good night, sweet prince. / And flights of angels sing thee to thy rest!" (V. ii. 359–60).

Comedy, as it must, strikes very different balances. Humanist moralization of Plautus and Terence, developed through centuries of adaptation and commentary, lead to a transformation of eros into romantic love. Shakespeare's only direct adaptation of classical comedy, *The Comedy of Errors*, from Plautus's *Menaechmi* and *Amphitruo*, accordingly, substitutes the bewildered confusion of the traveler for the lust of Plautus' denizen, invents the wife's sister and the lyrical love affair between her and Antipholus of Syracuse, downplays the courtesan, emphasizes marital love in the relations of Adriana and her husband and in the invented frame plot. Furthermore, the classical *virgo*, or maiden, normally unprivileged, sexually compliant, and often a *muta persona*, moves through Italian variations to reappear on Shakespeare's stage witty and chaste – Viola, Isabella, Hero, Marina, and Miranda.

Throughout his career, of course, Shakespeare worked with general traditions as well as specific texts. Ubiquitously present in various forms, self-consciously adapted or fully naturalized, ancient authors lived on in dramatic conventions, in stock characters (tyrants, maidens, angry fathers, bragging soldiers, clever servants), situations, or rhetorical forms, all of which excited certain expectations. Common practice, rather than a specific text, contributed the *senex iratus*, for example, that New Comic angry father who opposes his nubile daughter in the persons of Egeus, Capulet, Lear, Prospero, and others. The comparatively simple presentation of the type in Egeus sets off the more complex variations to follow – Juliet's well-meaning, volatile, stubborn, sincerely grieving father; Cordelia's childish, mad, wrathful, heroic, wrongheaded, magnificent, and finally, repentant, loving father; Miranda's magical *pater*, who feigns opposition to her beloved Ferdinand and grows beyond anger. Ancient texts also supplied familiar patterns of dramatic action, Hamlet and Horatio replay continually Seneca's *domina–nutrix* dialogue, for example, the conversation between passionate protagonist and restraining confidant; at the end they reverse roles as calm, dying Hamlet restrains the passionate Horatio from the rash action of suicide. The forms and models of classical rhetoric, learned by repetition and rote at school, also shape formal and informal writing in the Renaissance. The ideals of *copia* and eloquence, the practice of rhetoric formally divided into invention, disposition, elocution, memory, and utterance – all characterize early modern dramatic language. More specific formal inheritances for the drama include the use of prologue and epilogue, soliloquy, chorus, stichomythia, the construction of action in the form of *protasis* (introduction), *epitasis* (climax), and *catastrophe* (resolution), the emphasis on *anagnorisis*, or recognition, in both comedy and tragedy.

The humanists' reverence for antiquity and their habits of appropriation everywhere inform Shakespeare's reading of the classics. But Shakespeare can be a lighthearted reader of antiquity as well, at times even irreverent. The humorous Latin lessons in *Shrew* (III. i.) and *Wives* (IV. i, whence we began) are to the point here, as well as the portrait of the boy "creeping like snail / Unwillingly to school" (*As You Like It*, II. vii. 146–7) and the figures of ostentatious Latinity, Nathaniel and Holofernes, in *Love's Labor's Lost*. Putting praise of Ovid's "elegancy, facility, and golden cadence of poesy" in the mouth of that latter pedant, punning on Ovid's name, Naso, also meaning "nose," Shakespeare gently mocks the standard school line and, perhaps, humanist philology: "Ovidius Naso was the man. And why indeed

'Naso,' but for smelling out the odiferous flowers of fancy, the jerks of invention?" (IV. ii. 122–5). (One thinks as well of the terrible pun on *mollis aer* and *mulier* that enables plot resolution in *Cymbeline* (V. v. 446–8).) Upon arriving in Padua, Tranio advises against pursuing classical study at the expense of love, "Let's be no Stoics nor no stocks, I pray, / Or so devote to Aristotle's checks / As Ovid be an outcast quite abjur'd" (Shrew, I. i. 31–3). As usual in the period, the pun on Stoics/stocks suggests the perceived tedium and inhumanity of that ancient philosophical discipline. Falstaff alludes to Caesar as that "hook-nos'd fellow of Rome" and wittily renders the famous *veni, vidi, vici*, as "I came, saw, and overcame" (*2 Henry IV*, IV. iii. 41–2; cf. Rosalind on "Caesar's thrasonical brag," *As You Like It*, V. ii. 31–2). Fluellen ruminates on Alexander the Pig (*Henry V*, IV. vii. 13ff).

The cheeky playfulness evident here turns into something more serious elsewhere, as Shakespeare experiments with classical notions of genre. Among his strangest, most enigmatic works are three classical plays: *Troilus and Cressida, Timon of Athens*, and *Cymbeline. Troilus and Cressida* consistently evokes and upsets generic expectations. Shakespeare's fullest engagement with the great epic tale of Troy portrays a relatively minor amatory affair to question cynically human capacities for love and honor. Contemporaries too seemed puzzled: the play was advertised in the Stationers' Register entry and on both quarto title pages (the original and the replacement) as a history, an appellation that might mean simply "story"; the epistle to the quarto compares it to "the best comedy of Terence or Plautus"; the compositors of the first folio started setting it with the tragedies (after *Romeo and Juliet*), ran into legal difficulties, and then placed it, unpaginated, after *Henry VIII*, the last of the histories, and before *Coriolanus*, the first of the tragedies. In *Timon* Shakespeare casts a traditionally comic figure – self-important, inflexible, antifestive – in the role of Sophoclean hero. There results a bizarre and brittle tragedy of fulminating withdrawal, one that has rarely enjoyed theatrical or critical favor. In Timon, himself, Shakespeare seems also to experiment with the classical notion of *anagnorisis*, which Aristotle defined as the recognition of a friend in an enemy or of an enemy in a friend. Timon misperceives both friends and enemies, first wrongly thinking all Athenians his loving comrades, then wrongly reviling everyone in naïve misanthropy. That ragbag of plots and characters, *Cymbeline*, some have observed, is the only Shakespeare play to fit all of Polonius' categories: "tragedy, comedy, history, pastoral, pastoral-comical, historical-pastoral, tragical-historical, tragical-comical-historical-pastoral" (II. ii. 396–9).

Trained in humanist methods and curriculum, Shakespeare read the classics very much as a man of his age. As the humanists recommended, he read the ancients dynamically and competitively, boldly transforming texts and traditions. Attuned to rhetoric, analogical and eclectic in application, and moralizing in approach – Shakespeare's reading supplied material and form for his writing. Such reading in Greek and Latin writers may have commanded little respect from Ben Jonson or Richard Farmer; but to modern eyes it bespeaks considerable learning and an engagement with antiquity both serious and fruitful.

NOTE

References to Shakespeare are cited from *The Riverside Shakespeare*, ed. G. Blakemore Evans, 2nd edn (Boston: Houghton Mifflin, 1997).

REFERENCES AND FURTHER READING

Baldwin, T. W. 1944: *William Shakespeare's Small Latine and Lesse Greeke*, 2 vols. Urbana: University of Illinois Press.

Barkan, Leonard 1986: *The Gods Made Flesh: Metamorphosis and the Pursuit of Paganism*. New Haven: Yale University Press.

Bate, Jonathan (ed.) 1995: *Titus Andronicus*. The New Arden Shakespeare. London: Routledge.

Bolgar, R. R. 1954: *The Classical Heritage and its Beneficiaries*. Cambridge: Cambridge University Press.

Braden, Gordon 1985: *Renaissance Tragedy and the Senecan Tradition: Anger's Privilege*. New Haven: Yale University Press.

Bullough, Geoffrey (ed.) 1957–75: *Narrative and Dramatic Sources of Shakespeare*, 8 vols. London: Routledge and Kegan Paul.

Bush, Douglas 1932: *Mythology and the Renaissance Tradition in English Poetry*. Minneapolis: University of Minnesota Press.

——— 1952: *Classical Influences in Renaissance Literature*. Cambridge, Mass.: Harvard University Press.

Doran, Madeleine 1954: *Endeavors of Art: A Study of Form in Elizabethan Drama*. Madison: University of Wisconsin Press.

Grafton, Anthony and Jardine, Lisa 1986: *From Humanism to the Humanities: Education and the Liberal Arts in Fifteenth- and Sixteenth-Century Europe*. Cambridge, Mass.: Harvard University Press.

Jones, Emrys 1977: *The Origins of Shakespeare*. Oxford: Clarendon Press.

Kristeller, Paul Oskar et al. (eds) 1960–present: *Catalogus Translationum et Commentariorum: Mediaeval and Renaissance Latin Translations and Commentaries: Annotated Lists and Guides*. Washington, D.C.: Catholic University Press.

MacCallum, M. W. 1910: *Shakespeare's Roman Plays and their Background*. London: Macmillan.

Miola, Robert S. 1992: *Shakespeare and Classical Tragedy*. Oxford: Clarendon Press.

——— 1994: *Shakespeare and Classical Comedy*. Oxford: Clarendon Press.

Martindale, Charles and Martindale, Michelle 1990: *Shakespeare and the Uses of Antiquity: An Introductory Essay*. London: Routledge.

Muir, Kenneth 1977: *The Sources of Shakespeare's Plays*. London: Methuen.

Ovid 1632: *Ovid's Metamorphoses Englished, Mythologized, and Represented in Figures*, trans. George Sandys. Oxford: Clarendon Press.

——— 1977: *Metamorphoses with an English Translation*, trans. Frank Justus Miller. The Loeb Classical Library, 3rd edn, 2 vols. Cambridge, Mass.: Harvard University Press.

Reynolds, L. D. and Wilson, N. G. 1974: *Scribes and Scholars: A Guide to the Transmission of Latin and Greek Literature*. Oxford: Clarendon Press.

Salingar, Leo 1974: *Shakespeare and the Traditions of Comedy*. Cambridge: Cambridge University Press.

Seneca 1917: *Tragedies with an English Translation*, trans. Frank Justus Miller. The Loeb Classical Library, 2 vols. Cambridge, Mass.: Harvard University Press.

Smith, G. Gregory 1904: *Elizabethan Critical Essays*, 2 vols. Oxford: Clarendon Press.

Spencer, T. J. B. 1957: Shakespeare and the Elizabethan Romans. *Shakespeare Survey*, 10, 27–38.

Terence 1560: *Terentius, in Quem Triplex Edita est P. Antesignani Rapislagnensis Commentatio*. Lyon.

Velz, John W. 1968: *Shakespeare and the Classical Tradition: A Critical Guide to Commentary, 1660–1960*. Minneapolis: University of Minnesota Press.

——— 1971: Undular structure in *Julius Caesar*. *Modern Language Review*, 66, 1–12.

12

The Shapes of History

D. R. Woolf

These days we seem to be surrounded by history. Films treat historical subjects from imperial Rome to medieval Scotland to Vietnam; historical fiction remains popular in the pulp supermarket trade; film-makers churn out elaborate documentaries and dramatizations; and cable TV develops speciality channels. Museums, the major public forum for the exhibit of the physical remains of the past, remain enormously popular if chronically underfunded institutions. If one really gets ambitious to learn more about a particular event, there are always the public libraries and general interest bookstores, where works on military history and biography are easily available, and the newest addition to the pond of historical information, the Internet. If Shakespeare had written his plays today, they might well be lost amid the hundreds of titles available, and would of course run afoul of academic critics and amateur history buffs, who could easily point out the many 'howlers' in his representation of particular events or people.

It is easy to forget that the past was not so readily accessible in the late sixteenth and early seventeenth centuries. Then, only a small number of historical works of various sorts were available to a curious reader, and on a much more restricted range of subjects. The overwhelming majority of the populace knew little or nothing about the history of the world as a whole (episodes from the Bible being the most conspicuous exception), and had very sketchy impressions of their own national past, preferring the considerably more relevant local truths of oral tradition, folklore and custom. Among the educated élite, perhaps 10 per cent of the total population, knowledge of English or British history was only just becoming a mark of civility, and then mainly for practical purposes. It made sense to have a grasp of the customs and laws of the land and to know something of their origins; it was politically useful to know that ferocious civil wars had resulted from the deposition of a king in 1399, and to have a sense of the liberties granted under Magna Carta; and, under Elizabeth I, every Protestant needed to remember the awful consequences for godly religion of a popish queen as recently as the 1550s and the litany of Catholic atrocities and invasions of royal prerogative reaching back to John Lackland, Becket and Canossa. The biblical past – every bit as 'real' as secular history and more reliable, because divinely authorized – provided a common element in the education of both popular and élite culture, parcelled out in sermons on Sundays, holidays and anniversaries (Hutton 1994; Cressy 1989); scriptural figures like 'Gogmagog' were often transmuted via popular discourse into legends or toponyms (Thomas 1983; Woolf 1988a). Yet, by modern standards, one could get by without knowing very much history at all. The purpose of this essay is to digest a large quantity of writing, some of it very recent, on Renaissance English historiography and to offer some suggestions as to why the period between 1590 and 1620 can be considered, if not quite the full-blown 'historical revolution' that F. Smith Fussner deemed it (Fussner 1962; Preston 1977), then at least an important turning point in the ways in which history was presented to, and perceived by, the public. My concern here is principally with what I have elsewhere (Woolf 1997b) called 'historical culture', the level of knowledge of history, its uses and especially its 'social circulation' among individuals. Consequently, this chapter is only secondarily concerned with the historians themselves, and hardly at all with Shakespeare's plays *per se*, about which I am ill-qualified to comment. In particular, I shall be concerned with ascertaining what was available in print to the interested spectator of *Richard II, King Lear* or *Macbeth*, and with the rather sudden decline in the fortunes of the genre that lay behind the Renaissance history play, the Tudor chronicle.

The Early Tudor Background, 1485–1558

The age of the printed history book in England begins with William Caxton, who, as a small businessman rather than a scholar, was interested in producing what his reading clients wanted. It would not have entered Caxton's mind to write his own history, or even to commission another writer to do so (as would in fact become common practice within two centuries thereafter), so he simply selected for reprinting the two most familiar titles he could find, confident that his mechanical bride could churn out sufficient copies to keep the gentry happy. He chose, first of all, the *Brut*, a well-known 'urban chronicle' (that is, one mainly written in London and circulated there over the preceding century, in manuscript), dealing principally with ancient British history in a highly chivalric style reminiscent of the great chronicler of the Hundred Years War, Sir John Froissart (Kingsford 1913: 113–39; Levy 1967: 10–15; Gransden 1982: 220–48, 258). Although Caxton contributed little of his own material to the *Brut*, it soon became known as 'Caxton's Chronicle'. As a follow-up, since every Christian reader ought to have some knowledge of universal history, he published an established winner in that sub-genre, the famous *Polychronicon*. A world history *ab orbe condita*, but still with a considerable amount of material on Britain, this had been written in the mid-fourteenth century by a Chester monk named Ranulf Higden and translated into Middle English soon thereafter, proving very popular over the ensuing decades – it is one of the earliest non-religious books known to have circulated from late medieval cathedral libraries. Caxton added an eighth book to the *Polychronicon* in 1482 'to thentente that such thynges as have ben don syth the deth or ende of the sayd boke of polycronicon shold be had in remembraunce and not putte in oblyvyon ne forgetynge', in effect updating it and thereby setting the pattern for the republication of existing chronicles for the next century and a quarter.

Other chronicles, written *de novo* though using earlier ones as source material, were not long in coming. There are many surviving examples of minor urban chronicles that were commenced in the fifteenth and early sixteenth centuries, principally as records of civic events inserted as 'annals' next to the mayoral and shrieval year by good-willed citizens such as Bristol's Robert Ricart (*The Maire of Bristowe is Calendar*, initiated in 1479). More ambitiously, a London alderman named Robert Fabyan (d. 1513) wrote a full-length chronicle of England and France, whose histories had so intertwined over the preceding three centuries as to be nearly inseparable. Fabyan's work was published in 1516, and the tradition of Tudor chronicle writing which it may be said to have initiated would eventually include several works now generally believed to have been prominent among Shakespeare's sources: Edward Hall's chronicle (1548), the work of a minor Henrician official who saw a clear pattern in the disasters that had afflicted the kingdom between the deposition of Richard II and the 'union of the two illustre houses of York and Lancaster' under Henry VIII; mid-century works by Thomas Lanquet and Richard Grafton; Raphael Holinshed's gigantic *Chronicles*, which we will encounter at greater length below; and the several series of chronicles on London and wider English history by the prolific John Stow, who is also known to us as one of the leading antiquaries of the age through his magisterial *Survey of London* (1598).

For Londoners, knowing something of their history was practically useful, since the city's liberties had all at some point been granted by the Crown. The guilds and livery companies that dominated urban society took pride in their heritage, and annual mayoral installations recorded by Elizabethan writers frequently featured elaborate *tableaux* relating the trade of the new mayor to a historical or mythical figure. The same applied at major public events such as royal entries (that of Catherine of Aragon into London in 1502, for instance, or Queen Elizabeth's coronation in 1559). Often some object lesson like the need for submission and obedience to the sovereign was pointed out, though most people scarcely needed reminding of the awful pains inflicted on traitors and felons – the bloody quarters and parboiled piked heads of executed rebels provided throughout the sixteenth century a much more dreadful warning than any textual account.

On the other hand, the past regularly proved an extraordinarily potent tool for making points in an age which valued tradition over innovation, antiquity over recent times, an age in which an appeal to the past was always an effective argument. This made control of what was known and said about the dead and their deeds an imperative for the Tudor regime. Throughout Europe, Renaissance republics such as Florence and Venice and despotisms such as that of the Visconti and Sforza in Milan or the Aragonese in Naples made sure that the deeds of rulers were enshrined in history by commissioning histories of either recent or more remote times from their citizens (such as Florence's Leonardo Bruni or a long string of Venetian official historians) or by retaining the services of an intellectual hired gun, usually a product of the humanist schools (Ianziti 1988; Zimmermann 1995; Cochrane 1981). The Tudor monarchs were never as fully committed to this as some other European regimes – the office of 'Historiographer Royal' was not created until the 1660s (Hay 1951), and then in emulation of contemporary French practice – but despite this, the successive governments that ruled over the expanding sixteenth-century population still took great care to police the circulation of knowledge of the past. This was often done with a savagery that makes the most vitriolic book review in the *Times Literary Supplement* seem pale by comparison. When Henry Howard, earl of Surrey, dared to quarter his Howard family arms with those of Edward the Confessor, revered Anglo-Saxon monarch and lawgiver, a dying Henry VIII took it as a personal affront, and it was among the frivolous offences that brought Surrey to the block in 1547. The king's younger daughter, Elizabeth, was just as touchy, especially late in life. In the most famous instance of historical censorship in the entire period, she had an innocent but tactless historian, John Hayward, examined by her council and imprisoned because he had published a history of the deposition of Richard II that looked uncomfortably like a commentary on her own regime and which, worse still, was dedicated to the ambitious but disgraced courtier Robert Devereux, earl of Essex. The earl's head rolled in 1601, shortly after his abortive *coup* heralded by a dramatic restaging of Shakespeare's *Richard II*. Hayward was more fortunate, since, as the witty Francis Bacon observed, the budding historian could really only be charged with felony for stealing some of his best lines from the Roman historian, Tacitus, rather than with treason. Nevertheless, he spent several years imprisoned in the Tower until finding more gainful employment as a civil lawyer and historian under her successor (Manning 1991; Dowling 1930–1; Levy 1987).

The Hayward incident is so familiar to modern Shakespearians as to need little further comment here, but it bespeaks a mind-set that thought about the past in ways that now seem alien. Renaissance readers of history did not, in the first instance, consider episodes in the past from back to front, from cause to effect, so much as sideways, from event or person A to its analogue B. Centuries of typological analysis of Scripture had made this a mental habit, and the deeply held belief in an all-knowing and omnipotent Providence made the search for contingent, sublunary causes almost superfluous. The writings of some notorious continental students of history such as Machiavelli, though somewhat more sensitive to contingency (personified in the latter's *Il Principe* as fickle, female Fortune), had turned the search for comparisons and parallels from a general guide to morality into a more narrowly focused schoolroom of political wisdom, evincing the effects of particular actions, but not seeing history as an ongoing process whereby multiple past contingencies led, however indirectly, to a historian's own present. These habits of thought were further reinforced by certain oft-repeated classical descriptions of the nature and purpose of history, in particular those of Dionysius of Halicarnassus (who defined history as 'philosophy teaching by examples' long before Lord Bolingbroke appropriated that phrase in the eighteenth century), Lucian of Samosata and above all the great orator Cicero, whose widely repeated treatment of history in *De oratore* (II. ix. 36) had reduced it to the *testis temporum, lux veritatis, magistra vitae et nuncia vetustatis* topos echoed in many sixteenth-century works (Kelley 1988). The practical manifestation of such thinking can be found in numerous Elizabethan and Jacobean works of counsel like Robert Dallington's *Aphorismes Civill and Militarie* (1613), which drew explicitly from Francesco Guicciardini, or Bacon's more wide-ranging *Essays* (1597), in sermons making use of historical examples, and in innumerable commonplace books, where distinctions of time and place were intentionally eradicated. Those rare authors who questioned this rather mechanical comparison of events at one time and place with those at another were for the moment voices in the wilderness, whether Guicciardini himself (an accomplished historian widely read in England in Geoffrey Fenton's 1579 translation) or a home-grown sceptic, Sir Philip Sidney, whose attack on the historian by way of defending the poet revitalized the recurring argument between history and fiction, a point to which I shall return.

The Shapes of History

If knowledge of capital H History, in the sense of major events and personalities, was constrained by the limited number of works in print, the larger font of information from the past played a much more active role in daily life during the sixteenth century than at any time before or since, as can be seen by a straightforward comparison of the periods immediately preceding and following the Renaissance. The Middle Ages had great reverence for the past, but few tools with which to study it systematically, for all its massive generation of administrative and judicial records. By the early eighteenth century, in contrast, the tools were now in existence for critical study of the past, much more evidence was publicly accessible for study in books and printed editions of sources, and incomparably more people were interested in using them: but by then, paradoxically, the past had begun to lose some of its inherent authority over the conduct of personal and social life. A full account of why this happened cannot be offered here. It will have to suffice for the moment to suggest the following general influences on changing perceptions of the past, and with them the revised under-standing that contemporaries were evolving of the nature and use of history.

The relationship between the past as a whole (that which is to be represented) and history proper (its written representation) was itself in transition. For medieval and Renaissance writers, history was a literary record of events deemed worthy of com-memoration by historians, not the events themselves or their 'study'. History was thus a *genre*, not a *thing*, and still less (as it would become in the nineteenth century) a *discipline*. That the selection and arrangement of appropriate events, real or imagined, was rather different for twelfth-century authors like Geoffrey of Monmouth (legendary events, in his case) or William of Malmesbury than for those in the classical-humanist tradition of historiography (Thucydides, Leonardo Bruni or, in Shakespeare's time, Francis Bacon, John Hayward, Samuel Daniel and William Camden) is of less consequence than one might think. The humanists who would repudiate chronicle writing during the later English Renaissance did so because they wished to narrow, not to expand, the scope of subjects covered, focusing the historian's and reader's gaze on the *res gestae* of the great, those deeds from which lessons could most easily be drawn. I will have more to say a bit further on about the reasons for the Elizabethan chronicle's precipitous decline at the end of the sixteenth century. For the moment it should be noted that the late medieval and Tudor chroniclers regularly included apparently insignificant events such as monstrous births, shrieval appointments, destructive fires, salacious murders, wondrous frosts and notable price rises. Much of this is of course grist for the mill of the modern social historian, but it had scant appeal to those late Elizabethan historians weaned on Cicero, Thucydides and Tacitus. Such trivia were largely expunged from 'true' history, beginning in the 1590s (Patterson 1994; Helgerson 1997).

That this purification of history did not succeed in turning history forever into a political record of the high and mighty, used purely for didactic purposes, has to do in part with a major tension within humanism: the conflict between strict loyalty to classical language and its forms and the strong, almost visceral urge to apply lessons drawn from the painstaking reconstruction of ancient culture, excavated and cleaned up through rigorous philological study, to current political and social issues (Levine 1987) – a conflict between the past for its own sake and the past as ransackable source of precedent and example. In short, the very techniques for the analysis and restoration of texts from antiquity that were perfected by continental philologists from Lorenzo Valla and Desiderius Erasmus to Joseph Justus Scaliger and Isaac Casaubon could also be used to study other things. Late Elizabethan lawyers, for instance, some of whom were among the beneficiaries of humanist philological training, began to see their subject as a process of organic development as every successive present resulted from its cumulative past. It helped, too, that they were by professional training given to the orderly tracing and listing of legal precedents in chronological fashion, and it was not difficult to move beyond legal and parliamentary records to other sorts of evidence, including archaeological. The most sophisticated were able to trace the development of particular institutions and customs through the documents in which these were mentioned, and thus they soon began to see the past as not merely the analogue to, but the proximate cause *of*, the present.

In England, we can see this tendency at work embryonically in a group of historically minded scholars of Queen Elizabeth's time (some but not all of whom had common law training), especially those who met regularly in the short-lived Society of Antiquaries. Their 'discourses' – not, be it noted, 'histories' – concerning coins, land measurement, titles and other practices were collected by one of their number, Francis Tate, and were published in the early eighteenth century (Woolf 1990). We can see the same trend in one of the greatest of their number, William

Camden, whose *Remaines* (1605) was a much-read and frequently republished record of the linguistic heritage of the medieval past, and in another, Sir Henry Spelman, who used his knowledge of feudal tenures to demonstrate the profound impact that the Norman Conquest had had on English law and government, in contrast to those, such as his fellow lawyer Sir Edward Coke, who preferred the comforting bosom of an immutable 'ancient constitution' dating from time immemorial and untroubled by Roman, Anglo-Saxon, Viking or even Norman invaders (Pocock 1997; Burgess 1992). Finally, we can see it in the several scholars who followed another lawyer, William Lambarde (*A Perambulation of Kent*, 1576), in studying the antiquities of particular shires or even towns, with Stow's above-mentioned *Survey of London* and William Camden's own *Britannia* (1586 and later editions) furnishing a continuously revised and expanded guide to the landscape, families and antiquarian features (especially Roman) of the whole island (Mendyk 1989; Levy 1967: 147–61; Piggott 1989; Kendrick 1950; Parry 1995).

To put it another way, the social, linguistic, topographical and cultural features that the humanists found so repulsive in the chronicles were kicked out of narrative historiography, albeit temporarily, to find a home in various types of enquiry known collectively as 'antiquarianism'. Occasionally they could creep back into historical narrative by the back door. Shakespeare's slightly older contemporary, Samuel Daniel (1562–1619), is a good example. Daniel was a poet whose imagination ran well beyond the retelling of political lessons of great events – he had done that, and soon wearied of it, in his epic *Civil Warres* written between 1590 and 1609. In Daniel's *Collection of the Historie of England* (1618), which for a time was the most widely read general history of early medieval England (though it stopped rather abruptly at Edward III), the erstwhile poet took a broader view of his country's historical past, speculating on the process of legal and constitutional change. Daniel was no lawyer, but his interests show the influence of one of his patrons, James I's lord chancellor, Baron Ellesmere, and reveal a concern with contemporary discussions as to the nature of the English polity (Ferguson 1971; Levy 1987; Woolf 1990: 83–9). In the very same year as the first complete edition of Daniel's *Collection*, there also appeared an even more formidable work: the *Historie of Tithes* by the young barrister, antiquary and future parliamentarian John Selden (1584–1654). Selden's notorious *Historie* was significant both for its depth of learning and for the immediate controversy it sparked by threatening to subvert the clerical right to tithes. It showed with merciless philological rigour and unparalleled erudition in the sources that, historically at least, no *de jure* right to this tax had ever been asserted, and that the structure of ecclesiastical finance and of parochial administration had instead developed in a series of stages beginning in the early Middle Ages, the laws of the Church being in direct competition with the laws enacted by kings and parliaments. The *Historie* was also significant because both here and in his later works Selden asserted the freedom of the historian to study the past in its totality – its institutions and customs as well as its major events and people – with a view to explaining the origins of the present rather than deriving moral or political lessons (Berkowitz 1988; Christianson 1996: 63–79).

Selden was undoubtedly the greatest English-speaking scholar of his age, but he was a mediocre stylist and, like many of his modern successors, not much inclined to theorizing about the nature of history. If England produced anything approaching a philosopher of history during this period, that title must go to Francis Bacon (1561–1626), himself an aspiring lawyer under Elizabeth and Ellesmere's successor as lord chancellor under James I. Though much of it was borrowed from continental writers, Bacon's careful delineation of sub-genres of writing about the past in his *De augmentis scientiarum* established generic rubrics for 'history'. These certainly separated true or 'perfect' history (the political sort that he himself most admired and would have a go at in his history of Henry VII (1622)) from other, imperfect kinds; but it also preserved history's older sense, deriving from Herodotus, as an 'inventory' of things done *or* of things existent; the latter would eventually become the domain of 'natural history' (Wormald 1993; Clark 1974; Bushnell 1997). Bacon, Selden and Daniel between them subverted the very generic distinctions between true histories, chronicles, antiquarian discourses and other genres, a set of wobbly enclosing fences that had been only recently and rather hastily erected in the second half of the sixteenth century, mainly in a series of treatises usually known collectively as the *artes historicae* (arts of history), of which the most important English contributions were Thomas Blundeville's *True Order and Methode of Wryting and Reading Hystories* (1574), which was largely a translation of works by two Italians, Giacomo Aconcio and Francesco Patrizzi, and, half a century later, the *De ratione et methodo legendi historias dissertatio* (1623) by Degory Wheare, a minor classicist whom the great antiquary Camden picked to occupy the first endowed professorship of history at Oxford (Salmon 1997). Compared to the richer font of continental *artes historicae*, including the influential *Methodus* by the Frenchman Jean Bodin (much read in England during the 1580s and after), this was rather a poor showing on the face of things; but it has been characteristic of the English ever since to produce a great many first-rate historical scholars and precious few distinguished philosophers of history. Ben Jonson, who was friendly with a number of historians, may have been close to the mark, in *The Devil is an Ass*, when he had his character Fitzdottrel say, with regard to history plays, that they had a more 'authentic' understanding of the past than the prosaic account in the chronicles (Kamps 1996: p. xiii; cf. Worden 1994).

This leads us to a second notable development: namely, the shift in attitude toward the intrusion of fiction in history or, rather, the beginnings of that intrusion as an intellectual problem for the English (Nelson 1973; Levine 1997; Collinson 1997). This was not, as we have already seen, a new battle, having been fought long ago when Thucydides first questioned the veracity of his own immediate predecessor, Herodotus. It has certainly been engaged periodically ever since – we are fighting it again at the end of the millennium, as deconstruction and postmodernism threaten to undermine the 'reality' of the past by turning everything into discourse, reducing all 'fact' to rhetorical and social construction. But for the English of the late sixteenth century there was something new about the subject, since they had not previously had much reason to beat the bounds between two pasts, the real and the imagined. Medieval writers of course recognized a distinction between *storia* and *fabula*, but had difficulty mapping it with any precision, and in any case were more interested in evaluating the truth of a particular event (including miracles attested by worthy and credible witnesses) than in generalizing on the subject.

Like the shifting border territory between England and Scotland prior to 1603, that between history and fiction was a negotiated, not a natural, frontier. It was neither fixed nor impermeable. The further back one looked from the Tudor era, the murkier the border became, and as a result it was always much easier to doubt the historicity of a particular person or event than it was to come up with a true account. The fates of Geoffrey of Monmouth's legendary kings offer a case in point. Geoffrey's fictions had enjoyed virtually canonical status in the late Middle Ages (though he was not without sceptical critics at the time), but a truculent sixteenth-century Italian named Polydore Vergil, whose *Anglica historia* was written under the aegis of Henry VIII and published abroad, had little time for them. Yet, if Vergil did not come to praise Geoffrey, neither could he really bury him. The Italian could show that no external evidence survived of a line of British kings going back to Brutus (certainly no such references occur in the earliest Roman accounts by Caesar and, slightly later, Tacitus), but he was unable to prove that such kings had not existed. His opponents included some of the leading scholars of the age, such as the antiquary, John Leland, and although, in the longer term, Leland was proved wrong and Vergil right, he was correct to observe that the absence of reference to something in documents does not mean it never occurred (Levy 1967: 131), and his use of philology to defend Geoffrey is in many ways more impressive than Vergil's dogmatic scepticism.

Vergil's doubting of some time-hallowed truths opened a Pandora's box of deeper scepticism as to whether anything told about the past could – or should – be believed. A brief but important Elizabethan expression of this can be found in Sir Philip Sidney's *Apologie for Poetrie*, first published in 1595. This of course is a tract about poetry, not history, but its author's grumbling at the uncertainty of knowledge of the past – built upon 'the notable foundations of hearsay – gave voice to what everyone was already feeling rather uncomfortably: that the grounds of much of what was believed to have actually happened in the past was less a bedrock of verifiable fact than a sticky quicksand of belief and half-truth, likely to suck down the unwary traveller. Better, said Sidney, consistent with the 'pyrrhonist' tradition of continental scepticism emerging at about this time, to admit that the past was simply unverifiable anyway, and that even if it were, what it taught was principally what had happened (or was supposed to have happened), not what should be. The poet, unfettered by ties to a dubious historical reality, was in a far better position to teach moral and political lessons than the historian, 'loaden with old mouse-eaten records'. In articulating this view, Sidney was, of course, merely echoing a position that goes back to Greek antiquity. The *locus classicus* for a privileging of poetry over history is Aristotle's *Poetics*. In that work, the philosopher remarks that the real difference between history and poetry is not that one is in prose and the other in verse, but that one tells what happened and the other what might happen – the latter being preferable if one is concerned with truth in its wider sense. "For this reason poetry is something more scientific and serious than history, because poetry tends to give general truths while history gives particular facts" (*Poetics*, ix. 1).

By Sidney's day history had become a much more significant genre than it had been in the fourth century BC, and his preference for poetic truth, now overlaid with scepticism regarding those particular facts whose truth even Aristotle had grudgingly conceded, was potentially rather scary to those who saw such assertions as threatening the veracity of the past. Yet, perhaps surprisingly (and in contrast with the post-modern preoccupations of the 1990s), at this time very few people concerned themselves with such matters. Most historians and antiquaries went about their business as they had done before. What Sidney raised as a theoretical concern about the value of what history had to teach was still of less interest than concrete assaults on particular facts – there is no series of polemics against Sidney in the way that there had been, slightly earlier, against Polydore Vergil. Some practising historians even took such scepticism in stride. Samuel Daniel and William Camden – the former in his *Collection*, the latter in his *Annales* of Queen Elizabeth's reign (Latin, 1615–25; trans. 1625) – used private correspondence and government documents to reveal the motives of human actions more clearly and to demonstrate that some things could indeed be shown to have happened, some personalities to have existed outside the medieval imagination. Others (Brutus the Trojan, Albion, Lear and their murky successors, for instance) were better simply ignored or omitted, rather than argued about, and in fact there was not much overt argument among Elizabethan and early Stuart historians in any case prior to the ideologically fractious 1640s. Sir Walter Ralegh, a product of the same anti-Spanish, Protestant court culture that had produced Sidney, had just as sceptical a turn of mind, and accordingly emphasized the moral, religious and judgmental aspects of history, while retreating to the infallibility of Scripture as a historical source. Ralegh's *History of the World*, written during his long imprisonment by James I, is a grim but entertaining account of human folly and of the ineluctable hand of providence, which at times in his account looks less like beneficent divine wisdom than capricious Machiavellian fortune (McCrea 1997: 40–70).

Some years before Sidney's *Apologie* or Blundeville's *True Order*, the single most widely read historian of the late sixteenth and seventeenth centuries, John Foxe, also played on the ambiguities of the past. He used reliable documents and reliable eyewitness accounts where he could find them, but imposed a good deal of invention and rhetorical elaboration, practised in his earlier career as a Latin dramatist, and now given focus by the necessity of creating a Protestant martyrology (and parallel popish demonology) for the Reformed Church. Foxe's *Actes and Monuments of these Latter and Perilous Days*, the authoritative (and officially sanctioned) record of the survival of the Protestant Church and true religion through centuries of persecution culminating in the reign of Mary Tudor, had such longevity not only because of its semi-official status and its ubiquity in ecclesiastical and private libraries, but because it was well written and entertaining, its text accompanied by vivid if stereotypical woodcuts and engravings of martyrs going cheerfully to the stake or being examined, tortured and incinerated by sinister-looking English lackeys of Rome (Watt 1991; King 1989; Collinson 1997). As an aside, it should be mentioned that Foxe's book completed the sixteenth century's rehabilitation of King John, vilified in most medieval, clerically authored chronicles, and first restored to favour by John Bale's interlude, *King Johan* (Levin 1988: 85–92). Foxe turned John into one of many royal defenders of royal supremacy against popish incursions; it was left to Shakespeare, using these materials, to synthesize the good and evil King Johns, resistor of Rome but also murderer of his nephew, in his own play on the subject.

The Waning of the Chronicle

Mention of history plays brings us back to their immediate precursor, the chronicle, which by the middle years of Elizabeth I's reign was still the major vehicle for the written representation of secular history. The ancients had told their own history and were in no need of rewriting; their historical characters and episodes, because a common currency of Renaissance learned culture, were in any case transferred from text to text piecemeal, for purposes of exemplarity (Hampton 1990). So far as the history of England was concerned, no one save Vergil and to a lesser extent Hall, both of whom had used reigns as the basic units of narrative (in Hall's case superimposed on annals), had yet thought of writing a connected narrative history organized in chapters rather than by discrete years. Nor had more than a handful of authors like Sir Thomas More yet seen that biography (or 'lives', to give it its proper Renaissance appellation) could be put to use in depicting individual reigns in greater detail than was permitted by surveys (Anderson 1984; Conrad 1995). Thus the chronicle continued to rule by default, for the time being. Richard Grafton could conclude his *Chronicle at Large* in 1569 with an apology for his 'rude and unlearned woorke, not worthye the name of a Chronicle'. The word 'chronicle' itself remained in common parlance as a useful generic term for any historical writing, long after the writing of genuine chronicles had ceased. It was possible to use the word in such a way without pejorative associations – for example, as the physical embodiment of the collective human memory.

> Let me embrace thee, good old chronicle,
> That hast so long walk'd hand in hand with time.

Thus Hector greets the venerable Nestor in *Troilus and Cressida* (IV. v. 202). Among the men met by a speaker in an anonymous Jacobean dialogue is one 'so old that I should have had a Chronicle, to answer him'.

Recommendations on chronicle reading are frequent during the second half of the sixteenth century. The clergyman William Harrison praised the 'antient ladies' of Elizabeth's court who avoided idleness 'in continual reading either of the Holy

Scriptures or histories', and the Puritan Lady Grace Mildmay similarly urged 'under-standing and knowledge of the chronicles of the land' on young women as an exemplary encouragement to obedience (Woolf 1997a). At its peak in the later sixteenth century, the chronicle's popularity extended down to the lower levels of the literate. The Devon yeoman Robert Furse, in his family record book, advised his children to read and hear Scripture, be familiar with the laws of the realm, and to 'rede the old crownekeles and shuch like awnshyente hystoryes' (Woolf 1997b: 114).

By the end of the century, however, comments on the insufficiency of the chron-icles, the disparateness of their contents, or their lack of a good Latin style were becoming modish, particularly among those who believed that they themselves could write with greater eloquence or erudition. Polydore Vergil, unfortunately, was no help as a model, since through most of the second half of the sixteenth century and into the seventeenth he was a subject of derision. Bishop Francis Godwin proclaimed in 1616 the obsolescence of Vergil's *Anglica historia* and the urgent need (all the more so in a united 'Great Britain') for a new national history, a desire he shared with Bacon, his more distinguished contemporary. This call would go out several more times during the next century or so. More immediately dangerous objections to the chronicle as a form of historical writing would come from other quarters, in particular from humanist-trained Elizabethan and Jacobean historical writers, beginning with Sir Henry Savile's famous denunciation of medieval historiography in an edition of medieval chronicles (1596) and in his fervent praise of the ancients, especially Tacitus, whose *Histories* Savile translated in 1591, virtually inaugurating the English chapter of the late Renaissance fashion for 'Tacitism' (Burke 1969; Bradford 1983; Smuts 1994).

The insufficiency of the Elizabethan chronicles offered one of the very few issues on which the classically minded Gabriel Harvey found himself in agreement with his arch-enemy Thomas Nashe. Annotating his copy of Livy in or about 1590, Harvey wondered whether a British Livy, Tacitus or Frontinus would emerge, while com-plaining of the 'many asses who dare to compile histories, chronicles, annals, com-mentaries'. These include 'Grafton, Stow, Holinshed, and a few others like them who are not cognizant of law or politics, nor of the art of depicting character, nor are they in any way learned'. The minor verse historian Charles Aleyn, perhaps conscious of the weakness of his own claim to historical veracity, dismissed the chronicle accounts of Henry VII's defeat of the earl of Lincoln's rising as a superficial list of events:

> Chronicles doe it so lamely tell
> As if twere sayd, they came, they fought, they fell.

Most of all, it was easy to poke fun at the reliability of the chronicler by exposing the very disagreement of the sources on which he based his account and his failure to reconcile them – one of Sidney's major points, it will be recalled. The learned Lord Chancellor Ellesmere refused to cite evidence from Richard II's reign during the debate on the case of the post-nati in 1608, because 'some of our chroniclers doe talke idely [of it] and understand little'. And in Jonson's masque *News from the New World Discovered in the Moon* (1621) a chronicler despairs of being able to write the truth. 'I have been so cheated with false relations in my time, as I have found it a harder thing to correct my book than to collect it' (Woolf 1988b).

The genre that appealed to perhaps the broadest cross-section of Elizabethan and Jacobean society, though one primarily restricted to London, was the history play, which owed this social inclusivity both to an already existing late medieval tradition of popular drama and to its extremely close reliance on the Tudor chronicles for source material. Responsive both to late Tudor nationalism and to the sixteenth-century demand for visual spectacle, the plays took events out of the folio pages of the great chronicles of Grafton, Hall and Holinshed and from less voluminous works like Stow's *Summaries* and *Annales*, and literally brought them to life.

It is impossible to estimate precisely how much larger was the audience for plays than the readership of printed chronicles, but the effect of the chronicle play was probably analogous to that of the film or television dramatization today (hundreds may have seen Kenneth Branagh's *Henry V* or Ian McKellen's *Richard III* who have never read a word of Shakespeare). The performance of plays generally preceded their printing, but it is the printed versions that outlived the moment, to be read and re-performed in ensuing years. If the proportion of spectators who were sufficiently inspired by a performance to read the text in print was small, then the number who went further afield to read the chronicle sources must have been smaller still. The chronicle plays devoted to English history in particular enjoyed a relatively brief vogue between the 1560s and 1620s, their popularity falling off after that, though the explanation for this decline remains unclear (Kamps 1996). They would enjoy new life but a more socially exclusive audience in the second half of the seventeenth century, in the Restoration dramas of Orrery, Crowne, Tate and others. In the meantime they had introduced the contents of their sources, the chronicles themselves, to many more people than had ever before been exposed to history. They also provided new ways in which the past could be used to make critical comments about the present. According to recent literary scholars such as Phyllis Rackin, the plays permitted a kind of 'polyvocality', an opening to questioning of received wisdom and a doubting of orthodoxy not available to the author of single-voiced narrative histories (Rackin 1990; but cf. Patterson 1994: 279n). The price may have been to render the chronicles themselves less compelling, given that there were now other places to which the interested playgoer could turn, namely the 'politic history'.

The relation of the chronicles to these newer histories of the late Elizabethan and early Stuart period is somewhat different from the relation of either to the history plays. Stylistically, the prose histories departed from the chronicles much more self-consciously than did the plays (which as drama, rather than prose, were not in direct competition), asserting a pedigree from ancient historiography in which certain authors, Livy, Polybius, Sallust and especially Tacitus, figured as paragons of narrative eloquence, critical judgment and political acumen. Moreover, because the new histories existed publicly only in print, they reached a much more select audience, primarily of educated or at least relatively well-off gentry and aristocracy. In that very social exclusivity lay some of their appeal, that they contained worthwhile knowledge, told in an edifying and graceful prose better suited to the 'compleat gentleman' who was also frequently a courtier and politician. Whether Shakespeare wrote for the masses or reflected a 'popular voice' is a question that need not concern us here; it is pretty certain that John Hayward (on Henry IV, Williams I, II and III and Edward VI), Francis Godwin (on Henry VIII, Edward VI and Mary) and Francis Bacon (on Henry VII), on their own admission, did not. Moreover, these 'politic historians' were active just at the beginning of a period when genuinely popular beliefs about the past, often conveyed exclusively in unverifiable oral traditions, were beginning to be discounted by scholars as much for social as intellectual reasons. Drawing their inspiration from Tacitus, Bodin and Machiavelli, among others, Hayward, Bacon and their fellows mined from the chronicles the ore which they refined in their own works. They aspired to create unified, vivid characters out of the chroniclers' stylized descriptions and lists of names, to distil moral and political wisdom from the events that the chroniclers merely recorded, and to entertain the élite reader. They rarely contributed anything like a new interpretation of events, though they often corrected the chroniclers on points of detail or attempted to resolve contradictory reports. Rather, they translated the clipped, rough annals of the past into humanist Latin (in Godwin's case) or vigorous, readable English, sewing their fragmentary sources together into what one of their number, John Clapham, called a 'continued historie' and what Bacon designated as 'perfect history'. Only Camden, writing about very recent events in his *Annales*, saw the need to go beyond the chronicles themselves to base his account largely on original evidence in state papers, to which he was granted access by the Crown.

By 1632, the date of the last revision of Stow's *Annales*, the chronicle was a dead genre, though private individuals and corporations continued to keep chronologies and urban annals for some time to come. The sole example of a chronicle enjoying repeated republication in the later seventeenth century was that by Sir Richard Baker (1568–1645), which first appeared in 1643. It had the merit of both conciseness and comprehensiveness, furnishing Restoration readers with a digest of English history from remote times to the present (it was continuously updated as Stow had been, and went through a number of editions up to and after 1700). But it was already a throwback when first compiled, the pastime of an imprisoned and aged debtor who himself had grown up reading the likes of Holinshed and Stow. It was rather a whimpering exit for the genre that had spawned, among other things, Shakespeare's tetralogies.

The Reading of History

No account of the status of history in the age of Shakespeare would be complete without some attention to the 'end user' of history books (including plays), the reader, who seems to have been rather untroubled by the changing shape of the packages that the past came wrapped in. The evidence for reading practices, a matter explored more fully by Dr Brayman Hackel in chapter 9, is both more plentiful than that for writing and also more complex and of greater ambiguity, since the purposes of history reading could vary considerably, even for the same person at different times (Jardine and Grafton 1990). The same book could be a source of entertainment one day, of information the next, and of moral inspiration the day after. The places in which notes on reading were kept also vary considerably. Joseph Bufton, a Coggeshall, Essex, weaver of the mid-seventeenth century, took notes on historical and biographical works, together with his notes of funeral sermons, in ephemeral books ranging from his *British Merlin* and Goldsmith's *Almanack* to a copy of *The Compleat Tradesman*. Others used commonplace books to order their reading from various titles across many genres into usable topics, further reinforcing the analogizing tendencies noted above. Readers were not especially squeamish about cutting up their books in order to rearrange them for readier access. In an age before photocopying and with only rudimentary indexing, this was less sin than necessity, though it is still surprising how often expensive books, such as Camden's *Britannia*, fell victim to the knife, and not merely more disposable ephemera and octavos: one anonymous seventeenth-century collector cut out the entire section on Devon in the 1610 English edition of Camden, presumably to join it to other materials on that county. Any student of Tudor and Stuart antiquarianism will be familiar with the vast collections of transcripts from central and local documents that can be found not only in the archives of published historians like Foxe and Stow but also in the state papers of officers of the realm and scattered about the kingdom in family muniments, where they not infrequently offered a support for land claims or genealogical pretensions.

Diaries and journals are also useful, in a different way, because of what they reveal about the diarist's reading habits, his or her reactions to particular works, and, by the placing of remarks, the early modern thought processes that lead the pen sideways from one subject to the next. The Londoner Richard Stonley, a minor Elizabethan official, kept a diary (now in the Folger Shakespeare Library) that survives for three short periods in the 1580s and 1590s. This gives some indication as to his reading habits: for instance, 'This day after morning prayer I kept home at my books with thanks to God at nyght.' Although Stonley, in contrast to some later diarists, is unhelpful as to specific titles read, biblical stories featured prominently. A rhymed extract from the scriptural 'history' of Judith and Holofernes heads his daily entries at one point, and figures from ancient history with biblical associations, such as Artaxerxes, also intrude, the same sort of episodes commonly depicted in the tapestries and wall hangings then decorating many noble and gentry houses.

The variety of contexts of history reading (and perhaps of reading in general) can be illustrated at length from the miscellaneous notebooks (also at the Folger) of John Ward (c.1629–81), amateur physician and, from 1661 to his death, vicar of Stratford-upon-Avon – a suitably Shakespearian location at which to conclude this overview.

These contain, amid proverbs, recipes, medical notes and astrological comments, abundant references to historical episodes about which he had read, episodes which took his pen in surprising directions.

History, thought Ward, 'delivers to posterity an inventory of men's virtues', and throughout his volumes are scattered the traditional humanist injunctions about the gravity and seriousness of history, the need for truthfulness and the historian's duty to impartiality. He repeats familiar pieties about the limits of historical knowledge and the distinction between the fictions of poets and the verities recorded by historians. Ward trumpeted his faith in the existence of certain indisputable, irreducible historical facts and a limited form of scepticism.

> Believing is but opinion, if the evidence bee but probable, but if itt bee such that cannot be questioned, then 'tis as certaine as knowledge; for wee are no less certaine that there is a great towne called Constantinople, than that there is one called London; wee as little doubt that Queen Elizabeth once reigned, as that King Charles now reigns.

But his practice in extracting materials from history was quite at odds with such dicta and with the *gravitas* of humanist political historiography in general. Ward regularly blended the serious with the trivial, and conflated written sources with 'facts' he had heard casually in conversation. In other words, while he chanted the Ciceronian conventions of history's truth and dignity, picked up from the prefaces to the books he had read, Ward's usable past was much less orderly and homogeneous. It embraced biblical, classical, medieval and modern history, the low and humorous as well as the high matters of state and war to which historians were supposed to confine themselves. A series of extracts from a set of books on a particular subject typically includes Ward's efforts to digest his reading into at least one concise table or summary: several pages concerning ancient and biblical history, for instance, include a catalogue of all the kings of the twelve tribes of Israel as listed in the Bible, as if to save him the trouble of having to keep the other books close at hand.

Yet if Ward's reading was not tightly structured or devoted to a particular end, neither was it frivolous or chaotic. Present concerns, the matter of daily life, naturally weighed into his decision to pause over a particular passage in his reading. As a physician, he read his histories with an eye to past cases of disease, leading at one point to a discussion of the leprosy of 'Hugh de Orwal', William the Conqueror's archbishop of Canterbury. The parochial cleric's concern with monetary inflation arises from a casual remark in one of his books: 'Godwin of Bishops: p: 234: there says that 5 shillings hath now scarce so much silver in it, as 5 groates had formerly; no wonder then if things have treble the prices they were 300 years agoe.' A similar preoccupation inspired him to 'Remember most strictly to inquire how it came about that so much church land was alienated in the days of Edward the 6th and Queen Elizabeth'. Most of these plans for further research, urgent-sounding as they are, were stillborn, since they do not appear to have been pursued elsewhere in the notebooks.

Remember to search out the extent of the jurisdiction of our peculiar at Strat[ford] and that out of the auncient grant in K. Edward the 6ths time. Routing up the papers in the chamber and likewise searching in the Roles for the original graunt for it is graunted to us as the colledges had it, but the maine question is how it was graunted us the colledge at first, and whether it may not bee probable that it is wholy exempt even from the Bishop himself.

Ward's paging through Foxe's *Actes and Monuments* (still the most widely read of histories through the eight decades following its author's death) is certainly evident in at least one patch of several consecutive readings. During this period, he rifled through the 'Book of Martyrs' for material on English secular as well as religious history. In this case, Ward uncharacteristically read Foxe's work in chronological order. Blips of episodes from Foxe, and Foxe's sources, are sprinkled about, beginning with the heading 'ex lib: martyr: begins with the apostolic martyrs; 6–8 list of the successive persecutions'. Foxe's own comparison of himself with Livy is repeated in Ward's notes, and Ward largely adopts Foxe's periodization of church history into ages or periods in organizing his remarks. Arrival at the part of his text dealing with William the Conqueror creates a space in the notebook for a host of related facts peripherally connected with that king: 'King William the Conqueror died about the same time as did pope Hildebrand or Gregory the 7th the great sorceror. It is reported of William the Conqueror that he left but one bishop that was in before the land and that was Wolstan bishop of Worcester.' His shadowing of the text in his recording of it includes not only the chronology, but Foxe's own comparisons, for instance the martyrologist's use of the quasi-miraculous survival of Zwingli's heart after his body had been burnt to foreshadow the similar occurrence in the case of Archbishop Cranmer: 'Zwinglius slain amongst his citizens the Zuirickmen the enemies burn his bodie: his friends came the next day to see whether any part of him was remaining, where they found his heart in the ashes whole and unburnt, as is allso credibly reported of the heart of Cranmer.' Even the banderoles on Foxe's woodcuts, with their terse, godly declarations uttered amid the flames, were transferred holus-bolus into Ward's notes: 'Mr Rogers the 1st martyr in queen maries days.... Mr Saunders took up the stake and kissd it saying welcome the cross of X: welcome everlasting life.' And where Foxe resorts to dramatic dialogues in representing scenes between persecutors and martyrs, Ward follows suit. The notes on Foxe end abruptly, as Ward slides into a series of remarks on Roman history from a variety of authors: 'Nero never gave more than an hour for one to prepare for his mortal blow.'

The apparent randomness of all this is more easily explained if one grants a playful dimension to literacy and acknowledges that much early modern reading was browsing of a much less systematic sort than is practised now. If we accept that not everyone read in the highly structured, purposeful way that a paid professional like Gabriel Harvey or John Dee did (Sherman 1995), then a joke about the past like 'Gustavus and Augustus, are the same names only with a transposition of letters' begins to make sense, juxtaposed with serious discussions of war and policy. History, it seems, could free the mind to wander as much as fixing it upon important tasks; and the factual past, as much as the fictions and romances increasingly decried by moralists as frivolous time-wasters, could transport the reader of Foxe, Livy or Froissart into an imaginative landscape in which his or her mind could stroll about at random. This sort of literary consumption (sometimes called 'extensive' as opposed to the 'intensive' approach exemplified by a Harvey or a Dee) would increasingly be a mark of the readership of history, of both sexes, from the 1640s onward, a minority of scholars excepted. The greatest works of later seventeenth-century historiography, such as the earl of Clarendon's *History of the Rebellion* (first published 1702–4), were successful not merely because they dealt with great matters of state and successfully imitated Thucydides, but because they were also rhetorical masterpieces that kept the reader interested. By this time, too, the more traditional Renaissance manner of lifting episodes from their contexts for serious didactic purpose, in the manner of Machiavelli, is being challenged by a more holistic, leisurely experience of the historical text, in which entertainment, as much as utility or morality, can be found at the fingertips, whether that amusement lies in the joy of detailed information of the sort still to be gleaned from casual inspection of dusty copies of Holinshed and Stow or in the tautness of a gripping narrative enlivened by biographical vignettes, as in Clarendon (Hicks 1996). The pleasures of the past had been reconciled to its virtues.

REFERENCES

Anderson, Judith H. 1984: *Biographical Truth: The Representation of Historical Persons in Tudor–Stuart Writing*. New Haven: Yale University Press.

Berkowitz, David S. 1988: *John Selden's Formative Years: Politics and Society in Early Seventeenth-century England*. Washington, D.C.: Folger Shakespeare Library.

Bradford, Alan T. 1983: Stuart absolutism and the 'utility' of Tacitus. *Huntington Library Quarterly*, 46, 127–55.

Burgess, Glenn 1992: *The Politics of the Ancient Constitution: An Introduction to English Political Thought, 1603–1642*. Basingstoke: Macmillan.

Burke, Peter 1969: Tacitism. In T. A. Dorey (ed.), *Tacitus*, London: Routledge and Kegan Paul, 149–71.

Bushnell, Rebecca 1997: Experience, truth, and natural history in early English gardening books. In Donald R. Kelley and David Harris Sacks (eds), *The Historical Imagination in Early Modern Britain: History, Rhetoric, and Fiction, 1500–1800*. Cambridge: Cambridge University Press for the Woodrow Wilson Center, 179–209.

Christianson, Paul 1996: *Discourse on History, Law and Governance in the Public Career of John Selden, 1610–1635*. Toronto: University of Toronto Press.

Clark, Stuart 1974: Bacon's *Henry VII*: a case-study in the science of man. *History and Theory*, 13, 97–118.

Cochrane, Eric 1981: *Historians and Historiography in the Italian Renaissance*. Chicago: University of Chicago Press.

Collinson, Patrick 1997: Truth, lies, and fiction in sixteenth-century Protestant historiography. In Donald R. Kelley and David Harris Sacks (eds), *The Historical Imagination in Early Modern Britain: History, Rhetoric, and Fiction, 1500–1800*, Cambridge: Cambridge University Press for the Woodrow Wilson Center, 37–68.

Conrad, F. W. 1995: Manipulating reputations: Sir Thomas More, Sir Thomas Elyot, and the conclusion of William Roper's *Life of Sir Thomas Moore, Knighte*. In T. F. Mayer and D. R. Woolf (eds), *Rhetorics of Life-Writing in Early Modern Europe: Forms of Biography from Cassandra Fedele to Louis XIV*, Ann Arbor, Mich.: University of Michigan Press, 133–61.

Cressy, David 1989: *Bonfires and Bells: National Memory and the Protestant Calendar in Elizabethan and Stuart England*. London: Weidenfeld and Nicolson.

Dowling, Margaret 1930–1: Sir John Hayward's troubles over his life of Henry IV. *Library*, 4th ser., 11, 212–24.

Ferguson, Arthur B. 1971: The historical thought of Samuel Daniel: a study in Renaissance ambivalence. *Journal of the History of Ideas*, 32, 185–202.

—— 1979: *Clio Unbound: Perception of the Social and Cultural Past in Renaissance England*. Durham, NC: Duke University Press.

—— 1993: *Utter Antiquity: Perceptions of Prehistory in Renaissance England*. Durham, NC: Duke University Press.

Fussner, F. S. 1962: *The Historical Revolution: English Historical Writing and Thought, 1580–1640*. London: Routledge and Kegan Paul.

Gransden, Antonia 1982: *Historical Writing in England*, vol. 2. Ithaca, NY: Cornell University Press.

Hampton, Timothy 1990: *Writing from History: the Rhetoric of Exemplarity in Renaissance Literature*. Ithaca, NY: Cornell University Press.

Hay, Denys 1951: The historiographers royal in England and Scotland. *Scottish Historical Review*, 30, 15–29.

Helgerson, Richard 1997: Murder in Faversham: Holinshed's impertinent history. In Donald R. Kelley and David Harris Sacks (eds), *The Historical Imagination in Early Modern Britain: History, Rhetoric, and Fiction, 1500–1800*, Cambridge: Cambridge University Press for the Woodrow Wilson Center, 133–58.

Hicks, Philip 1996: *Neoclassical History and English Culture: from Clarendon to Hume*. London: Macmillan.

Hutton, Ronald 1994: *The Rise and Fall of Merry England: the Ritual Year, 1400–1700*. Oxford: Oxford University Press.

Ianziti, Gary 1988: *Humanistic Historiography under the Sforzas: Politics and Propaganda in Fifteenth-century Milan*. Oxford: Clarendon Press.

Jardine, Lisa and Grafton, Anthony 1990: 'Studied for action': how Gabriel Harvey read his Livy. *Past and Present*, 129, 30–78.

Kamps, Ivo 1996: *History and Ideology in Early Stuart Drama*. Cambridge: Cambridge University Press.

Kelley, Donald R. 1988: The theory of history. In Charles B. Schmitt and Quentin Skinner (eds), *The Cambridge History of Renaissance Philosophy*, Cambridge: Cambridge University Press, 746–61.

Kendrick, T. D. 1950: *British Antiquity*. London: Methuen.

King, John N. 1989: *Tudor Royal Iconography: Literature and Art in an Age of Religious Crisis*. Princeton: Princeton University Press.

Kingsford, Charles Lethbridge 1913: *English Historical Literature in the Fifteenth Century*. Oxford: Clarendon Press.

Levin, Carol 1988: *Propaganda in the English Reformation: Heroic and Villainous Images of King John*. Lewiston, NY: Edwin Mellen Press.

Levine, Joseph M. 1987: *Humanism and History*. Ithaca, NY: Cornell University Press.

—— 1997: Thomas More and the English Renaissance: history and fiction in *Utopia*. In Donald R. Kelley and David Harris Sacks (eds), *The Historical Imagination in Early Modern Britain: History, Rhetoric, and Fiction, 1500–1800*, Cambridge: Cambridge University Press for the Woodrow Wilson Center, 69–92.

Levy, F. J. 1967: *Tudor Historical Thought*. San Marino, Calif.: Huntington Library.

—— 1987: Hayward, Daniel, and the beginnings of politic history in England. *Huntington Library Quarterly*, 50, 1–34.

Manning, John J. 1991: Introduction to *The First Part of the Life and Raigne of King Henrie the IIII*. London: Royal Historical Society.

McCrea, Adriana A. N. 1997: *Constant Minds: Political Virtue and the Lipsian Paradigm in England, 1584–1650*. Toronto: University of Toronto Press.

McKisack, May 1971: *Medieval Historians and the Tudor Age*. Oxford: Clarendon Press.

Mendyk, Stanley 1989: *'Speculum Britanniae': Regional Study, Antiquarianism, and Science in Britain to 1700*. Toronto: University of Toronto Press.

Nelson, William 1973: *Fact or Fiction: The Dilemma of the Renaissance Storyteller*. Cambridge, Mass.: Harvard University Press.

Parry, Graham 1995: *The Trophies of Time: English Antiquariaus of the Seventeenth Century*. Oxford and New York: Oxford University Press.

Patterson, Annabel 1994: *Reading Holinshed's Chronicles*. Chicago: University of Chicago Press.

Piggott, Stuart 1989: *Ancient Britons and the Antiquarian Imagination: Ideas from the Renaissance to the Regency*. London: Thames and Hudson.

Pocock, J. G. A. 1997: *The Ancient Constitution and the Feudal Law: A Study of English Historical Thought in the Seventeenth Century: A Reissue with a Retrospect*. Cambridge: Cambridge University Press.

Preston, Joseph H. 1977: Was there an historical revolution? *Journal of the History of Ideas*, 38, 353–64.

Rackin, Phyllis 1990: *Stages of History: Shakespeare's English Chronicles*. Ithaca, NY: Cornell University Press.

Salmon, J. H. M. 1997: Precept, example, and truth: Degory Wheare and the *ars historica*. In Donald R. Kelley and David Harris Sacks (eds), *The Historical Imagination in Early Modern Britain: History, Rhetoric, and Fiction, 1500–1800*, Cambridge: Cambridge University Press for the Woodrow Wilson Center, 11–36.

Sherman, William H. 1995: *John Dee: The Politics of Reading and Writing in the English Renaissance*. Amherst: University of Massachusetts Press.

Smuts, R. Malcolm 1994: Court-centered politics and the use of Roman historians, *c.*1590–1630. In Kevin Sharpe and Peter Lake (eds), *Culture and Politics in Early Stuart England*, London: Macmillan, 21–45.

Thomas, Keith 1983: *The Perception of the Past in Early Modern England*. London: Creighton Trust Lecture.

Watt, Tessa 1991: *Cheap Print and Popular Piety, 1550–1640*. Cambridge: Cambridge University Press.

Woolf, D.R. 1988a: The 'common voice': history, folklore, and oral tradition in early modern England. *Past and Present*, 120, 26–52.

——1988b: Genre into artifact: the decline of the English chronicle in the sixteenth century. *Sixteenth Century Journal*, 19, 321–54.

——1990: *The Idea of History in Early Stuart England: Erudition, Ideology and the 'Light of Truth' from the Accession of James I to the Civil War*. Toronto: University of Toronto Press.

——1997a: A feminine past? Gender, genre, and historical knowledge in England, 1500–1800. *American Historical Review*, 102, 645–79.

——1997b: Little Crosby and the horizons of early modern historical culture. In Donald R. Kelley and David Harris Sacks (eds), *The Historical Imagination in Early Modern Britain: History, Rhetoric, and Fiction, 1500–1800*. Cambridge: Cambridge University Press for the Woodrow Wilson Center, 93–132.

Worden, Blair 1994: Ben Jonson among the historians. In Kevin Sharpe and Peter Lake (eds), *Culture and Politics in Early Stuart England*, London: Macmillan, 67–89.

Wormald, B. H. G. 1993: *Francis Bacon: History, Politics and Science, 1561–1626*. Cambridge: Cambridge University Press.

Zimmermann, T. C. Price 1995: *Paolo Giovio: The Historian and the Crisis of Sixteenth-century Italy*. Princeton: Princeton University Press.

13

Reading Vernacular Literature

Diana E. Henderson and James Siemon

I may boldely say it because I have seene it, that the Palace of Pleasure, the Golden Asse, the Ethiopian historie, Amadis of Fraunce, the Rounde table, baudie Comedies in Latin, French, Italian, and Spanish, have been throughly ransackt to furnish the Playe houses in London.
(Stephen Gosson, *Plays Confuted*)

Discussion of Shakespeare's relation to vernacular literature has focused predominantly on source study, especially his reinterpretation of particular narratives and phrases. Bullough (1957) and Muir (1978) have surveyed these debts, and others have investigated specific "high literary" cases, such as the relationship between Shakespeare and Chaucer (cf. Thompson 1978; Donaldson 1985). Much has thus been learned about the playwright's craft and suggested about Elizabethan audience reception, and much remains to be investigated. Here, however, we suggest other ways of situating Shakespeare's works.

One motivation for such inquiry arises from Shakespeare's practice of reading widely and combining scraps from many sources. Even when he worked predominantly from one text, such as Arthur Brooke's *Romeus and Juliet* (1562), that text was itself usually an adaptation and/or combination (in this case, from Boiastuau's French translation of Bandello's Italian tale, which drew on still earlier accounts). Specific, singular origins for Shakespeare's works are hard to find. Authorship meant something different in his time, allowing more fluid boundaries between writers' works – especially for those such as Shakespeare who wrote for the most collaborative of artistic venues, the theater. Written before the age of copyright and the individualist ideology of the solitary genius, Shakespeare's plays participate in what Greenblatt calls the "circulation of social energy," partly by recirculating specific genres and discourses current in the literature of his day. Limiting discussion to ascertainable cases of Shakespeare's borrowing often leads to an understanding of particular trees but not the literary forest, the larger generic shapes and recurrent topics found in text after text that the playwright surveyed. Thus we emphasize the kinds of literature when Shakespeare wrote; these genres would have shaped early modern assumptions about how narratives work and what they represent.

Moreover, we emphasize connections, rather than differences, between Shakespeare's writing and the literary landscape of his day. Even scholars such as Russ McDonald who agree that we should "expand our definition of *source*," continue to praise Shakespeare for exceptional artistry, "his unparalleled capacity for adapting, combining, and transmuting what he read" (1996: 101–2). While acknowledging the "outrageous and crude offerings of popular literature," McDonald sustains a dichotomy between such forms and "more elusive, less popular writing" such as Montaigne's, which provided Shakespeare "not stories or characters but ideas and philosophical viewpoints" (p. 111). These assumptions limit the kinds of texts we read carefully for ideas and value the playwright's innovations, his differences from other writing. But the boundaries between genres at the time were in flux, new forms colliding with old to challenge any easy categorization of "high" or "popular" culture; the downmarket possibilities of cheap print and the aspirations of non-aristocratic writers prompted debate over the values and morality of various kinds of vernacular writing. Within this contentious landscape, Shakespeare's plays exemplify the mingled modes and conflicting claims to authority characteristic of his era.

Recently, historicist scholarship interested in reading Shakespeare within his discursive and political contexts has challenged the boundaries of what counts as literature. "Vernacular" quite literally means popular, the native or indigenous language of the country, as opposed to scholarly or Church Latin. In the vernacular, one might read everything from self-consciously literary works such as Spenser's *Faerie Queene* to jestbooks and almanacs, texts making very different claims of authority and usefulness.

Although New Historicist accounts find specific connections between Shakespeare's plays and contemporary vernacular texts, such as ballads, anatomies, and court proceedings, they often resemble traditional source study in making Shakespeare's writing appear more subtle or rich than these other kinds of writing, though the difference is now measured in terms of ideology rather than aesthetics. For example, "The merry jest of a shrewd and curst wife lapped in Morel's skin, for her good behavior," a ballad frequently juxtaposed with *The Taming of the Shrew*, so enjoys the physical violence of wife-beating that it makes Shakespeare's play look sophisticated by comparison. Furthermore, the concentration on particular instances for comparison – such as this ballad with *Shrew*, Simon Forman's dream with *A Midsummer Night's Dream*, or Samuel Harsnett's *Discoverie of Witchcraft* with *Lear* – tends to keep the focus of inquiry narrow, detailing two treatments of a particular cultural problem. Reiterated reference to one or two outside texts per play not only increases the potential for arbitrariness in their selection but may also ossify what one thinks of as "the" cultural context. Examining the genres most widely read during Shakespeare's lifetime and considering their cultural functions relocates his work within wider contexts of vernacular literature.

What were the sixteenth-century bestsellers, and who read them? While lack of documentation makes these questions difficult to answer precisely, we do know some of the most popular works from printing records and widespread citation (see Febvre and Martin 1976; Esdaile 1912; O'Dell 1954; Watt 1991; Charlton 1987). They include religious tracts, including sermons, psalters, and pamphlets; almanacs and agricultural manuals (some, such as Thomas Tusser's, in verse); ballads; jestbooks; books combining mottoes and verse, such as Alciati's *Emblems* (1531); neo-chivalric romances; poetry-and-prose miscellanies such as George Pettie's *Petite Palace of Pettie his Pleasure*; prose fictions by Lyly, Lodge, and Greene; Richard Johnson's hybrid romance fictions; Dekker's pamphlets; Elyot's *The Boke Named the Governour*, Hoby's translation of Castiglione's *The Courtier*, and other "self-help" books for would-be gentlemen and ladies; and travel narratives such as the late-medieval *Voyages and Travels of Sir John Mandeville*. These works exhibit a great range of form and subject matter and also suggest the sixteenth-century expansion of a reading public to include not only lawyers, clergy, and aristocracy but also apprentices and merchants, and increasing numbers of yeoman and women (see Cressy 1980; Spufford 1982; Febvre and Martin 1976; Thomas 1986).

Perhaps consequently, this was also a time of linguistic play and social polyphony; writers repeatedly celebrate or decry the "gallimaufrey" of styles, the mixed genres, and polyglot character of contemporary writing. Without doubt, the expansion of vernacular writing and printing produced interest in the English language and injected new energy into its use (see Thomas 1986). Nowhere is this more evident than in John Lyly's widely imitated *Euphues: An Anatomy of Wit*, or its picaresque cousin, Thomas Nashe's *Unfortunate Traveller. Euphues* (published in 1578 and, indicating its remarkable popularity, again in 1579, 1580, 1581, 1585, 1587, 1590, 1592, 1595, 1606, and 1607) is usually cited for overusing antitheses and analogies to unnatural natural history, which Shakespeare is deemed to have transformed to better ends. But these rhetorical ticks signal a general enthusiasm for the play of words and ideas, a love of wit that *Euphues'* narrator concedes has sometimes superseded love of wisdom. Moreover, as Lyly elsewhere remarks, he writes in a time of change and innovation: "Traffic and travel hath woven the nature of all nations into ours, and made this land like arras, full of device, which was broadcloth, full of workmanship"; given this change, "If we present a mingle-mangle, our fault is to be excused, because the whole world is become a hodgepodge" (preface to *Midas*). Viewing *Euphues* as a set of static debates over the relative importance of love and friendship or shadow and substance (to cite two topics Shakespeare adapts in *Two Gentlemen of Verona* and *Richard II*) belies its dynamic qualities, both in its narrative and in its set-pieces. As its Greek hero is outwitted by a fickle Neopolitan mistress, *Euphues* transforms familiar *topoi* into an erotic contest between amorous disputants years before Beatrice meets Benedick in *Much Ado About Nothing*. Similarly, though with a far less courtly attitude, Nashe's *Unfortunate Traveller* presents its roguish hero as a savorer of words as well as pranks and exploits a wide range of the most popular genres within its roving narrative (prefiguring the mixture of genres and the foolery that Shakespeare dramatizes in *Henry IV*).

Lyly and Nashe owe a debt to George Gascoigne's *The Adventures of Master F.J.*, an adulterous fiction containing love sonnets which was included in his substantial poetic collection *A Hundreth Sundrie Flowres* (1573), soon repackaged as *The Posies* (1575). Adapting a form as old as Dante's *La Vita Nuova* but radically deflating its philosophical claims for love, Gascoigne's mingling of new and old, cynicism and sonneteering, provided an important precedent for the next generation of English writers. Whereas we tend to divide poets from prose-writers, the Elizabethans usually wrote in both forms or even combined them; surrounding prose narratives often framed courtly love poems in such a way as to mock their elevation of ladylove or to reveal the self-interested motives of the poet himself. These works in turn provided a model for Shakespeare's would-be courtier poets in *Two Gentlemen of Verona, Love's Labor's Lost, Romeo and Juliet*, and *As You Like It*.

Shakespeare's staging of sonnets and sonneteers also owes a debt to the most venerated Elizabethan courtly sonneteer and an equally important authorial model for balancing generic tradition with formal experimentation, Sir Philip Sidney. Incorporating elegantly crafted poems into his prose romance *Arcadia* (from which Shakespeare adapted narrative episodes as important as the Gloucester subplot in *King Lear*), Sidney also developed the narrative possibilities of the Petrarchan sonnet sequence by charting a lover's hopes and disappointment in *Astrophil and Stella*. Sidney's precocious intellect, thwarted political career, and untimely battlefield death all contributed to his charismatic image, and the posthumous publication of *Astrophil and Stella* in 1591 initiated a sonnet-publishing craze outside the court's manuscript culture. Commoners such as Spenser, Barnfield, and Chapman adapted the genre to their own ends, while Shakespeare's dramatization of fatuous courtly sonnet-eers for his public theater audience both circulated and mocked the sublimating aesthetics that had made the lyric so meaningful a device for political and personal pleading with Queen Elizabeth (see Henderson 1995).

Sonnets were among the most popular poetic forms, but they were just one among many in Tottel's *Songs and Sonnets* (1557), the anthology also known as Tottel's *Miscellany*, which included adaptations of Petrarch by the earlier Tudor courtiers Sir Thomas Wyatt and Sir Henry Howard, earl of Surrey. Including mid-century poems in poulter's measure and fourteeners alongside its sonnets, Tottel's *Miscellany* paved the way for other multi-author verse collections, such as *The Paradise of Daintie Devices*. The publication of such volumes confused distinctions between high and low culture, a confusion epitomized by the uncertain status of the sonnet itself: sonnets were "high" by association with self-proclaimed laureates (Petrarch, Spenser) and courtly culture, "low" by association with the "uncountable rabble of ryming Ballet makers and compylers of senceless sonnets, who be most busy to stuffe every stal full of grosse devices and unlearned Pamphlets," decried by William Webbe. Thomas Nashe, though professing admiration of Sidney's sonnets and including lyrics in his own fiction, still railed against "our babling Ballets and our new found Songs and Sonets, which every rednose Fidler hath at his fingers end, and every ignorant Ale Knight will breath foorth over the potte." Even Sir Philip Sidney dismissed the imitative work of poets who "coldly... apply fiery speeches, as men that had rather read lovers' writings, and so caught up certain swelling phrases" (see Henderson 1995). The conflict between a respected elite and what Pistol in *Henry V* dubs the "base, common, and popular" obviously held sway; but as in Pistol's case, the difficulty of distinguishing pots from kettles was one motivation for such attacks. Clergymen and humanist moralizers also condemned love sonnets alongside other forms perceived as potentially corrupting, including adulterous narratives and neo-chivalric romances (see Charlton 1987; Cressy 1980).

More immediately comprehensible was pious concern over Ovidian *epyllia*, erotic mini-epics informed by mythology but devoid of improving morals. Marlowe's *Hero and Leander* required Chapman's continuation to appear other than an aesthetic indulgence, and Shakespeare's own *Venus and Adonis* was famously condemned as an incentive to masturbation. But the dangers of print circulation were perceived as reaching beyond poetry directly encouraging sin to include works that might upset acceptance of the *status quo*. To challenge hierarchy through satire or simply by spreading news that might not fit the idealized notion of proper society, in other words, was not only a political challenge in our modern sense, but could be judged a moral affront to the inherited cosmology premised on God's orderly creation. As famously argued by Menenius Agrippa in *Coriolanus*, the social body was widely seen as analogous to the human body, with each stratum having its proper part, and upstart or mutinous members threatening the whole. Upstart genres of vernacular literature could also pose a social problem.

The one type of "poetic literature" in the vernacular that we can be certain was familiar and available to literally everyone in that social body was the ballad. Composed in a standard measure and stanza form, and usually printed on a single large sheet that frequently named the appropriate tune for singing and offered a rudimentary illustration, ballads were easily the cheapest, most widespread form of literature (usual price, from one halfpenny in the early sixteenth century to one penny by the mid seventeeth); they were sold widely, sung in parlor and market, pasted on walls of houses and taverns, read and reread, known at every social level. Already by 1520 John Dorne had approximately 190 "balets" for sale in his Oxford shop and at fairs, and ballads continued to be profitable well into the seventeenth century; estimates for the later sixteenth century suggest that roughly 3,000 distinct ballads were published. If we assume an average print run similar to that for books (roughly 1,000 to 1,250 copies), the total number of ballad copies circulating in the period could have been between three and four million; but even if we assume 200 copies as a minimum profitable print run, this would mean 600,000 copies circulating in Shakespeare's day (see Charlton 1987; Watt 1991).

Also widely available were chapbooks, cheap publications that sold for between one and three pennies and were usually no longer than twenty-four small pages. These inexpensive chapbooks and the new prose semi-fiction form of the pamphlet nearly rivaled the ballad in pervasiveness. Dorne sold fewer chapbooks than ballads in 1520, but he did sell one or two copies each of his two dozen or so titles (see Watt 1991).

Itinerant sellers of ballads, who sang extracts of what they sold, and pedlars of small books, with their boxes of wares hanging from their necks, were well-known figures in Tudor–Stuart London, and there is mention of countryside pedlars at least as early as the 1570s. Shakespeare's Autolycus in *The Winter's Tale* embodies their dubious reputation. In 1592 Henry Chettle warns that "pretty chapmen...spread more pamphlets by the state forbidden then all the booksellers in London." "Pamphleteers," as Thomas Nashe terms the authors of this "urban para-literature" (Hunter 1990: 169), offered news and advice to everyone on everything from eternal life to the practices of professional thieves and played a part in controversies political (the debates over enclosure of land), religious (the Martin Marprelate struggles of the late 1580s), and personal (the quarrel between Thomas Nashe and Gabriel Harvey).

As the cheapest, most widespread form of publication, ballads were frequently the subject of literate scorn even from sometime pamphleteers Nashe and Dekker for their low standards of execution and matter. Nashe observes that if one "loue good Poets hee must not countenance Ballet-makers," and among the worst insults he can find to utter against his enemy Gabriel Harvey is that Harvey aspired from childhood to be as "desperate a ballet-maker as the best of them" and to that end coined "pittifull Dittie[s]." However, much as some might denounce "babling Ballets" produced by "euery rednosed rimester" (*Martine Mar-sixtus* (1591)), there is evidence that they appealed to all levels of society. Indeed, as attested to by the derogatory comments linking sonnets and ballads, it was their very mingling of popular and elite audiences, undermining social distinctions, that may have made such forms worth denouncing. While many remain anonymous, we know the names of 200 Elizabethan ballad-writers, the most important being William Elderton, Thomas Churchyard, Anthony Munday, Leonard Gybson, Thomas Deloney, and Richard Johnson. Among those who mention ballads favorably is Sir Philip Sidney, who recalls his own positive reactions to the famous ballad of "Chevy chase," even when sung by a beggarly popular musician: "I must confesse my own barbarousness, I never heard the old song of Percy and Douglas that I found not my heart moved more than with a trumpet; and yet is it sung but by some blind crowder, with no rougher voice than rude style." Similarly, although Sir William Cornwallis suggests in his *Essays* (1600) that he uses ballads for toilet paper, he also observes that they provide useful objects of study for the cultural historian and for the moralist who can find in them "vice rebuked, and...see the power of Vertue that pierceth the head of such a base Historian, and vile Auditory."

Perhaps the predominant discursive impulse of the ballad is the tendency toward hyperbole, toward the best or the worst or the most extreme in anything; Shakespeare notes this tendency when one observer in *The Winter's Tale* says that "Such a deal of wonder is broken out" that even "ballad-makers cannot be able to express it." In subject matter ballads varied widely. Some well-known ballads shared with chapbooks material drawn from chivalric romances (Watt 1991: 14); many took up events or wonders (e.g., Thomas Deloney's "Lamentation of Beccles," which meditates piously on the fire that destroyed the town in 1586); but there was always official nervousness, regulation, or intervention when ballads treated prominent individuals or affairs of state. It was permissible to praise individuals – especially Queen Elizabeth – by name, but blame and attack usually had to be generalized, making it unlikely that Falstaff could fulfill his threat to avenge himself on Prince Hal in print by having "ballads made on you all, and sung to filthy tunes." Notoriously, ballads often included erotic subject matter, and the Stationers' Register records instances when ballads such as Thomas Gosson's "ballad of a yonge man that went a wooying" were not licensed because they contained "vndecentnes...in Diuerse verses" (Arber 1950: ii. 576). Sometimes this "undecentness" was a matter of rather simple double meaning, as in the physical allegory of songs like "Watkins Ale," but other ballads exploited sexual material in more complex narratives. One notable example is suggestively entitled "The swiming Lady, or a Wanton Discovered, being a true relation of a coy lady (betrayed by her lover) as she was stripping herself naked and swimming in a river near Oxford" (Charlton 1987: 460). Nevertheless, a significant percentage of ballads were pious or moralistic, with titles such as "The joyes of virginitie" or "The dying tears of a penitent sinner" (p. 461). Despite exceptions, it is generally true that even when there was eroticism in their subject matter, as in the ballads concerning fallen women such as Jane Shore, the mistress of Edward IV, there was also, as Patrick Collinson (1988: 94–126) has argued concerning Tudor–Stuart culture itself, a pervasive "moralistic" element which cautioned readers and listeners against sin and error.

Pamphlets were also intent upon teaching what was to be pursued or eschewed, and on teaching something to virtually everyone. Thomas Dekker's *The Bel-man of London* (1608), for example, claims no less than to be "Profitable for Gentlemen, Lawyers, Merchants, Citizens, Farmers, Masters of households, and all sorts of seruants, to marke, and delightfull for all men to reade," and scholars have argued that a good proportion of the pamphlets assume a fairly sophisticated reading audience, "capable of recognizing parody, burlesque, the use of rhetorical figures, who knew of Aristotle and Ramus, who appreciated, even if they could not necessarily understand, quotations in Latin and French, exempla, and marginal references to classical authorities" (Clark 1983: 20). Typically pamphlets take the form of the biographical life or confession, such as *The Historie of the damnable life, and deserued death of Doctor Iohn Faustus* or Robert Greene's autobiographical *Repentance* (both 1592); of complaints and satires directed against certain professions, especially the theatrical and legal professions, against Catholics and foreigners, or against disturbing social phenomena like usury, agricultural enclosure, urban crime, or changing female attire; and of reports of newsworthy occasions such as foreign warfare, domestic crime, or natural disaster. Frequently pamphlet titles suggest by their use of terms like "report," "news," and "true" along with "wonderful," "rare," and "dreadful," that whatever their subject, they will combine both the topical and the amazing, news and sensation, as in Alexander Gurth's *Most true and More Admirable news, Expressing the Miraculous Preservation of a Young Maiden of the towne of Glabbich in the Dukedom of Gulische* (1597). They also tend to relate individual instances to a larger general type and lesson, lumping together legend, history, and contemporary news on a single level of validity, so that even Thomas Twyne's "shorte and pithie" report on the earthquake of 1580 grandly promises to consider "all Earthquakes in general" (Clark 1983: 91). Furthermore, pamphlets keep a sharp lookout for the slightest threat to public order, frequently resorting to traditional moral-religious discourses that invoke sins and political crimes even in what might seem to us to be unlikely contexts. Thus, I. H. denounces the new vice of smoking as "first found out and inuented by the diuell, and first vsed and practised by the divels priests" (*Work for Chimny-sweepers: Or A warning for Tobacconists* (1602): Clark 1983: 196), and John Deacon excoriates tobacco for causing treason among its users, who, reduced to penury by their habit, "forthwith become professed malcontents against the well-setled peace of our public state: wishing and praying eftsoones for their long expected Iubilee: and hoping earnestly after a preposterous deliuerance from all dutifull subiection towards their holie Superiours" (*Tobacco Totuered, Or, The Filthie Fume of Tobacco Refined* 1616: Clark 1983: 195–6).

Sometimes pamphlets were officially produced, even written by high officials, when the matter at hand was some aspect of government policy or proceeding felt to need justification. Thus, there were such anonymous but by no means unofficial publications as *The Execution of Justice in England for maintenance of publique and Christian peace, against certeine stirrers of sedition* (1583), attributed to a "verrie honest gentleman" but now believed to have been written by no less a figure than Lord Burghley. The existence of some such obviously sanctioned publications and the fact that all printing was supposed to be under official control, with the Stationers of London charged to register all printed material as of the 1550s (although Hyder Rollins (1924) estimates that no more than half the surviving broadside ballads were in fact registered), actually had the effect of granting popular credibility to incredible or even dangerous material: according to Chettle, "the sellers swear these are published by authority; and people far off think nothing is printed but what is lawfully tolerated." This situation is reflected in the joke in *The Winter's Tale* on the credulousness of the rustics who assume the truthfulness of fantastic ballads, reasoning that it is right to love a ballad in print, "for then we are sure they are true." But no matter how officially sanctioned, how orthodox or unorthodox in morality and politics, pamphlet writing enjoyed little prestige, even among its most accomplished practitioners. Robert Greene, Thomas Nashe, Thomas Dekker, and Barnaby Rich all remarked upon the genre itself as windy, derivative, hypocritically moralistic, and dull (Clark 1983: 176). When he is not attacking Harvey as a would-be balladeer, Nashe derides his "pamphleting" about "births of monsters, horrible murders, and great burnings." Nevertheless, it might be wrong to go too far in joining in this condescension, since a case could be made that some instances of the form, such as the prison pamphlets of Luke Hutton (*The Blacke Dogge of Newgate* (1596), William Fennor (*The Compters Common-wealth* (1615)), and Dekker himself, no matter how sensationalistic or how derivative from Greene's fictionalized depiction of a criminal conspiracy in his conny-catching pamphlets, actually participated in forming a climate conducive to early penal reform (see Clark 1983). The treatment of harsh and arbitrary imprisonment in works such as *Measure for Measure* might appear differently if seen in the light of this contemporary prose material. Furthermore, from the standpoint of the later growth of an informed public sphere, there is no small historical interest in the early forms of news from unofficial sources, a fact which makes it especially interesting that Shakespeare's commoner gardener in *Richard II* is able to articulate and defend his evaluation of state politics against royal censure on the basis of his knowledge of "news" that is available to "everyone," even if unknown to Richard's hapless queen.

While pamphlet literature obviously addressed (or produced, according to its early modern critics) a desire for "news," that "itch in our natures to delight in newnes and varietie, be the subject never so grievous" (Hawkins's *Observations . . . in his voieage into the South Sea 1593* (1622), there are few news publications that do not also exhibit – as indeed does Shakespeare's pious, humanistic gardener – the religious values and discourse that permeated early modern English society under the continuing impetus of the Reformers' commitment to religious education for the laity. Not surprisingly, there was also a flourishing trade in specifically religious books. Some of these were clearly not designed for casual reading, as in the cases of the frequently reprinted but lengthy and hence quite costly *Plaine Man's Pathway to Heaven* (1601; similar works of over 300 pages cost at least ten pence unbound) or the more than 250 independent catechetical works appearing during Elizabeth's reign. These last comprised over 750,000 copies by the early seventeenth century, over and above the 500,000 copies printed of such officially prescribed forms as Alexander Nowell's *Cathecism* (1580; see Green 1996; Watt 1991). Their easily recognizable discursive form is evident when Shakespeare has the Bastard of *King John* conduct a question-and-answer dialogue with himself "like an Absey book" or has Falstaff meditate on the value of honor, answering a string of propositions with as many responses, only to conclude, "so ends my catechism." Obviously, in such cases, part of the dramatic effect comes from the paradox of hearing arguments for self-interested roguery mimic the pious abstractions of the catechisms.

Many books were intended for religious meditation rather than theological peda- gogy; these included devotions and countless meditations on Scripture such as Richard Taverner's *Commonplaces of Scripture* (1538) and John Norden's *Pensive Mans Practice* (1584), which eventually reached forty editions in as many years. So popular was this religious literature that arguably the most widely read of all books in the 1590s were the sermons of Henry Smith, rector of St Clement's Dane. As the number of entries in the *Short-Title Catalogue* attests (G. B. Harrison (1927) estimates 127 editions between 1591 and 1637), "silver-tongued Smith" was manifestly readable, but the sermons are also interesting for the sophistication of their thought. On the question of the humanity and culpability of monarchs, for example, Smith's religious meditations are every bit as alert to the potential differences between office and individual as Shakespeare's own more or less contemporary history plays. Less intel- lectual than the sermons, but just as popular, were the musical renderings of the biblical psalms in the version of Thomas Sternhold and John Hopkins, which set the

Bible text to ballad meter, with alternating lines of four and three beats; they went through more than forty printings between 1547 and 1600. Shakespeare draws on the language of Sternhold and Hopkins in *2 Henry VI*, when King Henry's deference to God – "For judgment only doth belong to Thee" (III. ii. 140) – echoes Psalm 3: 8: "Salvation onely doth belong / to thee O Lord aboue."

One form of vernacular literature that showed little evidence of religious sentiment or thinking and little interest in current events was the jestbook. Descended from material that had been around since the late medieval *facetiae*, the jestbooks usually focused their series of disconnected anecdotes on a fictionalized figure derived from a real person, like Scoggin (*The iestes of Skogyn* (ca. 1570)), Richard Tarleton (*Tarltons newes out of purgatorie* (1590)), or George Peele (*Merrie conceited jests* (1607). In this, the jestbook was not significantly different from the biographies of criminals such as *The Life and Pranks of Long Meg of Westminster* (1582) or *The Life and Death of Gamaliell Ratsey* (1605), which included similarly amusing anecdotes. It may be hard to get a religious moral out of stories like "How Scoggin let a fart and said it was worth forty pounds," but social lessons and prejudices were still there to be found in plenty. Scoggin and his ilk interacted with, and fooled with or alternatively were fooled by, representative and often unsavory figures from the worlds of tavern, market, and court, and their stories perhaps made the uncertainties of a newly urbanized population less unbearable by relativizing them.

Likely answering some similar need, but in a more embittered form, was a recurrent strand of more personalized satire in the nondramatic literature of the period. The targets and participants varied, from the exchanges between the largely anonymous Martinist and anti-Martinist writers of the late 1580s, through the quarrels of Thomas Nashe and Gabriel Harvey in the mid-1590s, to the intense melee of the late 1590s that involved Joseph Hall, John Marston, and Everard Guilpin, and even spilled over into the theater to Thomas Dekker and Ben Jonson. Although there is nothing overtly treasonous or as directly involving the prerogatives of the state in the Nashe–Harvey or Marston–Hall conflicts as there had been in the Marprelate conflict, the level of violence of language and matter, the vituperation, and the degree of popular engagement apparently registered as sufficiently alarming to require official intervention. The attacks of Nashe, Harvey, and later of Hall, Marston, and Guilpin upon one another and upon contemporary ignorance and folly disguised under classical settings and names prompted the famous June 1599 order from the archbishop of Canterbury and the bishop of London that lists works by these authors, insisting "that noe Satyres or Epigrams be printed hereafter" and "that none of [Nashe's and Harvey's] bokes bee euer printed hereafter" (S Register, Arber 1950: iii. 677). Reading Hall's *Virgidemiarum* (1597), Marston's two 1598 satirical collections (*Certaine Satyres* and *The Scourge of Villanie*), or Guilpin's *Skialetheia* (1598), it is difficult to quarrel with the judgment of W.I. in *The Whipping of Satyre* (1601), who accuses satirists generally of providing the reading public with salacious attacks on vice for their own profit and aggrandizement. The relation of this material, its tenor and its obsessive concerns, to the figure of Jaques in *As You Like It* or to the general atmosphere of *Troilus and Cressida* has long attracted critical attention. It might further suggest obvious ties to Prince Hamlet as well as to Timon.

Among the popular genres that would seem less threatening to the social order was the neo-chivalric romance, ranging from loosely structured, seemingly interminable prose sagas of adventuring knights to Ariosto's verse masterpiece, the *Orlando Furioso*, and Spenser's *Faerie Queene*. While Harington's complete translation of Ariosto did not appear until 1591, Ascham reported two decades earlier that the *Orlando Furioso* "was on sale at every street corner in London." And while chivalric romances might appear ideologically conservative to many (including modern social historians; see Thomas 1986; Capp 1985), by dint of length alone, if not the occasional adulterous representation, some argued that they led readers away from more godly pursuits. Henry Crosse refers to the romances, jestbooks, chapbooks, and ballads as all together amounting to "a universall deluge over all holy and godly conversation" (Charlton 1987: 461). Similarly, Francis Clement in *The Petie Schole* (1587) opposes "lovebooks" to "book-love": "Lovebooks, by which were meant romances and idle tales, 'be the enemies of virtue, nurses of vice, furtherers of ignorance, and hinderers of all good learning'. Booklove, by contrast, the love of good learning, 'embraceth virtue, abandoneth vice, expelleth ignorance, and nourisheth wisdom and learning'" (Cressy 1980: 22). Spenser's elaborate claims (and no doubt the belief) that his epic romance would be morally improving testify to anxiety even in the most self-conscious, allegorical, and formally elevated instance. Like the sonnet, the romance defied the boundaries between court and popular culture, respected literature and suspect entertainment.

Some of these romances closely imitated their medieval models. Early in the century, Lord Berners rendered two late medieval romances into English, *Huon de Bordeaux* and *Arthur of Little Britain*. *Huon* provided a source for Shakespeare's Oberon, but the impact of such romances goes far beyond specific citations. These stories and their English kin, including *Bevis of Hampton, Guy of Warwicke*, and Malory's *Morte d'Arthur*, were not only vastly popular in themselves, but the spur to composition of new romances, such as the Spanish sagas of Palmerin. They also inspired parodies, hybrids, and adaptations. The categorization and authorship of popular fictions is especially vexed, as tales were adapted, retold, and translated; often several closely related versions of a story were in circulation, causing grey hairs for scholars who seek to ascertain precisely which variants Shakespeare was using.

Most of the new sixteenth-century romances derived from Mediterranean countries. Near the start of the century Spain produced the most influential of all, *Amadis de Gaul*; in that country alone, there were sixty editions of it and its sequels during the next 100 years. No wonder Cervantes was driven to satirize its effects in *Don Quixote*. Extracts from the first book of *Amadis* were translated into English in 1567, with a new translation of books 1 and 2 by Anthony Munday appearing in 1595. Among the spin-offs from *Amadis* were *Esplandián* (a.k.a. son of Amadis); *Amadis of England*, and the Palmerin series with its own sequels: *Palmerin de Oliva* (1511), *Primaleon* (son of Palmerin), and *Palmerin of England*. This last, composed by the Portuguese Francisco de Moraes, was especially popular. The first book of *Palmerin de Oliva* was translated into English in 1588, part of a much more successful Mediterranean invasion than Philip of Spain managed by sea. The Amadis and Palmerin cycles "began to be translated with bewildering rapidity and profusion" (Esdaile 1912: p. xx). The first twenty books of *Primaleon* were published under the title *Palmendos* in 1589, with the rest following in three installments (*Primaleon of Greece*, 1595, 1596, and 1619). Thus the English popularity of the neo-chivalric romances was at its full height during Shakespeare's writing years, evidenced as well by their frequent reprinting (*Amadis* in 1589–90, *Palladine* and *Palmerin of England* in 1596, etc.).

Unlike works we now consider "high" literature, such as sonnet sequences and Spenser's epic, most of these expansive Mediterranean imports have seemed to scholars an odd, outmoded fad not worth discussing. As a result, we miss the extent to which those works we *have* canonized would have been perceived as part of this romance phenomenon, valued less for their individuated authorial perspectives than for their fulfillment and play with generic expectations. Moreover, while some romances were nostalgic invocations of chivalry, others manipulated the form to address audiences struggling with new appraisals of value, adventure, and social position.

The prolific Munday – also a playwright and thus part of Shakespeare's immediate milieu – helped sustain the taste, not only by translating many of the romances but also by penning his own derivatives. Others took up the challenge, including Forde (*Parismus, Prince of Bohemia*), Lodge (*Rosalynde*), and Greene (*Pandosto, Mamillia, Gydonius*, and more). These English fictions were shaped by the adventure narratives of the chivalric romances but also by the pastoral and amorous stories and verse that began to mingle and compete with them as the century progressed.

Closely related to the neo-chivalric adventures of knights and ladies were the sentimental novels popular in Spain, such as *Carcel de Amor* by Diego de San Pedro, based on Boccaccio's *Fiammetta* (an amorous text also translated into English), and the *Historia de Grisel y Mirabella* of Juan de Flores. As the chivalric tradition culminates in the sophisticated Italian epic romances of Pulci's *Morgante*, Boiardo's *Orlando Innamorato*, and especially the *Orlando Furioso*, so do the Spanish tales lead to Montemayor's masterpiece of pastoral romance, *Diana* (translated 1598). Both directly and through their inspiration for Spenser's *Faerie Queene* and Sidney's *Arcadia* respectively, these continental forms shaped the landscape of English storytelling. They also inspired a spate of extremely popular French romances, characterized by sentimental elaboration and subtlety. To survey the books printed in England during the last decades of the century is to realize through repetition the extent to which the continental neo-chivalric romances, pastoral romances, and their English derivatives constitute a canon of popular fiction. As Pettet remarks, romance fictions made a deeper impress upon Elizabethan drama than could classical or medieval drama, "for while only a small and later part of romantic literature was dramatic in form, this literature had been dominant in England and Europe for many centuries past. No Elizabethan writer could help absorbing it into his consciousness" (1949: 11).

What had knights rescuing damsels, illicit court *amours*, and lost princesses living among shepherds to do with the London merchants and civil servants who made up much of the reading public in the 1590s? How can we account for the continuing popularity of chivalric stories at a time when their contents had in many ways become anachronistic? One explanation, glaringly obvious to those who still make fantasy and popular romance bestsellers, may lure us to look no further: these were escapist entertainments, providing wish fulfillments and illusions of consequential action on a mythic scale. The romances were also less overtly didactic than most other reading matter available in the vernacular. But such a general answer glosses over the specific appeals and seeming contradictions of their Elizabethan popularity.

The landscape through which the questing figure wandered, ranging from fairytale distance through morally allegorized settings to historically specific locales, offered possibilities for variation in tone and commentary. The most traditional romances idealized sexual relations as true love matches or tests of fidelity and honor; Spenser's *Faerie Queene* interwove more cynical renditions of knightly behavior with these ideals, creating a cultural encyclopedia of amorous attitudes over and above its advertised moral instruction. The mythic resonance of wandering and return also allowed expressions of discontent with limited opportunities at home (an impetus for traveling apprentices in hybrid popular fictions as well) or, conversely, an occasion for xenophobic reminders of the dangers lurking in Mediterranean lands and beyond.

As Ferguson notes, the chivalric tradition allowed courtiers to romanticize the military function of their class; they "found in Amadis and Palmerin, in Orlando and the Arthurian knights, models especially to their taste" (1986: 71). Sir Philip Sidney averred that "*Orlando Furioso* or honest King Arthur, will never displease a soldier." But this enjoyment carried obvious ironies, as the type of warfare being prized had become obsolete (and dashing attempts to resemble knights of yore, such as Sir Philip's famed gallantry in sacrificing his leg armor at Zutphen, could be fatal). The escapist element of such fictions may mask the anxiety of an aristocracy losing real power as a more bureaucratized civil service began to displace old economies. Larger-than-life heroism and simple moral oppositions in some neo-chivalric tales functioned as a form of class nostalgia. *King Lear* might be viewed as the emergent nightmare of an early modern mind looking again at this mythic landscape knowing the system had gone awry.

An added irony appears in the shift of reading audience for these romances towards the century's end; while it remains hard to determine exactly who bought which books and who had access to them, nevertheless the repackaging of lengthy romances as chapbooks indicates that their readership was no longer confined to courtiers. Indeed, by Shakespeare's day such works were passé among the continental elite, but thriving among the English "middling sort," the tradesmen and yeomen whose increasing literacy and position encouraged the imitation of courtly tastes (Capp 1985).

Those buying the books, especially the cheaper versions of *Bevis of Hampton* or *Guy of Warwick* sold by itinerant pedlars, were among those whose trades, money, and numbers had helped to supplant the chivalric code and feudal relations based on static social positions, personal oaths of loyalty, and martial valor. Thus, whereas in the more aristocratic romances a turn to the supernatural or the workings of destiny usually brought families back together and revealed the coincidence between social hierarchy and divine order, in the hybrid forms generated for London merchants, more attention and honor was invested in the ingenious agency of its heroes, be they witty rogues (in Nashe's *Unfortunate Traveller*) or hard-working aspirers (in Thomas Deloney's *Jack of Newbury*). Capp sees in the energetic recitals of Robin Hood and Tom a Lincoln a reworking of traditional tales emphasizing boldness and physical strength, "male fantasies of toughness, adventure and fame" (1985: 207). Febvre and Martin (1976) argue that the romances encouraged readers to follow the Spanish conquistadors in exploring new worlds. Mixing the marvelous and the everyday made the romance form (like the lowly pamphlet) a capacious one, in which dangers both familiar and new, the products of fantasy or of economic flux, could be confronted within an ultimately comforting structure providing resolution and return.

These romances as a group reinforce our awareness that polyglot style permeated all popular forms of writing during Shakespeare's day, as it permeates his writing as well. More was involved than simply purveying "mouldy tales out of Boccaccio," as Ben Jonson would have had it (preface to *Volpone*). So it is not surprising that, alongside the neo-chivalric translations and intermingled with the tropes of medieval romance emerged hybrid forms of chivalric writing. One popular mixed-mode work was Richard Johnson's *Nine Worthies of London* (1592). Within a mythological frame, it presents the lives of nine English mayors and soldiers, each of whom is temporarily revived to tell his story, after the manner of *A Mirror for Magistrates* but for the purpose of celebration. If one is aware of the massive popularity of the chivalric exploits of the Amadis and Palmerin sequels, then the savviness of adapting those generic models to laud historical figures such as the mercenary leader Sir John Hawkwood or even a former lord mayor of London becomes more comprehensible. So too does the radical potential of such adaptation, in which birth is dissociated from the values and exploits praised. Like Deloney's upwardly mobile apprentices, Johnson's worthies are not noble by birth (indeed, Deloney's Jack of Newbury even refuses Henry VIII's offer of a knighthood). They achieve greatness – or have greatness thrust upon them.

Read in this context, *The Merchant of Venice*'s interweaving of the rescue of a fairytale princess with problems of finance appears less satirical; it addressed a generation of readers who enjoyed questing narratives with apprentices or merchants as heroes. Burke observes that the "emergence of the entrepreneur as popular hero, a type apparently without any contemporary European parallel" may be linked with the uniquely English category of the gentleman apprentice, an intermediary figure between popular and elite cultures (1985: 52–3). Just as significantly, knowledge of the neo-chivalric romances and their hybrids may help explain why the plays most overtly shaped by them (not coincidentally among the least venerated plays in the canon), *Cymbeline* and *Pericles*, were once popular. Posthumus Leonatus in *Cymbeline* provides an obvious case for comparison with Johnson's worthies, though Shakespeare is less sanguine about making a hero out of his non-aristocratic gentleman. (The most remarkable aspect of Posthumus's behavior, his repentance for killing his wife *prior* to learning of her innocence, in fact derives from Shakespeare's anonymous "lowly" source, *Frederycke of Jennen*, rather than from Boccaccio.)

We might look again at the initial encounter of Pericles with the incestuous king Antiochus, who simultaneously suppresses and reveals his corruption through a riddle. When, like Bassanio, young Pericles takes on the challenge of interpretation, he proclaims:

> Like a bold champion I assume the lists,
> Nor ask advice of any other thought
> But faithfulness and courage.
>
> (I. i. 61–3)

Whereas in *The Merchant of Venice* the chivalric language used by Portia at the similar moment of interpretive choice seems comically excessive but still hopeful, here the riddle sours the words of both Pericles and his would-be beloved. The king's relationship to his daughter perverts the ceremony of courtship, as if to announce how far from naïve this later version of romance will be. The play seems even less an escapist fantasy if we know that the status of speech we call "news" was not only the stuff of popular pamphlets but also a topic of vigorous legal debate. Stowe's historical *Survey* sympathetically recounts the plight of a bailiff who was hanged for spreading the word about an uprising in Essex that he himself opposed: simply speaking the truth could be seditious libel in the seventeenth century. In such a context, one had best take advantage of the distancing veil which chivalric romance provided if one wished to dramatize the dilemmas of truth telling. Clearly, *Pericles* is as much a hybrid as Johnson's *Nine Worthies of London*, using the knowledge of romance conventions to make a more jaded comment upon a social order far from fairyland. Similarly, in *Cymbeline*, an evil stepmother comments on state sovereignty; courtly slanders rather than shipwrecks cause familial disruption; and birth both is and is not a guarantor of value. If we recognize the marketability of romance and try to read in terms of the historical moment's narrative pleasures, attending not only to a particular verbal root but to the forests of romance from which these plays were cultivated, their mixed modes grow more substantial.

New forms of authority and value, then, can be discerned within the mixed genres of the 1590s, offering challenges in print to match any made at the theaters. But it is only by recognizing the dominant genres of the time, and noting variations within larger social and discursive fields, that such challenges as well as resemblances can appear. At the early modern moment of explorations, fluctuating values, and emergent technologies, literary genres suggested shapes and directives but also allowed more fluidity than we generally acknowledge. Old and innovative, popular and elite forms were jangling and mingling in the new marketplace of print. By relocating Shakespeare's writing within this welter of change and copia, we may gain a renewed sense of the narrative and discursive energy of vernacular culture, in which Shakespeare played one man's many parts.

References and Further Reading

Arber, Edward (ed.) 1950: *A Transcript of the Registers of the Company of Stationers of London, 1554–1640 A.D.* London: privately printed, 1875. Repr. New York: Peter Smith.

Bennet, H. S. 1965: *English Books and Readers, 1558–1603*. Cambridge: Cambridge University Press.

Bullough, Geoffrey 1957: *Narrative and Dramatic Sources of Shakespeare*. New York: Columbia University Press.

Burke, Peter 1985: Popular culture in seventeenth-century London. In Barry Reay (ed.), *Popular Culture in Seventeenth-century England*. London: Croom Helm, 31–58.

Capp, Bernard 1985: Popular literature. In Barry Reay (ed.), *Popular Culture in Seventeenth-century England*. London: Croom Helm, 198–243.

Charlton, Kenneth 1987: "False fonde bookes, ballades and rimes": an aspect of informal education in early modern England. *History of Education Quarterly*, 27, 449–71.

Clark, Sandra 1983: *The Elizabethan Pamphleteers: Popular Moralistic Pamphlets 1580–1640*. Rutherford, NJ: Fairleigh Dickinson University Press.

Collinson, Patrick 1988: *The Birthpangs of Protestant England: Religious and Cultural Change in the Sixteenth and Seventeenth Centuries*. New York: St Martin's Press.

Cressy, David 1980: *Literacy and the Social Order: Reading and Writing in Tudor and Stuart England*. Cambridge: Cambridge University Press.

Dean, John 1979: *Restless Wanderers: Shakespeare and the Pattern of Romance*. Salzburg Studies in English Literature, Elizabethan and Renaissance Studies, 86. Salzburg: Institut für Anglistik und Amerikanistik Universität Salzburg.

Donaldson, E. Talbot 1985: *The Swan at the Well: Shakespeare Reading Chaucer*. New Haven: Yale University Press.

Esdaile, Arundell 1912: *A List of English Tales and Prose Romances Printed before 1740. Part I: 1475–1642*. London: Bibliographical Society.

Febvre, Lucien and Martin, Henri-Jean 1976: *The Coming of the Book: The Impact of Printing 1450–1800*, Trans. David Gerard. London: NLB. (Orig. pub. 1958.)

Ferguson, Arthur B. 1986: *The Chivalric Tradition in Renaissance England*. Washington, D.C.: Folger Library.

Green, Ian 1996: *The Christian's ABC: Catechisms and Catechizing in England. c. 1530–1740*. Oxford: Clarendon Press.

Greenblatt, Stephen 1988: *Shakespearean Negotiations: The Circulation of Social Energy in Renaissance England*. Berkeley: University of California Press.

Harrison, G. B. 1927: Books and readers, 1591–4. *Library*, 4th ser., 8, 273–302.

—— 1934: Books and readers, 1599–1603. *Library*, 4th ser., 14, 1–33.

Henderson, Diana E. 1995: *Passion made Public: Elizabethan Lyric, Gender, and Performance*. Urbana: University of Illinois Press.

Hunter, Paul J. 1990: *Before Novels: The Cultural Contexts of Eighteenth-Century English Fiction*. New York: Norton.

McDonald, Russ 1996: *The Bedford Companion to Shakespeare: An Introduction with Documents*. Boston: Bedford Books of St Martin's Press.

Muir, Kenneth 1978: *The Sources of Shakespeare's Plays*. New Haven: Yale University Press.

O'Dell, Sterg 1954: *A Chronological List of Prose Fiction in English Printed in England and Other Countries 1475–1640*. Cambridge, Mass.: MIT Press.

Pettet, E. C. 1949: *Shakespeare and the Romance Tradition*. London: Staples Press.

Relihan, Constance C. 1994: *Fashioning Authority: The Development of Elizabethan Novelistic Discourse*. Kent, Oh.: Kent State University Press.

Rollins, Hyder E. 1919: The black-letter broadside ballad. *Proceedings of the Modern Language Association*, 34, 258–341.

—— 1924: An analytical index to the ballad-entries (1557–1709) in the registers of the Company of Stationers of London. *Studies in Philology*, 21, 1–324.

Salzman, Paul 1985: *English Prose Fiction, 1558–1700: A Critical History*. Oxford: Clarendon Press.

Spufford, Margaret 1982: *Small Books and Pleasant Histories: Popular Fiction and its Readership in*

Seventeenth-century England. Athens, G.: University of Georgia Press.

Stevenson, Laura Caroline 1984: *Praise and Paradox: Merchants and Craftsmen in Elizabethan Popular Literature*. Cambridge: Cambridge University Press.

Thomas, Keith 1986: The meaning of literacy in early modern England. In Gerd Baumann (ed.), *The Written Word: Literacy in Transition*. Oxford: Clarendon Press, 97–131.

Thompson, Ann 1978: *Shakespeare's Chaucer: A Study in Literary Origins*. New York: Barnes & Noble.

Watt, Tessa 1991: *Cheap Print and Popular Piety, 1550–1640*. Cambridge: Cambridge University Press.

PART FIVE
Writing

14
Professional Playwrighting
Scott McMillin

Writing for the Disreputable Theater

When Shakespeare first came to London and began to write for a living, he took up the least respectable, riskiest, and potentially most profitable medium – the common stage. Almost any kind of writing carried more esteem than turning out scripts for the players in their new theaters. The narrative poem on a classical topic was one avenue to respectability. So was the moral pamphlet on the evils of the day (which might well include those new theaters), or the translation of the Psalms or the classics of Greek and Roman literature. There was such a range of culturally important work to be done that parents, schoolmasters, and curates could only feel disappointment when a young man with a knack for writing wasted his gift on plays about legendary kings with unkind daughters, moneylenders who charged a pound of flesh for interest, or Danish princes with incestuous mothers.

Why would a young writer link up with the players? Part of the reason must be that the Danish prince with an incestuous mother is more interesting to young writers than the moral pamphlet, but in Shakespeare's case, the lure of the theater had something to do with the young writer's acting ability. As far as we know, Shakespeare got his start in the theater as an actor and became a writer as an outgrowth of this basic histrionic interest. I am restating the question of why the theater in the first place, but we are making gains. Think of the actor in Shakespeare, then think of the writer. To put oneself on display before crowds of spectators by pretending to be someone else – this is a special interest, with a touch of transgression about it, an element of the risqué. It also involves a special feeling for language and the way language can be spoken to crowds. If one thrives on impersonation, loves to speak poetry, loves to make poetry human by embodying the language and delivering it as though it were spontaneous, one will find the theater a blessing. If this is an approximation to the motive that drew Shakespeare to the theater in the first place (we really do not know), the second place does not come far behind, and it involves writing. For in seeking to be an actor in a theater of poetry, one might very well find that the greatest achievement lay in writing that poetry and giving it to the other actors to deliver. This would be especially tempting if one weren't a very good actor – no one ever said Shakespeare was good at it – and irresistible if one could write uncommonly well.

I am describing how a young actor/writer might take up the theater, but I am also getting to the deep reason of why the theater was thought to be immoral. Acting before the public was itself of questionable morality in the eyes of zealous Protestants, sometimes called (by stage-writers, mostly) "Puritans." A "Puritan" believed that you should present yourself as yourself in the world, not as someone else. The doubleness of identity involved in all theater ran counter to any moral code based on "integrity" (being one, not more than one). For boys to act as if they were women was especially reprehensible, as it crossed a strictly drawn gender line. Add to that the tendency toward plots tinged with sex and violence in a commercial theater that depended on drawing crowds, then add the propensity of plays staged in the afternoons to lure working people and apprentices away from their normal activities, and the complexity of the theater's "immorality" to the elders of London becomes apparent. The playhouses stood outside the city walls or across the river, just beyond reach of the London authorities, in areas long connected with sport, taverns, and brothels. The city fathers denounced them for drawing crowds away from work or from holy observances. Preachers denounced them for putting vice on display. Pamphleteers denounced them as sinks of iniquity. Little wonder the playhouses were crowded.

So one reason for choosing the theater over respectability was that the theater had a complex allurement. Another reason is that the theater paid a higher wage, at least for writers. There was a huge demand for new scripts. The major acting companies each changed the bill nearly every day. They rotated a repertory of over a dozen plays, so that any one title would be repeated only about every three or four days for the most popular items, and only about every nine or ten days for the ordinary piece. These companies were each trying to create a habit of playgoing among the London populace – not a habit of playgoing in general, but a habit of playgoing at *this* particular theater, Henslowe's Rose on the Bankside, say, where five or six different plays were staged each week, by Marlowe, or by Chettle and Dekker, in the hope of drawing spectators away from the five or six being staged each week at *that* theater, the one called the Theatre north of the city, where Shakespeare supplied some of his early scripts to the company to which he belonged from 1594 on, the Chamberlain's Men.

New plays were the key to success for the companies. Each of the adult troupes added a new piece to its repertory about every two weeks of an uninterrupted run. Moreover, specialized companies entirely composed of child actors operated now and then, and they required new plays too. The theater of Shakespeare's time was entirely made up of what we would call "contemporary drama." It had no classics to revive. Nothing the players were staging in the commercial theaters when Shakespeare first came to London (sometime between 1585 and 1590) would have gone back more than five years. Most of the active repertory had been written within the past year. That is how up to date the theater was, and how demanding of new plays from the relatively small number of writers who were turning out the scripts.

For the playwrights, this was a seller's market. The actors paid writers a better wage than did the Church, the university, the grammar school, or the noble family. The leading acting companies were paying £5 or £6 for a new play in 1598, with the price going up sharply to £10, even to £20 by 1613. This information comes from the accounts kept by Philip Henslowe in regard to the Admiral's Men, who were the chief rivals to Shakespeare's company, but there is no reason to suppose that Shakespeare's company paid less to the freelance dramatist. By contrast, the writer of the long narrative poem or the translator of Cicero was up against the cruel fact that most people in London did not buy books – they could not read. They could go to the theater, however, and that is one reason why the market for plays was potentially larger than the market for books. The publishers were not making large profits, and they paid no royalties – or, in a few cases, they *were* making large profits, and they paid no royalties anyhow. They paid a flat fee for the manuscript they would print and/or gave the writers several dozen free copies for them to sell on their own, and perhaps a bottle of wine.

In a year, a run-of-the-mill writer of "fine" literature might earn as much as the actors paid for a single play. Respectable writers hoped for position more than they hoped for what we would call royalties. They sought patronage from the great lords to whom they wrote ample dedications, the great lords whose children needed tutors perhaps, tutors who might also serve as secretaries to the great lords themselves. But great lords are not at their most predictable when it comes to the translator of Cicero, so the prospects of patronage were uncertain, and the writers were often forced to rely on the commercial marketplace. One nondramatic writer, Richard Robinson, who specialized in modernized versions of the Psalms, kept an account of his earnings between 1576 and 1596. In his best years he was earning £7 or £8 (see Miller 1959: 160–3 and Bentley 1971: 91). He averaged less than £3 per year. For *A Proceeding in the Harmony of King David's Harp* he netted £3 from Sir Christopher Hatton. This was one of his highest patronage rewards, but Sir Christopher did not come across with the clerical post which Robinson was seeking. Better writers than Robinson made more from their books, but not much more. Robert Greene (who also wrote plays) may have received £2 from the publisher for one of his racy autobiographical tales of the underworld. John Stow received £3 and fifty author's copies for a revised edition of one of the bestsellers of the day, his *Survey of London*.

Compare that to the income of the dramatists working for the Admiral's Men in the years covered by Henslowe. Both Henry Chettle and Thomas Dekker averaged about £25 a year during this period. George Chapman and Michael Drayton would both become well-known poets, but they turned to Henslowe and the Admiral's Men for stretches of time and income. Chapman earned more than £28 for contributing to seven plays in 14 months between May 1598 and July 1599. Drayton earned more than £32 compressed into 10 months in 1598–9 (Bentley 1971: 102–3).

Moreover, if one considers the other kinds of careers an educated man of literary ability might take up, one still finds the dramatists coming out ahead. Schoolmasters, tutors, and clerics were educated men, but £10 to £15 per year was normal for their callings. The schoolmaster in Stratford-upon-Avon, where Shakespeare grew up, was very well paid at £20 a year, but this still falls short of what Dekker and Chettle were averaging over their productive years for Henslowe, or what Chapman and Drayton were earning for their shorter stints. No other avenue for writers was as lucrative as this.

So much for the bright side. Freelance playwrighting was in fact a hard life, riddled with uncertainty. Schoolmasters and clerics could count on their wage from one year to the next, but the theaters were continually in danger of being closed, either by outbreaks of bubonic plague or by other government emergencies. When a dramatist was working, he was working very hard, and he was not setting his own schedule. He was not the lonely artist in his garret. In most cases, he was collaborating with two, three, or even four other writers, each of them taking an act or two of an outlined plot and working fast. The collaboration system forced the writers to keep to one another's pace and reminded them that they could easily be replaced. (It also taught the collaborators techniques and attitudes which the lonely artist in his garret does not learn.) And they did odd jobs of writing too, adding a prologue and an epilogue for a command performance at court, pasting in a scene here to allow time for costume changes, adding a speech for a speciality performer. Anyone who has worked on modern musical comedies knows about this kind of collaboration and patchwork, and has a sense of the excitement as well as the frustration of the business. But no one writing for the theater today will have worked on so many plays in such a short period of time as did Chettle, who had a hand in fifty plays over a period of five years, and Dekker, who had a hand in forty-four between 1598 and 1602 (a period during which he was in prison at least once).

Of all these plays, the writers involved in their composition owned not one. Once a play was sold to an acting company, the acting company owned it. It was the company's decision whether or not to publish a play, and usually the company did not publish. When a play did reach the bookstalls, its title page would name the acting company but usually not the playwright.

If this sounds like the setting for hackwork, it was. The average incomes given above for Dekker and Chettle disguise wide fluctuations from one year to another. They both spent time in debtors' prison. Outbreaks of bubonic plague shut the theaters for twenty months in 1593–4 and for sixty-eight months, off and on, between 1603 and 1611, the years when Shakespeare was writing his most famous tragedies. A riot led by apprentices would be seized upon by the city authorities to close the theaters, and a genuine government emergency such as the death of the queen would bring the industry to a halt. The market for new plays could easily come to a standstill. Richard Robinson peddling author's copies of his *Dial of Daily Contemplation* must have seemed at times to be on the fast track.

Writing Conditions

Let us imagine the concerns which Elizabethan playwrights had to keep in mind as they worked, by tracing an actual collaboration on a play. In 1599, Thomas Dekker, Henry Chettle, and William Haughton found an idea for a play in the old story of the Patient Griselda, told in Chaucer and elsewhere. They sought out the Admiral's Men as their market, perhaps because they had all sold plays to this company before, perhaps because they knew that the leading boy actor in this company would play the title role well, perhaps because they knew they could build in a Welsh-dialect role for one of the Admiral's Men who specialized in such things.

In October of 1599 they obtained an advance of £1 from the Admiral's Men, probably after showing the company an outline "plot" of the proposed play. At this point they would have parceled out a set of scenes for each writer to take away and write according to the "plot" outline. These writers were not following their artistic visions alone. They were keeping an eye on what the other writers were doing, counting the number of characters which the Admiral's Men could actually play, checking on whether there would be enough "offstage" time for an actor to change costume for a doubled role, heeding the requirements of the government censor, who was no rubber stamp, working on other collaborations with other writers (more than one iron in the fire) – *and* following their visions.

That means they were looking after two factors which the theater always insists on combining: economy and artistry. Every age has its assumptions about the economy of drama – how many main characters are needed to make a convincing drama, how large a supporting cast there should be, whether room should be made for music and dance, or detachable comic routines. The Greek drama developed out of choral dance and song, so the continuing prominence of a chorus seemed normal after a very small number of principal roles became the focal points of dramatic writing. Modern drama normally restricts itself to a small number of roles in an everyday setting, with no chorus and very few extras or walk-ons, this being one logic by which a commercial theater can be made economically viable. Smallness is not the only logic, however. The modern musical comedy uses singing and dancing choruses at great expense, characteristically takes up two or more love matches as principal plot lines, and adds in gangsters, bellboys, orphans, secretaries, and grandmothers as bit parts, as though a commercial theater should make money by abundance rather than by restraint. We know the aesthetic of abundance in our musical theater about as well as we know the aesthetic of restraint in our straight plays. The Elizabethan theater cared less than we do for restraint, and thrived on an aesthetic of abundance.

That is one reason why the writers looked to large-scale plots, involving a subplot or two and teeming with good parts for actors to double across the strands of the story. Economy came into play through the doubling. These big plays were performed by relatively small companies, with most of the actors taking on more than one role in each drama, sometimes five or six. Doubling was not forced upon the actors, as we might assume today. Doubling belonged to the actors' craft. Along with being elocutionists and acrobats, they were quick-change artists, and part of the pride of a good performer was his ability to play quite different kinds of roles on a single afternoon.

Writers had to learn how to write this kind of play. It did not come naturally to tailor a big plot exactly to the number of doubling actors the company had available. We will see in a moment that a cultural contest was being waged between writers who came from the ranks of actors and writers who had been to university. One reason why the most influential writers came from the actor group in the early years was that they knew this tricky combination of abundance and restraint from the inside. It is also a reason for the system of collaboration among writers. Collaboration brought new writers into contact with the veterans, who could teach them how to keep several dozen speaking parts in motion without losing track of the plot or the doubling pattern.

Those are some of the concerns faced by the writers of *Patient Grissell* (as the writers called it) during the fall of 1599. By December, they were piecing together their various contributions into a usable "book" of the play – what we today would call a "promptbook." Now that the company could see a stageable play taking shape, they made further payments to the authors, £3 on 19 December, £6 on 26 December, another five shillings on 28 December, another five shillings the next day. At some point during these later payments, the "book" of the play was turned over to the actors. If it was neatly prepared, the actors would have used it as it was. If a clean copy were needed, the actors would have hired a scribe. In either case, the text was now unified: a "book."

Or so it seemed. In truth, the text was about to be taken apart again. All play-wrights, then and now, must get used to the patch of agony that comes when the actors and the production team take hold of a text. This is the heart of theater, the joining together of various interpretations and sensibilities, but the process can take a toll on writers. In the Elizabethan theater, the "book" of *Patient Grissell* would now have been divided into parts and distributed to the actors. Sometimes the parts were copied onto long strips of paper which could be rolled up and carried about by the actors while they were memorizing their lines. Sometimes the manuscript was copied straight through and then chopped up into the separate parts, which would then have been pasted together to form the "rolls." These "rolls" (the word is related to "role") contained nothing but one actor's lines along with cue lines for each of his speeches. The "finished" text was now in an extreme state of distribution, each part being learned by an actor who would have only a sketchy idea of what the other actors were learning or what the overall play amounted to. Soon the text of the play had been committed to more than a dozen different memories, and when it came time to assemble everyone for a run-through, the parts belonged to the actors who had done the memorizing and had put their own stamps on their roles.

One problem the Elizabethan writer did not face was the actor who looks for the "subtext" of his role. The Elizabethan conception of "playing a role" was a far cry from ours. Searching for the subtext of a role would have been the farthest thing from the mind of a performer who was playing a daily repertory of fourteen or fifteen different plays at the same time as he was committing the text of this roll to memory. The job was to memorize this roll and keep it separate from the other memorized rolls he was playing at the same time. Because parts were frequently doubled in production, an actor may have been playing fifty different parts a month in twenty-five different plays. In the mornings he rehearsed with his fellows the new play that would get its first performance that week. In the afternoons he would perform with his fellows one of the fourteen or fifteen other plays now in repertory. After the performance, he would take up his roll for the new play that he would be rehearsing the following week and consign it to memory. The memories of Elizabethan actors are among the unexplained phenomena of human history – these were not short plays; the dialogue was among the most complex poetry ever written for the stage; there was nothing but candle light to work from at night; you could not know what the other roles consisted of while you learned yours; and on Sundays the preacher would be telling everyone you were doing something immoral. We do not know how these actors managed.

The dramatists would have seen their scripts undergo changes in this process, most of them unintended. Scribes would make mistakes copying out the parts. Actors would substitute fresh words here and there as memory played its tricks, and with so many other roles waiting in the memory, the tricks could at times have amounted to pulling in a line or, indeed, a few, from another play. By the time the actors had learned their roles, the acting company would have seen to it that the original text, or a copy of it, had been sent to the censor, the Master of the Revels, whose license was required for every play. (Ideally, the Master's license should have been obtained before the parts were learned, but the theater did not often have time for such orderliness.) If the censor wanted cuts or some words changed, the actors would have to learn them. Learning cuts is tricky, as all actors know, especially if cue lines for someone else's speeches disappear in the process. Further cuts might be introduced by the actors themselves, to reduce playing time or to save a few bit parts altogether. Additional passages might have to be written at this point, if it was found that more time was needed for backstage maneuvers, such as allowing actors who were doubling several parts to change costumes. Would the original authors have been called upon to write the additions? Would they have been consulted about the cuts? Not necessarily. If they were working for the Admiral's Men, they would have been writing at least one new play by then, and someone else might have written the patchwork: another writer hired for the job, or one of the actors, or the playhouse scribe.

Those are the conditions under which most dramatists worked in the later sixteenth century, when Shakespeare was getting started in the theater and building his career. It is not how he worked after he was established, as we will see, but it is the way most worked. The writers were hired hands, looking for large payments, caught up in the excitement of a new theater, and turning out scripts which might draw crowds to the highly competitive commercial playhouses.

Gradually over the years spanned by Shakespeare's career, the reputation of the theaters improved, and with it the reputation of playwrighting as a career. By the time Shakespeare retired from the theater, in about 1612, the modern sense of "authorship" in the theater was beginning to flicker into existence. This change was brought about by the achievements of a few stage-writers, and Shakespeare was the most important of the path-breakers. To see how this happened, we need to see something else first. Who were the dramatists? What backgrounds did they come from? Were they university graduates? Were they actors themselves?

Who did the Writing? Education and Class Backgrounds

The drama was about to make a permanent impact on English literature, and one sign of the change was the class background of the new dramatists. Respectable literature had always come mainly from the nobility or the landed gentry, or from the professional classes. Elizabethan literature was created by men and women of privilege. Raymond Williams once checked the class backgrounds of the writers listed in the *Cambridge Bibliography of English Literature* and found that of the thirty-six writers (of all kinds) who reached age ten between 1530 and 1580, two-thirds came from the nobility, the gentry, or the professional classes more or less related to the gentry. The other one-third were the sons of merchants, tradesmen, and craftsmen – but this is the group who wrote most of the new commercial drama. Williams called them "the radically new element" (Williams 1961: 232). They were men from what we would now think of as lower-middle-class families, men who did not have private incomes to fall back on, men who did not have a lot of status to lose in the first place.

Some of these playwrights were, like Shakespeare, actors themselves – it was their skill at performance that drew some sons of tradesmen to the theater. For those actors quick with a pen it would have been a normal corollary to write new scripts. Richard Tarlton, Robert Wilson, Anthony Munday, William Shakespeare, Ben Jonson, and Thomas Heywood all began their careers as actors, and became writers from within the theater, so to speak. Other dramatists, however, had been to Oxford or Cambridge, which were not simply bastions for those born to wealth and privilege. Thomas Lodge came from a tradesman family, but his father had risen to become lord mayor of London, and he could afford a university education. And it was quite possible for the son of a shoemaker like Christopher Marlowe to attain a university place on a scholarship. (Marlowe's scholarship was intended to prepare him for the clergy, but he became a spy, a playwright, and an atheist instead.) The result was that the writers of the new drama in London came mainly from the tradesman or lower-professional classes, but they were divided between those who had university degrees and those who had taken to playwrighting through some other route, often through being actors themselves.

This mixture of the university writers and the player-dramatists was not always smooth. In 1592 the well-known playwright Robert Greene, a Cambridge man before he became a writer, wrote an attack on actors, calling them "Puppets...that spake from our mouths" and "Anticks garnisht with our colours." He was especially vehement towards an actor who had shown the presumption to write plays himself, someone whom Greene calls "Shakescene" and insults by parodying a line from a Shakespeare play. There is no doubt that the lowly player who thought he could write plays as well as a university man was Shakespeare.

Greene's attack is contained in an open letter to certain "gentlemen" writers of his acquaintance, "that spend their wits in making plaies" – apparently Marlowe, George Peele, and either Thomas Nashe or Thomas Lodge – all university men. Obviously Greene meant to fire a salvo in some sort of battle between the university-educated playwrights and the players, especially those players who were competing with the university "wits" in writing plays, but why should he have singled out Shakespeare? And what was the real ground for his snobbish degradation of actors?

We have alluded to a tension between writers and actors built into the process of theater itself. Some writers thrive on this tension, but perhaps Greene was one of those for whom actors are a necessary evil. But something more than this is operating in Greene's 1592 attack, with its appeal to other university writers to join him in disparaging the players. There is a sign of educational snobbery here. Hardly any of the actors of the day had been to university. They were literate men, and they certainly acquired an education of a special sort through acting the complex and wide-ranging plays of the time; but they were not expected to have the aspirations for status which a university education could, and still can, arouse among snobs. The only university graduate who is known to have acted on the public stage was Stephen Gosson, who was at Oxford before he was a player. He did not make acting a long career, and while still a young man took to writing vociferous attacks on the immorality of the theater. Thomas Heywood, who was an actor for a time, claimed to have been at Cambridge, but this cannot be verified. The rest of the actors, as far as we know, gained their experience and training in the theater itself and set foot in Oxford and Cambridge only when on tour, where they were as often as not (especially at Cambridge) forbidden to put on their plays.

But why Shakespeare? There were other actor-dramatists at the time. Robert Wilson and Anthony Munday had been writing plays for longer than Shakespeare, and they were not university men. It is likely that Greene's attention was so sharply drawn to Shakespeare because Shakespeare had something the other actor-dramatists did not have, and that was a great facility in the medium Greene himself had learned to master, along with other university-educated writers (like Marlowe and Peele): dramatic language written in blank verse. Earlier actor-dramatists, like Tarlton, Wilson, and Munday, favored an assortment of styles, with blank verse one kind of dramatic speech among others. They wrote different forms for different kinds of actors and different kinds of scenes: fourteeners, prose, rhymed couplets, rhymed stanzas, *and* blank verse. They were not stretching the capabilities of any one kind of speech but practising them all. University-trained writers like Greene and Marlowe brought a passion for blank verse with them to London, however, Marlowe in particular becoming famous for the "mighty line" of this poetic method. They were experiment-ing with unrhymed iambic pentameter, learning how to break through the regularity of end-stopped lines to create verse paragraphs, and learning how actors could master these paragraphs to the point of making them seem like spontaneous speech. Shake-speare was one of two non-university men who was learning these same things about blank verse and was proving surprisingly good at it (the other was Thomas Kyd). That "surprisingly" comes from Greene's point of view. Most of the world's great poetry has been written by men and women who did not attend university, but to men who did, this fact is often obscure. Greene accused Shakespeare of only one actual fault, apart from his arrogance, and that consisted in supposing "he is as well able to bombast out a blanke verse as the best of you," the "best of you" being the university gentlemen addressed by the letter. The snobbery of the attack degrades players for being inferior to university-trained writers, but it also attacks *this* player, the "upstart Crow," for having the presumption to write in the very style the university writers were making a specialty.

So, if it had been up to Robert Greene, the answer to "Who did the writing?" would have been, "We did," and "We" would have been university men. But Greene was dead by the time his attack reached print in 1592. Marlowe was killed in a tavern fight a few months later. University men like Peele, Nashe, and Lodge wrote very little for the stage after 1593. The theaters were closed by a terrible epidemic of plague in 1593, and when they reopened in early 1594, the university writers whom Greene had thought to warn about the upstart crow were no longer part of the theater scene. As for the upstart crow, he had maneuvered his way through the disruptive playhouse closings by taking up respectable literature himself, turning out two long narrative poems dedicated to the earl of Southampton. But as soon as the theaters reopened in 1594, he returned to the stage and secured his future with the kind of position which Greene and Marlowe would never have imagined for themselves. He returned as one of the part-owners of an acting company – a "sharer" as the owners were called. It was the kind of position Tarlton and Wilson had held in their companies, only Shakespeare was going to make more of it than the others did, and he was going to become wealthy and respectable through his achievement.

Shakespeare's Career: The Writer as Sharer

As there were only some seven or eight sharers in the Chamberlain's Men, and as they were engaged in a risky but potentially profitable business, Shakespeare the sharer was staking a claim on prospects ranging from wealth to disaster. But the investment probably meant something else for a playwright. For a playwright to be a sharer meant that he did not have to find a market for his plays. He was writing for a group of actors who intended to hold together year after year, a group whose talents and specialties he knew well, a group virtually committed to staging his work. Now he even owned his plays – not because he wrote them, but because he shared in everything the company owned. We do not know if the company paid him separately for the plays, but we do know that as a sharer he was taking a part of the playhouse profits every day, whether or not he wrote the play being performed, and we also know that from 1599 on, some sharers of the Chamberlain's Men, including Shakespeare, owned the company's playhouse itself. Those sharers put up money for building the most famous of all London theaters, the Globe, which opened in 1599 on Bankside (across the Thames from the city proper, approximately where the reconstructed Globe stands today). This was the first time, and just about the last, that an acting company owned its own theater.

When a playwright gets to the point of owning the means of production too, he has passed beyond the ordinary income level of those who live by the pen. No one knows how much Shakespeare earned, but conservative scholars (Chambers 1930; Wells 1995) have estimated £180 to £200 per year. Remembering the Stratford schoolmaster's pay of £20, we may think even the conservative estimate for Shakespeare a little high, but this son of a glover was wealthy by the time he retired from the theater. It is on record that he purchased one of the two largest houses in Stratford-upon-Avon just three years after the new Chamberlain's Men were organized, and when he retired there about fifteen years later, he was a substantial landholder as well.

All Shakespeare's plays after 1594 were written for the same company of actors, who passed from the patronage of the lord chamberlain to that of the king himself when James I came to the throne in 1603. Because he knew the actors and stages he wrote for so well, he probably wrote his own plays more often than most writers did, and collaborated less. Still, the modern notion of the writer as lonely genius does not fit. The need for new plays was not so pressing in the latter half of his career as it had been earlier (because there were more successful older plays to repeat in the repertory), but this was still a theater built on original, contemporary work, and collaboration remained a useful way of increasing productivity. Some writers preferred collaboration, and there is no reason to think that Shakespeare turned his back on occasional opportunities. Late in his career, the team of Beaumont and Fletcher were collaborating for the King's Men and setting the fashion for the day. Shakespeare himself collaborated with Fletcher on at least two plays, and Thomas Middleton contributed to *Macbeth*. Very possibly Shakespeare was engaged in more teamwork than we are aware of, and pieces of other writers' work may remain undetected in Shakespeare texts.

One may detect an aura of respectability in the company's becoming the King's Men in 1603, but the degree of contact between royalty and the actors is a matter of scholarly debate. The King's Men gave more command performances at court than any other company – that much is certain. But in the growing tension between royalty and the citizenry of London – whose ideology was marked by a religious radicalism still hostile to the theater – acting remained a disreputable profession in the eyes of many.

Yet there was a gradual acceptance of common plays into the literary culture, and this was probably due less to royal patronage than to the role the theater itself played in circulating the literature of the day. The stage-writers mined the literary culture of the Renaissance in search of plots to satisfy the demand for new plays. They used prose romances, chronicle accounts of the history of England, classical literature, travel books, foreign bestsellers, long narrative poems. Shakespeare's earliest plays derived from English historians (Holinshed, Edward Hall, Sir Thomas More), from the classics (Ovid, Plautus, Seneca), and from continental writers (Montemayor, Ariosto, Bandello). With its choices of subject matter covering the range from Roman tragedy through English history to the popular prose romances of the day, the theater was gradually outdistancing its low-culture reputation and was in fact one of the forces driving English – the language itself, which was still regarded as faintly barbarous among the highly educated – into prominence as a major literary language. Many of the classical and European stories had already been translated into English when they were appropriated for the theater, but the theater put them into a language which could reach people of all classes and abilities, the quick listeners and spectators of Elizabethan London, for whom blank verse and good acting constituted a magnetic style. The playwrights who devoured the published literature of their own time and turned it into stage shows were forging a rich connection with the literary culture of the Renaissance. When Shakespeare turned the story of *Romeo and Juliet* into a play, it suddenly reached thousands of spectators, many of them unable to read the narrative sources on which it was based – a verse translation by Arthur Brooke of a French prose story which itself went back to the Italian writer Bandello, who was using earlier versions himself. As a result, *Romeo and Juliet*, a story deeply embedded in the continental Renaissance and for thirty years in England a "high culture" item in its poetic translation by Brooke (1562), was boosted into a widely popular plot when Londoners of all kinds were able to see Shakespeare's play in the theater in about 1595. (Something of the same sort is happening today, when most young people first see the Romeo and Juliet story in one of the film versions.)

The gradual acceptance of commercial drama into the literary culture can be seen in the emergence of Shakespeare's name as a valuable commodity in itself. Shakespeare was nobody in terms of class standing when his plays were first published, and the first two editions of *Romeo and Juliet* (1597 and 1599), no matter what a good job of circulating the story they were doing, did not mention his name. Playwrights with class standing had sometimes been named or initialed on title pages by then (Greene even listed his Master of Arts degree), but for the writer of common birth, the writer who had not been to university, the turning point came at about the turn of the century. Shakespeare's name was first given on published plays in 1598 (*Love's Labor's Lost*, his seventh or eighth to be published, plus some second editions of earlier plays). By 1600 his name obviously sold books – it appeared on four of his five plays first published in that year. Other common-born writers were making their mark by then or soon after. Ben Jonson's initials were carried on *Every Man Out of his Humour* in 1600, and Dekker made it onto a title page in 1602 (but not on *Patient Grissell*, which named no writers when it appeared in 1603). By the time Shakespeare retired, about half of his plays had been published, and over half of those bore his name.

Not that the author seems to have cared. The plays published during his lifetime contain so many printers' errors that we cannot suppose he even proofread them before they came out (those early narrative poems dedicated to Southampton were certainly proofed, though). It seems to be Shakespeare more than anyone else who made plays into a recognized form of literature; but this same Shakespeare seems to have disregarded this advance in status almost entirely. To gain a coat of arms for his family name, he would go out of his way, but there was not time in the day for proofreading his own published plays.

The dramatist who cared about literary status, and who made a campaign out of turning plays into respectable literature, was Ben Jonson. Jonson was careful to see his scripts through the press, and then, in 1616, the year of Shakespeare's death, he had the audacity to publish his writing to date in an expensive folio collection. This was a noteworthy piece of self-aggrandizement in itself, but the startling thing was that the bulk of Jonson's "works" were plays – plays being set forth as though they ranked with his poetry and commanded the highest attention. These two, Shakespeare and Jonson, the one acting as if he did not care, the other as though his career depended on it, were making plays into a permanent part of the established literary culture.

Jonson was ridiculed for his effort. "Pray tell me, Ben," wrote one wag, "where doth the mystery lurk / What others call a play, you call a work?" But the Jonson folio marked a cultural shift that had been under way for some time. Plays were now beginning to be known as "literature," and the definition was driven home seven years later when two actors from the King's Men published their late colleague Shakespeare's plays, in a folio version which went into four editions in the seventeenth century and eventually became one of the most famous books in the world. A Beaumont and Fletcher folio followed in 1647. Playwriting had shifted its image, and "works" written for the common stage were now available in fine books for the establishment.

Drama is still a suspect medium among the pious, but those who fret when the young and gifted head for Islington, Greenwich Village, or Hollywood to write scripts cannot possibly think that Shakespeare made a mistake when he went to London and found a place with the players. Writing plays for the fringe still comes second to writing A-levels for university placement in the minds of the influential and author-itative, but the A-level is bound to include searching questions about a Shakespeare script that was first written close to the fringe.

REFERENCES AND FURTHER READING

Bentley, G. E. 1971: *The Profession of Dramatist in Shakespeare's Time*. Princeton: Princeton University Press.

Blayney, Peter W. M. 1997: The publication of play-books. In John D. Cox and David Scott Kastan (eds), *A New History of Early English Drama*, New York: Columbia University Press, 383–422.

Carson, Neil 1988: *A Companion to Henslowe's Diary*. Cambridge: Cambridge University Press.

Chambers, E. K. 1923: *The Elizabethan Stage*, 4 vols. Oxford: Clarendon Press.

——1930: *William Shakespeare: A Study of Facts and Problems*, 2 vols. Oxford: Clarendon Press.

Gurr, Andrew 1996: *The Shakespearian Playing Companies*. Oxford: Clarendon Press.

Knutson, Roslyn 1991: *The Repertory of Shakespeare's Company, 1594–1613*. Fayetteville, Ark.: University of Arkansas Press.

Masten, Jeffrey 1996: *Textual Intercourse: Collaboration, Authorship, and Sexualities in Renaissance Drama*. Cambridge: Cambridge University Press.

Miller, Edward H. 1959: *The Professional Writer in Elizabethan England*. Cambridge, Mass.: Harvard University Press.

Mowat, Barbara 1997: The theatre and literary culture. In John D. Cox and David Scott Kastan (eds), *A New History of Early English Drama*, New York: Columbia University Press, 213–30.

Rasmussen, Eric 1997: The revision of scripts. In John D. Cox and David Scott Kastan (eds), *A New History of Early English Drama*, New York: Columbia University Press, 441–60.

Rutter, Carol 1985: *Documents of the Rose Playhouse*. Manchester: Manchester University Press.

Thomson, Peter 1992: *Shakespeare's Professional Career*. Cambridge: Cambridge University Press.

Wells, Stanley 1995: *Shakespeare: A Life in Drama*. New York: W. W. Norton.

Werstine, Paul 1997: Plays in manuscript. In John D. Cox and David Scott Kastan (eds), *A New History of Early English Drama*, New York: Columbia University Press, 481–97.

Williams, Raymond 1961: *The Long Revolution*. New York: Columbia University Press.

15

Shakespeare's 'Natiue English'

Jonathan Hope

In 1578, when Shakespeare was fourteen years old, John Florio, an Italian born and brought up in London, published a textbook for speakers of English who wanted to learn Italian. Called *Florio His firſte Fruites* (in modern English: 'Florio's First Fruits'), the book consists mainly of imaginary conversations which are printed in English and Italian for learners to copy. Like most foreign phrase-books, the work has its idiosyncrasies (the subject of buying gloves, and the vexed question of whether or not they should be perfumed, comes up more frequently than you would expect), but the dialogues offer us a version of the world in which Shakespeare grew up – a version all the more fascinating since Florio and Shakespeare later shared noble patrons, and almost certainly knew each other (perhaps uncomfortably well: it has been suggested that the Dark Lady of Shakespeare's *Sonnets* was Florio's wife). Chapter 13 of Florio's book offers its readers examples of 'Familiare talke' (everyday conversation); in it, several gentlemen chat about the situation in Europe, the realm of England and its queen. Florio's parents were Protestant refugees, so it is no surprise that his speakers praise England ('it is a good Realme') and Elizabeth, the Protestant monarch. She is 'learned, wyſe, gentle, courteous, noble, prudent, liberal, fayre, louyng, vertuous ... the laſt refuge, defenſe, and bulwarke of al baniſhed vertues' (fo.1 1r–v). This kind of hyperbolic idealization of Elizabeth is frequent in English texts of the late 1570s and 1580s: England felt itself isolated and threatened by the Catholic monarchies of Europe, and the fact that the latter tended to have male rulers hardly made the English any less anxious. As if by way of compensation, a cult of Elizabeth, celebrating her and her femininity – though significantly her femininity as a virgin queen – developed.

It is significant, however, that Florio's approval of England, and England's queen, does not extend to the English language. Asked 'what thinke you of the ſpeach?', an Italian visitor's answer is distinctly unflattering:

> Certis if you wyl beleeue me, it doth not like me at al, becauſe it is a language confuſed,
> bepeeſed with many tongues: it taketh many words of the latine, & mo frõ the French,

& mo frõ the Italian, and many mo frõ the Duitch, some alſo frõ the Greeke, & frõ the Britaine, ſo that if euery lãguage had his owne wordes againe, there woulde but a fewe remaine for Engliſh men, and yet euery day they adde . . . take a booke and reade, but marke well, and you ſhall not reade foure wordes togeather of true Engliſh. (fo. 50 v)

For Florio's imagined speaker, English is a confused language, pieced together ('bepeeſed') with words borrowed from six different languages, so that it hardly has any words of its own. Even with this motley heritage, English continues to borrow words daily, compounding the fault.

It may be surprising to encounter such a rejection of the mixed vocabulary of English, since today, English speakers tend to congratulate themselves on the cosmopolitan nature of English words; but Florio clearly values linguistic purity over widespread borrowing (a position held today by authorities within the French-speaking world, who see borrowing from English as a threat to the identity of French). Nor was this dismissive view of English based simply on linguistic theory. English was not, in 1578, much use if you wanted to travel:

> It is a language that wyl do you good in England, but paſſe Douer, it is woorth nothing.
> *Is it not vſed then in other coũtreyes?*
> No ſir . . . Engliſh merchantes, when they are out of England, it liketh them not, and they doo not ſpeake it
>
> (fo. 50 r–v)

Today English is the most widely spoken language in the world – soon more people will have it as a second language than learn it from birth. Scientific debates, inter-governmental discussions, and business deals are routinely transacted in English between people who speak different languages and use English as a *lingua franca*. At the end of the sixteenth century, however, it was true: English would barely get you past Dover.

Of course, Florio had an ulterior motive: as a teacher of Italian and French, it was hardly in his interest to promote English as a *lingua franca*. But the discussions of his fashionable gentlemen, as they move from the glover's shop to the tennis court, make it clear that in the late 1570s English was a language of small prestige and little use. So small was its prestige, indeed, that the word 'English' is not applied to the language when used outside the political boundaries of England. When asked of Queen Elizabeth '*Doth ſhe ſpeak many languages*', one of Florio's speakers replies:

> She ſpeaketh eight languages.
> Shee ſpeaketh Greeke, Latine, Italian, French, Spaniſh, Scottiſh, Flemiſh, and Engliſh: al theſe tongues ſhee ſpeaketh very wel, and eloquent
>
> (fo. 11 v)

'Scottiſh' and 'Engliſh' count as two languages, not because Florio means Gaelic (he calls that 'Britaine' when listing the languages English borrows from), but because these are equally historical developments from Old English, used in sovereign countries, just as French and Spanish are developments from Latin. When Florio wrote, Scottish English and English English had both developed somewhat different, but internally consistent, written norms. When Elizabeth I wrote to her 'cousin', James VI of Scotland, she wrote using English English norms, and he replied using Scottish English – the two were mutually comprehensible (at least on paper), but recognizably different.

Florio thus reminds us that Shakespeare grew up at a time when the status of English was uncertain. It had only relatively recently replaced French as the language of England's law courts and Parliament (the very words 'court' and 'parliament' are French), and it was still not the language in which serious scholars wrote (that was Latin). Nor could English boast a native literature to rival other European vernaculars like Italian or Spanish – never mind classical languages like Latin or Greek. A change in how the English viewed their language was under way, however: English represented the language of the major Protestant monarchy, which inevitably set it in opposition to the culturally fashionable, but religiously suspect, languages of Italy, France and Spain. It was difficult to maintain a rhetoric that celebrated England, and England's queen, as the last hope of Protestantism, while denigrating the English language. Furthermore, the emphasis which Protestantism placed on the translation of the Bible into the language of everyday use encouraged a rising of the prestige of English relative to that of Latin.

Consequently, while Florio was busy disparaging English, others were writing it up. In 1582, the schoolmaster Richard Mulcaster was prepared to admit that English was 'vncouth', but claimed that this was only because it was 'vnused'. There was no intrinsic linguistic reason why English should not be developed by writers so that it could deal with any type of material – and borrowing words was something all languages did: 'And tho we vse & must vse manie foren terms, when we deal with such arguments, we do not anie more then the brauest tungs do & and euen verie those, which crake of their cunning' (cited from Görlach 1991: 231). The tongues which 'craked' (boasted) of their 'cunning' (learning) were the classical languages and the more developed European vernaculars. If English lacked the vocabulary of other languages, words could be borrowed; if English lacked the literature of other languages, works could be written; if English lacked the historical depth of other languages, their classic texts could be translated, and thus subsumed into the English tradition.

In the 1590s, in the wake of the Armada victory, the mythologization of Elizabeth merged with specific poetic projects to raise English up to, and beyond, the status of other languages. Notable here is the work of one of Mulcaster's pupils, Edmund Spenser, who experimented with the vocabulary of English in his pastoral poem *The Shepheardes Calender* (1579), and set about deliberately to celebrate Elizabeth, and provide English literature with a native epic, in *The Faerie Queene* (1590). Florio attacked the mongrel vocabulary of English, but in the 1590s, Richard Carew wrote celebrating the 'bepeeſed' nature of English, even including a barbed thrust at Latin:

we borrowe (and that not shamfully) from the Dutch, the Breton, ye Romaine, the Dane, the French, Italyan, & Spanyard, how cann our stocke be other then exceeding plentifull...we imploye the borrowed ware soe far to our aduantadg that we raise a profitt of new woordes which yeat in their owne countrey are not merchantable, for example we deduce diuers woordes from the Latine which in the Latyne self cannot be yealded. (Cited from Görlach 1991: 242–3)

Florio's rhetoric of confusion has become an image of an abundantly, and profitably, stocked shop.

Such politically motivated shifts in the perception of English were matched in the early seventeenth century by shifts in its geographical distribution. In 1603, Elizabeth died, and her Scottish cousin became James I of England. James, a highly literate man, published many works during his lifetime, and after 1603 these appeared with London imprints and followed English English norms. The shifting of James's court to London effectively marked the end of official Scottish English, and, literary experiments aside, Scottish English ceased to be a written language. Had James decided to remain in Scotland, it is possible that Scottish English norms would have spread, and today, instead of 'which' we might write something like 'quhilk'.

As English English established itself in Britain, the language was also travelling to the Americas, in a series of speculative 'plantations', or colonizations. In 1621, the Mayflower Pilgrims, on the point of starvation, were saved by the help of two Native Americans, Squanto and Samoset, who taught the settlers how to live off the land. Communication was possible because both Native Americans already spoke English – Squanto had learned his in London. The spread of English as a second language had begun, along with the colonialism that was to guarantee the future linguistic dominance of English on the coat-tails of British and American economic power. Shakespeare, born in a country at times ashamed of its language, died in one actively exporting it.

Early Modern English: Variation and Standardization

The version of English used by Florio, Mulcaster, Squanto and Shakespeare is now called 'Early Modern English'. As the name suggests, this type of English is recognizably close to modern English – but with some significant differences. The Early Modern English period is conventionally dated from around 1400 to around 1700, which includes the whole of Shakespeare's lifetime (1564–1616); indeed, his career coincides with crucial stages in many of the most important changes in English during this period, a fact which has implications for the linguistic resources available to him.

The most obvious differences between Early Modern English and present-day Standard English are in spelling and printing conventions. In the extracts from Florio, there are 'long s' forms ('ſ'), and letters with bars over the top ('frõ' and 'lãguage'), as well as apparent confusion over the use of 'u' and 'v'. These features are relics of the manuscript tradition which lies behind printing: scribes used two different 's' forms to increase legibility in certain positions; letters with bars indicate that the following letter has been missed out (a useful device for speeding up writing and saving space), so 'frõ' is 'from' and 'lãguage' is 'language'; 'u' and 'v' are in fact used consistently – 'v' is always used at the start of words, and 'u' is always used in the middle (the usage derives from Latin inscriptions). Spelling varies considerably – in just four lines of Florio, the word *she* has four different spellings:

Doth ∫he ∫peak many languages?
She ∫peaketh eight languages.
Shee ∫peaketh Greeke.
∫hee ∫peaketh very wel.

Today, editors usually modernize such features of printing and spelling, so that early modern texts look more familiar, and can be read more easily. In this chapter, I have retained as many features of the original texts as possible, because they are evidence for the nature of Early Modern English. (Thus Shakespeare's texts are usually quoted from the first published version, quarto or folio, though in the cases of *Hamlet* and *The Merry Wives of Windsor*, I have used the second published text; line references are to the *Riverside* edition, however.)

The degree of variation we find in Early Modern English is typical of a language undergoing *standardization*. Standardization is a complex set of processes which occur when a language is written down and used for formal functions which require communication over distance or time (perhaps government or business). Pre-standardization written languages show a great deal of variation: in spelling, because people spell words as they pronounce them, and in grammar, because people use their own dialect grammars. Standardization identifies a single set of spellings, and delimits a restricted range of grammatical constructions for use in the written language, so that texts can be understood by anyone who speaks the language. Written English is now very highly standardized indeed. This means that anyone who can read English, wherever they were born, will be able to read this chapter: but it hides the fact that I pronounce the words 'written language' more like 'ri'en langwidch', and that in my casual speech the past tense of the verb *to treat* is not 'treated', but 'tret'.

By the end of the sixteenth century, English was rapidly developing a standardized written form. However, a great deal of variation in spelling and grammar remained. As we have seen, there was no 'right' way to spell 'she', and verb endings also varied – in Florio, Elizabeth '∫peake*th* eight languages', rather than 'speaks' them. We also find two ways of forming questions: one using the verb *to do*, as we would form it today – '*Doth* ∫he ∫peak many languages?' – and another changing the word order – '*What thinke you* of the queene?' (instead of 'What *do* you think of the queen?').

In these instances of grammatical variation we can see an important aspect of linguistic change during standardization: competition between linguistic forms for the same role. In the case of 'ʃpeak*eth*', we know from our knowledge of Present-day Standard English that -*eth* has now been completely replaced by -*s* as an ending for this form of the verb (the third person singular present tense). Historically, -*s* was the northern English ending, and -*eth* was southern; for hundreds of years before the early modern period -*s* had been gaining ground in the south, so that by the end of the sixteenth century it is common to find both endings in the same text, even in the same line: 'Who want*eth* food, and will not ʃay hee want*s* it' (*Pericles*, I. iv. 11).

How did early modern speakers decide which ending to use? It has been suggested that -*eth* carries a sense of formality or antiquity, and some early modern writers seem to use -*eth* for continuous states and -*s* for discrete or sudden events (so in the quotation from *Pericles*, -*eth* is used for the state of wanting something, which is a continuous state, and -*s* for the action of saying that you want it, a discrete event). At times, metrical considerations may prompt the use of one or other ending: 'Th'one ʃweetely flatter*s*, th'other fear*eth* harme' (*The Rape of Lucrece*, 172) is what appears in the text. If Shakespeare thought about 'Th'one sweetly flatter*eth*, th'other fears harm', he might have rejected it because of the way two light stresses come next to each other in 'flatter*eth*', and two strong stresses in 'fears harm'. Note, by the way, that once again we have the -*s* ending used for a discrete event (the flattering), and the -*eth* ending used for a state of mind (fear). Shakespeare generally prefers -*s* endings to -*eth*, which suggests that we should pay attention whenever he uses -*eth*, as there may be some special implication involved. However, with the common verbs *to do* and *to have*, he prefers -*eth*, using *hath* and *doth* more often than *has* and *does* (frequent words often resist change longer than less common ones).

Just as -*s* replaces -*eth*, so questions formed with *do* replace the older pattern of inversion (the 'What thinke you of the queene?' type). This change also affects negative sentences and orders, so that early modern writers have two ways of forming each of the following sentence types:

Questions
        without *do*:   *Liues he*[?] (*Antony and Cleopatra*, IV. xiv. 114)
        with *do*:   *doth he keepe* his bed? (*1 Henry IV*, IV. i. 21)
Negatives
        without *do*:   Cogitation / *Reʃides not* in that man, that do's not thinke (*The Winter's Tale*, I. ii. 272)
        with *do*:   Cogitation / Reʃides not in that man, that *do's not thinke* (*The Winter's Tale*, I. ii. 272)

(once again, we find both possible variants in a single line here: Shakespeare could have written, 'cogitation / Does not reside in that man that thinks not'.)

Orders
        without *do*:   *Deceaue me not* now (*Love's Labour's Lost*, II. i. 230)
        with *do*:   *do not deceiue* me (*The Rape of Lucrece*, 585)

Once again, Early Modern English offers its users choices which have now been standardized out of the language. In the early modern period, there are two distinct systems for forming questions and negatives – one using *do*, one without it. Speakers of Early Modern English thus had two sets of rules in their heads for the formation of such sentences: how did they decide which to use? To a large extent, speakers didn't decide consciously between the systems at all; everyone used both, usually favouring the modern system (the one with *do*) at a rate that was constant during their lifetime. In the population as a whole, the rate of usage of the modern system increased with time: each new generation of speakers was more likely to use *do* in forming negatives and questions than the last. Thus Shakespeare, born in 1564, uses the modern system 83 per cent of the time, while John Fletcher, born in 1579, uses the modern system 93 per cent of the time. As usage of the modern system increased with each generation, so the older system took on connotations of formality – potentially, users can distinguish between the systems on the basis of register, as some seem to do with *-eth* versus *-s*. There can also be technical reasons for choosing one system over another, as the following line from *The Rape of Lucrece* shows:

> Thou look'ſt not like deceipt, do not deceiue me (585)

Here Shakespeare first uses the old system ('Thou look'ſt not...'), then the new one ('do not deceiue...'), which may appear inconsistent – but try adapting the line so that the usages are consistent in use or non-use of *do*:

with *do*: Thou dost not look like deceit, do not deceive me

This produces a line with twelve syllables, and disrupts the stress pattern (if this explanation isn't clear, read chapter 16 on metrics, then reread the line). It is slightly harder to see why Shakespeare didn't use the old system for both forms:

without *do*: Thou look'st not like deceit, deceive me not

since this gives a regular iambic pentameter line (ten syllables), and brings 'deceit' and 'deceive' nicely together (it is characteristic of Shakespeare to play with the 'same' word in different grammatical roles: 'deceit' is a noun, 'deceive' a verb). So why did Shakespeare choose to mix the forms, and produce an irregular line (eleven syllables) in the process? The answer comes when we look at the line in context:

> My husband is thy friend, for his ſake ſpare me,
> Thy ſelfe art mightie, for thine own ſake leaue me:
> My ſelfe a weakling, do not then inſnare me.
> Thou look'ſt not like deceipt, do not deceiue me
>
> (582–5)

Shakespeare is building a rhetorical structure where each line ends with the pattern verb + pronoun ('ʃpare me / . . . leaue me / . . . inʃnare me / . . . deceiue me'); using the new system allows him to move the *not* forms in lines 584 and 585 so that the *me* forms come at the end, as they do in lines 582 and 583. Had he used the old system, this would not have been possible.

A third example of variation and replacement comes in the pronoun system. Present-day Standard English has a slightly curious feature: when we speak to one person, we use the pronoun *you*; but when we speak to more than one person, we use exactly the same pronoun: 'you'. We do this even though other pronouns distinguish between singular and plural ('I' versus 'we'; 'he' and 'she' versus 'they'). This strange situation is the result of several hundred years of change. Before 1200, English *did* distinguish between singular and plural in this pronoun. 'You' was used only to more than one person, and 'thou', was used for the singular. Sometime in the thirteenth century, however, people started using *you* to just one person when that person was powerful or commanded respect in some way. So kings, bishops and nobles started to be addressed with 'you'. During the thirteenth and fourteenth centuries this singular 'you' was comparatively rare, but as time went on, more and more people came to be addressed with it (much as today everyone in a company gets to be a vice-president, or all American academics get to be called 'professor'). Eventually, anyone in any kind of authority could be addressed as 'you': masters over workers, husbands over wives, parents over children.

The factors dictating usage of 'thou' and 'you' have been termed 'power' and 'solidarity': if someone was more powerful than you were, you used 'you' to them, and they used 'thou' to you; if you were of equal status with someone, you would exchange the same pronoun – 'thou' between lower-class speakers, and 'you' between upper-class speakers (solidarity). We can see this model at work in the following exchange between real early modern speakers, recounted as evidence in court around 1572. Here, three men are arguing about some stolen sheep. Two of them, Mr Antony and Mr Ratcliff, are of relatively high class; one, Roger Donn, is of relatively low class.

MR ANTONY.   Dyd not *thou* promess me that *thou* wold tell me . . . who sold George
                        Whitfeld sheep
ROGER DONN.   I need not unless I woll
MR RATCLIFF.   *Thou* breaks promess
ROGER DONN.   *You* will know yt soon enowgh for *your* man Nicoll Dixson stole them
                        . . . although *ye* be a gent. and I a poore man my honestye shalbe as
                        good as *yours*
MR RATCLIFF.   What saith *thou* liknes *thou thine* honestye to myn
                                                (cited from Hope 1993:86)

Note that Donn continues to use 'you' and its forms to Mr Ratcliff, even when he tries to assert his moral equality ('my honestye shalbe as good as *yours*'), but Mr Ratcliff's emphatic use of 'thou' forms in reply puts Donn firmly in his social place.

Such 'power' usages, prompted by the relative social statuses of speakers, are easy to find in Shakespeare. It is also possible to find instances where characters use both forms to the same person – for example, Prospero speaking to his treacherous brother at the end of *The Tempest*:

> For *you* (moſt wicked ſir) whom to call brother
> Would euen infect my mouth, I do forgiue
> *Thy* rankeſt fault
>
> (*Tempest*, V. i. 130–2)

Clearly something more than social status must be involved here in dictating which pronoun is used. Prospero's brother does not move up or down the social scale from one line to the next: but Prospero's emotional attitude to him may change. An actor playing Prospero might decide that, even as he says that he forgives his brother, Prospero becomes angry, thinking about what his brother has done to him – and so he shifts from the polite, or neutral, 'you', to a 'thou' of anger. In support of such an emotional reading of the forms, we find shifting pronouns in early modern court records. The following is an argument between two women, Bullman and Styllynge, from the late 1560s or early 1570s:

BULLMAN.   Noughtie pak
STYLLYNGE.   What nowtynes know *you* by me I am neyther goossteler nor steg
             [gander] steiler I would *you* knew ytt
BULLMAN.   What noughty hoore caull *thou* me goose steiler
STYLLYNGE.   Nay marry I know *thee* for no such but I thank *you* for *your* good reporte
             whills *you* and I talk further

> (cited from Hope 1993: 88)

Note here, that although Bullman insults Styllynge ('Noughtie pak' sounds funny now, but was caustic in its day), Styllynge replies with an apparently polite 'you'. While replying, however, she manages to accuse Bullman of stealing geese, and this so enrages Bullman that she insults Styllynge again, this time more forcefully ('hoore' – whore – was a very serious accusation at the time), and switches from her initial 'you' to an angry 'thou' ('caull *thou* me...'). Stung by this insult, Styllynge also switches from 'you' to 'thou' ('I know *thee*'), but then immediately switches back again as she tries to calm the situation ('I thank *you*...').

Choice of pronoun form can therefore mark not only social relationship (which is stable), but emotional attitude (which can change rapidly), and writers can vary their choice of form to communicate changes of register and emotion. Shakespeare makes extensive use of this feature of the language to map subtly shifting emotional attitudes, and paying attention to 'thou' and 'you' forms can often give clues to character and plot development. As with other grammatical choices, many factors have the potential to influence choice of form (even down to which sounds better), but if readers are aware of the range of possibilities, Shakespeare's texts become even richer in their possible meanings.

In each of the three examples of grammatical variation surveyed so far, standardization has subsequently removed the variation from English, hiding from readers the shades of meaning, and technical resources, available to early modern writers. Although a printed standard was emerging in the early modern period, it was not codified in dictionaries or grammars, or drummed into school children on pain of social ridicule. The linguistic fragments which would come together to form Standard English were drawn from the variety of English dialects slowly and haphazardly. From our point of view, Early Modern English is characterized by the choices it gives its writers where today we have none. Further, more detailed accounts of Early Modern English grammar can be found in Barber 1997, Görlach 1991 and Lass, forthcoming. Stein 1987 focuses on variation between *-th* and *-s* endings; Stein 1990 and Hope 1994: 11–26 have more detail on auxiliary *do*; Calvo 1992 and Hope 1993 are concerned with the use of *thou* and *you*.

While the grammar of standard written English was being formalized, change was also shaping the English vocabulary. As we have seen, the nature of the vocabulary of English was a matter for hot debate during Shakespeare's lifetime (few seem to have been aware of the grammatical changes in progress), and the diverse roots of English words were well known. Almost all commentators were agreed that English had to expand its vocabulary in order to challenge other languages, but there was controversy over how this should be done. Some, sharing Florio's unease at the notion of a 'mixed' vocabulary, felt that writers should go back to past states of the language, and revive lost native words. This 'purist' position was propounded by Spenser's tutor Richard Mulcaster – and his pupil put it into practice in his poetry. An alternative position, perhaps more in tune with the intellectual mood of the time, is represented by Richard Carew's comments, stressing the value of borrowing from other languages. Renaissance humanism celebrated 'copiousness' – the ability to present similar material within varying rhetorical structures and with contrasting stylistic tones. A rich vocabulary enabled writers of English to do this. Of course, it was possible to go too far in borrowing: early modern drama is full of characters like Armado in *Love's Labour's Lost* who speak as though they had swallowed a shelf of dictionaries ('go tendernes of yeeres . . . giue enlargement to the Swaine, bring him feʃtinatly hither' is how he says 'Go boy, let the swain out, and bring him here quickly': III. i. 4–6). Such words were pilloried as 'Ink-horn terms', because they savoured too much of the study, and characters like Dogberry (*Much Ado About Nothing*) are shown stumbling over their use.

To a large extent, however, the controversy over borrowing – native or foreign – is a false one. Whatever the theorists suggested, in practice the language did both. The most visible new words came from other languages – a process which had been going on since the Norman invasion. After the victory of William the Conqueror, French replaced English as the official language of government and the law, and a native version of French, Anglo-Norman, arose. Early in this *Middle English* period, English became much less common in the written record than Latin or French, although it continued as a spoken language. English did not become the most common written language again until after the late 1490s, and the written English of the late fifteenth century is very different from that found up to 1100, the most striking change being in its vocabulary. Having been spoken for hundreds of years alongside the more prestigious Anglo-Norman, we find that Middle English has taken on hundreds of French words – words for new things and new concepts, but also words which already had an equivalent in English, producing synonyms. Later in the Middle English period, and increasingly in the early modern period, writers turned to Latin as a source of new words, again borrowing to fill gaps in the English lexicon (for example, 'gorgon' and 'gladiator'), but also borrowing to produce synonyms ('depict', 'transcribe', and a range of words in some way synonymous with 'wit' or 'mind': 'ingenuity', 'intellect', 'intelligence').

The result of this increase in synonyms was an increase in the ability of writers to shift between registers, since Latin- or French-derived words tend in English to have a more formal register than native words, and Shakespeare frequently contrasts terms from different registers. Here is Macbeth, having just killed King Duncan, trying to blame Duncan's pages:

> Here lay *Duncan*,
> His Siluer skinne, lac'd with his Golden Blood,
>
> . . . .
>
> there the Murtherers,
> Steep'd in the Colours of their Trade; their Daggers
> Vnmannerly breech'd with gore
> (*Macbeth*, II. iii. 111–17)

The description of Duncan's skin as 'lac'd' with blood, contrasts with the verbs used of the blood on the supposed murderers, who are 'steep'd' in it, and their daggers, which are 'breech'd' (literally 'trousered'!) with it. 'Lace' comes from French, while 'steep' and 'breech' are native English terms. 'Lace' (in the sense of the fabric) was borrowed from French in the mid-sixteenth century – characteristically, Shakespeare seems to be one of the first people to convert the noun into a verb. 'Breech'd' ('to be trousered with') comes from a noun 'breech', which is Old English – it is recorded as a verb from 1468, and Shakespeare is given in the *Oxford English Dictionary* as the first writer to use it metaphorically. 'Steep'd' must also be an Old English word – because related words are found in the sister languages of Old English. It is not, however, found in any written text before 1400 – a useful reminder that the 'first use' dates given in the *OED* are dependent on the very patchy survival of texts and searches that were not comprehensive: we should always treat these as indicative, rather than absolute, especially for early words, where far fewer texts survive. We should also remember that the Victorian scholars who read texts for the first edition of the *OED* paid special attention to Shakespeare: his texts were read more thoroughly, and cited more often, so he is often credited with the first use of words, or senses of words, which can in fact be found earlier in other writers (Schäfer 1980).

First use is less relevant than effective use – and it should be noted here how Shakespeare plays on the registers of words, between English and French, but also within the native word-stock. 'Lace', along with 'gold' and 'silver', have connotations of nobility – the accused murderers, by contrast, are tradesmen, people who work for a living. There is also a careful shift from the relatively neutral 'Blood', when the blood is on the noble Duncan, to the repulsive 'gore', when it is on the grooms. Both are native English words, but 'gore' originally meant 'dung', and still carries shades of this meaning.

Newly borrowed words provoke admiring, and satiric, comment in plays (Armado is described as a man of 'fier new' words in *Love's Labour's Lost*, I. i. 178; Shallow is entranced by Bardolph's use of 'accommodated' in *2 Henry IV*, III. ii. 71), But we should remember that the great majority of new words in the period are produced by *derivation* rather than borrowing. That is, they are created by combining existing words ('fier new' is arguably an example) or adding affixes (looking for a synonym for 'killed', Shakespeare comes up with 'vnliued': *Lucrece*, 1754) or simply using a word in a different grammatical role – as Shakespeare seems to do above with 'lace', changing it from a noun, to a verb meaning 'decorate as if with lace'. Shakespeare is often represented as a major coiner of new words in English. In fact, it is probably safer, and certainly more interesting, to say that Shakespeare has a particular tendency to *derive* words – especially by adding negative prefixes (like *de-* and *un-*) and by shifting their grammatical role (*conversion*). The opening lines of 'A Lover's Complaint', the poem that accompanies the *Sonnets*, are a good example of this:

> From off a hill whose concaue wombe reworded,
> A plaintfull ſtory from a ſiſt'ring vale

The poem begins with the narrator overhearing the lover's voice echoing from the landscape, but instead of 'echoing' or 'reflecting' the voice, the hill 'rewords' it. Shakespeare creates a verb from the noun 'word', and the prefix *re-*. In the second line, instead of 'nearby', or perhaps 'similar', we have 'ſiſt'ring' – a verb ('to sister') created from a noun by conversion, and then used as an adjective. Shakespeare probably doesn't borrow words any more or less frequently than his contemporaries; but he does seem to be fascinated by the semantic possibilities of derivation, the way meanings can be refreshed and recombined by placing a familiar word in an unfamiliar role. There is an excellent discussion of the vocabulary of Early Modern English in Barber 1997: 219–59. Spevack 1985, drawing on the monumental Spevack 1968–80, focuses on Shakespeare's vocabulary. Elam 1984 explores the literary effects of Shakespeare's word play.

Phonology: The Sound of Early Modern English

There were no tape recorders in early modern England. This means that everything we 'know' about the sound of Early Modern English is a guess. We have good reasons for thinking our guesses are reasonably accurate, but they remain guesses. Our knowledge of Early Modern English pronunciation is based on the spelling of manuscripts and texts (one of the useful side-effects of not having a standard spelling system is that people often record their pronunciation of words when they write them) and the evidence of contemporary spelling reformers and orthoepists (writers who studied the sounds of their own language). The phonology of Early Modern English needs to be considered separately from spelling, grammar and vocabulary, since spoken English has not been standardized: written English today is much less variable than Early Modern written English; but current spoken English retains at least as much variation as would have been found in Early Modern spoken English (a fact sometimes glossed over by people who speculate about what 'Elizabethan English' would have sounded like – as if there was only one accent at the time). In reading Early Modern texts, it is useful to know, however, that many words had different pronunciations from today; some words had more than one possible pronunciation; and some words had different, or alternative, stress patterns.

During the Early Modern period, English was going through a process known as 'The Great Vowel Shift'. As the name suggests, phonologists see this as a major event in the history of English pronunciation. What seems to have happened is that during the period 1400–1700, the vowel sounds of English (especially southern English) changed. Words like 'house', 'mouse', 'down', 'town' and 'brown' in southern English now have the vowel sound /au/. Originally, though, these words all had the vowel sound /u:/, which made them rhyme with 'moose' – ([hu:s] [mu:s] [du:n] [tu:n]) – as they still do in some Scottish and northern English accents. Similarly, the vowel sound in 'ice', 'fly' and 'pie' originally made these words rhyme with modern /i:/ words like 'peace' and 'bee' – ([i:s], [fli:], [pi:]). During the Great Vowel Shift, these sounds, and others, moved towards those they have today in the south, but they did not all move together, and they did not move at the same time for all speakers – indeed, for some speakers, they still have not changed.

The Great Vowel Shift therefore increased the variety of possible pronunciations of the same word within early modern England. The words 'sea' and 'see', for example, were once pronounced differently, as their spellings suggest: 'see' had the /i:/ vowel it has today, but 'sea' had a vowel represented by /e:/, and probably sounded a bit like modern 'say'. During the Great Vowel Shift, some speakers changed the way they pronounced this /e:/ vowel in words like *sea*, so that eventually it merged with the /i:/ vowel. But this change was gradual – it probably began with lower-class speakers – and there were at least two possible early modern pronunciations of 'sea': [se:] and [si:] (rhyming with modern 'say' and 'see' respectively).

This may seem confusing, but as the 'sea'/'see' example shows, the spelling of a word is often a clue to an earlier pronunciation: most speakers of English now pronounce 'ale' and 'ail', 'meet' and 'meat', and 'write' and 'right' identically – but the differences in spelling indicate that they were once distinguished in pronunciation too. Most English English speakers don't pronounce the /r/ in 'heart' or 'bar' – but most Early Modern speakers, like most Americans today, did – as the spelling indicates.

Differences in possible pronunciations explain apparently 'bad' rhymes like the following lines from Shakespeare's Sonnet 49:

Againſt that time when thou ſhalt ſtrangely paſſe,
And ſcarcely greete me with that ſunne thine eye,
When loue conuerted from the thing it was
Shall reaſons finde of ſetled grauitie

Here 'paſſe' and 'eye' sound as they do today, and 'was' and 'grauitie' have different realizations that make them full rhymes.

Stress too has changed; most people reading the following lines find their usual stressing of 'complete' won't work:

What may this meane
That thou dead courſe, againe in compleat ſteele
Reuiſites thus the glimſes of the Moone,
Making night hideous?

(*Hamlet*, I. iv. 51–4)

The pattern of the line demands that we stress the first syllable of 'compleat', rather than the second: so '*com*pleat' rather than the expected 'com*pleat*'. Such differences arise because of early modern borrowing from French and Latin, where stress patterns were different. Often when a word was borrowed, a battle ensued between English stress (normally first syllable) and the word's original stress (second, or other syllable) – so that many borrowed words appear in Early Modern English with both stress placements (for example, '*ex*ile' and 'ex*ile*', '*cha*racter' and 'cha*rac*ter'). Giving words these alternative stresses when you read Early Modern English can make them sound strange and new – which of course they often were to speakers of Early Modern English –

Art thou ob*du*rate, flintie, hard as ſteele? (*Venus and Adonis*, 199)
A prodigie of feare, and a por*tent* (*1 Henry IV*, V. i. 20)
Foreſtall pre*ſci*ence, and eſteeme no act (*Troilus and Cressida*, I. iii. 199)
As twere tri*umph*ing at mine enemies (Q *Richard III*, III. iv. 91)

Further study of the sounds of Early Modern English should begin with Barber 1997: 103–41, from which I have stolen some of the examples here, as well as the point about modern spelling.

Shakespeare and 'English'

In Shakespeare's plays, the word 'English' is most frequently used as an adjective qualifying a noun (for example, 'an Engliſh Kerſey' – a type of cloth – in *Measure for Measure*, I. ii. 33; 'English coyne' in *King John*, II. i. 530); when it appears alone, as a noun, it usually means 'the English people': 'what Purgatiue drugge / Would ſcowre theſe Engliſh hence[?]', *Macbeth*, V. iii. 55–6. Not surprisingly, 'English', along with

'England', are most common in the history plays, especially *Henry V*, where the political identity of the nation is explored. 'English' in the sense of 'the English language' is also found in the history plays – comically in *Henry V* as Henry woos Katharine, and chillingly as Mowbray contemplates exile in *Richard II*:

> The language I haue learnt these forty yeeres,
> My natiue Englifh now I muft forgo
>
> . . . .
>
> Within my mouth you haue engaold my tongue,
> Doubly portculift with my teeth and lippes
>
> . . . .
>
> What is thy fentence but fpeechleffe death?
> Which robbes my tongue from breathing natiue breath
> *(Richard II*, I. iii. 159–73)

But the play which most consistently uses 'English' to mean 'the English language' is the only one Shakespeare set in an explicitly Elizabethan England: *The Merry Wives of Windsor*. Closer in style to the plays of Jonson and Middleton than to Shakespeare's other comedies, *Merry Wives* capitalizes on the English linguistic context, encompassing the legal Latin bandied about by the citizens of Windsor in the first scene; the Welsh English of Sir Hugh Evans, the parson; the imperfectly learned English of Dr Caius, the French physician; Mistress Quickly's battles with Latinate English words ('fhee's as fartuous a ciuill modeft wife' rather than 'virtuous' at II. i. 97–8) and misapprehensions of schoolboy Latin lessons ('*Genitiue* cafe' becomes 'Gynes cafe' – Jenny's vagina); Falstaff's often orotund diction; and the clear-sighted prose of the two heroines, Mistresses Page and Ford. In fact, there is more prose in *Merry Wives* than in any other play by Shakespeare, and it is studded with everyday phrases and references, many of them now obscure to us. In its diction and in its grammar (particularly the use of 'do' in questions and negatives), *Merry Wives* stands out as being rather modern when compared to Shakespeare's other plays. Paradoxically, it thus supports John Dryden's claim that by 1688 Shakespeare's English was 'a little obsolete' – something confirmed by today's historical linguistic studies, which show that, even in his own time, Shakespeare tended to lag behind grammatical change.

Writing as he was on the cusp of standardization, being a laggard in this respect had important implications for Shakespeare's linguistic resources: it meant that he was more able to exploit variation than most of his contemporaries. He was more able to use 'thou' (as he does in this play, subtly marking the relationship between Mistresses Page and Ford with shifts from 'you' to 'thou' and back), more able to exploit the old system of non-'do' use, perhaps more able to derive words because more tolerant of variation. He paid a price, in that his language appeared dated to generations immediately following (the plays of the slightly younger, far more standardized John Fletcher were revived about twice as often as Shakespeare's after 1660), but we reap the benefit now in terms of the range of linguistic experience to be found, even in one play like *Merry Wives*. There, although some characters struggle with English, all revel in synonyms and elaboration, in the texture of words. Asked if he wants an egg in his drink, Falstaff replies no, he wants it 'Simple of it ſelfe: Ile no Pullet-Sperſme in my brewage' (III. v. 31–2); asking Simple what he wants, and telling him to be quick about his answer, the Host luxuriates succinctly: 'What wouldſt thou haue? (Boore) what? (thick skin) ſpeake, breathe, diſcuſſe: breefe, ſhort, quicke, ſnap' (IV. v. 1–3). True to its setting, the play celebrates plain English as much as elevated puns or recondite allusions. Faced with the prospect of marrying Dr Caius, Anne Page retorts

> I had rather be set quick i'th earth,
> And bowl'd to death with Turnips
> (III. iv. 86–7)

Mistakenly anticipating success in his attempt to seduce Mistress Ford, Falstaff constructs a learned prose speech, citing the classical authority of Jove/Jupiter's transformations for the sake of adultery, but he is not afraid to pun in English:

> Remember Ioue, thou was't a Bull for thy *Europa* ... You were alſo (Iupiter) a Swan, for the loue of *Leda* ... a fault done firſt in the forme of a beaſt, (O Ioue, a beaſtly fault:) and then another fault, in the ſemblance of a Fowle, think on't (Ioue) a fowle-fault. (V. v. 3–11)

Or to end with a graphic image of himself as a stag growing thin in the mating season (when food is not on its mind): 'Send me a coole rut-time (Ioue) or who can blame me to piſſe my Tallow?' (ll. 13–15). Compared to the anxiety about Latin and classical learning to be found in some commentators on English, this suggests an alternative tradition, happy to set the two cultures and languages together, and thrash out a meaning. Overall, *Merry Wives* depicts a society with a striking toleration for variation within English, and a willingness to pursue meaning beyond apparently 'incorrect' surface forms. When Slender protests his determination to marry Anne Page, he aims at 'resolved' and 'resolutely', but falls unfortunately short – 'I am freely diſſolued, and diſſolutely' (I. i. 251–2) – unwittingly hinting at his own lack of resolution. It is Evans, of whom it is later said that he 'makes Fritters of Engliſh' (V. v. 143), who illustrates the robustness of meaning, even under duress: 'It is a fery diſcetion anſwere; ſaue the fall is in th'ord, diſſolutely: the ort is (according to our meaning) reſolutely: his meaning is good' (I. i. 253–6). The word is indeed 'resolutely'; his meaning is indeed good. In this version of the comic world, with this tolerance of linguistic variation, Evans can be laughed at for five acts; but in the final scene, Falstaff, elsewhere in Shakespeare one of the most adept handlers of language, must admit (albeit verbosely) that he has no words with which to answer the charges of the Welshman: 'Well, I am your Theame: you haue the ſtart of me, I am deiected: I am not able to anſwer the Welch Flannell ... vſe me as you will' (V. v. 161–4). Just as Captain Davy's professionalism survives his accent in *Henry V*, so Evans's insight is independent of the sounds he happens to use when putting it into speech, and his version of English is no bar to his inclusion in the diverse but unified society of Windsor which is reaffirmed at the end of *Merry Wives*. As Anne Barton notes in the introduction to the Riverside edition, no one, not even Falstaff, is excluded from the final moment – and that moment is striking in comparison with the other comedies in terms of the unadulterated and unproblematic solidarity it celebrates.

Such toleration of variation was about to disappear from English, as standardization gave way to prescriptivism, and linguistic difference came more and more to be associated with social and intellectual difference. Thanks to the date of his birth, and the place, Shakespeare was almost uniquely positioned to take advantage of the variation offered by Early Modern English. He was born early enough, and far enough away from the more standardized London dialect, to learn the older forms while they were still vital, but late enough also to have access to the features that entered the standard, and which we still use today. The resulting interplay between the old and the new, the strange and the familiar, is one of the least-known glories of Shakespeare's texts, and one of the few under-researched areas of Shakespeare studies. Its investigation is endlessly rewarding, and those wishing to pursue the topic should begin with Barber 1997, which achieves the admirable feat of being both a dear introduction to Early Modern English and a reliable reference tool. Elsewhere, Blake 1996 provides an overview of previous work on Shakespeare's language (to 1990); Lass, forthcoming, will, when it appears, be essential; and Salmon and Burness 1987 usefully collects articles published up to 1985.

REFERENCES AND FURTHER READING

Barber, C. 1997: *Early Modern English*. Edinburgh: Edinburgh University Press.

Blake, N. F. 1996: Shakespeare's language: some recent studies and future directions. In N. F. Blake, *Essays on Shakespeare's Language*, 1st series, Misterton: Language Press, 66–82.

Calvo, C. 1992: Pronouns of address and social negotiation in *As You Like It*. *Language and Literature*, 1, 5–27.

Elam, K. 1984: *Shakespeare's Universe of Discourse: Language-games in the Comedies*. Cambridge: Cambridge University Press.

Görlach, M. 1991: *Introduction to Early Modern English*. Cambridge: Cambridge University Press.

Hope, J. 1993: Second person singular pronouns in records of Early Modern 'spoken' English. *Neuphilologische Mitteilungen*, 94/1, 83–100.

—— 1994: *The Authorship of Shakespeare's Plays*. Cambridge: Cambridge University Press.

Lass, R. (ed.) forthcoming: *The Cambridge History of the English Language*, vol. 3: *Early Modern English*. Cambridge: Cambridge University Press.

Salmon, V. and Burness, E. (eds) 1987: *A Reader in the Language of Shakespearean Drama*. Amsterdam: John Benjamins.

Schäfer, J. 1980: *Documentation in the OED: Shakespeare and Nashe as Test Cases*. Oxford: Clarendon Press.

Spevack, M. 1968–80: *A Complete and Systematic Concordance to the Works of Shakespeare*, 9 vols. Hildersheim: Olms.

—— 1985: Shakespeare's language. In J. F. Andrews (ed.), *William Shakespeare: His World, his Work, his Influence*, New York: Charles Scribner's Sons, ii. 343–61.

Stein, D. 1987: At the crossroads of philology, linguistics and semiotics: notes on the replacement of *th* by *s* in the third person singular in English. *English Studies*, 5, 406–15.

—— 1990: *The Semantics of Syntactic Change*. Amsterdam: John Benjamins.

16

Hearing Shakespeare's Dramatic Verse

George T. Wright

Shakespeare wrote a verse that was standard for his time, yet innovative and even revolutionary because of the power with which features he added to it transformed it. In this sense, it was old but new; it was verse but not song, not singsong, not over-regular in its thump, though it lived by the beat; but it also had to be believable as speech, as the kind of language people might use in talking to each other on the stage. As verse speech, it had to be heightened at moments of tension; but in the theater all moments are moments of tension, so Shakespeare's verse language had to reflect the varying degrees and kinds of tension in the action of a play. If we listen to that language, we can hear how it achieves its drive and its color in part from the metrical system that Shakespeare received from older contemporaries (and Marlowe) but transmuted into a force of his own, edging and charging its effectiveness by devices and resources comparable in energy and grace to the tales of betrayal, revenge, romance, personal distress, and historical conflict they were designed to enact and express.

The plays show us remarkably different mixes of verse, prose, song, and spectacle: dances, disguises, masques, magic, even duels and battles. Unlike sonnets or stanzaic poems, they can change their audible forms as readily as the scenes and persons onstage give way to others. Some plays are written mainly in prose; some are entirely in verse. The verse includes doggerel, sonnets, and much rhyming in shorter (and some longer) lines, like that of the witches in *Macbeth* or of Puck in *A Midsummer Night's Dream*. But the basic metrical pattern Shakespeare uses in his plays and major poems is the line that has come to be called *iambic pentameter*: ten syllables, alternately unstressed and stressed.

This meter had been familiar to poets and readers in some form since the time of Chaucer, who had used its easy and graceful rhythmic design to tell a tale, explore a character's predicament, or unfold a feeling. The rhymed decasyllabic couplets of many of *The Canterbury Tales* provided a racy meter for Chaucer's subtle prologues and narratives. In his *Troilus and Criseyde*, on the other hand, and in many fifteenth-century poems, or in later massive works like *The Mirror for Magistrates* or *The Faerie Queene*, stanzas composed in this decorously varied meter (rime royal, Spenserian, or other) seemed almost like a series of enchanted rooms through which, one at a time, the unhurried, deliberate reader might make an elegant progress. Shakespeare's *Venus and Adonis* and *The Rape of Lucrece* belong to this narrative tradition, though their lively stanzas, like the rhymed couplets of Christopher Marlowe's unfinished *Hero and Leander*, move toward a more expressive or "mimetic" meter. That is, we are often likely to sense, as we read, that something in the rising rhythmic pattern and the varied departures from it corresponds to something happening in the action or in the feeling of one of the characters:

> (1)   And now this lustful lord *leapt from* his bed
> (*The Rape of Lucrece*, 169)

In the sixteenth century iambic pentameter came to be used widely for shorter poems, too, for sonnets and other lyric and elegiac poems. Sir Thomas Wyatt and the earl of Surrey had begun this practice with poems that were often metrically deft and inventive, but their mid-century imitators preferred to write a very mechanical meter, even for poems expressing strong feelings of love, longing, shame, or revulsion, like this one:

> (2)   The restless rage of deep devouring hell,
> The blazing brands, that never do consume,
> The roaring rout, in Pluto's den that dwell:
> The fiery breath, that from those imps doth fume...
> (from *Tottel's Miscellany* (1557), p. 131)

The images (and the alliteration) show that the writer wants to make the picture a frightening one, but it doesn't occur to him that some variation in the meter might help to convey the horror.

Still, the attraction of such regular lines should not be underestimated. Poets evidently enjoyed the experience of finding or fashioning English phrases that fitted the iambic pattern. A tragic play like *Gorboduc* (1561) might acquire a stately impressiveness from long speeches delivered in a wooden blank verse; and *The Mirror for Magistrates* (1559) could present in grim and regular stanzas the fearful consequences of ambition and pride. Even the gifted poets and playwrights who appeared in the 1580s and 1590s clearly enjoyed the way a regular line could crackle:

> (3)   I may, I must, I can, I will, I do
> (Sidney, *Astrophil and Stella*, 47. 10)

> (4)   One day I wrote her name upon the strand
> (Spenser, *Amoretti*, 75. 1)

(5)   There might you see the gods in sundry shapes,
       Committing heady riots, incest, rapes
                 (Marlowe, *Hero and Leander*, 143–4)

(6)   Methought I was enamor'd of an ass
                 (Shakespeare, *A Midsummer Night's Dream*, IV. i. 77)

Of course, English speech did not always fall neatly into iambic rhythm. A poet, however scrupulous in placing the words where their accents would chime with the meter, had also to maneuver the language a little to help it fit. Example 4 above sounds perfectly natural, but Spenser's next line doesn't. He wants to say, "But the waves came and wash'd it away," but that isn't iambic or pentameter. So he writes:

(7)   But came the waves and washéd it away

Spenser resorts here to two of the three devices Elizabethan poets regularly used to help the language fit the meter: (1) inversion of normal syntax ("came the waves"), and (2) pronunciation of a normally silent *-ed* ending of a past-tense verb or past participle. The other common device is (3) inclusion of an unnecessary *do, doth,* or *did* in phrases like "You *do* amaze her" (*Merry Wives of Windsor*, V. v. 220) or "I *did* consent, / And often *did* beguile her of her tears" (*Othello*, I. iii. 155–6). Once, at least, Shakespeare used all three devices in one line, asking, in Sonnet 37, which of his lover's attributes (beauty, birth, wealth, or wit) "Intitled in thy parts do crownéd sit."

These three devices, which poets continued to use for centuries, could make almost any English phrases sound the iambic pattern, especially when poets also took advantage of the ambiguities of contemporary pronunciation. Shakespeare and his fellow poets often heard words and phrases as having fewer or more syllables than we give them today, so that words like *heaven, seven, even, power, either, never, marry, sirrah, spirit,* and *being* could be monosyllabic, and words like *natural, general, eloquence,* and *innocent* might be pronounced as two syllables (*nat'ral, gen'ral, el'quence, in'cent*). Combinations like *in the, to the,* and *of the* are often reduced (to *i'th', to th',* and *o'th'*), but *-tion* is frequently but not consistently disyllabic. They might also give three syllables to some of our two-syllable words, such as *ocean, marriage, soldier, sergeant, entrance,* and *wrestler,* and sometimes *Henry, children,* and *England,* by inserting an extra vowel before the *r* or *l,* as some modern speakers do for words like *el-m, fil-m,* and *ath-lete.*

In writing iambic pentameter lines, poets were further aided by the ear's willingness to hear as iambic an alternating stress pattern that easily tolerates three conventional kinds of *metrical variation.* The three conventions we looked at above, along with syllabic compression and expansion, adjust the language to the meter; these three bend the meter a little to the language. The key to iambic pentameter is that both language and meter have to *give* a little; this mutual giving makes the verse more speechlike and the English more rhythmical. The three patterns that became standard variations on the basic, five-times-repeated iambic foot ($\cup$ /) are: (1) the *pyrrhic* ($\cup$ $\cup$),

(2) the *spondee* (\ /), and (3) the *trochee* (/ ◡). (At first these names may seem intimidating, but their wide currency makes it convenient to continue using them.).

(1)   In the pyrrhic, a strong (even) position in the line is filled by a minor syllable – e.g., *was* and *of* in example 6 – without disturbing our sense of the alternating rhythm. In fact, the pyrrhic, the most traditional variation, is essential to the easy flow and graceful movement of a line; it helps the poet avoid the impression of five great equal-sounding bumps – appropriate now and then, as in Hotspur's boisterous boast – "Till *fields*, and *blows*, and *groans* ap*plaud* our *sport*" (*I Henry IV*, I. iii. 302) – but tiresome if repeated often.

(2)   In the spondee, a weak (odd) position in the line is occupied by a rather important syllable but without attracting a beat in the five-beat line. Sparingly used in English verse before this period, the spondee became standard after Sir Philip Sidney's sonnet sequence, *Astrophil and Stella*, was published in 1591 and widely imitated. Sidney had realized how expressive a line could become if the poet placed important words in unstressed positions now and then. Instead of writing a rather blank and empty line like

(8)   To what a height the moon ascends the sky,

Sidney saw that a poet could augment some lesser syllables and make it harder for the voice to treat them as merely marking the intervals between the more prominent ones:

(9)   With how *sad* steps, O Moon, thou climb'st the skies
                    (*Astrophil and Stella*, 31. 1)

Here "sad" and "O" in unstressed positions encourage the voice to move slowly through the words, and that deliberate movement is likely to be shared by "thou." Whereas example 8 may be spoken as fast as one likes, a speedy reading of (9) is not a likely choice for any reader. Sidney could see, and other poets were quick to notice, that in lines where the matter has emotional resonance, the slightest increase in stress in an unstressed syllable here and there could make a notable difference in expressiveness. The alternating pattern is still audible, but now the line has a distinctive character and is no longer nearly identical to other lines with the same basic iambic structure.

(3)   Unlike the pyrrhic and the spondee, the trochee is a genuine structural deviation. In it the weak-strong pattern in pairs of syllables (◡ /) is reversed, a variation so frequent in iambic verse, especially to begin a line or after a midline break, that it has come to be accepted as integral to the meter. Poets frequently use it not only as an agreeable variation but also, as in example 1 above, to signal some dramatic turn in action, thought, or word.

Scanning the Verse

Shakespeare's skillful use of these variations keeps changing the sound pattern from line to line. If we *scan* some lines, we can see how variously the different pairs of syllables play out as "feet" (the root of "meter"). (To speak of feet should not suggest that we should hear or pronounce every two syllables separately or slowly and detach them from the body of the line; it merely helps us see how the alternating rhythm is subtly modified as the syllables run quickly by us.)

(10) How like | a win | ter hath | my ab | sence been
From thee, | the plea | sure of | the flee | ting year !
What free | zings have | I felt, | what dark | days seen !
What old | Decem | ber's bare | ness ev | erywhere!

(Sonnet 97. 1–4)

Shakespearian meter's prosperous ambiguities become evident in such a passage. Does one stress "How" or "like" in the opening phrase? The reader is free to decide, depending on how the phrase is interpreted – is the emphasis on absence (then stress "How") or on the comparison (then stress "like")? Lighter syllables in some stronger positions ("hath," "of," "have," and "-where") give the passage an air of modulation and variety. Besides, if some strong syllables are less emphatic, others ask for *more* emphasis. We sense this especially perhaps in "*freezings*" and "*everywhere*," and in the phrase, "*dark days seen*," where the important word "days" in an unstressed position does not attract a metrical beat but still is likely to be drawn out in the speaking and given considerable weight. On the other hand, the frequency of words with a trochaic cast *(winter, absence, pleasure, fleeting, freezings)* yields a counter-iambic current. We can even hear an amphibrachic (∪/∪) tune in "*a winter*," "*my absence*," "*the pleasure*," "*December's*," and elsewhere. (For a fuller analysis of this passage and further discussion and examples of most of the points made in this essay, see my *Shakespeare's Metrical Art* (1988).)

The pyrrhic and spondaic join either two weak (∪ ∪) or two strong or fairly strong (\ /, \\) syllables, but since the second syllable usually attracts (or is perceived as attracting) slightly stronger stress, they function in English poetry as variations of the iambic; they do not deeply change the line's alternating structure, but contribute to its rhythmical interest or its emotional expressiveness. The pyrrhic often lets the voice move lightly, sometimes speedily, through its syllables to intensify the next stressed syllable: "It is the *cause*, it is the *cause*, my soul" (*Othello*, V. ii.1); a pyrrhic before a spondee often gives the impression of four successive syllables with increasing stress:

(11) And on | just proof | surmise accumulate
(Sonnet 117. 10)

Such metrical nuances point up or inflect the iambic alternation, but they do not alter it in any essential way. Even when (rarely, and only at moments of great emotional intensity) a trochee follows the pyrrhic-spondaic combination, and we may seem to have *five* syllables with increasing stress, the iambic alternation is still not fatally disrupted. Perhaps that happens in these lines, though they might also be spoken differently:

$$\quad \breve{\ }\ \backslash\quad\ \backslash\quad /\quad /$$
(12)   Yet she | must die, | else she'll betray more men.
$$\qquad\qquad\qquad\qquad\quad (Othello, \text{V. ii. 6})$$

$$\quad\ \breve{\ }\ \backslash\quad\ \backslash\quad\ /\quad\ /$$
(13)   And his | gash'd stabs | look'd like a breach in nature
$$\qquad\qquad\qquad\qquad\quad (Macbeth, \text{II. iii. 113})$$

These familiar patterns, even in combination, can be heard not as disruptive of the basic meter but as graceful and/or dramatic variations on it. (In the examples below, only the pyrrhic, spondaic, and trochaic feet are marked; the others are probably iambic. Foot divisions should be thought of not as real walls but as similar to milestones; they are measuring markers and only help us see more clearly whether or not successive pairs of syllables are keeping or varying the iambic pattern.)

Pyrrhics and spondees

$$\qquad\qquad\qquad\ \backslash\quad /\qquad\quad \backslash\quad /$$
14)   The course of true | love ne | ver did | run smooth
$$\qquad\qquad\qquad (A\ Midsummer\ Night's\ Dream, \text{I. i. 134})$$

$$\quad\ \backslash\qquad /\quad\ \breve{\ }\ \breve{\ }\qquad \breve{\ }\ \breve{\ }$$
(15)   Makes mouths | at the | invi | sible | event
$$\qquad\qquad\qquad\qquad\ (Hamlet, \text{IV. iv. 50})$$

$$\qquad \breve{\ }\quad \breve{\ }\quad \backslash\quad /$$
(16)   And the | free maids | that weave their thread with bones
$$\qquad\qquad\qquad\qquad\ (Twelfth\ Night, \text{II. iv. 45})$$

$$\qquad\qquad\quad \backslash\quad /\quad \backslash\quad /$$
(17)   The death of each | day's life, | sore lab | or's bath
$$\qquad\qquad\qquad\qquad\ (Macbeth, \text{II. ii. 35})$$

Trochees (one or more in a line, or combined with pyrrhics and/or spondees)

$$\qquad /\ \breve{\ }$$
(18)   Walking | from watch to watch, from tent to tent
$$\qquad\qquad\qquad\quad (Henry\ V, \text{IV. Chorus, 30})$$

$$\qquad /\ \breve{\ }\qquad\qquad\ /\quad \breve{\ }$$
(19)   Nature | in you | stands on | the very verge
$$\qquad\qquad\qquad\quad (King\ Lear, \text{II. iv. 147})$$

$$\qquad\qquad /\quad \breve{\ }$$
(20)   The eye | wink at | the hand; yet let that be
$$\qquad\qquad\qquad\quad (Macbeth, \text{I. iv. 52})$$

(21)   Give me, | give me! | O, tell not me of fear!
                     (*Romeo and Juliet*, IV. i. 121)

(22)   Put strength enough to't.
                                   Wherefore, bold | peas ant
                     (*King Lear*, IV. vi. 231)

23)   Would harrow up thy soul, | freeze thy | young blood
                     (*Hamlet*, I. v. 16)

24)   O thou | foul thief, | where hast | thou stow'd my daughter?
                     (*Othello*, I. ii. 62)

25)   Shaking | their scratch'd | ears, bleed | ing as | they go
                     (*Venus and Adonis*, 924)

The first-foot trochee is very common; so is the midline trochee following a speech juncture (e.g., example 19). Much rarer are the second-foot trochee (example 20), the double trochee (example 21), and especially the fifth-foot trochee (example 22).

Some readers or actors might speak some of these lines a little differently, but in all of them we can probably hear five beats falling in a predominantly iambic pattern, though not all equally strongly or at equal intervals. Even in a pyrrhic foot we can usually hear one of the line's five beats on the second syllable. The variations enliven the music, assuring that the rhythmical interest of successive lines will take different forms and avoid the monotonous similarity of line after line that much earlier Elizabethan verse fell into.

In addition to these standard variations, the sense of a passage often puts special emphasis on certain focal words or syllables, which may belong to either minor or major grammatical categories and may fall either in stressed or unstressed positions:

Stressed

(26)   How *can* it? O how *can* love's eye be true
                     (Sonnet 148. 9)

(27)   Love? his affections do not *that* way tend
                     (*Hamlet*, III. i. 162)

(28)   O, *to* | him, *to* | him, wench! he will relent
                     (*Measure for Measure*, II. ii. 124)

Unstressed

29)   Your servant's servant is *your* servant, madam
                     (*Twelfth Night*, III. i. 102)

(30)   Upon my life, *she* finds (although *I* cannot)
(*Richard III*, I. ii. 253)

These last two (along with those noted in 78) I call examples of *contrary stress*, because the voice treats them in a singular way: it rises sharply in pitch, then immediately descends to give the next syllable its full stress, so that, despite the strong stress on an odd-numbered syllable, the pattern is not trochaic.

Number of Syllables

But there are other sources of variation in Shakespeare's lines. In particular, the *number* of syllables may exceed or fall short of the normal ten. Even when the pronunciation is unambiguous, lines occur that are plainly shorter or longer than pentameter.

1   Extra syllables

Double (or feminine) ending: an extra unstressed syllable at the end of a line. This presents no substantial change in the line pattern (the extra syllable is not a sixth foot), but it may introduce a note of hesitation, of subtlety, of casualness, or simply of difference, depending on the dramatic and the rhythmic context. The effect is of an amphibrach ($\cup / \cup$) at the line's end:

(31)   Unwillingly to school. And then | the lover,
Sighing like furnace, with a woe | ful ballad
Made to his mistress' eyebrow. Then | a soldier
(*As You Like It*, II. vii. 147–9)

In rhymed stanzas or rhymed dramatic verse, the rhyming disyllable in one line waits for its sometimes striking match in the next:

(32)   His taste delicious, in digestion *souring*,
Devours his will, that liv'd by foul *devouring*.
(*The Rape of Lucrece*, 699–700)

Several stanzas in Shakespeare's poems, and one entire sonnet, use double endings in *all* their lines, always for some expressive purpose.

Other variations: the *heavy ending*, in which the final syllable is unusually strong:

(33)   Sounds, and sweet airs, that give delight | *and hurt* not
(*Tempest*, III. ii. 136)

The *triple ending: two* extra unstressed syllables at line ending:

> ˘ / ˘ ˘
> (34)   What's Hecuba to him, or he | to Hecuba
> (*Hamlet*, II. ii. 559)

Shakespeare frequently uses this kind of ending with names like An*tony*, An*gelo*, Is*abel*, Lan*caster*, or Pa*dua*, and with other words whose two final unstressed syllables he evidently heard as (almost) compressed into one: ma*jesty*, gen*tlemen*, mess*enger*, Ca*pitol*, fol*lowers*; or with phrases to be spoken swiftly: *lovest me, warrant thee, able 'em*, and even *what's her name* (*Antony and Cleopatra*, III. xiii. 98).

Epic caesura: here the extra unstressed syllable occurs at midline, before a phrasal break.

> (35)   Lag of | a bro*ther*? | Why bastard? Wherefore base?
> (*King Lear*, I. ii. 6)

> (36)   Burnt on | the wa*ter*. | The poop was beaten gold
> (*Antony and Cleopatra*, II. ii. 192)

This variation dates back to a time in the fifteenth century when a phrasal break so frequently marked the pentameter line after the fourth or sixth syllable – see examples 2, 56, and 57 – that the line could seem composed of two short lines, one of four and the other of six syllables. When that first short "line" had a double ending, the line composed of both short segments showed an extra syllable that belonged to the first phrase, the one before the break, and a break of this kind was known as an epic caesura. Most later English poems, including Shakespeare's, avoid this extra midline syllable, but Shakespeare, much more than other playwrights, adopted it for use in his plays, evidently both to vary the rhythm with a midline amphibrach and to give some of his blank verse passages (especially in his mature plays) a feeling of hurry, of crowdedness, of meaning so abundant it seems to overflow the line. Until his last plays Shakespeare typically uses this formation where one sentence or clause ends and the next begins, or where there is a midline change of speakers, the second voice almost stepping on the heels of the first:

> (37)   LORENZO.   To come again | to Carthage. |
> JESSICA.   In such a night
> (*The Merchant of Venice*, V. i. 12)

Other variations: in lines with an epic caesura and a double ending, we may hear a distinctly amphibrachic "rhyme":

> ˘ / ˘   ˘ / ˘
> (38)   Nothing to be | were better. | This was | my master
> (*Cymbeline*, IV. ii. 368)

An epic caesura with *two* extra syllables at midline may seem to minimize (or fill) the pause between sentences:

(39)   Orsi | no's en*emy.* | A witchcraft drew me hither
(*Twelfth Night*, V. i. 76)

Very rare: two extra syllables both at the midline break and at the end:

(40)   In base | appli*ances.* | This outward-saint | ed de*puty*
(*Measure for Measure*, III. i. 88)

Double onset: an apparently extra syllable at the line's beginning:

(41)   *I am great* | with woe, and shall deliver weeping
(*Pericles*, V. i. 106)

But syllable combinations such as "I am," "I have," "Thou wilt," "you shall," would often be elided to a single syllable; so could words like *over, after, either, having,* or *father.* Still, genuine instances of double onset occur, especially when the first two syllables are evidently meant to be spoken quickly, even slurred, and lead up to a very important third one:

(42)   *Let's be sac* | rificers, but not butchers, Gaius
(*Julius Caesar*, II. i. 166)

Anapests: in nineteenth-century and later English verse, occasional anapests (∪ ∪ /) appear in iambic verse. Shakespeare and his contemporaries used them sparingly, usually to signal a rapid delivery:

(43)   You made | *in a day,* | my lord, whole towns to fly
(*2 Henry VI*, II. i. 160)

or to hurry the link between separate phrases:

(44)   But do not speak | *to me. Lead* | me to my chamber
(*Antony and Cleopatra*, II. v. 119)

2   Omitted syllables

If extra syllables imply an abundance of meaning compressed into limited space, the omission of expected syllables may suggest impatience, hurry, breathlessness, or other effects:

The headless line: this omits the first unstressed syllable (indicated by a caret):

> (45)   Jail | er, take him to thy custody
>   ∧   (*The Comedy of Errors*, I. i. 155)

The broken-backed line: this omits an expected unstressed syllable at the midline break:

> (46)   Horrible sight! | Now | I see 'tis true
>   ∧ (*Macbeth*, IV. i. 122)

The technique here suggests Macbeth's discomfiture at what the witches have shown him. In *Richard II*, on the other hand, the unctuous Northumberland, rebuked for referring to the king simply as Richard, tries to slither out of this charge of omission with the help of a syllable-omitting broken-backed line:

> (47)   Your Grace mistakes: | o | nly to be brief
>   ∧
>
>   Left I his title out.
>   (*Richard II*, III. iii. 10–11)

In *Measure for Measure*, Claudio's evident disdain for his sister's empty offer to lay down her *life* for him is registered in his laconic broken-backed ending to their common line:

> (48)   ISABEL.   O, were it but my life,
>   I'd throw it down for your deliverance
>   As frankly as a pin. |
>   CLAUDIO.   Thanks, | dear Isabel.
>   ∧
>   (*Measure for Measure*, III. i. 103–5)

Omitted unstressed syllable: when characters are greatly excited, they may omit an expected unstressed syllable anywhere in the line and more than once:

> (49)   Stay: | speak; | speak: | I charge thee, speak
>   ∧   ∧   ∧
>   (*Hamlet*, I. i. 51; Folio punctuation)

> (50)   Hear, | Na | ture, hear dear goddess, hear
>   ∧   ∧
>   (*King Lear*, I. iv. 275; Folio punctuation)

This pattern resembles a modern five-stress accentual line, especially when it is combined with an extra syllable at the line's end or at a midline break:

(51)   How? | traitor? |
     ∧   ∧

                 Nay, temperately: your promise

                    (*Coriolanus*, III. iii. 67)

(52)   Die, | perish! | Might but my bending down
      ∧   ∧

                 (*Measure for Measure*, III. i. 143)

Omitted stressed syllable: Finally, some lines sound as if they are missing an expected *stressed* syllable, usually at especially dramatic moments, as when Henry IV counters with caustic suspicion Worcester's pious assurance that "I have not sought the day of this dislike" and testily asks:

(53)   You have not sought | it, | how comes it then?
                         ∧

               (*1 Henry IV*, V. i. 26–7)

We can imagine Henry stamping, snorting, sniffing, or turning on Worcester to mark the audible gap in the line. A different effect may register when Iago delays for a moment before echoing Othello's pregnant question about Cassio:

(54)   Is he not hon | est?

               | Honest, my lord?

           ∧

          (*Othello*, III. iii. 103)

Even the tenth syllable may be omitted, especially when the speaker has some reason – distraction or impatience – not to finish his thought:

(55)   He writes me here, that inward sick | ness –

                             ∧

               (*1 Henry IV*, IV. i. 31)

All these metrical resources enhance rhythmic variety and heighten what would otherwise be the uninflected, level-toned, blockish verse of earlier Tudor poetry. But they are still only half the story. The other half, and the key to the new pentameter, is its new understanding of the relation between the phrase and the line.

Phrase and Line

Classical poetry, which was quantitative, and some kinds of accentual verse often show a *caesura* at a central point in a verse line's rhythmic structure. When English poets first began to write iambic pentameter, they usually employed a phrasal break which could be called a caesura because it typically came after the line's fourth syllable – see example 2 above – or sometimes after the sixth. But by Shakespeare's time, poets had begun to see the advantages of breaking the line occasionally in other places as well – after the fifth syllable or the seventh, and eventually anywhere in the line or not at all. Since such a variable placement of the midline phrasal break violates the structural rigidity that the caesura imposes on other kinds of verse, it seems best not to use that term to describe the much more flexible English practice. "Midline break" captures more clearly and accurately what happens in most lines of English iambic pentameter. But note that "midline pause" is equally inaccurate as a description of a phrasal juncture, because many lines composed of more than one phrase may be spoken in a single breath – e.g., examples 4 and 14.

Shorter lines of verse in English may be only one phrase long, but a line as long as ten syllables is likely to be composed of two phrases, perhaps more, and the border or hinge between them will be important to our sense of how we hear the whole line. Many of Shakespeare's lines follow the older procedure of combining a four-syllable phrase with a six-syllable phrase:

> (56)   Old men forget; | yet all shall be forgot
>   (*Henry V*, IV. iii. 49)

> (57)   And look upon myself | and curse my fate
>   (Sonnet 29. 4)

By the 1580s poets like Sidney and Spenser had discovered what a harmonious and variable music was made available when lines breaking after odd syllables, or not breaking at all, were mixed with these even-breaking ones. Shakespeare, too, learned to do it early:

> (58)   The ox hath therefore stretch'd his yoke in vain,
>   The ploughman lost his sweat, and the green corn
>   Hath rotted ere his youth attain'd a beard;
>   The fold stands empty in the drowned field
>   (*A Midsummer Night's Dream*, II. i. 93–6)

The phrasal boundaries occur variously after odd or even syllables, and some lines may break twice, or not at all. Lines written this way vary the iambic tune and embody the poets' new understanding that four lines written in the same meter need not seem monotonous if the poet makes sure that the phrases composing the line have different lengths and contours. The phrasing in one line may break after the fourth or sixth syllable and the phrasing in the next after the fifth or seventh or third. But the meter in both lines remains iambic:

> (59)   Nor Mars his sword nor war's quick fire shall burn
>   The living record of your memory
>   (Sonnet 55. 7–8)

(60)   Thus was I, sleeping, by a brother's hand
      Of life, of crown, of queen, at once dispatch'd
            (*Hamlet*, I. V. 74–5)

A line may even enclose four trochaic words between a first (unstressed) and a tenth (stressed) syllable that guarantee the iambic structure framing an interior trochaic rhythm:

(61)   Like strengthless hinges, buckle under life
         (*2 Henry IV*, I. i. 141)

Such a line places five syllables on either side of the midline break, but this does not divide the line in half, because its second half includes three metrical stresses, the first half only two. This essential imbalance in the line, its structural inability to divide into exact halves, is what gives iambic pentameter its chance to be more speechlike than any other English meter, what keeps it from falling into singsong, as four-beat and six-beat lines can easily do by splitting too neatly into halves. Shakespeare's plays include many six-beat, or *hexameter* lines, apparently as a way of changing the tune occasionally. Often, two three-beat half-lines answer one another.

(62)   PETRUCHIO.   I say it is the moon.
      KATHARINA.   I know it is the moon.
      (*The Taming of the Shrew*, IV. V. 16)

This is one of many variations Shakespeare learned to play on the classical *stichomythia* (sharp one-line exchanges between two characters) that appear occasionally in his early plays.

Such patterns are attractive now and then, but the pentameter is more durable, and all of Shakespeare's early poetry can be heard trying out ways in which pentameter lines of different rhythmical contours can combine variously and tunefully into stanzas and sonnets: the six-line stanza, rhyming *ababcc*, that takes its name from *Venus and Adonis*; the rime royal of *The Rape of Lucrece*, rhyming *ababbcc*; and the sonnets, almost always composed in three quatrains (*ababcdcdefef*) and a couplet (*gg*). But the *blank verse* that becomes increasingly prominent in his plays makes other choices available; in particular, blank verse makes it feasible to break the phrasing later in the line – even after the eighth or ninth syllable:

(63)   Give me my robe, put on my crown, I have
      (*Antony and Cleopatra*, V. ii. 280)

(64)   Methought I lay
    Worse than the mutines in the bilboes. Rashly –
           (*Hamlet*, V. ii. 5–6)

A late break in a non-rhyming line makes it more likely that a phrase will run over the line ending. Some poets (e.g., Donne and Browning) have written poems in run-on rhymed couplets, and Shakespeare in a few places did the same (e.g., *All's Well That Ends Well*, II. iii. 135–44), though without apparent enthusiasm. But blank verse that is breaking anywhere within the line can easily carry its phrases over the line endings. Shakespeare's early verse, whether rhymed or blank, tends to be end-stopped, like Marlowe's, but he more and more runs the sense of a sentence over the line, until in his more mature plays – from *Hamlet* on, essentially – the typical procedure in a speech of any length is to run a sentence (or a significant sentence segment) from midline to midline:

(65)   No! to be once in doubt
        Is once to be resolv'd.
                            (*Othello*, III. iii. 179–80)

(66)   You seem to understand me,
        By each at once her choppy finger laying
        Upon her skinny lips
                            (*Macbeth*, I. iii. 43–5)

Other sentences run from midline to full line, or from full line to midline:

(67)   If she must teem,
        Create her child of spleen, that it may live
        And be a thwart disnatur'd torment to her
                            (*King Lear*, I. iv. 281–3)

(68)   It was the lark, the herald of the morn,
        No nightingale.
                            (*Romeo and Juliet*, III. v. 6–7)

And a rhymed example, frequent at the end of Shakespearean scenes:

(69)   the play's the thing
        Wherein I'll catch the conscience of the King.
                            (*Hamlet*, II. ii. 604–5)

Longer speeches weave back and forth among these designs, which, with the help of the actors' sensitive speaking, can be heard in the theater. What we hear is a compound (almost a fugue-like) movement of phrase (or sentence) and line, in which by turns one continues while the other comes to an end.

To keep this kind of movement flowing, Shakespeare more and more ends characters' speeches at midline, letting another character complete the line with the first words of a new speech, as in examples 37, 48, 51, and 62. By the end of Shakespeare's career, this was so much his prevailing practice that all thirty-eight speeches in Act V, scene iii, of *The Winter's Tale* – or all but one? – are metrically linked either to the preceding or to the following speech; twenty-three are linked to both. For example:

<blockquote>

(70) PAULINA.   but then you'll think
(Which I protest against) I am assisted
By wicked powers.
    LEONTES.   What you can make her do,
I am content to look on; what to speak,
I am content to hear; for 'tis as easy
To make her speak as move.
    PAULINA.   It is requir'd
You do awake your faith.
                               (*The Winter's Tale*, V. iii. 89–95)

</blockquote>

If the actors help us hear these half-lines combining to form whole ones, the way the speeches dovetail into each other can be heard as a distinctive music, verifying the extent to which play production is an ensemble creation.

Shakespeare did not invent the technique of the shared line, but his frequent midline-to-midline versification led him to make use of it, sometimes in complex and even exotic patterns that stretch what one would imagine to be the structural possibilities of shared lines. The difference (and similarity) between nondramatic and dramatic verse is relevant here. In all verse, a rhyming line "answers" the line it rhymes with. A quatrain answers a quatrain, and in a Shakespearean sonnet (and sometimes a *Venus and Adonis* stanza or one of rime royal) a final couplet answers, or at least converses with, the differently structured lines it follows. Characteristically, in Shakespeare's verse, whether of the stage or of the page, every line's internal rhythmic structure answers the previous line's different one, but the *voice* of the lyric or narrative poem runs on, its speech uncontested, unless (as in the sonnets) from within. But in plays, not only must lines answer lines; speakers must answer speakers. A character's speech may be riddled with internal questions, but it usually has to be answered by an array of differently placed other speakers. As we study (or deliver) Shakespeare's metrical lines, then, we have to be sensitive to the ways in which speeches answer, evade, or parry other speeches. The shared line is an emblem of the shared stage, as dialogue is a microcosm of the theater.

Shakespeare must have realized not only that lines spoken onstage, in order to sound believably like words actual people might say to each other, should have some of the surge and ebb of ordinary intense talk, that people speak in phrases of varying lengths, not in ten-syllable lines, and that run-on blank verse lines built out of phrases varied in length and construction could imitate the movement of actual conversation. He must have judged, too, that lines shared by two (or more) characters could hurry the dialogue on and give the attentive listener in the theater something of the same sense of responsive music as was to be found in church litanies, madrigals, or other polyphonic compositions. For one character to complete another's blank verse line is a dramatic as well as a metrical obligation. It also seems normal, though some instances are extreme. Tense after the murder of King Duncan, the Macbeths speak four times in one line:

> (71)   Did not you speak?
>   When?
>   Now.
>   As I descended?
>   *(Macbeth*, II. ii. 16)

And even more elliptically, in *King John*:

> (72)   HUBERT.   My lord?
>   KING JOHN.   A grave.
>   HUBERT.   He shall not live.
>   KING JOHN.   Enough.
>   *(King John*, III. iii. 66)

The shared line was one device for intensifying the dramatic bond between lovers, antagonists, or other personages involved with each other on the stage. Lorenzo and Jessica (in example 37), Othello and Iago (in example 54), Lear and his daughters –

> (73)   LEAR.   I gave you all –
>   REGAN.   And in good time you gave it
>   *(King Lear*, II. iv. 250)

– are deeply joined by their verse. Some effects of this kind are quite extraordinary – inventions that seem right out of Mozart or Verdi. How, for example, do we hear (and interpret) the passage in *Macbeth* (I. ii) when Macbeth's words spoken aside, and Banquo's spoken to others out of Macbeth's hearing, compose between them perfectly metrical lines? Or the even more operatic scene in *Troilus and Cressida* (V. ii) that shows Troilus and Ulysses eavesdropping on Cressida and Diomede, who sometimes complete their eavesdroppers' lines, while Thersites listens to all of them and comments in prose?

Not that all short lines are shared; some are simply short. Ample speeches might end with a short blank line:

> (74)   Take physic, pomp,
> Expose thyself to feel what wretches feel,
> That thou mayst shake the superflux to them,
> And show the heavens more just.
>   *(King Lear*, III. iv. 33–6)

Even within a speech, Shakespeare sometimes allows a half-line of particular weight and interest to hold its own among longer lines:

> (75)   And a most instant tetter bark'd about,
>   Most lazar-like, with vile and loathsome crust,
>   *All my smooth body.*
>   Thus was I, sleeping, by a brother's hand . . .
>   (*Hamlet*, I. v. 71–4)

Sometimes short lines combine into *squinting lines*; that is, we may hear the middle of three half-lines as combining with *both* the one before and the one following:

> (76)   CLAUDIO.   The weariest and most loathed worldly life
>   That age, ache, penury, and imprisonment
>   Can lay on nature is a paradise
>   To what we fear of death.
>   ISABELLA.   *Alas, alas!*
>   CLAUDIO.   Sweet sister, let me live.
>   (*Measure for Measure*, III. i. 128–32)

Such squinting lines occur fairly often, but even the most scrupulous editors have not found a way to show their ambiguity in a printed text. The ear must hear it. In such a passage, the troubled situation of the characters appears to find an echo in the precariousness of the meter.

This is not to say that every metrical variation or anomaly has a specific dramatic function; most of them merely contribute to our sense that the verse in this passage or this play has a texture or character that we can fairly well describe or identify. It is easy to claim, for example, that metrical uncertainties are especially prominent in the later plays. As run-on lines more and more dominate the verse, it becomes harder in the theater to hear where lines begin and end. Squinting lines, short lines, and occasional hexameters keep jeopardizing our sense of the five-beat line; headless, broken-backed, and epic caesural formations may throw us off; so may an actor's blunders or a director's cuts; and so may the *weak and light endings* the playwright contrives in increasing numbers. Like other Elizabethan poets, Shakespeare had, from the beginning, found it acceptable to end lines with polysyllabic words whose final syllable falls on the line's fifth beat but is lightly stressed: *tapestry, Emperor, Plantagenet.* But his later plays take us much further in this direction: they frequently end lines with syllables we expect to *begin* phrases or clauses: prepositions (*to, by, from, with*); personal or relative pronouns (*I, you, we; which, that, who*); conjunctions (*when, if, as if*). They can even divide an auxiliary verb from the main one: *have / Done, would / Have, might / Be.* Few actors will pause at such junctures to signal the line ending; to do so would seem to violate realistic speech. It is more likely that, as we listen to the lines in the theater, we will lose track of the verse from time to time until an occasional clear pentameter, or just a few regular measures, help us catch the tune again. But in a line with many phrasal breaks (and such lines are common in the late plays), no matter how regular the meter, it may be hard to hear which is the *line* break.

> (77)   LEONTES.   Proceed;
>   No foot shall stir.
>   PAULINA.   Music! awake her! strike!
>   'Tis time; descend; be stone no more; approach
>   (*The Winter's Tale*, V. iii. 97–9)

Much of the time, however, this late verse often seems ravaged by sudden gusts of phrasing, self-interruptions, parenthetical rewordings and qualifications, subtle figures of repetition, inventive inversion, extreme syllabic compression and expansion, radical enjambment, and semantic balances often disturbingly off-center:

> (78)   A devil, a born devil, on whose nature
>   Nurture can never stick; on whom my pains,
>   Humanely taken, all, all lost, quite lost...
>   (*The Tempest*, IV. i. 188–90)

Notice the curious design of "nature / Nurture / never," the insignificant "a" in strong-stress position in line 1, and, after the regular (rational?) series of feet in lines 2–3, how the second "all" and "quite" (examples of contrary stress in successive feet!) seem almost to jump out of the line. Even so short a passage also illustrates Shakespeare's typically easy movement from one world of reference to another (*devil, nature, Nurture, lost,* among others, are all suggestive of other contexts), so that Prospero's lines, however firmly focused on matters at hand (here it is Caliban) evoke a range of meanings that go far beyond the immediate subject of meditation or dispute. (See Vendler, 1997: esp. 33ff.)

One of Shakespeare's gifts was for ferreting out the conflict or tension in any relation and dramatizing it. The counterpart of this in verse composition is to heighten the tension between lines, or portions of lines, that seem regular and those that depart from expected patterns, to make verbal music out of the tension between the natural-sounding phrases of English speech and the fairly regular beat of a metrical line. The early verse presents this tension in relatively simple terms that are almost wholly audible to any listening ear. But as the blank lines run their sense more and more over the line endings to pause in midline, the verse becomes more elusive and problematical, by turns dissonant and harmonious. One principal surprise in this late verse is the steadiness with which, in the midst of metrical eruptions of various dimensions, the verse keeps regaining its balance, often by letting the meter direct stress, and strong stress, to key words that bear powerful emphasis. Here is Leontes worried about his loss of sleep and imagining he can get it back again (or *half* of it, the "moiety") by burning his wife at the stake. (I have italicized the syllables –

almost all in strong-stress position – that seem to call for a degree of stress above that of the usual stressed syllable.)

> (79)   Nor night, nor day, no rest: It is but *weak*ness
>   To *bear* the matter thus, mere weakness, *if*
>   The *cause* were not in *being*: *part* o'th' cause,
>   *She*, th'Adultress; for the harlot-King
>   Is quite beyond mine Arm, out of the blank
>   And level of my brain, plot-*proof*: but *she*,
>   I *can* hook to me: say that she were *gone*,
>   Given to the *fire*, a *moi*ety of my rest
>   Might come to me again.
>   (*The Winter's Tale*, II. iii. 1–9; folio punctuation)

The syntax here, and often in this late verse, is so intricate and highly, though obscurely, patterned that it amounts almost to another elusive metrical arrangement superimposed on the meter. The three pairs of monosyllables (negatives and nouns) that begin the speech lead to three other reiterative pairs (*weakness–weakness, rest–rest*, and *if–say that*), but the heart of the meditation is carried by three reiterative triads, differently niched in the metrical lines:

(1)   "the cause"; "part o'th' cause"; "She, th'Adultress"
(2)   "beyond mine arm"; "out of the blank / And level of my brain"; "plot-proof"
        (= beyond arm, brain, and plot)
(3)   "not in being"; "gone"; "Given to the fire".

(See Houston 1988 for other fine examples.)

A rhetoric charged with such purposeful syntactic (and alliterative) patterning, and intended for incisive and speedy metrical delivery from the stage, presents a challenge to anyone's ear. The demanding charms of syntax, imagery, vowel and consonant repetition, and rhetorical figures, however much studied, have rarely been linked to the unfolding metrical lines and speeches we hear as we can in the theater, though Barton (1984), McDonald (1985, 1990) and Spain (1988) provide different kinds of assistance. We all might hear more than we do, if we learned how to listen better. The easy availability of texts (and of films and tapes) makes it possible nowadays to hear again, even to hear in silence but in near-simultaneity the sounds of lines and passages at some distance from each other in a play – or in Shakespeare's career – as photographs permit us to compare the look of buildings or artworks far removed from each other in space. If, respecting the unity of each play, we use this advantage to listen intently to the sounds being voiced in the theater of the printed page, to "hear with eyes," in Shakespeare's phrase (Sonnet 23. 14), we may hear more dimensions of the constantly flexible art of Shakespeare's dramatic verse – an art of which we may say to all fluent English speakers, as Paulina says to Leontes (*The Winter's Tale*, II. iii. 96) of the infant he refuses to acknowledge: "It is *yours*."

REFERENCES AND FURTHER READING

Abbott, E. A. 1879: *A Shakespearean Grammar*. London: Macmillan.

Barton, John 1984: *Playing Shakespeare*. London: Methuen.

Booth, Stephen 1969: *An Essay on Shakespeare's Sonnets*. New Haven: Yale University Press.

Booth, Stephen (ed.) 1977: *Shakespeare's Sonnets*. New Haven: Yale University Press.

Brogan, T. V. F. 1981: *English Versification, 1571–1980*. Baltimore: Johns Hopkins University Press.

Cercignani, Fausto 1981: *Shakespeare's Works and Elizabethan Pronunciation*. Oxford: Clarendon Press.

Clemen, Wolfgang 1961: *English Tragedy before Shakespeare: The Development of Dramatic Speech*, trans. T. S. Dorsch. New York: Barnes and Noble (orig. pub. 1955).

Freer, Coburn 1981: *The Poetics of Jacobean Drama*. Baltimore: Johns Hopkins University Press.

Hardison, O. B., Jr. 1989: *Prosody and Purpose in the English Renaissance*. Baltimore: Johns Hopkins University Press.

Hibbard, G. R. 1981: *The Making of Shakespeare's Dramatic Poetry*. Toronto: University of Toronto Press.

Houston, John Porter 1988: *Shakespearean Sentences: A Study in Style and Syntax*. Baton Rouge: Louisiana State University Press.

Howarth, Herbert 1965: Metre and emphasis: a conservative note. In Gordon Ross Smith (ed.), *Essays on Shakespeare*, University Park, Pa.: Penn State University Press, 221–7.

McDonald, Russ 1985: Poetry and plot in *The Winter's Tale*. *Shakespeare Quarterly*, 36, 315–29.

—— 1990: Reading *The Tempest*. *Shakespeare Survey*, 43, 15–28.

Partridge, A. C. 1964: *Orthography in Shakespeare and Elizabethan Drama*. London: Edward Arnold.

Shakespeare, William 1997: *The Riverside Shakespeare*, ed. G. Blakemore Evans, 2nd edn. Boston: Houghton Mifflin.

Spain, Delbert 1988: *Shakespeare Sounded Soundly*. Santa Barbara, Calif.: Garland–Clarke Editions.

Suhamy, Henri 1984: *Le Vers de Shakespeare*. Paris: Didier-Erudition.

Tarlinskaya, Marina 1987: *Shakespeare's Verse: Iambic Pentameter and the Poet's Idiosyncrasies*. New York: Peter Lang.

Thompson, John 1961: *The Founding of English Metre*. New York: Columbia University Press.

Vendler, Helen 1997: *The Art of Shakespeare's Sonnets*. Cambridge, Mass.: Harvard University Press.

Woods, Susanne 1985: *Natural Emphasis: English Versification from Chaucer to Dryden*. San Marina, Calif.: Huntington Library.

Wright, George T. 1985: Shakespeare's poetic techniques. In John F. Andrews (ed.), *William Shakespeare: His World, His Work, His Influence*, 3 vols, New York: Scribner's, ii. 363–87.

—— 1988: *Shakespeare's Metrical Art*. Berkeley: University of California Press.

—— 1993: Blank verse in the Elizabethan theatre: language that vanishes, language that keeps. In A. L. Magnusson and C. E. McGee (eds), *The Elizabethan Theatre*, vol. 12, Toronto: P. D. Meany, 1–18.

17
Shakespeare and Rhetorical Culture
Peter G. Platt

The effect of speech upon the condition of the soul is comparable to the power of drugs over the nature of bodies. For just as different drugs dispel different secretions from the body, and some bring an end to disease and others to life, so also in the case of speeches, some distress, others delight, some cause fears, others make the hearers bold, and some drug and bewitch the soul with a kind of evil persuasion.

(Gorgias 1972: 53)

Shakespeare wrote in a culture almost as rhetorical as our own. While American and English elementary schools no longer feature formal rhetorical training as a central part of their educational programs, our modern culture – suffused with seductive advertising and political "spin-doctors" – is deeply conversant with the art of persuasion. And persuasion was at the heart of definitions of rhetoric in the manuals that taught Shakespeare and his contemporaries the art. Rhetoric, according to Aristotle in his *Rhetoric*, was "the faculty of observing on any given case the available means of persuasion" (1355b; ii. 2155 in Barnes edn), while Cicero's *De oratore* tells students that "the duty of an orator is to speak in a style fitted to convince" (1. 31. 138; p. 97 in Sutton and Rackham trans.). But persuasion is never simple or wholly innocent, as Gorgias – one of the earliest commentators on rhetoric – suggests. There can never be a guarantee that rhetoric's tremendous power will be used or received in a constructive or healing fashion. Indeed, rhetoric's effect can be destructive, false, and harmful; the individual listening to the words – whatever their intent – can be bewitched by an "evil persuasion."

This potential to harm haunts the writings of Plato on oratory, and his attacks on rhetoric continued to reverberate in Shakespeare's day as they continue to in our own. In his *Gorgias*, Plato includes a discussion between Gorgias the Sophist and Socrates.

The latter asserts that rhetoric "has no need to discover the truth about things but merely to discover a technique of persuasion, so as to appear among the ignorant to have more knowledge than the expert" (459b–c; p. 242 in Hamilton and Cairns edn). Similarly, the Socratically influenced Phaedrus says, in the dialogue that bears his name, that "the intending orator is under no necessity of understanding what is truly just, but only what is likely to be thought just by the body of men who are to give judgment; nor need he know what is truly good or noble, but what will be thought so, since it is on the latter, not the former, that persuasion depends" (Phaedrus, 259e–260a; p. 505 in Hamilton and Cairns edn). Under the sway of the orator, there is nothing either good or noble but thinking makes it so. Plato sets up in these two dialogues what would become the key tenets of the anti-rhetorical prejudice: the philosopher is concerned with the true and the just, while the rhetorician strives only to *appear* just; persuasion is portrayed as inherently duplicitous and divorced from truth.

Aristotle's *Rhetoric* responds to this critique by admitting the doubleness of rhetoric and its essential strategy of arguing both sides of a question. Yet the goal of this approach, Aristotle argues, is to know the truth more fully: "we must be able to employ persuasion... on opposite sides of a question, not in order that we may employ it in both ways (for we must not make people believe what is wrong), but in order that we may see clearly what the facts are, and that, if another man argues unfairly, we on our part may better be able to confute him" (1355a; ii. 2154 in Barnes edn). Cicero goes a step further and claims that the rhetorical approach to language has a corresponding approach to knowledge: arguing on both sides of the question (*disputatio in utramque partem*) helps one acknowledge the difficulty of arriving at a single truth (see *Academica*, ii. 3. 7–9).

George Kennedy has suggested what is at stake in this debate between philosophy and rhetoric, truth and persuasion:

> The disagreement between Plato and the sophists over rhetoric was not simply an historical contingency, but reflects a fundamental cleavage between two irreconcilable ways of viewing the world. There have always been those, especially among philosophers and religious thinkers, who have emphasized goals and absolute standards and have talked much about truth, while there have been as many others to whom these concepts seem shadowy or imaginary and who find the only certain reality in the process of life and the present moment. In general, rhetoricians and orators, with certain distinguished exceptions, have held the latter view, which is the logical, if unconscious, basis of their common view of art as a response to a rhetorical challenge unconstrained by external principles. The difference is not only that between Plato and Gorgias, but between Demosthenes and Isocrates, Virgil and Ovid, Dante and Petrarch, and perhaps Milton and Shakespeare. (Kennedy 1963: 15)

This division, as Kennedy suggests, has implications that reach beyond speech and into the realms of knowledge and selfhood – into "ways of viewing the world."

Richard Lanham, sharing Kennedy's sense that rhetoric can shape the way a person comes to know the world and to conduct his or her life, has portrayed the tension as that between *homo seriosus* (serious man) and *homo rhetoricus* (rhetorical man). The former "possesses a central self, an irreducible identity. These selves combine into a single, homogeneously real society which constitutes a referent reality for the men living in it" (Lanham 1976: 1). The latter, though,

> is an actor; his reality public, dramatic. . . . The lowest common denominator of his life is a social situation. . . . He is thus committed to no single construction of the world; much rather, to prevailing in the game at hand. . . . Rhetorical man is trained not to discover reality but to manipulate it. Reality is what is accepted as reality, what is useful. (Ibid., 4; see Fish 1990)

There is something fictitious, constructed, and potentially false, then, about the rhetorical view of the world. Shakespeare's King Claudius certainly knows this, and in a rare moment of self-laceration, links his own general duplicity to the deception of rhetoric:

> The harlot's cheek, beautified with plas'tring art,
> Is not more ugly to the thing that helps it
> Than is my deed to my most painted word
> (Hamlet, III. i. 50–2[1]).

Gilding deed with word, Claudius shows us that Shakespeare understood what historians of rhetoric articulated centuries later: the gap between speaking and being. Shakespeare, trained in the fundamentals of the rhetorical tradition, both used rhetoric and examined the problems that rhetoric raised for his culture. Furthermore, because the bulk of his professional life was spent working in and writing for the theater, he had a knowledge of – and a perfect forum for exploring – the rhetorical, theatrical nature of being human.

What I hope to do in this essay is provide a sense of "the range of rhetoric" in Shakespeare's Europe (Burke 1950: 3). First, I will briefly survey the classical tradition that Shakespeare and his contemporaries would have been taught in school; the emphasis here will be on rhetoric as a process of speaking and writing. Next, I will turn to an expanded notion of the rhetorical, flexible self in the Renaissance, suggesting how rhetoric becomes connected to knowing and being. I will finish the essay by examining one scene from *The Merchant of Venice*, explicating the way in which Shakespeare not only employed but also interrogated the rhetorical system that he inherited.

The Classical Tradition of Rhetoric: A Sketch

An examination of classical rhetoric in an essay about Shakespeare is necessary because training in rhetoric was a central part of Shakespeare's and his contemporaries' educational program. Thanks largely to Erasmus and John Colet, who refounded St

Paul's School in 1508–10, English humanists had a scheme for education – laid out in Erasmus's *De ratione studii* (1511) – which facilitated the teaching of the classical texts that they had helped recover and disseminate. Many of the rhetorical manuals had been available only in parts until the fifteenth century; Quintilian's *Institutio oratoria*, for example, was not known in full until 1416, when it was discovered at St Gall, a monastery in present-day Switzerland. Valuing classical texts and having more complete ones at their disposal, humanist educators placed rhetoric at the heart of their curriculum, believing that eloquence in speech was linked to virtue in action (see Vickers 1988: 254–70).

While some rhetoric books published in England in the sixteenth century were undoubtedly developed for students and stemmed from the influence of continental humanism, the interest in them had other, more complex roots, as Frank Whigham has proposed. Outlining a superior sort of human being – the rhetorician – these texts also afforded anyone who could read "access to power and its assorted privileges"; mastering the art of rhetoric gave one "a power open to many applications" (Whigham 1984: 2). Whatever the complex, various sources of their appeal, rhetoric books began to emerge in England by the mid-sixteenth century, notably Leonard Coxes's *The Arte or Crafte of Rethoryke* (1530), Richard Sherry's *A Treatise on Schemes and Tropes* (1550), Thomas Wilson's *The Arte of Rhetorique* (1553), Gabriel Harvey's *Rhetor* (1575) and *Ciceronianus* (1576), Henry Peacham's *The Garden of Eloquence* (1577), Dudley Fenner's *The Artes of Logicke and Retorike* (1584), Abraham Fraunce's *A Lawier's Logike* and *The Arcadian Rhetoricke* (1588), and George Puttenham's *The Arte of English Poesie* (1589) (see Conley 1990: 133–43).

The classical writers who provided the sources for these English handbooks tell us that rhetoric had its origins in fifth-century BC Athens and Syracuse, as attempts were made to put into writing the various practices of law courts, political assemblies, and ceremonial occasions (see Kennedy 1994: 1; Conley 1990: 4–5). Surely, though, Richard Lanham is right to say that rhetoric did not begin in either Athens or Syracuse but in Eden, where "its basic techniques [were] first tried out against Eve – as Milton dramatizes" (Lanham 1991: 131). As soon as there was speech, a motive, and an audience, there was rhetoric.

Formal training in rhetoric certainly existed by the fourth century BC, when Isocrates came to prominence. It was Aristotle in this same century who most clearly articulated the three divisions of rhetoric, the three types of speeches, so important to Cicero and to the Renaissance humanists who were his apostles:

> Rhetoric falls into three divisions, determined by the three classes of listeners to speeches. For of the three elements in speech-making – speaker, subject, and person addressed – it is the last one, the hearer, that determines the speech's end and object. The hearer must be either a judge, with a decision to make about things past or future, or an observer. A member of the assembly decides about future events, a juryman about past events, while those who merely decide on the orator's skill are observers. From this list follows that there are three divisions of oratory – deliberative [political], forensic

[judicial], and epideictic [demonstrative]. Deliberative speaking urges us either to do or not to do something.... Forensic speaking either attacks or defends somebody.... Epideictic oratory either praises or censures somebody. (*Rhetoric*, 1358a–b; ii. 2159 in Barnes edn)

Besides emphasizing the power of the audience in any rhetorical performance, this passage links the type of speech to a particular mode of time: deliberative speeches, made in political assemblies, sought to shape future action; forensic speeches, made in law courts, commented on past actions (usually crimes); and epideictic speeches, made at public festivals or funerals, attempted to shape opinion in the present (which could, of course, lead to actions in the future).

For Shakespeare and other Renaissance writers, who lived under political and legal systems quite different from those of ancient Greece and Rome, epideictic was certainly the chief division of rhetoric. Indeed, Brian Vickers has claimed that "all literature became subsumed under epideictic, and all writing was perceived as occupying the related spheres of praise and blame" (1988: 54). For our purposes, Shakespeare's sonnets provide classic examples of epideictic oratory: the poet praises or blames the Young Man, the Dark Lady, and the Rival Poet throughout the sequence; analogues can be found throughout the Renaissance lyric tradition.

But what happened to an audience at a Shakespeare play? Surely, they experienced more than praise or blame (though they were certainly treated to epideixis in Marc Antony's funeral oration in Act III of *Julius Caesar*). The view of epideictic proposed by Vickers has been challenged by, among others, Victoria Kahn, who sees a blending of deliberative (political) and epideictic oratory in Renaissance rhetoric because, for the humanists so important to Shakespeare's education, "the deliberation involved in reading is itself understood as a form of the deliberation that leads to action" (Kahn 1985: 39). Because Kahn is primarily interested in reading – "the written text now takes on the functions of deliberative and judicial rhetoric" (p. 38) – she focuses on the power of the Renaissance dialogue as a site for this sort of rhetorical work. Building on her arguments, I would propose the theaters as another location of Renaissance deliberative rhetoric: a place where audiences could hear and deliberate on dialogues and debates staged almost daily, and where they heard speeches in a form and forum very close to those of their ancient forebears.

The importance of rhetoric in shaping an audience's moral actions was recognized by Renaissance humanists, who had learned practical applications for classical texts – "lessons applicable to warfare and administration as well as oratory and epic poetry" (Grafton 1991: 4). Using the claims made to defend rhetoric as a means of defending the poet, Sir Philip Sidney expresses a belief in the fashioning power of language in his *Apology for Poetry* (a. 1581/1595): "[poetry] worketh, not only to make a Cyrus, which had been but a particular excellency as Nature might have done, but to bestow a Cyrus upon the world to make many Cyruses, if they will learn aright why and how that maker made him" (Sidney 1965: 101). Alluding to Xenophon's *Cyropaedia*, Sidney defends the poet because he has the ability, through his rhetorical creation (Cyrus), to persuade his reading audience to emulate his fictive character and thereby help generate many actual, ethical citizens (the "many Cyruses"). This was the humanist ideal: rhetorical models could produce authentic moral individuals.

Sidney's defense of poetry, focusing as it does on the need for the practical application of rhetorical and poetic performances, has its roots in the work of the two great Roman defenders of rhetoric: Cicero and Quintilian. Influenced by Isocrates' emphasis on the link between virtuous action and eloquence, Cicero in turn influenced Quintilian, and both Romans shaped the humanist educational program. Justifying the social function of the rhetor, Cicero's Crassus says in *De oratore*:

> the wise control of the complete orator is that which chiefly upholds not only his own dignity, but the safety of countless individuals and of the entire State. Go forward therefore, my young friends, in your present course, and bend your energies to that study which engages you, that so it may be in your power to become a glory to yourselves, a source of service to your friends, and profitable members of the Republic. (1. 8. 34, p. 27 in Sutton and Rackham trans.)

Like Sidney's poet, Cicero's ideal orator studies in order to translate that knowledge into action, and for the orator this action is speech and persuasion; the contemplative life ultimately must give way to the active life.

Cicero most fully articulates these ideas in *De officiis* (*On Duties*):

> The very men, then, who have given their lives to the pursuit of teaching and wisdom, provide above all good sense and understanding for the benefit of mankind. Therefore it is better to speak at length, provided one does so wisely, than to think, however penetratingly, without eloquence. For speculation turns in on itself, but eloquence embraces those to whom we are joined by social life. (1. 156, pp. 60–1 in Griffin and Atkins edn)

Eloquence – or rhetoric – is proposed as the means by which speculation – or thought – leads to action. Further, rhetoric allows the orator both to embrace "those to whom we are joined by social life" and to instill in them a desire to perform socially significant deeds. Quintilian's entire *Institutio oratoria* is set up as a search for this sort of Ciceronian rhetor – "the orator of our quest." Refusing to cede the moral high ground to philosophy, Quintilian puts forth the orator as "the man who can guide a state by his counsels, give it a firm basis by his legislation, and purge its vices by his decisions as a judge" (1. Pr. 10; iv. 11 in Butler trans.).

Thus far we have seen that a central way of defending rhetoric was by emphasizing the rhetorician's ability to teach his audience how to be better citizens. But it is important to remember that delighting and moving were seen to be equally important goals of the effective rhetorical performance. Crassus tells us in *De oratore* that "for purposes of persuasion, the art of speaking relies wholly upon three things: the proof of our allegations, the winning of our hearers' favour, and the rousing of their feelings to whatever impulse our case may require" (2. 27. 115, p. 281 in Sutton and Rackham trans.). Or, as Thomas Sloane succinctly puts it, "One told people something that they didn't know and convinced them of it; one put them in a good mood; and one got them emotionally involved in one's subject" (Sloane 1985: 94).

Rhetoric was defended, then, because it could be shown to have positive goals that benefited a larger community; the motive – the end – of the persuasive act was crucial. What I would like to turn to now is *how* the rhetorician was supposed to achieve these positive ends. Both Isocrates and Aristotle divided up the rhetorical method into five divisions or stages. But Cicero in *De oratore* again provides the most influential (and concise) explanation of the stages:

> he must first hit on what to say [*inventio*]; then manage and marshal his discoveries, not merely in orderly fashion, but with a discriminating eye as it were of each argument [*dispositio*]; next go on to array them in the adornments of style [*elocutio*]; after that keep them guarded in memory [*memoria*]; and in the end deliver them with effect and charm [*actio*]. (1. 31. 142, p. 99 in Sutton and Rackham trans.)

The most important and most analyzed stages – in both classical and Renaissance rhetorical manuals – were the first three, and I will briefly suggest what was at stake in them for the rhetor and author.

As Cicero has told us, invention consisted of discovering a topic, of figuring out what to say. Aristotle listed twenty-eight "valid topics," or *topoi* (as well as ten invalid topics), in his *Rhetoric*. Invention also meant drawing on a storehouse of commonplaces. The court versus country debate that Shakespeare stages between Touchstone and Corin in Act III of *As You Like It* provides an example of such a commonplace in action. However, sometimes a trip to the storehouse could yield little – or perhaps too much – rhetorical sustenance, and we see a poet lost in the process of *inventio* at the beginning of Sidney's *Astrophil and Stella* sonnet sequence:

> But words came halting forth, wanting invention's stay;
> Invention, nature's child, fled step-dame study's blows;
> And others' feet still seemed but strangers in my way
> (Sidney 1973: 1. 9–11; p. 117).

Sidney's poet here is paralyzed by *topoi*, commonplaces, the "feet" or meter of earlier poets. And although Astrophil (or Sidney) may be presenting the difficulty as a way of enticing both the beloved and the reading audience into the sequence, this sonnet suggests that writer's block is not just a modern phenomenon; *inventio* has always been the most difficult part of composition.

Dispositio consisted of arranging the material decided on in the *inventio* stage and fashioning it into an effective structure. It is in the *dispositio* that the well-known six (or seven) parts of an oration came into play (see [Cicero], *Rhetorica ad Herennium*, 1. 3. 4; pp. 9–11 in Caplan trans.). Again, Sidney provides us with the most accessible example, as his *Apology for Poetry* was written according to this formula – one familiar from the rhetorical manuals, including Cicero's *De inventione* and Wilson's *The Arte of*

Rhetorique (1553) (see Sidney 1965: 11–17; Cicero, *De inventione*, book 1; Wilson 1962: book 1). The orator began with an introduction, an entrance into his topic (*exordium*), what we might now call a "hook." After laying out the facts in the *narratio* – and in some schemes taking a brief detour (*digressio*) – the rhetor would bring the terms of the dispute to the foreground in the *divisio*, informing the audience of the points of agreement and disagreement between him and his opponent. From there, he put forth the arguments that supported his case (*confirmatio*) and refuted the opponent's claims (*confutatio*). Finally, the orator rehearsed his arguments and sought to excite the audience into a lasting acceptance of his claims (*conclusio* or *peroratio*).

In order to win over this audience, though, rhetors needed more than just an important topic and a carefully structured speech: they needed, as Cicero said, "to array them [the arguments] in the adornments of style." I will address briefly three elements of style, or *elocutio*, here: the three styles, the figures of speech, and the notion of *copia*. Cicero's *Orator* provided the lasting divisions of style – low or plain, middle, and grand – and connected each to one of the goals of rhetoric discussed above: "To prove [*probare*] is the first necessity, to please [*delectare*] is charm, to sway [*flectere*] is victory. . . . For these three functions of the orator there are three styles, the plain style for proof, the middle style for pleasure, the vigorous style for persuasion; and in this last is summed up the entire virtue of the orator" (20. 69, p. 357 in Hendrickson and Hubbell trans.; see Burke 1950 73–4). The notion of style became much more complex and varied in the work of Hermogenes (*On Types of Style*, second century AD), but the central lesson for students of classical style is that different rhetorical goals were seen to require different linguistic presentations and modes (Shuger 1988; Biester 1997).

Another crucial weapon in the orator's arsenal was the figures of speech. This element of rhetoric is still very much with us, and few reading this essay will have had difficulty spotting the martial metaphors in the first sentence of this paragraph. Modern critics and students also have not only noted but also employed metonymy, synecdoche, paradox, oxymoron, and personification. But these are just a few of the literally hundreds of figures available to those trained in the rhetorical tradition ([Cicero], *Rhetorica ad Herennium*, Book 4; Quintilian, *Institutio oratoria*, Butler trans., vol. 4, book 9; Sonnino 1968; Lanham 1991). Most figures – often called tropes (from the Greek *tropos*, "turn") – involve a movement away from the standard meaning of a word, and it is this element of rhetoric and poetry that can inspire tremendous excitement at reality transformed or terror at reality disfigured. I will argue in the third section of this essay that the process of figuration – the transformation of literal meaning into figurative – is writ large in Shakespeare, as he constantly explores what is lost and gained in the translation from literal to figurative, true self to disguised self, being to seeming.

First, though, we need to examine one more area of *elocutio*: the concept of *copia*. Nearly all the classical manuals stress variety of expression: Cicero claimed in his *De partitione oratoria* that "eloquence is nothing else but wisdom delivering copious utterance" (23. 7; p. 369 in Rackham trans.), while Quintilian asserted that the orator "must accumulate a certain store of resources, to be employed whenever they are required. The resources of which I speak consist in a copious supply of words and matter" (*copia rerum ac verborum*) (Quintilian, *Institutio oratoria*, 10. 1. 5; iv. 5 in Butler trans.). These words of Quintilian inspired Erasmus to write one of the most influential rhetoric books of the Renaissance, *De duplici copia verborum ac rerum comentarii duo* (hereafter *De copia* (1512)). Following his classical teachers, Erasmus set out "to teach boys abundant Latin style in two ways, through copiousness of expression [*verborum*] and through copiousness of thought [*rerum*]" (Sloane 1985: 82). It was this love of verbal fecundity that engendered Rabelais' copious lists and catalogues, as well as the following exchange between Falstaff and Hal in *1 Henry IV* (II. iv. 244–51):

FALSTAFF 'Sblood, you starveling, you eel-skin, you dried neat's tongue, you bull's pizzle, you stock-fish! O for breath to utter what is like thee! you tailor's yard, you sheath, you bowcase, you vile standing tuck –

PRINCE.   Well, breathe awhile, and then to it again, and when thou hast tir'd thyself in base comparisons, hear me speak in this.

Falstaff's verbal variations on (mostly) phallic insults seem to have endless potential; both men suggest that only a shortness of breath or fatigue will silence him.

While the notion that language is abundant, multiple, and various may cause us anxiety in the late twentieth century, for Erasmus, Shakespeare, and the inheritors of the rhetorical tradition, this *copia* was usually a cause for celebration (Cave 1979: esp. 3–34). As Thomas Sloane nicely puts it, "The instability of language was to be revelled in, not fretted over. That language was plastic was shown in puns and in verbal ironies. But this plasticity... was no more cause for despair than the contrarieties of living in a fluid and changeable world" (Sloane 1985: 83) – in short, a rhetorical world. Or, as Erasmus says in *De copia*, the goal of his book is "to turn one idea into more shapes than Proteus himself is supposed to have turned into" (Erasmus 1978: 302).

Before turning to the connections between protean rhetoric and the protean self, I would like to comment briefly on the fourth and fifth divisions of rhetoric: *memoria* and *actio*. Because these two areas were necessarily limited to oral performance, they did not receive the same attention in the Renaissance as the first three divisions. Yet, as some pioneering work on *memoria* has shown, understanding the art of memory – both using mnemonic devices in delivering speeches and instilling these techniques in one's audience – allows crucial insights into conceptions of the imagination and psychology in the medieval and early modern periods ([Cicero] *Rhetorica ad Herennium*, 3. 16. 28–3. 24. 40; Yates 1966; Carruthers 1990). And although the classical manuals' historically contingent discussions of a speech's delivery and its accompanying gestures obviously have limited use for us, the notion of the body as an instrument of rhetoric is central to current discussions in gender and performance theory (Butler 1990; Turner 1988; Bulman 1996).

I would like to expand on one final element of rhetorical training, mentioned earlier in this essay, and use it as a bridge from rhetorical speaking and writing to rhetorical knowing and being: the strategy of *disputatio in utramque partem* – arguing on both sides of the question (Altman 1978; Trimpi 1983: esp. 287–95; Eden 1997). Cicero claims an essential link between speaking and knowledge – rhetoric and philosophy – when he tells us in his *Orator* that "whatever ability I possess as an orator comes, not from the workshops of the rhetoricians, but from the spacious grounds of the Academy. There indeed is the field for manifold and varied debate, which was first trodden by the feet of Plato" (3. 12; pp. 313–15 in Hendrickson and Hubbell trans.). Cicero goes on to note his departure from – as well as his debt to – Plato, by whom "the orator has been severely criticized but also [from whom he] has received assistance" (ibid. p. 315). Taking seriously the skepticism of Plato's teacher, Socrates, Cicero acknowledges that a search for the probable was the necessary office of both the rhetor and the philosopher. As Wesley Trimpi has observed,

> Recognizing the fallibility of sensory perception, these schools [the Academic schools of philosophy, to which Cicero belonged] claimed by means of such debate [*in utramque partem*] to be able to arrive at a degree of probability (*verisimile*) sufficiently great to permit choice and action. Their conclusions, though never certain, could be verified by experience to some extent and become grounds for deliberation about the future. (Trimpi 1983: 287)

For Cicero, this commitment to the probable was not an abandoning of knowledge altogether, just a recognition that truth could be known only contingently, as he claims in *De natura deorum*: "Our position is not that we hold that nothing is true, but that we assert that all true sensations are associated with false ones so closely resembling them that they contain no infallible mark to guide our judgement and assent." (1. 5. 12, p. 15 in Rackham trans.).

Elaborating on this point in the *Academica*, Cicero claims that "the sole object of our discussions is by arguing on both sides to draw out and give shape to some result that may be either true or the nearest possible approximation to the truth" (Cicero 1933: ii. 3. 7, p. 475 in Rackham trans.). Because knowing the world is so difficult – "true sensations are associated with false ones so closely resembling them" – it is through the skills of debating *in utramque partem* that the rhetorical philosopher can glimpse – and ultimately communicate – some partial truth.

I hope that this sense of the contingency of knowledge and truth already – without rhetorical prompting from me – sounds "Shakespearian." For there can be little doubt that the training in rhetoric that Shakespeare and his contemporaries received led to a "moral cultivation of ambivalence," as Joel Altman has called it, that found its ideal home in the drama (1978: 31). For in the theater the problematic issues could be staged if not ultimately resolved: "these plays did not merely raise questions, in the general sense, but literally were questions – or rather fictional realizations of questions" (p. 3). Before turning to an examination of this staging of questions in

Shakespeare, I would like to explore the implications of this Ciceronian "probabilism" for the Renaissance self. For if one accepts that, like language, selfhood can be shaped and manipulated, one has entered a world of tremendous possibility – for both exuberant self-fashioning and devious deception. This is the world that Malcolm – doing his best Cicero imitation – describes to Macduff in Act IV of *Macbeth*:

> That which you are, my thoughts cannot transpose:
> Angels are bright still, though the brightest fell.
> Though all things foul would wear the brows of grace,
> Yet grace must still look so.
>
> (*Macbeth*, IV. iii. 21–4)

Changing Shapes with Proteus for Advantages: The Flexible Renaissance Self

The importance of the rhetorical, mutable self to Renaissance literature has been helpfully laid out by some important articles and books in the last thirty years (Greene 1968; Giamatti 1968; Greenblatt 1973, 1980; Lanham 1976; Javitch 1978; Rebhorn 1978, 1995; Barish 1981; Whigham 1984; Bates 1992). What I would like to do here is provide a few key texts from the European and English Renaissance to suggest how the rules of the rhetoric books could be applied to the way individuals presented themselves to the world. These texts range from the exhilarating potential of Giovanni Pico della Mirandola's *Oration on the Dignity of Man* (1486) to the dark, potentially disturbing implications of Machiavelli's *The Prince* (1514). All suggest that the fluidity of speech and truth stressed in the Ciceronian vision have serious ramifications for the Renaissance self.

"Human beings are not born but fashioned," Erasmus said, and this is a statement that could serve as an epigraph for both humanism and *homo rhetoricus* (Greene 1968: 249). This idea presupposes – at least on the surface – a great deal of human freedom in molding the self. An important touchstone for this sense of human flexibility is Pico's *Oration*, in which Pico imagines God announcing to Adam – "a creature of indeterminate nature" – that he will give human beings "neither a fixed abode nor a form that is thine alone nor any function peculiar to thyself" (Pico 1948: 224). Because Adam has no pre-defined essence, God says, he has the power to shape himself:

> according to thy longing and according to thy judgment thou mayest have and possess what abode, what form, and what functions thou thyself shalt desire. The nature of all other beings is limited and constrained within the bounds of laws prescribed by Us. Thou, constrained by no limits, in accordance with thine own free will, in whose hand We have placed thee, shalt ordain for thyself the limits of thy nature. We have set thee at the world's center that thou mayest from thence more easily observe whatever is in the world. We have made thee neither of heaven nor of earth, neither mortal nor immortal,

so that with freedom of choice and with honor, as though the maker and molder of thyself, thou mayest fashion thyself in whatever shape thou shalt prefer. (Pico 1948: 225)

The "as though" constrains the Piconian individual somewhat, but the emphasis on personal self-fashioning is clear.

Pico concludes this part of the *Oration* by invoking the language and mythology of shape-shifting:

Who would not admire this our chameleon? . . . It is man who Asclepius of Athens, arguing from his mutability of character and from his self-transforming nature, on just grounds says was symbolized by Proteus in the mysteries. (Ibid.)

A chameleon, the Piconian self is also a Proteus – the Greek sea god noted for his ability to change shapes to avoid danger. Proteus was also invoked, as we have seen, by Erasmus in *De copia* in order to describe the rhetorical possibilites of copious language. According to Pico, there is a *copia* of selves available to human beings as well, and A. B. Giamatti (1968) has reminded us that the Proteus figure need not be a negative one for the Renaissance. Indeed, Erasmus – celebrator of the fashioning potential of rhetoric and selfhood – compared Christ to Proteus in his *Plan of True Theology* because of the "variety of his life and knowledge" (*varietate vitae atque doctrinae*) (see Sloane 1985: 84, 298, n. 19).

The notion that one individual could have an abundance of selves and roles was not, however, always portrayed as unequivocally positive or Christ-like. Although he clearly focuses on the potential good in treating, to use Burckhardt's phrase, "the self as a work of art," Baldessare Castiglione raises major questions about the ethical issues surrounding the protean, theatrical self in his *The Book of the Courtier*, a virtual handbook of self-fashioning. Limited space dictates that I focus on only the most famous example, the concept of *sprezzatura*, or effortlessness. As presented to the internal audience by Count Ludovico da Canossa in book 1, *sprezzatura* is the technique that allows the courtier

to conceal all art and make whatever is done or said appear to be without effort and almost without any thought about it. And I believe much grace comes of this: because everyone knows the difficulty of things that are rare and well done; wherefore facility in such things causes the greatest wonder; whereas, on the other hand, to labor and, as we say, drag forth by the hair of the head, shows an extreme want of grace, and causes everything, no matter how great it may be, to be held in little account. Therefore we may call that art true art which does not seem to be art. . . . And I remember having read of certain most excellent orators in ancient times who . . . tried to make everyone believe that they had no knowledge whatever of letters; and, dissembling their knowledge, they made their orations appear to be composed in the simplest manner and according to the dictates of nature and truth rather than of effort and art. (Castiglione 1959: 1. 26, pp. 43–4)

The count clearly links the art "which does not seem to be art" with oratory and reminds us why Plato feared rhetoric: it attempts to make the artful and constructed appear natural and effortless for a more persuasive effect.

The Book of the Courtier recognizes the danger of amoral self-fashioning, and its book 4 deals with "the end to which he [the courtier] is directed," an emphasis we will remember from defenses of rhetoric (Castiglione 1959: 4. 4, p. 288). The goal for Castiglione's courtier is to win favor with the prince, but the end is still idealistic: his courtier will "dissuade him [the prince] of every evil intent and bring him to the path of virtue" (4. 5, p. 289). But this noble end is not a given. George Puttenham, author of *The Arte of English Poesie* (1589), recognized the potential for dissembling in the courtier. In defining "*Allegoria*, which is when we speake one thing and thinke another, and that our wordes and our meanings meet not" (Puttenham 1936: 3. 18, p. 186), Puttenham "Englishes" the figure as "the Courtier" (3. 25, p. 299). Highlighting the moral ambiguity of the rhetoric and action of the courtier's protean self, Puttenham also calls *Allegoria* both "the figure of false semblant" (3. 18, p. 186) and "the figure of faire semblant" (3. 25, p. 299); the end, again, is crucial. For Puttenham recognizes that there will be times that "our courtly Poet do dissemble not onely his countenances & cōceits, but also all his ordinary actions of behauiour, or the most part of thē, whereby the better to winne his purposes & good aduantages" (3. 25, pp. 299–300). Using – indeed, becoming – *Allegoria* can be necessary to winning one's "purposes and good aduantages" (see Burke 1950: 60–1, 285–6).

As Puttenham's quotation suggests, the entire self has become rhetorical: the courtier who wants to win or persuade uses not only language ("conceits") but also "actions of behaviour." The emphasis on "countenances" – behaviors, appearances, shows (*OED*, 1a, 2a, 2b) – suggests that Frank Whigham is right when he notes that "public life at court was governed by a rhetorical imperative of performance. ... Elite status no longer rested upon the absolute, given base of birth, the received ontology of social being; instead it has increasingly become a matter of doing, and so of *showing*" (1984: 32–3). This rhetoric of both speaking and showing is crucial to Machiavelli's prince, a figure who, if he follows Machiavelli's instructions, will be the master of "the rhetoricality of politics" (Rebhorn 1995: 54). Like Plato's worst nightmare, the Prince

> need not necessarily have all the good qualities..., but he should certainly appear to have them. I would even go so far as to say that if he has these qualities and always behaves accordingly he will find them ruinous; if he only appears to have them they will render him service. He should appear to be compassionate, faithful to his word, guileless, and devout. And indeed he should be. But his disposition should be such that, if he needs to be the opposite, he knows how. You must realize this: that a prince, and especially a new prince, cannot observe all those things which give men a reputation for virtue, because in order to maintain his state he is often forced to act in defiance of good faith, of charity, of kindness, of religion. And he should have a flexible disposition, varying as fortune and circumstances dictate. (Machiavelli 1961: ch. 18, pp. 100–1)

Machiavelli adds moral flexibility to the "flexible disposition" of the rhetorical self, cutting off noble ends from rhetorical means. Seeming virtue and a reputation for goodness are as good – and at times better – than actual virtue.

That Shakespeare was aware of the problems of the rhetorical self – particularly the protean and Machiavellian strains – is revealed early in his career. I will finish this section, then, with a brief look at Richard of Gloucester's speech from Act III, scene ii, of *3 Henry VI*:

> Why, I can smile, and murther whiles I smile,
> And cry "content" to that which grieves my heart,
> And wet my cheeks with artificial tears,
> And frame my face to all occasions.
> I'll drown more sailors than the mermaid shall,
> I'll slay more gazers than the basilisk,
> I'll play the orator as well as Nestor,
> Deceive more slily than Ulysses could,
> And like Sinon, take another Troy.
> I can add colors to the chameleon,
> Change shapes with Proteus for advantages,
> And set the murtherous Machevil to school.
> Can I do this, and cannot get a crown?
> Tut, were it farther off, I'll pluck it down.

Richard tells us he is evil, shifting, seeming. He outdoes mermaids and basilisks, comparisons that suggest, despite his physical deformity, his deadly seductiveness; his comparison to Nestor hints at his tremendous rhetorical skills, skills that get people to do things seemingly impossible (particularly, in *Richard III*, convincing the woman whose father-in-law and husband he has killed to marry him). He notes his capacity to deceive in his allusions to Ulysses and Sinon, and he suggests how he does it with the allusions to a chameleon, Proteus, and Machiavelli. These last three figures, as we have seen, would have suggested to Shakespeare's audience the self-fashioning power of the Renaissance individual. A classic *homo rhetoricus*, Richard uses language and actions to persuade people and win the day. Like Machiavelli's prince, Shakespeare's evil king employs the talents of the flexible self for personal "advantages," while completely cutting himself off from the moorings of ethical ends.

Shakespeare and Rhetoric

Given the above example, this final section could be a catalog of protean characters in Shakespeare – good and bad – that would show Shakespeare's double response to the rhetorical self (Righter 1962; Giamatti 1968). Another method would be to reveal Shakespeare's use of specific rhetorical figures (see Vickers 1971). While these approaches have merit – and have been used to excellent effect – I would like to explore one passage from *The Merchant of Venice* with the aim of revealing rhetoric not so much as a linguistic tool or even as a method of self-fashioning but as a staged problem. In doing so, I would hope to uncover what Patricia Parker has called "the structural force of rhetorical figures" (1987: 96). Focusing in particular on "ornament," I hope to reveal how Shakespeare explores – using the Ciceronian ambivalence outlined in the first section – both rhetoric as problem and rhetoric as inevitability.

To adorn or not to adorn – that was the question. At the heart of the Reformation debates, the problem of ornamentation was also a central issue in the history of rhetoric. Shakespeare's approach was characteristically ambivalent, but this ambivalence exists in his rhetorical teachers as well. Quintilian tells us that "where ornament is concerned, vice and virtue are never far apart; those who employ a vicious style of embellishment disguise their vices with the name of virtue" *Institutio oratoria*, 8. 3. 7; iv. 215 in Butler trans.). Puttenham, who devotes an entire book of *The Arte* to the problem "of ornament," sees the issue in a similarly double fashion:

> But as it hath bene alwayes reputed a great fault to vse figuratiue speaches foolishly and indiscretly, so is it esteemed no lesse an imperfection in mans vtterance, to haue none vse of figure at all, specially in our writing and speaches publike, making them but as our ordinary talke, then which nothing can be more vnsauorie and farre from all ciuilitie. (Puttenham 1936: 3. 2, pp. 138–9)

Using ornament is a tricky enterprise: vice and virtue are perilously close together (Quintilian), but under-ornamenting is even more "vnsauorie" and uncivilized than over-ornamenting (Puttenham; and see Lanham 1976: 22–5).

Shakespeare explored this problem relentlessly through the motif of disguise, in both comic and tragic modes. Disguise afforded Shakespeare the means to examine what Stephen Greenblatt, speaking of Ralegh and his contemporaries, has called the "dramatic sense of life": a sense that had "two contradictory traditions, one that likened life to a play to express the emptiness and unreality of man's earthbound existence, the other that saw in playing an image of man's power to fashion the self" (1973: 44). But disguise also allows Shakespeare to look at a more rhetorical problem: that of ornament, of metaphor. As Patricia Parker reminds us, "the idea of metaphor itself as 'clothing' includes the possibility of a linguistic transvestism, a violation of boundaries which makes Shakespeare's plots – of changelings, exchangeable twins, disguises, usurpation, illegitimacy – virtual *mises-en-scène* of the activity of tropes" (Parker 1987: 38–9). This "violation of boundaries" is what Quintilian and Puttenham, as well as many others in the rhetorical tradition, isolated as a crucial issue in the use of ornament. What is at stake for Shakespeare is not just how we signify with words, but how we present meaningful selves to the world. As a result, the disguise motif allows Shakespeare to tackle problems not only of writing and theater but also of epistemology and ontology – knowing and being.

At the figurative (and nearly literal) center of *The Merchant of Venice* is Bassanio's soliloquy denouncing "outward shows" while observing that "the world is still deceiv'd with ornament" (III. ii. 73, 74). This speech represents Bassanio's thoughts before he ultimately chooses the lead casket, symbolic of the unadorned, simple truth that the other suitors cannot appreciate: "You that choose not by the view, / Chance as fair, and choose as true," he is told by the scroll that he finds inside the humble case (III. ii. 131–2).

The speech seems to be a straightforwardly anti-ornamental, anti-rhetorical one, firmly in the tradition of Plato rather than of Cicero. We are told that in law, "a tainted and corrupt plea" that "is seasoned with a gracious voice, / Obscures the show of evil" (lines 75–6); in religion, "damned error" is blessed "with a text, / Hiding the grossness with fair ornament" (lines 78–80). In short, "There is no vice so simple but assumes / Some mark of virtue on his outward parts" (lines 81–2). This is the danger pointed out by Plato and admitted to even by as staunch a defender of rhetoric as Quintilian.

Bassanio elaborates on this theme in increasingly metaphorical language, an irony I will return to below. First, he attacks cowards,

> whose hearts are all as false
> As stairs of sand, [who] wear yet upon their chins
> The beards of Hercules and frowning Mars,
> Who inward search'd, have livers white as milk,
> And these assume but valor's excrement
> To render them redoubted.
>
> (lines 83–8)

The cowardly heart crumbles and – like stairs of sand – causes a fall; cowards thrive on masks – here figured as godly beards – that hide the fear within. Most interestingly, the lily livers are hidden not only by beards-as-masks but also by the "excrement" of valor – valor's external appearance but also valor's waste. Ornament has been rendered figuratively as a piece of crap.

Beauty does not fare much better: it is "purchas'd by the weight" (line 89) and paradoxically makes "them lightest that wear most of it" (line 91). Beautiful-seeming hair – "those crisped snaky golden locks, / Which make such wanton gambols with the wind / Upon supposed fairness" (lines 92–4) – is actually a wig, the "dowry of a second head" (line 95). As Bassanio begins to conclude his diatribe against ornament, he uses more of it:

> Thus ornament is but the guiled shore
> To a most dangerous sea; the beauteous scarf
> Veiling an Indian beauty; in a word,
> The seeming truth which cunning times put on
> To entrap the wisest.

Ornament is figured – is ornamented – as both a deceptive shore masking a perilous sea and a scarf that hides an ironic, dark "Indian beauty" behind it. Bassanio brings the rhetorical issues to the front when he finishes his critique by telling us he will pick the lead casket – "the pale and common drudge" (line 103) – because its "paleness moves me more than eloquence" (line 106). We do not need to emend "paleness" to "plainness" the way the eighteenth-century editor Lewis Theobald did in order to see the rhetorical implications; "paleness" clearly contrasts with the "colors of rhetoric" that make up "eloquence" and that we saw earlier in Claudius's "painted word."

But we would be foolish to take this anti-rhetorical speech as the key or answer to the play as a whole, even if it seems set up to guide us in this direction. First, Bassanio is himself ornamented, affecting much more wealth than he has in his self-fashioned attempt to woo Portia; as he confesses to her later in the scene, "you shall see / How much I was the braggart" (lines 257–8). Second, as I have hinted above, this is a highly ornamented speech against ornament: Bassanio uses – among other figures – synecdoche (lines 78, 92), simile (lines 84, 86), allegory (line 85), personification (lines 88–9), paradox (lines 89–91), irony (lines 89–91, 99, 106), metaphor (lines 89, 95–6, 97, 98), and apostrophe (lines 101, 104). Third, beyond the range of this speech, the play seems both to attack the "paleness" of Shylock's language and thought and to celebrate the highly flexible Portia/Balthazar, who drives home the attack on Shylockian plainness. Ornamented as a man, Portia uses rhetorical maneuvering to expose the flaw in Shylock's literal interpretation:

> The words expressly are "a pound of flesh,"
> Take then thy bond, take thou thy pound of flesh,
> But in the cutting it, if thou dost shed
> One drop of Christian blood, thy lands and goods
> Are by the laws of Venice confiscate
> Unto the state of Venice.
>
> (IV. i. 307–12)

In extending Shylock's literalism *ad absurdum*, Portia makes a mockery of plainness.

It would be a mistake to swing back too far the other way, though, and see Shakespeare as unequivocally embracing Portia's method and end: there is something sinister in her treatment of Shylock, and though the fifth act tries to cover over the ugliness, there is a deep ambivalence at the heart of both this play's ending and its treatment of ornament and disguise. In *Merchant*, singleness – in language, interpretation, and thought – is punished as it usually is in Shakespeare. But it is not clear what we are supposed to embrace instead. Portia's duplicity is not without its moral troubles, and Shylock's approach to the bond – so clearly criticized – can be seen as actually double and thus as similar to the witches' manipulations of the literal that Macbeth finds so difficult to decipher: the "juggling fiends ... palter with us in a double sense" and "keep the word of promise to our ear, / And break it to our hope" (*Macbeth*, V. viii. 19, 20–2). The literal only *seems* single in meaning.

Rhetoric and the rhetorical self inspire such ambivalence because they can lead both to a solution – a new sort of truth – and to further error, falsehood, and cruelty. Rhetoric is not intrinsically either instructive or harmful – it is partly both – but it is inescapable. On some level, of course, Shakespeare is turning the technique of *disputatio in utramque partem* on rhetoric itself, showing that the very art that taught him his ambivalence – and one so connected to the drama – has an intrinsic doubleness to it. This recognition brings Shakespeare very close to Gorgias's position cited in the epigraph. But I would go further and suggest that Shakespeare ultimately sees rhetoric as a necessity.

This necessary quality of rhetoric is highlighted in an extremely influential passage of Cicero's *De inventione* (itself influenced by Isocrates' *Antidosis*), in which Cicero establishes what Wayne Rebhorn has called the "myth of the orator-civilizer" (1995: esp. 23–9): "There was a time," we are told, "when men wandered at large in the fields like animals and lived on wild fare . . . , did nothing by the guidance of reason, but relied chiefly on physical strength . . . ; and there was as yet no ordered system of religious worship and social duties" (Cicero, *De inventione*, 1. 2. 2; p. 5 in Hubbell trans.). Enter the orator, who introduced these people "to every useful and honourable occupation . . . [and] transformed them into a kind and gentle folk" (1. 2. 2, p. 7). This myth proved essential to defenses of rhetoric, appearing in Wilson and Puttenham in England, as well as in many other treatises throughout Europe (see Rebhorn 1995: 25, n. 1). Rhetoric is defended because it gives shape and culture to an unformed, inherently brutish humanity, because it has tremendous metamorphic power; rhetoric is defended not because it is natural – "a systematization of natural eloquence" (Vickers 1988: 296) – but because it is *not* natural. Rhetoric and fiction are necessary artifices that allow us to fashion ourselves and our cultures, transforming the raw and brutal into the "kind and gentle."

This tension between culture and nature – centered on language and rhetoric – will be familiar to any student or teacher of *The Tempest*. Shakespeare brings into question the sort of myth that Cicero promulgated by exploring the moral problems raised by the orator-civilizer Prospero. Yet he cannot fully embrace the strategies of the "natural" Caliban, either (see Platt 1997: 169–87). For Shakespeare, rhetoric is violent, artificial, and potentially distorting. Yet human experience would be brutal, bare, and amorphous without it. This Renaissance quest to define rhetoric with an eye toward condemning or celebrating its ornamental relation to truth has continued to modern times. As George Santayana (1922: 131–2) remarks in what can serve as a final defense of rhetoric:

> some philosophers seem to be angry with images for not being things, and with words for not being feelings. Words and images are like shells, no less integral parts of nature than are the substances they cover, but better addressed to the eye and more open to observation.

NOTE

1   All Shakespeare quotations are taken from *The Riverside Shakespeare*, ed. G. Blakemore Evans et al. Boston: Houghton Mifflin.

REFERENCES

Altman, J. B. 1978: *The Tudor Play of Mind: Rhetorical Inquiry and the Development of Elizabethan Drama*. Berkeley, Los Angeles, and London: University of California Press.

Aristotle, *Rhetoric*. In J. Barnes (ed)., *The Complete Works of Aristotle. The Revised Oxford Translation*, 2 vols. Princeton: Princeton University Press, 1984, ii. 2152–2269.

Barish, J. A. 1981: *The Antitheatrical Prejudice*. Berkeley, Los Angeles, and London: University of California Press.

Bates, C. 1992: *The Rhetoric of Courtship in Elizabethan Language and Literature*. Cambridge: Cambridge University Press.

Biester, J. 1997: *Lyric Wonder: Rhetoric and Wit in Renaissance English Poetry*. Ithaca, NY and London: Cornell University Press.

Burke, K. 1950: *A Rhetoric of Motives*. Berkeley, Los Angeles, and London: University of California Press.

Bulman, J. C. (ed.) 1996: *Shakespeare, Theory, and Performance*. London and New York: Routledge.

Butler, J. 1990: *Gender Trouble: Feminism and the Subversion of Identity*. New York and London: Routledge.

Carruthers, M. 1990: *The Book of Memory: The Study of Memory in Medieval Culture*. Cambridge: Cambridge University Press.

Castiglione, B. 1959: *The Book of the Courtier*, trans. C. S. Singleton. New York: Anchor Books.

Cave, T. C. 1979: *The Cornucopian Text: Problems of Writing in the French Renaissance*. Oxford: Clarendon Press.

Cicero, *De natura deorum* and *Academica*, trans. H. Rackham. London: William Heinemann Ltd, 1933.

——*Brutus* and *Orator*, trans. G. L. Hendrickson and H. M. Hubbell. London: William Heinemann Ltd, 1939.

——*De oratore*, trans. E. W. Sutton and H. Rackham. London: William Heinemann Ltd, 1942.

——*De oratore, Book 3. De fato. Paradoxa stoicorum. De partitione oratoria*, trans. H. Rackham. London: William Heinemann Ltd, 1942.

——*De inventione*, trans. H. M. Hubbell. Cambridge, Mass., and London: Harvard University Press, 1949.

——*On Duties*, ed. M. T. Griffin and E. M. Atkins, Cambridge: Cambridge University Press, 1991.

[Cicero], *Rhetorica ad Herennium*, trans. H. Caplan. London: William Heinemann Ltd, 1954.

Conley, T. M. 1990: *Rhetoric in the European Tradition*. Chicago and London: University of Chicago Press.

Eden, K. 1997: *Hermeneutics and the Rhetorical Tradition: Chapters in the Ancient Legacy and its Humanist Reception*. New Haven and London: Yale University Press.

Erasmus, D. 1978: *Collected Works of Erasmus*, vol. 24: *Literary and Educational Writings*, 2, including *De copia*, trans. B. I. Knott, and *De ratione studii*, trans. B. McGregor. Toronto, Buffalo, and London: University of Toronto Press.

Fish, S. E. 1990: Rhetoric. In F. Lentricchia and T. McLaughlin (eds), *Critical Terms for Literary Study*, Chicago and London: University of Chicago Press.

Giamatti, A. B. 1968: Proteus unbound: some versions of the sea god in the Renaissance. In P. Demetz, T. Greene, and L. Nelson, Jr. (eds), *The Disciplines of Criticism*, New Haven and London: Yale University Press, 437–75.

Gorgias 1972: Encomium of Helen. In R. K. Sprague (ed.), *The Older Sophists*, Columbia, SC: University of South Carolina Press, 50–4.

Grafton, A. 1991: *Defenders of the Text: The Tradition of Scholarship in an Age of Science, 1450–1800*. Cambridge, Mass., and London: Harvard University Press.

Greenblatt, S. J. 1973: *Sir Walter Ralegh: The Renaissance Man and his Roles*. New Haven and London: Yale University Press.

——1980: *Renaissance Self-fashioning: From More to Shakespeare*. Chicago and London: University of Chicago Press.

Greene, T. 1968: The flexibility of the self in Renaissance literature. In P. Demetz, T. Greene, and L. Nelson, Jr. (eds), *The Disciplines of Criticism*, New Haven and London: Yale University Press, 241–64.

Javitch, D. 1978: *Poetry and Courtliness in Renaissance England*. Princeton: Princeton University Press.

Kahn, V. A. 1985: *Rhetoric, Prudence, and Skepticism in the Renaissance*. Ithaca, NY, and London: Cornell University Press.

Kennedy, G. A. 1963: *The Art of Persuasion in Greece*. Princeton: Princeton University Press.

—— 1994: *A New History of Classical Rhetoric*. Princeton: Princeton University Press.

Lanham, R. A. 1976: *The Motives of Eloquence: Literary Rhetoric in the Renaissance*. New Haven: Yale University Press.

—— 1991: *A Handlist of Rhetorical Terms*, 2nd edn. Berkeley, Los Angeles, and London: University of California Press.

Machiavelli, N. 1961: *The Prince*, trans. G. Bull. Harmondsworth: Penguin.

Parker, P. 1987: *Literary Fat Ladies: Rhetoric, Gender, Property*. London and New York: Methuen.

Pico della Mirandola, G. 1948: *Oration on the Dignity of Man*, trans. E. L. Forbes. In E. Cassirer, P. O. Kristeller, and J. H. Randall, Jr. (eds), *The Renaissance Philosophy of Man*, Chicago and London: University of Chicago Press, 215–54.

Plato, *Gorgias*. In E. Hamilton and H. Cairns (eds), *The Collected Dialogues of Plato*, Princeton: Princeton University Press, 1961, 229–307.

——*Phaedrus*. In E. Hamilton and H. Cairns (eds), *The Collected Dialogues of Plato*, Princeton: Princeton University Press, 1961, 475–525.

Platt, P. G. 1997: *Reason Diminished: Shakespeare and the Marvelous*. Lincoln, Nebr., and London: University of Nebraska Press.

Puttenham, G. 1936: *The Arte of English Poesie*, ed. G. D. Willcock and A. Walker. Cambridge: Cambridge University Press.

Quintilian, *Institutio oratoria*, trans. H. E. Butler, 4 vols. London: William Heinemann Ltd, 1921–2.

Rebhorn, W. A. 1978: *Courtly Performances: Masking and Festivity in Castiglione's Book of the Courtier*. Detroit: Wayne State University Press.

—— 1995: *The Emperor of Men's Minds: Literature and the Renaissance Discourse of Rhetoric*.

Ithaca, NY, and London: Cornell University Press.

Righter, A. [Anne Barton] 1962: *Shakespeare and the Idea of the Play*. London: Chatto and Windus.

Santayana, G. 1922: *Soliloquies in England and Later Soliloquies*. New York: Charles Scribner's Sons.

Shuger, D. K. 1988: *Sacred Rhetoric: The Christian Grand Style in the Renaissance*. Princeton: Princeton University Press.

Sidney, P. 1965: *An Apology for Poetry*, ed. G. Shepherd. Manchester: Manchester University Press.

—— 1973: *Sir Philip Sidney: Selected Poems*, ed. K. Duncan-Jones. Oxford: Clarendon Press.

Sloane, T. O. 1985: *Donne, Milton, and the End of Humanist Rhetoric*. Berkeley, Los Angeles, and London: University of California Press.

Sonnino, L. A. 1968: *A Handbook to Sixteenth-Century Rhetoric*. London: Routledge and Kegan Paul.

Trimpi, W. 1983: *Muses of One Mind: The Literary Analysis of Experience and its Continuity*. Princeton: Princeton University Press.

Turner, V. 1988: *The Anthropology of Performance*. New York: PAJ Publications.

Vickers, B. 1971: Shakespeare's use of rhetoric. In K. Muir and S. Schoenbaum (eds), *A New Companion to Shakespeare Studies*, Cambridge: Cambridge University Press, 83–98.

—— 1988: *In Defence of Rhetoric*. Oxford: Clarendon Press.

Whigham, F. 1984: *Ambition and Privilege: The Social Tropes of Elizabethan Courtesy Theory*. Berkeley, Los Angeles, and London: University of California Press.

Wilson, T. 1962: *The Arte of Rhetorique*, ed. R. H. Bowers. Gainesville, Fla.: University of Florida Press.

Yates, F. A. 1966: *The Art of Memory*. London: Routledge and Kegan Paul.

18

Shakespeare and Genre

Jean E. Howard

Teachers of Shakespeare have typically chosen one of two routes when planning their undergraduate classes. Either they have organized their courses chronologically, beginning with the earliest plays Shakespeare wrote and progressing *seriatim* through to the last plays. Or they have organized their courses by genre, typically doing history plays and romantic comedies in one term and tragedies and "odd" comedies (problem plays and romances) in the second. Sometimes the two modes of organization are combined, with a few "immature" tragedies such as *Titus Andronicus* slipped into the first term to lay the groundwork for a "great" revenge tragedy such as *Hamlet*, or *Twelfth Night* or *Henry VIII* appearing on the second-term syllabus to show what happens to romantic comedy and the national history play after the turn of the century. While many teachers and scholars, I think, feel a little uncertain about the ontological status of the problem play and the romance as generic categories, very few are particularly troubled by using tragedy, history, and comedy as markers of some real categorical differences among groups of plays. The profession has reproduced these differences in its publishing practices. A number of books continue to be written that focus only on Shakespearian tragedy, on the Shakespearian history play, or on Shakespearian comedy. For many critics and students these categories have assumed the status of natural, not arbitrary, entities.

If one thinks seriously about these generic distinctions, of course, their status quickly becomes problematic. The authority for them often derives from the first folio, where in the prefatory matter to the volume the titles of the plays were displayed on a page headed "A Catalogue of the severall Comedies, Histories, and Tragedies contained in this Volume." Play titles follow in three groupings with unbroken lines surrounding each, in effect making generic corrals into which individual plays are herded. A good deal of scholarship has been devoted to thinking about what these boxes mean and about how particular plays got assigned to them. Immediately noticeable, of course, is the fact that neither problem plays nor romances appear as categories in this prefatory catalogue. *The Tempest* and *The Winter's Tale* are listed, respectively, as the first and last of the comedies. *Pericles* does not appear at all; and the fourth romance, *Cymbeline*, is placed as the last of the tragedies. Of those plays typically designated as "problem plays" in modern criticism, *Measure for Measure* and *All's Well That Ends Well* are entered as comedies, while *Troilus and Cressida* is absent from the catalogue, probably because of difficulties in getting title to the play until the last minute. In actual fact, under the title *The Tragedy of Troilus and Cressida*, the play itself does appear in the volume, right before *Coriolanus*, as a tragedy. In short, the three large groups in which Shakespeare's plays are arranged by this prefatory catalogue do not quite correspond to modern critical categories. If most critics feel that *Cymbeline*, *Pericles*, *The Winter's Tale*, and *The Tempest* share some important similarities and so can be grouped together as "late comedies," as "romances," or even as "tragicomedies," the catalogue questions this unity. It routes *Cymbeline* into the orbit of tragedy, leaving *The Tempest* and *The Winter's Tale* uneasily bracketing the domain of comedy.

If one ventures inside the volume, beyond the opening catalogue, new confusions emerge. Though *Richard III* is grouped with the histories in the catalogue under the title *The Life and Death of Richard the Third*, it appears inside the first folio under the title *The Tragedy of Richard the Third: with the Landing of Earl Richmond, and the Battle at Bosworth Field*. Instead of separate entities, history and tragedy here are super-imposed on one another, interpenetrate. Similarly, Francis Meres in his comments on "our English Poets" in *Palladis Tamia* (1598) praised Shakespeare for being the best among his peers for both tragedy and comedy. As examples of Shakespeare's excellence in tragedy, Meres cited his *Richard II*, *Richard III*, *Henry IV*, *King John*, *Titus Andronicus* and *Romeo and Juliet*. This list suggests that for Meres "histories" were not a category sharply distinct from "tragedies." If one examines the quarto versions of many of the plays later included in the first folio, a similar instability in generic labeling becomes equally apparent. In the first quarto, *Lear* is called *The History of King Lear*; in the folio, *The Tragedy of King Lear*. Similarly, the quarto title of *Richard II* was *The Tragedy of Richard II*, metamorphosing into *The Life and Death of King Richard the Second* in the folio. More such differences could be elaborated, but the point is obvious. The generic designations authorizing divisions within the Shakespearian canon are not as stable as it may appear, should one glance at the prefatory catalogue in the first folio. Some plays migrate from one generic grouping to another; some seem to inhabit more than one simultaneously; and late twentieth-century ways of parsing the canon overlap but do not totally coincide with those enshrined in the first folio.

So what are we to conclude about the role of genre in the study of Shakespeare once we recognize (1) the instability of generic designations and (2) the fact that some early modern people used them as organizing rubrics, if nothing else, and that we continue to do so today? Should we view genre as one more demystified entity and shake its dust from our feet? I think not. Clearly, then and now, the utility of generic categories is less ontological than provisional and productive; that is, generic schema do not so much map essential and immutable kinds of writing as describe the historically produced and mutable conventions by which a certain *kind* of text is distinguished from other *kinds*. These constructed distinctions serve several purposes. They help both in the writing and the reading of individual plays, and they aid in the production of dense networks of affiliated texts which collectively receive and shape the form and pressure of the times by mediating social change and contestation. I will return to each of these uses of genre in the course of this essay, even as I continue to argue against generic essentialism.

In regard to acts of reading, Wolfgang Iser and other reception critics have convincingly argued that the concept of genre is useful, as it creates one of the horizons of expectation which organize a reading act (1978: 79–81). Knowing that something is called a "tragedy" provides one framework for rendering it intelligible, and allows variations on the conventions of tragedy to become interpretively significant. It is not surprising, moreover, that a single work, such as *Richard III*, should fit into *two* generic categories, especially when at its original moment of production in the early 1590s the genre of the English history play was still an emergent one. In many cases, however, the conventions governing a particular genre do not encompass all the aspects of a given text. Some of those same features, along with others, become *significant in a new way* if mobilized under another generic banner. Thus, by 1623 when *Richard III* was presented with the histories in the folio's prefatory catalogue but was called a tragedy inside the volume, readers might genuinely have recognized the play as inhabiting two sets of generic conventions. It shared with other Elizabethan tragedies an emphasis on a single male protagonist of noble stature who is granted a degree of interiority and whose rise and fall evoke feelings of pity and terror in an audience. At the same time, the play shared with other Elizabethan history plays an emphasis on the representation of English medieval history, usually focusing on the events of a single monarch's reign, and concerning itself with questions of right rule and monarchical legitimacy. The generic doubleness of *Richard III* continues to be reproduced in twentieth-century critical practices. Nearly always discussed in books dealing with Shakespearian history plays, *Richard III* also appears in the first chapter of Janet Adelman's *Suffocating Mothers*, a study of Shakespearian tragedy from *Hamlet* on, which uses *Richard* as an example of what Adelman sees as many of the paradigmatic aspects of Shakespeare's mature utilization of the genre (1992: 1–4).

Genre, then, is a concept that lets critics and readers make productive connections between texts. Within an overarching literary system, genre allows the general expectation that certain topics will be matched with certain treatments – that the Pindaric ode will not only employ its characteristic formal pattern of strophe, antistrophe, epode, but will use it to depict events of unusual grandeur or emotional intensity. But knowledge of a generic repertoire not only serves readers; it also serves producers of texts. It provides them with forms and with matter for imitation: starting points for innovation, transformation, and critique. As E. H. Gombrich has argued, the vaunted imitation of life in any artistic medium paradoxically begins with the imitation of other works of art and generic models (1961: 3–30). A system of genres, then, can be an enabling resource drawn upon by readers and writers alike, though it can also be used to produce lifeless and unmotivated copies of prior work rather than creative refashionings of generic possibilities.

The early modern period was one of intense generic theorization and experimentation. This was partly due to widespread interest in imitating and surpassing classical models. As Rosalie Colie puts the case: "We may take it, then, that literary invention – both 'finding' and 'making' – in the Renaissance was largely generic, and that transfer of ancient values was largely in generic terms, accomplished by generic instruments and helps" (1973: 17). From the fourteenth to the sixteenth century Italian critics and writers were especially intensely involved in theorizing genre and in experimenting with different generic forms. Even in England, the desire to make the vernacular a fit medium for a national literature led to the production of rhetorical treatises, such as Puttenham's *The Arte of English Poetry*, and poetics, such as Sidney's *An Apology for Poetry*, which elaborated directives for Englishing classical tropes, meters, and generic forms. As is well known, Edmund Spenser consciously imitated the Virgilian progress from the lower to the higher poetic genres, though it is equally well known that such imitation did not keep him from hybridizing classical epic by joining it to Italian romance, or from making his poems fully answerable to the conditions of his historical time and place.

But while writers within early modern culture were very aware of a literary system dominated by the rules of "kind" or genre, at first blush the public stage does not seem a very classically oriented or rule-governed institution. Any notion of a strict "system" of dramatic genres must, in the context of this particular stage and its practices, be modified to take account of the experimentation, the collaborative production, and the competitive commercial pressures fueling dramatic production. Writers for the stage by and large did not write treatises about dramatic art, and so their programmatic comments on genre either don't exist or are confined to prefaces, prologues, or metadramatic comments within plays such as Polonius's famously fatuous speech about the actor troupe visiting Elsinore being the best in "tragedy, comedy, history, pastoral, pastorical-comical, historical-pastoral, tragical-historical, tragical-comical-historical-pastoral, scene individable or poem unlimited" (*Hamlet*, II. ii. 379–82).[1] A more systematic critic such as Sidney seemed appalled by the generic hybridity fostered by the stage. When considering poetic kinds in the abstract, he praised both comedy and tragedy and agreed that the mingling of generic forms was not necessarily bad, saying, "if severed they be good, the conjunction cannot be hurtful" (Shepherd 1973: 116). But when he actually described the public theater and its practices, his scorn for badly made plays (by which he meant those that failed to obey the classical unities or that violated generic forms) boiled over. For him the stage was a place where improbable events stretched the audience's credulity and where poetry was prostituted. In this context, mingling of forms became an act of mongrelization. As he wrote: "But besides these gross absurdities, how all their plays be neither right tragedies, nor right comedies, mingling kings and clowns, not because the matter so carrieth it, but thrust in clowns by head and shoulders, to play a part in majestical matters, with neither decency nor discretion, so as neither the admiration and commiseration, nor the right sportfulness, is by their mongrel tragi-comedy obtained" (ibid., 135). For him, the violations of the stage were both aesthetic and social. Improper genres correlated with the improper mixing of low and high personages and "matters."

Sidney's exasperation with the public stage in regard to the issue of generic purity was merited if one thinks of genre not as a fluid and productive starting point for reading and writing but as a set of prescriptive rules that must govern textual production. Judged by those criteria, the public stage often produced disorderly and unruly texts of mixed "kinds." In part, this was because many plays were mixed in their origins – that is, were produced by several hands. Writing for the stage was often a collaborative process (Masten 1997). This did not mean that the resulting plays were necessarily incoherent or built upon competing generic schema, but it *could* mean that. The multiple plot structure of many Tudor–Stuart plays juxtaposes generic conventions as well as characters and lines of action, as, for example, with the comic subplot and tragic main plot of Middleton and Rowley's *The Changeling* or with the more complex mixing of Italian revenge tragedy conventions and satiric city comedy conventions in Dekker and Webster's *Westward Ho*. The sort of mongrelization or mixedness to which Sidney objected lies at the heart of much of the most lively early modern drama. The existence of a repertoire of generic forms allowed for mixing and mingling in the service of new forms that could be read, despairingly, as curs of mixed blood or, more positively, as expressions of inevitable social and aesthetic change.[2]

The rough-and-tumble of the early modern theatrical world – its competitiveness and its precarious grip on both propriety and profit – makes it an interesting site for thinking about the productive uses of genre and their actual materialization on the stage and the page. The idea of "materialization" I take from Judith Butler's *Bodies that Matter*, where she uses it to indicate those processes by which bodies come into being through the operation of regulatory norms that over time "produce the effect of boundary, fixity, and surface we call matter" (1993: 9). In particular, she is interested in the processes by which bodies come to seem naturally to carry the marks of a primal sexual difference, even though it is only with enormous cultural labor and the reiterative performance of this difference that its arbitrary nature is effaced. A similar cultural labor is required to materialize a dramatic corpus and inscribe it with the marks of generic difference that eventually come to be taken as natural.

For Shakespeare, many of the practices through which generic categories were materialized into bounded categories were textual. As we have seen with the first folio, the retrospective grouping of the plays into a restricted set of categories was a powerful materialization of a differentiated canon, and it went hand in hand with various other kinds of standardization. It is in the first folio, for example, that what we now familiarly call "The Henry VI plays" were first naturalized into a group. In the folio they are entitled in the catalogue *The First Part of King Henry the Sixth*, *The Second Part of King Henry the Sixth*, and *The Third Part of King Henry the Sixth*, and are printed in that order. But in the 1590s *2 Henry VI* was printed in a quarto as *The First Part of the Contention betwixt the Two Famous Houses of York and Lancaster*, and *3 Henry VI* appeared in a considerably shorter version as *The True Tragedy of Richard Duke of York and the Death of Good King Henry the Sixth*. Dating these plays has proved difficult, but it is possible that both were written before *1 Henry VI*, and the quarto titles show some of the generic instability marking the early production of "the history play" as a category. The title *The True Tragedy of Richard Duke of York* places the play with tragedy, even though the titular Richard is dead by Act II; and *The First Part of the Contention* quite properly signals that the factionalization of England during the War of the Roses is the prime subject matter of the play. But by 1623, all three scripts have been chronologically ordered and homogenized under the name of the monarch within whose reign the events were all enacted. They have been textually materialized into "English histories" with the name of an English monarch in the title to advertise that fact.

The outpouring of work in the last decade on the material history of the book has made it apparent how the textualization of drama in the early modern period played a role in materializing the differentiated Shakespearian corpus we now take as fact. But what if we change the perspective and look not at historical outcomes – at the end point at which we have arrived – but at the moment of flux when audiences went to playhouses to see dramatic works not yet in print or, if in print, often not yet in their "final" textual embodiments? Did audiences know what "genre" of play they were seeing? Put another way, how was genre materialized at the site of performance, rather than at the site of publication? Here, I think, the evidence is more sketchy and difficult to interpret, partly because much of our knowledge of early modern perform-ance comes from texts, and those are never innocent or transparent representations of theatrical practice or experience. Certainly there were many classically educated theatergoers who, like Sidney, came to theatrical events with a definite sense of comedy and tragedy as dramatic forms with a long and distinguished heritage, a heritage he found bastardized on the Elizabethan public stage.

But literacy in generic kinds could also be achieved inductively. One would not have to see many plays, for example, to recognize the differences between comedy and tragedy in terms of the predominant social rank of the principal characters. But there is evidence that acquired generic literacy was a good deal more sophisticated and discriminating than the mere recognition of the class valences of certain genres. *The Knight of the Burning Pestle*, that hilarious metadramatic riff on theatrical practices and audience expectations, shows quite clearly that audiences often knew the conventions of different kinds of plays and had their favorites. For example, the grocer George and his wife Nell and her man Rafe who come to the theater to see a play proclaim that they *don't* want to see a satiric city comedy that "girds at citizens" (Beaumont 1967: 7; Induction, line 8). Instead, they demand a play about a London citizen-hero such as Dick Whittington or a romantic adventure such as *The Four Apprentices of London* in which men bearing shields embossed with the emblems of London's guilds conquer Jerusalem.

Various forms of foregrounded intertextuality or interperformance citationality were undoubtedly the means by which generic codes were materialized on the stage and made part of the theatergoer's generic repertoire. Titles, for example, sometimes indicated generic connections and affiliations: *Westward Ho, Eastward Ho, Northward Ho; The Revenger's Tragedy*; plays whose titles are the names of English monarchs. The repetition of specific internal performance elements also made it possible to produce "the effect of boundary, fixity, and surface" which Butler attributes to physical bodies and I am here attributing to a generic corpus. A ghost crying for revenge, a skull, a hero run mad, justice in the hands of criminals – repeated and varied, these enacted elements both materialized revenge tragedy and allowed variations of its citational codes to be meaningful to the generically literate audience they both counted on and helped to produce. In addition, at least by the second decade of the seventeenth century, generic expectations received other types of material reinforcement. Particular theaters and theater companies, for example, became known for performing certain types of plays (Gurr 1996: 105–36). A play's appearance at a certain venue would therefore by itself create expectations that it belonged to a certain dramatic kind. When the children's companies played at St Paul's, their repertoire included more witty and satirical comedies than one would have found, for example, at the Red Bull or the Fortune, which increasingly became associated with an old-fashioned, martial, and patriotic repertoire. The very difference between a children's company and an adult company was an important factor in materializing a play as of a certain kind.

Nonetheless, the rapidity of changes in theatrical forms must at times have outpaced both the descriptive vocabulary and the horizon of expectation of particular theatergoers. Consider Heywood's *Edward IV* (1599–1600). Its title makes it appear to us to be one of the decade's final English histories focusing on the reign of a particular monarch. But Edward IV plays a quite modest role in both Parts I and II of this work. Instead, primary attention focuses on the domestic tragedy of Jane Shore and her husband when Jane becomes Edward's mistress and on the guild culture of the city of London. Expecting an English history of the sort represented by *Richard II*, an audience would have found elements of Heywood's play puzzling: the emphasis on citizen life, the diminished role of the king and court, the foregrounding of the sentimental tale of a nonnoblewoman's personal suffering. Yet some of these elements would be beginning to be performatively materialized into another dramatic kind, the city comedy, a genre whose emergence has retrospectively been charted to the late 1590s. With Jonson's humors comedies the satiric city comedy begins to take shape; with Dekker, Heywood, and Haughton a more celebratory version of the city play emerges. *Edward IV* would probably have been intelligible first within the horizon of expectation created by the English history play, but with the monarchical and elite investments of the genre aggressively rewritten in the interests of the urban citizenry. It performs the conventions of the genre and simultaneously transforms them. At the same time, the play seems in conversation with the conventions of the emergent genre of city comedy with its densely plotted form and urban-based, nonmonarchical emphasis on civic nationalism, the politics of city marriage, and citizen-gentleman social, economic, and sexual rivalry. In retrospect, *Edward IV* looks like a hybrid form, and it is treated as such in certain modern criticism (Orlin 1991: 30). The variations in its performance of the history genre place it in conversation with both the middling sort of ethos that inflects both a domestic tragedy such as *Woman Killed with Kindness* (1603) and a city comedy such as *Westward Ho* (1604).

The emergence of these particular variants of comedy and tragedy raises the question of the motivation for changes in the overarching system of dramatic genres. I have argued that in the early modern theatrical milieu, the loosely differentiated system of dramatic kinds in play at any time was always in motion. But the emergence of new forms and their materialization into a set of conventions was implicated in social transformations and struggles as much as in the quest for a market niche or in purely aesthetic experimentation.[3] The emergence of city comedy was complexly interwoven with other phenomena at the end of the sixteenth century: the growing importance of the import business managed through the great trading companies (Brenner 1993); the ideological, if not yet actual, enclosure of city wives within the domestic sphere and the role of household manager and commodity consumer (Korda 1996); the influx of foreigners and strangers into the city space and the weakening of the hold of the traditional guilds over production and economic resources (Finlay and Shearer 1986). While the existence of Roman urban comedies, in particular, provided a precedent for the city plays written by Jonson, Marston, Middleton, and others in the first decade of the seventeenth century, the obvious popularity of the genre suggests that it would not have taken hold in such varied and sophisticated forms did it not address the particular anxieties and struggles of a specific historical juncture.

One of the consequences of the later textual materialization of the Shakespeare canon into the three categories of comedy, tragedy, and history is that such a materialization tends to occlude the way in which particular Shakespearian plays may have been in conversation with other genres or sub-genres during their performative lives. The popularity of New Historicist criticism has furthered this divide, since one of the peculiarities of New Historical critical practice is that it has more often encouraged the linking of Shakespeare's texts to nondramatic texts than to the plays of his fellow dramatists.[4] Consequently, the works of Dekker, Marston, and Beaumont and Fletcher remain oddly distanced from those of the Bard. Moreover, it is common practice to divide academic courses and job descriptions and journals in terms of Shakespearian and non-Shakespearian categories, as if the two never interconnected and as if the rich profusion of Tudor and Stuart drama could simply be homogenized under the rubric of "the non-Shakespearian."

If one wishes to create a new history of early modern drama, however, it may be useful to put Shakespeare's plays in conversation with those of other playwrights and sometimes to see them in relation to generic forms not foregrounded in the first folio. To explore this possibility, I would briefly like to think about *Measure for Measure* in relation to the city plays produced in considerable number in London theaters after the turn of the century, and, to be yet more specific, to a group written soon after James I's accession to the English throne. The new king had a vivid introduction to the problems of the city to which he was journeying when his projected arrival in

London had to be delayed by a devastating invasion of the plague (Barroll 1991: 70–116). One of James's first acts was to issue a proclamation calling for the razing of overcrowded, pestiferous suburban dwellings – including brothels – from which contagion was felt to issue (Larkin and Hughes 1973: 47). This proclamation signalled the new king's interest in curbing the disease and disorder that threatened his adopted city. Partly in response to the vast swelling of London's population in the second half of the sixteenth century, the city had already developed many structures, at the level of the ward and the neighborhood, for maintaining order and keeping an eye on its inhabitants (Archer 1991: 58–99). The Elizabethan poor laws and the establishment of the four great charitable hospitals of London were other aspects of a many-pronged attempt to manage the intractable problems of poverty, vagrancy, and disease.

Many city plays from the period echo James's concern with social disorder, and especially with the problem of how to regulate bodies within urban space. *The Shoemaker's Holiday*, for example, focuses on the submission of the laboring body to work regimes; *Measure for Measure* on the regulation of the sexual body; *A Chaste Maid in Cheapside* on the potential vagrancies of both the reproductive and the consuming body. Sometimes disorderly figures are shamed and brought to conform to social norms without judicial intervention, but many city comedies also acknowledge the carceral and violent aspects of social regulation. Officers of the law, law courts, and prisons appear all too frequently in city comedies. Recall, for example, the watchmen Haggis, Bristle, and Poacher, Justice Overdo, and the Court of Pie-powders in *Bartholomew Fair*, the Counter in *Eastward Ho*, the law court in Acts IV and V of *Volpone*, the sinister "promoters" in *Chaste Maid in Cheapside*, and the institutions of Bridewell and Bedlam that loom large at the end of *The Honest Whore, Parts I and II*. Many other city plays explore the use of force and juridical intervention in controlling the desires and movements of the urban populace.

Measure for Measure bears interesting intertextual connections to some of these plays, particularly to those produced in the years 1604–5 immediately following James's accession to the throne. *The Dutch Courtesan* (1605), *The Honest Whore* (1604), *Westward Ho* (1604), *Eastward Ho* (1605), and *Northward Ho* (1605) – all of them, like *Measure for Measure*, feature bawds and prostitutes among their cast of characters. All, like *Measure for Measure*, dramatize the disruptive effects of sexual desire on the stability of households and on the larger social order. Each, like *Measure for Measure*, is concerned with the regulation of bodies and desires within an urban milieu. And, as the directional signals embedded in the titles of the *Ho* plays suggest, anxiety about suburban spaces is, as in *Measure for Measure*, pronounced. East, west, or north – each marks a place (Cuckold's Haven, Brainford, Ware) where the sexual desires that overflow the city walls and the ordered households within them can potentially find satisfaction. Often, in these plays, only prison or the long arm of the law can properly discipline disorderly behavior.

It is not to commit Fluellenism, I think, to point out the many intertextual features that link *Measure for Measure* to a play such as *The Honest Whore*, the first part of which was played and published in 1604, the second of which was probably written shortly thereafter. Both display an apocalyptic view of urban vice, especially sexual disorder. Each depends absolutely upon the carceral institutions of the city and upon a problematical duke for the resolution of its plot. However, it is not with *The Honest Whore* and other city plays that *Measure for Measure* is most often discussed. Rather, since at least 1896, *Measure for Measure* has been designated a "problem play" or "problem comedy" and has most often been read against other plays in the Shakespearian canon which have been grouped under this label. This critical practice of reading Shakespeare's plays primarily in relation to other Shakespeare plays is one way in which faith in his uniqueness has been produced and reproduced. In effect, editors and commentators have kept the Shakespearian canon hermetically sealed from the theatrical world in which it was first performed, though the very creation of the category of "problem play" seems to signal a realization that a number of Shakespeare's early Jacobean productions do not quite fit into the generic groupings established in the first folio.

The term "problem play" deserves some attention as a designation for specific Shakespearian texts. When F. S. Boas (1896) originated the term, he included *Measure for Measure*, *All's Well*, *Hamlet*, and *Troilus and Cressida* within its catchment. Others have excluded *Hamlet*; Ernest Schanzer (1963) decided that the label should be applied to *Measure for Measure*, *Julius Caesar*, and *Antony and Cleopatra*. Whatever has been included in the category, definitions of it have centered largely on moral questions. In essence, the Shakespearian problem play has been defined as one in which the ethical course of action is unclear to the plays' characters and the contemplation of this dilemma causes the audience to lose its moral bearings. In focusing on moral ambiguities and complexities, Boas interestingly transformed the meaning which the term "problem play" actually carried in his own day. When applied to the drama of Ibsen and Shaw, it meant plays dealing with pressing social issues: war, poverty, prostitution, the woman question. If one returns to the definition of a problem play as one that deals with social problems, one is more easily led back to the various forms of city comedy with which *Measure for Measure* might have been linked at the original moment of production.

The Honest Whore is one such play. In each of its two parts urban vice is rampant and depicted in unsparing detail. Each has a two-plot structure. In one plot a whore, Bellafront, reforms and, despite many temptations, sticks with her reformation. This line of action involves a number of libertine figures who run the gamut of urban vices. They drink, smoke, whore, and spend quantities of money on luxury items they can't afford. In this libertine world the reformed whore ironically represents the spirit of self-regulation. Once she undergoes her moral transformation, she remains a model of virtuous, self-disciplining womanhood. She is, moreover, paralleled in the second plot by a linen draper, Candido, a self-regulating man. His hallmark, a feminine one, is patience. No matter how he is provoked, by unruly wife or demanding customer, he never loses his temper. Together the reformed whore and the patient shopkeeper seem to represent a desired social norm. In a world maddened by greed and lust, each retains his or her integrity. Yet each is also oddly vulnerable. Bellafront is abused by an out-of-control husband; Candido is abused by nearly everyone.

The logic of these plays seems to suggest that while the desired social norm is the self-regulating figure who will quietly tend to house or shop, such figures are vulnerable in the rapacious city they inhabit. Consequently, force must be used, not only to protect them from the violence they have eschewed, but also to regulate the many urban residents who will not regulate themselves. In both plays Candido finds himself having to call on others, often officers of the law, to protect or rescue him. However, *The Honest Whore's* central emblems of the city's power are Bedlam and Bridewell, those institutions whose representations dominate the fifth act of each play. In these settings, madmen and whores are made exemplary spectacles: they act out a dangerous lack of control and become the occasion for the imposition of carceral regulation. The inmates of both institutions are surrounded by signs of the state power that constrains them. The madmen are controlled by whips; the whores are accompanied by constables and beadles and are made to carry the blue gowns, spinning wheels, and mallets which are signs of the work regime to which the prison submits them.[5] Though self-regulating subjects are the ideal, those citizens act against a backdrop of governmental and quasi-governmental institutions that are now to monopolize the "legitimate" use of violence and by force impose discipline upon those who will not discipline themselves.

It is remarkable what *Measure for Measure* shares with *The Honest Whore* and as striking where it diverges. It shares with both parts, for example, a focus on pervasive social disorder, and it especially highlights the sexual crimes and misdemeanors rampant in Vienna. There are women pregnant before their lawful time, bawds and whores who do a thriving business in the flesh trade; taverns where wives can be accosted; and a hypocritical magistrate who harshly enforces the laws against sexual offenders while attempting to take the virginity of a woman sworn to the celibacy of the convent. Moreover, courts and prisons constitute the venue for many of the play's most memorable encounters. *Measure for Measure* thus shares with other city plays of its moment of production a peculiarly carceral imaginary.

But the differences are at least as striking as the similarities. Several things in particular stand out. One is Shakespeare's greater mystification of the duke's power and the duke's lesser reliance on the repressive state apparatuses to do the work of moral reform and social correction. While there are many prison scenes in *Measure for Measure*, the play does not end in the prison. Rather, it concludes by the gates of the city, where the duke, "like power divine" (V. i. 361), enters to dispense justice in his own person. In both parts of *The Honest Whore* the duke goes to Bridewell and Bedlam in Act V to bring order from chaos, and he does so against the powerful backdrop of the whips and the instruments of shaming and punishment that dominate these institutions. Shakespeare's duke, closer to an absolutist monarch than Dekker's, subsumes temporal and ecclesiastical powers in his own person and ultimately submits the legal institutions of Vienna to his authority.

Equally important is the absence of wives and artisans in *Measure for Measure* as compared to *The Honest Whore* plays. After her Act II reform, Bellafront is a model wife, a veritable patient Griselda who remains in the foreground of the action, as do Candido's several wives. There is nothing comparable in *Measure for Measure*. In Shakespeare's play the matrimonial state is singularly hard to attain. Juliet and Claudio's fraught union lacks social sanction; we never know if Isabella accepts the duke's proposal; Angelo and Lucio marry under duress. Another contrast is provided by the prominence of citizens in *The Honest Whore* and their virtual absence in *Measure for Measure*. Candido, the linen-draper-hero of *The Honest Whore's* second plot, embodies the supposed virtues of London's citizen class. Aspects of civic culture are everywhere dramatized: we see Candido's shop, see him go to take his seat in the Senate (probably the equivalent of the London Common Council), and listen to him conversing with his apprentices. In large measure the carceral institutions of Candido's city are there to protect those citizens who in their own persons have eschewed a violence dangerous to social order. As if to underscore Candido's symbolic centrality, at the end of each play the duke vows to take him to court to serve as a model of patience and self-restraint from whom his courtiers can learn.

Shakespeare's city, by contrast, is more markedly divided between the low and the high. Claudio must wait for Juliet's relatives to provide a dowry before they can marry, but there is no indication that he is anything but a gentleman. Though overrun with bawds and whores, Vienna seems to have no legitimate tradesmen and no civic culture separable from the person of the duke. To say that this is an unrealistic representation of an early modern city is an obvious point, but one that speaks to the play's class politics, just as the absence of married couples whose unions are both lawful and mutually chosen marks the play's distance from the culture of the middling sort so prominently displayed in *The Honest Whore* alongside the culture of gallants and courtiers.

Does this mean that Shakespeare secretly identified with the class position above him? That he eschewed the artisan culture from which he sprang and which surrounded him daily in his London existence? I have no idea, really, about the motives for the choices we see him having made in writing this play. What one *can* talk about, however, when *Measure for Measure* is juxtaposed with other city plays penned cotemporally by Shakespeare's fellow dramatists, is what his plays share with theirs and also what distinguishes them. He is both the same and different, in the case of *Measure for Measure* sharing a view of the city as disordered and in need of regulation, but also creating an urban representation that elides the middling sort and their marital and civic regimes, displacing both by the all-important figure of the duke. To say this is not so much to judge Shakespeare as simply to place him in a relational grid in which his are not the only texts in the conversation and the genres highlighted in the first folio are not the only organizing categories within which his plays can be construed. Genre, after all, is in part a useful concept precisely as it lets readers and theatergoers make productive connections among disparate texts. Theatergoers in Shakespeare's London would, I think, have recognized in *Measure for Measure* many elements of the city plays being written by Shakespeare's contemporaries in the years immediately following James's coronation. To follow up those connections allows us to materialize his corpus in a new way and re-position his plays within a theatrical milieu from which the first folio invites us to abstract them.

Notes

1 All quotations from the plays of Shakespeare are taken from *The Norton Shakespeare*, gen. ed. Stephen Greenblatt (1997).

2 John Lyly, for example, in the prologue to *Midas* (first published 1592), remarks on how quickly fashions in clothes, food, and plays alter and how in the present age once-distinct nationalities, foods, and generic forms all co-mingle. "... what heretofore hath been served in several dishes for a feast is now minced in a charger for a gallimaufrey. If we present a mingle-mangle, our fault is to be excused, because the whole world is become an hodge-podge" (Lyly 1969: 80).

3 The well-developed Marxist view of genres as sites for ideological contestation and class struggle is in the contemporary US academy best represented by Fredric Jameson (1981) and in Renaissance dramatic criticism by Walter Cohen (1985).

4 A partial exception to this generalization is Leonard Tennenhouse (1986), who approaches Shakespeare's plays generically and in some cases compares Shakespeare's uses of a genre to those of other playwrights.

5 J. A. Sharpe (1984) has argued that the creation of Bridewell represented a real shift in the state's attitudes toward punishment. In addition to retribution and deterrence, punishment was now meant to initiate the offender into the regime of labor discipline.

References

Adelman, Janet 1992: *Suffocating Mothers: Fantasies of Maternal Origin in Shakespeare's Plays, Hamlet to The Tempest*. New York: Routledge.

Archer, Ian 1991: *The Pursuit of Stability: Social Relations in Elizabethan London*. Cambridge: Cambridge University Press.

Barroll, Leeds 1991: *Politics, Plague, and Shakespeare's Theater: The Stuart Years*. Ithaca, NY: Cornell University Press.

Beaumont, Francis 1967: *The Knight of the Burning Pestle*, ed. John Doebler. Lincoln, Nebr.: University of Nebraska Press; orig. pub. 1607.

Boas, F. S. 1896: *Shakespeare and his Predecessors*. New York: Charles Scribner's Sons.

Brenner, Robert 1993: *Merchants and Revolution: Commercial Change, Political Conflict, and London's Overseas Traders 1550–1653*. Princeton: Princeton University Press.

Butler, Judith 1993: *Bodies that Matter: On the Discursive Limits of Sex*. New York: Routledge.

Cohen, Walter 1985: *Drama of a Nation: Public Theater in Renaissance England and Spain*. Ithaca, NY: Cornell University Press.

Colie, Rosalie 1973: *The Resources of Kind: Genre Theory in the Renaissance*. Berkeley: University of California Press.

Finlay, R. A. P. and Shearer, B. 1986: Population growth and suburban expansion. In A. L. Beier and R. A. P. Finlay (eds), *London, 1500–1700: The Making of the Metropolis*, New York: Longman, 37–59.

Gombrich, E. H. 1961: *Art and Illusion: A Study in the Psychology of Pictorial Representation*, Bollingen Series 35, 5, 2nd edn. Princeton: Princeton University Press.

Greenblatt, Stephen (gen. ed.) 1997: *The Norton Shakespeare*. New York: Norton.

Gurr, Andrew 1996: *The Shakespearean Playing Companies*. Oxford: Clarendon Press.

Iser, Wolfgang 1978: *The Act of Reading: A Theory*

of Aesthetic Response. Baltimore: Johns Hopkins University Press.

Jameson, Fredric 1981: *The Political Unconscious: Narrative as a Socially Symbolic Act*. Ithaca, NY: Cornell University Press.

Korda, Natasha 1996: Household Kates: domesticating commodities in *The Taming of the Shrew*. *Shakespeare Quarterly*, 47, 109–31.

Larkin, James F. and Hughes, Paul L. (eds) 1973: *Stuart Royal Proclamations*, vol. i. Oxford: Clarendon Press.

Lyly, John 1969: *Gallatea and Midas*, ed. Anne Begor Lancashire. Lincoln, Nebr.: University of Nebraska Press.

Masten, Jeffrey 1997: Playwrighting: authorship and collaboration. In John D. Cox and David Scott Kastan (eds), *A New History of English Drama*, New York: Columbia University Press, 357–82.

Orlin, Lena 1991: Familial transgressions, societal transition on the Elizabethan stage. In Carole Levin and Karen Robertson. (eds), *Sexuality and Politics in Renaissance Drama*, Lewiston, NY: Edwin Mellon Press, 27–55.

Schanzer, Ernest 1963: *The Problem Plays of Shakespeare: A Study of Julius Caesar, Measure for Measure, and Antony and Cleopatra*. New York: Schocken Books.

Sharpe, J. A. 1984: *Crime in Early Modern England 1550–1750*. London: Longman.

Shepherd, Geoffrey (ed.) 1973: *Sir Philip Sidney's An Apology for Poetry*. Manchester: Manchester University Press.

Tennenhouse, Leonard 1986: *Power on Display: The Politics of Shakespeare's Genres*. New York: Methuen.

PART SIX
Playing

19

The Economics of Playing

William Ingram

The latter part of England's sixteenth century was, like the latter part of America's twentieth century, a time of remarkable technical and psychological expansion. Burgeoning regional economies in the later sixteenth century created new markets for goods and services across Europe. A major catalyst was the growth of the book trade, which by the end of the century had created a smaller version of our own information explosion, along with a less tangible but equally important awareness explosion. In England, Richard Hakluyt's compendium of narratives about travel and exploration (popularly known as *Hakluyt's Voyages*) documented and popularized the success of new English ventures in opening foreign markets to English merchants; Sir Thomas Gresham's astuteness in strengthening English currency and in manipulating foreign exchange opened up a new world of financial adventurism for entrepreneurial Londoners; new strategies in the cloth trade brought prosperity (and some resentment) to rural clothiers and their London factors; and by the end of the century the book trade itself had created a market for commercial writers, exploited notably by Robert Greene and Thomas Nashe, men who for the first time could make a living in London by selling their prose and verse to printers.

The final decades of the sixteenth century also saw the emergence of stage playing as a viable trade in London. Prior to this time, stage playing in London had been largely an avocation, undertaken intermittently and in off-hours by people whose main source of income lay elsewhere; but the increasing popularity of stage plays in the city after the accession of Elizabeth in 1558 persuaded some performers that a living could be made wholly (or at least mainly) by playing. But it was a chancy move; as with any new or emerging trade, full-time financial stability was not easily arrived at. The early success of one or two groups of players was overinterpreted; other groups ventured their luck, the market was soon saturated, and ultimately more playing companies failed than succeeded. For all but the very best and most popular groups, economic survival was an ongoing and primary concern. Most stage players had wives and children, and if they could not make a living at playing – as most could not – they would need to give it up and find other lines of work. We know the names of close to a thousand people in London in Shakespeare's day who, at one time or another in their lives, were said to be stage players; no doubt there were many more whose names did not get into the records, and still more who never got further than wishing to be players. Of the players whose names survive, perhaps no more than fifty or sixty achieved what we would term success – that is, a steady, prolonged, and profitable career in playing. Until the recent past, our received assumptions about stage playing in Shakespeare's London were usually based on what we knew about these fifty or so men, or sometimes only on the most eminent dozen or sixteen of them. Fortunately we are past the point of thinking of such men, or especially of the two most famous of them, Richard Burbage and Edward Alleyn, as "representative." Burbage and Alleyn were by all accounts outstanding performers, and Alleyn was an exceptionally prosperous businessman; but these characteristics alone make them and their prosperous fellows utterly atypical. If we knew more about the lives of the men who made only a passable living, or a marginal living, or no living, as players, and could understand why this was their lot, we would have a fuller picture of the business as a whole.

But first we need to understand what it meant to "make a living" in Shakespeare's London. The Elizabethans had none of the standard economic measures we use today, no cost of living index, no notion of a minimum wage, so we have to approach the issue obliquely. It is always tricky making comparisons of money values from different historical periods, but we are on reasonably safe ground making approximate comparisons by referring to the series of statutes regulating wages in the period. One learns from these statutes that a London journeyman's annual wage – depending upon his trade and level of skill – was legislated to fall within carefully prescribed limits. For example, the statute for August 1585 specified the annual rate for journeyman painter-stainers to be £8, but if "meat and drink" were furnished, then the rate was to be half that amount. For coopers the annual rate was somewhat more than £8, but again only half that amount with meat and drink. As meat and drink were commonly furnished by employers (an economy for them, as it reduced cash wages by half), some of the annual rates specified in the statute – for example, for goldsmiths (£8); or broderers, joiners, and founders (£5); or skinners, linen weavers, and longbow string-makers (£4); or girdlers, horners, and barbers (£3) – presumed meat and drink and did not even specify an alternative annual wage without them.

Among the "best and most skilled workmen, journeymen, and hired servants" listed in this statute, the highest paid category was brewers, listed at £10 per year with meat and drink. This is twice the rate of a joiner, more than three times the rate of a barber. These figures, including their disparities, represent the legislated take-home pay with which various workers would have attempted to support their families, covering everything but their own workday food. Working six days a week, a journeyman near the top end of the scale with an £8 yearly wage would find his pay amounting to something under sixpence per day. (One pound (£1) = 20 shillings (20s.); one shilling = 12 pence (12d.).) In a world of annual wages where the bottom range was £3 to £4, a worker earning £8 to £10 a year should have been able to live quite adequately, perhaps even comfortably. We might therefore use £10 a year as our notion of a benchmark annual wage.

Stage players, because they were not "wage earners," were never subject to the regulation of these statutory lists, but one can presume that they, too, would have considered £8 to £10 a year as necessary to sustain themselves properly. As they were self-employed – except for the "hired men" they themselves engaged for particular plays or seasons, of whom more later – there was no one to furnish them meat and drink, so their annual earnings had to be all-inclusive. To do better than merely sustain themselves, to "succeed," they would have expected more than £10 a year. And some players did make more, considerably more, but most made less. Some common factors seem to have been present in the careers of those few who made more: one must presume that they had a real talent or skill at playing; that they were in a fellowship or company with other skilled players; that they had, as a company, a creditable patron; that they had access to people who could write good material for them to perform; and that they had a serviceable place to play. The first four of these went together: a company of players with sufficient skills would attract the attention of potential patrons (who might see benefit in having their name associated with the troupe and who would also confer the needed legitimation) as well as the notice of playwrights wishing to sell their texts. But finding a place to play was another matter. For the most part playing places, whether inn yards, parish halls, or specially built structures, were controlled by people who saw themselves as lessors, who were interested in profits at least as much as in players. The relations between companies of players and the owners or lessors of playing places were complex, and after 1576 they became even more complex.

The economic "big bang" in Elizabethan theater history is generally presumed to have occurred in 1576, with the unprecedented erection of three purpose-built play-houses in the London area, a collocation of events presumed to signal the sudden elevation of stage playing to the status of big business. But the fuse for this bang was probably lit five years earlier, in 1571, the year in which one of the most socially divisive issues of the Elizabethan age came to a head (though not to a conclusion) with the passage of the statute against usury. Like the *Roe v. Wade* decision in our own day, which brought legal focus but no social closure to the ongoing debate over abortion in the United States, the 1571 statute against usury served simultaneously to sanction and to limit certain manifestations of a much-disputed social practice, while at the same time ensuring that the already long-running dispute about its premises would continue. Those opposed to the lending of money at interest claimed to be waging God's war, and cited Scripture and scholastic arguments in defense of their positions; the opposite faction argued for freedom of conduct, common utility, and practical realities. The statute attempted, unsuccessfully, to satisfy both parties, and the debate it was intended to quell went on for nearly a full century more. But the 1571 statute was a landmark, in that it made both possible and feasible a market for the borrowing and lending of money in London. Provided that the statute's constraints were observed, arrangements for borrowing that had formerly been covert, and disguised as something else, could now be openly entered into. Moneylending was suddenly respectable, and borrowing no longer needed to be surreptitious.

Many reasons have been adduced by theater historians for the sudden florescence of playing activity, including the erection of playhouses, in the 1570s, but the relation of these phenomena to the open availability of credit after 1571 has still to be explored. Recent studies in the relation of "the theater" and "the market" (notably by J.-C. Agnew 1986) have been salutary in drawing attention to the symbolic and structural resemblances between these two enterprises; but the market referred to in these studies is invariably the market in goods and services, not the money market itself. Yet the Elizabethan money market, whose operations underlay both these other activities, has been little studied (see *Further reading* for suggested titles).

The social history of usury, in broad outline, resembles in many ways the social history of stage playing in the age of Shakespeare. From the early sixteenth century, partisan discourse denigrated both practices: requiring people to pay for the loan-use of money and asking them to pay to see a performance of a play. Though usury was seen as the more evil of the two, both were said to be reprehensible. That money, not a commodity but only a sterile medium of exchange, should generate more money of itself was on this view unnatural; equally unnatural was that stage players, idle drones whose stock-in-trade was mere public pretending (also no commodity), should think their behavior worthy of recompense. Despite such rhetoric, however, throughout this early period a broad range of noble, gentle, and otherwise well-to-do persons persisted in both practices, patronizing plays and borrowing money at interest, against the tide of published opinion.

By the middle of the sixteenth century, usury and stage playing had both found their public defenders, and each practice was endorsed and praised (perhaps self-servingly) by interested parties as being for the good of the commonwealth. Debate was immediately joined, at both the national and the local level, on both issues, and the public praise was quickly matched by public condemnation. By the early seventeenth century, much vituperation having been endured on each side, the contention was largely over, with both activities generally accepted as part of the new social fabric, though not without lingering resentment.

The foregoing is of course a gross oversimplification of the full course of events. But it allows me to suggest that the remarkable history of stage playing in the decade of the 1570s can be better understood in tandem with the history of moneylending in the same decade. Cuthbert Burbage is recorded in 1635, in a procedural dispute now known as the Sharers' Papers (PRO, L.C. 5/133, pp. 50, 51), as remembering how, a half-century earlier, his father James had built the Theatre in 1576 "with many hundred pounds taken up at interest," and how nearly a quarter-century after that he and his brother Richard "at like expense built the Globe, with more sums of money taken up at interest." Before 1571 it would have been foolish, and self-incriminating, to make such statements publicly; equally, before 1571 such sums of money would have been more difficult to find, and would have come on harder and more covert terms.

The usury debates in Parliament in 1571 marked out an important path between the Scylla of religious certitude and the Charybdis of nascent capitalism. The heated rhetoric engendered by stage playing, given vent not in Parliament but in public, moved along the same path. The religious arguments against playing were anchored in the same Church Fathers as the religious arguments against usury: playing is an abomination, only vicious men portray vices in public, only dissolute men dress boys as girls, only corrupt men show how treason and fraud might be effected, and so on, all such conduct being against God's will and therefore on the path to damnation.

But my analogy of stage playing with usury works only to a certain point. If it were a true parallel, the arguments from economics raised in defense of usury ought also to have been raised in defense of playing. But they were not. On the contrary, the economic arguments were as opposed to stage playing as were the religious arguments. Our modern histories of the Elizabethan theater often conflate the religious and economic attacks against the stage into a single anti-theatrical tradition, emanating from a presumed single center of discontent (though often given voice by opportunist professional writers exploiting the market). But complaints against stage players and their supposed prosperity arose from both ends of the ethical and political spectrum. It will be useful to consider the economics of playing by looking at some of the claims made against playing not by its religious opponents, but rather by those who objected to it on social and economic grounds.

In a tract published in 1574, three years after the passage of the usury statute, Geoffrey Fenton wrote that a principal aptitude of stage players was "juggling in good earnest the money out of other men's purses into their own hand" (*A Form of Christian Policy gathered out of French*, STC 10793a). A more opportunist position might have taken this skill as simple shrewd dealing and faulted the gullible spectators more than the entrepreneurial players for such a state of affairs. This is the approach John Northbrooke took in 1577; Northbrooke broadened Fenton's approach by blaming the audience too, defining "prodigality" as the propensity "to bestow money and goods [on] banqueting, feasting, rewards to players of interludes, dicing, and dancing, etc." But Northbrooke didn't let the players off the hook; he claimed that squandering money on interludes was especially discreditable, because the trade of stage player was "an idle loitering life" devoid of economic significance (*A Treatise wherein Dicing, Dancing, vain Plays or Interludes, with other idle Pastimes, etc., commonly used on the Sabbath Day, are reproved by the Authority of the Word of God and Ancient Writers*, STC 18670).

An anonymous writer, perhaps Anthony Munday, wrote in 1580 of the leech-like quality of players "which cannot live of themselves [but who] live at the devotion or alms of other men, passing from country to country, from one gentleman's house to another, offering their service, which is a kind of beggary." He observed correctly that "players in these days which exhibit their games for lucre's sake [are] held for vagabonds and infamous persons," and went on to moralize that "they may aptly be likened unto drones, which will not labor to bring in, but live off the labors of the painful gatherers" (*A Second and Third Blast of Retrait from Plays and Theatres*, STC 21677).

These are all strong assertions, and their main thrust is to imply a moral dimension – indeed, a moral imperative – to economic behavior. Stephen Gosson in 1582 rejected the claims of moral efficacy for stage plays, stating that "neither the poets which pen the plays, nor the actors that present them upon the stage, do seek to do any good unto such as they rebuke, for the poet's intent is to wreak his own anger; [and] the actors either hunt for their own profit, as the players in London; or follow the humour of their own fancies and youthful delights, as the students of the universities, and the inns of court." For the profit-hungry players of London the problem was compounded, said Gosson, by the very qualities of the stage players themselves, most of them being "either men of occupations, which they have forsaken to live by playing, or common minstrels, or trained up from their childhood to this abominable exercise and have now no other way to get their living" (*Plays Confuted in Five Actions*, STC 12095).

For Gosson, getting a living – that is, working – could in no way be made compatible with playing. Philip Stubbes made the same point even more succinctly when he wrote in 1583 that players were "idle persons, doing nothing but playing and loitering, having their livings of the sweat of other men's brows, much like unto dronets devouring the sweet honey of the poor labouring bees" (*The Anatomy of Abuses*, STC 23376).

The common theme of these complaints is economic; stage players are not honest earners of the money they take in, but are parasites, disrupting the economic balance of a society seeking to find its proper social equilibrium. Samuel Cox, in a letter to an unknown recipient dated 15 January 1590, brought the culpable spectator back into play when he wondered what could be more abominable than "To see rich men give more to a player for a song, which he shall sing in one hour, than to their faithful servants for serving them a whole year? To see infinite numbers of poor people go a begging about the streets for penury, when players and parasites wax rich by juggling and jesting?"; or what more lamentable than that "we should suffer men to make professions and occupations of plays all the year long, whereby to enrich idle loiterers with plenty, while many of our poor brethren lie pitifully gasping in the streets, ready to starve and die of penury?" (BL, MS Add. 15,891, fos. 184–5v).

Like the war on drugs in our own day, the secular war on stage plays in Shakespeare's day was presumed winnable by its proponents as soon as they altered the thinking of either the providers or the consumers of the wretched product; but victory was more likely with the latter, since members of the former group were beyond the pale. As late as 1615 a writer known only as I.G. asserted "That man that giveth money for the maintenance of [stage players] must needs incur the danger of . . . severe judgment, except they repent"; for "a true dealing man cannot endure deceit, but players get their living by craft and cozenage, for what greater cheating can there be than for money to render that which is not money's worth?" (*A Refutation of the Apology for Actors*, STC 12214).

"That which is not money's worth": an essentialist sentiment, to be sure, but historically legitimate; notions of absolute worth still underlay a variety of economic policies in the period, most notably as justification for the strict pricing regulations on basic commodities like bread and ale, and of the statutory controls on wages which we have already seen. Stage playing, because it could be neither weighed, measured, nor resold, was not a true commodity, and thus could have no just price affixed to it. Nor was it, in our modern terminology, a service profession; Elizabethan lawyers and doctors performed services, to be sure, but always left behind something tangible, a piece of parchment or a medication. Not so stage players, who left nothing behind but memories. Stage players who persisted in trying to "sell" the evanescence of their performances were thus, on this view, morally reprehensible.

The targets of this line of argument, the professional players whose livelihood lay in stage playing, seem to have understood both the origins of this logic and also its growing irrelevance in a society increasingly dominated by a market economy and able to afford the pursuits of leisure. The proponents of the just-price argument could not withstand the advance of the free-market entrepreneur, and the business of stage playing was a target of opportunity in this advance. The popular perception that there was money to be made in the playing business was in part well founded; but one didn't have to be a player to gain access to this money. There were people ready to undertake the presenting of plays as an investment, to spend money in order to make money from the mounting and marketing of performances. Some of these people were even willing to borrow money so that they could spend it in hopes of making more. Then, as now, the trajectory of such aspirations was often deflected into failure by unforeseen events. We are the beneficiaries of these failures, for they usually eventuated in lawsuits among the contending parties, by means of which many details that would otherwise be lost to us have been recorded and preserved. The success stories have left fewer traces.

As 1577 drew to a close, Londoners may have been aware not only that three new playhouses had been erected in the environs of their city within the previous twenty months, but also that their hero Francis Drake was about to set sail on a voyage around the world. Londoners who knew about such matters would have understood, as we ourselves sometimes forget, that Drake's circumnavigation was every bit as much about economics as was the erecting of playhouses and the merchandising of performances. Drake had been a regular privateer in the queen's service for several years, having received his commission in 1570; the proposed voyage round the world differed markedly in degree, but not at all in kind, from his earlier quests for plunder. But piracy, like playhouses and playing companies, requires seed money. Drake found a number of investors ready to accept his invitation to join financially in the undertaking, thereby becoming sharers in a form of investment increasingly popular in London during Elizabeth's reign, the joint-stock company. Drake raised some £5,000 from his investors, who bought "shares" in his venture; when he returned in 1580 with over £1,500,000 in booty, the sharers realized, even after the queen's percentage was skimmed off, a gross profit of some 4,700 percent, or close to 1,600 percent per year.

The notion of joining with other like-minded investors in "sharing out" the costs of a venture was of course not new to the sixteenth century; but, like mutual funds in our own day, it became the investment model of choice after 1550. The Merchant Adventurers were organized around this principle, as were the Muscovy Company, the Guinea Company, the Levant Company, the Eastland Company, the Virginia Company, the East India Company, the Mineral and Battery Works, and the Company of Mines Royal, among others. Some of these companies welcomed investments from the moneyed community at large; others accepted investments only from their own members. The model was simple and straightforward; a fixed number of shares was determined, usually one share for each interested party, and a price per share was determined that would furnish, in the aggregate, enough money to cover the cost of the venture. Shares in open-ended companies could be sold or transferred, and if the price of shares rose – that is, if the perceived value of the enterprise rose – trading in half-shares or quarter-shares became possible; the modern notion of accommodating growth by issuing additional shares was still on the horizon. Closed companies could restrict transfer of their shares to immediate heirs, or could prohibit alienation altogether. W. R. Scott (1910–12) estimates the total capital invested in joint stock companies in 1570 to have been about £100,000, but this figure may well be too low.

Companies of stage players were commonly structured on the joint-stock model. A nucleus of committed members would organize themselves both theatrically and financially into an entity, to secure both patronage and a patent and to share costs and profits. Surviving patents uniformly name the eight or ten principal men who were the sharers and thus who formally *were* the company. For example, the royal patent constituting the new King's players (formerly the Lord Chamberlain's players) in 1603 lists the sharers as Lawrence Fletcher, William Shakespeare, Richard Burbage, Augustine Phillips, John Heminges, Henry Condell, William Sly, Robert Armin, and Richard Cowley. Upon these men and their resources would fall the common expenses of the company, not only for play scripts and costumes and properties but also for hired men, musicians, and gatherers.

These costs were not inconsiderable. Play scripts cost from £4 to £10, with £6 being an average cost, and an active company would need anywhere from a dozen to two dozen new plays each season. We know a little about how much the "extra" players, men and boys, were paid. We learn from the records of Philip Henslowe, the entrepreneur who owned the Rose playhouse, that hired men – that is, contract players – might be paid in the range of 5s. to 10s weekly over the course of a year, with their wages to be reduced to half "when they lie still" – that is, when the company was for whatever reason not engaged in playing. This was a decent remuneration, averaging more than a shilling a day. Even in a poor playing year, composed equally of playing and non-playing days, the earnings of these hired men would match those of the better-paid London journeymen whose wages were specified in the statutes. A half-century later, in 1635, the King's players estimated that their operating costs – payment for play scripts and the cost of licensing fees, along with wages for hired men, for musicians, for the wardrobe keeper, the stage keeper, the book holder and the gatherers, as well as the boys – came in the aggregate to some £3, or 60*s*., for each performance day.

It is harder to amortize the daily or annual cost of costumes and properties; such a reckoning is probably beyond us at this stage of our knowledge, but it seems likely that costumes were the single largest expense in a company's budget. We know from Henslowe's records and other sources that it was fairly common for the cost of certain individual costumes to exceed the cost of the plays they were to be used in. This is in distinct contrast to the practice a half-century earlier. In the early years of the sixteenth century, performers in London, all of whom had other trades, organized themselves into small troupes, acquired play texts that could be performed by their own small number, hired costumes as needed from haberdashers or other purveyors, and operated with far less overhead than did their successors in the Elizabethan and Jacobean periods. The later burgeoning of expenses for hired men, musicians, costumes, and so on, afford an insight into one of the principal by-products of the professionalization of stage playing: the escalation and proliferation of costs.

These expenses were met by a combination of sharers' investments and company income. Some fragments of information about shares have survived. In 1597 Edward Alleyn is said to have received £50 upon redemption of his share in the Admiral's company when he "leafte playinge" for a time. In 1612 the redemption of a share in Queen Anne's company was worth £80. Three years later a redeemed share in Prince Charles's company was worth £70. In the mid-1630s a share in Prince Charles II's Company cost £100. Theophilus Bird, a player and manager, claimed in 1655 that the net value of his company in 1640 – playbooks, costumes, properties, "hangings," etc. – was £3,000, suggesting a valuation of some £300 per share. Other instances of shares and their costs can be found in Chambers (1923) and Bentley (1984).

The one expense not yet discussed was perhaps the most crucial one of all for a playing company: the expense of hiring a playing place. In London before 1576 the conventional playing space was an inn yard. The appearance of purpose-built playhouses after 1576 should be understood as a shrewd and profitable response to an already present need; there were more groups of players wishing to perform in London than there were playing spaces able to accommodate them. After 1576 inn yards continued to serve as playing venues, and there was no shortage of playing companies prepared to negotiate for access to them as well as to the new playhouses.

But a playhouse was a different kind of venture. The joint-stock approach to financing a playing company did not translate very well to the financing of a playhouse. We know of only two playhouses erected and paid for on this model: the Globe, whose joint sharers were Richard and Cuthbert Burbage, William Shakespeare, Augustine Phillips, Thomas Pope, John Heminges, and William Kemp; and the Blackfriars playhouse, whose sharers were Richard and Cuthbert Burbage, William Shakespeare, Henry Condell, William Sly, John Heminges, and Thomas Evans. Many of these names will be familiar as sharers also in the King's company of players. But the two ventures were separate, and a careful distinction was kept between being a sharer in the playing company and a sharer (or "housekeeper") in a playhouse. When the housekeepers negotiated with the playing company over the terms of tenancy, men like Shakespeare found themselves negotiating with themselves. More importantly, they found themselves profiting from both sides of the undertaking.

Playhouse shares in both the Globe and Blackfriars could be negotiated within the company. In his will in 1635 the player John Shank described his share in the King's company of players as being worth £50 (a figure which suggests a half-share), which he asked his fellows to pay to his widow "according to the old custom and agreement amongst us." But in addition to owning a share in the company, Shank had also purchased, in the year or two before his death, three shares in the Globe and two shares in Blackfriars from William Heminges (son of John) for a total of £506.

To the best of our knowledge, no other playhouse in London was financed on this model; though the evidence, especially for the earliest of them, is so scant that we can only guess at how they were financed. The playhouse at Newington Butts was built by Jerome Savage, a stage player, and the Curtain playhouse by Henry Laneman, a yeoman of the queen's guard; but nothing is known about the source of funding for either enterprise. Savage is identified in a lawsuit in 1577 as the sole owner of the former, and Laneman acted as sole owner of the latter when he sold his interest to James Burbage in 1585. Such actions suggest the absence of investment syndicates behind either man.

We know more about later playhouses, all of which seem to have been financed by individuals or partnerships, undoubtedly through the borrowing of money. That is, in any event, the present state of our knowledge about Francis Langley, the builder of the Swan; Oliver Woodliffe and Richard Samwell, builders of the Boar's Head; Aaron Holland, owner of the Red Bull; Philip Rosseter, builder of the playhouse at Puddle Wharf; and, preeminently, Christopher Beeston at the Phoenix or Cockpit.

One cannot discuss the particularities of issues such as these, however, apart from the larger economic envelope in which they functioned. Then, as now, ventures that succeed in one year might well fail in another. We know in some detail about the Spanish depredations in the Low Countries beginning in 1569, and about the rebellion of the northern earls in 1570, events that destabilized the foreign and domestic sides of the economy for almost a decade. The usury debate in 1571 was in part a response to the monetary crisis engendered by this disruption. But trade worsened, and the economy of London was struck an especially grievous blow by the collapse of the Antwerp market in 1576. Antwerp had been the London merchants' principal gateway to European trade, and its loss must have made 1576 seem a bleak year indeed, hardly a good time to risk the construction of even one playhouse, let alone three. Yet three were built.

There was another crisis in the mid-1580s, precipitated by plots against the queen's life, defined by heavy expenses in the Netherlands (Sir Philip Sidney being one of the costs), and perhaps best remembered for the casket letters and the trial of Mary Stuart – a curiously poor time for Philip Henslowe to have risked the erection of the Rose. Social unrest precipitated by a series of bad harvests from 1594 to 1597 coincided with Francis Langley's building of the Swan; and so on. Considering the economic odds, all these ventures should have failed; yet we know they did not.

By contrast, the opening years of King James's reign were, despite some parliamentary quarreling over impositions, a time of relative calm and prosperity, marked by what seemed an auspicious peace with Spain. In that economic climate – a climate in which the Red Bull playhouse, opening in 1605, prospered – the Whitefriars venture of 1607 should have had an easy entry into the market. But it did not. Nor did Christopher Beeston's Phoenix playhouse fare any better a decade later; erected in 1617, it was trashed by rioters almost as soon as it opened. These instances of failure where success was expected – like the earlier instances of success where there could easily have been failure – require a fuller understanding than we can bring to them at present. Even the seemingly straightforward events of 1625, a year of peaceful royal succession but also of plague, when all the London playing companies except the King's players went bankrupt, are more complex than it might appear. What is clear is that the economy of stage playing cannot be wholly understood in isolation from an awareness of its relation to the larger economies of London and of the nation.

Such a study remains to be written. In its absence, however, we can profitably retreat to the particularities of what we do know – or what we have collectively come to believe – about the economic aspect of stage playing in the Elizabethan and Jacobean period. The largest single sums of money associated with stage playing had to do, of course, with the construction of playhouses. For the most part this money came from people who were not stage players. Though the evidence of costs and charges, here as elsewhere, is not nearly as complete as one would wish, there is enough data for us to be able to assemble bits of information.

According to some documents found by C. W. Wallace, putting up the Theatre in 1576 cost James Burbage, a stage player, and his brother-in-law John Brayne about £700; the money came largely from Brayne, a grocer, some from his own resources but most from loans he took out. Ten years later, Philip Henslowe's partnership contract with John Cholmley for the erection of the Rose playhouse in 1587 called for payments totalling £816. Cholmley, a tanner, died shortly after the contract was drawn up, leaving Henslowe to bear the costs himself, but Henslowe, a dyer and pawnbroker, seems to have managed, and a figure in the vicinity of £800 is probably close to correct. Francis Langley, a draper, may have spent as much as £1,000 erecting the Swan in 1597, a playhouse remarked upon at the time for its opulence. In 1600 Edward Alleyn, a stage player, joined more frugally with Philip Henslowe (who was his father-in-law) to build the Fortune playhouse at a cost of £520; but in 1622, when the Fortune was rebuilt, the cost had inflated to £1,000, probably because of more ambitious plans for the newer building. In 1635 one of the sharers in the Globe syndicate professed to recall, during a legal controversy, that the cost of rebuilding the Globe, after the disastrous fire in 1613, had been £1,400; but this figure has been greeted with skepticism by modern scholars as being too high, inflated by legal posturing. In 1613 Philip Henslowe paid some £360 to convert an existing structure, the bearbaiting pit called the Bear Garden, into a playhouse called the Hope.

From these figures we can get some sense of the average cost of an average play-house in the later sixteenth and earlier seventeenth centuries in London. Clearly, investments in playhouses on the order of £500 or £1,000 were not made by people earning £10 a year. But for people who were somewhat better off than that, it was not necessary to have £1,000 of one's own funds ready at hand in order to finance a playhouse. Money was available for borrowing on the open market after 1571, at the statutory legal rate of 10 percent per annum. Anyone who needed money and who was not a clear credit risk could find a moneylender, or usurer, willing to serve him. The aptly named Security, the usurer in *Eastward Ho*, is at everyone's service, as he repeatedly makes clear throughout the play. Moneylending was itself a form of speculation, by which persons with available funds could virtually assure themselves of a 10 percent annual return, made almost foolproof through the services of a usurer as middleman and by the mechanism of sureties and penalties built into the debtor's bond, as well as by the new right to take a defaulting debtor to court. The usurer's own fees, supplemental to the publicly acknowledged 10 percent, went unrecorded.

There were, then, two kinds of people for whom £1,000 might not have been an insurmountable sum. There were those who *had* money, who could be lenders if they so chose, who might prefer to invest their money in some project (such as a playhouse) rather than risking it in a joint-stock venture or making it available to a usurer for lending out on the open market. And there were those who could *get* money, by borrowing it from the same usurers in the same market. For both potential lenders and potential borrowers, the viability of any proposed investment would turn upon its prospect of safely returning a profit greater than 10 percent per annum: for if the investment returned less than that, the loan would be a net loss for the borrower, and such a diversion of resources would be, for the lender, less profitable than lending through a usurer.

But, despite its fluctuations, London's economy was strong in the later sixteenth and early seventeenth centuries, and there were many investment opportunities that promised, and often delivered, profits considerably in excess of 10 percent per year. We know that those who preferred to invest in the various venturing companies, such as the Levant Company or the Muscovy Company, enjoyed a healthy return on their capital. Those who bought shares in privateering ventures, or who speculated in commodities, often became quite wealthy. There were of course risks attached to such investments; but there were risks as well in being financially responsible for a play-house. Plague (as Philip Henslowe learned in 1592) could shut down a playhouse for as much as two years. Official disfavor, for whatever reason (as Francis Langley discovered in 1597), could shut one down indefinitely. Natural calamities such as fire (as Shakespeare's fellows discovered in 1613) or riot (as Christopher Beeston discovered in 1617) could seriously damage or even destroy a playhouse.

Yet we know that playhouses appeared attractive to at least a small handful of speculators, whose principal motivation was profit rather than love of the drama. Philip Henslowe, owner of the Rose playhouse, has left more comprehensive records of his day-to-day business than has any other playhouse owner, so by default one is obliged to take his evidence as a starting point. By reading through his account book (the so-called Diary), one can make estimates of the annual earnings he was able to pocket. For the 1594–5 playing season, for example, Henslowe recorded some 275 performances of plays. His share of the paid admissions came to an average of thirty-three shillings on each of these days, for an annual total of some £450. At that level of profit, it would have taken Henslowe only two years to recoup the whole cost of building his playhouse. But 1594–5 was a very good year, the first full year of playing after two years of disastrous plague; other years were less profitable. E. K. Chambers reckoned that, over the long haul, Henslowe's total annual receipts averaged about £350. Even using this figure, and factoring in the cost of periodic refurbishment and remodeling of the structure, Henslowe's annual return on his investment seems to have been on the order of 25–30 percent.

Against these figures for the Rose, we have a few – very few – figures available for the Globe. Unlike the Rose, which was Henslowe's own project, the first and second Globe theaters were built and owned by a syndicate – Richard Burbage and William Shakespeare among them – who were first and foremost stage players. Chambers reckoned that the Globe returned about £280 to this group of owners, or householders, in 1615. John Witter, who had married the widow of the stage player Augustine Phillips, claimed in a lawsuit in 1619 that the annual revenues from the Globe were £420 to £560 before the 1613 fire, and higher afterwards. In a 1635 legal dispute it was claimed that the Globe returned 54*s*. each playing day to its collective householders or sharers, nearly twice as much as Henslowe's earnings in 1594–5. In the same dispute, it was claimed that the Blackfriars playhouse, which had returned perhaps £140 in 1615, was now worth £700 to £800 a year. The 1635 dispute was over the control of shares in the playhouse, and from its claims and counterclaims one might reasonably conclude that in the early seventeenth century each member of the King's players who was also both a Globe householder and a Blackfriars householder received some £120 to £150 a year as his share of earnings. This is well in excess of our benchmark living wage of £10 a year; the moral may be – as G. E. Bentley (1984) has claimed – that the true path to prosperity on the stage was to be both a sharer and a householder; which meant, in essence, to be a King's player. Shakespeare would have understood this.

But the Globe and Blackfriars were special enterprises. The normative paradigm for producing a busy and active playhouse presumed that the playhouse owner, or lessor, and the company of stage players, or lessees, were different entities. The players, needing a playhouse, and the owner, needing tenants, would come to terms. This was the arrangement understood by such owners as Philip Henslowe at the Rose, Francis Langley at the Swan, Aaron Holland at the Red Bull, and others. Surviving documents indicate that from early on the system was predicated upon a flexible rent; that is, instead of paying a fixed weekly sum for a playhouse without regard to the success of the tenancy, the members of the playing company shared with the owner of the playhouse a certain fixed part of their takings at each performance.

The normative paradigm worked as follows. Spectators paid at the door for their initial entrance to the playhouse, and these receipts went wholly to the company of players. Admission was one penny at the early public playhouses, more at the private playhouses. Remembering that the average journeyman earned five or six pence a day, and that the average apprentice had far less than that at his disposal, we may better understand the significance of a one penny admission charge to see a play (not to mention the much steeper sixpence cost of purchasing a play text in quarto). Once inside the playhouse, spectators wishing access to the galleries, or to the tiring house, would have had to pay again, another penny or more, depending on the house; these additional receipts were shared between the players and the owner. The money-collectors at these various levels were called "gatherers"; their honesty in reporting all their takings each day was a crucial part of the operation, and playhouse owners and playing companies contended over who had the right to appoint them.

The prosperity of the select group of King's players who were both company sharers and householders did not go unremarked. One might wonder why, with this exemplar as their model, other companies of players did not take their livelihoods more into their own hands, as the King's players had done. Perhaps other groups of players were less entrepreneurial – a possible but not very persuasive answer. Perhaps tradition or habit sustained the assumption that the single-investor model or the partnership model for playhouse ownership really did assure better success – an untestable hypothesis. Or perhaps further efforts in this direction were constricted by the Privy Council, which was determined from the 1590s onward to limit the number of playhouses in the city and its environs. Prevented from building new playhouses of their own, however, entrepreneurial playing companies might still have negotiated with owners of existing playhouses in an effort to buy them out. There is no surviving evidence that any playing company attempted to do so.

We are left, then, once the anomalies are discounted, with two modes of organization: the joint-stock model for playing companies and the single-owner or partnership model for playhouses. Efforts to bridge these two models are almost as old as the models themselves; the emergence of the theatrical manager, whose roots go back to Philip Henslowe and Edward Alleyn but whose preeminent early exemplar is Christopher Beeston, set the pattern for further development in theatrical affairs. There was, after the closing of the playhouses in 1642, an extended time for reflection about good and bad forms of business organization; and when playing resumed in 1660, the managerial model was dominant.

REFERENCES AND FURTHER READING

Agnew, Jean-Christophe 1986: *Worlds Apart: The Market and the Theater in Anglo-American Thought, 1550–1750*. Cambridge: Cambridge University Press.

Appleby, Joyce Oldham 1978: *Economic Thought and Ideology in Seventeenth-century England*. Princeton: Princeton University Press.

Barish, Jonas 1981: *The Antitheatrical Prejudice*. Berkeley and Los Angeles: University of California Press.

Bentley, Gerald Eades 1984: *The Profession of Player in Shakespeare's Time 1590–1642*. Princeton: Princeton University Press.

Cerasano, Susan 1985: The "business" of shareholding, the Fortune playhouses, and Francis Grace's will. *Medieval & Renaissance Drama in England*, 2, 231–51.

Chambers, Edmund K. 1923: *The Elizabethan Stage*, 4 vols. Oxford: Clarendon Press. (See especially vol. 1.)

Coleman, D. C. and John, A. H. (eds) 1976: *Trade, Government, and Economy in Pre-industrial England: Essays Presented to F. J. Fisher*. London: Weidenfeld & Nicolson.

Fisher, Frederick Jack 1935: Development of the London food market 1540–1640. *Economic History Review*, 5, 46–64.

—— 1940: Commercial trends and policy in sixteenth-century England. *Economic History Review*, 10, 95–117.

—— 1948: *The Development of London as a Centre of Conspicuous Consumption in the Sixteenth and Seventeenth Centuries*. London: Royal Historical Society.

—— 1957: The sixteenth and seventeenth centuries: the Dark Ages in English economic history? *Economica*, n.s. 24, 1–18.

—— 1990: *London and the English Economy, 1500–1700*, ed. P. J. Corfield and N. B. Harte. London: Hambledon Press.

Fisher, Frederick Jack (ed.) 1961: *Essays in the Economic and Social History of Tudor and Stuart England in Honour of R. H. Tawney*. Cambridge: Cambridge University Press.

Ingram, William 1985: The playhouse as an investment, 1607–1614: Thomas Woodford and Whitefriars. *Medieval & Renaissance Drama in England*, 2, 209–30.

—— 1986: Robert Keysar, playhouse speculator. *Shakespeare Quarterly*, 37, 476–85.

—— 1992: *The Business of Playing: The Beginnings of the Adult Professional Theater in Elizabethan London*. Ithaca, NY: Cornell University Press.

Jones, Norman Leslie 1989: *God and the Money-lenders: Usury and Law in Early Modern England*. Oxford: Blackwell.

Kerridge, Eric 1988: *Trade and Banking in Early Modern England*. Manchester: Manchester University Press.

Knutson, Roslyn Lander 1991: *The Repertory of Shakespeare's Company 1594–1613*. Fayetteville, Ark.: University of Arkansas Press.

MacPherson, David 1805: *Annals of Commerce, Manufactures, Fisheries and Navigation*, 4 vols. London: Nichols and Son. (See especially vol. 2.)

Nelson, Benjamin 1969: *The Idea of Usury, from Tribal Brotherhood to Universal Otherhood*. Princeton: Princeton University Press, 1949. 2nd edn, enlarged: Chicago: University of Chicago Press.

Noonan, John Thomas 1957: *The Scholastic Analysis of Usury*. Cambridge, Mass.: Harvard University Press.

Rabb, Theodore K. 1967: *Enterprise and Empire: Merchant and Gentry Investment in the Expansion of England, 1575–1630*. Cambridge, Mass.: Harvard University Press.

de Roover, Raymond Adrien 1949: *Gresham on Foreign Exchange: An Essay on Early English Mercantilism with the Text of Sir Thomas Gresham's Memorandum: For the Understanding of the Exchange*. Cambridge, Mass.: Harvard University Press.

Scott, William Robert 1910–12: *The Constitution and Finance of English, Scottish and Irish Joint-stock Companies to 1720*, 2 vols. Cambridge: Cambridge University Press.

Shatzmiller, Joseph 1990: *Shylock Reconsidered: Jews, Moneylending, and Medieval Society*. Berkeley: University of California Press.

The Theatrical Manager in England and America; Player of a Perilous Game: Philip Henslowe, Tate Wilkinson, Stephen Price, Edwin Booth, Charles Wyndham, ed. Joseph W. Donohue, Jr. Princeton: Princeton University Press, 1971.

Tudor Royal Proclamations, ed. Paul L. Hughes and James F. Larkin, 3 vols. New Haven: Yale University Press, 1964–9.

Wilson, Thomas 1925: *A Discourse upon Usury by Way of Dialogue and Orations, for the Better Variety and More Delight of all those that shall Read this Treatise* (1572), with a historical introduction by R. H. Tawney. Repr. New York: A. M. Kelley, 1965.

—— 1936: *The State of England, anno Dom. 1600, by Thomas Wilson*, ed. from the manuscripts among the state papers in the Public Record Office by F. J. Fisher. London: Royal Historical Society (Great Britain) Publications, Camden series, 3rd ser., 52.

20

The Chamberlain's–King's Men

S. P. Cerasano

When Isaac Jaggard printed the first folio in 1623, he prefaced the plays with several dedications, a portrait of Shakespeare, and a list of "Principall Actors" (Figure 20.1). Historians have inferred that Heminges and Condell prepared the actors' list with the same care that seems to have surrounded the rest of the folio. Nevertheless, as one document defining Shakespeare's companies, the list poses many unanswered questions. What does the list represent, and what characteristics, if any, did the players share? Why did the compilers include some players who had short careers with the company alongside those who had invested the greater part of their careers in that group? What, if anything, is implied by the order of the players' names in the list? What questions does the list not answer? Perhaps most surprising are the many issues that interest contemporary historians, but which didn't somehow seem worth preserving to Heminges and Condell, who knew the players best.[1]

The Players' Status, Servitude, "Companies"

The acting company that has become known to posterity as the Lord Chamberlain's–King's Men was a group of professional actors who, during their shared existence, benefited from the license of two aristocratic patrons and the talents of many distinctive, charismatic actors. Yet, at the most basic level, playing companies were professional units founded upon traditional notions of servitude. Actors wore the livery of a nobleman who, in return for certain services, granted them a license to perform in public in order to make a living. Beyond this, however, most patrons seemed to be relatively disinterested. They worried little, if at all, about the artistic or financial side of company life.

Despite this neat formula, the question of the actor's status is complicated by a variety of artistic, professional, and political issues. As David Loades points out, the wearing of livery brought honor to the receiver of the patronage, but there was also a

The Workes of William Shakefpeare,
containing all his Comedies, Hiftories, and
Tragedies: Truely fet forth, according to their firft
ORIGINALL.

The Names of the Principall Actors
in all thefe Playes.

Illiam Shakefpeare.	*Samuel Gilburne.*
Richard Burbadge.	*Robert Armin.*
John Hemmings.	*William Oftler.*
Auguftine Phillips.	*Nathan Field.*
William Kempt.	*John Underwood.*
Thomas Poope.	*Nicholas Tooley.*
George Bryan.	*William Eccleftone.*
Henry Condell.	*Jofeph Taylor.*
William Slye.	*Robert Benfield.*
Richard Cowly.	*Robert Goughe.*
John Lowine.	*Richard Robinfon.*
Samuell Croffe.	*Iohn Shancke.*
Alexander Cooke.	*Iohn Rice.*

Figure 20.1   Page showing "Principall Actors" (first folio, 1623). Used by permission of the Department of Special Collections, Everett Needham Case Library, Colgate University.

shared expectation that the patron would enhance his own dignity, magnificence, and power by bestowing such a privilege. Concurrently, the receipt of livery contained both a practical and an aesthetic component. In part, a nobleman built his household on individuals who could be trusted and who would also participate in the actual operation of that household.[2] Early on, this was probably the case for players: they were working members of a nobleman's household who were allowed, several times per year, to provide entertainment for the household. But in the course of the sixteenth century this balance shifted so that increasingly the players became professional entertainers. What remained in place was the expectation that the patron granted livery and privilege in return for a continuing exchange of benefits.[3] Therefore players both were, and were not, liveried servants in the traditional sense of that arrangement.

In *The Rise of the Common Player*, M. C. Bradbrook noted that the status of players is difficult to define, her assessment based largely on the shifting terminology applied to entertainers ("minstrels," "retainers") and the indeterminate quality and character of early performances: "Medieval playing took many forms and was seasonal and festive …What happened in the theatre of the Hall – whether a Lord's Hall or a College Hall – is harder to establish."[4] Like so many historians, Bradbrook views the players' settlement in London as the determining factor that facilitated their "rise" in status.[5] In particular, she cites the formation of Leicester's Men and the playhouse enterprise of James Burbage as key factors that finally allowed the players to separate themselves not only from the "rogues and vagabonds" to which they were so commonly compared, but also from the household retainers and occasional performers of the early sixteenth century.[6]

The narrative of the Chamberlain's–King's Men is mired in a history of unusual antecedents. James Burbage, the titular father of the Elizabethan theatre, was actually a joiner by trade. Although he never performed in the Chamberlain's Men, it was his enterprising spirit that created the conditions in which they would eventually thrive. At some unspecified time before 1574 Burbage transformed himself into a player, his name appearing first in a patent for Leicester's Men. This document authorized the company – traceable primarily as a touring company – to perform throughout the "Realm of England" (10 May 1574). Within a few years, however, Burbage seems to have become tired of the touring life, and he decided to establish a more permanent playing place in London. Borrowing a substantial amount of money from his brother-in-law, he constructed the Theatre in Shoreditch in 1576. In the beginning, it is unclear as to who performed there. Yet the playhouse seems to have been in constant use, relatively unimpeded, for many years, until the late 1590s, when a dispute with the lessee of the grounds on which the playhouse stood forced Burbage's sons, Richard (an actor) and Cuthbert (the playhouse manager), into litigation. In the meantime, sometime around March 1583, Leicester's Men had disbanded, several of the senior players moving into the newly formed Queen's Men. Therefore it is improbable that James Burbage's performing career was a long one; however, he worked hard to maintain his aristocratic connections. In 1584 he declared himself a Hunsdon's Man, having attached himself to Henry Carey, who was created Lord Chamberlain the next year. In this manner Burbage paved the road for his son and the rest of his company to eventually become the Lord Chamberlain's–King's Men.

But regardless of his ambition and his eminence as an actor-manager, James Burbage is not amongst the players in the first folio's register of "principall actors," largely because the inventory of actors concentrates on "players" as performers. What Heminges and Condell seemed primarily interested in were those who made an artistic mark on the company's history.

Charismatic Actors

With few exceptions, the lead actors in the Chamberlain's–King's Men were coincidentally the chief shareholders in the company, although this does not enlighten us in matters relating to their acting styles or the roles in which they distinguished themselves. In fact, extant records convey much less information about individual performances than we would like. Interestingly, at the head of the 1623 actors' list is William Shakespeare, about whose histrionic talents there is only speculation. Nevertheless, his position, first on the list of "principall actors," reminds us that – at least to Heminges and Condell – he was as deeply invested in acting as he was in writing for the stage.[7]

The twenty-five actors who follow Shakespeare on the Folio list performed a variety of roles within the company's repertory. Some were clowns, while others made their mark primarily as tragic actors. Although the compilers chose to arrange the actors in two parallel lists on the page, when read by column, the order of names suggests roughly four "generations" of players, just over half of whom were still living when the folio was published in 1623.

The first nine players in the inventory (William Shakespeare, Richard Burbage, John Heminges, Augustine Phillips, William Kempe, Thomas Pope, George Bryan, Henry Condell, William Sly) are those who comprised the company in August 1597, plus George Bryan who seems to have left late in the previous year. With the exception of Sly, Bryan, and Condell, all seem to have held shares; so the compilers of the 1623 list placed the nonsharers last on the list. This is the "generation" that built the first Globe playhouse in 1599.

The second generation (Richard Cowley, John Lowin, Samuel Cross, Alexander Cooke, Samuel Gilborne, and Robert Armin) are those who saw the company develop into the King's Men in 1603, when it assumed royal patronage. Five additional players (William Ostler, Nathan Field, John Underwood, Nicholas Tooley, and William Ecclestone) were employed by 1611, some of them replacing others who had died or dropped out of the company. This is the generation that witnessed the company's acquisition and operation of a private playhouse, the second Blackfriars, in 1609. They were also present when the first Globe burned down during a performance of *All is True* (*Henry VIII*) in 1613, and they were the players who built the second Globe in its place. It is also likely that they were present when Shakespeare retired to Stratford-upon-Avon.

The fourth "generation" (Joseph Taylor, Robert Benfield, Robert Goughe, Richard Robinson, John Shank, and John Rice) were members of the company in 1619, when its final patent was issued. All were alive when the first folio was published, and several (Robinson, Benfield, and Taylor) were alive when the Puritans finally closed the London playhouses in 1642.

A close examination of the actors in the first generation of the Chamberlain's Men reveals that each contributed a unique expertise and versatility; and although none received the acclaim of Richard Burbage, the founders represented a range of professional and social backgrounds and performed many different signature roles. William Kempe – actor, clown, and dancer – has been conjectured to have been the son of a printer or a gentleman's servant. He made his mark in Shakespearian roles such as Dogberry (*Much Ado About Nothing*) and Peter (*Romeo and Juliet*). However,

much of his career was spent peregrinating among several acting companies and at
least several countries, including Denmark, where he was on the king's payroll at
Elsinore. In his early years Kempe was characterized in a letter written by Sir Philip
Sidney as "my lord of Leicester's jesting player." (Sidney was godfather to one of
Kempe's sons, named Philip.) By 1590 he was established in London as a clown.
Kempe left the Chamberlain's Men just after the lease to the first Globe playhouse was
signed in 1599. Following this, in response to a bet, he agreed to dance his way from
London to Norwich, which is recorded in a contemporary account, *Kempe's Nine Daies
Wonder* (1600). Kempe's career continued on the Continent and in Italy. At his death
he was best known on the public stage for his jigs (short sketches accompanied by
song and dance, often obscene) and "merriments" (improvised passages of witty
repartee). His career with the Chamberlain's Men had lasted only six years; but his
inclusion in the actors' list suggests that while his career was short, it was very
distinguished.

Like Kempe, Thomas Pope spent time in Danish service in the mid-1580s, leaving
that appointment eventually to assume another at the court of the elector of Saxony at
Dresden, in Germany. None of his Shakespearian or Jonsonian roles are identifiable;
however, Pope was business manager of the Chamberlain's Men, serving as joint payee
with Heminges for court performances from November 1597 to early October 1599.
Pope apparently retired before the 1603 patent for the King's Men was drawn up. His
position in the middle of the actors' list suggests that, whilst in service with the
company, he served an important role, though perhaps primarily as more of an actor-
entrepreneur than solely a performer.

Augustine Phillips was consistently listed in the documents associated with the
Chamberlain's Men, but no specific role can be attributed to him. He might have been
a dancer, like Kempe, for the Stationers' Register records a lost piece: "Phillips gigg of
the slyppers" in May 1595. With the rest of the company Phillips performed in both
Jonson's *Every Man in his Humour* (1598) and *Every Man out of his Humour* (1599) and
in *Sejanus* (1603); and he participated in the coronation procession for King James on
15 March 1604. Phillips also seems to have been one of the players who was
responsible for managing the Lord Chamberlain's Men; he apparently served as
business manager for the troupe. It was Phillips who was contacted by the conspirators involved in the Essex uprising (1601) when they hired the Chamberlain's Men to
perform *Richard II* on the eve of the rebellion.

John Heminges and Henry Condell entered the company as young men and lived
to see it change patrons and playhouses several times. They were the obvious company
historians and guardians of its reputation; but all they were obviously interested in
preserving were the good names of their colleagues and the rehabilitated texts of their
chief dramatist, their "friend and fellow" as they characterized him. It has been
thought that Heminges played Falstaff or, alternatively, that he was primarily a
tragedian.[8] Venus, in Jonson's *Masque of Christmas* (1616), refers to "old master
Heminges," and some verses written to commemorate the burning of the Globe,
three years earlier, refer to "old stuttering Heminges." Heminges's artistic roles cannot

be identified with exactitude, and it is possible that he ceased playing altogether around 1611 when he was last mentioned in Jonson's actors' list for *Sejanus*.

Henry Condell's career is equally sketchy. He played the role of the cardinal in *The Duchess of Malfi* (ca. 1611) and took part in at least thirteen other plays performed by the Chamberlain's–King's Men. Similarly, George Bryan's career with the company was short-lived and obscure, William Sly performed in several Jonson plays, but the specifics of this involvement are totally unknown.

Of all the players in the Chamberlain's–King's Men, none was applauded more than Richard Burbage. At Christmas 1594, he was summoned with two other players (Kempe and Shakespeare) to perform in several interludes before the queen at Greenwich Palace. Following this he played a prominent role in the formation of the Chamberlain's Men, and it seems to have been for Burbage that many of the lead roles in Shakespeare's plays were written. Contemporaries concurred in assigning to Burbage the roles of Hamlet, King Lear, and Othello. To this some have added Richard III, Romeo, King Gorboduc, Hieronimo (*The Spanish Tragedy*), and Ferdinand (*The Duchess of Malfi*). Doubtless there were many others, but they are also difficult to trace with any certainty.

Even though Heminges's and Condell's list clearly suggests that the players were remembered for their acting ability, the heading "principall actors" does not suggest the range and diversity of their origins, professional interests, or the many complex interrelationships amongst them, factors which, if taken into account, would create a rather different narrative of the Lord Chamberlain's–King's Men. To begin with, the account would underscore the fact that there were several different "generations" of actors in the company, that the performers made up several "companies" throughout the period from the mid-1590s to 1642. In all cases the actors seem to have been taken into the company because of their abilities as stage performers; however, some positions within the company seem to have been reserved for actors who were adept at performing specific types of roles. For instance, the company always recruited a clown who was capable of improvisation and who perhaps could provide jigs at the ends of plays. First this was Robert Armin, whose career can be traced to 1599, the brief period during which the Chamberlain's Men performed at the Curtain. Later came Will Kempe, who replaced him. But even Armin stood within a tradition of clowns, having been trained by another comedian, Richard Tarlton, who performed with the Queen's Men in the 1580s, and who was called "the wonder of his time" for his "wondrous plentifull pleasant extemporall wit." And if every company required a clown, there was also an actor whose forte lay in the performance of tragic roles. In fact, so pressing was the demand for actors who could perform certain types of roles that a clear sense of generationality runs throughout the company's history. Joseph Taylor, whose performances included Hamlet and Mosca in *Volpone*, seems to have been drafted into the company upon Richard Burbage's death specifically to replace Burbage. Similarly, Richard Robinson picked up the cardinal's role in *The Duchess of Malfi* from Henry Condell; William Ostler passed the role of Antonio, from the same play, to Robert Benfield.

The actors' training also helped to foster a sense of generationality within the company. Bryan, Pope, and Kempe all performed foreign service at Elsinore. Several players (who eventually grew to maturity as Chamberlain's–King's Men) were recruited as young boys from the Children of the Chapel Royal (Nathan Field, Richard Robinson, and John Underwood); and some (for instance, John Shank and Alexander Goughe) were originally sought out as young men to play female roles. When evaluated in retrospect, the genealogy of young men who were apprenticed, throughout the company's history, is impressive: Nicholas Tooley to Richard Burbage; James Sands and Samuel Gilborne to Augustine Phillips; Alexander Cooke and John Rice to John Heminges; Nicholas Burt and Thomas Pollard to John Shank; Charles Hart to Robinson. Nathan Field received instruction from Ben Jonson, who taught him to read Horace and Martial in Latin and might well have taught him something of writing drama and acting as well.[9]

Another subset of the actors listed in the folio would comprise those who held shares in the Globe and, later, in the Blackfriars. These, like artistic roles, were passed from one player to another. A different subset of actors – particularly Condell, Lowin, and Taylor – distinguished themselves as business managers for the company, and a complementary group (Heminges, Pope, Bryan, and Phillips) served as payees for court performances.[10]

However, playing the role of Feste or Lear was not the only factor determining a player's identity. A few, such as Robert Armin, identified themselves as tradesmen, probably because they wished to maintain their status as goldsmiths and grocers. In terms of their origins, some members of the company were of working-class families, whilst others were from more substantial backgrounds. The material rewards of performing, as well as the visibility achieved by certain player-sharers, allowed some to purchase sizable houses outside London (Shakespeare in Stratford-upon-Avon; Phillips in Mortlake, Surrey; Condell in Fulham). Condell was said to be "of great living, wealth, and power" upon his death. Heminges received a confirmation of arms in 1629 as a "long tyme Servant to Queen Elizabeth of happie Memory, also to King James hir Royal Successor and to King Charles his Sonne now raigning."

Although the players invested in the company and their playhouses with the intention of making a living, it is clear that they reaped other, less tangible benefits, in terms of both close personal friendships and more binding, domestic ties. Within the circle of the Lord Chamberlain's–King's Men were several marriages, and there were others across company lines. Richard Robinson married Richard Burbage's widow, Winifred, after her husband died in 1619. John Heminges's daughter Thomasine married William Ostler (and Heminges had formerly married the widow of another actor, William Knell, a former Queen's Man who died in 1588). Robert Goughe married Augustine Phillips's sister in 1603, and another of Phillips's sisters is probably the Margery who married William Borne, a lead actor with the Lord Admiral's Men.

But even if the actors were not literally related to one another, the close contact fostered by rehearsing, performing, and touring bred a sense of the acting company as an extended family. This is supported by the numerous mentions of players and their families in probate documents, particularly wills. To cite only a few, Augustine Phillips bequeathed to "my late apprentice," Samuel Gilburne, "the some of ffortye shilling*es*, and my mouse Colloured velvit hose, and a white Taffety doublet, A blacke Taffety sute, my purple Cloke, sword, and dagger, And my base viall."[11] Another apprentice received "the some of ffortye shilling*es* and a Citterne a Bandore and a Lute." Other bequests went to Shakespeare, Condell, Armin, Richard Cowley, Christopher Beeston (who performed with the company a short time), Nicholas Tooley, and Alexander Cooke. Shakespeare remembered Heminges, Burbage, and Condell in his last will and testament, and Robinson and Tooley stood witness to Burbage's will, which was written out by the scrivener to the King's Men, Ralph Crane.[12] Nicholas Tooley, who had once been Burbage's apprentice, left various sums of money to friends, including members of Burbage's family, Condell's wife and daughter, and fellow player Joseph Taylor. Tooley forgave debts owed by two other King's Men, John Underwood and William Ecclestone, and left a further £10 to Cuthbert Burbage's wife in whose house Tooley died.

When establishing their places of residence, the players often gravitated toward the neighborhoods near the playhouses; or if not, to neighborhoods where they were close to other members of the company. Three locations were especially popular: the parish of St Leonard's Shoreditch, northeast of the city wall (near to the Theatre and the Curtain, where many of the early Lord Chamberlain's Men started their professional lives), the parish of St Saviour's, Southwark, on Bankside (in which both the first and second Globe playhouses stood), and the parish of St Mary, Aldermanbury (located on the western side of London within the wall, northeast of St Paul's Cathedral and a modest walk from the Blackfriars playhouse). The players in St Leonard's included the Burbages and Richard Cowley. Theirs was a tightly knit group. Richard and Cuthbert lived as close neighbors on Halliwell Street, and Cowley named his two sons Cuthbert and Richard after the brothers. St Mary Aldermanbury, near to the Guildhall, was the parish of both Heminges and Condell. Later, William Ostler married into the Heminges family and took up residence in the same parish where he baptized his son, Beaumont, presumably named after the dramatist.

Players in St Saviour's, Southwark, included William Shakespeare, Alexander Cooke, Richard Goughe, John Lowin, Augustine Phillips, William Sly, and Joseph Taylor, who together represent the Chamberlain's–King's Men from their earliest days to their latest. Other players tended to congregate in Cripplegate, just to the north of St Mary Aldermanbury, without the city wall, in the neighborhood of another public playhouse, the Fortune; and some of these players seem briefly to have been associated with the Prince's Men, who performed there, or with their financier, Philip Henslowe. John Shank appeared in the 1610 list of Prince's players, and Benfield was contracted to Henslowe as one of Lady Elizabeth's players in 1613. In addition to placing the actors close to their places of employment, their residences in specific neighborhoods doubtless assisted them in professional matters – rehearsing, the readings of new plays, contracting for costumes and playbooks, training apprentices, keeping up the physical fabric of the playhouse and the grounds on which it stood – all which entered into the business of company management and playhouse ownership. In the case of the Globe, this was a complex set of responsibilities, because the players were in charge of every detail, from repairing the roof and stage to paying for sewer maintenance.

Perhaps because of the many personal benefits they enjoyed, the core of the Chamberlain's–King's Men was relatively stable. However, players occasionally left the company of their own volition, and those who were young enough to continue working found alternative occupations. John Rice took holy orders and became clerk of St Saviour's, Southwark. Lowin was rumored to have become an innkeeper. Alexander Goughe worked as a publisher during the Commonwealth. But, perhaps owing to the connections they enjoyed through aristocratic patronage, many sought and received court appointments. George Bryan held the office of an ordinary groom of the chamber (ca. 1603–13), and Robert Goughe was last identified in 1624 as "one of the Messengers of his Majesties Chamber." Around 1637 Joseph Taylor petitioned for the next king waiter's place "which shall void in the Custom House, London," and two years later he was appointed to the office of Yeoman of the Revels.

Quite apart from their professional responsibilities, a surprising number of players managed to distinguish themselves in other ways. John Lowin served as overseer of Paris Garden (1617–18). John Shank became famous first as the author of a jig, which was licensed by the Master of the Revels for performance by the King's Men (*Shank's Ordinary*, 1624), and later he was noted as the composer of at least one song ("Now Chrecht me save, Poor Irish knave"). Not least of all, Richard Burbage was admired as an excellent painter; John Davies of Hereford mentioned him specifically in *Microcosmos* (1603) as a player he admired for painting, and Thomas Overbury reported that Burbage was "much affected to painting." The dramatist Thomas Middleton wrote an elegy for Burbage entitled "On the death of that great master in his art and quality, painting and playing, R. Burbage." Finally, the accounts of the earl of Rutland for the tilt of 1613 contain one particularly significant entry. In the first part Shakespeare was paid "about my Lorde's impreso, 44s." In the second Richard Burbage was rewarded "for paynting and making yt." In the earl's 1616 accounts Burbage was paid again "for my Lorde's shelde and for the embleance, £4 18s." Moreover, there is every possibility that the well-known portrait of Burbage was a self-portrait. Other players from the company whose portraits survive include Lowin (figure 20.2), Field, and Shakespeare. It would be tempting to attribute these to Burbage's hand; however, unhappily, there is little evidence to corroborate such a claim.

Touring

In addition to their ability to mount productions quickly, the players exhibited a flexibility in relation to the arenas in which they performed. The Chamberlain's–King's Men enjoyed a variety of playing places during their history. First were the

Figure 20.2. Portrait of the actor John Lowin (1640). Used by permission of the Ashmolean Museum, Oxford.

Theatre and the Curtain, and later on, the two Globes and the private playhouse in the Blackfriars. Contrary to established opinion, recent research into provincial records suggests that the companies had seasonal homes and that they chose to tour in the provinces both for profit and for reputation, to advertise themselves and create an interest in the company amongst those who might, at some time, travel to London for business or pleasure. Surprisingly, perhaps, there seems to have been no increase in provincial performances during plague periods in London. Consequently, it would appear that James Burbage's chief contribution was in supplying a London home where profits could be increased due largely to the sizable, proximate audience. However, touring predated Shakespeare's companies by centuries and was considered standard professional practice.[13]

The Lord Chamberlain's–King's Men are known to have traveled to Shrewsbury, Ipswich, Oxford, Bath, Faversham, Maidstone, and Marlborough, amongst other places. A few – Oxford and Barnstaple (Devon) – seem to have been regular stops.[14] Although it is impossible to estimate precisely what a company's profits for a summer's worth of provincial performing would be, touring appears to have been lucrative enough to return a sizable profit. When the players stopped in a town, they applied to the lord mayor for permission to perform. If granted, they were generally in residence for several days, earning part-profit from the mayor (in the form of a fee); but additional income was probably derived from the audience who, formally or informally, donated at the door. The players apparently also received bed and board, sometimes from acquaintances. In fact, there is every probability that the players planned their tour routes taking into consideration where they thought that they would be welcomed, where the rewards were good, and where they would be provided for while in residence.

In addition to the town halls in which the players performed, they also stopped at aristocratic households where they not only entertained, but advertised the name of their patron. Thus, wittingly or not, the players became employed as symbols of royal and aristocratic authority, much as they were when they performed at court or at the Inns of Court. In these venues the Chamberlain's–King's Men were well known. During the Christmas season 1594, the Gray's Inn revels included a performance of *The Comedy of Errors*; and John Manningham's diary records a performance of *Twelfth Night* at the Middle Temple in February 1602 for Candlemas. Between 1594 and 1603, the Chamberlain's Men performed at court over thirty times, and, as the King's Men, they performed equally as much in the first five years of their existence. Hampton Court, Windsor, and Whitehall (both the great hall at the palace and the Banqueting House) all saw performances by Shakespeare's company. These included *Othello*, *The Merchant of Venice*, *King Lear*, *The Merry Wives of Windsor*, *Measure for Measure*, *Henry V*, *Every Man In/Every Man Out*, and *The Devil's Charter*. Still, as is so often the case in the record keeping of Shakespeare's contemporaries, the majority of the plays performed were not named by the Lord Chamberlain in whose household accounts the payments to the companies were preserved.

Patronage and Politics

Whether performing on the public stage, touring under their patron's patent, painting for the duke of Rutland, or (like Alexander Goughe) helping to organize surreptitious performances during the Commonwealth, the players were "servants" of many dimensions. Their performances at court or service as grooms of the chamber placed them in proximity to the seats of political power. Nonetheless, whether this allowed the players to acquire political influence has been hotly debated.

Some players were born into families whose names brought social and political connections with them, especially those such as Richard Burbage whose father would have had city and guild connections in addition to those he cultivated with the earl of Leicester and Lord Hunsdon. Such players would have enjoyed a certain personal status that placed them above others of their fellow actors. Another small group of players, such as John Heminges, were granted coats of arms during their lifetime. However, this should not be confused with a company's quest for political favor. Nor should we confuse the political interests expressed in a certain subgroup of Shakespeare's plays (*Henry V* and *Macbeth* are often discussed in this vein) with a company's interest in cultivating and maintaining the pleasure of its patron. Certainly the players were aware of the necessity for acquiring influence. But, apart from currying favor with their patrons, this they accomplished on a local level – in order to secure good will for their playhouse – by serving as minor church officials and contributing significantly to poor relief through their local parishes.[15]

In the larger arena, it is difficult to discuss the political allegiances of the Chamberlain's–King's Men. Some critics have seen their performance of *Richard II* on the eve of the Essex rebellion as an indication that the company was covertly involved in the insurrection, that part of the company's repertory demonstrates a tendency to subvert authority.[16] Others have argued that the grant of the 1603 patent (bestowing royal patronage on the King's Men) placed the company squarely in the camp of conservative authority. Of the two possibilities, the latter is the likelier scenario because, throughout Shakespeare's lifetime (and for some years before and beyond), the players ultimately depended upon aristocratic pleasure for their existence. Although the players performed *Richard II* at the request of Essex's conspirators, Augustine Phillips testified that they had no knowledge of the plot; the players had simply been offered a sizable fee (40s. more than the ordinary amount) and so had decided to take advantage of the opportunity to make some extra money.[17] The formidable panel of judges who examined Phillips accepted his testimony and made no more of the incident.

Additional corroboration supporting the link between the Chamberlain's Men and conservative authority is provided by a connection about which little is known – that between the Burbages and Sir Walter Cope, the long-standing friend and political ally of Sir Robert Cecil. Cope appears early on, in 1589, in the midst of the controversy between James Burbage and his sister over money owed for the construction of the Theatre. Here, another man owed money by Burbage – John Hyde – was approached by Cope concerning a plan for repayment. Cope, acting as an informal mediator in the conflict, was then master of the young Cuthbert Burbage.[18] Many years later, Cope reentered the scene, in 1604, when Cecil put him in charge of arranging for entertainments for Queen Anne at Cecil House in the Strand. Cope apparently had a difficult time locating the King's Men and wrote, in palpable annoyance, to Cecil:

> I have sent and been all this morning hunting for players, jugglers, and such kind of creatures, but find them hard to find. Wherefore leaving notes for them to seek me, Burbage is come, and says there is no play that the Queen has not seen; but they have received an old one called *Love's Labour Lost*, which for wit and mirth he says will please

her exceedingly. And this is appointed to be played to-morrow night at my Lord of Southampton's unless you send a write to remove the *corpus cum causa* to your house in Strand. Burbage is my messenger ready attending your pleasure.[19]

Although it is unclear whether Cope is referring to Richard or Cuthbert Burbage, such evidence establishes the Burbages and their fellows as connected to, and very much at the behest of, established authority.

Shareholding Arrangements

The Carey family seems to have patronized an acting company periodically from the middle of the sixteenth century. Consequently, for some time prior to the establishment of Shakespeare's company, at least several different groups of players identified themselves as Lord Hunsdon's Men, mostly in provincial records. The version of the Lord Chamberlain's Men to which Shakespeare belonged emerged during the autumn of 1594, at the Cross Keys, when they were identified by Henry Carey as "my nowe company."[20]

The company – throughout its existence – was rarely documented, except in the patents of 1603 and 1619, and in the cast lists of some of Ben Jonson's plays. As a result, how the membership of the company overlaps with the shareholding system remains open to some speculation. Because the sharers were those who purchased a share and then received a portion of the company's profits, several types of information can be used to build a larger picture. For instance, those players who served as payees at court doubtless had a financial stake in the company, while the cast lists provide a fuller picture of the company's members. However, no shareholders' agreements exist, and the lists of players in the patents – whose purpose was to identify only the performing members of the company – do not always coincide precisely with the sharers. Also, it is clear that shareholding arrangements changed radically throughout the companies' histories. In their earlier days, when some of the actors resided at James Burbage's Theatre, the sharers doubtless "shared" the expenses of playbooks, costumes, and props; but there is no indication that they also shared financial ownership of the playhouse. (They probably paid rent for using it. Along this line there is some indication that the Chamberlain's Men rented the Curtain for two years.) By 1600, however, the actors had acquired both the privilege and the financial responsibility of the Globe playhouse; and in 1609 seven players became lessees in the private playhouse called the Blackfriars.[21]

Reconstructing the shareholders' arrangements from company membership presents a changing, often incomplete picture. Prior to 1599, company payees included Richard Burbage, William Shakespeare, Will Kempe, Thomas Pope, John Heminge, and George Bryan.[22] By this time conflicts over the lease of the property on which the Theatre stood prompted the players to seek a new site on Bankside. On 21 February 1599 a lease was signed by the same group minus George Bryan (whose share was purchased by Augustine Phillips) and with the addition of Cuthbert Burbage, Richard's brother, who was not a performer but performed managerial duties for the company. Under this arrangement the Burbage brothers retained 55 percent of the profits, while the five player-lessees shared the remaining half. By 1603 the company's circumstances had changed radically. Henry Carey, the players' first patron, had died, and his son George (first Lord Hunsdon and later Lord Chamberlain) had also passed on. Finally, through arrangements that are still not fully clear, a royal patent was issued for the company on 19 May 1603. It named Shakespeare, Burbage, Phillips, and Heminges along with five new members – Lawrence Fletcher, Henry Condell, William Sly, Robert Armin, and Richard Cowley. (It would appear that Thomas Pope and Lawrence Fletcher had dropped out of the company. Pope, who had joined the company after the 1599 lease, was near death. Lawrence Fletcher seems to have been a temporary member of the company, having made his reputation leading companies of English actors on tour in Scotland. There is no reason to believe that Fletcher ever performed at the Globe or was allowed to purchase a share in the company.) Additionally, it is clear that Cuthbert Burbage retained his share even though he is not named in the patent. Moreover, other factors shaped the company's history in unpredictable ways. In the usual course of events it was common for there to be some movement in and out of the ranks of the company, and not all performers became sharers.

By 1606 Augustine Phillips had also died, so the principal actors listed in Jonson's *Alchemist* (1610) were yet a different group: Burbage, Armin, Heminges, and Condell from the old company and John Lowin, Alexander Cooke, William Ostler, John Underwood, Nicholas Tooley, and William Ecclestone as newer recruits. Of this newer set only William Ostler (probably because he had married one of Heminges's daughters) became fully invested as a shareholder within a short time. By contrast, Lowin, who had served in the King's Men since 1603, held no financial interest in the Globe and Blackfriars playhouses for many years, until after the death of Heminges in 1630.[23]

The 1619 patent records the final documentation of the King's Men before the 1623 folio. While it was going through its final stages of authorization, Burbage died, leaving "better than £300 land to his heirs." Presumably much of this was tied up in his shares of the Globe and Blackfriars playhouses. (His brother Cuthbert lived until 1636 and carried on with the company.) Gone from the company identified in 1603 were Shakespeare, Phillips, Sly, Cowley, Armin, and Fletcher. Cooke had died in 1614, leaving Heminges, Condell, Underwood, Tooley, and Ecclestone to continue. They had moved quickly to cut their losses, and the 1619 patent showed the addition of five new players – Robert Goughe, Richard Robinson, Nathan Field, Robert Benfield, and John Shank.[24]

If, as some theater historians have concluded, most of the players either named in the patents or referred to as "fellows," or those referred to in Jonson's cast lists were also sharers, then we would want to add a few other names to the previous lists.[25] However, we can only speculate as to what details finally characterized the shareholders' arrangements. After 1600 it seems that players who were with the company only for a short period weren't allowed to purchase shares, in large part because the physical structures that were the Globe and Blackfriars were at stake, and the company was probably unwilling to risk such a large investment. The lessees who appear to have been involved in these arrangements were few, rather than many; and it is possible that as some of these sharers died, only players who were committed to the company for the long haul were allowed to acquire their "vacated shares," as did William Ostler. On the other hand, it is equally possible that the expense of owning and maintaining the theaters, as well as money laid out for playbooks, costumes, and the rest, necessitated the largest group of shareholders possible. But it is difficult to know which alternative more clearly reflects the company's financial practices.

Acting Styles and Traditions

No overview of actors and companies would be complete without at least a brief discussion of acting as a craft. Even now, following years of studying Shakespeare's plays and the theater, historians are uncertain as to what particular acting style was employed by most players. Although contemporaries honored the memory of Richard Burbage and others of the company by writing commemorative verse, their descriptions convey little substantive information concerning acting. The notable actor – whether Burbage or William Ostler – was simply described as the "Roscius of his age."

Amidst the speculation surrounding this area of inquiry it has been common to display a bias towards Shakespeare's actors, to associate Burbage with a naturalistic, subtle form of performing, whilst it has been customary to attribute more stylized, bombastic features to his rivals. However, as R. A. Foakes has pointed out, the roles played by Burbage contained many features that would lend themselves to a strong, even perhaps slightly exaggerated form of portrayal; and key roles performed by popular actors in other companies often suggest a restrained style of presentation. Therefore, this simple division is probably not the most useful means by which to conceive of the style adopted by Elizabethan actors.[26]

Suffice it to say that a mixture of acting styles, some more stylized than others, seems to have been employed. Thus, the actor's purpose was not to move in the direction of "realism" as we understand the term today, in an age in which Stanislavsky has made such an impact. Shakespeare's actors did not attempt to *become* a character, but to *represent* a character, to convey emotion in such a way that the spectator could relate to a character's joy or grief.[27] Acting was about inspiring the audience.

Moreover, actors' styles seem to have been as individualistic as the actors themselves, and they obviously showcased particular talents. Thus, the "Funeral Elegy" on Burbage noted that he could draw a specific type of sorrow "so truly to the life." "Oft have I seen him," the narrator continues, "leap into the grave / Suiting the person."

But the narrator, invoking many different roles that Burbage played, makes it clear that the roles were not simply the same, but distinctive, the actor "suiting the person." It is understandable, then, that John Davies of Hereford printed an epigram about Robert Armin in which the poet commented that "most men over-act, miss-act, or miss / The action which to them peculiar is." But Armin apparently didn't. He knew what his strengths were and "with harmless mirth / Dost please the world."[28]

The actor's training is, similarly, an area that has generated many conflicting theories. The Chamberlain's–King's Men seem always to have had several boy players in the company, all participating in apprenticeships. While the terms of these apprenticeships are a mystery, it was common for boy players to perform the roles of both women and boys. Still, the specifics of the actor's training are unknown. It would seem that the players studied oratory, though they might not have been put through the same formal rhetorical training – pertaining to oral declamation and physical bearing – as others. Bertram Joseph summarizes: "the speaker who was to express emotion must be able to mime"; and "he had to enable his listeners to experience the literary quality of what was pronounced."[29] The art of miming was, according to some scholars, learned through formal handbooks of gestures, such as John Bulwer's *Chirologia, or the Naturall Language of the Hand* (1644), in which threats are created through the shaking of a clinched fist, or silence is mimed by placing the index finger on the lips. But apart from this, there is no concrete evidence to suggest that whatever shorthand of gestures was employed was copied from printed manuals. Rather, conventions of gesture were probably learned through imitation of the best actors who employed them, a method that allowed the apprentices to learn their craft quickly. Bernard Beckerman reminds us that a quickly changing repertory limited the possibilities for rehearsal, forcing an actor to "systematize his methods of portrayal."[30] This is not to say that acting had the staid, wooden quality that we associate with pantomime, but that some emotional modes might well have been portrayed in a more stylized manner than others.

Although it was not the norm, in Shakespeare's printed texts, to identify the actors – either as a company or in relation to the roles they performed – many dramatists were fastidious about such details. In the 1616 Jonson folio the "principal comedians / tragedians" are identified, as a group, preceding each play in the collection. Webster included actor lists for *The Duchess of Malfi*; Fletcher for *The Captain, Valentinian, Bonduca, The Queen of Corinth*, and other plays in the 1647 folio. Therefore the fact that Heminges and Condell included an actors' list is not unusual, in and of itself.

However, the actors' list in the Shakespearean folio conveys many complex impressions. It is, above all, a memorial record, enshrining the names of key players but in no way characterizing the qualities that made them distinctive. In this, the compilers conferred a sort of "democratic status" on the players, as though performance alone was the reason for their inclusion, and all players were somehow equal. Yet an exploration of issues connected with company organization and management, the qualities of specific players, and their individual careers prompts us to consider the distinctiveness of the actors who comprised the Lord Chamberlain's–King's Men. Certainly, they were, in the parlance of the time, "gentlemen of a company." But, concurrently, they were masters and apprentices, trained and self-made men, managers and investors, servants and politicians. Contrary to the one-dimensional characterizations of Samuel Butler or Sir Thomas Overbury, the player's profession was hardly homogeneous, but richly varied in nuance and detail.

Notes

1   Many theater historians have written about the Chamberlain's–King's Men. See E. K. Chambers, *The Elizabethan Stage* (Oxford: Clarendon Press, 1923), vol. 2, pp. 192–220; G. E. Bentley, *The Jacobean and Caroline Stage* (Oxford: Clarendon Press, 1941–68), vol. 1, pp. 1–134; G. B. Harrison, "Shakespeare's company," in *Introducing Shakespeare* (London: Penguin, 1966), pp. 106–19; Peter Thomson, "The Lord Chamberlain's servants," in *Shakespeare's Theatre* (London: Routledge, 1983), pp. 3–18; and, most recently, Andrew Gurr, "Hunsdon's/ Chamberlain's/King's Men, 1594–1608," in *The Shakespearian Playing Companies* (Oxford: Clarendon Press, 1996), pp. 278–305.

2   David Loades, *The Tudor Court* (London: Batsford, 1986), pp. 3, 6, 17, 111. Suzanne R. Westfall also comments: "The patron exercised ownership over his revels ... which were designed to glorify him by representing his ideas, his wealth, and his artistic tastes" (*Patrons and Performance: Early Tudor Household Revels* (Oxford: Clarendon Press, 1990), p. 2).

3   Linda Levy Peck, *Court Patronage and Corruption in Early Stuart England* (London: Routledge, 1993), p. 17.

4   M. C. Bradbrook, *The Rise of the Common Player* (Cambridge: Cambridge University Press, 1979), p. 18.

5   Bradbrook characterizes the players as being "under the protective shield of their lord's badge, invoking a declining, obsolescent form of service, which was in their case sometimes little better than a legal fiction" (ibid., p. 39).

6   Bradbrook (ibid., pp. 39–95) discusses the "new estate" of Leicester's Men and the construction of the Theatre, together with the controversy concerning the social status of the "common player."

7   S. Schoenbaum, *William Shakespeare: a Compact Documentary Life* (Oxford: Oxford University Press, 1977), pp. 111–17, 200–3.

8   Chambers, *Elizabethan Stage*, vol. 2, pp. 321.

9   Jonson's attachment to a young player, Salathiel Pavy, who performed in *Cynthia's Revels* and *The Poetaster*, is celebrated in an epitaph written by Jonson, "An Epitaph on Salathiel Pavy, a child of Queen Elizabeth's chapel." Jonson states that Pavy, "scarce thirteen," was "the stage's jewel," and that occasionally he played old men.

10 Mary Susan Steele, *Plays and Masques at Court 1558–1642* (New York: Russell and Russell, 1968), p. 107, *passim*.

11 All wills are quoted from E. A. J. Honigmann and Susan Brock, *Playhouse Wills, 1558–1642* (Manchester: Manchester University Press, 1993), pp. 72–5.

12 Ibid., pp. 113–14.

13 For information on touring, see Peter H. Greenfield, "Touring," in *A New History of Early English Drama*, ed. John D. Cox and David Scott Kastan (New York: Columbia University Press, 1997), pp. 251–68; J. A. B. Somerset, "'How chances it they travel?': provincial touring, playing places, and the King's Men," *Shakespeare Survey*, 47 (1994), pp. 45–60, and Sally-Beth MacLean, "Tour routes: 'provincial wanderings' or traditional circuits?," *Medieval and Renaissance Drama in England*, 6 (1993), pp. 1–14.

14 Companies actually seem to have developed a customary circuit. Doubtless more patterns will emerge in the future as the Records of Early English Drama project is able to make additional data available.

15 For discussion of economics and influence during the early years of professional theatre

see William Ingram, *The Business of Playing: The Beginnings of Adult Professional Theater in Elizabethan London* (Ithaca, NY: Cornell University Press, 1992). The intersection between local service and theatrical endeavor is more clearly seen in the histories of the Rose and Fortune playhouses, owned by Philip Henslowe and Edward Alleyn. (See S. P. Cerasano, "Edward Alleyn," in *Edward Alleyn: Elizabethan Actor, Jacobean Gentleman*, ed. Aileen Reid and Robert Maniura (Dulwich: Dulwich Picture Gallery, 1994), pp. 11–31.) Henslowe and Alleyn regularly served as churchwardens in St Saviour's parish; their contribution to poor relief in St Giles's, Cripplegate, became a significant factor in the Privy Council's support of the construction of the Fortune playhouse.

16 For a discussion of the *Richard II* controversy, see Leeds Barroll, "A new history for Shakespeare and his time," *Shakespeare Quarterly*, 39 (1988), pp. 441–64, and Gurr, *Shakespearian Playing Companies*, pp. 288–9.

17 Only the examination of Augustine Phillips is extant amongst the State Papers Domestic (PRO, SP12/278/85). In the "examination" Phillips states that Sir Charles Percy, Sir Joscelyn Percy, and Lord Monteagle came to him and some of the other players to make arrangements for the play. The players tried to talk them out of it, "holding that play of King Richard to be so old and so long out of use as that they should have small or no company at it" (modernized spelling).

18 Chambers, *Elizabethan Stage*, vol. 2, p. 389.

19 Historical Manuscripts Commission, Salisbury Papers, vol. 16 (1604), p. 415.

20 Chambers, *Elizabethan Stage*, vol. 2, pp. 192–3, and Gurr, *Shakespearian Playing Companies*, pp. 278–9.

21 Chambers, *Elizabethan Stage*, vol. 2, pp. 509–10.

22 Steele, *Plays and Masques*, pp. 107–17.

23 Chambers, *Elizabethan Stage*, vol. 2, pp. 328–9, 331.

24 Ibid., pp. 218–19.

25 Gurr, in *Shakespearian Playing Companies*, pp. 303–4, refers to "playing sharers" and so includes Christopher Beeston and John Duke amongst the potential sharers. Yet the distinction between players and sharers is fraught with difficulty. Sometimes wills allow us to identify shareholders, especially for players who died starting in the early 1620s, when shares began to be treated more as property than they had been previously, and so they were often bequeathed to relatives. Unhappily, Duke's will doesn't identify any shares that he might have owned, and Christopher Beeston who, by the time of his death had taken up with a different company, mentions only shares in Beeston's Boys.

26 R. A. Foakes, "Shakespeare's Elizabethan stages," in *Shakespeare: An Illustrated Stage History*, ed. Jonathan Bate and Russell Jackson (Oxford: Oxford University Press), esp. pp. 14–19.

27 For a survey of the spectrum of opinion on this see ibid.; Andrew Gurr, "Styles of acting," in *The Shakespearean Stage, 1574–1642* (Cambridge: Cambridge University Press, 1992), pp. 95–103; Bertram Joseph, "The Elizabethan stage and acting," in *The Age of Shakespeare*, ed. Boris Ford (Harmondsworth: Penguin, 1976), pp. 147–61; David Mann, *The Elizabethan Player: Contemporary Stage Representation* (London: Routledge, 1991); Daniel Seltzer, "The actors and staging," in *A New Companion to Shakespeare Studies*, ed. Kenneth Muir and S. Schoenbaum (Cambridge: Cambridge University Press, 1971), pp. 35–54; Peter Thomson, "Rogues and rhetoricians: acting styles in early English drama," in *A New History of the Early English Drama*, ed. John Cox and David Scott Kastan (New York: Columbia University Press, 1997); David Wiles, *Shakespeare's Clown* (Cambridge: Cambridge University Press, 1987).

28 Edwin Nungezer, *A Dictionary of Actors and other Persons Associated with the Public Representation of Plays in England before 1642* (New Haven, Conn.: Greenwood Press, 1927), pp. 20, 74–6.

29 Joseph, "Elizabethan stage," p. 152.

30 Bernard Beckerman, *Shakespeare at the Globe, 1599–1609* (New York: Macmillan, 1962), p. 130.

21

Shakespeare's Repertory

Roslyn L. Knutson

Every play written by Shakespeare was performed in a repertory of other plays owned by his company, the Chamberlain's–King's Men. And it was this battery of offerings that attracted playgoers. Scholars in the nineteenth and early twentieth centuries had the texts of many of the company's non-Shakespearian plays and knew the titles of more; but they were so concerned with Shakespeare that they assessed the repertory largely on the basis of his plays alone. This bias led them to conclude that the repertory of the Chamberlain's–King's Men was smaller, more upmarket in subject matter and genre, and more attractive to a higher class of playgoer than the repertories of other companies. But issues of size, variety, quality, and audience taste look different when we put Shakespeare's plays where they belong, in a calendar of performances with the rest of the company's annual offerings. From this perspective, we see not only how Shakespeare's plays contributed to the commercial appeal of the company's offerings, but also how the Chamberlain's–King's Men matched and bettered the offerings of other companies.

Unfortunately, we do not have such a calendar of performances; in fact, no records of the company's daily business survive. If Shakespeare had joined the Admiral's Men in June 1594 instead of the Chamberlain's Men, we would have had not only schedules of daily performances but also other details of repertorial management from the diary kept by Philip Henslowe, owner of the Rose playhouse. Henslowe built the playhouse in 1587 and remodeled the interior in 1592. At that time he began to keep a book of accounts, now popularly called "Henslowe's Diary," in which he entered information about companies playing at the Rose. From 1592 to 1597 he recorded the stage runs of companies, including titles of plays, dates of performances, and his receipts at each show (half the takings of the galleries). From 1597 to 1603 he entered payments for expenses such as playbooks and apparel.

There is one moment when Shakespeare's company turns up in Henslowe's Diary: for a ten-day period in June 1594, the newly formed Chamberlain's Men joined with the newly formed Admiral's Men for performances at the playhouse in Newington Butts. Henslowe, recording the event, listed the following performances:

3 of June 1594		Rd at heaster & asheweros	viijs
4 of June 1594		Rd at the Jewe of malta	xs
5 of June 1594		Rd at andronicous	xijs
6 of June 1594		Rd at cvtlacke	xjs
8 of June 1594	ne	Rd at bellendon	xvijs
9 of June 1594		Rd at hamlet	viijs
10 of June 1594		Rd at heaster	vs
11 of June 1594		Rd at the tamynge of A shrowe	ixs
12 of June 1594		Rd at andronicous	vijs
13 of June 1594		Rd at the Jewe	iiijs

Four of these plays – *Hester and Ahasuerus* ("heaster & asheweros"), *Titus Andronicus* ("andronicous"), "Hamlet," and *The Taming of the Shrew* ("the tamynge of A shrowe") – do not appear subsequently in Henslowe's play lists for the Admiral's Men. Theater historians therefore assign them to the Chamberlain's Men, starting with these four to make a list of the company's repertory. Reliable documents such as the title pages of published quartos, records from the court, and allusions to performances in private letters enable us to add the names of several dozen plays not by Shakespeare, and we add the titles of all of those wholly or partially Shakespearian. Conjecture based on substantial evidence provides perhaps another dozen titles. Conjecture based on far flimsier stuff provides another few.

A study of the repertory might stop here, with a partial play list, but the entries in Henslowe's Diary – those for all companies at the Rose, including the run of the Chamberlain's Men and Admiral's Men at Newington Butts – provide evidence on another aspect of the repertory. The entries suggest the mechanics of offering a repertory of plays. Obvious even from the brief Newington entry is that a play was presented nearly every day of the week. Also, the offerings changed daily. Longer sets of entries in Henslowe's Diary reveal more features of the repertory system. A repeat showing of a play might not occur for a week, or a month, or even several months. Plays marketed as new (as a rule, those marked "ne") entered the list of offerings every two to three weeks. Sequels and serials were often scheduled on consecutive days. In a given fall, winter, or spring season (e.g., August–October, All Hallows to Lent, Eastertide to summer), a company might have twelve to twenty-four plays in performance, perhaps one-third of which were new. In a year of performance that included a stint of summer touring but was otherwise uninterrupted by plague or governmental injunctions, a company might have thirty to thirty-six plays in performance, perhaps with nearly half new.

Given a play list (even one incomplete) and the mechanics of scheduling and marketing a battery of offerings, we may evaluate the repertory of the Chamberlain's–King's Men as a commercial entity. In the sections below, I begin an evaluation by dividing the years of Shakespeare's tenure with the company into five-year units. I assemble a list of the plays acquired by the company, based on evidence considered generally reliable. I add to the list conjectural attributions, conjectural continuations of the stage runs of no longer new plays, and revivals. I then suggest ways in which various combinations of offerings from that repertory might have been marketed according to commercial strategies implied in the performance calendars of Henslowe's Diary, strategies I take to have been in use by the playing companies generally in Shakespeare's time. I set these suggested combinations in the context of plays being offered at other playhouses at the same time. I am confident that most of the plays I discuss here were owned by the Chamberlain's–King's Men, because most of the attributions are based on solid evidence, but no doubt some are wrong. I may also be wrong on the chronology. Having no better guide, I assume here that a play was staged shortly after it was composed (for dates of composition of Shakespeare's plays, I rely largely on those suggested in *The Riverside Shakespeare*; for non-Shakespearian plays, I rely on dates suggested by Chambers 1923). I am less confident that the combination of new, revived, and continued plays in any particular season is accurate, because there are no documents on which to base calendars of performance. Nonetheless, I will argue that the repertory of the Chamberlain's–King's Men, whatever the configuration of its offerings in a given season, was crucial to the financial success of the company. The repertory was large and diverse in subject matter and genre; it reflected theatrical fashions and the popular material in the offerings at other playhouses. By thus appealing to a wide range of playgoers, the repertory enabled Shakespeare's company to flourish.

The Repertory of the Chamberlain's Men, 1594–1599

After June 1594, the Chamberlain's Men toured in the provinces and spent part of the winter playing at the Cross Keys Inn before settling down in Shoreditch at the Theatre, the playhouse built under the supervision of James Burbage. The lease on the Theatre expired in 1597, and the company moved to the adjacent Curtain playhouse.

Henslowe's entry for the Newington Butts run suggests that the Chamberlain's Men had already acquired at least four plays: *Hester and Ahasuerus*, *Titus Andronicus*, "Hamlet" (presumably the *Ur*-Hamlet, putatively by Thomas Kyd), and *The Taming of the Shrew* (Henslowe recorded "A shrowe," but theater historians assume that the company played Shakespeare's version). When Shakespeare joined the company in 1594, the company presumably acquired the plays that he had already written: *Titus Andronicus* and *The Taming of the Shrew* plus *Henry VI* (part one), *The First Part of the Contention of the Two Famous Houses of York and Lancaster* (2 Henry VI), *The True Tragedy of Richard Duke of York* (3 Henry VI), *Richard III*, and *Two Gentlemen of Verona*. During the next repertory year (1594–5), Shakespeare contributed *The Comedy of Errors*, *Love's Labour's Lost*, and *Romeo and Juliet*. In the next four years, he supplied *Love's Labour's Won* (now lost), *Richard II*, and *A Midsummer Night's Dream* (1595–6); *The Merchant of Venice*, *1 Henry IV*, and *King John* (1596–7); *2 Henry IV* and *The Merry Wives of Windsor* (1597–8); and *Much Ado About Nothing* and *Henry V* (1598–9).

Three more plays belong to the Chamberlain's repertory list for 1594–9 on the basis of documentary evidence. One is Ben Jonson's *Every Man in his Humour*, the quarto of which in 1601 advertised ownership by the Chamberlain's Men on the title page. The second is *Mucedorus*. Its first quarto in 1598 does not name a company, but its third in 1610 advertises Shakespeare's company, which presumably had owned the play from the start. The third is *A Warning for Fair Women*, which appeared in quarto in 1599 with a title page advertisement of the Chamberlain's Men.

There is some evidence, variously persuasive, that another six plays belonged to the Chamberlain's Men in 1594. The best case can be made for *Fair Em*, which was bound in a volume with *The Merry Devil of Edmonton* and *Mucedorus*, both Chamberlain's plays. *Fair Em*, which has the subtitle "*With the loue of* William the Conqueror" (Greg 1950: no. 113), may be the "william the conkerer" played by Sussex's Men in January 1594 at the Rose playhouse; by that subtitle, it seems further connected to the Chamberlain's Men through an anecdote that attributes a role of William the Conqueror to Shakespeare. The anecdote, told by John Manningham (a student at Middle Temple in 1602), is about a woman playgoer who invites Richard Burbage to visit her after a play and to come in the costume of Richard III. But when Burbage arrives, Shakespeare is already there and (in Manningham's words) "at his game." Burbage learns this when a servant, who had carried his message of arrival, returns with Shakespeare's message that "William the Conquerour was before Rich. the 3" (Manningham 1976: 75).

Weaker cases can be made for assigning *A Knack to Know a Knave*, *Edward II*, *Arden of Faversham*, *Edward III*, and *The Tartarian Cripple* to the Chamberlain's Men. These plays seem to have had some kind of stage life in 1594 or later, yet they do not show up in the repertory lists of other companies (the exception is *Edward II*, published in 1622 with a title-page advertisement of Queen Anne's Men). *A Knack to Know a Knave* was published in 1594 with an advertisement on the title page of its featured performers: "as it hath sundrie tymes bene played by Ed. ALLEN and his Companie. *With KEMPS applauded Merrimentes*" (Greg 1950: no. 115). If Alleyn and the Admiral's Men had acquired the play, it would have shown up in Henslowe's Diary, and it does not. If Kempe had acquired it, he would have passed it on to the Chamberlain's Men when he joined the company in 1594. *Edward II* and *Arden of Faversham* belonged to Pembroke's Men in 1593 (Wentersdorf 1977: 85). Both were printed after 1593, and *Edward II* was still being staged after 1603 (for how it might have moved from the Chamberlain's Men to Queen Anne's Men, see Knutson 1989: 75–8). Because the Chamberlain's Men acquired both players (John Sincler) and texts (Shakespeare's 2, 3 *Henry VI*) from Pembroke's Men, it is reasonable to assume that they acquired other texts from them also. *Edward II* and *Arden of Feversham*, because of their survival in print and on the stage, are likely candidates. The attribution of *Edward III* rests entirely on two suppositions: that the Chamberlain's Men acquired all of Shakespeare's plays, and that Shakespeare wrote some or all of *Edward III*. The attribution of *The Tartarian Cripple* rests entirely on the coincidence of its having been entered in the Stationers' Register on 14 August 1600 immediately after an entry of the

Chamberlain's play *Every Man in his Humour*; the coincidence is heightened by the fact that one of the stationers who had signed the registration of *Every Man in his Humour* also registered *The Tartarian Cripple* (ibid., 78–83).

This list of plays (including conjectural attributions) gives us more insight into the first year of the Chamberlain's Men's business than into subsequent years, simply because we know the titles of more of the plays the company was likely to have acquired from incoming players. We do not know how many of those plays went into immediate production or the order in which the offerings were presented. None-theless, the play list suggests numerous marketing possibilities. To explore those possibilities, I exercise scholarly license below and imagine a calendar of performances for the winter of 1594. By this time the Chamberlain's Men might have brought all of their old plays into performance and added a new play or two. Their schedule might have looked something like the following (I use the calendar format of Henslowe's Diary but modernize the titles of plays for easy reading; I indicate the conjectural attributions from the discussion above in strike-through type):

A conjectural performance calendar, October–November 1594

11 of October 1594	Rd at
12 of October 1594	Rd at Two Gentlemen of Verona
14 of October 1594	Rd at
15 of October 1594	Rd at Comedy of Errors
16 of October 1594	Rd at Titus Andronicus
17 of October 1594	Rd at Henry VI (part one)
18 of October 1594	Rd at Hester and Ahasuerus
19 of October 1594	Rd at Hamlet
20 of October 1594	Rd at
21 of October 1594	Rd at Comedy of Errors
22 of October 1594	Rd at
23 of October 1594	Rd at The Taming of the Shrew
24 of October 1594	Rd at
25 of October 1594	Rd at
26 of October 1594	Rd at
28 of October 1594	Rd at Henry VI
29 of October 1594	Rd at
30 of October 1594	Rd at
1 of November 1594	Rd at Henry VI, part 2 (The Contention)
2 of November 1594	Rd at Henry VI, part 3 (The True Tragedy)
3 of November 1594	Rd at Love's Labour's Lost
4 of November 1594	Rd at Richard III

This calendar – a fictional construct here for the purpose of discussing marketing strategies – gives the company a large repertory with which to start business. That size is not really a surprise. The Chamberlain's Men acquired players from several defunct companies, and they very likely acquired plays along with the players.

This large repertory provides diversity. The three tragedies on the 1594 play list represent two popular formulas: the revenge play (*Titus Andronicus*, "Hamlet") and the true domestic crime (*Arden of Faversham*). In 1595 the company added a third formula, the romantic tragedy (*Romeo and Juliet*), and in 1598 they added a second true domestic crime play, *A Warning for Fair Women*.

The comedies in 1594 and subsequently were also diverse in formulaic materials. *Two Gentlemen of Verona* and *Love's Labour's Lost*, in addition to having Petrarchan motifs, treat the issue of male friendship. *The Comedy of Errors* contributed the frame structure of Greek romance and Roman conventions of mistaken identity and the clever servant. *The Taming of the Shrew* exploited a folk stereotype. The comedies acquired after 1595 provided diversity as well as additional marketing opportunities. *A Midsummer Night's Dream* and *Mucedorus* were pastorals. *The Merchant of Venice* used the pastoral for its love story but city streets for its revenge story. *Love's Labour's Won*, if played in sequence with *Love's Labour's Lost*, gave the company a comedic serial. In 1597–8 and 1598–9, *The Merry Wives of Windsor*, *Every Man in his Humour*, and *Much Ado About Nothing* provided comedies based on the psychology of humors, a new fashion generated by *The Comedy of Humours* in the repertory of the Admiral's Men, 1596–7.

The history plays, likewise diverse, illustrate also the opportunity of the repertory system to market plays as sequels and serials. The set of *Henry VI* plays, culminating in the death of Richard III at Bosworth Field and the triumph of Henry Richmond, illustrates not only the function of chronicle plays as Elizabethan epic, but also the scheduling of the plays as serials (hence my choice in the conjectural calendar above to pair *The Contention* and *The True Tragedy* on the consecutive dates of 1 and 2 November, with *1 Henry VI* and *Richard III* nearby). The *Henry VI* plays anticipated the tetralogy of *Henry V*, which the company acquired from 1595 to 1599. The two parts of *Henry IV* would surely have been scheduled consecutively, like the two-part *Tamburlaine, Hercules, Tamar Cham*, and *Caesar and Pompey* in the repertory of the Admiral's Men. And, like second parts in the Admiral's repertory, the second part of *Henry IV* probably made its debut while the run of its first part continued. The company had additional options, such as carrying over one or both parts of *Henry IV* to play in concert with *Henry V*; and scheduling the prequel, *Richard II*, and the spin-off, *The Merry Wives of Windsor*, to accompany one or more of the trilogy directly about Hal/King Henry.

In the Chamberlain's performance calendar conjectured above, *Edward II* is scheduled on 24 October and *Edward III* on 25 October. This pairing extends the principle of marketing serials on consecutive days to plays with titles that merely sound like serials. *Edward II* and *Edward III* provided also a generic diversity. *Edward II*, like *Richard III* in 1594 and like *Richard II* to be staged in 1595–6, gave the repertory a tragical history. *Edward III* gave it a comical history that was focused as much on wooing as fighting. In this, *Edward III* is similar to *Fair Em*, which gives more stage time to the miller's daughter than to William the Conqueror. A *Knack to Know a Knave*, a moral play starring King Edgar and a knave-spotting "plain man of the country," also mixes historical and comedic material. *Hester and Ahasuerus*, now lost, might have privileged the love story over politics and religion.

In addition, the repertory of the Chamberlain's Men in 1594–9 capitalized on subject matter in the holdings of other companies. The play lists in Henslowe's Diary show these connections in more detail for the offerings of the Admiral's Men in 1594–9 than for the offerings of companies at the Swan and Boar's Head playhouses (for which there are no play lists), but such referencing appears to have been common-place. Some of these parallels are familiar: for example, echoes of *The Jew of Malta* (Admiral's Men, 1594 and 1596) in *Romeo and Juliet* (1594–5) and *The Merchant of Venice* (1596). There are other instances among the history plays. Shakespeare provided his company with the two parts of *Henry IV* and *Henry V* between 1596 and 1599; in 1595 the Admiral's Men gave the first performance of *Henry V*, which received thirteen performances in all from 28 November 1595 to 15 July 1596. If the Queen's Men were at the Swan in 1595 and 1596 (as some company must have been (Ingram 1978: 115–20)), their repertory might have included two old plays known to have been Queen's property at one time: *The Famous Victories of Henry V* and *The Troublesome Reign of King John*. The revival of the former play added to the number of plays on Henry V onstage in 1595–6, and a revival of the latter provided a motive for Shakespeare to have written (or revived) his own *King John* for the Chamberlain's Men in 1596. Still another instance is *The Tartarian Cripple*. The Chamberlain's Men might have scheduled this "Tamburlaine" clone when the Admiral's Men were playing either the *Tamburlaine* or *Tamar Cham* plays, which followed one another onstage at the Rose during the 1590s and probably thereafter at the Fortune (Knutson, 1989: 83–4). There is the appearance of similar subject matter in the Chamberlain's Men's *A Knack to Know a Knave* and the Admiral's Men's *A Knack to Know an Honest Man*. This appearance might have invited the companies to schedule their sequel-sounding plays responsively. To illustrate these possibilities in the conjectural performance calendar above, I schedule *A Knack to Know a Knave* near days when Henslowe's Diary shows that the Admiral's Men were performing *A Knack to Know an Honest Man*.

The Repertory of the Chamberlain's Men, 1599–1603

In 1599 the Chamberlain's Men dismantled the building of the Theatre and erected it on the South Bank as the Globe playhouse. The construction coincided with a period of growth in the theatrical industry generally. The playhouse at Paul's reopened in 1599 (with a company of boys), and the Boar's Head playhouse was enlarged. In 1600 the Admiral's Men built the Fortune, and Blackfriars playhouse reopened (with a company of boys). In response to these events, the Chamberlain's Men apparently did not change their strategy of acquiring a large and generically diverse repertory, keeping up with the latest theatrical fashions, and appropriating popular materials in the offerings of competitor companies. However, they might have employed this strategy with fresh zeal.

Shakespeare's contributions to the repertory were not only new plays but old plays in revival. The new plays included *As You Like It* and *Julius Caesar* in 1599–1600; *Hamlet* in 1600–1; *Twelfth Night* in 1601–2; and *Troilus and Cressida* and *All's Well That Ends Well* in 1602–3. It is likely that *Richard III* was revived; its appearance in quarto in 1597, 1598, and 1602 suggests great popularity. With *Richard III*, the company might also have revived some or all of the *Henry VI* trilogy, the second two parts of which were republished in 1600. Another possibility is *Romeo and Juliet*, the second quarto of which advertised an enlarged and revised text (1599). *Richard II* was revived, but for one performance only. Supporters of the earl of Essex requested that the play be performed on Saturday, 7 February, 1601. The next day, the earl led a rebellion against Queen Elizabeth for which he was speedily executed (Ash Wednesday, 25 February). The player Augustine Phillips, who testified on behalf of the Chamberlain's Men about the event before Lord Chief Justice Popham, claimed that the company's players had protested the choice of *Richard II* because it was "so old and so long out of use that they should have small company at it," but that they agreed to perform it with the guarantee of "40s. more than their ordinary" (*Calendar*, v. 578).

Stationers' records indicate that the following plays were owned by the Chamberlain's Men, 1599–1603: *Cloth Breeches and Velvet Hose*, *A Larum for London*, *Thomas Lord Cromwell*, *Satiromastix*, *The Merry Devil of Edmonton*, *Every Man out of his Humour*, and *The Freeman's Honour*. Less trustworthy documents suggest that the Chamberlain's Men also owned *Oldcastle*, *Stuhlweissenburg*, and *Jeronimo*. Evidence for *Oldcastle* comes from a letter to Sir Robert Sidney in 1600, in which Rowland Whyte says that Louis Verreyken, a Dutch diplomat, was entertained by the lord chamberlain on 6 March with an afternoon performance of "Sir *John Old Castell*" (Collins 1746: ii. 175). The assignment of *Stuhlweissenburg* is based on an entry in the diary recording the visit to London in 1602 of Duke Philip Julius of Stettin-Pomerania, who saw the play in September, presumably at the Globe (Chambers 1923: ii. 367). A quip in the Induction of *The Malcontent* by John Marston, which the Chamberlain's Men acquired in 1603, suggests that a play named *Jeronimo* had been in their repertory (Knutson 1991: 189–90).

To these repertory assignments I make a whimsical addition: a play called *The Labours of Hercules*. I suggest that the Chamberlain's Men acquired such a play to advertise their playhouse, which reputedly had a sign that depicted Hercules holding a globe on his shoulder. In 1600 the Admiral's Men used the marketing strategy of advertising their new playhouse in play titles by performing *Fortunatus* and *Fortune's Tennis*. It is reasonable to assume a similar strategy by the Chamberlain's Men. They certainly acquired plays with witty allusions to globes and worlds (e.g., *As You Like It*: "All the world's a stage"). With a *Labours of Hercules*, they would have had in addition a play that capitalized on the two-part *Hercules* in the repertory of the Admiral's Men (1595–6, 1598, 1601).

Given this list for 1599–1603 (both the certain items and those conjectured), I suggest that the company was continuing to acquire a diverse body of plays with appeal to both existing tastes and the newest theatrical fashions. The new comedies in 1599 and those purchased over the next few years represent a diversity of formulas: *Cloth Breeches and Velvet Hose* was probably an updated estates satire; *The Freeman's Honour* was evidently a guild play like *The Shoemaker's Holiday* (Admiral's Men, 1599–1600); *Every Man out of his Humour* and *Twelfth Night* continued the fashion of humors comedies; *Satiromastix*, like Jonson's new plays at Blackfriars, extended the humors comedy into comical satire. *All's Well That Ends Well* followed the new trend in prodigal plays; and *The Merry Devil of Edmonton* repeated the old motif of magician as matchmaker. In histories and tragedies, the repertory for 1599–1603 likewise shows a mix of old favorites and new fashions. *Julius Caesar* met a long-established taste for Roman narrative (e.g., Admiral's Men: *1* and *2 Caesar and Pompey* (1594–5), *Hannibal & Scipio* (1601), *Caesar's Fall* (1602), and the revival of *Romeo and Juliet* illustrates the popularity of that tragic love story. The soon to be available Shakespearian *Hamlet*, which duplicated the earlier Chamberlain's own earlier "Hamlet," continued the interest in revenge tragedies. One new history in 1599, *A Larum for London*, and one new in 1602, *Stuhlweissenburg*, exploited the general taste for foreign history plays (e.g., the Admiral's Men: *Massacre at Paris* (1594) and the four-part *Civil Wars of France* (1598–9; Oxford's Men: *George Scanderbeg* (1601). Another of the new histories in 1599, *Oldcastle*, and one in 1600–1, *Thomas Lord Cromwell*, show the interest in relatively current political figures (e.g., the Admiral's Men: *Cardinal Wolsey* (1601). With *Henry V*, the company completed a second epic serial. The stage run of *2 Henry IV* might have been lengthened so that it could accompany *Henry V* to the stage; likewise, the run of *Every Man in his Humour* might have been extended to accompany the serial-sounding *Every Man out of his Humour*.

In 1599–1603 the Chamberlain's Men continued to capitalize on popular and fashionable plays in the repertories of other companies. In 1601 Ben Jonson ridiculed public-theater dramatists in *Poetaster*, which was played at Blackfriars. Thomas Dekker, in *Satiromastix* at the Globe, appropriated and twisted Jonson's ridiculous characters into likable pragmatists whose retaliation was more a defense of their profession than personal spite. Scholars have fastened on this instance of repertorial competition, which Dekker himself called a *Poetomachia*, and interpreted it as proof of commercial war among the companies (the so-called War of the Theaters, or Stage Quarrel). However, the competitive scheduling of *Poetaster* at Blackfriars and *Satiromastix* at the Globe is an instance of the now-familiar game of matching and/or bettering others' offerings. In another instance, in terms of revenge tragedies, the Chamberlain's Men had *Hamlet* to offer to playgoers not long after Paul's Boys opened at the playhouse at Paul's with the two-part revenge play by John Marston, *Antonio and Mellida* and *Antonio's Revenge*. Not long after that, the Admiral's Men paid Ben Jonson for revisions to *The Spanish Tragedy* (25 December 1601). And perhaps during this time the Chamberlain's Men played their own *Jeronimo*, which the Children of the Queen's Revels at Blackfriars stole (or cloned).

Still other repertorial competitions occurred with plays on historical figures. One sequence concerns plays on the War of the Roses, if the *Henry VI* plays and *Richard III* were revived (as conjectured here). The sequence runs from 8 November 1599, when the Admiral's Men bought the second part of *Henry Richmond* (which implies a first part), to May 1603, when Worcester's Men made an initial payment for *Shore's Wife*. In the months between, Derby's Men were playing the two-part *Edward IV* (perhaps at the Boar's Head). Even if the Chamberlain's Men were not reviving some or all of their *Henry VI* plays, two were available in new editions in 1600: *The Contention* and *The True Tragedy*. *Richard III* was republished in 1602, and on 22 June of that year the Admiral's Men paid Ben Jonson for *Richard Crookback*.

A second sequence concerns the character of Oldcastle, a spin-off from Shakespeare's serial on King Henry V. The Admiral's Men commissioned a two-part *Sir John Oldcastle* in October 1604; the prologue of the first part specifically reminds audiences that its hero is not the fat knight and tempter-to-riot of the Chamberlain's *1 Henry IV*, which was published in a new edition in 1604. Both parts of the Admiral's *Oldcastle* were registered at Stationers' Hall on 11 August 1600, and the first part was printed that year with a title page advertising the Admiral's Men. The Chamberlain's *Oldcastle* was in repertory in March 1600, when the company performed it at their patron's residence for the Dutch diplomat. Worcester's Men paid 50s. to Thomas Dekker on 7 December 1602 for additions to *Oldcastle* (presumably the Admiral's old two-part text). Behind these activities lies a story – much of which is now lost – about currying favor with important noblemen (Cobham had been lord chamberlain in 1596–7 when *1 Henry IV* first came out) and cloning heavyweight entries in a competitor's repertory.

The Repertory of the Chamberlain's Men, 1603–1608

The plague returned to London in the spring of 1603, shortly after Queen Elizabeth died. The playing companies toured in the provinces during the summer, as was their custom regardless of plague. Sporadic performances were probably given throughout the winter, but officially the playhouses did not reopen until 9 April 1604. In the interim the Chamberlain's Men became the King's Men. But from the point of view of the repertory and our ability to evaluate its competitiveness with other companies' offerings, a more momentous event was Henslowe's decision to "cast vp all the acowntes" of the Admiral's Men (now the Prince's Men) "from the begininge of the world vntell this daye beinge the 14 daye of marche 1604" (Henslowe's Diary, 209), for with that decision Henslowe stopped entering repertorial data in the Diary. Now, for all the companies, we must rely on title-page advertisements, records from court performances, and the odd document to provide repertory information for evidence on ownership and stage runs. This evidence for 1603–8 suggests that the King's Men continued the repertorial practices that had characterized their business and that of the other companies in the previous decade.

From Shakespeare in these years, the King's Men received *Othello, Measure for Measure, King Lear, Macbeth, Antony and Cleopatra, Pericles, Coriolanus*, and *Timon of*

Athens. From other sources they acquired *Sejanus* (Ben Jonson), *The Fair Maid of Bristow, Robin Goodfellow, The London Prodigal, The Malcontent* (John Marston), *The Spanish Maze, Gowrie, The Revenger's Tragedy* (Cyril Tourneur?), *Volpone* (Ben Jonson), *A Yorkshire Tragedy, The Miseries of Enforced Marriage* (George Wilkins), and *The Devil's Charter* (Barnabe Barnes). An account from the Office of the Revels for the holiday period of 1604–5 names a few old plays that obviously were in revival: *The Merry Wives of Windsor, The Comedy of Errors, Love's Labour's Lost, Henry V, Every Man in his Humour, Every Man out of his Humour,* and *The Merchant of Venice.* Other likely revivals are *As You Like It, Mucedorus,* and *Richard II* (Knutson, 1991: 110–11).

Given this list of repertory items for 1603–8 (certain items as well as conjectural), I suggest that the King's Men, as they had done while enjoying the patronage of the lord chamberlain, offered far more comedies each season than history plays or tragedies. Among those comedies, there is a familiar diversity, achieved in large part through revivals: the Lylian comedy in *Love's Labour's Lost,* the Greek romance–Roman street comedy in *Comedy of Errors,* the old-fashioned pastoral in *As You Like It* and *Mucedorus,* the hybrid urban world-pastoral in *Merchant of Venice,* and the humors comedy in *The Merry Wives of Windsor, Every Man in his Humour,* and *Every Man out of his Humour.* Two newish comedies reprise the role of magic figure as matchmaker: *Robin Goodfellow, Merry Devil of Edmonton.* The remaining four belong to the continuing fashion for plays about domestic relations, specifically the prodigal husband and patient wife: *All's Well That Ends Well, Measure for Measure, The Fair Maid of Bristow,* and *The London Prodigal.* The one known new history play, *Gowrie,* shows an interest in the politics of Scotland, specifically the plot by the Gowrie brothers to murder James I; the revival of *Henry V* celebrates again a victorious heroic moment in English history. The tragedies in the King's repertory – *Othello, The Malcontent* – emphasize domestic fidelity in the revenge play, marking a new direction in the genre. (The story of *The Spanish Maze* is anyone's guess.)

An unusually large number of plays appear to have been available for performance in 1604–5. In part, this number is due to the change in monarchs. James I, having lived in Scotland rather than England, had not seen the company's old repertory. Thus for the ten dates at court (from All Hallows to Shrove Tuesday 1604–5), the King's Men could schedule seven old plays confident that the offerings were new to their new patron. Another reason for the large repertory is the long period of interrupted playing. Plays new in May 1603, such as *The Merry Devil of Edmonton* and *All's Well That Ends Well,* were still new in April 1604. Likewise, plays acquired during the period of closure – *Robin Goodfellow, The Fair Maid of Bristow,* and *The London Prodigal* – would swell the offerings, along with plays that were literally new in the fall of 1604, such as *Gowrie.* Also, though it cannot in any sense be considered "new" when acquired in 1603, because of its history with the Queen's Revels at Blackfriars, *The Malcontent* might have remained in repertory in 1604 for the simple reason that the King's Men might not have had time during the plague year to have got back in receipts the money they spent on textual emendations by John Webster and John Marston. In addition to these new and old but not exhausted repertory items, there were plays in revival. Yet the repertory of 1604–5 was not as large as it might have been. *Sejanus*, according to Jonson himself, was new in 1603 but unpopular, and thus soon withdrawn.

In the number and variety of plays about domestic relations, the King's Men joined other companies in satisfying playgoers' appetite for this fashion, but also developed variations. The Admiral's–Prince's Men may be given credit for launching the formula with mythic and folkloric materials in *Patient Grissell* and *The Golden Ass and Cupid and Psyche* (1599–1600). Their two-part *Honest Whore* (1604–5), with the humors of the patient man and the longing wife (according to its subtitle), capitalized on a realism introduced in plays performed by Worcester's–Queen Anne's Men: *How a Man May Choose a Good Wife from a Bad* (1600–2); Thomas Heywood's *A Woman Killed with Kindness* (1603) and *The Wise Woman of Hogsdon* (1604); and the anonymous *How to Learn of a Woman to Woo*, which was given at court on 30 December 1604. The King's Men, having the relatively new *Fair Maid of Bristow* and *London Prodigal* still in production in 1604, and giving both *Othello* and *Measure for Measure* during the winter season at court, moved domestic drama further into realism and tragedy by purchases in the next few years of *The Miseries of Enforced Marriage* and *The Yorkshire Tragedy*.

The presence of *Othello* and *The Malcontent* in the repertory of 1604 anticipates the acquisition of increasingly lurid tragedies. *The Devil's Charter* (1607) owes its connection with the revenge tradition to Marlowe's *Jew of Malta* and also to *Doctor Faustus*, which was revived in 1602–3. Vindice in *The Revenger's Tragedy* (1607) looks back to the Chamberlain's–King's Hamlet and Malvolio (previously onstage at Blackfriars), as well as to Antonio (Paul's playhouse) and the vengeful son in Henry Chettle's *Hoffman* (at the Rose and later at the Phoenix); it looks ahead to the melodramatic revenge plays of the King's repertory in 1608–13.

Gowrie, the one known new history play in 1604, and *Henry V*, the one revival, seem not to anticipate the tragical histories and classical tragedies that enter the King's repertory from 1605 to 1608. The few histories that survive in the repertories of other companies – *Bussy D'Ambois* (Paul's) and Heywood's plays for Worcester's – Queen's (*Sir Thomas Wyatt*, the two-part *If You Know Not Me, You Know Nobody*, and *Fortune by Land and Sea*) – suggest a focus like that in *Gowrie* on contemporary figures, a focus not echoed in *King Lear* or *Macbeth* (the Admiral's Men had had a play called *Robert King of Scots* in September 1599 and another, *Malcolm King of Scots*, in April 1602). Perhaps some of the lost plays by dramatists other than Shakespeare filled this niche in the company's offerings. Shakespeare's *Timon of Athens* and *Coriolanus* continue an interest in portraits of Roman generals illustrated by the Admiral's Men's *Catiline* (1598–9), as do the Chamberlain's own *Julius Caesar* and *Sejanus*.

The Repertory of the Chamberlain's Men, 1608–1613

In August 1608, as in early summer 1603, plague returned to London, interrupting business at the playhouses until the fall of 1609. Indeed, according to Leeds Barroll

(1991), plague had disrupted playing frequently since mid-1605. In 1608 also, the King's Men reacquired the lease of Blackfriars playhouse, a circumstance that no doubt made the closure in 1608 more frustrating. Lacking any precedent for a company's having two playhouses at its disposal, most theater historians have accepted G. E. Bentley's (1948) thesis that the company would divide its time between the open-air Globe (summer) and enclosed Blackfriars (winter), selecting its offerings accordingly: the new plays by true poets would be reserved for Blackfriars; revivals of potboilers and new fillers by hacks would be offered at the Globe. Andrew Gurr asserts that the King's Men were so rich by 1608 that they could afford the "proud, exclusive, and uneconomical choice" to leave one playhouse vacant while they performed in the other (1996: 297). A substantial repertory list can be assembled for 1608–13, but unfortunately it does not reveal how the company used two playhouses or scheduled its offerings.

Much of our information on the company repertory comes from two documents from the court: an account from the Revels Office for 1611–12 and accounts from the Office of the Chamber for 1612–13. The Revels Account provides the following titles and dates of performance for the holiday period 1611–12: *The Tempest*, 1 November; *The Winter's Tale*, 5 November; *A King and No King*, 26 December; *The Twins Tragedy*, 1 January; and *The Nobleman*, Shrove Sunday (23 February). These plays were apparently new in 1611–12 except for *The Winter's Tale*, which was new in 1610–11. The Chamber Accounts provide the titles of the plays given at court in 1612–13, but not the dates of performance. The plays apparently new that year were *The Knot of Fools, A Bad Beginning Makes a Good Ending, The Captain*, and *Cardenio*; those being continued or revived were *Philaster, Much Ado About Nothing, The Maid's Tragedy, The Merry Devil of Edmonton, Sir John Falstaff* (*Merry Wives of Windsor?*), *Othello, Caesar's Tragedy* (*Julius Caesar?*), *The Alchemist, The Hotspurr* (*1 Henry IV?*), and the five plays named in the Revels Account of 1611–12. The revival of *Othello* for the court in 1612–13 was not its first; Prince Lewis Frederick of Württemberg had seen the play at the Globe on 30 April 1610 (Chambers 1923: ii. 419).

Another important repertory document from this period is the diary kept by Simon Forman, a physician and fortune-teller of dubious reputation. In April and May 1611 Forman went to the Globe and saw *The Winter's Tale* (new), a play that he called *Richard the 2* (apparently new), *Macbeth* (in revival), and *Cymbeline* (new in 1609–10). Other new plays in this period were *Bonduca* and *Valentinian* by Francis Beaumont and John Fletcher (1610–11), Ben Jonson's *Catiline* (1611), the anonymous *Second Maiden's Tragedy* (1611–12), Shakespeare's *Henry VIII* (1613), and Shakespeare and Fletcher's *Two Noble Kinsmen* (1613).

Beyond those indicated by court records and Forman's diary, continuations and revivals in 1608–13 cannot be identified with certainty. However, there are clues in the publication of quartos, the popularity of genres, and the interruption of playing seasons by plague. The King's Men had all three reasons to continue *Pericles* into 1609–10 and beyond: a first quarto in two editions in 1609 and a second quarto in 1611 attest to its popularity; its genre of romance was increasingly fashionable; and its maiden run had been interrupted by plague in 1608. Publications of *Mucedorus* in a third (1610), fourth (1611), and fifth quarto (1613) suggest it was revived at this time. Recurrence of plague might have interrupted runs of *Antony and Cleopatra*, *Timon of Athens*, and *Coriolanus* from 1607–8. One or more, if continued into 1609 or revived, might have motivated revivals of *Troilus and Cressida* (Q1, 1609) and *Titus Andronicus* (Q3, 1611). *Romeo and Juliet* was reprinted in 1609 (Q3), and *The Miseries of Enforced Marriage* was printed in 1611 (Q2); either or both might have been revived. *The Troublesome Reign of King John* was also reprinted (Q2, 1611), a possible sign that *King John* was revived. Many scholars think that *Every Man in his Humour* was revised by Jonson in conjunction with his writing of *The Alchemist*. Thus it is reasonable to suppose a revival some time in 1609–12.

Simon Forman's diary entries on *Richard the 2*, *Cymbeline*, *The Winter's Tale*, and *Macbeth* are valuable not only for the names of plays onstage in the spring of 1611 but also for insight into audience taste. Forman's comments suggest that the plays he saw contained motifs long popular, as well as changes in familiar genres. In *Richard the 2*, Forman noticed the folly of Jack Straw in exposing himself to authority, the duplicity of the king and nobles in their maneuvers against one another, and the unjust treatment of the soothsayer; but the fact that the King's Men would acquire a new play on the subject of Richard II suggests that the old genre of historical tragedy remained popular. In this environment, the King's Men might well have revived *King John*. The presence of *The Hotspurr* in the King's 1612–13 offerings at court is further evidence that the taste for chronicle materials continued unabated.

In *Cymbeline* and *The Winter's Tale*, Forman noted the swift turns of plot, the reign of unreason, providential interventions, and the trickster-rogue. These features, characteristic of the hybrid forms of romance and tragicomedy, are present as well in the new comedies supplied to the King's Men in this period by Beaumont and Fletcher (*Philaster*, *A King and No King*), and by Shakespeare and Fletcher (*Cardenio*, *Two Noble Kinsmen*). Of the revivals conjectured above, *Mucedorus* is most like the tragicomedy in its romance plot and pastoral setting. However, the offerings at court in 1612–13 show that the hybrids did not supplant old forms. There was still a market for the comedy of humors as illustrated by revivals of *Much Ado About Nothing* and *The Merry Wives of Windsor* (if it is the "Sir John Falstaff" in the Chamber Accounts). There was also still a market for magician plays, as illustrated by the revival of *The Merry Devil of Edmonton*. Perhaps its stage life was renewed by the successes of *The Alchemist* and *The Tempest*. *The Alchemist* updates the satire of humorous characters with a London setting, and *Every Man in his Humour* complements love comedies of the period in the repertories of other companies: for example, *Humour out of Breath* and *Ram Alley* (King's Revels, 1608–9); *The Roaring Girl* (Prince's Men, 1610); and *Greene's Tu Quoque, or The City Gallant* (Queen Anne's Men, 1611). Two of the King's Men's new plays in 1612–13 – *A Bad Beginning Makes a Good Ending* and *The Knot of Fools* – are now lost, but both sound like they were made of long-familiar materials.

Forman's summary of the plot of *Cymbeline* makes clear that the play is set in a Romanized Britain and a Englished Rome. To the average playgoer, the settings of

Bonduca, *Catiline*, and *Titus Andronicus* must have looked similar. The naming of titles in the Revels Account for 1611–12, which documents performances of *The Rape of Lucrece* ("Lucrecia") and *The Silver Age*, both by Heywood, confirms a continuing appetite for Roman materials (since Heywood wrote both plays, scholars assume that both belonged to Queen Anne's Men, even though in the Revels Account of 1611–12 the performances are attributed to the Queen's Men and King's Men together). *The Silver Age* and its serial pieces (*Golden Age*, *Brazen Age*, and *Iron Age*, 1611–13) complement this Roman material, using myth to tell history. The Chamber Accounts of 1612–13 further confirm the popularity of Roman materials in the King's Men's performance of *Caesar's Tragedy* (presumably *Julius Caesar* in revival).

Forman knew *Macbeth* to be Scottish history, but he liked best the supernatural events: the appearance of the "3 women feiries or Nimphes," the blood that Macbeth could not wash off his hands, the "prodigies" of nature on the night of the murder, the appearance of Banquo's ghost, and the sleepwalking of Lady Macbeth. These details invite a comparison with *The Second Maiden's Tragedy*, in which the Lady commits suicide rather than be ravished by the Tyrant. The Lady appears as a ghost in the scene where the Tyrant steals her body from the tomb; the Lady-ghost reappears in a court scene that features the Tyrant's wooing of her stolen corpse. By its title, however, *The Second Maiden's Tragedy* sounds like the second part of *The Maid's Tragedy*, a pairing that might have enabled the two plays to be scheduled on successive afternoons, as sequels. Unlike the two-part *Knaves* in the Prince's Men's 1612–13 repertory (now lost), the two "maiden" tragedies are not literally sequels, but they share a lurid theatricality and a hysterical morality that is expressed in attempted rape and revenge. *Valentinian* transports these elements to a Roman setting (as does *The Rape of Lucrece* in the repertory of Queen Anne's Men). Other companies had similar materials, as illustrated by *The White Devil* in the repertory of Queen Anne's Men (after 1612) and *The Proud Maid's Tragedy* in that of Lady Elizabeth's Men (1611–12). In the context of these repertory offerings, therefore, the King's Men's decision to revive *Othello* in 1610 and 1612–13 made good sense; its motifs of chastity and revenge not only had not aged, but were newly popular.

By making a list of the repertory of the Chamberlain's–King's Men and imagining configurations of that repertory in seasonal offerings, we cannot answer questions about the commerce of the Chamberlain's–King's Men, such as whether they routinely scheduled serial plays on sequential days, whether they alternated between Blackfriars and the Globe, or whether they attracted a higher class of playgoer than did other companies. But with a list and a sense of the marketing principles of play scheduling, we may agree that the repertory of Shakespeare's company looks very much like the repertories of other companies in size, variety, and distribution of plays by genre; that, like other companies, they acquired plays in fashionable genres; and that they and other companies echoed their own and each other's plays in duplicate subject matter, serials, sequels, and spin-offs. It is therefore reasonable to conclude that the role of the repertory in the commercial success of the Chamberlain's–King's

Men during Shakespeare's tenure was not in its difference from other repertories or in its appeal to a narrow category of playgoers but in the shrewdness of its managers to manipulate the industry-wide repertory system to their own financial advantage.

REFERENCES

Much of the subject matter in this essay appeared first in *The Repertory of Shakespeare's Company, 1594–1613*. I gratefully acknowledge the permission of the University of Arkansas Press to use that information in this essay.

Barroll, J. Leeds 1991: *Politics, Plague, and Shakespeare's Theater*. Ithaca, NY: Cornell University Press.

Bentley, Gerald Eades 1948: Shakespeare and the Blackfriars theatre. *Shakespeare Survey*, 1, 38–50.

Calendar of State Papers, Domestic 1856–72: ed. Mary Anne Everett Green, 12 vols. London: Longmans.

Chambers, E. K. 1923: *The Elizabethan Stage*, 4 vols. Oxford: Clarendon Press.

Collins, Arthur (ed.) 1746: *Letters and Memorials of State*, 3 vols. London: T. Osborne.

Foakes, R. A. and Rickert, R. T. 1962: *Henslowe's Diary*. Cambridge: Cambridge University Press.

Greg, W. W. 1950: *A Bibliography of the English Printed Drama*, vol. 1. London: Bibliographic Society.

Gurr, Andrew 1996: *The Shakespearian Playing Companies*. Oxford: Clarendon Press.

Ingram, William 1978: *A London Life in the Brazen Age*. Cambridge, Mass.: Harvard University Press.

Knutson, Roslyn L. 1989: Evidence for the assignment of plays to the repertory of Shakespeare's company. *Medieval and Renaissance Drama in England*, 4, 63–89.

—— 1991: *The Repertory of Shakespeare's Company, 1594–1613*. Fayetteville, Ark.: University of Arkansas Press.

Manningham, John 1976: *The Diary of John Manningham of the Middle Temple 1602–1603*, ed. Robert P. Sorlien. Hanover, NH: University Press of New England.

Wentersdorf, Karl P. 1977: The repertory and size of Pembroke's company. *Theatre Annual*, 33, 71–85.

22

Shakespeare's Playhouses

Andrew Gurr

The Development of Playing Places

Until 1594 the professional playing groups could never expect to perform in one place for any length of time. They had only recently acquired the use of the large amphitheatres that were custom-built for their use in London. Mostly they toured, performing at inn yards or in the upper rooms of inns even inside London. Settling to perform in one space was not their practice. Even the Queen's Men, during the years when they were England's leading company, from 1583 to the early 1590s, played at four different inns inside the city as well as at all three of the open playhouses located in the suburbs: the Theatre, the Curtain and the Rose.

The inns were an improvement on the places where professional playing first developed. Unlike the free space of a town market, where the stage was open to all, the inns could prevent access to the performance until the customer had paid his or her cash for it. The first playhouses developed that idea, enclosing the stage inside a circuit of scaffolding for seats, where extra spectators could be piled up high. They were built more for the profit that could be made from the auditorium than the new resource of a permanent stage structure that they also permitted. Not until the first playhouses started to become the regular places where the professional companies liked to perform, at the end of the 1580s, did writers begin to exploit the additional staging facilities that the permanent playing places offered them.

The players' own preferences conditioned all playhouse building through this period. Starting from a tradition of touring, and adapting every performance to whatever stage and resources happened to be available, their staging was always simple and portable. Since even in London each play was staged only once at a time, to keep the repertory fresh, they had no use for scenery or other time-consuming property structures to amplify their words and actions. Staging developed only very gradually from touring companies using market-places towards the kind of theatre we are used to now, in roofed structures with the audience seated passively. The desire to move plays indoors manifested itself quite early, in 1596, soon after the professional companies were stopped from using the city inns with their large rooms for winter performances, but it was not until 1609 and after, in Shakespeare's last years of writing for the stage, that his company could start playing indoors. Almost all of his plays, like those of his contemporaries, were composed to be performed on the large open-air stages of London's suburbs, and to be taken on tour every year for playing at whatever sort of stage a local guild-hall or inn might offer.

The Rose

In 1594 two playhouses in the suburbs of London were licensed for two professional companies to use. Both companies were new, and were set up under the patronage of senior Privy Councillors: the lord chamberlain, who was the licenser of plays, and his son-in-law, the lord admiral. They were allocated the Theatre and the Rose to perform in. This was the first time that any playing companies had gained official approval to play at a specific place in London. Up to 1989 information about these first two officially sanctioned playing venues was scanty. It amounted to little more than a few unreliable pictures engraved in panoramas of the city, plus a sketch of the interior of one of the unauthorized playhouses and builder's contracts for two more. The only contemporary picture of the Rose showed it as a tall, narrow, six-sided polygon like a broad tower, taller than it was wide, comprising a circuit of galleries round an open space, with an interior tower or hut jutting forward from the northernmost face and a flag flying from its top. Then in 1989, in a hurried dig carried out before a new office block filled the site, archaeologists uncovered two-thirds of its ground-plan (see figure 22.1). It was not six-sided. It appeared to have been originally a fourteen-sided polygon, later stretched out at the stage end to the north into a form we might call tulip-shaped. In both forms, it was twice as broad as it was high. This material evidence about the structure of the early building which stood on these foundations prompted an immediate and drastic clarification of ideas about London's first playhouses.

The Rose was built in 1587 on marshy land on the south bank of the Thames a quarter of a mile to the west of London Bridge. It adjoined two bearbaiting and bullbaiting houses, the only alternative source of recreation for Londoners to the two playhouses that already existed in the northern suburbs. It had a similar structure to the baiting houses, sharing the three levels of scaffolding for the galleries that gave seating to spectators. The galleries rose more than thirty feet in all to the roof ridge. To this structure the playhouse added only a section of the galleries closed off to make a dressing-room or 'tiring house', with a stage protruding forward from it into the middle of the central arena or 'yard'. In its original polygonal form the Rose measured roughly seventy-four feet in outside diameter, each of the fourteen bays in the timber frame of the galleries measuring ten feet six inches in depth and an average of fourteen feet across (each of the outer walls seems to have been roughly one rod, or

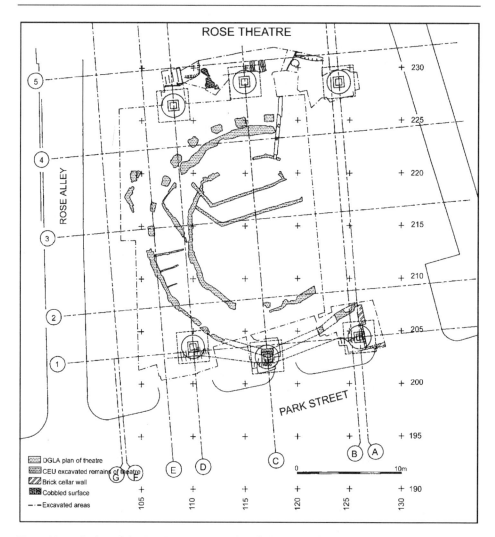

Figure 22.1   A plan of the Rose's remains, as identified in 1989 by English Heritage. Copyright ©
English Heritage 1989.

sixteen feet six inches). The extension, which other evidence indicates was made in
1592, pushed the stage itself back by six feet six inches, providing an extra gallery bay
on each side and extending the yard's capacity to accommodate those who chose to
watch the plays from a standing position around the stage.

The stage itself was tapered, stretching in both its 1587 and its 1592 forms roughly
twenty-five feet (one and a half rods) across the yard and thirty-seven feet (two and a
half rods) to the rear. It was a little more than one rod in depth. The yard itself sloped
downwards from the galleries towards its centre, where a barrel-head provided a sump
for water drainage, probably with an underground pipe to take the run-off northwards
to the river. It was covered in mortar, over which was laid a thick deposit of ash,

clinker and hazel-nut shells, a porous by-product of the local soap factories used for road surfacing. This provided a hard yet dry surface for the standing spectators who had to watch the plays through London's rain. The spectators in the three levels of galleries were sheltered by a roof of thatch, which dripped down on to the standers in the yard when it rained. Entrance to the lowest gallery was from the yard. No evidence has yet been found to show how the wealthier spectators gained access to the upper galleries at the Rose. There may have been an internal stairway, or more likely a stairway built outside the frame, as at the baiting-houses and the northern playhouses, located on the not yet excavated eastern portion of the site. The lowest level of galleries was associated with the yard, and provided shelter (at a price) for the standers, or 'groundlings' as Hamlet called them, when the rain became too heavy. The upper galleries were quite literally superior, used by the wealthier playgoers who could afford a seat and a roof over their heads.

Along with the Rose's foundations, the most remarkable survival from the 1590s is the record of its use kept by its owner, Philip Henslowe. From 1592 onwards he listed the companies that performed there, the titles of their plays, and the takings from their performances. His accounts include both the costs of his rebuilding of the Rose early in 1592 and his later dealings with the company that was licensed to perform there from mid-1594, the Lord Admiral's Men. His so-called Diary (Foakes and Rickert 1961) includes entries for performances of two of Shakespeare's plays, *1 Henry VI* and *Titus Andronicus*. The former, known to Henslowe as 'harey the vj', began a profitable run on 3 March 1592, performed by Lord Strange's Men, who had Edward Alleyn of the Lord Admiral's Men as their leading player. It was played again on 7, 11, 16, 28 March; 5, 13, 21 April; 4, 7, 14, 19 and 25 May, all with very good takings at the gate. It recurred in the repertory up to 1594. *Titus Andronicus* was performed as a new, or as the records put it a 'ne', play on 23 January 1594 by Lord Sussex's company, later merged with part of the Queen's Men. It had another four performances up to June 1594, when along with *1 Henry VI* it was probably transferred to the newly formed Lord Chamberlain's Men, Shakespeare's company, playing at the other licensed playhouse, the Theatre. The new Chamberlain's Men seems to have taken on all of Shakespeare's plays, staging them at the Theatre and its successors.

The Theatre

The first open-air playhouse specially built in London's suburbs that had an extended life was called the Theatre by its builder, the player James Burbage. He chose the name at a time when a 'theatre' was the word not for a playhouse but for an atlas, a book of maps. Burbage chose the name as a reminder of Rome's theatres and amphitheatres, and as a reminder of the classical grandeur that was Rome which he was now trying to re-create in London. That was in 1576, when the professional travelling companies were making their first major attempt to establish a bridgehead in London.

Burbage's design for the Theatre was as prescient as its intended successor, the second Blackfriars theatre. Possibly learning from an earlier project financed by his brother-in-law John Brayne in Whitechapel in 1567, the Red Lion playhouse, Burbage built his own venture as a twenty-sided polygon, nearly one hundred feet in outside diameter – markedly bigger than the Rose – with three levels of galleries, a pair of flanking stair towers for access to the upper galleries, and a covered stage. Its success made its design a precedent for all eight of the other amphitheatres built subsequently in London's suburbs (see figure 22.2). Not all were as big as the Theatre, and some were made square rather than polygonal, but they all followed Burbage's idea of surrounding the stage by ranks of galleries which themselves surrounded and contained the standers gathered in the yard on three sides of the stage. It set comfort and protection from the weather at a higher price than proximity to the players, but it allowed those who could afford the price to be quite literally overlookers of the crowd standing in the yard under the stage. Above all, the two entrances into the yard and up to the galleries made it easy for the players and their landlord to charge for admission. To the travelling companies used to taking a hat around the bystanders in the market-places where they set up their temporary stages, it gave a reassuring air of permanence, and a much more secure source of income.

Figure 22.2   Detail from the Utrecht 'View of London from the North', showing the Theatre on the left and the Curtain with its flag on the right. (University Library, Utrecht, Ms. 1198.)

In the first years of his new playhouse, Burbage hired it out to various travelling companies. They came to work in London for longer periods than the country towns allowed. That gave them stability, as well as the extra custom from London's thousands of playgoers. Performing in only the one place, though, demanded far more plays than were needed for the brief visits to country towns. To keep audiences coming, they had to stage a different play each afternoon. In the early years of playing at the Theatre and its neighbours, once a company's repertoire had been thoroughly exhausted, it had to move on, and take its plays back to the country.

In 1594, however, the Privy Council assigned one company to the Theatre, and their rivals to the Rose, as their only performance venues. The Rose, on Bankside in Surrey, became the home for the reconstituted Lord Admiral's Men, while the Theatre, to the north in Shoreditch, became home to Shakespeare's new company, the Lord Chamberlain's Men. These two nobles, the company patrons, had great power over playing. The lord chamberlain was the official responsible for licensing plays and performances at court. He was secure at court as the queen's cousin. The lord admiral was his son-in-law, husband to Elizabeth's closest friend at court.

The Theatre soon became a problem. It had been built eleven years before the Rose, on land held on a twenty-one-year lease, and it was due to expire in less than three years' time, in April 1597. Its owner, James Burbage, was father to the new company's leading actor, and had ambitious plans for his son's company. Giles Allen, owner of the freehold of the land on which the Theatre stood, refused to extend Burbage's lease beyond its first twenty-one years, so Burbage knew that he would soon have to find a replacement. In 1596, therefore, he bought a set of tenements in the Blackfriars, tore the partitions down and converted the property into a roofed playhouse. Another part of the same building had been used as a theatre before, when the choirmaster of the Chapel Children had built his boy players a playhouse there in 1576. That had closed down after only eight years, but the memory of its wonderfully convenient location probably lingered on. Situated next door to the office of the Master of the Revels, who worked for the lord chamberlain as controller of the playing companies, it was in the centre of the best neighbourhood in town, just below St Paul's, the main gathering place for London's idlers. Its indoor setting made it weatherproof, and it was inside the city walls yet free from the lord mayor's disapproval because it was in an old 'liberty', once a monastic precinct. Burbage constructed it as a smaller version of the Theatre, building curved galleries around the front of the stage, with benches in the pit to replace the standing room of the Theatre's yard, boxes for grandees on each side of the stage, and a central music room plus seating for more grandees on the stage balcony.

No doubt Burbage expected that the much smaller size and capacity of the new Blackfriars could be offset by the higher prices he could charge for this all-seat auditorium and the more affluent clientele in the West End of the city. But he miscalculated, and his long-term patron, the lord chamberlain, whose support was vital for the new move, died in July 1596 before the new theatre was complete. In November 1596 over a hundred of the senior inhabitants of the Blackfriars precinct, including the lord chamberlain's son, the new patron of Burbage's company, sent a petition to the Privy Council asking that the new venture be stopped. On the advice of the new lord chamberlain, who also happened to live in the Blackfriars, the Privy Council accepted the residents' plea. Burbage's capital was now locked into a project he could not use. He died a month later, and in April 1597 when the lease expired, the owner of the land evicted the company. For the next two years Burbage's sons, one of them the company's leading player, had to rent the Curtain to play in.

The Curtain

Burbage's Theatre in Shoreditch, built in 1576, acquired a neighbour in the following year, the Curtain. Ultimately it became the longest-serving of all the playhouses in London of this era, still being used for performances as late as the 1620s. Overshadowed at first by its neighbour, and later by the other amphitheatres in the northern suburbs, it never gained the favour that most of the others enjoyed at one time or another. In 1613 a member of the Florentine embassy in London rated it 'an infamous place, in which no good citizen or gentleman would show his face'. That estimation was made when the roofed halls were in the ascendant and the northern playhouses were getting a reputation as inferior theatres with a 'citizen' or populist repertoire. Similar in structure to its neighbour the Theatre, by the time it had been offering plays for more than fifty years it must have shown its age.

The Blackfriars

By July 1596 James Burbage had purchased most of a large building in the Blackfriars precinct, and largely finished converting it into an indoor hall theater. In many ways this new design marked the beginnings of modern theatre in England. Instead of allowing the poorest payers to stand nearest to the stage, in the yard, it put them at the back in the topmost galleries. Prices rose the closer you got to the stage, a principle followed in all subsequent theatre design. Like the amphitheatres, it grouped its audience all around the stage except for the music room, which was sometimes used for the 'above' when plays demanded one. The balcony had audience seating adjacent to the music room, and the highly prized and highly priced boxes were at stage level on each flank. In addition, it was possible for the most self-assured of the nobles and gentry to enter the theatre through the tiring house, where they could hire a stool and then sit on the stage itself to watch the play.

The Blackfriars stage had similar features to those at the amphitheatres. The *frons scenae*, the wall fronting the tiring house, through which the players entered, had a broad central opening covered by cloth hangings and two flanking doors. Above the central opening, on the stage balcony, the music room doubled as Juliet's balcony. It differed from the Theatre chiefly in the much smaller size of the stage area and in not having the two large pillars which supported the stage cover at the amphitheatres. Unlike the amphitheatres, which at first used their stage balconies only for playing and perhaps for the company's trumpeters, the music room at the Blackfriars could house a full orchestra or broken consort of six or seven musicians. The indoor setting allowed them to play stringed instruments and woodwinds instead of the noisy brass used at the open-air playhouses.

James Burbage's sons could do nothing with their inheritance in the Blackfriars precinct for some time. Eventually they rented it to the manager of a new boys' company. Boy players performed only once a week, under the rather dubious pretence of doing 'private' rather than the 'public' officially licensed performances that companies of adults players were held to. Presumably that pretence allowed them to bypass the objections of the local residents. For eight years from 1600 the boys staged plays once a week, gaining increasing notoriety for the sophisticated satires in their repertory. They ran into several scandals up to 1608, when, during a long closure of theatres because of the plague, their manager surrendered his lease to the Burbages.

The Globe

The Globe was built as an attempt to retrieve something out of the disasters of the Theatre's closure and the ban on the use of the Blackfriars hall playhouse. It grew as the rather despairing outcome of nearly two years of unsuccessful negotiations with Giles Allen to renew the lease on the Theatre. Allen hated playing, and declared that he would pull it down and use its materials 'for a better purpose'. During those years, while Richard Burbage and his company rented the Curtain for their performances, its predecessor stood nearby in what Everard Guilpin called 'darke silence, and vast solitude', a constant reminder of what they had lost. Finally, in December 1598, the Burbages hired a builder to pull down the Theatre and take its framing timbers to be reconstructed on Bankside, on a site which they were optimistic enough to lease for thirty-five years instead of the twenty-one their father had taken for the Theatre. The reconstructed playhouse became the Globe. Allen took them to court, but never retrieved his lost timbers.

The Globe's name was a logical extension of its predecessor, the Theatre. In its three-dimensional form an atlas or 'theatre' of the world was indeed a globe, and just as the stage was said to mirror the world, so the theatre of the world could become a globe. Iconic images were a constant feature of Elizabethan decoration. In 1613 the earl of Rutland commissioned Shakespeare to devise an 'impresa' or badge for his role in a court tourney, and paid Richard Burbage to paint it for him. A similar assemblage of skills probably generated the Globe's 'impresa', an image of Hercules carrying the Globe on his shoulders. Depicted on its flag, and in the decoration on the stage's *frons scenae*, the impresa of Hercules and his globe prompted the three references that Hamlet makes to it, contrasting himself to the mythical man of action Hercules, and actually calling the throbbing head on his own shoulders 'this distracted globe'.

The Globe's basic structure was predetermined by the massive oak framing timbers taken from the old Theatre. A twenty-sided polygon, its circumference was twenty rods, or three hundred and thirty feet, its outside diameter almost one hundred feet (see figure 22.3). It had three levels of galleries, its twenty main outer posts each made from an oak tree trunk trimmed off into a twelve-inch square section, weighing two tons and rising thirty-two feet vertically to the top of the outer walls. Inside, the galleries were stepped forward, or juttied, so that each level overhung the one beneath it. The lowest of its vertical posts on the inside was eleven feet high, the next ten, and the highest nine. This timber frame was fitted on a foundation wall made of brick. The lowest of the timbers were thick wooden beams or groundsills which provided the structure's damp course. All the framing timbers were made of oak, each beam

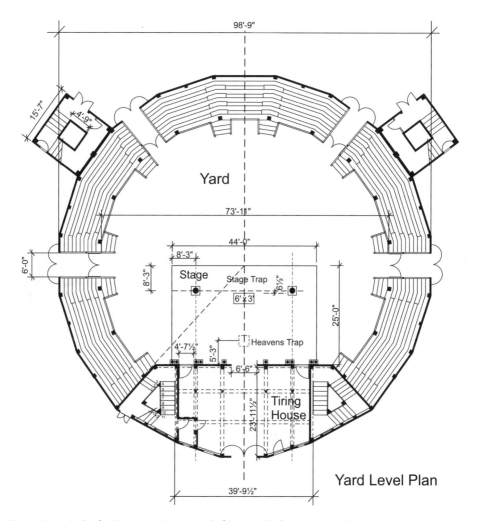

Figure 22.3 A plan by Pentagram Design Ltd of the new Globe in Southwark at ground level. For safety reasons, it has extra entry ways for modern audiences. Used by permission of Pentagram Design Ltd.

locked into its neighbour by mortise and tenon joints held with elm pegs. The walls were infilled with panels of lath and plaster. The circuit of galleries was roofed with thatch, so that all the audience who bought seats were protected from London's rain. Inside the galleries the yard had a one-in-ten slope towards the centre, where an underground wooden pipe took water out of the building northwards, as at the Rose. The yard's mortar surface was, like the Rose, covered in a mix of ash, clinker and hazel-nut shells. Conveniently porous, the same mix was used to surface the local roads, trampling down into a hard core which freed the passageways from London's pervasive mud.

Unlike the Rose's, the Globe's stage was positioned like its adjacent and expensive seating for the nobles and gentry with its back to the sun. Ultra-violet light is as damaging to expensive clothing of silk or satin as is rain. The players, who invested more of their capital in their costumes than in their playbooks, needed to play in shadow. Henslowe built the Rose's stage facing south, but the Globe's, by facing north, helped the players economically by preserving their costumes from damage by the sun. The Globe's stage cover, or 'shadow', had a gable-fronted thatched ridge running out into the middle of the yard from the gallery ridge at the back of the tiring house. This 'hut', with its triangular gable front, housed the chambers or cannon used in plays like *Henry V, Hamlet* and *Henry VIII*. It was an ember from a celebratory cannon-shot during a performance of the new *Henry VIII* in July 1613 that set the gallery thatch alight, and burned the first Globe down. Its replacement, built in a much more costly fashion, was roofed in tiles and had not one but two gables across the front of its stage cover, presumably fronting a wider storage area above the 'heavens' to allow larger and more elaborate devices to be flown from the trap in the painted and gilded surface of the stage ceiling.

Pairing off the Globe and Blackfriars

By 1613 Shakespeare's company, now the King's Men, had far greater ambitions than they were able to afford when they built the cut-price first Globe in 1599. From 1608, they had two playhouses, the Globe and the Blackfriars. With the arrogance that went with being the country's leading players, they chose, in spite of a distinct shortage of good playhouses, to keep both for their own use. They played in the open-air Globe throughout the summer, leaving it empty through the months of cold and shorter daylight. For the winter season they played at the indoor Blackfriars. Through the summer the court and most of the gentry, including London's large and affluent population of lawyers, lived out of town. They did this partly because country estates were more pleasurable in the warmer weather, and partly because the warmer conditions of summer encouraged the bubonic plague bacillus, carried by a rat flea, to flourish in well-populated areas like London.

Gradually plays staged in summer at the Globe began to cater for the citizenry who could not afford lengthy escapes from town, while the innovatory plays in the repertory were kept for the Blackfriars and for the long season of Christmas celebrations at court. Under King James the court expected to enjoy their Christmas plays in the festivities that ran from soon after Michaelmas (the end of October) until the general close-down in Lent (the six weeks up to Easter). Since the Master of the Revels chose the plays for the court out of the current repertory of the leading companies, they had to plan their schedule so that their new plays were available for the master to choose from throughout the fall. From 1615 onwards the master only ever chose plays for performance at court that came from the indoor playhouses. The King's Men at the Blackfriars rarely supplied the court with less than 50 per cent of its performances each season. Gradually the open-air playhouses in the northern suburbs, the Fortune and the Red Bull, and to a large extent the Globe as well, came to be thought of as the standard venues for the citizenry, not for the gentry. The plays and perhaps the acting styles came to vary accordingly.

The Plays Written for Specific Playhouses

While the playwrights certainly wrote with specific stage conditions and even specific playhouses in mind, the expectation that plays would go on tour and therefore have to be staged in any venue must always have conditioned what they wrote. For a short time, from the late 1580s until 1594, the availability of custom-built playhouses seems to have broadened their ambitions. Plays written in this period, including Shakespeare's, were delivered to the players with high expectations of the facilities available for their staging. After 1594, Shakespeare's own ambitions seem to have become more modest, staging practices standardized, the other writers also began to show more modest expectations. The chief variations the writers put into their texts seem to reflect much less any differences in the stage's features of the playhouses than what they thought the audiences at the different kinds of playhouse would expect. Jonson's plays vary according to whether he was writing for the Chamberlain's Men at the Curtain and the Globe or for the Blackfriars boys' company at their indoor playhouse. *Cynthia's Revels* and *Epicene*, written for the Blackfriars, differ from *Every Man Out of his Humour*, *Sejanus* and *Volpone*, written for the Globe, as much by their verbal witplay and their prose as in any distinct requirements laid down by the smaller stages. *The Alchemist*, written for the adult company on their arrival at the Blackfriars, featured special games to mark the innovation. Middleton wrote one kind of play for the Paul's Boys, a rather different kind for the Blackfriars Boys, and plays demanding different staging again for the King's Men and the other adult companies. They all, however, seem to reflect the standardized tastes of the audiences at each playhouse rather than any variation in the possible forms of staging. Behind every new play was the expectation that it had to be portable, and might have to be staged in a wide variety of different locations.

Some plays, notably Shakespeare's and Jonson's, were certainly written with one playhouse chiefly in mind. They provide good evidence that their writers wanted the players to use the specific features in their staging. But so many of the other plays also written for such venues have been lost that it is not easy to see just how specific or localized Shakespeare's and Jonson's expectations really were. A clear majority of the plays written for the stages through this period have not survived, either in print or in manuscript. Philip Henslowe's records list all the plays performed at the Rose between 1592 and 1597, and a selection of later plays, barely one-third of which have survived. Of the plays performed by Shakespeare's company from 1594, even fewer have come down to us.

For a play to get into print was still rare, and gave only a marginal source of income to its sponsors. Most of the plays that were staged, especially in the earlier years, have disappeared without trace. A letter from Sir John Harington tells of one such play. Writing to his friend Thomas Sutton on 5 February 1610, he expressed regret at the miserable end of an enemy of Sutton's: "that he should dye in such miserie as ys reported, under the arrest of the sheriffs baylfes; and that in his life tyme hee should bee played uppon the stage soe extreme scornfully" (Harington 1930: 140). The stage censor made it an offence to have any living man mocked onstage, but it certainly happened. The victim in this case was a man called Sir John Skinner, whose mishaps survive only in legal papers, and whose brief fame in the playhouses has left no more record than this reference to the play that mocked him. Many others besides the one that scorned him on the stage have vanished.

One set of unique records does survive, about the plays that may have been written for staging at the Rose theatre, in Philip Henslowe's Diary. Once the Rose had been designated by the Privy Council as the official place for the Lord Admiral's Men to perform their plays in London, in the summer of 1594, they ran an intensive programme of plays there. As owner of the Rose and later the company's financial manager, Henslowe's so-called Diary gives tangible evidence for the work his tenant company did at the Rose. In the month of November 1594, for instance (Foakes and Rickert: 25–6), they staged twenty-five performances of thirteen different plays, on every afternoon of the week except Sundays. *A Knack to Know an Honest Man*, which opened on 22 October, had its third performance on 1 November, and was offered three more times, on 7, 21 and 29 November. *Caesar and Pompey* was staged for the first time that month. It appeared three times, on 8, 14 and 25 November. Another new play, *Diocletian*, appeared twice, on 16 and 22 November. In addition to these innovations the first part of *Tamburlaine* appeared twice, on 4 and 27 November, *Faustus* on 5 and 20 November, and four other plays also twice. Four were given a single performance. Considering that the same players performed in every play, this was a considerable feat of productivity.

Charges for new plays seem to have been higher than for repeats, because they almost always brought in more money. On average the company introduced one or two a month to the repertory. All but a few of the favourites, most notably Marlowe's two *Tamburlaine* plays, *Faustus* and *The Jew of Malta*, generated less and less income as their runs continued. Takings for the fourth performance of *A Knack* were less than one-third of its first November performance. Two-part plays were quite popular, and were usually staged together in sequence, although *1 Tamburlaine* appeared much more frequently than its sequel.

Shakespeare wrote plays for staging at the Rose, the Theatre, the Curtain, the Globe and finally the Blackfriars. Generally his demands for props and stage features were minimal, certainly less than the few other playwrights known to have written for the Globe while he was in the company and whose texts have survived. For some of the earlier plays, notably *Titus Andronicus* and *Romeo and Juliet*, he used the stage balcony and a trapdoor. Few of the later plays were as demanding, although *Hamlet* does need a stage trapdoor for the ghost's initial entry and for Ophelia's grave. Not until *Antony and Cleopatra* in 1608, with Antony's monument, and *Cymbeline* in 1609 or 1610, when he asked for a flight by Jupiter from the stage 'heavens', did he make many demands of the Globe stage's resources. *The Tempest*, an even later play, demands a flight for Juno in the masque, and makes substantial use of the Blackfriars musicians.

The known repertory of Shakespeare's company is far smaller than its actual range of plays. In its first twenty years the company staged at least thirty-eight of Shakespeare's plays (*Timon of Athens* is the only doubtful candidate from the thirty-six in the First Folio, plus *Pericles*, which was omitted from that edition, and the lost *Cardenio*). Forty other plays are known, by Ben Jonson, Barnabe Barnes, Beaumont and Fletcher, and several unknown authors. Only twenty-five of these plays survive in print or in manuscript (see Knutson 1991: 179–209). The reality was far more crowded than we can tell today from the few survivors of this experience. In the rush of such repertories, with a change of play daily on six days of each week, the first performers can have taken little note of the careful details about staging which subsequent centuries of editors have taken so much trouble to supply in place of the cryptic stage directions of the original texts.

Visible Audiences and Metatheatrical Staging

The use of artificial lighting, whether to illuminate the stage or the audience, is a relatively new feature of theatres and of playgoing. In Shakespeare's time the theatres all used natural daylight. Even the enclosed playhouses performed their plays in the afternoons. The principal effect of this was to emphasize the fact that the whole exercise was a game of deceit. In broad daylight it was not easy to forget that the player now posing as Hamlet had died yesterday as Brutus in *Julius Caesar*. However costly the king's dress, the crown on his head was visibly no more than a gilded wooden O. Only the least sophisticated in such audiences, standing amongst their fellows in the playhouse yard by taking time off from their day's work, could forget that what they were watching was an illusion, a pretence. The pulpits insisted that illusion was the devil's chief instrument, and the use of illusion as deceit became a major part of the religious indictment against plays and playgoing. Many of the playwrights, Shakespeare above all, insisted on the 'metatheatrical' character of their work by including devices like the 'play within the play' and breaking the realistic mode of presentation that generated the illusionism which so many commentators openly feared.

It might almost be said that staging in Shakespeare's time was not just less realistic but positively anti-realistic. The players had every reason not to seek much of the illusionism on which modern cinema is based. Playgoers could be credulous about the stories depicted on stage, yet some of them openly preferred plays done by companies of boy actors to those of the adults. Part of that preference came from their suspicion of illusionism, along with the fact that boys playing men (or women) could not so readily be mistaken for real people as could adult players.

Elizabethan credulity over realism on the early stages is an elusive concept. There is evidence for the popularity of 'theatre of enchantment', the illusive art of spectacle, that prevailed well beyond the 1590s, alongside the new 'theatre of estrangement' which began to exploit its own metatheatricality, like Brecht's alienation effect, his *Verfremdungseffekt*, in the early seventeenth century. *Faustus* was exciting to the more ignorant in its audiences chiefly because it put on show the terrifyingly real prospect of being dragged down to hell. Anecdotes about the actors in *Faustus* finding too many devils onstage and spending the night in prayer, and Middleton's claim that a frightened man 'had a head of hayre like one of my Divells in Dr. Faustus when the old Theater crackt and frighted the audience' (*The Black Book*, ed. A. H. Bullen, in *Works*, viii. 13), indicate the tension that such subjects could generate. The court room at the trial of Ann Turner, the alleged witch who Frances Howard employed to get poisons, gave even a gentrified audience a similar fright when the court room's timbers creaked. William Prynne (*Histriomastix* (1633), fo. 556) gleefully cited 'the visible apparition of the Devill on the Stage at the Belsavage Playhouse, in Queen Elizabeth's dayes (to the great amazement both of the actors and spectators) while they were there prophanely playing the History of Faustus (the truth of which I have heard from many now alive who well remember it) there being some distracted with that fearful sight'. According to Samuel Rowlands (*The Knave of Clubs* (1609), p. 29), when Edward Alleyn played Faustus at the Rose, he took out an insurance by wearing a cross round his neck. Such a public token acknowledged the fear that God might punish the deceptions of the stage. That fear remained a constant pressure on writers and players and on audiences. It put a heavy emphasis on the need for overt metatheatricality in the performances.

The preference of the more educated in Shakespeare's time for boy companies over adult players may have been not just social snobbery but suspicion of stage realism. The history of boy playing in Tudor times is a long one. Its roots were in the new grammar school system, when schoolmasters staged plays to teach their pupils how to speak in public. Choirmasters used their songsters to entertain their patrons and the court. In the later sixteenth century some of them began to offer their productions to a wider market, and at the end of the century two companies of boys, set up for plainly commercial profit, became a new feature of London playing. This kind of playing, respectable in its school origins and using what were claimed to be 'private' playhouses, free from the controls that the Master of the Revels exercised over the adult companies, was for a time in serious competition with the adult companies amongst the richer patrons of the stage. It was anti-realistic because boys could not be confused with real people. But their more emblematic playing survived for only a few years, as the fear of illusion gradually ebbed, and the more realistic mode began to triumph with the rise of the adult companies. The fear of playing as devilish deception was never far out of any audience's mind, however. The suspicion of illusion was another part of the reason why the playing companies kept their plays portable, and never went to the trouble and expense of stage scenery and deep illusionism. Stage costumes which advertised that the actors were playing roles well above their own social status were bad enough, attracting diatribes about their deceptions and counterfeiting from pulpits all over London. They performed in daylight, and their audiences were never expected to forget where they were, in daylight amongst thousands of other Londoners, standing in the rain to watch a game of obvious pretence.

References and Further Reading

Astington, John 1985: Descent machinery in the playhouses. *Medieval and Renaissance Drama in English*, 2, 119–33.

Berry, Herbert 1986: *The Boar's Head Playhouse*. Washington, D.C.: Folger Shakespeare Library.

—— 1987: *Shakespeare's Playhouses*. New York: AMS Press.

Berry, Herbert (ed.) 1979: *The First Public Playhouse: The Theatre in Shoreditch 1576–1598*. Montreal: McGill–Queen's University Press.

Carson, Neil 1978: John Webster: the apprentice years. *Elizabethan Theatre*, 6, 76–87.

Dutton, Richard 1989: Hamlet, An Apology for Actors, and the sign of the Globe. *Shakespeare Survey*, 41, 35–43.

Foakes, R. A. 1985: *Illustrations of the English Stage 1580–1642*. Stanford, Calif.: Stanford University Press.

Foakes, R. A. (ed.) 1978: *The Henslowe Papers*, 2 vols. London: Scolar Press.

Foakes, R. A. and Rickert, R. T. (eds) 1961: *Henslowe's Diary*. Cambridge: Cambridge University Press.

Gurr, Andrew 1988: Money or audiences: the impact of Shakespeare's Globe. *Theatre Notebook*, 42, 3–14.

—— 1996: *The Shakespearian Playing Companies*. Oxford: Clarendon Press.

Gurr, Andrew and Orrell, John 1989: What the Rose can tell us. *Antiquity*, 63, 421–9.

Harington, Sir John 1930: *Letters and Epigrams*, ed. Norman Egbert McClure. Philadelphia: University of Pennsylvania Press.

Hildy, Franklin J. 1991: *New Issues in the Reconstruction of Shakespeare's Theater*. New York: Peter Lang.

Ingram, William 1992: *The Business of Playing: The Beginnings of the Adult Professional Theater in Elizabethan London*. Ithaca, NY: Cornell University Press.

Knutson, Roslyn Lander 1991: *The Repertory of Shakespeare's Company, 1594–1613*. Fayetteville, Ark.: University of Arkansas Press.

Loengard, Janet 1984: An Elizabethan lawsuit: John Brayne, his carpenter, and the building of the Red Lion playhouse. *Shakespeare Quarterly*, 35, 298–310.

Middleton, Thomas 1885: *Works*, ed. A. H. Bullen, 8 vols. London: John C. Nimmo.

Orrell, John 1977–8: The London stage in the Florentine correspondence, 1604–1618. *Theatre Research International*, 3, 155–81.

—— 1982: *The Quest for Shakespeare's Globe*. Cambridge: Cambridge University Press.

—— 1985: *The Theatres of Inigo Jones and John Webb*. Cambridge: Cambridge University Press.

—— 1988: *The Human Stage: English Theatre Design, 1567–1640*. Cambridge: Cambridge University Press.

Rutter, Carol Chillington (ed.) 1984: *Documents of the Rose Playhouse*. Manchester: Manchester University Press.

Wickham, Glynne 1959–81: *Early English Stages 1300–1660*, 3 vols. London: Routledge.

23

Licensing and Censorship

Richard Dutton

KING.	Have you heard the argument? is there no offense in't?
HAMLET.	No, no, they do but jest; poison in jest – no offense i'th'world.
KING.	What do you call the play?
HAMLET.	'The Mouse-trap.' Marry, how? tropically: this play is the image of a murther done in Vienna; Gonzago is the duke's name, his wife, Baptista. You shall see anon. 'Tis a knavish piece of work, but what of that? Your Majesty, and we that have free souls, it touches us not.

(Hamlet, III. ii. 232–42[1])

Hamlet plays many roles, several of them quite explicitly theatrical, including that of Master of the Revels. He determines that the actors shall play *The Murder of Gonzago* at court, and when Claudius shrewdly suspects that it may contain 'offense' (i.e., offensive material), he assures him that it contains 'no offense i'the'world' (i.e., no crime of any sort) – because the poisoning it depicts is only fictional, not the real thing. It is a sophisticated piece of quibbling, going to the heart of the role of the Master of the Revels, the key figure in the licensing and censorship of professional drama in the time of Shakespeare and down to the closing of the theatres in 1642.

He was primarily an official in the lord chamberlain's office, charged with providing suitable entertainment at court. When Theseus in *A Midsummer Night's Dream* demands a 'play / To ease the anguish of a torturing hour' (V. i. 36–7), Philostrate is on hand as his 'usual manager of mirth' (line 35).[2] Yet he can only outline a sorry list of options for the wedding night. As Theseus warms to *Pyramus and Thisbe*, Philostrate insists: 'It is not for you. I have heard it over, / And it is nothing, nothing in the world' (lines 77–8). That is, he has done his proper job as Master of the Revels – he has seen a dress rehearsal of the production and knows it is not fit for the court. In the real world, it would not even have been on a list of options, but in the freedom of comedy Theseus insists, 'never anything can be amiss, / When simpleness and duty tender it' (lines 82–3). If we strip away the fictional packaging, Shakespeare is obliquely addressing his own situation as a commoner in a troupe of 'mechanicals', frequently called upon to play before royalty, but at all times required to attest 'simpleness and duty' (Wilson 1993).[3] The structure of licensing and censorship that grew up around the Master of the Revels was precisely one that enabled professional actors to become adjuncts of the court and aristocracy, while also providing them with a relatively stable environment within which they could ply their trade for a more diffuse audience in the public theatres.

In 1581 the queen gave the serving master, Edmond Tilney, a special commission, which authorized him:

> to warne commaunde and appointe in all places within this our Realme of England, as well within francheses and liberties as without, all and every plaier or plaiers with their playmakers, either belonging to any noble man or otherwise, bearinge the name or names of using the facultie of playmakers or plaiers of Comedies, Tragedies, Enterludes or whatever other showes soever, from tyme to tyme and at all tymes to appeare before him with all such plaies, Tragedies, Comedies or showes as they shall in readines or meane to sett forth, and them to recite before our said Servant or his sufficient deputie, whom we ordeyne appointe and aucthorise by these presentes of all suche showes, plaies, plaiers and playmakers, together with their playing places, to order and reforme, auctorise and put downe, as shalbe thought meete or unmeete unto himself or his said deputie in that behalf. (Chambers 1923: iv. 285–7)

He was also given powers to enforce this authority.

This commission was the basis of what became Tilney's role as licenser and censor of the professional theatre in the London region. Some scholars have seen it as a next step towards absolute state control of players and playing, in the wake of concerted efforts in the provinces to eradicate the mystery cycles and other religious drama closely associated with Roman Catholicism (Wickham 1959–81: ii. 1. 94). But W. R. Streitberger (1978) has shown that Tilney was given these powers specifically to aid him in his primary role as the provider of theatrical entertainment at court, and the social dynamics which governed the control of professional theatre in London were actually very different from those operating in other spheres of early modern life. Prior to his appointment (in 1579), the Office of the Revels had been in disarray: it was expensive to run, some of the shows it sponsored were not satisfactory, and there were problems with the aristocrats who patronized acting companies competing to have their own 'servants' perform at court. The commission was aimed at dealing with the first two problems, by drawing on what was still a relatively recent resource – a professional theatre industry semi-permanently resident in London, signalled by purpose-built theatres like the Red Lion (1567), the Theatre and the Curtain (both 1576).

Tilney's commission gave him the power to compel these troupes to rehearse their repertoire before him, with a view to the most satisfactory pieces being performed at court during the festive season. Until 1607 he had capacious quarters in the old palace of St John's, where, as Thomas Heywood recalled in *An Apology for Actors*, 'our Court playes have been in late daies yearely rehersed, perfected, and corrected before they come to the publike view of the Prince and the Nobility'. The quality of drama at court duly improved, and it was provided more economically than hitherto. The problem of competition at court between influential patrons of the actors was largely resolved for a decade in 1583 by a decision to create a new royal troupe, the Queen's Men (Gurr 1996: 196ff). Tilney was instructed to create this élite company, drawing on players from existing companies; it was clear that they were specifically subject to his authority, and they received the lion's share of performances at court over the next several years.

Tilney, however, remained only one figure in a complex array of authorities. The key competing authorities in respect of the theatres were, on one side, the court itself, usually represented by the Privy Council: one member, the lord chamberlain, had a particular brief for acting matters, though Lord Admiral Howard (Tilney's patron) also took a particular interest in them; and on the other side, the City of London, variously represented by its lord mayor, its Common Hall, Court of Common Council and Court of Aldermen. The received picture of this competition has it that the court staunchly supported the actors, while the Puritan-inclined city resented their presence and tried to put them out of business. But this is misleading. The court was only ever interested in supporting actors patronized by its own senior members, often regarding their commercial activities as in effect rehearsals for performance before the queen; it readily followed Parliament in stigmatizing unlicensed actors as rogues and vaga-bonds. In the city there were legitimate concerns about the maintenance of order and the threat of disease (which the Privy Council sometimes shared), as well as the promotion of crime and lewd behaviour; but there was also a shrewd sense that these enterprises could be licensed and so taxed to support the hospitals for the poor and diseased (Ingram 1992: 119–49). At times negotiations between the parties boiled down to a contestation over their respective prerogatives, in which the theatres were almost an incidental issue.

As a result of such tensions – financial as much as ideological – all the early purpose-built theatres were constructed outside the jurisdiction of the city author-ities, in the liberties to the north and south, where they came under the authority of the magistrates for Middlesex and Surrey. But until around 1596 – and perhaps even after that – there was also regular playing at inns within the City's jurisdiction, notably the Bell, the Bull, the Cross Keys and the Bel Savage (Ingram 1978: 140–1). The role of the Master of the Revels evolved in the midst of these conflicting authorities and agendas, and not without competition. As early as 1574 the Common Council of London sought to establish that playing places in the city should be licensed, and that plays performed there should be 'first perused and allowed', by persons appointed by the lord mayor and the Court of Aldermen. This was partly to rebut the Lord Chamberlain's proposal that 'one Mr Holmes' should undertake such a role. They wanted to preserve the city's own authority and to control profits from the licensing, rather than promote 'the benefit of any private person' (Ingram 1992: 127, 142). There is no evidence, however, that such persons were ever appointed.

In 1589, the Privy Council instructed Tilney to act in consort with nominees of both the lord mayor and the archbishop of Canterbury in a commission for the censoring of all plays to be performed 'in and about the City of London'; but the articles setting it up are all we ever hear of this commission. By 1592 Tilney's importance was such that the city authorities saw his office as an impediment to the kinds of restraint they wanted to exert themselves, and they sought (though without success) to buy him out. By then, he was certainly receiving regular fees from Philip Henslowe. Aspects of Henslowe's accountancy remain inscrutable, but it seems that Tilney was receiving separate fees for licensing the theatres, the acting companies and each play – which he would 'peruse' (that is, read rather than see in rehearsal) and then 'allow' when he was satisfied with it, appending his signature at the end of what became the only 'allowed copy' for performance purposes. Tilney kept records of licences in his office-book, but the office-books of both Tilney and his successor, Sir George Buc, have been lost. Only from the time of Sir John Astley (1622), who quickly sold his office to Sir Henry Herbert (1623), do we have information, from their shared office-book – but even that is patchy and second-hand, since the original long since disappeared (Bawcutt, 1996: 13–26). We often have to infer from this what may have been earlier practice. The precise nature and rate of fees changed a good deal over the period as a whole, but a significant economic symbiosis between the Master of the Revels and those whose livelihood he licensed remained throughout (Dutton 1991: 52, 116; Bawcutt 1996: 38–40).

Precisely which companies Tilney licensed in the 1580s and early 1590s we do not know, apart from the Queen's Men: probably only those who actually performed at court, notably Leicester's, Strange's, the Admiral's and the boy companies (Chapel Royal/Oxford's and Paul's) closely associated with the court, though their licences as adjuncts of choir schools were different from those of the adult players. As early as 1574, Leicester's Men had received a patent which gave them the right to perform anywhere in the country, providing that their plays had been 'sene and allowed' by the Master of the Revels (Chambers 1923: ii. 87–8; Gurr 1996: 187–8). This was probably sought by the company as defence against civic authorities (including London) who tried to prevent them from playing; the Master's licence certified that their plays were fit for court, and ought not to be challenged elsewhere. This reinforced the status they claimed as servants of a patron like Leicester, whose livery they wore. In practice, patronage by an influential aristocrat was an important adjunct to commercial viability for any company, and a form of control in as much as loss of patronage could have important consequences. Earlier in Elizabeth's reign members of the gentry had patronized the actors, but from 1572 this privilege was restricted to the aristocracy (barons and those of higher degree), though companies could locally get permission to perform from two justices of the peace. Those without patronage or permission were subject to the harsh laws against rogues, vagabonds and sturdy beggars (Chambers 1923: iv. 270).

In such a context we can see why some (including the city authorities) might see the Master of the Revels as the protector of the most successful actors, as much as their regulator. And we may suppose that the actors appreciated this themselves; his licence gave them protection against unwelcoming authorities, an opportunity for lucrative performances at court, and the sole right to perform plays 'allowed' to them – a version of performing copyright. As a censor, it seems that each of the Masters was scrupulous, could on occasion be strict, but on the whole applied relatively broad criteria of what was permissible, determined largely by their position within the court. In the years before Elizabeth's reign a number of edicts specifically restricted plays in English, but tacitly permitted those in Latin in privileged contexts, such as the universities, Inns of Court and noble households. At the start of her reign Elizabeth issued a proclamation (16 May 1559) which instructed royal officers everywhere on what was not acceptable in plays performed within their jurisdictions:

> And for instruction to every one of the sayde officers, her majestie doth likewise charge every one of them, as they will aunswere: that they permyt none to be played wherein either matters of religion or of the governaunce of the estate of the common weale shalbe handled or treated, beyng no meete matters to be wrytten or treated upon, but by menne of aucthoritie, learning and wisedome, nor to be handled before any audience, but of grave and discreete persons. (Chambers 1923: iv. 263–4)

Here too there is an assumption that such matters *might* be put onstage (even in English) in privileged contexts, an implicit court standard of what was acceptable. This explains how a play like *Gorboduc*, which clearly, if mythologically, treats of matters 'of the governaunce of the estate of the common weale' (the need for the queen to marry, beget heirs or otherwise provide for the succession), could be performed in the Inns of Court. But the play passed into the professional repertoire after it was published, circumventing notional restrictions.

Similarly, Masters of the Revels, who were supposed to be reviewing plays for possible performance before the monarch, implicitly applied a court standard in their licences. One of the clearest demonstrations of this comes in Herbert's office-book (January 1631): 'I did refuse to allow of a play of Massinger's, because itt did contain dangerous matter, as the deposing of Sebastian king of Portugal by Philip the <Second,> and ther being a peace sworen twixte the kings of England and Spayne' (Bawcutt 1996: 171–2). So he refused to licence a play he deemed overtly hostile to the king's current foreign policy. Yet five months later he licensed a play called *Believe as You List* which is transparently a reworking of the play he had turned down, merely transposed to classical antiquity. It could be an oversight, but this is unlikely. All the Masters were literate, sophisticated men – Tilney a diplomatic genealogist, Buc a highly respected historian, and Herbert the brother of the poets Edward and George Herbert. I suspect, rather, that Herbert was well aware that this was the same play, reworked, but judged that it was no longer an overt affront to the royal prerogative or to a friendly foreign power. In that context, it was acceptable. It was not for him to second-guess either Massinger's *intentions* or what audiences might *infer* from material that was not openly provocative. There is something very patrician about all this –

Herbert, as representative of the privileged classes, not deigning to notice what did not strictly require to be noticed. As Annabel Patterson puts it: 'there were conventions that both sides accepted as to how far a writer could go in explicit address to the contentious issues of his day, how he could encode his opinions so that nobody would be _required_ to make an example of him' (1984: 11).

To return for a moment to _Hamlet: The Murder of Gonzago_ was an entirely innocent piece of work, doubtless duly licensed (in the fictional world) by Tilney's counterpart in Elsinore. Hamlet's appreciation of its aptness for a particular audience was provocative but not strictly an 'offense' – just as the aptness of _Richard II_ performed on the eve of the Essex Rebellion was suspicious but not in itself punishable (Barroll 1988).[4] But his insertion of a passage not cleared by the licenser was an 'offense' in itself.[5] While we do not strictly know what was in that passage, it seems almost certain to have been something that, for one critical member of the audience, breached the art–life boundary. Claudius is unmoved by the sight of his own crimes in the dumb show, but reacts intemperately to hearing that the poisoner ('nephew to the king') will woo the dead king's widow. The king/nephew/widow triangle revolves, and in that moment all the fictional veils are down: a tacit accusation of guilt has become a pointed promise of revenge.

It was normally the Master's function precisely to ensure that the fictional veiling was adequate, so that serious offence might not be offered to members of the court or friendly foreign dignitaries. They also needed to be alert to immediately contentious issues, with possible public order implications; but in other respects they could take quite a relaxed approach to their remit. So the only extant manuscript of a play that shows Tilney's attentions is _Sir Thomas More_, about a man seen by many as a Catholic martyr to Elizabeth's father, Henry VIII; the play depicts More going to his death for refusing to accept the Act of Supremacy – though it tactfully does not go into detail about this extremely delicate subject. We might have supposed that Tilney would ban the play outright, but his markings suggest that he was careful about its main theme, though not overly disturbed. On the other hand, the opening scenes, depicting riots against aliens in London, brought this strict warning: 'Leave out the insurrection wholy and the Cause ther off and begin with Sr Tho: Moore att the mayors sessions with a reportt afterwardes off his good service don being Shrive [Sheriff] of London upon a mutiny Agaynst the Lumbardes only by A Shortt reporte and nott otherwise at your perilles. E. Tyllney' (Dutton 1991: plate 7). His concern is almost certainly similar anti-alien riots in London at the time the play was first drafted (Long 1989). Feelings against French immigrants were running particularly high, so references to the Lombards might be less inflammatory; but the main thrust is to replace graphic scenes of rioting with a short _report_ of More's actions. In short, Tilney seems much more concerned by the immediate public order resonances of the play than by its broader ideological implications.

We may see something analogous in the censorship of the 1597 quarto of _Richard II_. We do not know if the abdication scene was cut by Tilney (either when it was first licensed or later) or by the press censor (Dutton 1991: 124–7). But we have the apparent anomaly of censorship which allows the murder of a king to be shown openly, while cutting the very stylized, non-inflammatory abdication. The most compelling explanation of this is that the scene specifically shows Richard's abdication being sanctioned by Parliament, suggesting that parliamentary authority might outweigh that of the monarch (Clegg, 1997). In the context of 1597, with no agreed successor to Elizabeth and no agreed mechanism for finding one, this was highly contentious. Again, the censor's attention seems to be on a matter that was immediately provocative rather than on *potentially* subversive subtexts in the play as a whole.

The fraught situation as the reign neared its uncertain end did play its part in a sequence of Privy Council initiatives concerning the theatres, which finally installed the Master of the Revels centre-stage. In July 1597 they issued an extraordinary order, which has never been fully explained, that the theatres should be 'plucked down' (Wickham 1969; Ingram 1978: 167–86). But it was never enforced. Instead, it restricted the number of companies authorized to play in the London area to two (February 1598), both licensed by Tilney and patronized by two of their own number, the lord chamberlain and lord admiral, both cousins of the queen.[6] At the same time Parliament removed the right of justices of the peace to authorize playing: patronage was restricted exclusively to the peerage, while the penalties against masterless men were made even more Draconian. In June 1600 the two companies were restricted to playing (in the London area) to their 'usual houses' – for the Chamberlain's Men the new Globe, for the Admiral's Men (after a short delay) the new Fortune. And the number of performances they could give was strictly limited. The intention was clear: to restrict London playing to two select companies, both patronized by Privy Councillors, in fixed locations and at known times, conditions which Tilney could easily police.

The reality was a little different: first the Children of the Chapel, then Paul's Boys, both defunct for a decade or more, were revived under their different licensing arrangements. Then Derby's Men started playing at the Boar's Head, and even performed at court. When they failed to achieve a permanent place among the 'allowed' companies, they were replaced by Worcester's Men. Worcester, as Master of the Horse and a Privy Councillor, secured them a place among the 'allowed' companies – making three adult and two boys, companies. This was as many companies as the Master of the Revels was ever directly responsible for – usually four and sometimes five – as companies and patronage possibilities fluctuated. Tilney and his successors sought to expand their authority (and revenue) by licensing firstly non-theatrical shows and latterly actors travelling in the provinces (Dutton 1991: 116, 235–6). But their central concern was always those London-based companies who, in the nature of things, were the most successful of their time and bequeathed the overwhelming majority of plays which have survived to posterity.

When James I finally succeeded Elizabeth, he took four of the five London companies into royal patronage: the Chamberlain's became the King's Men, the Admiral's Prince Henry's, and Worcester's Queen Anne's. The Children of the Chapel became the Children of the Queen's Revels.[7] This has commonly been seen as a decisive act of royal absolutism, pulling the theatres away from their popular roots and redirecting their repertoires towards courtly tastes and political perspectives. In fact, it was only a logical development of the policy of the Elizabethan Privy Council, taking into account the fact of multiple royal households, which had not been an issue before, and it very probably only reinforced the economic instincts of the companies affected. The adult companies remained answerable to Tilney, but the Queen's Revels Boys were given their own licenser, Samuel Daniel, and for the next few years this company (under a variety of titles but until 1608 always at the Blackfriars theatre) was responsible for some of the most notable theatrical scandals of the era. First, Daniel's own play, *Philotas* (1604), was seen as commenting on the Essex rebellion, and he was questioned by the Privy Council. In 1605 *Eastward Ho!* landed Jonson and Chapman in prison and under threat of mutilation; their provocative satire of mercenary Scots courtiers proved to be compounded by failure to have the play licensed at all – a serious omission when much could be overlooked within the circle of licensed authority, but the flouting of that authority might be unforgivable. It seems that only representations to some of the most powerful people at court effected their release. Day's *Isle of Gulls* (1606), also unlicensed, also caused offence to the Scots, and reheated the old scandal over *The Isle of Dogs* (see n. 6).

We presume Daniel lost his post as licenser. Andrew Gurr states: 'By the end of 1606, like all the other companies, the Blackfriars company was under the orders of the Master of the Revels' (1996: 352). This is plausible, but more than we know, and the company continued to cause scandal, with Chapman's *Byron* plays (1607/8) and other works. The fact is that the company had fostered a repertoire of politically charged satirical drama from the time they were resuscitated; this may well have found encouragement under Queen Anne's patronage, and they continued to be controversial whoever was licensing them, at least until they lost the use of the Blackfriars (Lewalski 1993: 24). There is evidence that other parts of the profession resented the threat to their collective livelihood; Heywood in his *Apology for Actors*, urges them 'to curbe and limit this presumed liberty', while the 'little eyases' additions to the folio *Hamlet* have been convincingly linked to this period (Knutson 1995).

The lines of authority in the Revels Office seem further confused by the fact that in 1606 Sir George Buc took over the licensing of plays *for the press*; these powers were formerly held by clerics of the Court of High Commission, who licensed all other printed books. Buc had held the office of Master in reversion since 1603, but we do not know how he acquired this new authority. It has been supposed that he acted as the ageing Tilney's deputy, but there is no evidence of this, and Tilney continued to collect his allowance for attendance at court until his death. Only then, in 1610, can we be confident that one man, Buc, was licensing all the London companies, as well as play texts for the press. He inherited from Tilney a system of licensing and control that did not change in essence until the closing of the theatres. From 1606 this included the need to attend to the provisions of Parliament's 'Acte to restrain the

Abuses of Players', which sought to put an end to blasphemous language on the stage. Most, though not all, texts licensed or re-licensed after this are more careful (see, for example, the differences between the quarto and folio *Volpone* and *Othello*); the manuscript of *The Second Maiden's Tragedy* (1611), which bears Buc's licence, shows that he was alert to the issue, marking a number of places where such changes were necessary, perhaps expecting the actors to change the others (Dutton 1991: 194–209). Herbert later felt that his predecessors had not been as scrupulous on these matters as he was, but his changes to William Davenant's *The Wits* caused problems. Davenant had influence at court, and so Herbert reviewed it with King Charles himself: 'The king is pleasd to take *faith, death, slight,* for asseverations, and no oaths, to which I doe humbly submit as my masters judgment; but under favour conceive them to be oaths, and enter them here, to declare my opinion and submission' (Bawcutt 1996: 186).

Sir John Van Olden Barnavelt (1618) is another manuscript where Buc's hand is visible; we see a careful system of lightly pencilled markings, some of which are later reinforced in heavy ink, with warning crosses in margins where he perhaps intended to consult the actors (Howard-Hill, 'Buc'). Where he finds objectionable material, he tries to find acceptable alternatives, and seems only to cross it out altogether as a last resort. He is particularly alert to depictions of the prince of Orange, whom he had encountered in his earlier career as a diplomat; he loses patience in an initialled note: 'I like not this: neithr do I think that the prince was thus disgracefully used, besides he is too much presented' (Dutton 1991: 208–17 and plate 9). We learn during the *Game at Chess* controversy that at some point 'there was a commandment and restraint given against the representing of any modern Christian kings in those stage-plays' (ibid., 242). On the whole, however, Buc seems patient and constructive, drawing a line only when faced with outright provocation, as in a strongly anti-monarchist passage which contains the loaded suggestion (ostensibly meant for those onstage, but equally likely to be picked up by an audience) 'you can apply this' (ibid., 214–15). Buc tinkered, redrafted, but finally crossed out the whole passage. In all probability the play (rather like Chapman's *Byron* plays) was doubly problematic, since it depicts recent Dutch history, and so might be diplomatically sensitive; but it was probably read as a commentary on the death of Walter Ralegh, who, like Barnavelt, was a 'patriot' who had fallen from royal favour and been executed.

Buc finally went mad, probably from the pressures of trying to run an office in a court that was all but bankrupt. This perhaps explains how some actors managed to circumvent the Revels Office, and obtained licences by other routes – a situation which Lord Chamberlain Pembroke tried to rectify with a special warrant of November 1622, confirming the exclusive authority of the Revels Office in such matters throughout the country (ibid., 225–6). Perhaps because of such problems, Buc's successor, Sir John Astley, quickly sold the post to Sir Henry Herbert (Dutton 1990; Bawcutt 1992). The outcome was a situation in which Herbert was the client and kinsman of his lord chamberlain, the powerful third earl of Pembroke; even when Pembroke vacated his office in 1626, in favour of his brother the earl of Montgomery (later fourth earl of Pembroke), the essential ties of patronage and kinship remained.

This perhaps helped to maintain a continuity of emphasis and practice in the Revels Office (in particular, helping to extend a recognition of his authority into the provinces), at a time when the supremacy of Buckingham and later the personal government of Charles I made for a very different political atmosphere from that in which the largely consensual role of the Master of the Revels had evolved.

Herbert had been in office only a year when the most resonant theatrical scandal of the era occurred. Middleton's *A Game at Chess* was performed to packed houses for an unprecedented nine days in a row, before the protests of the Spanish ambassador had it stopped.[8] The play is a lively satire on Jesuit wiles and the machinations of the previous Spanish ambassador, Gondomar, contriving to review recent Anglo–Spanish relations in unusually close detail. Gondomar and the archbishop of Spalato were impersonated in some detail, and while other characters were shrouded in the allegory of chess-pieces, it was evident that they represented, among others, the kings of Spain and England, Prince Charles and Buckingham. We know that Herbert gave the play a licence in the usual way, but commentators then, and some scholars since, have supposed that the play may have been specially sponsored at the highest level (Heinemann 1980; Limon 1986; Howard-Hill 1991; Dutton, forthcoming). This is unprovable, and probably not a necessary conjecture. England and Spain were on the brink of war, a context in which Herbert would have felt no need to protect Spanish sensitivities (as he did over *Believe as You List*), and may have felt that the depiction of the English court was acceptably patriotic. Perhaps the lengths to which the actors went to impersonate Gondomar (acquiring a cast suit of clothes and a 'chair of ease' for his anal fistula) created more of a stir than he anticipated, and breached the fictional veiling on which he normally insisted (*Believe as You List* is again instructive). In 1632 he recorded: 'In the play of *The Ball*, written by Sherley, and acted by the Queens players, ther were divers personated so naturally, both of lords and others of the court, that I took it ill' (Bawcutt 1996: 177). The chess allegory may have looked adequate veiling on paper, but as with *The Ball*, performance was a different matter.[9]

Middleton may have spent some time in prison over *A Game at Chess*, but the King's Men suffered no more than a brief suspension of playing.[10] The business clearly did not over-awe them, since in December 1624 they staged *The Spanish Viceroy* (now lost, but clearly exploiting the same anti-Spanish sentiments) without Herbert's licence. He was so incensed – and so sensitive to the implications for his own standing – that he got all the patented members of the company to subscribe to a letter (transcribed in his office-book), acknowledging their fault, promising not to repeat it, and submitting to his authority (ibid., 183). Yet again, however, no one actually suffered the harsh penalties which potentially lay in store either for libelling someone important onstage or for flouting the licensing regulations. Although dramatists and actors spent relatively brief periods in prison, no one involved in the theatre in the period suffered the grim mutilations of John Stubbes or William Prynne or the prolonged imprisonment of John Hayward, for their transgressions in print (Finkelpearl 1986). Which is a testament of sorts to the effectiveness of the Revels Office as an instrument of regulation, but also to the general good will of the court towards the actors it patronized.

In October 1633 something about a revival of Fletcher's *The Woman's Prize* (or *The Tamer Tamed*, c.1611) aroused Herbert's particular indignation and severely strained his relations with the actors (Bawcutt 1996: 182–3). Normally, where the actors still had the 'allowed copy' and were performing it unaltered, they did not require it to be re-licensed. Yet Herbert stopped a performance of this play at short notice, which 'raysed some discourse in the players, though no disobedience'. His recorded objections were to 'oaths, prophaness and ribaldrye', which he certainly did take seriously. Yet something more specific and serious probably caused him to react as he did, perhaps an 'application' of the play to Queen Henrietta Maria's openly practised Roman Catholicism. Whatever the case, Herbert now insisted that old plays should be re-licensed, 'since they may be full of offensive things against church and state, ye rather that in former time the poetts tooke greater liberty than is allowed them by me'. The actors concerned later apologized for their 'ill manners'; they knew how things stood.[11]

One effect of the growing identification of the leading companies with the court, which clearly affected Astley and Herbert's terms of office, was the emergence of gentlemen or courtier playwrights, who were in a position to challenge the authority of the Master of the Revels.[12] Davenant's challenge over *The Wits* is an example of this. Astley had problems with a play by Lodowick Carlell, a courtier with connections. His office-book records: '6 Sep. 1622, for perusing and allowing of a new play called *Osmond the Great Turk*, which Mr Hemmings and Mr Rice affirmed to me that Lord Chamberlain gave order to allow of it because I refused to allow it <? at> first . . . 20s' (Bawcutt 1996: 137). Was it Astley's own idea to refer the play to Pembroke, or had these veterans of the King's Men presumed on Carlell's influence to go behind his back? We do not know, though it must be significant that the normal machinery of perusal and allowance (and payment) is followed, despite Astley's misgivings.

Herbert more fully recorded his own referral of *The King and the Subject* (1638), by the professional dramatist Massinger, to the ultimate authority, the king himself: 'who, readinge over the play at Newmarket, set his marke upon the place with his owne hande, and in thes words: "This is too insolent, and to bee changed". Note, that the poett makes it the speech of a king, Don Pedro kinge of Spayne, and spoken to his subjects' (Bawcutt 1996: 204). The passage in question (which Herbert carefully transcribed) concerns royal taxation without parliamentary sanction, transparently a very sensitive issue during Charles I's personal rule. The wonder is that Herbert did not simply rule the passage, or even the entire play, out of court. In fact, he followed Tilney and Buc in doing his best to make it playable – his allowance was on the condition that 'the reformations [be] most strictly observed, and not otherwise', including that the highly provocative title be changed. Yet he still took the precaution of referring it to the king – whose own reaction is also instructive. The phrase 'too insolent' almost suggests that he was used to tolerating insolence, but that this crossed the limits of toleration. (And Herbert carefully notes for future reference that the format of the passage – a king speaking to his subjects – constitutes part of the insolence.) Even so, there were no recriminations: Massinger was not to be punished for what he very likely thought. There is no evidence of *any* dramatist of the period being punished for his ideas, opinions or intentions. If this seems suspiciously liberal, we may have to settle for a truth unpalatable to many modern scholars: that in early modern England, players and playwrights were too insignificant for those in power to take all that seriously, except when they were 'too insolent' or contrived to offend someone with influence (Yachnin 1991). And the Masters of the Revels were adept at preventing that from happening too often. It is that which made them, perhaps paradoxically, such an important element in the cultural formula which produced early modern drama. Without their protective presence, giving the theatrical profession a degree of creative and expressive space (albeit within well-defined limits), it is unlikely that the plays they licensed could have been as intellectually, socially and politically vigorous as so many of them actually were.

Tensions surrounding *The King and the Subject* clearly foreshadow the Civil War and the closing of the theatres. But, just as it was misleading to see the survival of the Elizabethan theatres simply as an assertion of courtly tastes over entrenched Puritan attitudes in the city, so it is a mistake to see what happened in 1642 as the revenge of parliamentary Puritans, now able to impose their will. The critical ordinance for the cessation of playing was passed by Parliament, which by then controlled London, on 2 September 1642. Earlier, on 26 January (before the final breach with the king), an order was moved in the Commons 'that the lord chamberlain be desired to move his majesty that in these times of calamity in Ireland and the distractions in this kingdom, that all interludes and plays be suppressed for a season'. But that motion was 'laid aside by Mr Pym his seconding of Mr Waller in alleging it was their trade' (Coates et al. 1982: 182). If a leading parliamentarian like John Pym resisted a ban on playing as an infringement of the players' trade, and the House backed him, it is difficult to see what finally happened as the act of a vengeful Puritan Parliament.

In fact, the September ordinance requires only that 'while these sad Causes and set times of Humiliation doe continue, publike Stage-Playes shall cease' – the 'sad Causes' apparently being the rebellion in Ireland, the most important matter before the Commons that day. There was no move against the playhouses themselves, and it is likely that 'the prohibition was intended to be a temporary one, to last as long as the crisis which occasioned it' (Roberts 1997). In all probability it was the reaction of the actors themselves to the loss of courtly patronage and protection which turned a temporary prohibition into a state of affairs that lasted eighteen years. As Andrew Gurr observes of the King's Men, 'even before the actual closure ... the company seems to have started to disintegrate' (Gurr 1996: 385–6). Those who had controlled them also parted company in ways that underline how complex were the affiliations in the Civil War. Henry Herbert joined the royalist parliament at Oxford, though it is not true (as some accounts assert) that he fought for the king. By 1648, however, he had at some cost made his peace with the Westminster Parliament. But his kinsman and superior, Lord Chamberlain Pembroke, sided (however reluctantly) with the Westminister Parliament from the outset. Only as positions hardened did a vindictive anti-theatricality overtake Parliament: in 1647 it chose to regard the old legislation against *masterless* players as applying to all of them; the next year it ordered the demolition of all the playhouses.

NOTES

1 References to Shakespeare are to *The Riverside Shakespeare*, textual editor G. Blakemore Evans (Boston: Houghton Mifflin, 1974).

2 Only in the 1599 quarto text; most of his role is redistributed among other characters in the 1623 Folio.

3 The precise social status of the actors was always a moot point in their anomalous profession. Shakespeare himself professed to be a gentleman, untainted by 'mechanical' trade or labour. Many of his fellows, however, were members of trade guilds which had no bearing on their theatrical work but gave them secure standing as citizens of London; John Heminge, for example, was a grocer, and Robert Armin a goldsmith. Similarly, Ben Jonson retained his formal status as a bricklayer long after he ceased to ply that trade.

4 Augustine Phillips, the actor, was questioned about the performance, and insisted that the play (probably Shakespeare's) was an old one – and so, probably, duly licensed. The Chamberlain's Men received no penalty, and performed at court within the month, on the eve of Essex's execution.

5 The actors were accused of adding unlicensed material to the 'allowed' text of *A Game at Chess*, but denied it; they were, however, found guilty of doing it to Jonson's *The Magnetic Lady* in an exceptional instance where both Jonson and Sir Henry Herbert were taken before the Court of High Commission over some offensive material (Butler 1992).

6 The Queen's Men had lost prestige by the early 1590s, and never really recovered from the break in playing caused by the plague of 1593–4. It remains unclear whether the scandalous *Isle of Dogs* (1597), written by Thomas Nashe and Ben Jonson, and performed by Pembroke's Men at the Swan, had a bearing on the new restrictions. The fact that Tilney was apparently not involved – they seem to have been licensed by the Surrey justices – reinforced the case for making him the key figure in the new provisions.

7 The much smaller Paul's Boys were in decline, and disappeared around 1606.

8 It ran from 5 to 14 August, barring only 8 August, since performances were not allowed on Sundays. Performances were normally also suspended for much of Lent, though in later years dispensations could be bought from the Master of the Revels (Bawcutt 1996: 213). Playing was also stopped when the weekly plague bills exceeded a given number – the years of 1593–4, 1603 and 1608–9 were particularly bad (Barroll 1988). There is evidence that the Privy Council sometimes exploited this excuse for other reasons, even when plague deaths did not warrant it (Freedman 1996).

9 Only people of substance could expect to be protected from malicious 'personation'. We know that Chapman's lost *The Old Joiner of Aldgate* (Paul's Boys, 1603) shadowed real events, and that key participants saw 'themselves' onstage, though they chose not to complain. Anne Elsden complained about the portrayal of herself in *The Late Murder in the White Chapel, or Keepe the Widow Waking* (1624), by Dekker, Rowley, Ford and Webster, and paid Herbert's deputy to prevent its performance, but he did nothing (Dutton 1991: 129–32).

10 Dramatists (rather than actors) often carried the blame for offensive impersonations, perhaps as convenient scapegoats; over *The Ball*, Herbert records the assurance of Christopher Beeston, manager of the Queen's Men, 'that he would not suffer it to be done by the poett any more, who deserves to be punisht' (Bawcutt 1996: 177). The actors surely knew what they were doing.

11 Herbert appears to have had a very strained year with the actors in 1632/3. It was in November 1632 that his licensing of Jonson's *The Magnetic Lady* was referred to the Court of High Commission (see 5); the incident over *The Ball* occurred in January 1633, the problems over *The Woman's Prize* in October 1633, and it was only then that Herbert inserted in his office-book the 1624 submission of the King's Men to his authority after *The Spanish Viceroy* affair; the actors apologized for their response to his banning of *The Woman's Prize* one day before the Court of High Commission finally exonerated Herbert over *The Magnetic Lady* – and blamed the actors (Dutton, forthcoming).

12 In arguing that the leading companies were increasingly identified with the court, I do not suggest either that the court was itself a monolithic entity or that the actors and their dramatists readily endorsed (e.g.) Stuart absolutist government but rather that the economic and social dependence of the companies on the court affected their theatrical styles and strategies. Within this, however – as Massinger's *The King and the Subject*, written for the King's Men themselves, amply demonstrates – there remained room for a considerable range of political views (Butler 1984).

REFERENCES AND FURTHER READING

Adams, Joseph Quincy (ed.) 1917: *The Dramatic Records of Sir Henry Herbert*. New Haven: Yale University Press.

Ashton, Robert 1983: Popular entertainment and social control in later Elizabethan and early Stuart England. *London Journal*, 9, 1–11.

Barroll, Leeds 1988: A new history for Shakespeare and his time. *Shakespeare Quarterly*, 39, 441–64.

Bawcutt, N. W. 1992: Evidence and conjecture in literary scholarship: the case of Sir John Astley reconsidered. *English Literary Renaissance*, 22, 333–46.

—— 1996: *The Control and Censorship of Caroline Drama: The Records of Sir Henry Herbert, Master of the Revels 1623–73*. Oxford: Clarendon Press.

Bevington, David 1968: *Tudor Drama and Politics: A Critical Approach to Topical Meaning*. Cambridge, Mass.: Harvard University Press.

Burt, Richard 1987: 'Licensed by authority': Ben Jonson and the politics of early Stuart theater. *ELH*, 54, 529–60.

—— 1993: *Licensed by Authority: Ben Jonson and the Discourses of Censorship*. Ithaca, NY: Cornell University Press.

Butler, Martin 1984: *Theatre and Crisis, 1632–1642*. Cambridge: Cambridge University Press.

—— 1992: Ecclesiastical censorship of early Stuart drama: the case of Jonson's *The Magnetic Lady*. *Modern Philology*, 89, 469–81.

Chambers, E. K. 1923: *The Elizabethan Stage*, 4 vols. Oxford: Clarendon Press.

Charles, Amy M. 1982: Sir Henry Herbert: the Master of the Revels as a man of letters. *Modern Philology*, 80, 1–12.

Clare, Janet 1990: *Art Made Tongue-tied by Authority: Elizabethan and Jacobean Dramatic Censorship*. Manchester: Manchester University Press.

Clegg, Cyndia 1997: 'By the choise and invitation of al the realme': *Richard II* and Elizabethan press censorship. *Shakespeare Quarterly*, 48, 432–48.

Coates, W. H., Young, A. S. and Snow, V. F. (eds) 1982: *The Private Journals of the Long Parliament: 3 Jan to 5 March 1642*. New Haven: Yale University Press.

Dutton, Richard 1990: Patronage, politics, and the Master of the Revels, 1622–40: the case of Sir John Astley. *English Literary Renaissance*, 20, 287–331.

—— 1991: *Mastering the Revels: The Regulation and Censorship of English Renaissance Drama*. Basingstoke: Macmillan.

—— forthcoming: *Buggeswords: Censorship and Authorship in Early Modern England*. Basingstoke: Macmillan.

Eccles, Mark 1938: Sir George Buc, Master of the Revels. In C. J. Sisson (ed.), *Sir Thomas Lodge and Other Elizabethans*. Cambridge, Mass.: Harvard University Press, 409–506.

Finkelpearl, Philip J. 1986: 'The comedians' liberty': censorship of the Jacobean stage reconsidered. *English Literary Renaissance*, 16, 123–38.

Freedman, Barbara 1996: Elizabethan protest, plague, and plays: rereading the 'documents of control'. *English Literary Renaissance*, 26, 17–45.

Gildersleeve, Virginia Crocheron 1908: *Government Regulation of the Elizabethan Drama*. New York: Columbia University Press.

Gurr, Andrew 1996: *The Shakespearian Playing Companies*. Oxford: Clarendon Press.

Heinemann, Margot 1980: *Puritanism and Theatre: Thomas Middleton and Opposition Drama under the Early Stuarts*. Cambridge: Past and Present.

Hill, Christopher 1985: Censorship and English literature. In *The Collected Essays of Christopher Hill*, Vol. 1: *Writing and Revolution in Seventeenth-Century England*. Brighton: Harvester Press, 32–71.

Howard-Hill, T. H. 1983: Marginal markings: the censor and the editing of four English prompt-books. *Studies in Bibliography*, 36, 168–77.

—— 1988: Buc and the censorship of *Sir John Van Olden Barnavelt* in 1619. *Review of English Studies*, n.s. 39, 39–63.

—— 1991: Political interpretations of Middleton's *A Game at Chess*. *Yearbook of English Studies*, 21, 274–85.

Ingram, William 1978: *A London Life in the Brazen Age: Francis Langley, 1548–1602*. Cambridge, Mass.: Harvard University Press.

—— 1992: *The Business of Playing: The Beginnings of the Adult Professional Theater in Elizabethan London*. Ithaca, NY: Cornell University Press.

Knutson, Roslyn L. 1995: Falconer to the little eyases: a new date and commercial agenda for the 'little eyases'. *Shakespeare Quarterly*, 46, 1–31.

Lewalski, Barbara K. 1993: *Writing Women in Jacobean England*. Cambridge, Mass.: Harvard University Press.

Limon, Jerzy 1986: *Dangerous Matter: English Drama and Politics 1623/24*. Cambridge: Cambridge University Press.

Long, William B. 1989: The occasion of *Sir Thomas More*. In T. H. Howard-Hill (ed.), *Shakespeare and 'Sir Thomas More': Essays on the Play and its Shakespearian Interest*. Cambridge: Cambridge University Press, 45–56.

Patterson, Annabel 1984: *Censorship and Interpretation: The Conditions of Reading and Writing in Early Modern England*. Madison: University of Wisconsin Press.

Roberts, Peter 1997: William Prynne, the legal status of the players, and the closure of the playhouses by the Long Parliament. Unpublished paper given at the Shakespeare Association of America conference, Washington, D. C., April 1997.

Streitberger, W. R. 1978: On Edmond Tyllney's biography. *Review of English Studies*, n.s. 29, 11–35.

—— 1986: *Edmond Tyllney, Master of the Revels and Censor of Plays: A Descriptive Index to his Diplomatic Manual on Europe*. New York: AMS Press.

Tricomi, A. H. 1986: Philip, earl of Pembroke, and the analogical way of reading political tragedy. *Journal of English and Germanic Philology*, 85, 332–45.

Wickham, Glynne 1959–81: *Early English Stages 1300–1600*, 3 vols. London: Routledge and Kegan Paul.

—— 1969: The Privy Council order of 1597 for the destruction of all London's theatres. In David Galloway (ed.), *The Elizabethan Theatre*, Toronto: Macmillan, 21–44.

Wilson, Richard 1993: The kindly ones: the death of the author in Shakespearian Athens. *Essays and Studies*, 46, 1–24.

Worden, Blair 1988: Literature and political censorship in early modern England. In *Too Mighty to be Free: Censorship and the Press in Britain and the Netherlands*. Zutphen: De Walburg Press, 45–62.

Yachnin, Paul 1991: The powerless theater. *English Literary Renaissance*, 21, 49–74.

PART SEVEN
Printing

24

Shakespeare in Print, 1593–1640

Thomas L. Berger and Jesse M. Lander

Introduction

We know Shakespeare through print. While writers of every sort – poets, dramatists, essayists, satirists – left behind manuscripts, the only "manuscript" in Shakespeare's hand may be the 147 lines in *Sir Thomas More*, a play in manuscript in the British Library (Harleian 7368). It is to print and to a developing culture of print that we must turn to piece out Shakespeare's works. And it is through print that our narrative will unfold, using the facts of print culture to speculate on the author and his literary and dramatic pursuits. In its own fashion, that culture, following the dictates of early modern capitalism, put Shakespeare into print surely for its profit, even perhaps for its readers' pleasure. The texts it put before the book-buying public varied greatly.[1] Although scholars a decade ago could with some confidence have presented a hierarchy of Shakespearian texts, ranging from the "bad," "mutilated" first edition of *Hamlet* in 1603, to its "good" edition in 1604, to its "theatrical" edition in the first folio of 1623, today scholars are less sure; and while they may in some cases prefer one early printed version of a Shakespearian text to another, they do not reject other printed versions. Rather than dismissing variant editions as "spurious" or "corrupt" and clinging to those deemed "authorial" or "theatrical," this essay seeks to understand the cultural forces – social, literary, theatrical – that put in motion the processes that gave these editions life in print.

The existence of multiple editions of certain works by Shakespeare, an opportunity for the cultural historian, is for the textual scholar a challenge. Part of the textual scholar's task is to determine what kind(s) of manuscript(s) lay behind a particular printed text. The case of *Hamlet* is notorious. A short (or shortened, depending on one's perspective) version of the play appeared in 1603, a greatly expanded version in 1604–5, and a third version in the first folio of 1623. In each the play as it has come down to us is more or less recognizable. But what were the origins of each? Was the 1603 quarto a version stolen ("pirated") by actors or scribes? Or was it Shakespeare's first version of what he later expanded? Is the 1604–5 quarto the "full" text derived from Shakespeare's foul papers? Does the folio text represent a revised version of the play, based on the way it played in the theater? On which text(s) should an editor base his or her edition? If an editor chooses the 1604–5 quarto, then he or she may well have selected the text closest to the author but furthest from the theatrical performance. If the editor selects the folio text, then the author is put at a further remove, and the theater, the company, is foregrounded. Who, then, is Shakespeare the author? Is he the isolated (romantic) figure working alone to compose a poetic work, or is he the collaborator, working with actors, prompters, and others to produce a piece for the stage? As this essay is co-authored, we would suggest that the author is both of these creatures.

The Poems

When Shakespeare came to London from Stratford we do not know. When he began acting in plays and when he began writing them, we do not know. We do know that in 1592 and 1593 the plague was intense enough to cause the closing of the theaters, leaving actors and playwrights out of work. And we do know that on 18 April 1593, the printer Richard Field, like Shakespeare a native of Stratford, entered in the Stationers' Register "a booke intituled *Venus and Adonis*" (Arber 1875–9: ii. 630) and that Field printed it in the same year. If popularity can be measured, then Shakespeare's Ovidian poem, dedicated to Henry Wriothesley, earl of Southampton and baron of Titchfield, was his most popular work. But it was not, we must point out, his most profitable.[2] If Richard Field paid Shakespeare for *Venus and Adonis*, that payment was the only payment he received for the poem. Generally speaking, once an author received payment for his manuscript, he had sold his "rights" to the publisher or printer. The "copyright" belonged to Field, who in turn sold ("transferred") it to John Harrison, the bookseller of the first edition. Thereafter the right to print passed (was sold) to William Leake, to William Barret, to John Parker, and finally to John Haviland and John Wright. While the publication of Shakespeare's plays may have been intense at some times, spotty at others, *Venus and Adonis*, with fifteen editions following the 1593 quarto in the sixteenth and seventeenth centuries, was reprinted regularly until 1638, then finally in 1675. It should be noted that in none of these editions does the author's name appear on the title page, though the dedication to Southampton is signed "William Shakespeare."

In the following year, on 9 May 1594, was entered in the Stationers' Register "a booke intituled *the Ravyshement of Lucrece*." This poem, which we now call *The Rape of Lucrece*, was also originally printed by Richard Field, simply as *Lucrece*. Like *Venus and Adonis*, it was dedicated to Henry Wriothesley. Though not as popular in print as *Venus and Adonis*, it was printed eight times in the sixteenth and seventeenth centuries, making it as popular in print as any of Shakespeare's plays. Shakespeare's name is not on the title page of the first edition, but, as with *Venus and Adonis*, it appears at the close of the dedication. In 1616, however, the year of Shakespeare's death, changes appear. The title *Lucrece* becomes *The Rape of Lucrece*. "Mr. *William Shake-speare*" is on the title page. There appears a "Contents" page dividing the poem into twelve parts and summarizing each part. At various points in the poem marginal notes appear to gloss the action of the poem. The "Contents" and marginal notes appear in the editions of 1624 and 1632. For the last edition of the seventeenth century, that of 1655, the marketing of Shakespeare, especially during a period of no theatrical activity, intensifies. The title of this edition reads:

> The Rape of | LUCRECE, | Committed by | TARQUIN the Sixt; | *AND* | *The remarkable judgments that befel him for it.* | BY | The incomparable Master of our *English Poetry,* | WILL: SHAKESPEARE Gent.| —— | *Where-unto is annexed,* | *The Banishment of* TARQUIN: | Or, *the Reward of Lust.* | By J. QUARLES.

While the "Contents" of the three previous quartos has been omitted, into the text have been inserted thirteen notes which divide the poem into sections. There is a frontispiece, an engraving by William Faithorne of Shakespeare, adapted from the Droeshout engraving in the first folio of 1623. Under this are full-length figures of Collatine and of Lucrece stabbing herself. At the very bottom is the moral:

> The Fates decree, that tis a mighty wrong
> To Weomen Kinde, to have more Griefe, then Tongue
> Will: Gilbirson: John Stafford, excud.

While the text of *Lucrece* remains pretty much the same, the window dressing, the apparatus that surrounds and disposes that text, has changed drastically sixty years, three monarchs, no theaters, and one regicide later. Is it the same poem?

The third, and surely the most puzzling, of Shakespeare's purely poetic works are his sonnets. Two narratives have emerged surrounding their publication. The first has Shakespeare composing his sonnets around the same time as *Venus and Adonis* and *The Rape of Lucrece*, in the heyday of the Elizabethan sonnet sequences, and circulating them among courtly and literary circles but avoiding making them public in print. When they were printed in 1609, by George Eld for Thomas Thorpe, and sold by William Aspley and John Wright, Shakespeare was not involved. By 1609, the story goes, the vogue of the sonnet was over, and Shakespeare had established himself as the leading playwright of the leading company in London. By then he had no need of the patron he sought in 1593 and 1594. By 1609 Shakespeare had turned his back on nondramatic poetry and had long since committed himself to the theater, a world which, however unstable, he had discovered was far less fickle than the court.

A second narrative appears to be emerging. It sees a revival of the sonnet shortly after the accession of James I in 1603. In this narrative Shakespeare plays a role, though probably not a major one, in an emerging court culture and in the poetry of that culture. This narrative has Shakespeare revising his earlier sonnets and writing new ones in a culture less homophobic than that of Elizabeth's court, certainly in a culture less homophobic than the nineteenth-century culture that promulgated the first narrative. Far from being "pirated," as if they were not fit for public consumption, the sonnets were prepared for publication by the author himself, a poet at least as concerned in 1608–9 with the immortality of his verse as with a fair young man and a Dark Lady (Duncan-Jones 1997: 29–45).

Shakespeare the Playmaker

With plays, the question of authorship is complex. Indeed, what exactly "authorship" was and what a "work" was had not been settled.[3] Theater is, of course, always a collaborative enterprise, and rarely does all that an "author" writes actually make it onto the stage in performance. Actors and managers adapt and change what an author writes to suit the conditions of the stage, the abilities of the actors, the composition of the audience, the dictates of a monarchical (and thus despotic) government, and even the weather.

Shakespeare was an actor, a part of the collaborative enterprise, even as he became a playmaker. The title pages of early editions of Shakespeare's plays reflect the collaborative nature of the craft. To illustrate, we have chosen the title page of the first quarto (Q1) of *The Merchant of Venice* (Fig. 24.1). The title page is packed with information.

First, the play's title:

> The most excellent | Historie of the *Merchant* | *of Venice*.

Then the subtitle:

> VVith the extreame crueltie of *Shylocke* the Iewe | towards the sayd Merchant, in cutting a iust pound | of his flesh:

Then another subtitle:

> and the obtayning of *Portia* | by the choyse of three | chests.

Then information about performance:

> *As it hath beene diuers times acted by the Lord | Chamberlaine his Seruants.*

Then the author:

> Written by William Shakespeare.

Then the place of publication:

> AT LONDON

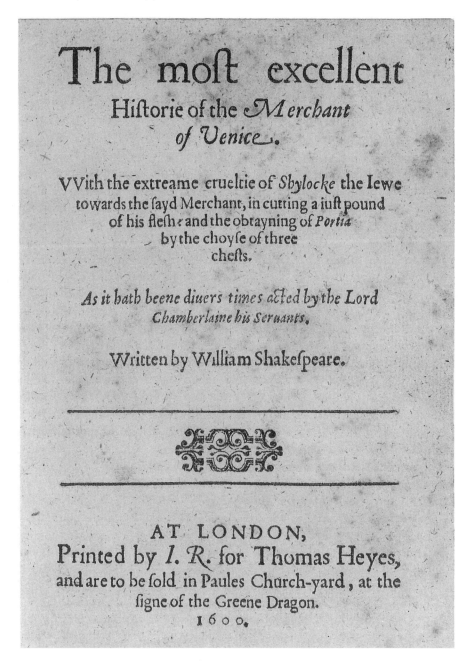

Figure 24.1 *The Merchant of Venice*, Q1 (1600). Used by permission of the Folger Shakespeare Library.

Then details of printing, publishing, and bookselling:

> Printed by *I. R.* for Thomas Heyes, | and are to be sold in Paules Church-yard, at the | signe of the Greene Dragon.

And finally the date:

> 1600.

Acknowledging Shakespeare's composition as well as the shaping influences of the theater and the print shop, this is a "typical" title page for a Shakespearian play printed around the turn of the century. However, the publication of some of Shakespeare's early plays reflects both the collaborative nature of the theatrical venture and the non-authorial status that Shakespeare, a playmaker among other playmakers, merited early in his career. *Titus Andronicus* is Shakespeare's first play in print, printed in 1594 by John Danter and sold by Edward White and Thomas Millington. We are told the play's title: "THE MOST LA-| mentable Romaine | Tragedie of Titus Andronicus." We are denied a subtitle but are given information about performance: "As it was Plaide by the Right Ho-| nourable the Earle of *Darbie*, Earle of *Pembrooke*, | and Earle of *Sussex* their Seruants." There is no mention of an author, but the publication information is intact: "LONDON, | Printed by Iohn Danter, and are | to be sold by *Edward White & Thomas Millington*, | at the little North doore of Paules at the | signe of the Gunne. | 1594." When the play was reprinted in 1600, the Lord Chamberlain's Men (the acting company in which Shakespeare was a "sharer," or partner) was added, but there is still no author. Nor is there an author in the 1611 reprint, where *"the Kings* | Maiesties Seruants"* displace the earlier acting companies.[4]

If the first play of Shakespeare to appear in print lacked what were to become standard features of title pages, the second play, which would appear in the first folio and would come to be called *2 Henry VI*, appeared in 1594 as "THE | First part of the Con-| tention betwixt the two famous Houses of Yorke | and Lancaster." Shakespeare's name is nowhere to be found; nor is there any information about an acting company. Rather than focus on the theatrical or authorial origin of the play, the title page concentrates on the play's apparently sprawling plot. There are upwards of five subtitles: "Lancaster" in the title is followed by "with the death of the good | Duke Humphrey," which is followed by "And the banishment and death of the Duke of | *Suffolke*," which is followed by "and the Tragicall end of the proud Cardinall | of *Winchester*," which is followed by "with the notable Rebellion | of *Iacke Cade*," which is followed, lastly, by *"And the Duke of Yorkes first claime vnto the | Crowne."*

The title page of the first play to carry at least the suggestion of Shakespeare as the author also delineates plot points: "THE | Lamentable Tragedie of | *Locrine*, the eldest sonne of King *Brutus*, discour-| sing the warres of the *Britaines*, and *Hunnes*, | with their discomfiture: | *The* Britaines *victorie with their Accidents, and the | death of* Albanact. *No lesse pleasant then | profitable.*" Though scholars dispute its authorship,

Locrine is said to be "Newly set foorth, ouerseene and corrected, | By *VV. S.*" on its first appearance from the press of Thomas Creede in 1595. Thereafter it languished until it reappeared in the third folio of 1664, to be reprinted in the fourth folio of 1685 and to become part of the "Shakespeare Apocrypha."

What we now call *3 Henry VI* appeared first in 1595. Its title, "The true Tragedie of Richard | *Duke of Yorke*," is followed by two subtitles: "*and the death of* | good King Henrie the Sixt" and "*with the whole contention betweene* | the two Houses Lancaster | and Yorke." We are told who acted the play, and where, by whom, for whom, and when it was printed, as well as where it could be purchased. All that is missing is the author's name, missing as well in the second edition of 1600. Indeed, this is true for all the plays of Shakespeare published before 1598.

That year, the first play whose first edition includes Shakespeare's name on the title page, *Love's Labour's Lost*, is published. Interestingly, however, rather than making a claim for Shakespeare's authorship in any simple sense, the title page asserts instead that the play has been "Newly corrected and augmented | By *W. Shakespeare*." In 1599, the third edition of what we now know as *1 Henry IV* was published with Shakespeare's name on the title page, but the following year the first edition of *Henry V* makes no mention of Shakespeare's authorship (nor for that matter do subsequent editions in 1602 and 1619). Later that year, however, *2 Henry IV, Much Ado About Nothing, A Midsummer Night's Dream*, and *The Merchant of Venice* appeared, all bearing Shakespeare's name. Thus, twelve or thirteen years after he came to London, seven years after the publication *Venus and Adonis*, with more than half of his "*oeuvre*" complete, William Shakespeare had arrived.

Shakespeare the Author

Authorship has value; authorship has cachet. We have spoken of *Locrine*, published in 1595 as "Newly set foorth, ouerseene and corrected, | By *VV. S.*" After Shakespeare's "arrival" as an author/playmaker in 1600, other plays joined *Locrine*. In 1602 appeared "THE | True Chronicle Hi-| storie of the whole life and death | of *Thomas* Lord Cromwell. | As it hath beene sundrie times pub-| *likely Acted by the Right Hono-*| rable the Lord Chamberlaine | *his Seruants*. | Written by W.S." *Thomas Lord Cromwell* was reprinted in 1613, with the "W.S." attribution, and it appeared next in the third folio of 1664 as one of the plays, along with *Locrine*, added as being Shakespearian. Joining that group in 1605 is "*THE* | LONDON | Prodigall. | As it was plaide by the Kings Maie-| sties seruants. | By *VVilliam Shakespeare*." It too appeared in the third folio, as did "THE | PVRITAINE | Or | THE VVIDDOVV | of Watling-street. | *Acted by the Children of Paules*. | Written by W. S," published in 1607. In 1608 appeared "A | YORKSHIRE | Tragedy. | *Not so New as Lamentable* | and true. | *Acted by his Maiesties Players at* | the *Globe*. | *VVritten by* VV. Shakespeare." *A Yorkshire Tragedy* was reprinted in 1619 and joined those plays added to the third folio in 1664. *Pericles* (THE LATE, | And much admired Play, | Called | Pericles, Prince | of Tyre. | With the true Relation of the whole Historie, | aduentures, and fortunes of the said Prince: | As also, | The no lesse strange, and worthy accidents, | in the Birth and Life, of his Daughter | *MARIANA*. | As it hath been diuers and sundry times acted by his Maiesties Seruants, at the Globe on | the Banck-side. | By William Shakespeare) was first published in 1609 and saw two editions in that year and editions in 1611, 1619, 1630, and 1635. It too found its way into the folio of 1664. Unlike its neighbors in the third folio, *Pericles* has found its way into the canon, part of all one-volume editions of Shakespeare.

At the same time as the above plays, some now more canonical than others, were being published with Shakespeare as their implied or stated author, the "real" Shakespeare continued to find its way into print. As in so much else, *Hamlet* seems to be a turning point. The first quarto of *Hamlet* was published in 1603: "THE | Tragicall Historie of | HAMLET | *Prince of Denmark* | By Williams Shake-speare. | As it hath beene diuerse times acted by his Highnesse ser- | uants in the Cittie of London: as also in the two V-| niuersities of Cambridge and Oxford, and else-where." This "bad" quarto, or "short" quarto, or quarto whose text is considerably shorter than the texts of *Hamlet* that follow it, this *Hamlet* with its emphasis on the play's productions on the title page – this *Hamlet* was replaced by a second, "good," "long" quarto in 1604, with the information about the play's staging replaced by information about the play's text: "Newly imprinted and enlarged to almost as much | againe as it was, according to the true and perfect | Coppie." The stage has given way to the study, the action to the word. That enlarged edition of 1604 reappeared in 1611 and again in an undated edition, then in 1637, in 1676, in an undated edition, in 1683, and finally in 1695. For the most part these texts resisted influence from the first folio's version of the play.

The title page of the first edition of *King Lear* (1608) conjoins the author to his text and both to the court, the stage, and a religion that permitted plays to be staged: "M. William Shak-speare: | *HIS* | True Chronicle Historie of the life and | death of King Lear and his three | Daughters. | *With the vnfortunate life of* Edgar, *sonne* | and heire to the Earle of Gloster, and his | sullen and assumed humor of | TOM of Bedlam: | *As it was played before the Kings Maiesties at Whitehall vpon* | S. Stephans *night in Christmas Hollidayes*. | By his Maiesties seruants playing vsually at the Gloabe | on the Bancke-side." This same information was reprinted in 1619 for the Pavier quarto (dated 1608) of that year. More tantalizing is the edition which Jane Bell published in 1655, the same year that *Lucrece* appeared in a drastically modified form, a year in which the afterglow of the revolution may have been waning. The 1655 quarto has the same information as its 1608 ancestor. In a nation whose king had been executed in 1649, in a nation ruled by a Commonwealth headed by Oliver Cromwell, how would readers have responded to "*As it was plaid before the Kings Maiesty at Whit-hall, vp-*| *on S. Stephens night, in Christmas Holllidaies*. | By his Maiesties Servants, playing vsually at the | *Globe* on the *Bank-side*"? There was no king's majesty; Whitehall would not have been used for theatrical events; and the Globe (built in 1599, destroyed by fire on 13 June 1613 during a performance of *Henry VIII*, and rebuilt in 1614) had been pulled down in 1644. This is not to say that title pages need be political. It is to suggest, however, that history sometimes pushes them in that direction.

As if designed to confound, the title pages of the two issues of the first edition of *Troilus and Cressida*, both printed in 1609, are every bit as vexing as this problematic "problem" play. The play was entered in the Stationers' Register on 7 February 1603: "*Ent. (J.) Roberts in full Court, to print when he hath gotten sufficient authority: the booke of Troilus and Cressida, as yt is acted by my Lord Chamberlens men.*" But Roberts never printed "*the booke...as yt is acted.*" On 28 January 1609 Richard Bonian and Henry Walley entered "*a booke called the history of Troylus and Cressida.*" A quarto edition was printed in that year, in two issues. The first issue entitles the play "THE | Historie of Troylus | and Cresseida. | *As it was acted by the Kings Maiesties* | seruants at the Globe. | *Written by* William Shakespeare." Information about the place, date, printer, publishers, and place of purchase follows. The verso of the title page is blank, and the text of the play itself commences on the next page, concluding some ninety pages later. Of this issue four copies survive. But this issue was cancelled – which is to say, its title page was removed and replaced with another title page, reading: "THE | Famous Historie of | Troylus *and* Cresseid. | *Excellently expressing the beginning* | of their loues, with the conceited wooing | of *Pandarus* Prince of *Licia.* | *Written* by William Shakespeare." The verso of that new title page is blank, but another leaf has been added. Called "The Epistle" and addressed "A neuer writer, to an euer reader. Newes," the epistle states that the play was never performed ("neuer stal'd with the Stage"), suggesting that it was published against "the grand possessors wills." The movement from stage to page, from print as record of a performance to print as separate from and superior to performance, offers a striking conclusion to those plays of Shakespeare that appeared in print in his lifetime.

The Pavier Quartos

Shakespeare's death in 1616 was initially met with silence. No elegies were published, nor was there any immediate attempt to memorialize his work as a playwright. Indeed, his retirement to Stratford in 1611 coincided with the beginning of a lull in the publication of his plays (see table on p. 411). Editions of *Hamlet*, *Titus Andronicus*, and *Pericles* appeared in 1611. A sixth edition of *1 Henry IV*, a consistently popular play, was published in 1613, a sixth edition of *Richard II*, another strong seller, in 1615. These five editions, however, are the only extant plays by Shakespeare published between 1610 and 1618 (another nine-year span, 1597–1605, by comparison, saw the publication of twenty-four editions), suggesting that the period of Shakespeare's retirement and death saw a decline in demand for his plays. No longer fashionable, but not yet taken up as objects of nostalgia or recognized as classics, Shakespeare's plays existed in something of a limbo in the three years after his death. This was, of course, soon to change.

The year 1619 witnessed one of the most fascinating and mysterious episodes in the long and complicated history of Shakespeare in print. It was in this year that Thomas Pavier produced an unprecedented ten separate titles, attributing all to Shakespeare.

The first in this series was a volume comprised of *The First Part of the Contention* (now known as *2 Henry VI*), *The Second Part of the Contention* (initially published as *The True Tragedie of Richard duke of Yorke* in 1595 and now referred to as *3 Henry VI*), and *Pericles*. Though each of these three plays has its own title page, the use of continuous signatures is evidence that they were intended to form the beginning (Pavier may well have envisioned a larger book including all ten titles) or the entirety of a single volume. The opening title page for the first time asserts Shakespeare's authorship of *1 Contention*: "Written by W. Shakespeare, Gent." This is also the first title page to claim the status of gentleman for Shakespeare. Pavier thus began his series with an overt attempt to reconstitute Shakespeare by combining two discrete and anonymous publications into an author(iz)ed and aesthetic, if turbulent, unity: *The Whole Contention*. A different dynamic is visible in the next playbook produced by Pavier. *A Yorkshire Tragedy*, discussed above, was entered in the Stationers' Register by Pavier in 1608, where it is identified as having been written by "Wylliam Shakespere." Pavier immediately published an edition in 1608 with a title page again claiming Shakespeare's authorship. Unlike *The Whole Contention*, which makes a new claim for authorship, the 1619 edition of *The Yorkshire Tragedy* simply repeats the assertion made in 1608.

The titles that followed in this series of playbooks – and it is evident that these several publications were conceived as a series – were *The Excellent History of the Merchant of Venice*; *A Most pleasaunt and excellent conceited Comedy, of Sir John Falstaffe, and the merrie VVives of VVindsor*; *M. William Shake-speare, his True Chronicle History of the life and death of King Lear, and his three Daughters*; *The Chronicle History of Henry the Fift*; *The first part of the true & honorable history, of the Life of Sir John Old-castle*; and, finally, *A Midsommer nights dreame*. Of these ten plays, Pavier had a clearly legitimate claim to only four: *1 Oldcastle, 1 Contention, Yorkshire Tragedy*, and *Henry V*. It is more than possible, however, that Pavier made arrangements with the owners of the other plays (Johnson 1992). Leaving aside the rather murky question of property rights, it is clear that something unusual happened. After the initial four offerings, the plays appeared with false imprints intended to disguise the date of publication and/or the publisher's name.

All these plays were printed in the shop of William Jaggard, a printer with whom Pavier had worked before. But there is some uncertainty over whether Pavier was dealing with William or his son Isaac. In any case, it seems clear that something occurred that caused the publisher to shift strategies, abandoning the plan for a single volume, and then abandoning the very idea of open publication. This change in direction is usually attributed to the intervention of William Herbert, earl of Pembroke and lord chamberlain. The Court of the Stationers' Company registers receipt of a letter from the lord chamberlain and endorses its demand with an entry stating that: "It is thought fitt & so ordered That no playes that his Ma^{tyes} players do play shalbe printed w^{th}out consent of som*me* of them" (Jackson 1957: 110). As lord chamberlain, Herbert supervised the King's Men, who were considered liveried servants of the royal household, and it has been assumed that he intervened in order to protect the interests of Shakespeare's former acting company. It is not clear, however, whether Herbert's letter was an attempt to protect the theatrical repertory of the company or to forestall the appearance of a book that would compete with an as yet unpublished collection of Shakespeare's dramatic works. Indeed, it is possible that the Pavier quartos galvanized others into conceiving an even more ambitious project, the first folio. While the precise motive underlying Herbert's letter remains obscure, one of its consequences at least appears incontestable: Pavier felt compelled to disguise several of his quartos by providing them with false imprints, perhaps in order to allow them to be passed off and sold as "old" stock.

If these false imprints were an attempt to fool the officers of the Stationers' Company or the copyright-holders, they were remarkably sloppy: they make no effort to replicate precisely the title pages of earlier editions. It may be, as Gerald Johnson (1992) has suggested, that the wardens of the Stationers' Company were themselves satisfied with the appearance of compliance. Indeed, whoever felt their interests damaged by the quartos may have been willing to countenance the appearance of apparently old playbooks on the grounds that they might actually help create a market for a new, authoritative edition. Whether the Pavier quartos are evidence of renewed interest in Shakespeare's plays or whether they are themselves in part the cause of a revival of interest, there is little question that the period immediately following this strange episode saw the production of the most important single book in the long publication history of Shakespearian drama.

Before considering the first folio, however, we must pause over the first edition of *Othello*, published by Thomas Walkley in 1622. Apparently Walkley felt no pressure to disguise this publication, despite the ruling of the Stationers' court. *Othello* appears with an accurate imprint; "Printed by N.O. for *Thomas Walkley*, and are to be sold at his shop, at the Eagle and Child, in Brittans Bursse. 1622." However, perhaps, the most striking aspect of this quarto is Walkley's short preface in which he asserts that "the Authors name is sufficient to vent his worke" (A2^r). If this was not true at the end of the sixteenth century, seemingly it has become true in the seventeenth. The appearance of this preface is highly unusual; indeed, the only other Shakespeare quarto that has a preface is the second issue of *Troilus and Cressida* (1609), discussed above. Interestingly, Walkley explains that no book should appear without an epistle, "and the Author being dead, I thought good to take that piece of worke vpon mee." Death becomes an author, freeing editors and publishers to shape that author's image without fear of contradictions or troublesome new developments. It is perhaps not surprising that Walkley engages directly with the problem posed by dead Shake-speare's dramatic legacy, for at the very moment in which his quarto of *Othello* appears, others are hard at work producing the first folio.

The First Folio

The first folio distinguishes itself from Pavier's collection in two important respects. While there is no evidence to suggest that Pavier intended a complete collection of

Shakespeare's plays, the producers of the folio clearly aimed to be, or at least to appear, comprehensive. Secondly, whereas Pavier was content to use the quarto format that had traditionally been employed for the printing of plays, the publishers of this book opted for the luxurious folio format, usually reserved for reference works and canonical literature, classical or modern. Indeed, the one precedent for printing contemporary drama in folio format is Ben Jonson's *Workes*, published in 1616, the year of Shakespeare's death. Unlike that book, however, the Shakespeare folio does not include poetic works.

What it does include is thirty-six plays, eighteen never before published (see figure 24.2). Of the eighteen that had been printed before, only two appear unaltered: *Much Ado* and Q2 *Romeo and Juliet*. Four – the "bad" quartos of *The Merry Wives, Henry V, 1 Contention, Richard Duke of York* – were replaced by versions presumably based on authoritative manuscripts. Of the remaining twelve, six were printed from edited copies of the printed text, and six were printed from manuscripts. In all, this means that the folio provides twenty-two texts that are either new or substantive departures from their predecessors and another twelve that offer significant textual variants (Blayney 1991: 1). Excluded from the folio are *Pericles* and *Two Noble Kinsmen*, as well as *A Yorkshire Tragedy* and *1 Sir John Oldcastle*, two of the plays that Pavier had attributed to Shakespeare.

The folio was a complicated project, requiring the cooperation of a broad cast of characters. The two main publishers, Edward Blount and Isaac Jaggard, were responsible for collecting the various texts and negotiating with the owners of previously published plays. For unpublished material they turned to Shakespeare's old colleagues John Heminges and Henry Condell, who, as principal actors and shareholders of the King's Men, were in a position to provide authorial manuscripts, transcriptions, and promptbooks from the playhouse. Dealing with the owners of previously printed plays could be more complicated. The simplest solution would have been to purchase the plays outright from their current owners, but it is clear that this was not always possible, and that therefore the publishers may have arranged for the right to publish a given play only in the folio. Presumably, *Troilus and Cressida* was considered unattainable at the time that the folio's table of contents was printed, for it makes no mention of the play. However, an arrangement with Henry Walley, the play's owner, must have been reached sometime shortly afterwards, because most copies of the folio do indeed include the play. Yet its place within the volume – inserted in front of the other tragedies without pagination – reveals that it was only added at the very last minute. Alternatively, there is the case of Walkley to consider. *Othello* appears in the folio, but it seems unlikely that Walkley actually sold all his rights to the play, for in 1628 he assigned *Othello* to another stationer, Richard Hawkins, who published a quarto edition of it in 1630. The publishers also appear to have run into difficulties in their negotiations with Matthew Law, who owned *Richard II, Richard III*, and *1 Henry IV*. The irregular pagination of the section of history plays presumably indicates that the acquisition of these plays was not untroubled. Again, like Walkley, Law appears to have retained the rights to his plays, because he himself published an

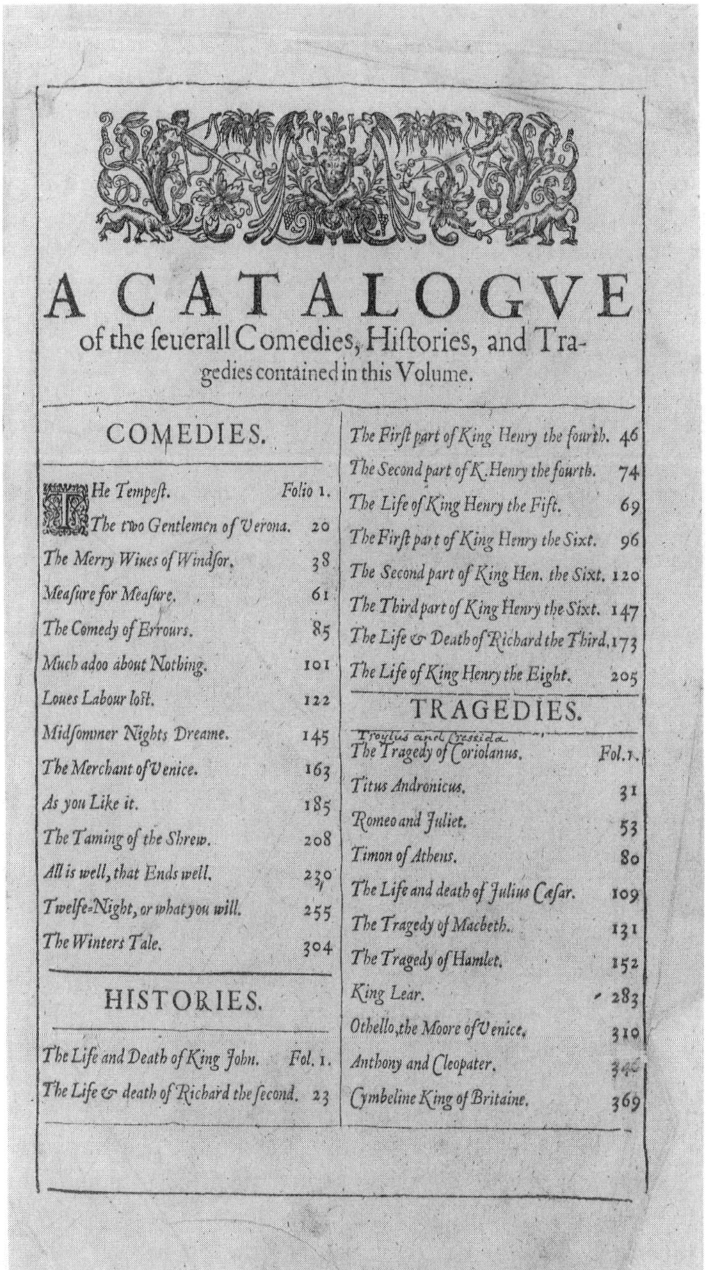

A CATALOGVE

of the ſeuerall Comedies, Hiſtories, and Tragedies contained in this Volume.

COMEDIES.

The Tempeſt. Folio 1.
The two Gentlemen of Verona. 20
The Merry Wiues of Windſor. 38
Meaſure for Meaſure. 61
The Comedy of Errours. 85
Much adoo about Nothing. 101
Loues Labour loſt. 122
Midſommer Nights Dreame. 145
The Merchant of Venice. 163
As you Like it. 185
The Taming of the Shrew. 208
All is well, that Ends well. 230
Twelfe-Night, or what you will. 255
The Winters Tale. 304

HISTORIES.

The Life and Death of King John. Fol. 1.
The Life & death of Richard the ſecond. 23
The Firſt part of King Henry the fourth. 46
The Second part of K. Henry the fourth. 74
The Life of King Henry the Fift. 69
The Firſt part of King Henry the Sixt. 96
The Second part of King Hen. the Sixt. 120
The Third part of King Henry the Sixt. 147
The Life & Death of Richard the Third. 173
The Life of King Henry the Eight. 205

TRAGEDIES.

Troylus and Cressida
The Tragedy of Coriolanus. Fol. 1.
Titus Andronicus. 31
Romeo and Juliet. 53
Timon of Athens. 80
The Life and death of Julius Cæſar. 109
The Tragedy of Macbeth. 131
The Tragedy of Hamlet. 152
King Lear. 283
Othello, the Moore of Venice. 310
Anthony and Cleopater. 346
Cymbeline King of Britaine. 369

Figure 24.2 Catalogue of plays from the Shakespeare folio (1623). Used by permission of the Folger Shakespeare Library.

edition of *Richard III* in 1629. Another approach was used with John Smethwick and William Aspley, who together held the rights to six plays. Perhaps unwilling to sell or lease their rights, they were allowed to join Blount and Jaggard in the role of publishers, though presumably as lesser partners in the undertaking.

The rather mundane machinations of these men of business led, in time, to the production of a striking, if not exceptionally handsome, volume. The title page is dominated by Martin Droeshout's engraving of Shakespeare, which provides an icon of authorial authenticity. This image serves as visual verification of the title's claim: "MR. WILLIAM | SHAKESPEARES | COMEDIES, | HISTORIES, & | TRAGEDIES. | Published according to the True Originall Copies." On the opposite page, a short poem, "To the Reader" by Ben Jonson, urges the reader to "looke / Not on his Picture, but his Booke." But it is, of course, far from clear in what sense it is *his* book. Most obviously it belongs to the syndicate led by Blount and Jaggard; or, more accurately, it belongs to a specific reader who has paid the steep purchase price of about a pound. Publication of the volume was an expensive undertaking; it is no wonder that Heminges and Condell implore the reader: "What euer you do, Buy."

Nonetheless, Heminges and Condell, in their dedication to the earls of Pembroke and Montgomery, insist that because death deprived Shakespeare of the opportunity "to be exequutor to his writings" (A2^r), they, his friends, must take up the responsibility: "We have but collected them, and done an office to the dead, to procure his Orphanes, Guardians; without ambition either of selfe-profit, or fame: onely to keepe the memory of so worthy a Friend, & Fellow aliue, as was our SHAKESPEARE" (A2^v). Their work is simultaneously an act of memorialization and a mere collecting of that which already exists. In their address, "To the great Variety of Readers," Heminges and Condell again express regret over the fact that death has kept Shakespeare from overseeing the publication of his own writings. Yet, whereas before readers "were abus'd with diuerse stolne, and surreptitious copies, maimed, and deformed by the frauds and stealthes of iniurious imposters, that expos'd them: euen those, are now offer'd to your view cur'd, and perfect of their limbes; and all the rest, absolute in their numbers, as he conceiued the*m*" (A3^r). Heminges and Condell here distinguish between plays that have been published ("surreptitious copies") and those that have not ("all the rest"). Though many scholars have argued that "stolen and surreptitious copies" refers to a more restrictive class, the so-called bad quartos, the rhetoric works to identify "exposure" in print with corruption itself. Like attentive surgeons, Heminges and Condell have "cured" these maimed books. Indeed, the more expansive understanding of this designation accords well with what we know of the texts used in the production of the folio. The fact that two plays that had been exposed in print are included without correction actually helps to explain the somewhat ambiguous language of the address: Heminges and Condell would discredit all pre-folio publications; yet for them to declare flatly that every one of these plays is corrupt would involve an obvious contradiction (either that claim is itself false or the assertion that the folio offers only perfect plays is).[5]

Indeed, the whole range of Shakespeare quartos is conveniently available for repudiation; this repudiation gives substance to Heminges and Condell's claim to have published Shakespeare's plays "as he conceiued the*m*." Here, Shakespeare, who never showed the least bit of interest in being a dramatic author while he lived, is identified as the privileged and singular source of literary meaning – an assertion that quite obviously flies in the face of the collaborative fluidity that typified playhouse practices. Rather than being pictured as a literary worker who cooperated with his fellows and responded to a diverse range of pressures, Shakespeare is imagined to have created effortlessly and alone: "His mind and hand went together: And what he thought, he vttered with that easinesse, that wee haue scarce receiued from him a blot in his papers" (A3^r). Not only does this serve to romanticize Shakespeare's artistry, it also works to render the role of the publishers unproblematic: unblotted papers do not require editorial intervention. The whole complicated, and necessarily material, process of textual transmission is made to appear simple and transparent.

It would be both convenient and tidy if the first folio were the culminating and final event in the publication of Shakespeare's works. Such, alas, is definitely not the case. As the table at the end of this essay indicates, Shakespeare's works continued to be published in quarto editions well after his death, well after the first folio. Plays as varied as *1 Henry IV, The Merry Wives of Windsor, Othello, Richard II, Hamlet,* and *Love's Labour's Lost* reappeared, as well as *Two Noble Kinsmen,* which was first published as a quarto in 1634 with a title page attributing its authorship to both John Fletcher and William Shakespeare.

1640 *Poems*

In 1640, John Benson published *POEMS: WRITTEN BY WIL. SHAKE-SPEARE. Gent.,* a volume that, like so many of the Caroline editions of Shakespeare (Berger 1996), reveals a nostalgia for a lost "Elizabethan" world. This octavo volume was printed for Benson by Thomas Cotes, the printer of the second folio, and, as Margreta de Grazia has pointed out, it mimics the appearance of that larger book (1991: 166). Like the folio, Benson's *Poems* has an engraved portrait of the author facing the title page, an address to the reader, and prefatory poems praising Shakespeare. This volume attempts to do with the poems what the folio did with the plays. Like the folio, it offers itself as a memorial designed to fix and perpetuate the reputation of Shakespeare: Benson assures his readers that the poems "appeare of the same purity, the Authour himselfe then liuing auouched" (*2^r) and expresses satisfaction at the thought that his own effort has been "serviceable for the continuance of glory to the deserved Author in these his Poems" (*2^v).

At the same time, Benson's volume reveals that Shakespeare's poetry has not yet achieved a canonical fixity. At the center of the volume are 146 of Shakespeare's 154 sonnets, but they have been grouped together and printed as 72 single poems comprised of one, two, three, four, and even five sonnets. Benson's apparent textual intervention was not, however, limited to rearranging the sonnets: in several cases pronouns were switched from masculine to feminine, and nouns were changed in order to obscure the gender of the addressee. To these modified sonnets have been added another twenty-nine poems taken from *The Passionate Pilgrim* (1612), a miscellany that had claimed, in its 1599 edition and in some states of the 1612 edition, Shakespeare's authorship. All these poems are set off by horizontal rules and short titles. Thus one finds Sonnet 20, addressed to "the Master Mistris of my passion," titled, "The Exchange" (B4^r). Sonnet 116, "Let me not to the marriage of true mindes / Admit impediments," is designated, "The Picture of true love" (D3^v–D4^r). This series of "Shakespearian" poems concludes with three elegies for Shakespeare, followed by a section entitled "An Addition of some Excellent Poems, to those precedent, of Renowned *Shakespeare*, By other Gentlemen" (L2^r). These editorial choices have more or less guaranteed that Benson's volume is looked upon as little more than a curiosity. Though scholars no longer insist that the volume was an illegal reprint of the sonnets (according to this theory, the rearrangement of the sonnets is merely an attempt to disguise illicit material), the taint of illegitimacy lingers. After all, Benson's own claim is demonstrably false – the poems presented are not all Shakespeare's, and those that are have been tampered with.

While it is certainly true that Benson did not trouble to authenticate (however that might have been done) the various poems he attributed to Shakespeare, those that he did include had appeared in print earlier under Shakespeare's name. To accuse Benson of duplicity is to mistake his principle of selection. Benson is actually attempting to capture an entire poetic milieu, an Elizabethan age of unfettered and limpid eloquence that goes, synecdochically, by the name of "Shakespeare." The introduction of poem titles is part of a strategy that would insist on the clarity and universal applicability of these poems and secure the legibility of a particular aesthetic. This strategy is not dictated by an unadulterated nostalgia; as always, nostalgia finds its motives in the contemporary scene. Benson's address describes Shakespeare's poetry as "*Seren*, cleere and elegantly plaine, such gentle straines as shall recreate and not perplexe your braine, no intricate or cloudy stuffe to puzzell intellect, but perfect eloquence" (*2^v). The obvious target here is Donne and his imitators. Indeed, Benson's volume bears more than a slight resemblance to the 1635 edition of *POEMS, By J. D. With Elegies on the Authors Death*, which also included an accurate engraving of the author, John Donne, facing the title page. Benson, in turn, offers his readers an alternative to the new obscurity, a chance to experience the poetic beauties of an earlier, and presumably simpler, age.

Other Folio Editions

If the first folio of 1623 was the major event in the publication of Shakespeare's plays, by comparison, the second folio of 1632, the third folio of 1663/4, and the fourth folio of 1684 are of little importance in the history of the texts of Shakespeare. Indeed, the

Table: Chronology of publication

Date	Comedy	Tragedy	History	Poetry	Other
1593				V&A	
1594			2HVI	Luc., V&A	
1595		Tit.	3HVI	V&A	
1596				V&A	
1597		R&J	RII, RIII		
1598	LLL		1HIV, RII, RIII	Luc., V&A	
1599		R&J	1HIV	PP, V&A	
1600	MV, MND, AD0	Tit.	2HIV, HV	Luc.	
1601				P&T	
1602	MWW		HV, RIII	V&A(?)	
1603		Ham.	RII		
1604		Ham.	1HIV		
1605		Ham.	RIII		
1606					
1607				Luc., V&A?	
1608		Lr.	1HIV, RII		
1609		R&J, T&C		Son.	Per.
1610				V&A?	
1611		Ham., Tit.			Per.
1612					
1613			1HIV		
1614					
1615			RII		
1616				Luc.	
1617				V&A	
1618					
1619	MV, MWW, MND		HV, 2HVI, Lr.		Per.
1620				V&A	
1621					
1622		Oth., R&J(?)	1HIV, RIII		
1623	F1	F1	F1	F1	
1624				Luc.	
1625		Ham.			
1626					
1627				V&A	
1628					
1629			RIII		
1630	MWW	Oth.		V&A	Per.
1631	LLL, Shr.				
1632	F2	F2	F2, 1HIV	Luc.	F2
1633				V&A(+/− 3)	
1634			RII, RIII		TNK
1635					Per.
1636				V&A	
1637	MV	Ham., R&J			
1638					
1639			1HIV		
1640				Poems	

second folio based its texts on the first, the third folio on the second, and the fourth folio on the third. These folios, then, possess no textual "authority." In terms of the marketing of Shakespeare, however, they bear some consideration. The second folio's six variant title pages, each bearing the name of a different publisher, are worth noting, the impression being that each of the investors was getting his "share" of the publication through his exclusive appearance on a title page. Do these variant imprints indicate that the project was a risky investment that needed to be shared by many? Or does it indicate that Shakespeare was such a sure-fire favorite that willing investors could be found, thus lowering the risks and improving the profits?

England welcomed Charles II back to its shores in 1660, as the monarchy was restored. It took another three years for a London publisher to welcome the king with a new folio edition of the playwright who, though still shakily, was on his way to becoming the national author. Shortly after this 1663 folio was published, another issue of it appeared, bearing a 1664 imprint, and adding "seven Playes, never before Printed in Folio": *Pericles, The London Prodigal, Thomas Lord Cromwell, Sir John Old-castle, The Puritan, A Yorkshire Tragedy*, and *Locrine*. Of these, only *The Puritan* does not have Shakespeare or "W.S." indicated as the author in an earlier edition. But only *Pericles* has been accepted into the Shakespeare canon. As England welcomed Charles II, so too did London publishing welcome seven new plays into the Shakespeare fold, where they would remain for the rest of the seventeenth century and, for the most part, for all of the eighteenth.

Evidently it took quite some time before print successfully stabilized Shakespeare. Indeed, perfect stability has never been achieved. One has only to examine some of the multitudinous Shakespeare editions now in print to notice that there exist serious and consequential disagreements over not only textual variants but entire plays. Acknowledging the complexity of this situation along with its complicated history does not lead inevitably to a corrosive skepticism toward modern editions of Shakespeare. Editing is a necessary process of mediation that prepares a text for reception at a particular historical moment, and this is why no edition is ever definitive: new circumstances bring new needs and interests, and, therefore, new editions. However, we would urge students and scholars alike to compare their modern editions of Shakespeare with readily available facsimiles, such as the Norton first folio (1968, 1996) and Allen's and Muir's collection of quartos (1981). Just look. The vagaries of print offer a wide world of variety – a multiplicity not to be lamented but explored.

NOTES

1 For the burgeoning world of print in early modern England, see Pollard and Redgrave 1976, a gold mine of information.

2 This presumes not only that we know what *was* Shakespeare's most profitable work but

wherein profit lies. Shakespeare made his living, on which he became a prosperous "Gent." of Stratford, not by writing plays but by being a "sharer" (a partner) in the Lord Chamberlain's Men, which, on the death of Queen

Elizabeth and the accession of King James I, became the King's Men. His major concern in that enterprise was writing plays for the company to act.

3 Whether it has been settled at the end of the twentieth century is debatable. Who are the "authors" of, among other programs, "Cheers," "The Mary Tyler Moore Show," "Seinfeld," and "The Simpsons"? How many literary critics would call them "Works"? Thus, when Ben Jonson published plays among his "Works" in 1616, he was the subject of ridicule is some quarters.

4 *Titus Andronicus* was entered in the Stationers' Register on 6 February 1594 by John Danter, who would print the play that year. No author is given, only *"a noble roman historye of Tytus Andronicus."* The next play entered in the Stationers' Register is *A Looking-Glass for London and England*. Thomas Creede, the printer, entered the play, but of some interest is that

the play's authors, Thomas Lodge and Robert Greene, also appear in the entry. Their names also appear on the title pages of all the early editions (1594, 1598, 1602, and 1617), along with their titles ("Gentleman" for Lodge, *"In Artibus Magister"* for Greene), suggesting that authorship (at least for plays) and social status are closely linked. In the first edition of Christopher Marlowe's *Edward II* (1594), the title page is careful to note that Marlowe is a *"Gent."* Later that year, however, Marlowe's name stands alone on the title page of *The Massacre at Paris*.

5 W. W. Greg criticizes earlier bibliographers who, noticing this apparent contradiction, accused Heminges and Condell of "branding themselves as frauds and liars" (1955: 83). Greg follows Pollard (1909) in reading "stolen and surreptitious copies" as designating only "bad" quartos, thus insisting that the two men are, in fact, honorable and pious editors.

REFERENCES

Arber, Edward (ed.) 1875–9: *A Transcript of the Registers of the Company of Stationers of London: 1554–1640 A.D.* 5 vols. London: n. p. Repr. Birmingham: n. p., 1894.

Berger, Thomas L. 1996: Looking for Shakespeare in Caroline England. *Viator*, 27, 323–59.

Blayney, Peter W. M. 1991: *The First Folio of Shakespeare*. Washington, D.C.: Folger Library Publications.

de Grazia, Margreta 1991: *Shakespeare Verbatim: The Reproduction of Authenticity and the 1790 Apparatus*. Oxford: Clarendon Press.

Duncan-Jones, Katherine (ed.) 1997: *Shakespeare's Sonnets*. Nashville, Tenn.: Thomas Nelson.

Greg, W. W. 1939–59: *A Bibliography of the English Printed Drama to the Restoration*, 4 vols. London: Bibliographical Society.

—— 1955: *The Shakespeare First Folio: Its Bibliographical and Textual History*. Oxford: Clarendon Press.

Jackson, William A. (ed.) 1957: *Records of the Court of the Stationers' Company, 1602 to 1640*. London: Bibliographical Society.

Johnson, Gerald D. 1992: Thomas Pavier, publisher, 1600–25. *Library*, 14, 12–50.

Marcus, Leah S. 1996: *Unediting the Renaissance: Shakespeare, Marlowe, Milton*. New York: Routledge.

Pollard, A. W. 1909: *Shakespeare Folios and Quartos*. London: Methuen.

Pollard, A. W. and Redgrave, G. R. 1976–91: *A Short-Title Catalogue of Books Printed in England, Scotland, and Ireland and of English Books Printed Abroad, 1475–1640*, 2nd edn rev. W. A. Jackson, F. S. Ferguson, and Katharine Pantzer, 3 vols. London: Bibliographical Society.

Shakespeare, William 1968: *The Norton Facsimile: The First Folio of Shakespeare*, ed. Charlton Hinman. New York: Norton.

—— 1981: *Shakespeare's Plays in Quarto: A Facsimile Edition of Copies Primarily from the Henry E. Huntington Library*, ed. with introduction and notes by Michael J. B. Allen and Kenneth Muir. Berkeley: University of California Press.

25

"Precious Few": English Manuscript Playbooks

William B. Long

I refer to surviving English manuscript playbooks as "Precious Few" in two senses: there are "precious few" of them, because only eighteen survive out of probably 3,000, and these few are precious because they comprise our chief repository for knowing what kinds of manuscripts playwrights delivered to the playing companies and for finding out how the players altered these manuscripts in putting plays into production. These manuscripts thus are not merely antiquarian curiosities; they comprise the major source for theater researchers into staging and production and for revealing to editors what was likely to happen to a manuscript in the playhouse.

Given their seminal and vital importance, it might well be assumed that much research had been done on them, that their features had been well examined, and their significance and implications become the commonplaces of scholarly papers on theater practice and in textual introductions to the plays of William Shakespeare and his contemporaries. If such were the case, there would be no need to write this essay. Alas, these "precious few" generally have been ignored: theater researchers regularly make suppositions about staging and "directing" without referring to surviving manuscripts; in seeking to establish the nature of the manuscripts which lay behind printed editions, editors expend great quantities of ink discussing "promptbooks" and what they should reveal as they babble on, constructing a screen of flimflam, weaving explanations out of their imaginations while ignorantly (or arrogantly or both) ignoring even the mention of the existence of these surviving playbooks. One can read textual introduction after textual introduction to the plays of William Shakespeare, for example, without finding a single mention of these playbooks, while these same editors have no qualms whatsoever about inventing features which "promptbooks" would be expected to contain. It is obviously much easier (and probably more fun) to conjure up explanations of the provenance of a text without being fettered by surviving historical evidence.

It is into this sorry state of affairs, then, that this essay comes as, essentially, a piece of advertising. For those who do not know about them, here is a brief survey of the eighteen surviving manuscript playbooks and at least some of the kinds of things they reveal – information to be found nowhere else among the bits and pieces of evidence surviving from the Elizabethan–Jacobean–Caroline theaters.

Let us begin with the label "promptbook," which editors invariably use when referring to what I have called "manuscript playbooks." "Promptbook" is not an innocuous descriptive identification of a kind of play text; it is a highly judgmental label connoting the function of playwrights, players, theater personnel, their relation to each other, and assumptions of how these people worked to get plays on the stage. The term "promptbook" is not used in the Elizabethan–Jacobean–Caroline theater; to use it in discussing pre-1660 play manuscripts is anachronistic, teleological, and very confusing, if not deliberately obfuscating. The term used in pre-Restoration playhouses to refer to these manuscript plays used in the theater is "playbook" – sometimes referred to as "the book"; they are never called "promptbooks." Those who use such a book, hold it, keep it, and occasionally make a mark in it are called, most commonly, "bookkeeper" and occasionally "bookholder." They are never referred to as "prompter." The issue is not a pedantic one of nomenclature. The two sets of terms reflect radically different sets of assumptions about how playwrights tailored their manuscripts for acting companies and how the players used these manuscript plays. Thus these attitudes in turn radically condition how one regards early printed editions. "Promptbook" connotes an authoritarian document with heavy extra-authorial alterations and a managerial direction of players. "Playbook" connotes a cooperative venture in which the playwright and the players collaborate by contributing separate, complementary elements to create a play production. Since many investigators now admit that certain choices must be made in assembling their narratives of the origin of printed books, attitude is vital. Insistence on using earlier, historical terms keeps reminding both the commentators and their readers that the earlier theaters were in many very important ways much different from their successors; and they must be thought about and dealt with differently.

Understanding playbooks and how they functioned begins with understanding how they were constructed – even before anything was written on the paper. All surviving manuscripts that were constructed into playbooks started out as sheets of paper measuring approximately twelve inches by sixteen inches. Initially such a sheet was folded in half, making a longitudinal page of about eight inches by twelve inches which could carry fifty to eighty lines, depending upon the size of the handwriting and the desire or need of the writer to save space. For the sake of convenience, the bookkeepers seem to have folded the books so that only one page would be visible at a time – the leaves in turn being folded back against each other – an easy thing to do with unbound stitched sheets. The advantage of having tall, thin books rather than short, fat ones or horizontally oriented ones should be obvious; they are easier to handle and to read. In trying to find directions or lines of text, the fewer times one has to turn a page, the better; for each turning creates possibilities of loss or confusion.

And all page turnings are not equal. Given the shape of the book, except for the initial page, two pages were available almost simultaneously; the bookkeeper merely had to flip the book to execute a turning from a reverse page to the obverse page of the next leaf, a "b" to "a" turning; but to turn a page from an obverse to its reverse, an "a" to "b" turning was needed – a much more time-consuming and difficult maneuver because a leaf had to be turned, rather than flipping the book itself. This took more effort and was subject to error. Several playbooks display instances showing book-keepers insuring against errors (usually in timing of music or sensitive entrances) by copying stage directions originally appearing at the top of a "b" (reverse) page to the bottom of the preceding "a" (obverse) page so that something important would not be missed in the turning of the page.

Once the playwright or scribe made this initial fold in his sheet, he then made two more equal longitudinal folds, thus producing a sheet of four pages, each divided into four equal columns. Whether composing or copying, whether playwright or scribe, the writers of these playbooks inscribed their texts in the center two columns, reserving the left column for speech headings and the right for long prose lines, the occasional exit, and even rarer stage directions. Most entrances were placed in the center columns. It was a practical and sensible arrangement: everything has its place. Anyone looking for something, even in a manuscript from a playwright or a company with which he was unfamiliar, would know where to look. Sometimes, of course, in the hurly-burly, some writings would be out of place; but I think that it is important to know that there were assumed places where certain things were expected to be found. There was a system; there was even a pattern. A playwright setting about to craft a play did not have to invent the wheel.

Critics, and even theater historians, while acknowledging that the players and playwrights were professionals because they were paid for their efforts, often fail to explore other aspects of what their professionalism meant. One of the results of studying these playbooks is a realization and an appreciation of some of the many aspects of professionalism displayed there.

When writing (or copying) a play, playwrights and scribes did not copy line for line across the page from one edge to the other as most modern writers would be prone to do. Rather, they regularly copied the play text first, carefully ticking off the end of each speech (however long or short) with a speech rule of approximately one inch beginning slightly into the left column. When the text of the page, several pages, or sometimes the entire play was complete, the speech headings were then added, a phenomenon I call "the ease of copying habit" because it is easier and faster to copy play texts in this manner. The speech rules would show their proper locations; but often in copying them, speech headings are slightly misaligned, appearing slightly ahead of the speech rules. This is an accident of (probably too rapid) copying; it is not a sign of "anticipated" entries as is often assumed.

For those accustomed to more modern directorial practices, these manuscript playbooks are far more sparsely marked than one might expect. A 2,500-line playbook might bear twenty-five theatrical alterations, or ten, or none – but certainly not the

dozens or hundreds which modern expectations assume were added. Elizabethan–
Jacobean–Caroline theatrical notation was a reaction to a problem, not an end in itself;
nothing was done to a playwright's directions unless the players found it to be
necessary. There was no marking for regularity or thoroughness, no set group of
alterations made to a manuscript once it got to a theater. There was no "tidying up" or
"regularization" that modern editors are so fond of claiming surely must be signs of a
"promptbook." So infrequently do theatrical alterations occur that if a stage direction
exists in a late sixteenth- or early seventeenth-century play text, manuscript or
printed, it is most likely a playwright's. If a rule is needed for judging what happened
to a playwright's manuscript in the theater, it must be "as little was done as was
possible." When playhouse notations are added, they solve problems – generally that
of ensuring proper timing. Regularity of marking is not to be expected from play
to play or even within the same play. What may have caused a problem at one point
in a play often did not in a similar situation at another point in the same play. Nearly
all playhouse markings were made to insure the smoothness of a production, but there
is no infallible checklist of such situations.

Nor can it be assumed that all directions inscribed by playwrights necessarily were
followed. However sensible such a proposition may seem, it does not reckon with the
fact that the players were remarkably casual (by modern expectations) about how they
regarded what was written in the playbook and what they wanted and/or were able to
do with it. Again and again it becomes obvious that these manuscripts cannot be used
to reconstruct a performance with the relative assurance that a modern promptbook
can. Great caution needs to be exercised also in treating what I have labeled "playwright's advisory directions" – directions in which the playwright details a player's
location, or movement, or expressions. These do not include mere entrances and exits,
nor do they include indications of costumes or properties; rather, a playwright's
advisory direction is a direction in which the playwright tells the player *what* to do
and/or *how* to do it.

In general, playwrights tend to over-advise – to include stage business in entrance
directions, to add directions for actions implicit in the dialogue; but the more
experienced the professional playwright, the fewer such directions he adds and the
more of the enacting of his play he leaves in what he assumes or knows to be the
capable hands of the players. It is thus hardly surprising – albeit frustrating – to find
so few stage directions in the plays of William Shakespeare, not only a professional
playwright, but also a player and a shareholder in the playing company. The extant
playbooks show that amateur playwrights add far more playwrights' advisory directions than do the professionals, presumably because the amateur is less well
acquainted with the backstage workings of the theater and thus does not always
understand the abilities of the players to handle his play. The amateurs, as a rule, will
tell *how*, not just *what*.

Players add or delete according to their needs, not because of custom or habit. They
apparently saw no need to change or to delete playwrights' minutiae if they were not
observing them. And they almost never change a playwright's call for an unspecified

number of extras. A call for "others" or something similar obviously was a signal for two, or three, or however many, and no specification was needed for the book. Thus modern scholarly predispositions can lead to great difficulty if they expect not only word-for-word fidelity to playwrights' instructions, but also that players would clarify theatrical details by carefully inscribing them in the book. None of the theatrical personnel who add notations to the surviving playbooks shows any inclination to clarify, particularize, or regularize either stage directions or speech headings. We must never forget that playbooks were of, by, and for the theater; they existed solely for use by players and theater personnel. It is only by occasional accident (and great good fortune for us) that any found their way to the printing house and thus to not only a vastly wider, but also a very, very different readership.

This survey, then, necessarily, only skims the mountaintops of the available material. My aim is to note the general features of each book and to discuss some features in each that are particularly valuable in helping to understand how playwrights and players used the books to produce their plays. The danger with this approach is that readers will take what is exceptional as the rule and look to find such entries far more frequently than they occur. Both detailed directions by playwrights and additions by playhouse personnel are always the exception, never the rule.

The earliest surviving playbook is Anthony Munday's holograph of *John a Kent and John a Cumber* (Huntington Library, MS 500), its *terminus ad quem* firmly fixed by the bookkeeper's inscription on the last leaf, the partially deleted "Decembris 1590." Munday folded his sheets into four equal columns, wrote his text in Elizabethan secretary hand, and his speech headings and stage directions in his version of Italian script – the normal pattern for the writing of playbooks. This change of hand is obviously valuable in the theater for telling quickly what was what.

Munday has divided his text into acts; no effort was made to delete these breaks, possibly indicating that they were observed. Considerable caution also must be used in deciding if a playwright's indications of act breaks were followed by the players, who rarely delete matter that they consider extraneous. Here there is no effort to indicate scenes even though the centered act breaks for all but the third add "Scene Prima." The reason for the playwright's notation of the original scene probably came, like the five-act structure itself, from school-text familiarity with Latin drama, which, of course, did indicate scene division. Act and scene divisions in playbooks arise mostly from the playwrights, and, not surprisingly, are not regularized.

There are but seven additions by the bookkeeper, three of which concern calls for music. Munday had entered a call for music in the right-hand column and one as part of a centered entrance: thus they are difficult to see at a glance, and they must be performed at the time specified (fo. 6b, l. 776; fo. 7b, l. 916; and fo. 9a, l. 1138). In each case, the bookkeeper has added "musique" in the left column – making the calls hard to miss. Three markings concern entrances – all quite different, but all concerned with getting a player in to position at a particular, important time, where lateness would skew the dialogue. At fo. 2b, l. 211, the bookkeeper places the word "Enter" followed by a line of one and one-half inches in the left column a line after the entrance of John a Kent to make sense of the last line before his entry: "But what olde man is this comes toward vs?" On fo. 8b, ll. 1048–9, Munday placed a direction in the right column "Ent Iohn / a Ken>t listning." Four lines earlier the bookkeeper wrote in the left column "Enter Iohn / a Kent" so that Kent is onstage long enough that his eavesdropping will justify his soliloquy that shortly ends the act. This is one of the very many instances in playbooks demonstrating the cooperative nature of play production. The contributions of both the playwright and the bookkeeper combine to produce an effective production.

On fo. 11b between lines 1435 and 1436, the bookkeeper has added "Enter" followed by a line about an inch and a half into the text between the lines to bring on John a Cumber in time to hear a reference to him spoken onstage. The most unusual playhouse addition in the manuscript was occasioned by an "a to b" turning where the accident of spacing had placed the entrance of the boy Shrimp at the top of fo. 8b. It was important for this character to be noted by the figure onstage at the proper moment. Most likely because Shrimp was played by a boy, the bookkeeper wrote "Enter Shrimp" in the right column three lines from the bottom of fo. 8a to be sure to see that the boy was in place at the proper time.

At one point Munday entered a series of stage directions calling for players to enter from different places: "ffrom one end of the Stage . . . queintly disguysde," followed by another "ffrom the other end of the Stage," then a third "ffrom vnder the Stage," and yet "The fourth out of a tree, if possible it may be" (fo. 6b, ll. 780, 798; fo. 7a, ll. 819, 836). Munday shows what he wants, to a degree (the costume is marvelously vague), and leaves the carrying out of his suggestions/plans to the players. They will choose for costumes what they can or will; and they will use a "tree" if they can or if they wish. The bookkeeper adds nothing here whatsoever; neither does he delete anything. We as readers and researchers do not know what the audience saw. Thus the book-keeper was moved to intervene only seven times in adapting this manuscript for the playhouse – a cautionary tale in itself for those expecting a heavily marked "prompt-book."

The best-known manuscript playbook is the next earliest, *The Book of Sir Thomas More* (BL, MS Harley 7368). It is, of course, because three leaves of a revision are in the hand of a playwright that a number of scholars think (or wish to think) it is that of William Shakespeare. Indeed, this possibility is usually the only thing discussed about this manuscript, and even these three leaves are usually not investigated in terms of what they can reveal about the writing and staging of plays. Munday wrote a fair copy, with no act and scene divisions indicated, of what looks to be a collaborative writing effort. The play was written during (and I believe conceived for) a time (1592–3) of intense domestic political turmoil – indeed, of the threat of civil riot. Master of the Revels Edmond Tilney inscribed directions for changes; playwrights contributed changes, but it would seem that political conditions worsened, and the play was not publicly acted. But the book was certainly prepared for production – both before and after Tilney wrote in the left column alongside the opening lines of the play the longest surviving memo from a Master of the Revels:

<Leaue out> / ye insur<rection> / wholy & / ye Cause ther off and / <b>egin wt Sr Tho:
/ Moore att ye mayors sessions / wt a reportt afterwards / off his good servic' / don being'
Shriue off London / vppon a mutiny Agaynst ye Lumbards only by A Short / reportt &
nott otherwise / att your own perrilles / E Tyllney

This has often been taken as a prohibition of performing this play, but it patently is
not. Tilney elaborately here and more simply elsewhere in other instances – "Mend
Yis" (fo. 5a, l. 316), "All [] Alter" (fo. 17b, l. 1256) – is aiding the players in
"mending" the play so that it *can* be played. Because several playwrights and the
bookkeeper were working to rush *More* onto the stage, the manuscript contains more
additions and patches than most likely would have been usual; the company seems
willing to accept this book as their playbook with all its confusions. Near the
beginning of addition II (fo. 8a), the patching playwright some would like to believe
was Shakespeare is building to the entry and big speeches of More; he seemingly does
not know (or much care about) the names of minor characters for some lines; so he
adds succeeding speech headings for them as: "other," "other," "oth," and "o." The
bookkeeper later has filled in the names of the minor characters – another good
example of the complementary interworkings of playwright and bookkeeper. Munday,
as in *Kent*, tends to make directions detailed:

> An Arras is drawne, and behinde it (as in Sessions)
> sit the L. Maior,
> Iustice *Suresbie*, and other Iustices, Sheriffe Moore
> and the other Sherife
> sitting by, *Smart* is the Plaintife, *Lifter* the prisoner
> at the barre.
> (fo. 3b, ll. 104–6)

> Enter *Lincolne, Betses, Williamson, Sherwin* and other
> armed, doll in a shirt<
> of Maile, a head piece, sword and Buckler, a crewe
> attending.
> (fo. 5b, ll. 410–11)

> ———— :ex. some seuerally, others
> set vp the Iibbit
> (fo. 10b, ll. 582–3)

The bookkeeper does not particularize the vague number of extras, nor does he add
directions about the large properties. We do not know how the trial was staged; a
"Iibbit" presumably was there, because later More is directed to speak from a ladder.
Unspecified numbers of extras remain unparticularized. Munday centered the second
entry but began about a third of the way into the column; in this section of long prose
lines, this direction as written is not easily seen at a glance. Accordingly, in the left
column the bookkeeper had added "Enter Lincoln / Betts Williamson / Doll,"

surrounded by rules on all sides but the outer page margin. Now it is easily seen. "Noticeability" is deemed important for the bookkeeper. Here and in many other books, additional notations are made by bookkeepers so that an entry would be noticed easily by glancing at a page. Other "problems" posed by stage directions in *More* will be handled by others or perhaps by the bookkeeper in other ways that do not require inscription in the book. At one point in the additions, the bookkeeper has attached the name of a minor player who took the role of a messenger to his speech heading: "Mess / T Goodal" (fo. 13*a, ll. 1–2); why he should do this here and not elsewhere is not known. Often we can observe but cannot tease out the explanations. For all the things going on in this disrupted playbook, the bookkeeper aids both the playwrights and the players in their tasks but adds very little.

John of Bordeaux or The Second Part of Friar Bacon (Duke of Northumberland's Library, Alnwick Castle, MS 507[2]) is anonymous and difficult to locate. It was probably written as a sequel to Robert Greene's *Friar Bacon and Friar Bungay* and thus produced by Philip Henslowe at the Rose between 1590 and 1593. The inscription of the play generally follows that of other plays except that the scribe was very pressed for space and wrote two or more short speeches and their speech headings into a single line proceeding across a page (fos 3a, 7a, 7b, 9a).

There are two bookkeepers at work here; one would seem to be the same person as was bookkeeper for *The Two Noble Ladies* (1619–23), *The Welsh Embassador* (ca. 1623), *The Parliament of Love* (1624), *The Captives* (1624), all for the Lady Elizabeth's Company at the Phoenix, as well as for a revival of *Edmond Ironside* (ca. 1632) for the Prince Charles's (II) Men playing at the Salisbury Court. This identification of bookkeeper would seem to locate this playbook of *John of Bordeaux* into the 1623–32 dating, obviously for a revival. The hand of the second bookkeeper would seem to be that of the bookkeeper of *Kent* and *More*, apparently still working in theater thirty-odd years later.

The bookkeepers here have done much what they and others did elsewhere, but in *John of Bordeaux* their task was much enlarged and complicated by having to add many speech headings which were left out by the scribe. But even so, bookkeepers here did no more than was needed. There is no indication that things had to be added for "completeness."

The First Part of the Reign of King Richard the Second, or Thomas of Woodstock (BL, MS Egerton 1994[8], fos 165–86) was most likely composed and produced for the season 1594–5; playwrights, company, and theater of the original performance are unknown. The play evidently was popular, because it is thumbed and stained from playhouse use. Probably all of the speech headings were added after the text was written, most by the writer of the book, but many by two other hands. The leaves have been folded for margins, and the basic text is written in a very readable English secretary hand with stage directions and speech headings in a finely formed Italian script; speech rules are regularly in place. Minor differences in the inscription of speech headings add to the supposition that *Woodstock* is a collaboration – the most common way of writing plays during the period.

There are markedly fewer playwright's advisory directions in *Woodstock* than in *Kent* and *More*. Such less frequent use strongly indicates the habits of professional playwrights, who were more familiar with the professional abilities of the players than those, like Munday, who wrote only occasionally for the stage. It is said frequently that directions appearing in the left column were inscribed by playhouse personnel. And this is often the case, but by no means necessarily so. Hand A, one of the playwrights of *Woodstock*, occasionally heightens his own actions by adding stage directions in the left column: "A Drome afare of" (fo. 179a, l. 2152) and "Drom Collours" (fo. 185b, l. 2957). Then too, occasionally directions are repeated in left or right columns just so that they would not be missed – another kind of "noticeability."

On fo. 184b, both a playwright and a bookkeeper, on different occasions, added the name ("Arrondell", "Ar:") of a character already identified by a quite noticeable speech heading: "Enter Arondell." Such duplication would seem pointless; yet evidently some difficulty or confusion moved both playwright and bookkeeper on separate occasions to add the name. They did not want to miss this entry. Why it was so problematic eludes us. What we do know is that the additions were needed. If *Woodstock* had been printed in its day and if a compositor had set what was in front of him, and if this manuscript had disappeared (as nearly all playbooks have), textual scholars might well be moved to label these additions as sloppy or careless when they patently are just the opposite.

The bookkeeper has added two notations in the left column that warrant particular notice; both are highly unusual. Thirteen lines before a centered direction bringing on "the Shreues of Kent & Northumberland" (fo. 179b, l. 2221), the bookkeeper added "Shrevs Ready." Why this notation was needed is unknown. This may be the sort of "warning direction" that theorists would have "prompters" making continually in order to thrust the players on the stage at the proper point. Yet this is the only time in the play that such a notation occurs, and the entrance is not nearly so complicated as many others, nor is there any particular delicacy of timing. It might also very well be viewed as resulting from the players' noting a need for "Shreues" – that is, for supplying the persons in the roles with whatever properties or elements of costuming needed to indicate their office to the audience – in which case, this usage would be not unlike the following note for a bed.

In the left column of fo. 180b (ll. 2377–8) the bookkeeper has written an even rarer note: "A bed / for woodstock." The ensuing dialogue shows that this was a curtained Tudor bed, with Woodstock in it onstage. What is curious here is that the notation does not seem to have any bearing on stage action or the need to get this very large property onstage. This notation occurs just a few lines before one of the collaborating playwright's indication of an act break. Whether or not the act break was observed, this inscription merely notes its need. It is a large, cumbersome, yet vital property for which special measures would be needed, and I believe that this is the reason for its existence. "A bed / for woodstock" seems to have been written by a member of the company reading through the play to see if it demanded any unusual properties. Noting such items in the left column is a convenience that would make them easy to find when needed. Assuming that any and all inscriptions bear directly upon the literal acting of a play – that every word inscribed in the book is for the guidance of stage action – is dangerous. Such a regularization and compartmentalization of processes patently is not supplied by the surviving evidence.

The bookkeeper has added only seven notations to the very well-marked directions of *Woodstock* – again, precise but sparing alteration. The continuity of playing and annotating practices cannot be stressed too strongly. As late as the middle of the final decade of the sixteenth century, new plays were being written to be performed in a playing area essentially unchanged from its medieval antecedents, and players were marking their books in the same sparse manner so as not to limit their playing to a particular place; and these practices continued until the closing of the theaters.

Woodstock was apparently revived ca. 1604, approximately ten years after the original production; and it is significant that the players have found nothing either unusable or in need of change. The customs of staging and of making books continued unaltered. The few new notations facilitate smooth presentation but offer no divergences. In this revival, two separate hands appear as bookkeepers. The second, who added a few annotations in the last two-thirds of the play, is identifiable as the bookkeeper of the anonymous *Charlemagne* (ca. 1604) played by the Children of the Queen's Revels at the second Blackfriars.

That *Woodstock* was again revived, most likely around 1633, is ascertained by its third bookkeeper, who also appears as bookkeeper in Walter Mountfort's *The Launching of the Mary*, licensed by Sir Henry Herbert on 27 June 1633, and presented by an unidentified company in a private theater. The bookkeepers of both the original production and the last revival add players' names, the letters of which are now too fragmentary for positive identification. What is to be noted is that the later bookkeepers did not make any attempt to delete earlier players' names even though the latter had nothing to do with the new production. Apparently these names did not bother them; if they had, striking them through would have been an easy matter.

The endurance of these names brings attention to a feature of the playbooks that might otherwise go unnoticed: no succeeding bookkeeper seems to have found any difficulty in guiding a play with additions made by others in an earlier production. In preparing an old play, the new companies add a few notations; but they do not delete. I should like to suggest that this is the result of another, previously unnamed, custom: the ease of transmission. Bookkeepers and players deliberately, albeit probably unconsciously, left markings in the side columns alone, because there was no habit of tidying them up. There was no need for such extra work, since the book itself was not nearly as important a directional tool as it was to become in later centuries. *Woodstock* is important not only for the kinds of adaptation which it does and does not show, but also in documenting the continuity of the customs of ease of adaptability and sparse marking that have continued through three quite different decades.

Similar attitudes influencing the marking of the playbook can be seen in the anonymous *Edmond Ironside, or War Hath Made All Friends* (BL, MS Egerton 1994[5], fos 96–118), which can be dated no more precisely than the final decade of the century; the company and theater are also unknown. The hand is that of a scribe, one evidently not well acquainted with working with players, for his speech headings are not only misaligned, but also slightly incised into the text, the first word of a speech being slightly indented to accommodate it as he copies line for line across the whole page. Not surprisingly, he does not seem to use or to understand speech rules. Act breaks were added later, probably when the play was revived at Salisbury Court by the company under the "sponsorship" of the infant Prince Charles (II). The bookkeeper is the one whose hand is seen in the anonymous *Two Noble Ladies* (ca. 1622–3) and in Thomas Heywood's *The Captives* (1624). All playhouse additions seem to be from this revival. Problems and solutions bring no surprises.

An "a to b" turning brings the same response that it had in *Woodstock* for the boy Shrimp. Centered at the top of fo. 107b is "*Enter a Messenger*"; at the bottom of fo. 107a, the bookkeeper has added in the left column "*Enter / H: Gibs*," while in the right column another theatrical hand has added "*assayle the walls.*" This is a complicated and important scene. It is vital that the messenger arrive at the proper time. That these two additions were made at different times by different people should not be surprising. As a company familiarized itself with a play, the need for additional inscriptions could easily arise. There are six places where the names of minor players have been added to small roles.

Again, the bookkeeper actually does very little. The tradition of sparse marking observable in *Kent, More, John of Bordeaux,* and *Woodstock* continues in *Ironside,* with the resulting flexibility of production and ease of adaptability again proved with the revival. Markings by hands other than the bookkeeper were not exceptional, and playhouse additions by no means need be expected to relate to the immediate problems of stage action. The playing practices involving the marking and use of the books of public theater companies in the mid-1590s were apparently still generally current in a public house about 1632.

The anonymous *Charlemagne or the Distracted Emperor* (BL, MS Egerton 1994[6], fos. 119–35) is written by a scribe who crams eighty English secretary lines to a page, making particularly noticeable the Italian hand used for speech headings, stage directions, and proper names. He has copied the text in columns and emphasizes the playwright's act breaks by adding his own in the left column just above the playwright's. To save more space, the playwright has added a number of stage directions in the right column, often boxed by two lines for added noticeability.

The representative of the acting company saw fit to alter very little, even though the chief peculiarity of this playbook is that most of the stage directions are entered in the right column. Instead of laboriously switching these to the left column for regularity, what the bookkeeper has done throughout the play is to emphasize the playwright's right-column directions to make them more noticeable; the playwright had underscored each direction and added a bar on the left to mark them off from the text. The bookkeeper has added a strong line over each entry, leaving other directions to stand unemphasized. He has also particularized the playwright's right-column calls for music in three instances, adding his decisions in the left: "Hoboyes" for "Loud

Musique" (fo. 119b, ll. 151, 154), "softe musique" for "Musique" (fo. 125a, ll. 1070, 1071), "Dead marche" for "Funerall sounde" (fo. 135a, l. 2721), and adding calls for flourishes to embellish royal entrances (fo. 119a, l. 73; fo. 134b, l. 2620).

This bookkeeper also cut extensively; to do this he used the accustomed method of drawing a horizontal line in the left column next to the lines not to be played; they are not crossed out or defaced, leaving them available to be used at a different production. These cuts may have been made to shorten the play; but removing these lines does make Orlando a more active and a more interesting character. I suggest that this is a more theatrically valid reason for the cuts than that of sheer length. So much is heard of players' damaging a playwright's text; here is a case that proves directly the opposite. Here the players have made a theatrically better role.

Another hand in *Charlemagne* is little seen, but is worthy of notice. At line 1420 of fo. 127a, Sir George Buc struck through "reverend p'latt" (prelate) and interlined "preist." Carefully marking his insertion with a cross and duplicating the cross in the left column next to the text, he then moved farther into the left column to add "Read Preist." The attitude in which this was done, whether helpful or restrictive or repressive, is impossible to ascertain. The usual interpretation is the latter. Each Master of the Revels differed, of course, answering the dictates both of his personality and of his times; but in light of Tilney's work on *More*, the possibility of this being intended as helpful is a more than logical interpretation. To limit the Revels Office to being merely an agency of censorship is both to ignore its primary function as the provider of royal entertainment as well as to view the sensitivities and ideas of propriety of another age from a distinctly modern vantage point. Masters of the Revels must have realized that their careful exercise of watchful restraint was mutually advantageous to themselves and to the companies from whom they received the greater part of their incomes.

I have brought in a number of details from these early playbooks to establish how the books were constructed by the playwrights and the theater personnel, in order to establish their usual *modus operandi*, because one of the problems in looking at play-books singly is that it is impossible to tell what is customary and what is exceptional. With the playbooks that follow, I shall limit myself to noting particulars which distinguish these books from the others.

The Second Maiden's Tragedy (BL, MS Lansdowne 807[2], fos. 29–56), written by Thomas Middleton and bearing Sir George Buc's license dated 31 October 1611, was performed by the King's Men, presumably at the second Globe and the second Blackfriars. This is a fair copy written by a scrivener who folded his sheets for columns and used speech rules; the book contains some corrections and revisions by Middleton. Theatrically the most interesting aspect of this manuscript is the thirty-two play-wright's advisory directions in 2,410 lines of dialogue, ranging from simple "withins" to very elaborate ones; all are left untouched by the bookkeeper except that he adds the names of two players to roles. *The Second Maiden's Tragedy* reveals Middleton, the scrivener, the bookkeeper, Sir George Buc, and another, unidentified playhouse person at work on the manuscript at much the same time. Thus the often assumed pattern of passage of the book from playwright to scrivener to players to censor and back has to be considered as at the very least variable. *The Second Maiden's Tragedy* demonstrates again and again that all cuts are not censoring. At least half a dozen stock speeches were deleted by the players (as they also were in *Sir John van Olden Barnavelt* in 1619 and in *The Honest Man's Fortune* in 1625), tightening the roles and making them more theatrically effective. In short, this bookkeeper did what his counterparts were to do later, responding to difficulties as he found them, and "difficulties" encompasses a surprisingly wide range.

Sir John van Olden Barnavelt (BL, MS Add. 18653) by John Fletcher and Philip Massinger was first performed by the King's Men at the second Globe between 14 and 16 August 1619. The chief hand in the manuscript is that of Ralph Crane, the company's long-time scrivener. The play is fully divided into acts and scenes. Some revisions have been made on two odd leaves and on three inserted slips of paper, none of which seem to have bothered the players in running their production. It is to be noted that Crane here follows theatrical conventions by placing speech headings in the left column, using speech rules, and copying by columns, customs he does not observe in extant copies of plays that he made for non-theatrical eyes.

Barnavelt is by far the most sparsely marked of the surviving playbooks – leaving great amounts of the decision making in the hands of the players. The bookkeeper is not concerned with offstage sounds except for several calls for horns. Twice (fo. 13a, l. 1142, and fo. 19a, l. 1656) Crane enters changes in stage directions in the left column (over- and underscored) that bring Barnavelt's son onstage, thus significantly altering the dramatic action in making for a livelier performance. Fletcher and Massinger, of course, were both professional playwrights closely involved with the King's Men. Their work with the players shows them all cooperating to refine the production.

The bookkeeper in *Barnavelt* is the same one who had worked on *Woodstock*, where he had added "A bed / for woodstock"; here he adds in the left column the words "Barre" and "Table" on fo. 21b, l. 2159, and "Scaffold" (fo. 27b, l. 2851) as notations for large properties that would be needed; like "A bed / for woodstock," the bookkeeper does not over- or underscore them as he does for markings pertaining to the actual acting of the play.

Censorship is significant in *Barnavelt*. There is no way that a play about the downfall of the Arminian Barnavelt and the triumph of Maurice, prince of Nassau, would not be fraught with problems. James I detested both the Arminians and Barnavelt; Master of the Revels Sir George Buc had been James's diplomatic representative in Holland and knew the figures personally. As with *More*, to put on a play about controversial figures, players had to have a "friend at court," and even then the going could be tricky. Buc here, like Tilney in *More*, is careful, advisory, yet strict. No one was looking to upset the apple cart. Buc read the play carefully, making many crosses in the left column next to problematic passages, many of which were altered. Making dramatic capital out of politically inflammatory material was a dangerous game, played without a formal rule book. The considerable evidence of censorship in *Barnavelt* is most revealing in terms of the relation of officialdom to the play, of the interaction between Master and company, of the players' indifference to having a particularly clean playbook, and in demonstrating the considerable dangers involved in scholars' prejudgments about matters theatrical in the period.

The Two Noble Ladies (BL, MS Egerton 1994[11], fos 224–44) is anonymous but comes from the Players of the Revels at the Red Bull sometime between 1619 and 1623. The play would seem to have been written by an amateur, because he knows very little about the customs of writing for professional players; thus he makes extra work for himself and the players simply by not knowing how a playbook is usually put together. He does not distinguish the different uses of English and Italian scripts; he surrounds almost all his stage directions in the right column with rules to make them easily noticeable; he provides a complete division into scenes; acts are distinctly separated by a row of dots enclosed in rules running across the entire page – easy to see, but not necessary.

He is almost compulsively complete, even writing out the full name in every speech heading, apparently unaware of the almost universal theatrical practice of abbreviation. Similarly, each line is written *in toto* across the page, as in *Ironside*, not inscribed in columns; he does not know about speech rules either. His failings are clearly a matter of ignorance, not of unwillingness to aid the players. He is all too ready to do that – according to how he felt this should be accomplished. In his view, the way to aid the players was to tell them how to do their jobs. To this end, he provided 128 playwright's advisory directions plus a dumb show – or almost one for every sixteen lines of dialogue; they are particularly heavy in the action-packed fourth and fifth acts.

The bookkeeper here is the one whose work has survived in the largest quantity, in *Ironside*, *Captives*, *Welsh Embassador*, and *Parliament of Love*. And here he works as he usually did, clarifying and smoothing. He had to do rather more here because he was working with an amateur playwright; he adds the names of two minor players, as well as clarifying and emphasizing things as in the other books. His changes here are in no way untypical of the usual practices of his contemporaries.

The Welsh Embassador (Cardiff Public Library MS) would be remarkable chiefly for its relative lack of marking were it not for one highly unusual feature: of the fifty-four entrances which do not begin acts, thirty-nine are anticipated in the left column by the formulaic "bee redy...." Although an occasional unusual circumstance caused somewhat analogous occasional markings in other books, *The Welsh Embassador*, *The Lady Mother*, and *The Wasp* are the only ones where this is done with regularity. *The Welsh Embassador* is generally attributed to Thomas Dekker and most likely was performed by the Lady Elizabeth's Men at the Phoenix (Cockpit) in Drury Lane.

The manuscript has been copied by a scribe after marginal notations were added by the bookkeeper of *The Captives* and *The Two Noble Ladies*. Other than the anticipatory notations, *The Welsh Embassador* is much what might be expected: folded for columns, speech rules, division into acts only, a generally careful copy. There are very few playwright's advisory directions, bespeaking a professional playwright. The curious warning directions are precisely done; for whatever reason they were made, the person who added them knew what was being done onstage.

Thomas Heywood's *The Captives* (BL, MS Egerton 1994[3], fos. 52–73) is holograph, which presents its chief difficulty, and this is in itself a corrective to popular impressions about what playbooks should look like. The problem is Heywood's penmanship. He did not form letters well, and thus it is a difficult manuscript to read. Nonetheless, what is important theatrically is that the players accepted it and readied it for production as their playbook – no fair copy was apparently needed or wanted. The bookkeeper's none-too-neat inscriptions are mixed with the text, because Heywood's long prose lines very often take over the right columns and because his curiously atypical insistence on writing out the full names in speech headings limits space in the left columns which might have been used by the bookkeeper.

Indeed, the vast majority of the bookkeeper's markings here would not have been needed if he had had a fair copy and would not have been made if he had been expecting to have one supplied to him. Any legible book would not require asterisks to mark entrances, "clere" to indicate an empty stage, and the addition of characters' names (often accompanied by such words as "to them"). It is abundantly clear that the bookkeeper is planning to use this manuscript as his playbook.

Heywood folded his manuscript, used speech rules, divided his work into acts and scenes, entered only fifteen playwright's advisory directions, and actually is neat and orderly in his own fashion. Any man who testified that he had a hand in 220 plays surely qualifies as a professional; and he inscribes his book like one. And as a professional, he certainly knew that he could trust professional players, providing a stage direction that is the *locus classicus* of leaving an artistic decision up to the players. A character is instructed "Eather strykes him / wth a staffe or / Casts a stone" (fo. 68a, ll. 2432–4); this left-column direction is untouched by the bookkeeper. Readers and performance reconstructors do not know what happened at this point.

The bookkeeper added the names of minor players on three occasions and a number of notations for clarity and timing. The workings of Heywood and the bookkeeper are valuable contributions both to theatrical knowledge and to understanding the work-ings of playwrights and players.

Philip Massinger's *The Parliament of Love* (Victoria and Albert Museum, MS Dyce 39), in great contrast to *The Captives*, has almost no markings. Herbert records that he licensed the play for the Lady Elizabeth's Men at the Cockpit (Phoenix) 3 November 1624. There has been damage to this manuscript (probably the first two leaves have been lost and all the page bottoms have some loss) made by the hand who also copied *The Welsh Embassador*. It would seem that these now rather frail leaves had been folded; the play is divided into acts but not scenes; speech headings are abbreviated and are shoved almost right up to the text; speech rules touch speech headings to the text. The bookkeeper on fo. 102 emphasized by repetition a stage direction because the play-wright's direction followed the text with little break, leaving it difficult to see. Even though there are no directions other than simple entries, the players found this manuscript playable too, with almost no annotation.

The Honest Man's Fortune (Victoria and Albert Museum, MS Dyce 9) by John Fletcher was originally produced in 1613. This playbook is endorsed by Master of the Revels Sir

Henry Herbert 8 February 1624/5 for the King's Men. The book is in the hand of Edward Knight, bookkeeper for the King's Men for many years and the only book-keeper to whom a name can be assigned. Here, too, players have edited, taking out lines which they felt detracted from theatrical effectiveness, tightening and shaping dialogue (fos 16b, 17a, 20b, 22a, 24a, and 25a). On three occasions Knight adds abbreviations of the names of three players who were members of the King's Men in 1625. A theatrical hand other than Knight has added a few markings, demonstrating that the old custom of various hands adding annotations to the book was still operative.

The Honest Man's Fortune demonstrates that although play companies were becoming more prosperous and leaving more records for theater historians to document their existence, they continued the conservative nature of playbook marking. In the middle of the third decade of the seventeenth century, plays were still being crafted for a simple stage and for companies of relatively limited resources, leaving open the possibilities of playing in different venues, important both for traveling companies and also for the King's Men who were operating both the second Globe and the second Blackfriars. Playhouse additions remain very few and are limited to unusual situations.

John Clavell's *The Soddered Citizen* (privately owned) was written for the King's Men ca. 1630 and annotated by Edward Knight. Clavell was an amateur, but the manuscript was written by a scribe who folded the pages in columns. At least four other playing company hands often make alterations *currente calamo*. Clavell apparently had no idea of what a theatrical manuscript looked like and conceived of his manuscript as if it were a printed play. Folio 3 bears on its verso the earliest known manuscript *dramatis personae*; it is unique in extant playbooks and is a key document in dating the play. *The Soddered Citizen* has only thirteen speaking parts, four of them assigned to boys. The old habit of keeping the company small yet diverse is patently still functioning at this late and prosperous time for the King's Men.

Clavell's unfamiliarity with theatrical customs is readily observable in his stage directions. In 2,826 lines of text, he supplied eighty playwright's advisory directions – one for every thirty-one lines. Players are instructed specifically what actions to take and how to comport themselves at certain moments – just the sort of advice no professional needs from an amateur, especially one composing his first play. In their customary actions of not doing more to a book than they deemed necessary, the company and Knight let Clavell's directions stand.

Often called the "most complete" and "the most scientifically marked" of the playbooks, Philip Massinger's *Believe as You List* (BL, MS Egerton 2828), produced by the King's Men, licensed by Sir Henry Herbert 6 May 1631, and heavily annotated by bookkeeper Edward Knight, is also the most baffling. *Believe as You List* is everything that the other playbooks are not. It is highly atypical in the extreme. It contains features that no other surviving manuscript playbooks possess, and it contains in profusion some that others have only most sparingly. The explanation for such differences is moot. Something made Knight act differently here from every other known playhouse bookkeeper, as well as differently from his own work in *The Honest*

Man's Fortune (1625) and *The Soddered Citizen* (ca. 1630). We know what Knight did (he almost literally left no direction untouched); we do not know why he did it.

The play had been refused a license in 1630 because it dealt openly with Spain's deposing of the king of Portugal. Massinger reset the play in ancient Bithynia, recopied it, and presumably renamed it. Probably little else was done; indeed, several of the original names have survived in speech headings despite its recopying. But surface transposition of locale was good enough for Herbert, a man of known anti-Spanish bias. Compliance to the letter went a long way in dramatic censorship; the spirit was more debatable.

Knight is over-active. He deletes all Massinger's act and scene divisions and adds his own; he marks the beginning of each act with a short line to the exact beginning line in the text. These alterations for Acts II and IV are accompanied by "Long," referring to the duration of the act break during which music was played. Knight adds to every notation where property pieces of paper (various letters and writings) were needed, and even provides a list of the six times when these were needed, as well as the names of the players who carried them onstage. Knight adds players' names to entrances – for principals as well as for minor players and boys: "Harry / Wilson: & / Boy ready for the song at ye Arras:" boxed in the left column (fo. 20a, ll. 1968–71), and even for the chief player in the company, Joseph Taylor: "Antiochus—— / ready: *vnder* / the stage" in the left column (fo. 19a, ll. 1877–9). Larger properties are noted in the left column to be ready: "Table ready: / & .6. chairs / to sett out" over- and underscored (fo. 9a, ll. 654–6).

Everything and everybody is readied and in the proper place at the proper time so that nothing would be missed – to insure that nothing would go wrong. What has caused this radical departure from all surviving theatrical custom and habit is unknown. It would seem that something happened, or threatened to happen, that made the players want to be extra cautious, to guard every step. From these exceptions, much is to be learned about theater history and playhouse functioning; the danger is that, as in the past, these highly atypical markings are assumed to be what was, or should have been, the normal pattern. They were not.

The Launching of the Mary (BL, MS Egerton 1994[15], fos. 317–49) was written by the amateur Walter Mountfort for what was probably a private theater. Mountfort seems even more unfamiliar with the ways of the theater: he does not make the customary use of Italian script for speech headings and stage directions; nor does he make act and scene divisions in any distinctive way. He generally follows a number of writing customs, apparently without understanding their rationale, and thus fails to exploit the advantages they provide. He seems not to understand the very practical adaptation that theater people made of the widespread habit of folding a sheet into four long, equal columns. Mountfort folded his sheets, but not into equal columns. Not realizing the convenience of wide outside columns for constructing playbooks, he has come up with narrow columns, half the normal theatrical size – and less than half as useful.

He uses no speech rules and writes speech headings and some stage directions continuously in the text. He has divided the play into acts and somewhat irregularly into scenes. As in *The Soddered Citizen*, there is a heavy reliance on playwright's advisory directions. The bookkeeper, not surprisingly, marked only what he felt needed to be highlighted into noticeability. But the major non-authorial feature here is the activity of the Master of the Revels, Sir Henry Herbert, whose license is dated 27 June 1633 – a time of increasing difficulty for Charles I; and Herbert is very cautious, even though the ship being launched is named in tribute to his queen "Mary" – that is, Henrietta Maria. Herbert's actions here counterpoint those of Tilney in *More* and Buc in *Barnavelt*; all three Masters demonstrate their concern and their determination to salvage the plays on which they have expended so much time and effort.

Mountfort's indication of entrances is also regularly rudimentary. Like other amateurs, he is needlessly helpful. He is "directional" rather than "notational"; that is, he believes that he must tell the players what to do and what properties to bring on, rather than merely providing integral suggestions. Thus he frequently belabors the obvious. The bookkeeper, who also worked on the 1630s revival of *Woodstock*, added music calls and a few tidyings, but did very little here.

The Launching of the Mary is remarkable in two major ways. It further demonstrates and substantiates the differences between amateur and professional playwrights, and in so doing it adds to the store of knowledge about how the professionals regularly functioned. And this playbook provides considerable illumination of the attitudes and consequent activities of Sir Henry Herbert.

Henry Glapthorne's *The Lady Mother* (BL, MS Egerton 1994[7], fos 186–211) was licensed by Herbert's deputy, William Blagrave, on 15 October 1635, and was produced by the company of the King's Revels at Salisbury Court. It is to be noted that in 1635 Blagrave was also the financial agent of the King's Revels as well as one of the builders of the Salisbury Court, and thus further ties the Revels Office to an active, positive role in promoting plays. Glapthorne was not a professional playwright; but as the author of eleven plays, he was not exactly unfamiliar with the stage. Thus it is not surprising to find that in 2,575 lines of dialogue, Glapthorne added only twenty playwright's advisory directions, one for every 129 lines – a ratio much closer to those of professionals.

Glapthorne's assumptions about what directions a playwright should add are themselves professional. Not only does he add few, but the obvious directions like "aside," "within," and "kneels" so dwelt upon by Clavell, Mountfort, and the anonymous playwright of *The Two Noble Ladies* are either absent or present only in drastically reduced numbers. In his more complex directions, Glapthorne does the same sort of thing he does in the simple ones. He keys them carefully to the dialogue; and though they are precisely timed, they are still general enough to allow the players to handle them on their own. The explicitness and over-detailing which Clavell and Mountfort often use give a sense of the playwright's wishing to hover over his manuscript – to tell the players *how*. Glapthorne's approach tells them only a much more professional *what*. Glapthorne also works very closely with his scribe, correcting and revising in cooperation.

No bookkeeper can be assigned because there simply are no alterations or additions certifiably made by any playhouse personnel. The play qualifies as a playbook because it bears Blagrave's license. Another important feature of this book is the most curious. All entrances which do not begin a new act are "anticipated" by inscribing in the left column the names of characters coming onstage eight to twenty lines before their actual entrance. The names are connected to where the characters enter by vertical lines in the left column; there are at least thirty such sets. This phenomenon, of course, is much like similar additions in *The Welsh Embassador*, where "bee ready" and the characters' names were similarly positioned.

The leaves have not been folded for columns (resulting in narrow outer margins); there is a normal use of rules, and the play is divided into acts only. The name of one of the King's Revels players is added to one entrance. Blagrave is much less fussy than Herbert, but also helpful, once even correcting an omission.

The Wasp or Subject's Precedent (Duke of Northumberland's Library, Alnwick Castle, MS 507[1]) is in the hand of its anonymous playwright, who was both competent and familiar with the usual proceedings involved in fulfilling a theatrical company's expectations. The playwright uses speech rules and fills in the speech headings after writing the text of a page; he uses vague numbers of extras (leaving the company to deal with them as they see fit). There is one curious difference from most playbooks, in the inscription of warnings for entrances some twelve to twenty lines before entry and connecting these to the entry with lines, as in *The Lady Mother*. This also occurred in *The Welsh Embassador* – an anomaly that is both atypical and inexplicable. Why it was felt to be needed is simply unknown.

The names of six players taking minor roles have been added to their roles, tying the play to the King's Revels at Salisbury Court either shortly before the theaters closed because of plague in May 1636 or shortly after their reopening in October 1637. Of particular interest are two occasions (fos 7a, 13b) on which it looks very much as if the playwright and the bookkeeper were working on the book at the same time, showing that close relationships, documented first in *More*, were still operating in a theatrical enterprise which most likely dates between 1636 and 1639, within a few years of the closing of the theaters and the end of the theatrical era.

Understanding the playbooks necessarily involves understanding the contexts in which they were created. This often involves sorting out a great mass of evidence and trying to find the reasons for many markings. Basic to this attempt at understanding is the perspective from which the researcher approaches these playbooks. My perspective is that these playbooks are the product of professional players in the process of bringing a play to life on the stage. My basic assumption is that they knew what they were doing. My task is to find out how they accomplished this and why they made the kind of annotations they did.

This paper is intended as an enticement to others to explore these few documents and their precious treasures. There is much to be learned. Those readers who wish to look at some more detailed explorations and/or to see some of the assumptions and the unsubstantiated claims made by editors about what "promptbooks" did and did not contain could look at my "Stage-directions: a misunderstood factor in determining textual provenance," *TEXT: Transactions of the Society for Textual Scholarship*, 2 (1985), pp. 121–37; "'A bed / for woodstock': a warning for the unwary," *Medieval & Renaissance Drama in England*, 2 (1985), pp. 91–118; and *"John a Kent and John a Cumber*: an Elizabethan playbook and its implications," in *Shakespeare and Dramatic Tradition: Essays in Honor of S. F. Johnson*, ed. W. R. Elton and William B. Long (Newark, Del.: University of Delaware Press, 1989), pp. 125–43.

26

The Craft of Printing (1600)

Laurie E. Maguire

In 1594 John Danter published *Titus Andronicus*, the first Shakespeare play to reach print. The title page of the edition provides succinctly salient marketing details. It defines the play's genre ('the most lamentable Roman Tragedie of Titus Andronicus'); it advertises the play's recent stage history ('As it was Plaide by the Right Honorable the Earle of *Darbie*, Earl of *Pembrooke*, and Earle of *Sussex* their Seruants'); it names the printer and publisher (who, in this instance, are one and the same: John Danter); and it indicates the wholesaler: 'Edward White & Thomas Millington, at the little North doore of Paules at the signe of the Gunne'.[1] St Paul's churchyard (and precincts) was the centre of the bookselling trade, both wholesale and retail. Cathedral premises were administrative centres and, consequently, had been associated throughout Europe with bookbinding and bookselling since before the era of the printed book: the keeping of registers, ledgers, records, etc. required parchment, paper, inks and bindings. In addition, the scribes, clerks and clergy involved in this clerical work constituted a large literate population for enterprising stationers (Blayney 1990: 18). Then, as now, businesses thrived in colonies of competitors, the geographical concentration of specialists drawing custom to the area. In London, as elsewhere in Europe, print culture simply expanded the cathedral precinct as a centre of the booktrade.

Prospective book purchasers, eager for the latest publication ('the first question at every Stacioners shoppe is, what new thing?', laments Thomas Jackson in 1603 in *David's Pastoral Poem*, STC 14299, sig. ¶ 5ᵛ), would see not just sheets of complete printed books in the booksellers' shops in St Paul's churchyard but title pages of new publications hung up as advertisements on posts and available surfaces. Ben Jonson's Epigram III, 'To My Booke-seller', reveals that Jonson finds such advertising demeaning, as if the book 'made sute to be bought'. Jonson asks his bookseller not to display his title leaf 'on posts, or walls, / Or in cleft-sticks', admonishing: 'If, without these vile arts, it will not sell, / Send it to *Bucklers-bury*, there 'twill, well' (see Jonson 1947). Bucklersbury was a popular market area, characterized by 'Peperers and Grocers' and

'Apothecaries' (Stow 1971: i, 81, 260), and the implication is that Jonson's book will make ideal wrapping paper for herbs, spices and provisions.

Sometimes title pages advertise that a text was printed by **A** (printer) for **B** (publisher) to be sold by **C** (bookseller). All three men (almost always men) are identified more generally by the blanket term 'stationer' (from the medieval Latin *stationarius*, used to distinguish a vendor with a station or shop from an itinerant tradesman; for no known reason, the term came to be associated primarily with booksellers, and, by extension, with 'anyone engaged in any of the trades connected with books' (*OED*, 1a)).

Booksellers were often publishers, and publishers were often printers. (There were at least a hundred active publishers in 1600, of whom nineteen were also printers; there is no way of determining how many booksellers there were.) Confusion is easily created by failure to keep the terms and functions of printer/publisher/bookseller distinct – and this confusion is not limited to the twentieth century: sixteenth- and seventeenth-century epistles to printed texts, headed 'From the Printer to the Reader', often mean 'From the Publisher to the Reader', 'printer' being used simply in the sense of 'the one who caused the text to be printed'. In the academic play *2 Return from Parnassus* (*c*. 1600, published 1606), an impecunious writer, Ingenioso, is shown negotiating the sale of a manuscript to John Danter. Danter demurs ('good faith M. *Ingenioso*, I lost by your last booke'), but offers '40. Shillings and an odde pottle of wine'. Ingenioso is insulted, dismissing the fee as 'a fit reward for one of your reumaticke Poets', and, when he describes the tantalizingly commercial content of his work, 'a Chronicle of Cambridge cuckolds', Danter becomes enthusiastic: 'Oh this will sell gallantly: ile have it whatsoever it cost' (B3r–v). Despite his identification in the stage direction as '*Danter the Printer*', Danter is here negotiating in his function as publisher (no printer would say 'I lost by your last booke' unless he were also a publisher, for printers were paid by the publisher who employed them for the job in hand). Richard Jugge was also clearly negotiating as a publisher rather than a printer when he met Richard Eden, whose translation of *The Booke of Marten Curtes of the Art of Navigation* he had 'many yeeres before . . . printed'. Eden tells us that 'having with him [Jugge] some conference, [Jugge] declared that he woulde prynt that booke agayne, yf I woulde take the paynes to deuise some addition touchyng the same mater, that myght be joyned thereto' (STC 23659: J. Taisnier, *A very necessarie and profitable Booke concerning Navigation* (1579?), trans. R. Eden sig. $*_*^*$ 2ʳ). Thus, the professions of publisher and printer often coincided. However, despite such overlap and symbiosis, my focus here is the printer, printing, and the print-shop.

When a publisher buys a text from a source, he immediately needs to print it or have it printed. If he is not himself a printer, he must first choose one from the twenty-two operating in London in 1600.[2] Whereas publishers specialized (e.g., in news pamphlets or sermons), printers (with a couple of exceptions) didn't. (The exceptions were for technical subjects: Thomas East was known for music printing, and William Jaggard for heraldry, for instance, although these men by no means confined themselves to such specialist material.) A publisher's choice of printer was very much determined by who he knew, who he happened to meet, who was currently available, and who had done work for him previously at a reasonable price and standard. In 1608 Nicholas Okes printed Q1 *King Lear* for Nathaniel Butter. Nicholas Okes had never printed a play before, and play printing presented special technical difficulties (see below). But Okes had printed six books for Butter in the last months of 1607 and the first months of 1608, and it was probably this current association that encouraged Butter to approach him about *King Lear*, which he, Butter, had bought in November 1607. The printer would supply an estimate, and the publisher would (often) supply the paper. Then the printing process could begin.

The shortest seventeeth-century description of printing is provided by Joannes Comenius (*Orbis Sensualium Pictus*, 1658) in a picture-book designed to teach Latin to German children. I quote from the Latin–English version (first published in 1659 and reprinted in 1664 and 1672); the narrative simplicity represents the language teacher's need to introduce key nouns and verbs:

> The *Printer* hath *Copper Letters* in a great number put into *Boxes*. The *Compositor* taketh them out one by one, and (according to the *Copy* which he hath fastened before him in a *Visorum*) composeth words in a *composing-stick*, till a *Line* be made, he putteth these in a *Galley*, till a *Page* be made, and these again in a *Form*, and he locketh them up in *Iron Chases*, with *coyns*, lest they should drop out, and putteth them under the *Press*.
>
> Then the *Press-man* beateth it ouer with *Printers-ink* by means of *Balls*, spreadeth upon it the papers, put in the *Frisket*, which being put under the *Spindle*, on the *Coffin*, and pressed down with the *Bar* he maketh to take *Impression*. (Comenius 1970: 123, pp. 190–1; I have omitted the numbers that key the relevant terms to the diagram)

From brevity to mind-numbing detail: at this other extreme lies Joseph Moxon's *Mechanick Exercises on the Whole Art of Printing*, first published in 1683–4 (see Moxon 1958). Moxon was a Yorkshireman who printed his first book in London in 1647. Although the 'Whole Art of Printing' (with movable metal type at least) was over 200 years old by the time Moxon described it, it had changed little (and would continue to change little until mechanization in the nineteenth century). The London printer of 1600 and Joseph Moxon in 1683 both lived in the age of the hand press; Moxon's book supplements Comenius's succinct summary, and can reliably guide us through the process of printing.

Whereas publishers and booksellers congregated, as we have seen, in one area, St Paul's churchyard, for the purpose of marketing, printers set up business wherever was convenient for them, often in their own dwelling. The necessary equipment was fitted in as and where possible. In rare circumstances impecunious or pressurized authors lodged with the printer (as did Gabriel Harvey with John Wolfe, and Thomas Nashe with John Danter). Depending on its size and affluence, the printing house personnel comprised the master-printer, two or more pressmen, six or more compositors, apprentices, and 'devils' (also known as 'spirits' or 'flies'). The master-printer owned and supervised the business; the compositors and pressmen were hired by the week and paid by the hour (they presented their bill for labour on Saturday night), although a pressman's hour was not a temporal unit but a physical quota: 250 impressions (Moxon explains: 'If two men work at the Press ten Quires is an Hour; if one man, five Quires is an Hour' 1958: 344); the apprentices (if any) were attached to the establishment for seven years; and the devils (so called because they became black with ink dust in the course of the day) were boys hired to fetch and carry, stack paper, deliver printed sheets to the corrector, and do odd jobs. A small Elizabethan printing house would have had two or three presses (McKenzie 1969: 54–7), one of them being a press for proofs and/or spare parts. Moxon calls such a press an 'Empty Press': 'Most commonly every *Printing-House* has one of them for a *Proof-Press*' (1958: 339). Usually three compositors were employed for every press.

Elizabethan printing was a relief process, which means that the surface to be printed was raised higher than the other parts. History credits Johann Gensfleisch von Hofe zum Gutenberg (1394–1486) with the invention of printing. In fact, relief printing was already known in China, Japan and Korea (the Chinese, for instance, used woodcuts to print books with text and illustration, carving entire pages on wooden blocks: *block books*), but Gutenberg's major innovation was the invention of movable type.

Letters of movable type were made in a foundry in three stages: the punch, the matrix and the type. The *punch* was a long steel bar at the tip of which was cut a letter in relief; the letter end of the punch was then hit with a hammer into a copper block, leaving an impression of the letter in mirror image. This copper-block impression, known as the *matrix*, was clamped into a cast, and molten metal was poured into it from a ladle. This formed a small metal block with the mirror-image letter at the tip: the *type*. The metal composition of the type varied with date. Around 1580 the composition was 83 per cent lead, 9 per cent tin, 6 per cent antimony, and 1 per cent copper and iron (Nave 1989: 20). A century later Moxon (1958: 167) provides a recipe for equal weights of iron and antimony, plus 25 lbs of lead to every 3 lbs of iron. He follows this with a beverage of sack and salad oil for the metal founders 'intended for an Antidote against the Poysonous Fumes of the *Antimony*, and to restore the spirits that so violent a Fire and hard Labour may have exhausted'.

The type letters were cast in different *founts*, or *fonts* (e.g., italic, roman, black letter, Greek, Arabic) and in different sizes. Not only did letters – in both upper and lower case – have to be cast, but abbreviations (e.g., ampersand), ligatures ('tied letters'), spaces of varying widths, accents, punctuation marks and numbers. The average Roman fount had a minimum of 130 types; a Greek fount required a minimum of 450 types.

If he bought a complete fount, the printer received a discount from the foundry on his purchase, bulk being cheaper than individual types; however, he still received a preferential rate if he supplemented the fount with extra types within three months of his initial purchase. The Plantin–Moretus Museum in Antwerp (a printing house from the sixteenth century to the eighteenth, before being bequeathed to the city as a

museum) contains packets of unopened supplementary type in their original wrap-
pings, all carefully labeled according to sort and size. (A *sort* is an individual letter: a,
b, c, etc.) The type was then arranged in two sloping cases (a *pair* of cases) on a table in
front of the compositor. Each case was divided into small compartments (ninety-eight
boxes of equal size in the upper case, fifty-six boxes of fourteen different sizes in the
lower case), and the compartments were lined with paper to prevent the thin type
lodging itself in the cracks. Lining was the responsibility of the compositor. Like the
modern QWERTY keyboard, the layout of letters represented the frequency of use in
English; unlike the modern keyboard, however, the layout differed from printing
house to printing house, and any compositor who changed employer or worked in two
printing houses at a time ('Workmen when they are out of constant Work, do
sometimes accept of a day or twos Work, or a Weeks Work at another Printing-
house: this By-Work they call *Smouting*,' explains Moxon 1958: 351–2) had to
familiarize himself with the new layout of the case. As with all repetitive digital
actions, position is crucial to comfort and well-being; with typical thoroughness,
Moxon gives instructions for adjusting the height of the cases to accommodate a man
who was uncommonly tall or short.

Light is also crucial in the printing house. Moxon's ideal printing house has 'a clear,
free and pretty lofty Light, not impeded with the shadow of other Houses, or with
Trees, nor so low that the Sky-light will not reach into every part of the Room: But
yet not too high, lest the violence of *Winter* (*Printers* using generally but paper-
windows) gain too great advantage of Freesing the paper and Letter, and so both Work
and Workman stand still' (p. 17).

Some compositors pinned their manuscript copy in front of them in a *visorum*. With
a *composing stick* (a wooden rule which held a few sentences of type) in his left hand, the
compositor began to select type, letter by letter, which he placed in his composing
stick. Since it was easier to lay one line of type on *top* of another, and since, in the
printed text, line 3 follows line 2 follows line 1, the compositor set the sentence
upside down; and since the individual types were mirror-image letters, he conveniently worked in the way that comes most naturally to the Western mind: from left to
right. Here, as elsewhere, Moxon is full of helpful hints and explanations. For
example, he explains how and why to use a *composing rule* ('a *Brass-Rule* cut to the
length of the *Measure*') as a useful supplement to the composing stick. The compositor
lays it 'upon the *Compos'd Line*, to *Set* successively a succession of *Lines* upon . . . [T]he
Letter slides easier and smoother down to the *Back* of the *Stick*, than it will upon a *Line*
of *Letters*' (p. 205).

Compositors are identified primarily with typesetting, but their job begins with
deciphering the manuscript hand of their copy. In the Elizabethan period this was
often a difficult task, as many authors did not prepare their manuscripts for the press,
and, on several occasions, their texts were printed without their knowledge (as
printers and publishers sometimes acknowledged in prefatory epistles or on title
pages – see, for example, the title page of STC 6282: *A brief apologie prouing the
possession of W. Summers: written by J. Darrell but published without his knowledge*). In the

preface to *Kind-Hart's Dreame* (not dated, but probably 1593) Henry Chettle explains that he transcribed the manuscript of his friend Greene's *Groatsworth of Wit* for the press as Greene's handwriting was difficult for compositors to read. (There is a possibility, however, that Chettle composed the entire text himself, and cited Greene's alleged bad autograph as a justification for the text being in his own handwriting.) At the end of *The Exemplary Lives and Memorable Acts of Nine the Most Worthy Women* Heywood asks us to excuse the compositor, 'who received this Coppy in a difficult and unacquainted hand', the second adjective implying that compositorial accuracy is naturally enhanced by familiarity with authorial autograph. (This was the first and only Heywood text printed by Thomas Cotes.) Hieronymus Hornschuch, a German medical student who supplemented his finances by working as a professional proof-reader in Leipzig, wrote in 1608, in a tone of weary irritation that can only be due to personal experience of the phenomenon he is describing: 'It is particularly bothersome if someone submits his writings to their press not neatly written.' He offers advice to authors, concluding with a vivid image: 'If good seed has been scattered in the typographical field, it will be a hard job for wretched weedy errors to grow there' (1972: 33–4).

Often the compositor received a manuscript in more than one hand. Richard Brome wrote not only new plays for the Salisbury Court Theatre but 'divers scenes in auld revived playes for them and many prologues and Epilogues . . . songs and one Intro-duccon'. The printer of the second issue of the first quarto of Middleton and Rowley's *A Fair Quarrel* printed the additions as he received them, 'bound in at the end and not distributed through the play, as it would have been when acted' (Bentley 1971: 244). Eric Rasmussen (1993) has identified unusual compositor divisions in the first quarto of *Dr Faustus* (1604), where compositor stints change mid-page usually at 'scene breaks or important entrances'; Rasmussen attributes these divisions to the different manuscript pages of an authorial collaboration which presented difficulties. Moxon refers to difficult manuscript copy ('bad copy') as *'Bad, Heavy, Hard Work'*, in contrast to *'Light, Easie Work'* from 'good copy', and laments that 'if a Price be already made for a whole Book, the Good and Bad is done at the same Price' (1958: 203).

The compositor held about five to six words or one sentence from his copy in his memory at one time. The composing stick held approximately three lines of type (depending on fount size). When the stick was full, the compositor emptied it, placing the lines on a *galley* – a flat wooden board with a handle, like a paddle – until he had completed a page. Compositors were punningly known as 'galley slaves'. The compositor tied the page in the galley securely with packthread and transferred it to the correcting stone; he then repeated the process until he had set the necessary number of pages for a *sheet* (or *forme*).

Page size varied, although the sheet size was uniform. The page size was deter-mined by how often the sheet was folded. One fold created two leaves (a folio); each leaf had a recto and a verso (hence two leaves constituted four pages); two folds created four leaves (eight pages – a quarto); four folds created eight leaves (sixteen pages – an octavo); and so on. The compositor placed an identifying alphabetical signature, in upper or lower case, on each sheet; if the book was longer than the alphabet, he began again with a doubled alphabet (aa or Aa). These signatures ensured that the sheets were correctly collated. To help the binder fold the sheets correctly, a number was added to the signature on each leaf: A1, A2, A3, A4 for a quarto (A1–A4 is the short way in which modern bibliographers designate the collation), A1–A8 for an octavo, and so on. The numbered signatures were placed on odd-numbered pages (i.e., the recto of a leaf). The reason for signatures and numbers, Moxon explains, is that 'the *Gatherer, Collater* and *Bookbinder* may the readier lay *Sheets* right, if they be turned wrong'. However, he admonishes: 'This Rule is not among *Compositers* so well observed as it ought to be: For in Quarto's [*sic*] they not only leave the *Signature* 4 out, but rarely put in *Signature* 3' (p. 211).

The forme now has to be imposed. *Imposition* refers to 'the placing of the Pages that belong to a Sheet . . . in such an order as when the Sheet is wrought off at the Press, all the Pages may be folded into an orderly succession' (Moxon 1958: 223). The first side of the sheet to be printed, the inner forme, was known as the 'white side', and the second side, or outer forme, was called 'reiteration'. Obviously it was most efficient in time and type to compose the pages in the order in which they were to be printed (forme printing), which was not the order in which they would be read (seriatim). Single plays were usually printed in quarto. Since the eight pages in any sheet of a quarto were created by folding, the imposition for a quarto sheet is as shown in figure 26.1. Thus, it makes sense for a compositor to compose pages in the order 1, 4, 5 and 8 (since they were printed together), and then to compose pages 2, 3, 6, and 7. If two compositors were setting the same book, these units might also represent the division of compositorial labour.

Whether working alone or with a partner, it is clear that the compositor needed to estimate how his manuscript copy would translate to page sizes. He accordingly 'cast off' his copy. In the case of verse lines, casting off was easy, for one verse line equals one type line. In the case of a play whose dialogue was in a mix of prose and verse, the process was more complicated. Moxon offers various techniques for casting off. The first is a process of calculation, based on a sample setting of a manuscript line which the compositor judges 'indifferently written, between wide and close'; the second method, devised by Moxon himself, uses compasses; the third method is a sequence of arithmetical calculations based on the number of letters in a standard line of the manuscript, the number of lines on a page, and the number of pages in the manuscript.

Casting off copy required care to ensure that the dialogue on page 7 (say) would meet up perfectly with that on page 8; miscalculations were difficult to remedy at later stages. Later-stage remedies included the adjustment of spacing ('botching'). Moxon, ever the perfectionist, disapproves of botching, but allows that 'if it is in any case excusable – it is in this: for with too great *Spacing-out* or too *Close Setting*, [the compositor] many times may save himself a great deal of Labour, besides the vexation of mind, and other accidental mischiefs that attend *Ouer-running*' (p. 237). It is sometimes claimed that, in extreme cases, compositors would set prose as verse (to

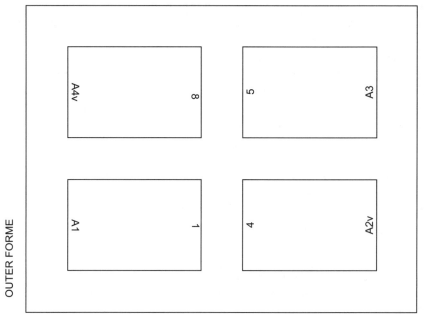

OUTER FORME

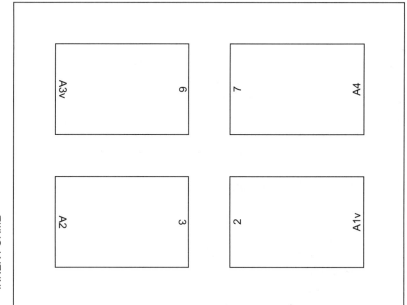

INNER FORME

Figure 26.1 Imposition for a quarto sheet.

use up space) or verse as prose (to save space), or even omit lines for which they had no room. It is unlikely that compositors would resort to such desperate expedients. Adjustments in the amount of blank space would fill up a page more conscientiously and as efficiently as the conversion of prose to verse; the saving in space is negligible in converting verse to prose; and Moxon is specific on where a compositor must follow or may deviate from his copy. Obviously, Moxon is unlikely to advertise a major compositorial peccadillo and its remedy. But earlier this century John Dover Wilson (1923) showed that compositors conscientiously, even slavishly, followed the author's spelling of proper names, at least in speech prefixes, in dramatic texts (e.g., Justice Scilens in *2 Henry* IV). A compositor who conscientiously follows his author's orthography is unlikely to take liberties with his prosody.

Having composed the pages and imposed the sheet, the compositor now laid an iron *Chase* – a frame with crossbars – over the imposed sheet on the composing slab. Gaskell (1972: 78–80) describes the next step:

> The spaces between the type pages and the bars of the chase were filled up with wooden furniture, and long wedges were fitted round the edges. Short wedges, or quoins, were then put in between the long wedges and the inside of the chase, loosely at first so that the string with which the pages were tied up could be unwound and removed, and so that any pieces of type that were sticking up above the rest could be knocked down with a wooden planer. Finally the quoins were driven home with a mallet and 'shooting stick' to lock the forme up tightly. . . . If the job had been done properly . . . the forme was now virtually a solid slab of wood and metal . . . and could be moved about or lifted without the type falling out.

Comenius's brief description of this process (see above) streamlines the complexity of Moxon's (1958: 223–33), but Gaskell's account is not only unmatched for clarity but is usefully supplemented by a photograph (1972: 79).

Before locking the chase, the compositor checked the forme for evenness of height (unevenness led to uneven inking). Some raised letters could be *patted down* (Moxon 1958: 230); others required hard knocks with the fist or a stick. Once satisfied, the compositor handed the locked chase to the pressmen, who inked the pages and pulled a trial proof-sheet.

Compositors were employed to compose; all compositors did the same thing, even when working together on a single book: they read copy; they set type; and they *un*-set type (*distributed* it: see below). Pressmen tended to work in pairs (two men was a full press; when operated by one man, a press was working at *half press*), but they alternated activities in shifts of three or six hours. While one man inked (*beat*), the other pulled sheets. Both activities were physically arduous; the sheer physical labour earned pressmen the nickname 'horses'.

Inking was done by means of two large hemispherical leather balls, about seven inches in diameter, filled with carding wool or horsehair. It was the pressman's job to make these balls and to maintain their condition: the leather had to be soaked at lunch-time and at the end of the day. (In England it was soaked in urine, and even

Moxon is at a loss to explain why. However, urine was used in laundry as a water-softener, and perhaps this was its purpose here too.) The pressman massaged the ink balls together to spread the ink, and then, with an ink ball in each hand, he inked the composition thoroughly. Moxon tells us that an inking of the balls lasted only three sheets before the ink had to be reapplied to the leather. Black ink was made from linseed oil (used as suspension and for binding), soot (as pigment) and pitch (also for pigment, obtained by burning fatty oils); vermilion was used instead of soot and pitch to make red ink.

Before printing it was necessary to wet the paper to make it more pliable and hence more receptive to the type. Moxon used a butcher's tray as a receptacle for soaking. The wet paper was then weighted and left to stand overnight ('for *Press-men* generally Wet their Paper after they have left Work at Night': p. 281). The next day the pressmen placed a sheet of paper on the printing press's *tympan*, a square iron frame covered with a piece of taut cloth. A hinged attachment to the tympan, called the *frisket*, was covered with a sheet of paper in which pieces were cut out which exactly matched the size and shape of the imposed pages; this prevented the edges of the paper becoming blotchy with ink during printing. The frisket was folded over the composition, and both tympan and frisket were rolled under the *platen* (the flat printing plate). A sharp pull on a handle ensured that the platen applied pressure to the paper and inked type, and so printed the sheet.

This sheet was a trial, a 'proof' sheet, and now required proof-reading. Moxon provides for three stages of proofing. This may be wishful thinking, and, in some respects, Moxon describes an ideal printing house. But he was also a practical printer, and though he may have overstated the process, his description is unlikely to be sheer invention. In fact, many woodcuts of the period show a proof-reader (known as a 'corrector') in the printing house. In *2 Return from Parnassus* Iudicio warns Ingenioso: 'what ere befalls thee, keepe thee from the trade of the corrector of the presse' (A4^v). Heywood's *Exemplary Lives and Memorable Acts of Nine the Most Worthy Women of the World* explains that his book contains an errata list because the 'corrector... could not bee always ready in regard of some necessary employment'. Topsell's letter 'To the Reader' at the beginning of his *History of Serpents* acknowledges the errors in his previous book, *Four-footed Beasts*, and blames the printer for his lack of Latin, himself for his absence from the printing house, and 'both of vs together, because we were not so thoroughly estated as to maintaine a sufficient Scholler to attend only vpon the presse'. In his book on proof correction, *Orthotypographia*, Hornschuch states (with an obvious degree of exasperated exaggeration) that the entire burden of seventeenth-century printing fell on the corrector: a sloppy authorial manuscript led to faulty typesetting, and it was the corrector who had to set all to rights.

Alternatively, or additionally, correction might be done by the author who, if not in the printing house himself, received proofs. That it was usual for authors to correct proofs is indicated by the apologies for their failure to do so. Marston explains that his 'enforced absence' from the printing house obliged him to 'rely upon the printer's discretion' in the first quarto of *The Malcontent* (1604), and he requests the reader to overlook the consequent errors. The second quarto of his *Fawn* (1606) corrects faults which 'by reason of the author's absence were let slip in the first edition'. The printer of Reginald Scot's *A perfite platforme of a Hoppe Garden* (1574) reveals that 'M. Scot could not be present at the printing of this his Booke whereby I might have used his advice in the correction of the same'. In 'Author to the Reader', Thomas Wilson lists the 'faults escaped' in the printing of his book *A Christian Dictionary* (1612); these errors, he explains, were caused by the 'badnesse of the Copy, *and by absence*, as also partly by forgetfulnes of the Author' (6^r; my emphasis). In Middleton and Fletcher's *The Nice Valour* (*c.* 1615), an author is shown receiving proofs of his book ('Here's your last proof Sir. / You shal have perfect Books now in a twinkling': IV. i. 303–4), and in Augustine Vincent's book *A Discoverie of Errours in the First Edition of the Catalogue of Nobility published* [i.e., written] *by Raphe Brooke, Yorke Herald, 1619*, the printer, William Jaggard, tells the reader that 'in the time of this his [Ralph Brooke's] unhappy sicknesse, though hee came not in person to over-looke the Presse, yet the *Proofe*, and *Reviewes* duly attended him, and he perused them . . . in the maner he did before' (¶, 6^v).

Such references must surely dispose of the prevalent view that the Elizabethan printing house did not trouble with correctors or careful proof-reading. The New Bibliographers, who were responsible for this belief, liked to measure, to quantify, to demonstrate what had gone wrong in the process of textual transmission. Proof-reading (like authorial revision) is unquantifiable, and hence it suited the New Bibliographers to argue that it did not usually take place. The evidence of printed texts points in the opposite direction. As Blayney admonishes, 'A Jacobean printer could no more have contemplated taking the financial risk of printing a forme from unchecked and freshly set type than a textual scholar could consider publishing the first draft of an article without even reading it' (1982: 201). According to Moxon, the corrector in the printing house was assisted by a reader who read the manuscript copy aloud. Editors may note that this introduces *two* additional (and unquantifiable) stages of mediation between manuscript and print.

Proof-reading was also undertaken for aesthetic infelicities: *pigeonholes* (wide white spaces), *hangs* (type is said to hang if it is not upright on its feet), *friars* (uninked white places), *monks* (black splodges) and *squabbling* (misaligned type). Sheets that were damaged – torn, stained or marred by printing errors – were called *naughty sheets*, and type that was worn or damaged was called *naughty type*. Proof-reading generally took place in a side-room, 'some little Closet adjoyning to the *Composing-room*' (Moxon 1958: 247). Errors spotted immediately by the corrector could be rectified, although unlocking the chase and adjusting or replacing type was a tricky business, and Moxon outlines techniques for making sure that one doesn't dislodge correctly set type. Once the printing process was under way, errors could still be corrected, simply by stopping the press and making a 'stop press' correction. In this instance the defective sheets already printed were not discarded but bound up with the newly corrected sheets. Thomas Tymme conscientiously prefaces his translation of *The Three Partes of Commentaries* (1574) thus: 'Note here (good Reader) that these faultes escaped in

Printing, are not so escaped in al the Bokes of this impression, but in some. Least therefore they to whome those should happen, might be troubled in the reading with obscure sense, I thought it good to make a general note of all' (STC 22242, sig. Mm4).

Once a sheet was printed, the type was distributed by the compositor. The printing of plays strained the supplies of type: the frequency of character's names in speech prefixes put pressure on supplies of italic capitals, as did the frequent stage directions 'Enter' and 'Exit', and if one encountered a scene with characters named *Edgar* and *Edmund* the problems were compounded. Thus, it was necessary to get the type back into circulation as soon as possible after one forme was printed: the technical name for this was *distribution*. The composition had first to be cleared of ink. It was washed and rinsed, quadrant by quadrant, several times until the water ran clear. Moxon (1958: 198) explains how to loosen type without removing it for thoroughness of rinsing, noting that this is best done at the end of the day so that the type may dry overnight; in winter it was necessary to dry it by the fire. The clean, dry type was then returned to its compartments in the case. If a printing error was noticed after the distribution of type, it could be corrected only by the inclusion of an errata list, or, more desperately, by the insertion of a paste-on slip or cancel.

Typographical errors were not the only errors that could befall the printing process. The pages had to be imposed on the forme in the right sequence. To most compositors correct imposition was probably automatic, but the fact that Moxon provides a mnemonic to ensure that pages 1 and 4, 2 and 3, go together in quarto layout (for example) suggests that even the most experienced compositor could err. Furthermore, even when the pages are in the right order, they have to be in the correct plane of rotation, otherwise the folding process will not work. Again, this might be automatic (although anyone who has repeatedly put letterhead in the laser printer or photocopier the wrong way round might demur), but the fact that printing houses had penalties for getting the pages the wrong way round suggests the very real possibility of mistakes. Once the white side was printed, the reverse side, the reiteration, was printed ('perfecting the sheet'), and like double-sided photocopying, the process of aligning the formes was open to error. A pressman who wrongly perfected a heap of sheets had to compensate the master for the loss out of his own pocket (p. 265).

The time-consuming care required at each stage of the operation, both artistically and technically, meant that printing was neither a rapid nor a simple operation. The title page demanded particular attention, for it was the first item to be seen by the reader and, as we have seen, was used independently as advertising. Moxon outlines the artistic decisions that went into its composition (pp. 212–14). Furthermore, the compositor's job was to 'correct' the punctuation of his author, to impose accuracy. Moxon is specific about the compositor's responsibility for correcting the punctuation of his author.

However, he elsewhere acknowledges that in dealing with difficult manuscript copy and the potential errors arising from it, the compositor is caught between Scylla and Charybdis. On the one hand, slavish adherence to the manuscript copy with all its imperfections is advisable, because it provides refuge from the blame of errata: the author can be held responsible. But following an author's errors, imperfections, and infelicities brings shame on the compositor and the printer for whom he works. Thus, although on page 192 Moxon writes: '*a* Compositor *is strictly to follow his* Copy, viz. to *observe and do just so much and no more than his* Copy *will bear him out for; so that his* Copy *is to be his Rule and Authority*,' on page 219 he modifies this position: 'Nor (as afore was hinted) is a *Compositer* bound to all these Circumstances and Punctilio's . . . [;] it is necessary the *Compositers* Judgment should know where the Author has been deficient, that so his care may not suffer such Work to go out of his Hands as may bring Scandal upon himself, and Scandal and prejudice upon the *Master Printer*.'

The kind of scandal that could result is illustrated in Thomas Heywood's vituperative attack on the printer William Jaggard (by name!) at the end of book 3 of *An Apologie for Actors* (1612). *An Apologie for Actors* was printed by Nicholas Okes, whose care Heywood praises in comparison to the negligence of Jaggard, who had printed *Troia Britanica* by Heywood with 'misquotations, mistaking of sillables, misplacing halfe lines, coining of strange and never heard of words, these being without number', When Heywood desired to list the errata, 'the printer answered me, hee would not publish his owne disworkemanship, but rather let his own fault lye upon the necke of the author'. Seven years later Jaggard's printing was again castigated, this time by Ralph Brooke, whose *Catalogue and Succession* Jaggard printed the same year. In the errata list to this volume, Brooke blamed Jaggard for errors that, as Jaggard later pointed out, it is difficult to attribute to a printer: genealogical errors, 'Mesnomers' (as Margaret for Katherine, Chancellor for Treasurer, Lady Dorothy for Lady Luce), and 'mispricions of place' (the Tower of London for Hampton Court). Brooke then prepared a revised edition, further attacking Jaggard; the book, printed by William Stansby (at Brooke's expense, with Stansby's presses working day and night), was published in 1622. Jaggard responded to Brooke by printing Augustine Vincent's *A Discoverie of Errours in the First Edition of the Catalogue of Nobility Published by Raphe Brooke* (1622), essentially a reprint of Brooke's folio of 1619, but with a 'caustic commentary' by Vincent (see Willoughby 1934: 151). Jaggard himself wrote a long and eloquent defence of his reputation at the front of this volume, providing fascinating details of the quarrel between himself and Brooke and of attitudes in the printing house. Listing the alleged printer's errors, he states: '[T]hough I ascribe no such infallibility to the Presse, as Master *Yorke* doth to his Pen, yet I am confident, that these Errors, or the most part of them, looke so like the Author, as no man of judgement will father them upon the Printer, inasmuch as they rather savour of Ignorance then Neglect' (¶ 6ʳ). The workmen who produced the book are offended by Brooke's allegations, Jaggard says, and it seems to them that Brooke's 'Clerkship' failed him, either in his source reading or in transcription. In support of this claim the workmen cite the numerous errors they received in Brooke's manuscript copy 'which if the Worke-men had bene so madly disposed to tye themselves too, and have given him leave to print his owne English (which they now repent they did not) hee would (they say) have made his Reader, as good sport in his Catalogue, as ever *Tarleton* did his Audience, in a Clownes parte' (¶ 6^r). The only error the printing house made, Jaggard says, was the error of dealing with Brooke in the first place.

Once sheets were printed, they had to be removed from the press and hung up to dry. The warehouse or other adjoining room was used to dry sheets. They were hung up on double wooden racks extending the length of the room, raised carefully by a wooden peel (a sort of oar). Although contemporary woodcuts show sheets hanging up to dry in the printing room, this almost certainly never happened (the air was dusty with specks of ink, and if ink dust adhered to the skin and clothes of the 'devils', it would inevitably be attracted to the moist paper). Once dry, the sheets were placed on benches in an orderly succession of signatures ready for collation (*laying the heaps*). After collation the sheets were *pressed*: flattened by weights and left to stand for approximately 24 hours. Sheets were delivered unbound and sometimes even uncut to the publisher; since it was necessary to trim them for binding, cutting could be left to the binder. Prospective buyers browsed through books whose ordered sequence of sheets was stabbed and stitched on the side (an Elizabethan form of stapling). Having made their choice of book, customers were free to select their own binding.

The working week in the printing house was long (six-day weeks, with the length of the day varying according to summer and winter light), but the work was rarely continuous; nor were the days unsociable. In his section on *Ancient Customs used in a Printing-house* Moxon paints a picture of community and camaraderie. The paper windows in the printing house were to be replaced by the journeymen every year, 'whether the old will serve again or no; Because that day they make them, the Master Printer gives them a Waygoose; that is, he makes them a good Feast, and not only entertains them at his own House, but besides, gives them Money to spend at the Ale-house or Tavern at Night' (1958: 327). The Waygoose took place about St Bartholomew's Feast (24 August). Such sociability was not confined to official feasts or after-hours gatherings. For example, 'in discourse, when any of the Workmen affirm any thing that is not belieued, the *Compositer* knocks with the back corner of his *Composing-stick* against the lower edge of his *Lower Case*, and the *Presseman* knocks the Handles of his *Ball-stocks* together: Thereby signifying the discredit they give to his story' (pp. 326–7). A hierarchical system of fines – for swearing, fighting, abusive language, drunkenness, dropping a composing stick or ink ball – indicates an orderly work-place, but the purpose of some fines seems to have been less behaviour modification than the fostering of community (and the easy furnishing of a petty cash kitty): 'If a Journey-man marry, he pays half a Crown to the *Chappel* [slang for printing-house]. When his Wife comes to the *Chappel*, she pays six Pence; and then all the Journey-men joyn their two Pence apiece to Welcome her. If a Journey-man have a Son born, he pays one Shilling. If a Daughter born, six Pence' (p. 328).

The date of the Waygoose also marked the resumption of candlelight in the printing house after the brighter days of summer. Each compositor was allotted one candle, and a fine was levied for any workman who left his candle burning at night. At the Oxford University Press multiple candles were permitted for any compositor working with three pairs of cases, in which event the compositor positioned his candles in the compartments of his case. However, when only one candle was allotted, the Oxford University Press compositor had to carry it with him. A woodcut on the title page of *Yet More Work for a Mass Priest* (1622) shows pressmen utilizing a single candle each. The technique depicted was probably as efficient as it now seems amusing: the pressmen wore the candle on their head.

There is nothing in Moxon to suggest that the social atmosphere in the printing house led to that cartoon stereotype invoked by bibliographers: the inebriated English compositor. Certainly ale was the thirst-quenching drink of choice, in the printing house as elsewhere, in England as on the Continent (a flagon of liquid is represented in the Dutch woodcut of a printing house in *Orbus Pictus*). Even so, it is a big step from drinking and merriment to drunkenness and incapacity. Moxon specifies a fine for drunkenness, and in Germany, Hornschuch is similarly appalled at the possibility of inebriation: 'let those whose business it is to do the job [do it] soberly, not through a screen of expiring vapours from excess of alcohol.' It generally suits most nations to view others as less responsible than their own, and Gaskell (1972: 141) hints that the tradition of viewing English compositors as drunk originated with Benjamin Franklin in the eighteenth century.

Larger transgressions of master-printers, not their journeymen, are better documented. The records of the court of the Stationers' Company list infractions of printers and publishers. In 1671 the fictional but quasi-autobiographical picaresque narrative of Richard Head devoted a few chapters to the hero's activities as an apprentice printer (1928: 376–84). The master-printer printed lucrative titles (such as school-books) that were owned legally by other printers; buying 300 of the legitimate copies from a wholesaler, he mingled his own pirated imprints with them. The manuscript commonplace book of Sir Roger Wilbraham (1902: 37) records the (possibly apocryphal) story of the printer/publisher of Rabelais: he 'was a loser by his first impression of Rables: then he caused a preacher in his sermon to inveigh against the vanitie thereof: since which it hath ben 6 tymes under presse: so much it was in request'. It seems that the craft of printing, as of every profession, has the potential to become 'craftiness'.[3]

NOTES

1   This imprint, like twentieth-century imprints, is of primary use to retailers. Any sixteenth-century stationer, like any twentieth-century bookshop, could, of course, *sell* a book. See Blayney 1997: 390.

2   The university presses at Oxford and Cambridge were sometimes also patronized by London publishers. The only other printing houses in England – also in London – were

illegal. Outside England there were two printing houses: one in Dublin and one in Edinburgh.

3   This essay could not have been written without the help of Peter W. M. Blayney, who has once again confirmed his status as the most valuable reference source in the Folger Shakespeare Library.

REFERENCES AND FURTHER READING

Abbott, Craig S. and Williams, William P. 1985: *Textual and Bibliographical Studies: An Introduction*. New York: Modern Language Association.

Beaumont and Fletcher 1989: *The Nice Valour*. In Fredson Bowers (gen. ed.), *The Dramatic Works in the Beaumont and Fletcher Canon*, vol. 7, Cambridge: Cambridge University Press, 425–51.

Bentley, Gerald Eades 1971: *The Profession of Dramatist*. Princeton: Princeton University Press.

Bevington, David and Rasmussen, Eric (eds) 1993: *Dr Faustus: A and B Texts by Christopher Marlowe, his Collaborator and Revisers*. Manchester and New York: Manchester University Press.

Blayney, Peter W. M. 1982: *The Texts of 'King Lear' and their Origins*, vol. 1: *Nicholas Okes and the First Quarto*. Cambridge: Cambridge University Press.

—— 1990: *The Bookshops in Paul's Cross Churchyard*. London: Bibliographical Society.

—— 1997: The publication of playbooks. In John D. Cox and David Scott Kastan (eds), *A New History of Early English Drama*, New York: Columbia University Press, 383–422.

Comenius, Joannes 1970: *Orbis Sensualium Pictus* (1659), trans. Charles Hoole. Menston, England: Scolar Press.

Gaskell, Philip 1972: *A New Introduction to Bibliography*. Oxford: Clarendon Press.

Head, Richard and Kirkman, Francis 1928: *The English Rogue (1665–1671)*. London: Routledge.

Hornschuch, Hieronymus 1972: *Orthotypographia* (1608), ed. and trans. Philip Gaskell and Patricia Bradford. Cambridge: University Library.

Jonson, Ben 1947: *The Poems*, ed. C. H. Herford, Percy and Evelyn Simpson. Oxford: Clarendon Press, vol. 8.

McKenzie, D. F. 1969: Printers of the mind. *Studies in Bibliography*, 22, 1–76.

McKerrow, R. B. 1927: *An Introduction to Bibliography for Literary Students*. Oxford: Oxford University Press.

Moxon, Joseph 1958: *Mechanick Exercises on the Whole Art of Printing* (1683–4), ed. Herbert Davis and Harry Carter. London: Oxford University Press.

Nave, F. de et al. 1989: *About Types, Books and Prints*. Antwerp: Plantin–Moretus Museum and City Prints Gallery.

Rasmussen, Eric 1993: *A Textual Companion to 'Doctor Faustus'*. Manchester: Manchester University Press.

Stow, John 1971: *Survey of London*, intro. by Charles Lethbridge Kingsford, 2 vols. Oxford: Clarendon Press.

Taylor, Gary and Wells, Stanley et al. 1987: *William Shakespeare: A Textual Companion*. Oxford: Clarendon Press.

Wilbraham, Sir Roger 1902: *The Journal of Sir Roger Wilbraham*, in *The Camden Miscellany*, vol. 10, London: Royal Historical Society, 1–139.

Williams, George Walton 1985: *The Craft of Printing and the Publication of Shakespeare's Works*. Washington, D.C.: The Folger Shakespeare Library,

Willoughby, Edwin Elliott 1934: *A Printer of Shakespeare*. London: Philip Allan.

Wilson, J. Dover 1923: Bibliographical links in the three pages and the good quartos. In A. W. Pollard et al., *Shakespeare's Hand in the Play of Sir Thomas More*, Cambridge: Cambridge University Press, 113–41.

27

The London Book-Trade in 1600

Mark Bland

The London book-trade in 1600 was, at once, more sophisticated in the diversity of its products and much smaller than we might assume. It was neither entirely a trade in printed books, nor were the printed books always English in origin. This broader perspective is important, for narratives of the book-trade commonly privilege the trade in printed books over manuscripts and construct their histories within national boundaries. Yet, as Sir William Cornwallis was to observe in his *Essayes*: 'The Worlde is a booke: the words and action*s* of men Co*m*mentaries vpon that volume: The former lyke manuscriptes priuate: the latter common, lyke things printed.' The ambivalence that Cornwallis registers between words and actions, manuscript and print, the private and the public, is suggestive also of the way in which the book-trade in 1600 was poised between these competing interests. The books produced by London printing-houses catered to a large but specific segment of the overall market. Much material continued to circulate in manuscript, however, not only for religious and political reasons (and the two were often contiguous), but because the trade in printed books had yet to displace manuscripts as a primary source for the transmission of knowledge. Equally, the Latin trade (as it was called) in continental books catered for a learned clientele. This material, some of it extremely erudite and obscure, could be imported in limited quantities but provided far greater diversity in a bookseller's stock than it is now possible entirely to recover. For such publications the London book-trade rarely had either the resources or the necessary economies of scale to compete against the leading producers in Paris, Lyons, Antwerp, Frankfurt, Basle, Geneva, Venice and the other major centres of European book production. Approximately 80 per cent of the books that survive from the libraries of Ben Jonson and John Donne, for instance, were printed on the Continent. This is not untypical of the libraries of English intellectuals in the sixteenth and seventeenth centuries.

The London book-trade was concentrated around Paul's churchyard but spread to Holborn in the west, Aldersgate in the east, and down to the river along Thames Street. It was relatively small, tightly controlled, and largely self-regulated. By 1600, the Company of Stationers had been in existence for forty-three years, though its establishment and incorporation had a long pre-history. The Star Chamber decree of 1586, which regulated the number of printers and the trade more generally, had consolidated the Company's control. Such forms of trade protection and regulation were largely intended to ensure that everyone involved in the book-trade survived. Like every such attempt, it was only partially successful, and those who repeatedly infringed the rules were punished as refractory and, at worst, might have their right to trade withdrawn. Furthermore, the Stationers' Company had been engaged in a long-running dispute with the Company of Drapers, which was finally resolved in May 1600, when twelve Drapers were translated to the Stationers'. As Gerald Johnson (1988) has described, this was an event that the Drapers' had resisted for many years as against the freedoms of the City, but it was an inevitable consequence of the consolidation of trade practices.

The choice of any year as a snapshot of the book-trade is arbitrary, of course, but it does help to bring a variety of issues into focus. Conveniently, 1600 is a peak year for playbook production. It was also a year that might be characterized by political and therefore official nervousness. The problem of an ageing queen and an undeclared succession remained an insistent undercurrent to other concerns. More obviously, English domestic politics was coloured by the first imprisonment and trial of the earl of Essex, whilst internationally the papal jubilee was scarcely a matter that the authorities would wish to celebrate, despite its importance and attraction to such English and Welsh Catholics as William Stanley, sixth earl of Derby, and Hugh Holland. Neither event is mentioned in Stow's *Annales*, which instead records the extremely cold winter and spring (it snowed in April) known as the Great Frost, the scarcity and hoarding of corn, the departure of Mountjoy for Ireland, the Gowrie Conspiracy in Scotland, and various diplomatic negotiations, including an abortive peace treaty with Spain. Stow's silence on Essex was not necessarily imposed upon him: he may have preferred not to discuss a subject that had yet, finally, to resolve itself (when he subsequently did, his account was sympathetic). It is true, however, that the authorities were clearly concerned about the political situation and the press as a mechanism for the dissemination of potentially inconvenient material.

The previous year, the literary fad for epigrams and satire had resulted in both a ban (which was partially ignored) and a token *auto-da fé* of the offending material in Stationers' Hall. A similar instruction for *The Letting of Humours Blood in the Vaine* was made in October 1600. Yet censorship and political control were neither coherent nor effective. So convoluted was the political situation that Robert Southwell's *A Humble Supplication to her Majestie* was surreptitiously published, not by Catholic sympathizers, but by the government in order to embarrass the Jesuits. As this illustrates, changed political circumstances and retrospective reinterpretation might equally legitimize an opposition text that had previously circulated in manuscript, or it might render an innocent text guilty by insinuation as Sir John Hayward discovered with *The Historie of Henry IIII*. Hayward was to spend 1600 in the Tower writing one of the most popular pocket-books of godly piety, *The Sanctuarie of a Troubled Soule,* while Sir Edward Coke attempted to prove his guilt by association because he wrote a dedication to Essex.

For the book-trade as a whole these were unpleasant but not significant events. The vast majority of domestically printed output – Bibles, Books of Common Prayer, works of piety, sermons, law-books, proclamations, schoolbooks, translations of the classics, and most works of literature or history – were not likely to be subject to official interference beyond the ordinary mechanisms of licensing or sanction. What concerned the authorities more were secret press books and the Puritan and Catholic tracts that were printed on the Continent. Yet the fact that so many illegal books survive indicates that official attempts at control were arbitrary and ineffective. To minimize the impact of such illicit material, the government relied on the co-operation of the Stationers' Company. It was equally in the Company's interest to help, as co-operation with the government helped to consolidate its authority. Yet, by and large, the Company was more concerned about its relationships with other London guilds and the regulation of its members, if only to reduce political inter-ference and maintain the existing methods of trade association, than with the problems that might possibly be generated by any particular book – unless it infringed someone else's right to the copy.

With its limited resources, the book-trade tried to cater to everyone, from the barely literate to the deeply learned. Single-sheet items, whether broadsides or pamphlets, in English or Latin (for instance, Aesop) were quickly consumed, and in some cases the only evidence for the existence of these popular texts is through inference from earlier and later editions. At the other extreme, there were sixteen books printed over eighty sheets in length (the number of pages depended on the format) and a further twelve that were between forty-one and eighty sheets in length. These substantial books were obviously the most expensive items produced in London, and their readership was therefore restricted to those either able to afford them or to borrow a copy from someone who could. The expensive end of the trade, however, primarily relied on imports. An educated reader might acquire books as varied as the Des Planches Cicero that Jonson bought at this time, books by intellectuals such as Lipsius, Brisson, Bodin or Scaliger, and on topics as diverse as hieroglyphics and inscriptions, alchemy, witchcraft, Hebraica and Cabalistic texts, medicine, jurisprudence, military theory, near contemporary political history, math-ematics and architecture. The libraries of Dee and Selden are suggestive of just how esoteric some of this material could be. Simply because the London trade did not print this material does not mean that it was not part of a bookseller's stock.

English vernacular literature was, in this context, a very small (though politically sensitive) part of the overall market. There were twenty plays, four miscellanies, thirty-one volumes of verse (including translations), sixteen volumes of essays, prose romances and other forms of popular literature, and nine music books published in 1600. Such material was predominantly slight and inexpensive. Peter Blayney (1997) has described the financial calculations involved in producing a typical play quarto, and the same calculations would have been true of books of verse or of prose romance.

What equally needs to be emphasized is the economic insignificance of English literature to the book-trade. With twenty plays printed during 1600, including six by Shakespeare and three editions of Jonson's *Every Man out of his Humour*, the year is notable for the production of this material. Yet there was less composition and press-work involved in the production of all of these plays than there was in a single octavo edition of the Bible. Simply counting the number of plays or volumes of verse that were printed in a given year is a very misleading way of representing the economic importance of this material to the trade.

Furthermore, English literature was only part of the broader literary culture. Neo-Latin poetry, contemporary European literature and editions of the classical authors were among the most popular books both printed domestically and imported into England. The interest in this literature is most obviously seen in the translations that were published for local consumption. For books that were imported from Europe, however, the mechanisms for distribution and control were inevitably different from domestically produced material, with the Latin trade controlled by the partnership of John Norton and his former apprentice John Bill. These books were not licensed, and the privileged trade was to be one of the Puritans' main matters of complaint at the Hampton Court conference. The government simply relied on language (and, therefore, education) as a barrier. For the Latinate reader (such as Jonson), the available literature included not only Martial, Euripides and Apicius, but such contemporary European authors as Pierre Pithou and Baltasar de Beaujoyeulx.

The intellectual life of London, and therefore the book-trade, was strongly influenced by its connections to Europe. Editions of Tasso, Aretino, Montaigne, Montmayor and others were both available in their original languages and, increasingly, translated. Major intellectual figures such as Camden also maintained important contacts with Europe: Camden's network of private correspondents included François Hotman, Jacques Auguste de Thou, Nicolas Fabri de Peiresc and Jacob Ortelius. The correspondence of English intellectuals with their continental contemporaries often alludes to the private circulation of books, with gifts exchanged and copies procured of difficult-to-get material. Amongst the most deeply educated groups, literacy was multi-lingual.

Although the number of Latin books, other than schoolbooks, printed in London was small, they were culturally significant. Gilbert's *De Magnete* is one of the foundation texts of the new science, and was later reprinted in Europe. Similarly, the sixth and penultimate Latin edition of Camden's *Britannia* was clearly meant not only for local consumption, but for the international trade. It had already been printed in Frankfurt, but Camden revised his material continually over a period of twenty-one years, expanding his original work by more than six times. The other significant Latin texts were by Matthew Sutcliffe, dean of Exeter and one of the royal chaplains, and Thomas James. Sutcliffe's *De Vera Christi Ecclesia* was a ninety-sheet Latin response to Cardinal Bellarmine and followed on another similar response from the previous year. Similarly, James's *Bellum Papale* reflected his very strong views on religion, while his *Ecloga Oxonio-Cantabrigiensis* is a catalogue of manuscripts held in Oxford and Cambridge libraries. James was a noted theologian and Bodley's first librarian.

Many of the largest books were works of history. The largest book published, at 363 sheets, was Philemon Holland's translation of Livy; but several other folios appeared, including translations of Conestaggio's *A Historie of the Uniting of the Kingdom of Portugall to the Crowne of Castill*, Fumée's *The Historie of the Troubles of Hungarie* and *The Geographical Historie of Africa* by Leo Africanus. Three history books were also printed in quarto: Thomas Danett's *A Continuation of the Historie of France*, *The Mahumatane or Turkish Historie* translated by Robert Carr and Stow's *Annales*. As well as these, the third volume of Hakluyt's *Voyages* appeared. The extensiveness of the list emphasizes the diversity and wide range of contemporary history that was available. More recent political events, such as the papal jubilee and events in France and the Low Countries, as well as earthquakes and other news stories, were printed in news-books of two or three sheets.

Likewise, the book-trade in English theology was dominated by the third edition of John Willet's *Synopsis Papismi*, Mornay's *Fowre Bookes on the Institution, Use and Doctrine of the Holy Sacrament*, and another work by the ever prolix Matthew Sutcliffe: Sutcliffe's *A Briefe Replie* proved instead to be an immodest fifty-six-sheet (448-page) harangue. Sutcliffe maintained such an output on an annual basis, and clearly found a market for his work and royal favour (under both Elizabeth and James) for his efforts. Willet's *Synopsis Papismi* was an even more ambitious work, and was the second largest book published in London. It sought to list and confute 500 errors attributed to the Catholic faith. It was probably subsidized by Lambeth Palace. In contrast to the insularity of Willet's work, the publication of Mornay's *Fowre Bookes*, together with his *Discourse of Life and Death*, reinforced the English connections with the broader discourse of European Protestantism. Such publishing activity was only further encouraged by the papal jubilee, and the Church went to considerable trouble to bolster its position in response.

During 1600, there was also printed a substantial amount of controversial pocket literature, godly pocket-books and sermons, including reprints of Arthur Dent's *A Sermon of Repentance*, Bishop Jewell's *The Apologie of the Church of Englande*, John Norden's *A Pensive Mans Practice*, St Augustine's *A Pretious Booke of Heavenly Meditations* and *The Imitation of Christ* by Thomas à Kempis. New production included such items as Francis Bradley's *A Godly Sermon*, John Downame's *Spiritual Physicke*, Luca Pinelli's *Breife Meditations*, Gabriel Powell's *The Resolved Christian*, Adrian Polanus's *The Substance of the Christian Religion* and Johann Habermann's *The Enemie of Securitie*. Godliness also found its way into domestic literature with such books as Robert Cleaver's *A Godly Forme of Housholde Government* and into political literature with Thomas Floyd's *The Picture of a Perfit Common Wealth*, which described both 'the offices of Princes' as well as 'the dueties of subiects'. These items were staples of the press and were designed to be portable. Few copies survive.

Other forms of domestic literature covered such issues as estate management, health and cookery. Many of these books were heavily used. The largest book produced was a translation of Charles Estienne and Jean Thibault's *Maison Rustique or the Countrie Farme*. This compendious work was intended to serve a variety of purposes and be a useful reference work. Other books with similar though less wide-ranging themes included Conrad Heresbach's *Fowre Bookes of Husbandry*, a reprint of Leonard Mascall's *The Firste Booke of Cattell* (Mascall wrote several works on these subjects), and John Partridge's *The Treasurie of Commodious Conceits*, which was a guide to health.

Other books served professional needs, not least the law. Editions of the statutes and yearbooks, Littleton's *Tenures*, William Fulbecke's *A Direction or Preparative to the Study of the Law*, Dyer's *Reports* and those of Sir Edward Coke are all representative of the legal book-trade. Some also catered specifically to the need for manuscript annotation: Coke's *Reports*, for instance, was printed with a foreshortened page and to a shorter measure so that the annotations of lawyers could be accommodated in the margins. Most surviving copies have marginalia.

Occasional evidence also survives both about book prices and contemporary readers. A note on the rear endpaper of the Cambridge copy of Camden's *Reges, Reginae, Nobiles, & alij Ecclesia Collegiata B. Petri Westmonasterij Sepulti* records that it was bought on 28 July for 10*d.* – a price that presumably included the vellum binding. Francis Meres bought the Folger copy of George Abbott's *A Briefe Description of the Whole World*, while the parliamentarian Sir Peter Manwood acquired the second Folger copy of Thomas Danett's *A Continuation of the Historie of France*, and subsequently gave it to his son in 1605. John Manwood similarly acquired the first Folger copy of the 1596 edition of Spenser's *Faerie Queene* on 29 March for 7*s.* The other Folger copy was owned by John Shelburye, and has notes on other contemporary book prices. Jonson's friend Sir John Roe acquired the Folger copy of *The Lawes and Statutes of the Stannaries of Devon*, while Thomas Knyvett bought one of the Cambridge copies of *Ecloga Oxonio-Cantabrigiensis* for 2*s.* 6*d.* on 27 October. John Golburne had the Huntington copy of Cipriano de Valera's *Two Treatises* elaborately bound in vellum and gilt for the dedicatee, Thomas Egerton. Other less datable, but early readers include Richard Lewis, who owned the Huntington copy of Fumée's *The Historie of the Troubles of Hungarie*, and Elizabeth Warner, who owned the Huntington copy of Drayton's *Englands Heroicall Epistles*. Perhaps most interestingly, Susan Risley (or Riley) owned the Folger copy of Dowland's *First Booke of Songes*. Susan was dyslexic, and reversed her initial S to a curved Z.

Many other women found themselves the subjects of an admiring dedication, particularly of literature, piety or household books. Henry Olney dedicated the *Essayes* of Sir William Cornwallis to the author's circle of women friends: Lady Sara Hastings, Lady Theodosia Dudley, Lady Mary Wingfield and Lady Mary Dudley. Though Olney claimed to have pirated the book, the dedication probably has more to do with Cornwallis's modesty. Simon Stafford dedicated 'the tithe of my poore Printing-presse', Richard Curteys's *The Care of a Christian Conscience*, to Lady Dorothea Stafford. John Dowland dedicated *The Second Booke of Songes* to Lucy, countess of Bedford. William Hunnis dedicated *Seven Sobs of a Sorrowful Soule* to Frances, countess of Sussex. Mathias Leius dedicated his *Certamen Elegiacum* to the queen. More generally, John Partridge prefaced *The Treasurie of Commodious Conceits* to his women readers, while William Vaughan dedicated *Natural and Artificial Directions for Health* to his sister-in-law Lady Margaret Vaughan. Vaughan's book is quite suggestive of the different values of the early seventeenth century to those of our own time. He advised the reader, and therefore primarily Margaret, that during spring 'Venerie [i.e., lustfulness or promiscuity] will doe no great harme', and, because it was important to keep warm in winter, 'To vse carnall copulation is expedient'. In fact, Vaughan was probably more embarrassed by his dedication than his advice, for he praised Margaret's father as a man 'who for integritie of life, prudence, magnaminitie, and liberall behauiour, is inferiour to no man of what qualitie soeuer'. Unfortunately, Margaret's father, Sir Gelly Meyrick, was executed the following February for his part in the Essex Rebellion.

If these outer witnesses to the history of reading are informative, so is some of the internal evidence to be found in the books. The care and attention that was given to the printing of various books have been a matter of some contention, as the surviving evidence is uncommon. Perhaps the most written-about proof-sheet from the period is to be found in the Bridgwater copy at the Huntington Library of *The First Part of the Contention Betwixt the Two Famous Houses of Yorke and Lancaster*, printed by Valentine Simmes. This shows Simmes's corrector making changes to spelling and punctuation. Other books reinforce evidence about contemporary printing-house activity, including concurrent production and shared printing. For instance, the first edition of Jonson's *Every Man out of his Humour* was printed by Adam Islip, the second was shared between Islip and Peter Short, and the third was shared among four printing-houses. Other volumes also reveal the subtle changes in font between sheets which indicate shared work.

Similarly, distinctions in format, type-face and type-size indicate something about the nature of the material, the audience for which it was intended, its portability and use, and the conventions of the trade. There are no exact boundaries, but rather a series of generally observed practices: plays were set as quartos in pica roman, prose romances in blackletter, schoolbooks and godly pocket-books in the smaller formats of octavo and duodecimo, larger more learned works in folio or quarto in eights. The more elegantly printed books were often set in English roman, those for which the economic use of paper was expedient (schoolbooks, Bibles and psalm-books) in the smaller fonts of brevier and long primer. These distinctions not only catered to the expectations of the reading public but allowed for flexibility in the printing-house. A book set in English roman, for instance, could be proofed and printed while another set in pica black letter was being set.

Evidence relating to format, typography and readership is a primary source of information about the history of the book as a social document. This cultural context has also been of interest to literary scholars, who have engaged in a series of speculations about power, privilege, censorship and the emergence of print as a significant material witness to the culture of the early modern period. These accounts, however, have typically relied on traditional narratives that begin with a series of unstated assumptions. A literary text is held to be a self-evidently important witness to intellectual and cultural history. Its value is often reinforced by its material rarity. The histories of these objects have also been held to be typical of the book-trade in general. It would be helpful, therefore, to try and describe the extent of what we do not know and to question the assumptions that have been made about the books and literary culture in the early modern period. Often the reason given for poorly produced texts has been piracy, commercial opportunism, memorial reconstruction ('I write this', Sir William Cornwallis remarked, 'in an Alehouse') and so forth. The lure of a quick profit has frequently been attributed to the mercenary printer.

When the assumptions about the primacy of literary documents are weighed against all the surviving evidence, a series of questions naturally arise. How big was the trade in printed books? How many books were sold? What was the turnover of the trade? How profitable was it? How many people did this support? How large was the trade in printed books compared to that in manuscripts? And what might this suggest about literacy and the importance of literary texts? Any attempt to answer such questions must be avowedly speculative, but a study of the surviving evidence is suggestive. The calculations made for this exercise are typically based on a combination of the evidence that McKenzie records in 'Printers of the Mind' (1969), the collation and description of at least one copy of every book published in 1600, and some informed speculation about edition sizes and book-prices. By definition, the figures that will be produced must be inaccurate, but not by more than a reasonable margin of error. I simply wish to overstate the importance of the printed book-trade in order to demonstrate its insignificance.

Excluding almanacs and the very approximately dated Act Verses from Cambridge, the *Short-Title Catalogue* lists 342 books published either during 1600 or in a few cases approximately dated to that year. To this can be added a unique copy of the folio edition of the Psalms in the Library Company of Philadelphia. Clearly, many ephemeral items do not survive at all, but the figure is suggestive of the more obvious activities of the trade. Of the 343 items, sixteen are either variant imprints or issues where one or two sheets have been reset. One item, Marlowe's *Hero and Leander*, reissues another item (Marlowe's translation of Lucan). A further sixteen items were printed in Europe, twenty in Scotland, eleven in Cambridge, seven in Oxford, nine at secret presses (one of which may have been printed in 1604) and one in Ireland. The remaining 262 items were printed in London: eight are ballads, seven are proclamations, two are maps, and six are other forms of single-sheet broadside ephemera. Thus, there are 239 books and pamphlets that range from single-sheet news-books to Livy's *Historie*. They include two schoolbooks: Culmann's *Pueriles Sententiae* and Record's *Arithmeticke*. To these must be added more than two dozen other schoolbooks and catechisms, including Aesop's *Fabulae*, Aphthonius's *Praeexercitamenta*, Castalio's *Dialogi*, Cato, Cicero's *Epistolae, De Officiis,* and *Sententiae*, Cordier's *Colloquia Scholastica*, Erasmus's *Colloquia*, Evaldus Gallus's *Puerile Confabulatiunculae*, a volume of *Poemata* by Horace, Juvenal and Persius, Lily's *Grammar*, Mancinus's *De Quatuor Virtutibus*, Aldo Manuzio's *Phrases Linguae Latinae*, Paulo Manuzio's *Epistolae*, Nowell's *Catechism*, Ovid's *Heroidum Epistolae* and *Fabularum*, the *Zodiacus Vitae* of Palingenius, Ravisius Textor's *Epistolae* and *Epithetorum Epitome*, Sallust, Seton's *Dialectica*, Spagnuoli's *Bucolica*, Susenbrotus's *Figurae*, Talaeus's *Rhetorica*, Terence's *Comedia* and Virgil's *Opera*.

One or two other items might also be included. All these books exist in other editions and were reprinted throughout the late sixteenth and seventeenth centuries by the London (and later the university) trade. Other missing items probably include the second edition of Lewis Thomas's *Seaven Sermons, or, the Exercises of Seven Sabbaoths*.

Of these, some books (Bibles, the Book of Common Prayer, schoolbooks) were protected by privilege, and would have been printed in edition runs of approximately 2,000 copies. For some other material, the edition would be unlikely to be more than 500 copies, while the earl of Essex's *Apologie* was printed in a short run of 200. For present purposes, edition sizes have been estimated both by genre and by the number of sheets, with privileged books and godly pocket-books estimated towards the high end of legal production and playbooks, verse, music, sermons and very large books estimated with print runs of 500. Other books have been estimated with print runs somewhere in between. The figure, though highly speculative, is unlikely to be seriously misleading, and probably overstates the actual facts. Based on these figures, the London book-trade in 1600 set approximately 5,400 sheets of type, produced approximately 240,000 books and pamphlets, and used 4.8 million sheets of paper. The list of new titles was growing on average by eight to twelve titles a year.

As McKenzie (1969) has also shown, there were 'a prodigious number' of ephemeral texts produced that do not survive. If the Cambridge figures for the 1630s are any guide, almanac production must have used at least 250,000 sheets of paper. There must have been abcedariums and hornbooks, and the ballad trade must have been far larger than the eight items that survive. There may have been other forms of street literature for which we now have no record. Such broadsides as *The Groome-Porters Lawes at Cards* and *A Description of a New Kind of Artificiall Bathes* are suggestive of what this material was like. Finally, some allowance also needs to be made for small-scale batch printing for businesses, such as Bevis Bulmer's contract and other forms of advertising. Apart from Bulmer's contract, there is almost no evidence for work of this kind, but Cornwallis's comment about every post in the alehouse being pasted with the text 'Feare God' must have had some basis. Such material would have provided the daily grist for the compositors in particular: it could have been almost as important as the almanac trade. An estimate of six to eight hundred thousand sheets of paper for printed ephemera probably overstates the case but would not be significantly inaccurate.

When all these figures are added together, the London book-trade starts to look quite large. This is an illusion. The point, however, is not so much the size of the estimates, but the kinds of evidence and speculation that inform any attempt at understanding literary culture in all its complexity. Many historians of the book would regard the production estimates that have been given as quite high, yet on a micro level much greater levels of production are commonly assumed. So either the book-trade is larger than we have any evidence for, or the size of edition runs are commonly overestimated. That the latter must be true becomes apparent when we try to estimate not the volume of new production but the stock of the London trade.

Once it was printed and used, ephemeral material had no commercial resale value. Similarly, schoolbooks were used very quickly. Other books would reappear for sale over the years, and copies would be more gradually destroyed. The rate of attrition must have depended on the nature of the book, the value attached to it and so forth. In the scientific sense, each edition must have had something like a half-life. Until the twentieth century, when a serious attempt was made to record and preserve the surviving evidence, the average half-life of an edition seems to have been about sixty years. Obviously, some books from the sixteenth and seventeenth centuries, like Spagnuoli's *Bucolica*, disappeared more quickly, others like Holland's Livy survive in fairly large quantities. Depending on the assumptions that one makes about the half-life of printed texts, the average time between purchase and subsequent dispersal of books and libraries, the average period of time that an edition takes to sell, and the slant of the demand curve, it is possible to make an estimate about the stock of London booksellers. A conservative calculation might suggest that the stock of the London book-trade was probably between four and five hundred thousand books. Annual sales would have included new stock, older items, imports and second-hand material. To this should be added the production of ephemera and the turnover of the bookbinders. On a generous estimate, the trade in printed texts was worth, at most, £22,000–24,000 a year.

The next step is to estimate the number of people this supported. With twenty-two printing-houses and fifty-four licensed presses, we might be tempted to conclude that there were about 200 journeymen compositors and pressmen working in London. It is difficult to estimate exactly how many people were members of the Company in 1600, for the Stationers' were more than a company of printers. The twenty-two printing-houses variously required journeymen compositors and pressmen, apprentices who may not have yet been involved in such activities (known as 'monkeys'), correctors, servants, warehouse and shop managers and, depending on the size of the establishment, overseers and other staff. Clearly, not all of these people were necessarily members of the Company. Equally, there were publishers, booksellers (new and second-hand), binders, typefounders, engravers, and, in the sense we would now use the word, stationers – people whose principal trade was paper. Again, many of these people were members of the Stationers' Company, but some were not.

McKenzie (1969) has shown that estimates for the daily activity of compositors and pressmen have been substantially overstated, but even his lower figures show that fewer people were employed by the trade than we might expect. There were nearly 300 working days a year. If we take the second and third most productive employees at Cambridge as a reliable average, then the printed book trade provided enough work for thirty-six full-time compositors and sixteen press crews. This underlines the importance of ephemera as a source of extra work for the trade. It must equally be true that underemployment was the norm, and that the workmen did not work as hard as we might suppose, but even then it is difficult to imagine that there were more than 100 journeymen who sustained a living as compositors and pressmen. In all, perhaps 200–300 people were directly involved in the printed book-trade in London in 1600, and perhaps as many again earned at least part of their living from ancillary activities. At the time, London had an estimated population of 250,000.

One of the more enduring fallacies is that the trade in printed books had displaced the commercial production of manuscripts by 1600. In part, this is because a fragment of a printed text is proof of an entire print run, but a manuscript bears witness only to itself, and therefore we tend to overemphasize the importance of the evidence that survives. Consequently, it would help to be able to make some estimate of manuscript activity. We can do this, because customs records for the importation of paper survive, and because there was almost no domestic production of paper for writing or printing. If anything, these figures will understate the quantity of paper being imported into England. Thus, if we add the press production at Oxford and Cambridge and by the secret presses to the fairly generous estimate of the London trade, then printing-house activity in England probably used six million sheets of paper a year. Compared to this, white paper imports rose from approximately 45,000 reams in the 1580s, to approximately 63,000 reams in 1600, to 80,000 reams a year in the 1620s, and nearly 115,000 reams a year in the 1670s. A smaller quantity of brown, and some blue, paper was also imported. In itself this is an interesting witness to the spread of literacy, as paper use was growing much more rapidly than the population. There was on average 480 usable sheets of paper in a ream. Allowing for a little extra wastage, paper use in England in 1600 was approximately 30 million sheets of paper per annum. By definition, paper not used for printed books was used for manuscripts. Manuscripts consumed some four times the amount of paper as the trade in printed books.

In order to estimate how much of this was commercial, we need to know how much paper was used for private, educational, ecclesiastical, business, official and secretarial purposes. Allowance must be made for the grammar schools, the universities, the Inns of Court, the Crown and Parliament, the court, personal political papers, local political administration, literary, scientific and antiquarian accounts, the law courts and the legal system, the parish churches and the central ecclesiastical administration, the guild organizations, commercial activity and bills of exchange, estate and household records, conveyancing and legal records, surreptitious material, street literature and other forms of ephemera as well as blank commonplace books, personal correspondence, drawings and private manuscript circulation. Those estimates need to be made with an understanding of the size of the population, estimates for written literacy, and the size of the institutions for which these various types of manuscripts might be prepared. Any figures generated are simply speculative, no matter how well informed, but it would be surprising if the commercial manuscript trade (which worked mainly on commission) were not as large (or used as much paper) as the trade in printed books.

This is not the usual account of the relationship between manuscript and print in the period, yet provincial cities must have been heavily dependent on the activities of scriveners; in Oxford and Cambridge they would have catered to the universities, and in London to administrative and legal, as well as personal, needs. At least some scriptoriums are likely to have been linked to book-trade publishers and the printing-houses. The evidence for this is tenuous and fragmentary, but from a practical and commercial point of view it made a great deal of sense. Apart from the six or seven largest printing-houses and publishers, like Waterson and Ponsonby (who was also a book-binder), most businesses would not have been able to survive if they had dealt simply in printed books. Manuscript production would have provided for these businesses an alternative source of income. One possibility therefore arises. Despite the considerable evidence for their activity, the presence of a full-time corrector has sometimes been questioned as a regular feature of the printing-house. It would make rather more sense if the corrector also served as the principal printing-house scrivener. William Stansby, for instance, indentured Randall Booth at a scrivener's and was fined accordingly: this may be simply a matter of contractual convenience, but it is equally suggestive of something else. Stansby's cousin, John Stansby, was a professional scribe.

The trade in printed books was active and growing, but in some respects its importance was social rather than economic. Southampton, Egerton, Pembroke and Cecil probably each had a greater personal net worth than the entire net asset value of the London book-trade: that places their relationship with Shakespeare, Donne, Daniel and Jonson in a rather different perspective. Printers and publishers, as well as scriveners, must all have been open to opportunities for immediate work, and even the accumulation of small profits, but very few made more than an adequate living in the book-trade. Given the limited size of the market and the power of individual patrons, forms of external regulation only usually affected those without protection and political influence and, at any rate, existed more as a token form of oversight. Some books did find their way to the kitchen fire in Stationers' Hall, but more than 80 per cent of all written documents existed in manuscript, and most printed books required little supervision. It certainly was dangerous to be caught with questionable books (less so in manuscript than printed), but most literate people did not deal in matters of that nature.

What the evidence from the book-trade also suggests is that literary values of the time were different from those that we now attribute to that culture. Since 1981, more than 11,600 articles have been written on Shakespeare, a little more and a little less than 900 have been written about Donne and Jonson, and 21 have been written about Samuel Daniel. To an Elizabethan in 1600, this would have seemed absurd. Following the death of Spenser, Daniel was unquestionably the most important and respected literary figure of his day. By the end of 1600, Daniel's *Works* were already at the press, he had been repeatedly reprinted throughout the 1590s, and anecdotal evidence points to his considerable popularity with woman readers. Similarly, Nicholas Breton was perhaps the most popular contemporary poet, and Shakespeare was also most admired for his poetry, with both *Venus and Adonis* and *Lucrece* going through multiple editions. Of the six plays by Shakespeare that appeared in 1600, *Titus Andronicus* was a reprint of the 1594 edition and was reprinted again in 1611, *Henry V* was reprinted in 1602, *The Merchant of Venice* and *A Midsummer Night's Dream* were not reprinted until the Pavier forgeries in 1619, and *Much Ado About Nothing* and *2 Henry IV* were not reprinted until 1623. Only *Henry V* and *Titus Andronicus* could be described as popular. The gross value of Shakespeare to the book-trade in 1600 was probably no more than £40, and after production expenses his publishers might well have made a loss. Of the well-known dramatists, Jonson probably turned the quickest profit for the book-trade, with *Every Man out of his Humour* going through an unprecedented three editions for a play-book in a single year. Even then, the sums involved cannot have been large. The book-trade published Shakespeare's plays because of the popularity of his poetry, but Shakespeare made his money through patronage and the theatre.

Both the trade in printed books and manuscript culture bear witness to a widespread interest in contemporary literature, but very few poems or plays were reprinted, and many remain largely unknown. Some typical examples from 1600 would include C. G.'s *The Minte of Deformities*, John Lane's *Tom Tel-Troths Message*, Christopher Middleton's *The Legend of Humphrey Duke of Glocester* (with a prefatory poem by Drayton), and John Weever's *Faunus and Melliflora*. For such books the investments and returns involved were small, and the political implications of publication were non-existent. Of course, some works of literature did occasionally broach politically sensitive issues (not least those by Shakespeare and Jonson), but the mechanisms of control existed more to assuage official and public concern than to enforce an ideology. The ultimate arbiter of literary success was whether a printer or publisher was willing to finance a second and subsequent editions, or a scrivener was willing to engage in speculative serial copying. In commercial terms, this is what interested the book-trade. It is easy to take something out of context and misrepresent its significance, but a publisher cared little for the meanings and indirections of a text unless it was likely to cost him his livelihood. For such material, there was always unrestricted circulation through manuscript, or publication abroad. It is this larger reality that is the true context of the London book-trade and intellectual life in early modern England. To write of 'the hermeneutics of censorship' and 'the displacement by print of manuscript culture' is not only to misunderstand the nature of the evidence relating to the book-trade; in their understanding and representation of the past, such tropes have been as fabulous as the volumes of prose romance in the library of Don Quixote.

REFERENCES AND FURTHER READING

Arber, E. (ed.) 1875–94: *A Transcript of the Registers of the Company of Stationers of London 1554–1640 A.D.*, 5 vols. London and Birmingham: Privately Printed.

Barnard, J. and Bell, M. 1991: The inventory of Henry Bynneman (1583): a preliminary survey. *Publishing History*, 29, 5–46.

——1994: *The Early Seventeenth-Century York Book Trade and John Foster's Inventory of 1616.* Leeds: Leeds Philosophical and Literary Society.

Beal, P. (comp.) 1980: *Index of English Literary Manuscripts*, vol. 1: *1450–1625*, 2 parts. New York: Mansell and Bowker.

——1998: *In Praise of Scribes*. Oxford: Clarendon Press.

Binns, J. W. 1990: *Intellectual Culture in Elizabethan and Jacobean England: The Latin Writings of the Age*. Leeds: Francis Cairns.

Bland, M. B. 1996: 'Invisible Dangers': censorship and the subversion of authority in early modern England. *Papers of the Bibliographical Society of America*, 90, 151–93.

——1998: The appearance of the text in early modern England. *TEXT*, 11, 67–130.

Blayney, P. W. M. 1982: *The Texts of* King Lear *and their Origins*, vol. 1: *Nicholas Okes and the First*

Quarto. Cambridge: Cambridge University Press.

—— 1990: *The Bookshops in Paul's Cross Church-yard*. London: Occasional Papers of the Bibliographical Society.

—— 1997: The publication of playbooks. In J. D. Cox and D. S. Kastan (eds), *A New History of the Early English Drama*, New York: Columbia University Press, 383–422.

—— forthcoming: *A History of the Stationers' Company to 1616*.

Chartier, R. 1994: *The Order of Books: Readers, Authors, and Libraries in Europe between the Fourteenth and Eighteenth Centuries*, trans. L. G. Cochrane. Oxford: Polity Press.

Clegg, C. S. 1997: *Press Censorship in Elizabethan England*. Cambridge: Cambridge University Press.

Coleman, D. C. 1958: *The British Paper Industry 1495–1860: A Study in Industrial Growth*. Oxford: Clarendon Press.

Cressy, D. 1980: *Literacy and the Social Order: Reading and Writing in Tudor and Stuart England*. Cambridge: Cambridge University Press.

Gaskell, P. 1974: *A New Introduction to Bibliography*, rev. edn. Oxford: Clarendon Press.

Greg, W. W. 1939–59: *A Bibliography of the English Printed Drama*, 4 vols. London: The Bibliographical Society.

—— 1962: *Licensers of the Press, &c. to 1640*. Oxford: Oxford University Bibliographical Society.

—— 1967: *A Companion to Arber*. Oxford: Clarendon Press.

Greg, W. W. and Boswell, E. 1930: *Records of the Court of the Stationers' Company 1576 to 1602 – from Register B*. London: The Bibliographical Society.

Johnson, G. D. 1988: The Stationers versus the Drapers: control of the press in the late sixteenth century. *The Library*, 6 (10), 1–17.

Love, H. 1993: *Scribal Publication in Seventeenth-Century England*. Oxford: Clarendon Press.

McKenzie, D. F. 1966: *The Cambridge University Press 1696–1712: A Bibliographical Study*, 2 vols. Cambridge: Cambridge University Press.

—— 1969: Printers of the mind: some notes on bibliographical theories and printing-house practices. *Studies in Bibliography*, 22, 1–75.

—— 1974: The London book trade in 1668. *WORDS*, 4, 75–92.

—— 1976: The London Book Trade in the Later Seventeenth Century, Sandars Lectures 1976, unpublished (on deposit at selected libraries).

—— 1986: *Bibliography and the Sociology of Texts*. London: The British Library.

—— 1990: Speech–manuscript–print. In D. Oliphant and R. Bradford (eds), *New Directions in Textual Studies*, Austin: Tex.: Harry Ransom Centre for the Humanities, 89–109.

—— 1992: The London book-trade in 1644. In J. Horden (ed.), *Bibliographia: The Mark Fitch Lectures 1975–1988*, Oxford: Leopard's Head Press, 130–52.

McKitterick, D. J. 1992: *A History of the Cambridge University Press*, vol. 1: *Printing and the Book Trade in Cambridge, 1534–1698*. Cambridge: Cambridge University Press.

—— 1997: Ovid with a Littleton': the cost of English books in the early seventeenth century. *Transactions of the Cambridge Bibliographical Society*, 11, 184–234.

Moore, J. K. 1992: *Primary Materials Relating to Copy and Print in English Books of the Sixteenth and Seventeenth Centuries*. Oxford: Oxford University Bibliographical Society.

Pollard, A. W. and Redgrave, G. R. (W. A. Jackson, F. S. Ferguson and K. F. Pantzer) 1976–90: *A Short-Title Catalogue of Books Printed in England, Scotland, & Ireland and of English Books Printed Abroad 1475–1640*, 2nd edn., 3 vols. London: The Bibliographical Society.

Roberts, R. J. and Watson, A. G. 1990: *John Dee's Library Catalogue*. London: The Bibliographical Society.

Watt, T. 1991: *Cheap Print and Popular Piety, 1550–1640*. Cambridge: Cambridge University Press.

Woodfield, D. B. 1973: *Surreptitious Printing in England 1550–1640*. New York: The Bibliographical Society of America.

Woudhuysen, H. 1996: *Sir Philip Sidney and the Circulation of Manuscripts*. Oxford: Clarendon Press.

28

Liberty, License, and Authority: Press Censorship and Shakespeare

Cyndia Susan Clegg

Early in Shakespeare's lifetime in an epistle to the reader, a printer describes the English reader's relatively free access to printed texts. Assuming the persona of a Scot, the printer writes:

> Ye Englishmen our good neighbors, friends, brethren, and patrons, I pray you consider rightly our labour... my purpose is ... to set before you a store as I found it, referring the confirmation thereof to truth and prooves, as in all historicall cases is lawfully used. How many histories written in Latine, Italian & French ... are printed in Italie, France and Flanders, and published & freely had and read in your land, although they contain matter expressly to the sclander of your state and princes? Matters of that nature are published, the burden of prouing resteth vpon the author, the iudgement pertaineth to the reader, there is no preiudice to anye part, Bokes are extant on both parts. The very treatises of diuinitie are not al warranted that be printed, you must take it as it is, onely for matter of reporte on the one parte, so faire to binde credit as it carieth evidence to furnish your understandings, as other bokes do that make rehearsals of the actes & states of princes, common weales, and peoples. (*A true and plaine report of the furious outrages in Fraunce* (1573), A1ᵛ–A2ᵛ)

This epistle alludes to some important and contradictory conditions governing printing. It expresses some anxiety about the reception of the text it is introducing – both about its bias as a "matter of reporte on the one parte" and about its "rehearsals of the actes & states of princes, common weales, and peoples." At the same time, however, it makes it clear that books with "matters of that nature" are widely available, certainly from continental presses and implicitly from English ones. It refers to a system of official authorization – "warranting" – (particularly for books on divinity), but says that not all theological treatises are reviewed prior to printing.

Finally, it argues that readers are accustomed to having access to information on "both parts" of an issue, and they expect to test arguments for their historical veracity. Despite England's alleged environment of free inquiry, this book presents itself as being "Scottish" rather than English. To further complicate this vexed picture of an English print culture not so free after all are the conditions under which this history of the St Bartholomew's Day Massacre is actually being printed. Its Scottish imprint ("AT STRIVELING in Scotlande") and authorial attribution ("By ERNEST VARA- MUND OF FRESELAND") are both false. Henry Bynneman, a reputable member of the London Company of Stationers, surreptitiously printed the English translation of François Hotman's *A true and plaine report of the Furious outrages of Fraunce* after he had printed the book in French and Latin under his imprint. The text's political nature – its appeal to the English Crown and commoner to lend support to French Protestants – may have suggested to Bynneman the need for caution in a version accessible to a wider readership. Whether Bynneman's caution stood the book in good stead, or whether the conditions of relative freedom the printer described in his preface indeed prevailed, *Furious outrages* was not suppressed by the government, nor was Bynneman censured by the London Company of Stationers for printing in violation of company licensing regulations. This text and the circumstances of its printing point to the complex and often contradictory conditions affecting the liberty of print in England in the early years of Shakespeare's lifetime – conditions that are no less contradictory a few years after Shakespeare's death when King James took pride in his state's "open- nesse, and liberty of discourse, even concerning matters of State," in a proclamation calling for increased restraint.[1] Both Bynneman's epistle and James's proclamation acknowledge a system in which the state controls discourse, particularly political and ecclesiastical expression, at the same time that they testify to the ability of writers, publishers, and printers to subvert or ignore altogether the system of controls. Understanding both printing-trade practices and the mechanisms the governments of Elizabeth I and James I instituted to control the press will allow us to assess the impact which press censorship had on Shakespeare's writing.

During the reigns of Elizabeth and James, the London Company of Stationers and printers at Oxford and Cambridge universities exercised a monopoly on printing in England.[2] Besides the policies the Stationers adopted to govern Company business, its most important regulations related to publishing rights the Company conferred on its members – the license to print. Company regulations required that Stationers obtain the Company's license for any work they printed. When a Stationer obtained this license, he was assured the exclusive right to print – or have printed – the title for which he held the license. The license was conferred by the master and wardens of the Company for a fee, and should the Stationer wish to pay an additional fee, the record of that license was entered in the Company's Register book (Blayney 1997). The Company's Court of Assistants met regularly to hear cases of license violation, its fines assuring the license's integrity. Even though the Company's license was distinct from the approval of a text by a church or government official – which the Stationers usually referred to as "authorization" – the two have often been confused. While "authorization" of every book seems to have been expected by the state, entries in the Stationers' Registers indicate that the Stationers' wardens could choose whether or not to insist upon ecclesiastical authorization as a condition for the Company's license.[3]

The Stationers' Company's licensing of printing should not be understood as much more of an extension of state authority than the self-regulation of, say, the Grocers' Company. Certainly, the London companies cooperated with the state, but the companies were not the principal means the state employed to control the supply of goods – material or intellectual. The state looked to its own creations to achieve these ends. State control and censorship of the press took two forms in sixteenth-century England. The first was pre-publication review and authorization, which sought to prevent objectionable texts from being printed; the second was censorship of offensive printed texts, by either parliamentary statute or royal prerogative. Each was affected not only by immediately contemporary political and religious events, but by the changing tempers of monarchs. Such changes, taken together with the inconsistent administration of controls, mean that censorship contributed less to cultural hege-mony than scholars have maintained.

Pre-publication review and authorization was born of the Elizabethan Church settlement. The 1559 Act of Supremacy, which gave the queen both the authority to visit and reform the "ecclesiastical state" and the means to execute this authority, authorized the queen to employ royal letters patent to create an ecclesiastical commis-sion to administer her authority over the ecclesiastical state (*Statutes of the Realm, 1 Eliz.* ca. 1). Sometime before 19 July 1559, Elizabeth I issued letters patent for an ecclesiastical commission for London headed by the archbishop of Canterbury and the bishop of London, which came to be known as the High Commission. The letters patent empowered the commission "to put in execution throughout the realm the Acts (1 Elizabeth) of Uniformity and Supremacy and to inquire touching all heretical opinions, seditious books, contempts, false rumours and the like and hear and determine the same" (*CPR, Eliz.*, i. 118). The queen's 1559 Injunctions, which set forth to the clergy the form and substance of Elizabethan Church reform, included one item (no. 51) that required approval of texts for print by the ecclesiastical commis-sioners. Authorization for print, then, was clearly ecclesiastical in its administration and predominantly ecclesiastical in its intent. The practice of official authorization during the reign of Elizabeth suggests that preprint censorship "according to her majesty's injunctions" was principally concerned with texts that might conceivably oppose the queen's authority as it was expressed in the Acts of Supremacy and Uniformity. Prior to 1586, printers and publishers sought pre-licensing review largely for texts in modern foreign languages, translations of these texts, and religious materials – theological tracts, scriptural commentary, and apologetics. This effectively restricted the printing of any "popish" texts (except some devotional works) and forced them and the most radical of Protestant texts "underground." When the Stationers did seek authorization, they went to local clerics as often as they appealed to the heads of the High Commission – the bishop of London and the archbishop of Canterbury.

In 1586, in response to challenges in the Court of Star Chamber to the Stationers' printing monopoly, the court issued its decrees for order in printing that, among numerous other printing trade regulations, called for authorization "according to her majesty's injunctions" of all books by either the archbishop of Canterbury or the bishop of London. To facilitate this demand, Archbishop of Canterbury John Whitgift created a board of authorizers, principally minor clerics whose interests were largely religious. James's government appears to have understood preprint authorization somewhat differently from Elizabeth's. A 1604 letter from Robert Cecil to the Stationers' Company officials reveals the king's concern that preprint authorization should be secular as well as ecclesiastical.

> His Majesty, considering the abuses more and more arising by the indiscreet publishing of books containing matters of much offence, tending to the corruption of manners, the spreading of false rumours, the seducing of people by propositions of new invention, to personal defamation, and to intermeddling in affairs of government, has directed his letters to the writer, which he encloses; according to the tenor whereof he has chosen E.F., T.W., and —— P. to whom he has referred the perusal and allowance of all books not handling divinity, law or physic. He charges them to take a course for the due executing of this order by "you[r] whole company." The King has by other letters given charge to my Lord of Canterbury to provide against like disorders in setting forth treatises of divinity. (*HMC, Salisbury*, 427, no. 16)

This expands the motives for control from suppressing opposition to the monarch's ecclesiastical state to regulating a variety of kinds of discourse. While Elizabethan preprint authorization was ecclesiastical in its administration and intent, Jacobean authorization was intended to be moral, cultural, and political as well. It is perhaps to this interest that we can attribute the appointment in 1606 of George Buc as the official press authorizer for dramatic texts.[4] James's intentions for preprint control appear to have continued throughout his reign. In 1624 he issued a proclamation that reiterated the need for efficient and extensive authorization of texts for print.[5]

Regardless of government intentions, preprint authorization never achieved pervasive control of printed texts. Even in years immediately following the 1586 Star Chamber decrees, pre-publication authorization never accounted for more than half the books published, and the average between 1558 and 1625 was more like 30 percent, with authorization being more regular – though no more reliable – during the reign of James than during that of Elizabeth. Besides the Stationers' Company wardens' leniency in requiring authorization, certain anomalous practices kept many texts out of the hands of official authorizers. Books printed under royal patents – and there were many (including all Bibles, psalters, private prayer books, catechisms, Latin texts, dictionaries, chronicle histories, law books and schoolbooks) – were not usually entered in the Stationers' Company Registers, and hence they did not necessarily receive ecclesiastical review. When in 1603 King James transferred many of these patents to the Stationers' Company and they became the basis of the Company's English stock, title ownership belonged to the Company, and thus entrance in the registers continued to remain unnecessary. Furthermore, once a book was printed, subsequent editions did not require entrance unless their changes were substantial; hence later editions saw review infrequently. As P. J. Olander has pointed out, such a practice made Calvinist catechisms widely available even when the Jacobean church was anti-Calvinist (1976: 138–9). These idiosyncrasies affected Shakespeare's printed poems. Only *Venus and Adonis* (1593) was entered in the Stationers' Registers with notice of ecclesiastical authorization (the archbishop of Canterbury's, 18 April 1593), so it is the only poetic work that we may be certain received official scrutiny. *Lucrece* (1594) and the *Sonnets* (1609) were entered without notice of authorization. It is unlikely, then, not only that censorship would have affected variants in Shakespeare's poems, but that most of the poetry was reviewed at all.

Besides these anomalies in the system of authorization, individual authorizers could be idiosyncratic. The circumstances of Samuel Harsnett's notorious approbation of John Hayward's *The first part of the life and raigne of King Henrie IIII* upon the recommendation of "a gentleman in my Lord of London his house" without even reading it are well documented (Dutton 1991: 199–222). Less familiar are the practices of authorizers approving their own ecclesiastical texts and printers employing authorizers they knew to be sympathetic to their authors' political or religious views (Olander 1976: 68). All of these factors combined to make preprint authorization effective for preventing the legal publication of only the most blatantly oppositional texts; authorization, however, could not touch illegal publications. The laws of England were required to suppress works like Gregory Martin's treasonous *Treatise of Schism*,[6] John Stubbs's libelous *Discoverie of a Gaping Gulf*, John Udall's seditious *Demonstration of Discipline*, or the works of Martin Marprelate.

A second means which the early modern English state employed to control printed discourse was parliamentary statute. During Elizabeth's reign Parliament passed no fewer than eleven treason statutes that included in their definitions of treason and sedition some form of the phrase "by Wryting Pryntinge Preaching Speache expresse Wordes or Sayinges." During the reign of James, Parliament neither rescinded nor augmented the Elizabethan statutes.[7] The statutory grounds for press censorship are clear. Writing or printing texts denying the monarch's right to govern England or the English Church, advocating the rights of anyone else to that government, advocating rebellion, calling the monarch a heretic or a usurper, or "compassing" bodily harm to the ruler – that is, attacks on the queen or king's authority – came within the compass of the treason statutes. The statutes against treasonous writing provided the grounds for prosecuting the Protestant separatist preachers and authors John Penry, John Udall, Henry Barrow, and John Greenwood, and the Catholic printer William Carter. In other cases, possessing treasonous books became part of the evidence in treason trials rather than the cause itself. Furthermore, writing, publishing, or printing texts with rumors, libels, or slanders against the monarch – that is, attacks on his or her dignity – while not high treason, were defined as seditious and invoked painful but not mortal sanctions as the author and publisher of *A Gaping Gulf* discovered.[8] The most remarkable aspect of statutory press control is that it did not go beyond protecting the authority and dignity of Elizabeth and James.[9] In measures more restrictive on the press than those that would protect the authority and dignity of the reigning monarch, Parliament was largely uninterested.

Although Parliament did not enact measures to control the press, Elizabeth and James acted to suppress certain books through the royal prerogative, principally by royal proclamation or Privy Council order. During the reign of Elizabeth, the majority of texts suppressed were censored by eleven royal proclamations, and her Privy Council called in texts on two occasions, once for each edition of Holinshed's *Chronicles*. James employed royal proclamation only once to suppress a printed text – in 1610, in response to Parliament's objections to Dr John Cowell's *The Interpreter*[10] – though he employed proclamations to control "discourse" twice and to reaffirm official authorization once. James, however, frequently called upon members of his Privy Council to summon the authors of objectionable texts to court and to order books burned at the king's request. Government press censorship, for the most part, proceeded *ad hoc*, reflecting the interests of the monarch and responding to religious and political discourses as they arose.

Of the eleven Elizabethan censorship proclamations, six addressed Catholic texts. Of these six only the first, issued in 1569 to call in Catholic texts that responded to Bishop Jewel's challenge, concerned itself with apologetics.[11] The remaining five addressed texts clearly political in nature, which included the writings of Bishop John Leslie which supported the claim of Mary Queen of Scots to the English throne, those of Cardinal William Allen and Robert Parsons which opposed Elizabeth's ecclesiastical and political supremacy,[12] and books like *A Treatise of Treasons against Q. Elizabeth and the Crowne of England* and *Leicester's Commonwealth* that libeled Elizabeth's ministers. Elizabeth and her Privy Council acted four times to suppress texts associated with radical Protestant reform and once to suppress a political book that has been associated with the interests of the Protestant left. The writings of the Protestant left that proclamations ordered suppressed included the *Admonition to the Parliament* and the pamphlets defending it,[13] the Marprelate tracts, and books associated with two religious sects that the proclamations also outlawed: the Family of Love and the Brownists.[14] The proclamation against John Stubbs's book, *The Discoverie of a Gaping Gulf*, stands alone as a government act to suppress an English book regarded as seditious on entirely political grounds, and the proclamation's claim of seditious libel went a long way in laying the groundwork for the trial of the book's author, "publisher," and printer.[15] The only book censored by James's proclamation was John Cowell's *The Interpreter*, a law book written in the king's cause at Archbishop Bancroft's insistence but vigorously opposed by Parliament.

The effectiveness of censorship by royal proclamation was limited by the nature of proclamations themselves. Royal proclamations were restricted by English common law, and, according to Geoffrey H. Elton, "They could not (and did not) touch life or member; though they might create offences with penalties, they could not create felonies or treasons" (1960: 22). Proclamations held no force in the common law courts and required for their effective administration provisions within the proclamation for their enactment. The royal proclamation was, in short, an administrative tool as effective as its own provisions made it. Elizabeth's censorship proclamations ordered that illegal books be taken to local and state officials, but provided no means to discover or apprehend illegal texts. Any effectiveness at all that they possessed rested in their appeal to the statutes. Even James could offer nothing more than the "paine of our high displeasure" to those who did not submit copies of *The Interpreter* to the authorities.

While royal proclamations may not have been very effective for conveying to James's subjects the pain of his displeasure with regard to the printed word, his use of personal government was. James's governing style reflected his understanding of the superiority of royal authority over the institutions of Parliament and the common law. According to Louis A. Knafla, "King James defined his prerogative to rule as absolute, and he believed that all institutions of government and law existed solely by his grace. Even though he fully accepted the proposition of governing in partnership with the Privy Council, Parliament, and the courts of law, he spoke continually of his exalted role" (1977: 65). This led to repeated conflict between the Crown and Parliament and the common lawyers, on one hand, and among factions in the king's council and household, on the other. (These conflicts, of course, make up the histories of the reign of James.) With regard to press control, this had an important consequence. Common law courts increasingly challenged the actions of the High Commission, which, given its efforts to control Nonconformity in the 1590s, had become increasingly unpopular. Conflict between the common law and ecclesiastical courts came to a crisis in 1611, which led James to issue letters patent to reconstitute the High Commission on 29 August, something that had not been done since the reign of Elizabeth (ibid., 141). Reissued and expanded in 1613, these letters patent, though they imposed some desired limitations on the court, strengthened the High Commission's authority over the press. The king's 1613 patent gave to the commission full authority to

> enquire and search for all heretical, schismatical and seditious books, libels and writing and all other books, pamphlets and portraitures offensive to the state or set forth without sufficient and lawful authority in that behalf and their procurers, counsellors and abettors; and the same books and the printing presses themselves likewise to seize and so to order and dispose of them . . . as they may not after serve or be employed for any such unlawful . . . and also to take, apprehend and imprison . . . the offenders in that behalf and also all persons which shall offend against any decree heretofore made by the high court of Star-Chamber . . . or hereafter to be there made touching the reformation of divers disorders in the printing and uttering of books. (*Prothero's Select Statutes*, 427–8)

It is difficult to assess the degree to which increasing the High Commission's authority over the press from Elizabethan "inquiry" to Jacobean search and seizure altered the High Commission's practice of press control. Records of the High Commission's proceedings no longer exist, but by the end of the reign of Charles I, the High Commission had acquired a reputation for exercising Draconian control. Its history suggests why this might be so.

During the reign of Elizabeth the limited evidence available suggests that the High Commission as a whole exercised its power over the press infrequently.[16] During the 1590s, however, the head of the High Commission, Archbishop of Canterbury John Whitgift assumed considerable authority over the London press. Although Whitgift has been erroneously credited with personally enacting the 1586 Star Chamber decrees to achieve his ends, it was not the decrees themselves but Whitgift's appropriation of authority from them that enabled his practice of personal censorship. Subsequent to the decrees he assumed full responsibility for licensing new presses and overseeing ecclesiastical authorization. As we have seen, in 1588 Whitgift appointed a board of licensers to regularly "peruse and allow" books. He also served as a liaison between the Privy Council and the stationers. In 1587 the Privy Council called upon him to oversee the review and reform of Holinshed's *Chronicles* (Dasent 1890–1964:, 311). He also extended his authority from licensing to suppressing books. A 1587 entry in the Stationers' Register for *A Commission sent to the pope and Convenres of freres by Sathen* is crossed out with a notation that the archbishop of Canterbury ordered the book burnt on 27 February 1587. On 15 August 1595 at Whitgift's command, five books (all apparently foreign) were burnt at Stationers' Hall.[17] In 1599 Whitgift suppressed John Hayward's *Henry IV*, in 1600 the earl of Essex's, and in 1599, together with the bishop of London, he banned satires, ordered the authorization of all plays, and called for Privy Council authorization of histories.[18] With the exception of staying the sales and overseeing the revision of the 1587 edition of Holinshed's *Chronicles*, all these actions appear to have been independent of Privy Council orders.

While no subsequent archbishop of Canterbury appears to have exercised the kind of personal control over the press that Whitgift did, the office retained some of its authority, particularly because the archbishop of Canterbury led the High Commission. In 1614 Archbishop Abbot relayed to the Stationers the king's direction that Ralegh's *History of the World* be seized from booksellers' shops (Greg 1967: 52). In 1622 the archbishop detained Nathaniel Butter for twenty-eight days before inquiring into his role in printing a book about the unlawful succession of Ferdinand II (ibid., 61, 187). The High Commission assumed responsibility for licensing new presses, and it also acquired jurisdiction for royal printing patent violations (ibid., 55, 58, 69–71).

While James protected the High Commission as an extension of his royal prerogative, he depended on neither the High Commission or the archbishop of Canterbury to exercise his personal control over the printed word. Several books were censored at the king's order because he personally opposed their political or religious views. Among these were: in 1609 books opposing the Oath of Allegiance, in 1612 Conrad Vorstius's *Tractatus*, in 1613 Francis Suarez's *Defensio Catholicae Fiede contra Anglicannae Sectae errores*, in 1617 Richard Mocket's *Doctrina Et Politia Ecclesiae Anglicanae*, in 1622 the works of Daniel Paraeus, and in 1625 Edward Elton's *God's Holy Minde* (Gillett 1932: i. 99–113). Most of these books were burned ceremoniously at Paul's Cross and equally public squares at the universities. Other books were left to the king's "beagle," Robert Cecil, whose papers are full of letters to and from his agents about the seizure of unnamed offensive texts and the illegal presses that printed them.

Press censorship during Shakespeare's lifetime primarily affected printed books that contained overtly political and religious materials, regardless of the means of control. On one occasion, however, a furor over printed books may have spread to the stage. Church officials employed writers to counter Martin Marprelate's satiric attack in a group of pamphlets. The satiric attack on Martin spread to the London stage and provoked the ire of Church officials and theatrical licenser Edmund Tilney, probably because the plays were performed without license and possibly because they engaged in overt religious comment (Dutton 1991: 74–80). One must be very cautious, however, not to generalize this particular circumstance to a general condition for theatrical writing and publishing. Richard Dutton's statement that theatrical censorship tended to be "more pragmatic than doctrinaire" (p. 86) is equally applicable to press censorship, as I have suggested here. It cannot, then, be argued that press censorship affected the works of Shakespeare in any pervasive and consistent way beyond the most blatant. Shakespeare did not write about contemporary religious controversy or about ruling monarchs or members of their governments. It is at the level of allusion to such matters, however, that arguments have been made for official interference. And given the pragmatic nature of this interference, arguments for censorship need to be considered on an individual basis.

The historical record does not show any clear evidence that any play or poem by Shakespeare was censored for the press. That we may even consider the possibility that a text was censored derives from discrepancies among printed editions, principally between early play quartos and the 1623 folio edition of the collected works. Besides political censorship, textual variants can derive from the printing house, from a text's transmission (copying or reporting),[19] or from the nature of the copy text (authorial foul papers, a fair copy of these, a copy of the allowed book, a promptbook derived from the allowed book, or a promptbook altered for a special or provincial performance). When a printer acquired a play for publication, the source for his printed version could thus derive from a number of different kinds of manuscript. Until recently scholars have been reluctant to ascribe authorial revision as a viable source of textual variants, preferring, instead, to attribute textual variants to faulty textual transmission or censorship (Wells 1985). In recent years what Stanley Wells describes as "a substantial and growing, body of opinion" has allowed us to view different substantive texts of a play as "different stages of its composition," thus allowing for authorial revision (p. 93). Any manuscript of a play could be altered over time, as easily by the author in his lifetime as by an authorial collaborator or the actors. The printed edition, however, fixed the play in a particular textual state at a particular historical moment. Different printed editions of a play could (and often did) represent entirely or in part a different manuscript state. This can be most simply illustrated by *Richard II*. The play, probably written in 1595, was first printed in 1597, most likely from Shakespeare's foul papers or a transcription of them. Two editions of substantively the same text followed in 1599. In 1608 the play was reprinted, only this time 163 lines were added, in which Richard relinquished the symbols of his kingship before Parliament. The added lines are generally regarded as deriving from aural reconstruction, probably a transcribed performance. A 1614 edition substantively reprinted this. The 1623 folio, probably printed from a prompt copy, contains a version of the "deposition scene" that textual scholars generally regard as superior to that in the 1608/1614 editions. Q1, as a whole, is judged to be the best witness to Shakespeare's text; F provides the best witness to the deposition scene. The presence of the deposition scene in the seventeenth century has been explained in the following ways. It never existed prior to 1608 and was added by authorial revision then. It was part of the play originally and was censored for later performance because the representation of deposition became politically dangerous (hence the Stationers' Company had a copy of the play containing the scene that could be put back in 1608, and which could serve as the source for the folio version). It was always part of the play but was cut by the ecclesiastical censors for print in 1597. This example of *Richard II* reveals problems that derive from the multiple manuscript sources. Furthermore, it points to the potential for a play being censored by different authorities. (I will return to the question of the play's censorship later.)

While the acting companies both preserved and proliferated plays in manuscript, printers acted differently. After the printer purchased his source copy, it was presented first to the ecclesiastical authorizer and then to the Stationers' Company officials for licensing and entry. The manuscript then went to the printing house, where it was marked up for the compositor, to serve as the compositor's working source. The existence of few manuscripts that bear witness to the ecclesiastical censor's cuts or authorization suggests that printers may have regarded manuscripts as disposable once the text was printed. Since subsequent editions did not require re-licensing or reauthorizing, one must be very cautious in attributing later variants to a print censor.

Discerning censorship at all and discriminating between the hands of the theatrical and press censors for theatrical texts poses some special problems. First of all, in the case of any play that has been performed, regardless of the kind of manuscript used for the printer's copytext, the play has potentially already been censored by the Revels Office. While there were certainly lapses and mixed motivations in Revels licensing practices, as Richard Dutton has shown, plays were more regularly licensed for performance than books were authorized for print. So any variant that appears that can be seen to reflect censorship has greater probability of deriving from the Master of the Revels. Furthermore, the Revels Office's interests are clear. According to Dutton, "a high proportion of the interventions made by Tilney and his successors seem to relate to matters of immediate moment, to the over-specific shadowing of particular people and current events, rather than to considerations of doctrine" (1991: 85). Despite evidence of the focused nature of the censor's interest, scholars have been more ready to attribute variants with any political allusions to the censors than to the author or his agents. John Jowett and Gary Taylor suggest a useful "rule of thumb" for evaluating the censor's (theatrical or ecclesiastical) role: when authorial revision can account for any change in the text (that is, it is a change made with an eye to poetics, character, or plot development, or performance), then every change in that text must be regarded as potentially authorial (1987: 39). Non-authorial interference becomes likely, however, when a change mars the text – substance appears to be missing, rhyme schemes are interrupted, or sentences are incomplete. Where the omitted material is "sensitive," political interference – censorship – is possible (p. 42). Censorship, according to Taylor, "imposes the political restraints of a particular time and place upon a potentially timeless work of art" (1983: 76). Taylor here concurs with Dutton that the occasion for censorship must involve, but somehow be greater than, topical reference. Taylor's discussion of censorship with regard to *King Lear* offers an excellent illustration of the difference between mere topical allusion and sensitive political reference. In *Lear* the mock trial indicts the administration of justice in a very general way, but its omission from the folio may be attributed as well to artistic considerations as to censorship. On the other hand, having the Fool directly call the king a fool, or ascribing to Lear some of James's errors and frivolities (a passion for hunting, giving away titles, abusing monopolies) engaged in particular reference to sensitive political issues that could provide grounds for censorship. It seems likely that the theatrical censor would pay close attention to offense to James, particularly since the play was performed at court on 26 December 1606.

The existence of Revels Office censorship vastly complicates the discernment of press censorship, as can be seen with regard to *2 Henry IV*. In 1934 Alfred Hart identified five variants between the folio and first quarto that he attributed to censorship because they entailed "covert references to the events, politics and persons of the day" (p. 180). In their discussion of *2 Henry IV*, Jowett and Taylor (1987) eliminate censorship as the cause of all but two of the variants between the quarto and folio texts.[20] These two variants they attribute to the press censor, because they find topical reference to political events in 1600 (Q1's printing date) rather than 1597. The difficulty in attributing variants of this kind to the press censor rests first in how the problematic passage is understood to refer to historical events, and, second, in how the historical events are themselves understood. Jowett and Taylor encounter both of these problems. The two passages they finally attribute to censorship rationalize the archbishop's rebellion. In the first example (I. i. 189–209) Mourton recounts the rebellion's religious character; in the second (IV. i. 55–79), the archbishop finds in the king's refusal to receive him at court a motive for his rebellion.

Jowett and Taylor (1987) fall into some dangerous traps in identifying the topicality of the two passages and therefore attributing to censorship their omission from the quarto. They follow Alfred Hart in seeing a parallel (and thus an offense) between the bishop's actions – "religion white-washing rebellion" – and events in Ireland in 1600, when, by Hart's account, Bishop Oviedo came from Spain to serve as the bishop of Dublin, gave the Irish £6,000, and promised them Spanish aid (Jowett and Taylor 1987: 41–2). Documents in the State Papers do record Oviedo's arrival but they do not mention him "leading" a rebellion. At the time that *2 Henry IV* was being printed in August 1600, Oviedo was not a major concern. State Papers contemporaneous with his arrival reveal far more interest in Lord Mountjoy's successes in Ireland than in the Spanish effort. Even if the state had been anxious about a passage alluding to rebellion in religious dress, its concerns cannot be confined to the summer of 1600: outrage over this had been the theme (book, chapter, and verse) of Burghley and Walsingham throughout Elizabeth's reign. The case for censorship in the summer of 1600 is weak, both because the historical event supposedly referred to was relatively unimportant and because a larger general anxiety about religion and rebellion cannot be confined to 1600.

The problems are much the same for the second passage. According to Jowett and Taylor, a "Bishop" justifies rebellion, first in the most general terms, and they by a specific complaint which would have been, late in 1600, even more embarrassing. The primary complaint of the earl of Essex, and what eventually provoked his abortive "rebellion," was that he was "deny'd accesse vnto" Elizabeth (p. 43). This refers to the following Shakespearian passage:

> [Wee] . . . have the summarie of all our Griefes
> (When time shall serve) to shew in Articles;
> Which long ere this, wee offer'd to the King
> And might, by no Suit, gayne Audience
> When we are wrong'd, and would unfold our Griefes
> Wee are deny'd accesse unto his Person
> *(2 Henry IV, IV. i. 73–8)*

Assigning to censorship the suppression of this has two problems. First, eliminating the passage did not remove the cause. Only a few lines later Westmerland asks, "When ever yet was your appeale denied? / Wherein haue you beene galled by the King?" (IV. i. 88–9). And again in the next scene, in reply to Prince John's query about his motives, the archbishop replies, "I sent your grace, / The parcells and particulars of our griefe, / The which hath beene with scorne shoved from the court" (IV. ii. 35–7). Second, the historical parallel is nonexistent. Any allegations about government anxiety regarding Essex during the summer of 1600 are unfounded. At the end of June, Essex had been exonerated for his misconduct in Ireland; indeed, Gelly Meyricke, Essex's steward, indicated in a 11 June 1600 letter to the earl of Southampton that the York House proceedings against Essex had resolved matters fairly well: "The Lords and the rest freed his Lordship from any disloyalty . . . all had one counsel which was fitting to clear the Queen's honour, which, God be thanked, I hear she is well satisfied . . . (*HMC, Salisbury*, X. 178). During the summer Essex became insignificant compared to Mountjoy's Irish campaign. And by late October John Chamberlain wrote to Dudley Carleton that "The Earl of Essex is much in town, fed with hope" (SP 12/275/196 PRO). No censor could possibly have known in the late summer or fall of 1600 that in February 1601 the earl of Essex would lead a rebellion because he was denied access to the queen.

This close scrutiny of the misreading of topical allusion should suggest a further difficulty: the violence that reading for a particular topical illusion may do to the reading of the passage as a whole. In their efforts to attach the cuts to the press censor, Jowett and Taylor read the passages only from the perspective of 1600, the year of Q1's printing, and thereby isolate the allusions, which in turn, slant their reading of the passages. In each case a few lines become the focus, decontextualizing the topical allusions from the play's wider significance. In doing so, Jowett and Taylor neglect the much larger point that both passages exist in scenes that *as a whole* represent the archbishop's causes for rebellion. Removing the allegedly suppressed passage in no way eliminates or diminishes the play's representation of rebellion. With or without the reference to religion whitewashing rebellion, the play represents the archbishop's participation. The second passage does contain censorable material (but material that was as censorsable in 1597 as it would have been in 1600): it argues a subject's right to rebel when conditions are intolerable and describes a land in torment under present rule as the justification for rebellion. We have clear evidence that both a theatrical manuscript and two printed books were censored for similar matters. In 1584 William Cardinal Allen's *A True, Sincere and Modest Defence of English Catholiques* justified rebellion on religious grounds, and in 1595 Robert Parsons's *A Conference about the Next Succession to the Crowne of England* supported the subject's right to depose a tyrannical monarch. Likewise, the manuscript of "Sir Thomas More" shows Edmund Tilney's concern about passages on rebellion. Richard Dutton has located this anxiety specifically in London riots in 1593 and 1595 and suggested that "the effect of the censorship he proposed would have been both to suppress potentially inflammatory scenes of rioting and to keep the depiction of More's rise and fall at a more restrained, less contentious pitch" (Dutton, 1991: 84–6).

In 1597, the year *2 Henry IV* was probably written, the representation of the archbishop's cause may have been deemed objectionable, first because it appeared broadly popular ("And more, and lesse, do flocke to follow him"), and second, because it presented rebellion as an inevitable and just recourse ("Wee are all diseas'd, / Have brought our selves into a burning Fever, / And wee must bleede for it"). In 1597 the government was anxious enough about conditions in England that the Crown sought remedies in Parliament. In notes prepared to defend the Crown's proposal, Lord Burghley wrote:

> They complain of many how they are not able to keep hospitality, although they be well inclined therunto, is in respect of the dearness and high prices of corn.... The lamentable cry of the poor who are like to perish by means hereof is chiefly or principally to be considered, how the same may be provided for... That it doth not proceed upon scarcity or want is generally reported, but rather of the insatiable desire of such as do forestall and in gross for their particular lucre, which persons in all ages have been accounted ...odious to the commonwealth. (*HMC, Salisbury*, vii. 497)

Further along in his notes Burghley's assessment of cause and effect sounds a lot like the archbishop's "And wee must bleede for it":

These late few wet years, whereby many sheep have died which have been kept upon such grounds as were formerly employed to tillage and now kept for sheep, have manifested that Almighty God is displeased herewith, so as there is not only some less corn than formerly hath been but also fewer sheep. (Ibid., 498)

The parallel between conditions in 1597 and the bearing they might have upon passages cut from *2 Henry IV* and the conditions Dutton described as influencing the censor in his treatment of "Sir Thomas More" are striking. It is not my interest, however, to argue here for theatrical censorship based on this evidence from 1597. But this example should indicate that as long as alternative historical parallels may be drawn to the year a play is written, arguments for press censorship become suspect. Furthermore, given that the kinds of books that were actually censored did not merely *refer* to political matters but libeled government officials (either at home or abroad), denied the ruling monarch's ecclesiastical or political authority or the authority of Parliament, or advocated successors to the monarch, it seems unwise to credit the press censors with eliminating even sensitive topical allusions unless all other possibilities have been ruled out. Jowett and Taylor's arguments that *2 Henry IV* was censored for the press are too easily refuted.

Similar problems in correlating literary allusions with contemporary events may be found in Annabel Patterson's argument for the censorship of *Henry V* (1989: ch. 4). Although Patterson never maintains that press censorship alone was responsible for the differences between the folio and the 1600 quarto (Q1) of *Henry V*, her emphasis on the relationship between the play and a censored book, together with attention to the heightened climate of scrutiny brought about by the 1599 Bishops' Ban, implicates press censorship. Q1 lacks the folio's choruses (one of which has an allusion to the earl of Essex's anticipated triumphal return from Ireland), the first scene in which the archbishop of Canterbury and the bishop of Ely propose a French war to distract the king and prevent Parliament from passing a bill that would allow the seizure of certain church lands, and Henry's soliloquy on the eve of Agincourt.[21] Patterson contends that the "censored" quarto version eliminates any possibility that Henry V might be read as representing and favoring the earl of Essex. The 1599 uncensored play, Patterson maintains, would have allowed parallels to be drawn between the earl and Henry V that would have been objectionable to Elizabeth on several grounds – because she liked the benefits of the popular Henry V mythos to accrue to herself; because she was in competition with the earl, whose enormous popularity threatened her authority; and because there was a long-standing breach between the queen and Essex. When Essex not only failed to fulfill the uncensored chorus's prophecy that he would return from Ireland with "Rebellion broached on his Sword" but was disgraced for mismanaging the Irish campaign, it would not have been enough to eliminate the chorus's single reference to the earl, since this would not remove the text's larger offense to the queen. Patterson maintains that *Henry V* was censored on grounds similar to those that provoked the 1599 censorship of John Hayward's history of Henry IV – both indicated a connection between "the popular local hero Essex had become" and a popular Lancastrian monarch. Patterson further argues the probability that the play was censored for the press by pointing out that the 1599 Bishop's Ban required that plays be authorized for the press and that histories be authorized by a member of the Privy Council. On two grounds, then, *Henry V* would have been closely scrutinized for anything that might offend.

On its own terms, Patterson's argument fits my criteria for the likelihood of press censorship – that the censored text resemble a book certainly censored and that topical allusions refer to specific and significant political events. A few pieces of evidence, however, argue against her. First, John Hayward's *The first part of the life and raigne of Henrie IIII*, the book so reputedly offensive to Elizabeth, was censored in 1599 at the request of the earl of Essex.[22] Second, arguments that Elizabeth was threatened by the earl of Essex's popularity are perplexing. Why would the queen have accepted Essex to lead the expedition to Ireland – indeed, why would she have given him any military authority and power – if he threatened her? In the summer of 1600, as we have seen, Elizabeth hardly needed to fear Essex; she held the trump card, her favor. Furthermore, in the summer of 1600 the humiliated Essex little resembled Henry V in either political or military acumen, so it is difficult to say why a simple cut of the Essex allusion would not have been sufficient to prevent the play from being read allegorically. Nor did Essex in 1600 (or Henry V, for that matter) resemble the hero of Hayward's book, Henry IV, who led the rebellion against Richard II. One should not, then, as Patterson does, argue 1600 censorship backwards to the 1599 censorship of Hayward's book (at Essex's request), or forward, to the earl of Essex's 1601 rebellion.

Even if we were to allow the conflation of Essex–Henry IV–Henry V, Essex's two rebellions and two trials, and the censorship of Hayward's book, the problem still remains of who would have detected the play's offense. Patterson believes that the censors would have been particularly sensitive to *Henry V*'s political implications, given the 1599 Bishops' Ban. We do not, however, have any evidence that the play was reviewed and authorized. Indeed, it may not even have been entered in the Stationers' Register. On 14 August 1600 *Henry V* appeared among a list of titles being assigned to Thomas Pavier. In this listing, *Henry V* appears as having already been printed. *Henry V* also appears to have been one of four titles whose license was stayed on 4 August, probably, according to Peter Blayney, because it lacked ecclesiastical authorization or the wardens were not present to waive that authorization. More important, however, as Blayney has suggested, the 4 August notice may not have been for *Henry V* at all, since it was either already in print or being printed, given the proximity to the 14 August transfer of title. Instead, the 4 August reference was to *2 Henry IV*, whose title page closely resembled that of *Henry V* (Blayney 1989: 11). *Henry V* may have appeared under an entirely different licensing scenario. *The Famous Victories of Henry the Fifth* had been licensed to Thomas Creed, so the booksellers Thomas Millington and John Busby would have required his permission to publish Shakespeare's *Henry V*. According to Blayney, Creede presumably gave his consent "on condition that he be hired (and therefore paid) to print the rival play" (p. 32). If

Shakespeare's *Henry V* rode in on the coattails of *The Famous Victories*, Millington and Busby were probably saved the fee to the ecclesiastical authorizer.

With *Henry V*, then, we have a play that was probably not perused by the ecclesiastical censor, that lacks authentic parallels to a book actually censored for the press, and that relates only tangentially to contemporary events in an epic simile. Even so, conflicting evidence does not conclusively prove that the play was not censored. Indeed, if there were no other possible explanation for the variants, Patterson's argument for censorship would look quite convincing. Gary Taylor, however, has persuasively argued that the shorter version reflected in Q1 would be appropriate for a provincial performance by a smaller touring company (1982: 22). Furthermore, the high correlation between scenes in Q1 and the folio where the actors playing Gower and Exeter are onstage and the extensive variation where they are absent argues that the text for Q1 was memorially reconstructed by the actors playing these parts. However valuable Q1 may be as what Taylor calls "a historical document of far more authority than the hypotheses of any twentieth-century scholar" (p. 23), even an eye untrained in the sophisticated nuances of textual scholarship can recognize Q1's uneven quality, and, hence, the possibility that theatrical cuts and reporters' memories are as likely a source of the variants that exist between the two texts as is censorship.

While I am reluctant to credit press censorship with variants among the texts of Shakespeare's plays, there is one instance where press censorship seems altogether likely – namely, in the case of *Richard II*. Most arguments favoring censorship have pointed to the discomfort of Elizabeth's government with the representation of rebellion. This kind of general motive is obviously inconsistent with everything that I have suggested here about the kinds of things press censors regarded as objectionable. Furthermore, remembering that the absence of the deposition scene does not remove from the play its representation of bad government, rebellion, deposition, or, indeed, "bodily harm" to the king, argues against the scene's censorship. Although not censored for its representation of misguided kingship, rebellion, or deposition, the "deposition" scene may have provoked suppression because its representation of Parliament apparently corroborated *A Conference about the Next Succession* (1595) by Robert Doleman (Robert Parsons), a work which Elizabeth's government regarded as highly offensive on many grounds – and to many parties.[23] As J. H. M. Salmon has recognized, Parsons's work subscribed to the central tenets of continental Catholic resistance theory, particularly the secular nature of political society and the monarch's subjugation under law (1991: 243). Its offense in the 1590s, however, rested more on its particular arguments about the English succession than on its general subscription to resistance theory. Parsons's book effectively denied the validity of the entire Tudor line by claiming the primacy of the Spanish claim by way of John of Gaunt and arguing for the strength of the Lancastrian line by demonstrating that Richard II was legally deposed:

> First for that it was done by the choise and invitation of al the realme or greater and better parte therof as hath bin said. Secondly for that it was done without slaughter, and

thirdly for that the king was deposed by act of parlament, and himselfe convinced of his
unworthy government, and brought to confesse that he was worthely deprived, and that
he willingly and freely resigned the same . . . (Doleman, ii, 67)

The 1608 quarto's reenactment of the ritual of Richard's abdication conflates three
parliamentary events which in Holinshed's *Chronicles* (Shakespeare's source) represent
Parliament's voice (both Lords and Commons) as *consenting* to Richard's abdication and
Henry's accession. While these events remained distinct in the source, when Shakespeare compressed them into one scene that inverts the order of the events, the scene
suggests that the Commons *urged* Richard's deposition. While "May it please you
Lords, to graunt the common suit" is separated from Bolingbroke's "Fetch hither
Richard, that in common view / He may surrender, so we shall proceed without
suspition" in the folio, the 1608 quarto makes this one continuous speech by Northumberland, which represents that the common suit is to summon the king and call for
his deposition.[24] Northumberland's insistence on Richard responding to the Commons' suit implies that Parliament can and does act without the king, and, indeed,
that Parliament takes precedence over the king and can dictate to him its terms. Such
apparent corroboration of views expressed in a text that genuinely offended the state
suggests why *Richard II*'s Parliament/deposition scene may have been censored.
While such offense could have been to the Master of the Revels as well as to the
ecclesiastical censor, this looks more like press censorship, because it relates to
particular interests of the ecclesiastical establishment to which the authorizers
belonged. In 1597 leading Anglican clerics – men like John Aylmer, Thomas Bilson,
and John Bridges – were actively engaged in refuting papal claims to authority over
secular rulers and rejecting Catholic views of resistance. Cognizant of Parsons's book,
the clerics would have been attentive to any text that appeared to subscribe to his
views. It is, then, not difficult to imagine that an ecclesiastical authorizer, reading
quickly through Shakespeare's *Richard II* while someone from the Lord Chamberlain's
Men or the printing house stood by, would require summarily that the play be printed
without the Parliament scene. This has little to do with the kind of close reading
required for the censorship of *King Lear* or *2 Henry IV*; nor does it resemble the kind of
close attention to detail apparent in Tilney's censorship of the manuscript of "Sir
Thomas More."

Besides alleging that specific Shakespearian texts were censored, scholars have
posited censorship's general effect on Shakespeare. O. J. Campbell says of the genre
"Comicall Satyre" that its "immediate inspiration came from the satiric movement of
the last decade of the sixteenth century, which ended abruptly through the interposi-
tion of ecclesiastical authorities acting in the interest of offended morality." Campbell
posits a kind of literary transference from verse to theatrical satire. The playing and
printing of *Troilus and Cressida* may have been prevented, others have claimed, because
of associations that might be made with the 1601 Essex Rebellion. The suggestion
frequently appears that the 1599 Bishops' Ban and the censorship of Hayward's *Henry
IV* constituted the deathblow for the history play. All these possibilities assume a

climate of state authority that has not been substantiated by recent historical studies. Furthermore, they envision censorship practices extraordinarily sensitive to general offense rather than to the kind of local and particular events that recent scholarship has discerned.

While I have been skeptical here about the degree to which press censorship affected the texts of Shakespeare's plays, I do not mean to suggest that censorship did not occur – that the "authorities" did not act to control what appeared in print. They did. "Authority," however, resided in many entities in early modern England. Indeed, multiple kinds of "authorities" acted upon the texts of plays that were performed and that appeared in print. Stationers' economic interests dictated the Company's authority over licensing. Monarchs retained the authority to issue mono-polies (privileges) to individual authors and printers despite the Stationers' authority over their trade. The Elizabethan High Commission had authority to "enquire" for seditious books and to authorize books for print "according to her Majesties Injunc-tions." Parliament granted to the law courts the authority to try authors, printers, and publishers for treasonous writing. The archbishop of Canterbury, John Whitgift, exercised personal authority and suppressed books. The 1599 Bishops' Ban conferred authority on the Privy Council to authorize histories (which, by the way, they did not assume). James I exercised personal authority to burn books that countered his religious and political positions. Parliament demanded that the king call in a book that challenged parliamentary authority which had been written to honor the king. Plays, subject first to the authority of the Revels Office, depended on popular audiences to authorize their success both in the theater and at the bookseller's stall. Authority in Elizabethan and Jacobean England was multiple; all authorities' interests were special, and the exercise of these authorities was local. A model of binary opposition between Shakespeare and authority simply does not suffice to explain the varied and conflicting influences that can explain why texts of the plays printed at different times vary. The production of each text is intimately tied to its local aesthetic, theatrical, social, economic, and political contexts, and these, not infre-quently, exerted contradictory demands. The binary model upon which we have based our understanding of early modern English culture has led us to assume a hegemony that ties the tongue of literary creativity. The multiple interests that influenced print culture, including specific events and specific books written by specific people, were never so unanimous that we should assume that writing was subject to clear and consistently controlled conditions. We should, then, be as ready to accept that Shakespeare or a collaborator or someone in the acting company was as likely to be the source of an altered line or scene in a play as we are to attribute any variant with possible political associations to the censor. Would it not, then, be possible that the speaker of Sonnet 66 who "cried" for "restful death" because he "Tir'd with all these" – faith forsworn, honor misplaced, virtue strumpeted, perfection disgraced, and "art made tongue-tied by authority" – was not referring to the censor at all, but to the demands placed on the poet by the authorities of popular taste, theatrical perform-ance, classical models, or literary rivals?

NOTES

1   James's 24 Dec. 1620 proclamation calls for restraint in discourse, because the limits have been exceeded: "there is at this time a more licentious passage of lavish discourse, and bold Censure in matters of State, then hath been heretofore, or is fit to be suffered" (Hughes and Larkin 1973: i, 495–6).

2   The London Company of Stationers, which had been in existence since the fifteenth century, received the royal charter that assured its monopoly in 1557. While the charter conferred upon the Stationers the exclusive right to print, the Crown could still confer on individual printers – stationers or not – the exclusive right to print a work or class of work.

3   This does not mean that the Company officials themselves served as official authorizers. Instead, the presence in Company Registers of the authorizer's name appears to be an added documentary protection to the Company and its members; i.e., should any question ever arise surrounding the official legality of a text, the presence of the authorizer's name in the entry would displace any stigma of illegal printing from the Company or its member.

4   Prior to his appointment, as Peter Blayney (1997: 397) points out, plays were "usually allowed for printing by the same ecclesiastical authorities who allowed books of all kinds." Although Buc had secured the reversion for the Mastership of the Revels in 1603, his office as dramatic licenser appears to have been distinct, even though he continued licensing plays for print after he assumed the Mastership. After 1613 ecclesiastical authorities started allowing plays again.

5   "We doe straitly charge and command, That from henceforth no person or persons whatsoever, presume to print any Booke or Pamphlet, touching, or concerning matters of Religion, Church governement, or State, within any Our owne Dominions, which shall not first be perused, corrected, and allowed, under the hand of the Lord Archbishop of Canterburie, the Lord Archbishop of Yorke, the Bishop of London, the Vicechancelour of one of the Universitites, of Oxford, or Cambridge, for the time being, or one of them, or some other learned person or persons, to that purpose appointed by them, or one of them" (Hughes and Larkin 1973: i, 599–600).

6   On 20 Jan. 1584 London printer William Carter was executed for treason for printing a London edition of Gregory Martin's *A Treatise of Schism* (Douay, 1578), which contained passages inciting the women of the court to assassinate the queen.

7   The exception might be made that in 1606 Parliament imposed censorship on oaths and blasphemy, but this was primarily directed to the "Playing."

8   On 30 Oct. 1579, the book's author, John Stubbs, its printer, Hugh Singleton, and William Page were tried before the King's Bench under the statute against "seditious libel" passed by Parliament (1 and 2 Philip and Mary, ca. 3) and extended to Elizabeth by her first Parliament (1 Eliz. ca. 6). The jury found them guilty; Stubbs and Page, according to the statute's designated punishment, lost their right hands on 4 Nov. 1579. Singleton was apparently pardoned. Kenneth Barnes has convincingly demonstrated that William Page, the "dispenser" of copies, was William Page M.P., the gentleman servant to the second earl of Bedford, who enabled Page to be returned for Elizabeth's first four parliaments. Rather then "publishing" *A Gaping Gulf* (as some have asserted), Page sent to Sir Richard Grenville, probably with Bedford's knowledge, fifty copies for circulation (Barnes 1991).

9   Libel itself, however, was still a serious matter throughout Elizabeth's reign. Slander and libel belonged to ecclesiastical moral law, and cases in these matters were tried in the Church courts. According to Ingram (1987), libel was the single most prevalent cause tried in Elizabethan England. These, however, were not cases brought by the Church against individuals, but by those libeled against the libeler. Libel cases were also heard in the common law courts, and many of these had to do with "lewd words" against the government or

nobility. Between 1558 and 1603, the Privy Council addressed reports of such slander, usually by remanding investigation to local officials, with most cases being heard in the common law courts. Press control does not appear to have been the issue in any of these actions. Suppression of rumor and libel, constituting as it does a kind of censorship, requires independent consideration beyond the scope of this project.

10 According to Hughes and Larkin, "On 2 Mar 1610, upon a motion in the Commons, a joint conference was appointed 'concerning Dr. Cowell's book containing scandalous and dangerous matter against the authority of Parliament, which see in the titles of 'Subsidy', 'Parliament', and 'Prerogative', in that book of his called the Interpreter... That the King might make laws of himself and demand subsidies *de jure* without consent of Parliament' (Debates 1610, 26)." Six days later, Cecil informed the Lords that James would suppress the book by proclamation, (Hughes and Larkin 1973: i. 244, n. 2).

11 Bishop Jewel's challenge for evidence from Scripture or the early Church Fathers justifying transubstantiation, communion in one kind, nonvernacular service, and papal authority. The challenge made in 1559 had by 1569 produced sixty-two texts, forty-four by Catholics finally judged in 1569 as "enemies to God's truth and the quiet government of the Queen, in maintenance of the usurped jurisdiction of the Papistical See of Rome."

12 Allen's *A True, Sincere and Modest Defence of English Catholique* (1584) and *Admonition to the Nobility and People of England and Ireland* (1588) and Parsons's *A Conference about the Next Succession to the Crowne of England* (1594).

13 The *Admonition* having been written and printed in three editions in 1572, this proclamation represents a response from the Crown after other efforts to control the controversy had failed. By April 1573, Thomas Cartwright's *A Replye to An Answere made of M. Doctor Whitgifte Agaynste the Admonition to the Parliament by T. C.* appeared, advocating presbyterian governance and criticizing both the episcopacy and the Book of Common Prayer. The 11 June 1573 proclamation

appears more in response to this escalation and the bishops' efforts than to the original *Admonition*. Public response (or, rather, nonresponse) to the proclamation is notorious. After the twenty-day grace period had expired, Archbishop Parker complained to Burghley: "Her Majesty's proclamation took none effect: not one book brought in" (Collinson 1967: 149).

14 The Familists' offense, according to the proclamation, was in declaring themselves saved and all others damned. To justify actions against the Familists, the proclamation makes it clear that the sect is "an evil by the malice of the devil first begun and practiced in other countrie to be now brought into this her realm" (Hughes and Larkin 1969: ii, 474–5). The 30 June 1583 proclamation declaring Brownist writings seditious and schismatic was probably prompted by the action of two followers of Brown, Elias Thacker and John Coppin, who had been brought before the assizes for denying the queen's supremacy. The indictment included the offense of conspiring to dispose of Browne and Harrison's books (ibid. ii, 502).

15 The censorship proclamation is less concerned with the book's attempt to discourage Elizabeth's marriage to the duke of Anjou than in characterizing the book as a "a heap of slanders and reproaches of the said prince bolstered up with manifest lies and despiteful speeches of him, and therewith also seditiously and rebelliously stirring up all estates of her majesty's subjects to fear their own utter ruin and change of government."

16 In 1576 ecclesiastical commissioners ordered that extant copies of three texts, including George Gascoigne's *Poesies*, be sent to Stationers' Hall. In 1587 they suppressed John Knox's *The first booke of the history of the reformation of religion within the realm of Scotland*. By warrant of "his grace and other high commissioners," dated 2 December 1594, "one barrell and ii firkers of books of Alexander Humes' Doing" were ordered seized. Hume was a Scottish poet and radical Puritan.

17 Among these were *Thesaurus Principium, Ministromachia* (by Cardinal Stanislaus Rescius, Cologne, 1592), Rosseus (William Rainolds),

De justa Republicae Chrestianae (Douay, 1590; Antwerp, 1592), "Little French bookes in 8 and Surius Chronicle" (Laurentius Surius, probably his hagiographical history, Cologne, 1572) (Arber 1875–94: ii, 40). Religio-political interests probably motivated this censorship, since Rosseus's book addressed the English succession.

18 See Clegg 1997b: ch. 7 for a detailed discussion of the censorship of Holinshed's *Chronicles* and ibid., ch. 9, for a discussion of *Henry IV* and the satires.

19 Blayney has persuasively argued against the idea that "good" and "bad" quartos of Shakespeare's plays reflect the "piracy" of copytexts. That the copy for some quartos of Shakespeare's plays derived from "performance texts written down by actors who took part in them," however, is inescapable. According to Blayney, "the quality of such texts would vary greatly (both from each other and from scene to scene within a single text)." If the actor had to write down the play partly or wholly from memory "those parts of the performance he had least opportunity to observe might prove extremely difficult to reconstruct, and might emerge noticeably garbled" (1997: 394).

20 In this case, the folio contains lines not present in the first quarto, but Taylor establishes that the quarto comes from earlier foul papers and the folio from a later manuscript.

21 Q2 (1602) reprints the 1600 text without substantive changes.

22 Early in 1600 Hayward's book was quarried for its seditious potential by Edward Coke to establish a case of treason against Essex for his conduct in Ireland in 1599. See Clegg 1997b: ch. 9.

23 My full argument for the press censorship of *Richard II*, summarized briefly here, appears in Clegg 1997a.

24 Most modern editors accept the folio text, which reads:

[NORTHUMBERLAND]. May it please you, Lords, to grant the Commons Suit?
BULLINGBROOKE.   Fetch hither Richard, that in common view
                                    He may surrender: so we shall proceede
                                    Without suspition.

REFERENCES

Arber, Edward (ed.) 1875–94: *A Transcript of the Registers of the Company of Stationers of London*, 5 vols. London and Birmingham.

Barnes, Kenneth 1991: John Stubbe, 1579, the French ambassador's account, *Historical Research*, 64, 421–6.

Blayney, Peter W. M. 1989: Exeunt pirates. April 1989 version of an unpublished manuscript.

—— 1997: The publication of playbooks. In John D. Cox and David Scott Kastan (eds), *A New History of Early English Drama*. New York: Columbia University Press, 383–422.

Calendar of the Manuscripts of the Marquis of Salisbury. London: Historical Manuscript Commission, 1883–1976. Cited as *HMC, Salisbury*.

Calendar of the Patent Rolls in the Public Record Office, Elizabeth. London: H. M. Stationery Office, 1939–86. Cited as *CPR, Eliz.*

Campbell, Oscar J. 1938: *Comicall Satyre and Shakespeare's Troilus and Cressida*. San Marino, Calif.: The Huntington Library.

Clegg, Cyndia Susan 1997a: "By the choise and inuitation of al the realme": *Richard II* and Elizabethan press censorship. *Shakespeare Quarterly*, 48, 432–48.

—— 1997b: *Press Censorship in Elizabethan England*. Cambridge: Cambridge University Press.

Collinson, Patrick 1967: *The Elizabethan Puritan Movement*. Berkeley and Los Angeles: University of California Press.

Dasent, Sir John Roche (ed.) 1890–1964: *Acts of the Privy Council, 1542–1631*, 46 vols. London: H. M. Stationery Office.

Doleman, R. 1595: *A Conference about the Next Succession to the Crowne of Ingland. Where unto is added a Genealogie*. Published by R. Doleman. [R. Parsons, R. Rowlands, and others.]

Imprinted at N. [Antwerp, A Conincx], 1594 [1595].

Dutton, Richard 1991: *Mastering the Revels*. Iowa City: University of Iowa Press.

Elton, Geoffrey H. 1960: *The Tudor Constitution*. Cambridge: Cambridge University Press.

Gillett, Charles R. 1932: *Burned Books*, 2 vols. New York: Columbia University Press.

Greg, W. W. 1967: *Companion to Arber*. Oxford: Oxford Bibliographical Society.

Hart, Alfred 1934: *Shakespeare and the Homilies and other Pieces of Research into the Elizabethan Drama*. Melbourne: Melbourne University Press.

Hughes, Paul L. and Larkin, James F. 1969: *Tudor Royal Proclamations*, 3 vols. New Haven and London: Yale University Press.

——1973: *Stuart Royal Proclamations*, 2 vols. Oxford: Clarendon Press.

Ingram, Martin 1987: *Church Courts, Sex, and Marriage in England, 1570–1640*. Cambridge: Cambridge University Press.

Jowett, John and Taylor, Gary 1987: The three texts of *2 Henry IV, Studies in Bibliography*, 40, 31–50.

Knafla, Louis A. 1977: *Law and Politics in Jacobean England: The Tracts of Lord Chancellor Ellesmere*. Cambridge: Cambridge University Press.

Olander, Philip Mark 1976: Changes in the mechanism and procedure for control of the London press, 1625–37. B. Litt. thesis, Oxford University.

Patterson, Annabel 1989: *Shakespeare and the Popular Voice*. Oxford: Blackwell.

Prothero's Select Statutes, ed. George Aller. Oxford, 1894.

Salmon, J. H. M. 1991: Catholic resistance theory, ultramontanism, and the royalist responses, 1580–1620. In J. H. Burns, with assistance from Mark Goldie (eds), *The Cambridge History of Political Thought, 1450–1700*, Cambridge: Cambridge University Press, 219–53.

Statutes of the Realm. London, 1810.

Taylor, Gary (ed.) 1982: *Henry V*. Oxford: Clarendon Press.

——1983: Monopolies, show trials, disaster, and invasion: *King Lear* and censorship, In Gary Taylor and Michael Warren (eds), *The Division of the Kingdoms*, Oxford: Clarendon Press, 75–119.

Wells, Stanley 1985: Revision in Shakespeare's plays. In Richard Landon (ed.), *Editing and Editors: A Retrospective*, New York: AMS Press, 67–97.

PART EIGHT
Shakespeare II

29

Shakespeare: The Myth

Michael D. Bristol

Santa Claus is a myth. He serves as the embodiment of a spirit of conviviality, expenditure, and gift exchange that has been traditionally associated with Christmas and the winter solstice time out of mind. A department store Santa Claus is a concrete social institution, complete with tedious lines, tense parents, and cheery photographers. Realizing that the man in the Santa Claus suit is not the real Santa Claus is an important step in growing up. Understanding the sad fact that Santa Claus doesn't exist at all is a further, and no doubt more difficult, achievement in reaching maturity. In the long run, however, one does not go around muttering "bah humbug"; people discover that Santa Claus is an indispensable part of the Christmas holiday, even if he doesn't exist for real. What's real about Santa Claus has nothing to do with the actual existence of a generous fat man with a fondness for children living at the North Pole. Teaching children to believe in Santa Claus is a way for people to express an affiliation with the social institution of Christmas, and especially with the secular tradition of gift exchange.

It goes against common sense to say that Shakespeare is a myth. Santa Claus, the Tooth Fairy, and Jack Frost are myths. William Shakespeare, on the other hand, was a real person, a man born in the small market-town of Stratford-upon-Avon in 1564. He grew up in Stratford, went to school, married a woman named Ann Hathaway, and fathered three children. As a young man he moved to London, where he became an actor, wrote poetry, and participated in various business ventures. When he died, in 1616, he was just fifty-three years old. This William Shakespeare really existed; he is the man who wrote the poems and plays that have made his name so famous. But actual existence is hardly an obstacle to the formation and propagation of a myth. To speak of Shakespeare as a myth is not to deny the existence or the dignity or the practical significance of the man from Stratford. It is, however, a convenient way to highlight the socially effective afterlife of his work in the various successor cultures of early modern England. Shakespeare's works, together with various ways which people have invented to interact with them, have become durable features in the cultural landscape of contemporary society. The myth of Shakespeare appears as a complex narrative that orients and guides the social activity generated by these remarkable artifacts.

Believing in Shakespeare is not altogether different from believing in Santa Claus: such belief articulates a deep sense of affiliation with a tradition of expressive forms and institutional practices. "I sit with Shakespeare and he winces not" (DuBois 1986: 438). W. E. B. DuBois discovered in Shakespeare's works a sense of belonging and of full social acceptance that was simply not available to him as a black man in the everyday life of early twentieth-century America. To "sit with Shakespeare" is to come into possession of full personhood. But William Shakespeare the actual man is just another dead white person. The Shakespeare who "sits with us" and enables us to recognize our own human dignity, our own deeper and fuller aspirations, is in fact a myth, projected and sustained through multiple institutional practices – department store Santa Clauses if you will. These institutional artifacts are not the "real Shakespeare," but neither is the man buried in the parish churchyard in Stratford-upon-Avon. The real Shakespeare – like the real Santa Claus – doesn't actually exist at all, except as the imaginary projection of an important tradition of social desire.

The institutional, mythic Shakespeare is a vital, durable social fact, something that many people have worked hard to sustain over time. In the long run, then, Shakespeare the myth is what really counts in contemporary culture. But for many people such a statement seems a craven betrayal of what is uniquely valuable about Shakespeare. He is, after all, the genius whose unique achievement transcends the banal pettiness of institutional life. There may be a structure of institutional practice that surround the plays, but the real brilliance of Shakespeare's originality is a scandal and a reproach to the small-time efforts of educational bureaucrats or crass show-business promoters. This common view of Shakespeare as a unique, transcendent genius is a kind of just-so story that finds its greatest importance, paradoxically, as the enabling narrative of the Shakespeare institution. It is not altogether untrue, but it is a myth. Like all socially important myths, it expresses an important intuition in uncritical and pre-theoretical form.

Shakespeare's mythical identity is given its typical, enduring shape by men who actually knew him. The most resonant themes of the myth are those set out by his friend and rival Ben Jonson in his dedicatory verse for the first folio: *To the memory of my beloued, The Author, Mr. William Shakespeare: and what he hath left us.* Shakespeare is remembered as an author who has left something – for us. And he is beloved. Jonson's poem expresses the fully contradictory aspects of the myth. Shakespeare is a "monument without a tomb." He is both the greatest of dramatic poets and the object of homely, familiar affection. His work is fully expressive of his own lived social reality – he is "the Soule of the age" – and at the same time it transcends the local concerns of a particular historical moment – he is "not for an age but for all time." Finally, Shakespeare's poetry figures forth the reconciliation of form and content, "nature" and "art."

> Nature her selfe was proud of his designes,
>   And joy'd to weare the dressing of his lines!
> Which were so nicely spun, and woven so fit,
>   As since, she will vouchsafe no other wit.
>
>   . . . .
>
> Yet must I not give Nature all: Thy Art,
>   My gentle Shakespeare, must enjoy a part.
> For though the poet's matter, Nature be,
>   His Art doth give the fashion.

The outline of a Shakespeare of mythical proportions is already fully delineated in Jonson's verse. Certain of his phrases here are continually invoked as a way to characterize Shakespeare's achievement. And Jonson seems uncannily prophetic in forecasting Shakespeare's perdurable fame in diverse cultural settings all over the world.

Ben Jonson saw in Shakespeare a remarkable creative spontaneity. His genius was of a natural kind, derived from an immediate responsiveness to lived experience.

> He was (indeed) honest, and of an open, and free nature: had an excellent *Phantsie*; brave notions, and gentle expressions: wherein he flow'd with that facility, that sometimes it was necessary he should be stopp'd: . . . His wit was in his own power; would the rule of it had been so too.

This view of Shakespeare as both abundantly inventive but also undisciplined has been central in the formation of the cultural mythology that continues to surround his work. What distinguishes his art is not its formal perfection but rather an intuitive sympathy with the claims of everyday life. Shakespeare is not a classical artist who observes the formal rules of dramatic composition. He is, however, the great poet of the vernacular.

Jonson's memoir of Shakespeare articulates a powerful myth of reconciled wholeness. Like every important and enduring myth, Jonson's commemorative recollection is an attempt to harmonize contradictory impulses in a single, unified narrative. Shakespeare's poetry represents the fusion of nature and art. More fundamentally, however, what is most natural in Shakespeare himself as a poet finds perfect expression in his writing, which is simultaneously artless – "he never blotted a line" – "and artful" – "nicely spun, and woven so fit." He is a man closely embedded in the concrete particularity of his own time and place, but he is also the transcendent genius of a universal human nature. And Shakespeare's genius is at one with his geniality – on top of everything else, he is a really nice person.

The editors of the first folio, John Heminge and Henry Condell, complicate Jonson's memoir by integrating his praise of Shakespeare with a narrative of loss and recovery. Shakespeare's legacy is an art composed of words, but words are fragile, insubstantial, and easily forgotten.

> It had been a thing, we confesse, worthie to have bene wished, that the Author himself
> had liv'd to have set forth, and overseen his owne writings; But since it hath bin
> ordain'd otherwise, and he by death departed from that right, we pray you do not envie
> his Friends, the office of their care, and paine, to have collected & publish'd them; and so
> to have publish'd them, as where (before) you were abus'd with diverse stolne, and
> surreptitious copies, maimed, and deformed by the frauds and stealthes of iniurious
> impostors, that expos'd them: even those, are now offered to your view cur'd, and perfect
> of their limbes; and all the rest, absolute in their numbers, as he conceived them.

The publication of the first folio is the founding event in the articulation of the
Shakespeare myth. The editors of this volume are somehow able to restore the
plenitude and the singularity of Shakespeare's achievement out of the fragmentary
remains of "stolne, and surreptitious copies." Two further elements are thus added to
the myth. The first folio assigns ethical precedence to the written text over any
possible tradition of theatrical performance. But the brilliance and the integrity of
Shakespeare's word will be continually shadowed not just by the possibility of
accidental loss or erosion, but by a more deliberate malevolence, fraud, or masquerade
that would deny posterity its full entitlement to Shakespeare's legacy.

The grand cultural narrative sketched out by Ben Jonson and the editors of the first
folio has had an extraordinary persistence. According to this narrative, the decisive
achievement exhibited in Shakespeare's collected plays is a powerful, circumstantial
realism of attitude, motive, and behaviour. This, of course, is, all the more remarkable
because Shakespeare could only have observed a historically specific form of social life.
The greatest of eighteenth-century critics, Samuel Johnson, saw the concreteness of
Shakespearian representation, its sympathetic correspondence with ordinary everyday
social reality, as at once its most characteristic excellence and at the same time the
source of its crucial difficulties.

> It is the great excellence of Shakespeare, that he drew his scenes from nature, and from
> life. He copied the manners of the world then passing before him, and has more
> allusions than other poets to the traditions and superstition of the vulgar; which must
> therefore be traced before he can be understood . . . . If Shakespeare has difficulties above
> other writers, it is to be imputed to the nature of his work, which required the use of the
> common colloquial language, and consequently admitted many phrases allusive, ellip-
> tical, and proverbial, such as we speak and hear every hour without observing them.
> (Johnson 1968: 58)

For Johnson the heterogeneity of Shakespeare's language, its wide-ranging familiarity
with obsolete, common, and colloquial idioms as well as with foreign languages, is
something of an "embarrassment for the reader." Nevertheless, he was astute enough
to recognize that Shakespeare's use of colloquial speech is integral to his achievement
as a writer of lasting value.

As the compiler of the *English Dictionary* Johnson appreciated with perhaps unusual
sensitivity that Shakespeare's language was an immense, shared resource, equally

important for the "common workmen" and the "critick." Shakespeare's works are, for Johnson, a rich and varied printed archive of popular usage that continues to shape the language of everyday social interaction. Beginning sometime in the middle of the eighteenth century, an explanation of Shakespeare's distinctive achievement begins to be developed based on his sympathetic affinity with the common people. Johnson's highly qualified admission that Shakespeare can be understood only against a background of colloquial idiom and popular culture is developed and expanded in an influential volume by Lady Elizabeth Montagu called *An Essay on the Writings and Genius of Shakespeare, Compared with the Greek and French Dramatic Poets, with Some Remarks upon the Misrepresentations of Mons. de Voltaire.*

The "essay" is a remarkable performance in a number of ways, not least for its broad and lasting impact. The book, first published in 1769, went through a total of six editions, with the latest appearing in 1810, a long run for a work of literary criticism. Although Montagu's reputation as a critic has now declined, the *Essay* was widely admired and praised by her contemporaries. It was translated into German (1771), French (1777), and Italian (1828). Lady Montagu's essay lays out a format for scholarly and critical commentary that remains standard right up to the present. The book consists of two expository chapters setting out interpretive and theoretical principles, followed by six lengthy, detailed discussions of individual plays. Even more important, however, is Montagu's control of her problematic and her keen awareness of the adversarial nature of her task.

Lady Montagu begins with an acknowledgement of the contributions of Shakespeare's editors, who have created the possibility for a fuller and more accurate criticism of "this celebrated Author." Her real indebtedness, however, is not to her English authorities, notably Pope and Johnson, but rather to her French antagonist, Voltaire. For Voltaire, the English admiration for Shakespeare was not simply a matter of bad taste, or a lack of aesthetic discrimination. English enthusiasm for Shakespeare reveals a nostalgia or even tacit approval for what Voltaire calls "barbarism," by which he means a preference for archaic repression, violence and ignorance. His *Appel a toutes les nations de l'Europe* (1761) was a call for general resistance to a regressive, backward-looking England in the name of progress, order, civilization, and the Enlightenment. Shakespeare, on this account, is symptomatic of England's reactionary ignorance, its entrenched opposition to the project of Enlightenment modernity.

Elizabeth Montagu has a pronounced sense of her own culture's "modernity" and a corresponding sense of the antiquity of the culture in which Shakespeare's work was first produced. Although Shakespeare had lived only about two centuries earlier, there is an emphatic stress in Montagu's essay on the feeling of contrast and difference produced in modern readers by these works written in a historically distant context. For Mrs Montagu, as for Voltaire, that earlier culture had been uncultivated, unsophisticated, "rude." Voltaire attacked Shakespeare as a drunken lout and argued that enthusiasm for his work was evidence both of a lamentable absence of cultural standards in England and an equally lamentable lack of aspirations for enlightened social order. Mrs Montagu would defend him as an instance of vernacular artistry as well as for the wealth of realistic psychological and moral insights his work provides. This defence begins with an open, candid acknowledgement of the vernacular and popular sources of Shakespeare's achievement, in order to affirm that "he is certainly one the greatest moral philosophers that ever lived" (p. 37). What Elizabeth Montagu evidently had in view with her claim that Shakespeare was a great moral philosopher was an attempt to redefine and re-articulate both the subject matter of morality and the community in which moral inquiry would be pursued.

It is clear that for Montagu the central question of character is closely linked to the exploration of moral problems. Furthermore, the "moral philosophy" found in Shakespeare is a realistic and practical knowledge founded in concrete, contingent social circumstances. Moral inquiry, then, necessarily entails an affirmation of ordinary life.

> The dramatis personae of Shakespeare are men, frail by constitution, hurt by ill habits, faulty and unequal: but they speak with human voices, are actuated by human passions, and are engaged in the common affairs of human life. We are interested in what they do, or say, by feeling, every moment, that they are of the same nature as ourselves. Their precepts therefore are an instruction, their fates and fortunes an experience, their testimony an authority, and their misfortunes a warning. (p. 60)

The moral force of these depictions arises from an immediate sympathy between the dramatic character and the spectator. What makes such sympathy possible is a shared background in the complex and contradictory experience of everyday life. Shakespeare's characters are non-heroic, and even at times anti-heroic; but it is precisely the modest human scale of their depiction that makes them morally significant.

For Elizabeth Montagu, and for many of her eighteenth-century contemporaries, morality is not a schedule of virtues, but rather a matter of more or less vivid, well-defined feelings, inclinations, and dispositions. Shakespeare's "moral philosophy" on this account is indistinguishable from his understanding of the emotional sources of will and action, or, to use the eighteenth-century vocabulary, the passions. Montagu's formulation of this idea incorporates an interesting discussion of the relationship between social rank and the accessibility of the affective and expressive dimensions of everyday experience.

> Shakespeare was born into a rank of life, in which men indulge themselves in a free expression of their passions, with little regard to exterior appearance. This perhaps made him more acquainted with the emotions of the heart, and less knowing or observant of outward forms: against the one he offends, he very rarely misrepresents the other. (p. 15)

Montagu introduces the no doubt romantic idea here that people of lower social standing have more immediate, and therefore more reliable, intuitions about "the emotions of the heart" than their more decorous and no doubt more powerful social superiors. For Montagu the subject matter of morality cannot be grasped as a system of constraints, duties, and imperatives administered to a subordinated population through institutions of tutelage. The maxims of morality simply make explicit a certain element of benevolence or good will, "tender impulses" that appear to be a natural endowment of all human subjects. On this view, morality is not a property defined by hierarchical status; nor is the achievement of moral dignity confined to men of a particular social class. To the contrary, morality, whatever substantive forms it may take, is both universal and universally binding. Men *and* women, irrespective of social position, have the capacity to express moral feeling in their everyday lives, and also to articulate moral understanding through a vernacular idiom of maxims and customary practices.

Ralph Waldo Emerson proposes an even more expansive view of Shakespeare's pervasive influence in shaping everyday life.

> He [Shakespeare] wrote the text of modern life; the text of manners: he drew the man of England and Europe; the father of the man in America; he drew the man, and described the day, and what is done in it: he read the hearts of men and women, their probity, and their second thoughts and wiles; ... he knew the laws of repression which make the police of nature. (Emerson 1968: 211)

For Emerson, Shakespeare is one of the great "representative men," and his "originality" is precisely his ability to absorb and give voice to the experience of a diverse social collectivity. "In the composition of such works the time thinks, the market thinks, the mason, the carpenter, the merchant, the farmer, the fop, all think for us" (p. 201). Emerson makes an extremely bold claim for Shakespeare's representative power here. It's not just that Shakespeare was a shrewd observer of the varied social types that populated his world. There is a sense that Shakespeare came to possess the ability to speak for large, diffuse collectivities. The greatest and most durable works are in a sense created anonymously, not by one person, but by many. Two examples of great works produced collectively in this way are the English Bible and the English Common Law. Shakespeare is in one sense the local surrogate of a similar process of anonymous social creativity, except of course that he also actually existed as an individual. What Shakespeare "represents," then, is the reconciliation of singular individuality with the contradictory totality of social life.

Emerson's views are more fully theorized in Virginia Woolf's *A Room of One's Own*. Woolf's account of Shakespeare's authority and its relation to everyday life suggests that literary creativity is sustained through broad social participation, that it is an effect of communal life. Shakespeare's works are built up from comprehensive borrowing from preceding literary works and from an unselfconscious absorption of the speech types of the common people.

> For masterpieces are not single and solitary births; they are the outcome of many years of thinking in common, of thinking by the body of the people, so that the experience of the mass is behind the single voice. Without ... forerunners, Jane Austen and the Brontes and George Eliot could no more have written than Shakespeare could have written without Marlowe, or Marlowe without Chaucer, or Chaucer without those

forgotten poets who paved the ways and tamed the natural savagery of the tongue. (Woolf 1929: 98)

Woolf's immediate concern is with the revolutionary, epochal emergence of the institution of women writing, an event she thinks of "greater importance than the Crusades or the Wars of the Roses" (p. 97). Such an emergence takes place through the initiative of an exceptional singular agent, but the precondition of such originality is the existence of a shared expressive life among the socially excluded and unvoiced.

The most powerful figure for the silenced, subordinated community in *A Room of One's Own* is Woolf's description of Judith, Shakespeare's "wonderfully gifted sister" (pp. 70ff). As Woolf has no doubt correctly insisted, a woman with a Shakespearian capacity for expressivity and a determination to use that capacity publicly would almost certainly have been denounced and punished as a witch or demon. Judith Shakespeare is a casualty of the patriarchal order and its violent policing of language. William Shakespeare himself is not, however, indicted for the generic persecution of Judith or of any of his anonymous sisters. Furthermore, the voice of the doomed sister can in fact be heard resonating through the work of the brother.

One of the fullest, most confident accounts of Shakespeare as the universal poet of ordinary life is the entry on Shakespeare written by the editor-in-chief of the ninth edition of the *Encyclopaedia Brittanica* (1886), Thomas Spencer Baynes. The article begins by situating Shakespeare in the geographical and cultural milieu of the Warwickshire countryside, specifically in the small town of Stratford-upon-Avon. There is a section on the Rother market, a long discussion of holiday spectacles and festivities, and a very detailed account of Shakespeare's family background. On the basis of this quite exhaustive history, Baynes feels justified in concluding that

> ...all the best known facts of Shakespeare's personal history bring into vivid relief the simplicity and naturalness of his tastes, his love of the country, the strength of his domestic affections, and the singularly firm hold which the conception of family life had upon his imagination, his sympathies, and his schemes of active labour....it is clear that the unity and continuity of family life possessed Shakespeare's imagination with the strength of a dominant passion and largely determined the scope and direction of his practical activities. (p. 766)

Shakespeare's "practical activities" were orientated by the strong evaluations of family life and social continuity that were normative for his society. These traditions of conviviality and mutual aid were enabled to flourish within the communal life of the Warwickshire villages in which Shakespeare was reared. His plays are only fully intelligible from within this moral horizon. The great genius of Baynes's account is in the way it develops a picture of Shakespeare as the "soul of the age" of Elizabethan England. But it is precisely by means of this delineation of a historically specific context that Shakespeare can be recognized as familiar, contemporary, and representative. Small-town life in sixteenth-century Stratford-upon-Avon is not remote and distant from the experience of Baynes's readers. It is at once a convincing reflection of the everyday life of ordinary English neighborhoods and a powerful image of social desire.

Any socially productive myth will have the power to generate innumerable variants over time, and Shakespeare is no exception to this principle. The myth of Shakespeare continues to circulate throughout contemporary society, where it informs an extraordinary range of cultural practices. It is commonly encountered at various levels in public education. Students first become familiar with the basic tenets of the myth when they study Shakespeare in English classes, when they participate in school productions, and when they are taken to a local festival to see one of his plays performed. These experiences provide people with important pre-theoretical intuitions about Shakespeare's larger significance, and these intuitions then reappear as new variants of the myth. I once met a man on the subway who told me that his son was performing a leading role in a high-school production of *Romeo and Juliet*. "This is going to make him really popular with the girls," he said, with obvious enthusiasm. The idea here is that simply by learning to recite Shakespeare's lines, one somehow becomes more amiable, more sensitive, and therefore more attractive to the opposite sex. Girls like poetry, therefore girls like boys who can recite poetry; Shakespeare's is the most seductive poetry of all. This incident suggests that in its most basic form, the Shakespeare myth is an idea of enhanced and heightened sympathy, a way to become more fully attuned to the feelings of others. But the myth as it is articulated here also has more sinister valences as a story about self-aggrandizement and the instrumental utility of poetic language. Shakespeare is recruited to provide this young man with more effective resources for the pursuit of his desires.

More fully developed, formal versions of the Shakespeare myth are reproduced in any number of discursive genres. Shakespeare's genius is a recurrent topic in the editorial pages of newspapers and in reviews of his plays.

> What would the English language be without Shakespeare, a cab driver once asked me. Indeed it would be the poorer, and more than we might think. The world's greatest playwright has so imbued our life and thought with the imagery of his works that even now, more than four centuries after his birth, his words have a direct effect on the way we say things. (George Neavoll, 23 April, 1993)

In a side-bar to this piece, Neavoll, editor of the *Portland Press Herald*, invites the public to a birthday party for Shakespeare where free cake and coffee will be served. Neavoll's policy of annual celebrations of this kind expresses his belief in Shakespeare as a promoter of conviviality and social equality. It's interesting that Neavoll's "informant" should have been a cab-driver. In fact, cab-drivers who quote or interpret the significance of Shakespeare have become a standard feature in contemporary variants of the myth. The cabbie is, of course, a modern embodiment of the popular voice, and the cab itself a privileged space where the barriers of social difference are more easily crossed. Again, the Shakespeare myth is closely tied to ideas of a broad sympathy that reconciles and reunites otherwise divided fragments of the social world.

Important variants of the myth also inform much contemporary scholarship and criticism. There is a significant sense in which contemporary scholarship is continuous with a tradition of inquiry and critical reflection on Shakespeare which began in the eighteenth century and was further articulated and expanded by Ralph Waldo Emerson, Virginia Woolf, and Thomas Spencer Baynes, as well as many others. What characterizes this tradition is the way various critics are similarly oriented within a moral or evaluative framework in which the dignity and significance of everyday life is preeminent. The reconciliatory valences of Shakespeare's plays receive prominent attention in the influential writings of Northrop Frye. In its most recent manifestations this tradition takes the form of an intense preoccupation with the experience of family life. This concern is given a particularly clear and moving articulation in *The Whole Journey* by C. L. Barber and Richard Wheeler:

> "The family in Shakespeare" refers at once to the handling of the family in his works and to the internalizing of the family situation in his own sensibility, which actively informs his works. Shakespeare's art is distinguished by the intensity of its investment in the human family and especially in the continuity of the family across generations. (1986: 2)

Concern with the ethical and psychological dimensions of the family is important for philosophical critics like Stanley Cavell (1987), for feminists like Carol Neely (1985), for psychoanalytic critics like Janet Adelman (1992), and for those scholars who are now deeply concerned with sexuality and the body, such as Valerie Traub (1992) and Gail Paster (1993).

Critical scholarship of the kind I have just summarized tends to reproduce variants of the Shakespeare myth, even as it struggles to distance itself from the practice of naive idealization or vulgar "bardolatry." This is also apparent in the extremely stylized genre of general introductions to collected editions of Shakespeare's works. Harry Levin provides an eloquent summary of the myth in his "General Introduction" to the widely used Riverside edition of Shakespeare's works. But his language is measured, cautious and reserved. Clearly Levin believes that it is important to acknowledge the myth on behalf of his prospective readers, but he also feels obliged to withhold full commitment. Instead he tries to maintain an attitude of cool detachment towards the myth's more emotionally overheated variants. Stephen Greenblatt, in his "General Introduction" to *The Norton Shakespeare*, presents his readers with a brilliant, deeply ironic condensation of the great man's legend.

> The celebration of Shakespeare's genius, eloquently initiated by his friend and rival Ben Jonson, has over the centuries become an institutionalized rite of civility. The person who does not love Shakespeare has made, the rite implies, an incomplete adjustment not simply to a particular culture – English culture of the late sixteenth and early seventeenth centuries – but to "culture" as a whole, the dense network of constraints and entitlements, dreams and practices that links us to nature. Indeed, so absolute is Shakespeare's achievement that he has himself come to seem like great creating nature:

the common bond of humankind, the principle of hope, the symbol of the imagination's power to transcend time-bound beliefs, and assumptions. (p. 1)

All the traditional themes are still powerfully operative here: Shakespeare's identification with nature, his deep human sympathy, the transcendent power of his imagination. It is apparent that Greenblatt himself is wised-up about this story, and wants to alert his readers to the mythic status of these beliefs. Yet at the same time it is simply not possible to "introduce" Shakespeare without invoking the myth in its standard form.

The contemporary vitality of the Shakespeare myth is perhaps most dramatically manifested in a series of comic books "suggested for mature readers," written by Neil Gaiman and published by D.C. comics. The character of Shakespeare first appears in "Men of Good Fortune," volume 13 of *The Sandman*. In 1589 Christopher Marlowe meets with a mediocre but ambitious young actor named Will Shaxberd at the White Horse Tavern, somewhere near London. Shaxberd's desire is to become a playwright, and to that end he asks Marlowe for his opinion on his first play. Marlowe is appalled at a dreadful passage invoking "comets" to "scourge the bad, revolting stars" (*I Henry VI*, I. i. 4). He tells his aspiring younger colleague that he lacks the talent to be a successful poet. Shaxberd, discouraged at the fading of his dream, laments that his aptitude falls so far short of Marlowe's: "I would give anything to have your gifts. Or more than anything to give men dreams that would live on long after I am dead. I'd bargain, like your Faustus, for that boon" (Gaiman 1989: 13). Also present in the tavern at this moment is Lord Morpheus, King of Dreams, who overhears the conversation. He approaches Will Shaxberd and makes him an offer. As a result of the ensuing discussion, Shaxberd embarks on his wished-for career as the poet of men's enduring dreams.

Neil Gaiman's brilliantly rendered account of this important meeting confirms the mythic belief that Shakespeare's genius comes into being through the intervention of a supernatural power. The exact terms of the bargain Shakespeare makes with Lord Morpheus are not revealed, however, until volume 19 of *The Sandman*, "A Midsummer Night's Dream," which appeared in February 1990. Here we learn that Shakespeare has agreed to write two plays in repayment of Lord Morpheus. The first is *A Midsummer Night's Dream*, first performed by Lord Strange's Men, in Gaiman's version of events, on the Sussex Downs near Wilmington, on Midsummer's Eve in 1593. The audience consists of Lord Morpheus, now known as "Prince of Stories," along with none other than Oberon, Titania, Robin Goodfellow, and the entire fairy *entourage*. Titania is attracted to an eight-year-old child in the acting troupe, young Hamnet Shakespeare, who plays the part of the Indian boy. In the morning after the play is performed, he tells his father: "I had such a strange dream. There was a great lady, who wanted me to go with her to a distant land." In the book's final panel there is a brief text: "Hamnet Shakespeare died in 1596, aged eleven. Robin Goodfellow's present whereabouts are unknown."

The final chapter in this story appeared in *The Sandman*, volume 75, for March 1996, "The Tempest." In this extraordinary mythopoetic text, written by Neil

Gaiman, illustrated by Charles Vess, and lettered by Todd Klein, a sadder but wiser Shakespeare is depicted writing the second of the two plays he promised Lord Morpheus during the winter months of 1610–11. He is represented as gentle, forbearing, and deeply melancholy, a man who is kind to his neighbors and patient with his reproachful wife. As the story unfolds, it becomes clear that Shakespeare's genius as a poet is closely tied to his ordinariness as a man. His art records the various fragments of his own day-to-day experience, ranging from his feelings for his daughter Judith to his encounter in a local inn with two drunken sailors. These provide the materials for "The Tempest." It is difficult to do justice to the richness of this text in the limited space available here. However, two particularly notable episodes are especially relevant to Gaiman's novel retelling of the Shakespeare myth.

On Guy Fawkes' Day in 1610 Shakespeare receives a visit from his old friend Ben Jonson. Jonson is buoyant and expansive, Shakespeare pensive and withdrawn. Ben is critical of Shakespeare's evident carelessness as a writer: "You write with such facility, Will. For me I anguish over every word. I am convinced that your work would be improved if you took more time over it." Later the ambitious Jonson taunts Shakespeare for the mundane life he has led. "In my time I've been a soldier, a scholar, a pauper, a duelist, an actor, a translator and a spy. I've killed a man in a duel. I've thrice been imprisoned. . . . I have met all sorts of people . . . from the lowest to the most high. Thus, I understand 'em." Shakespeare's reply to this is brief and to the point. "I would have thought that all one needs to understand people is to be a person. And I have that honor." Jonson has trouble understanding Shakespeare's quiet resignation, his willingness to settle for an ordinary life in a provincial town. But it is clear from the visual framing and the way his facial expressions are rendered by Charles Vess's drawing that Jonson is something of a vain, pompous fool. Shakespeare's face, by contrast, clearly hints at a much deeper, more complex inner life concealed by his plain, unprepossessing surface.

On the night *The Tempest* is completed, Shakespeare is taken by Lord Morpheus to his castle for a glass of wine in honor of the fulfillment of their bargain. Morpheus recalls their agreement and explains why Shakespeare was chosen to receive "the power to give men dreams that would live on." There are several reasons: "Because you had a gift, and the talent. Because you were no worse a man that many another. Because you had a good heart. And because you wanted it . . . so much." Prompted by this, Shakespeare remembers how his experience was transformed into his art. "My son died, and I was hurt; but I watched my hurt, and even relished it, a little, for now I could write a real death, a true loss." In Gaiman's text the story of Shakespeare is reshaped as a modern myth of self-realization. Shakespeare's genius is the gift of a supernatural power, but the gift itself consists of nothing more than the ability to feel more keenly and to record one's own experience more vividly than other people do. For Gaiman and his associates, however, the myth has consistently dark, melancholy overtones. An individual subjectivity is fully and perfectly actualized by perdurable works of art. But Shakespeare's expressive genius is purchased at the cost of a deep sorrow and loneliness. As Titania says, "he did not understand the price. Mortals never do."

A myth is not a description of things as they are. In fact, a myth can be used to bully people and intimidate them, to make them feel ashamed of what they feel and of who they are. The Shakespeare myth is no exception to this. Shakespeare's works may be a "common endowment" of Western civilization; but they have by no means been an unambiguous benefit to every member of society. In fact, the Shakespeare myth of geniality, of universal sympathy for ordinary human beings, has more often than not been used to reinforce invidious social distinctions and exclusionary privileges. At the same time, however, there is a larger cogency to the Shakespeare myth as an enduring image of important forms of social desire. The idea of a great vernacular poetry endowed with the power to shape our dreams represents a deferred or unrealized hope for the possibility of expressive unity and completeness. Shakespeare, as he is imagined in this folk narrative, is the image of unalienated labor. The individual gift, nurtured in a broad social engagement, is fully rendered back as the expression of a lived collective life. The Shakespeare myth is one of the great stories, continually rewritten over time as a form of "thinking in common" that creates and sustains a society's fullest aspirations for each of its members. It is a complex, ironic, and potentially deceptive story. But as stories go, it's not a bad one to hold on to.

REFERENCES AND FURTHER READING

Adelman, Janet 1992: *Suffocating Mothers*. London: Routledge.

Babcock, Robert Witbeck 1931: *The Genesis of Shakespeare Idolatry, 1766–1799*. Chapel Hill: University of North Carolina Press.

Barber, C. L. and Wheeler, Richard 1986: *The Whole Journey: Shakespeare's Power of Development*. Berkeley: University of California Press.

Bate, Jonathan 1989: *Shakespearean Constitutions: Politics, Theatre, Criticism 1730–1830*. Oxford: Oxford University Press.

Baynes, Thomas Spencer 1886: Shakespeare. In *Encyclopaedia Brittanica*, 9th edn, vol. 21.

Bristol, Michael 1996: *Big-Time Shakespeare*. London: Routledge.

Cavell, Stanley 1987: *Disowning Knowledge in Six Plays of Shakespeare*. Cambridge: Cambridge University Press.

DeGrazia, Margreta 1991: *Shakespeare Verbatim: The Reproduction of Authenticity and the 1790 Apparatus*. Oxford: Clarendon Press.

Dobson, Michael 1992: *The Making of the National Poet: Shakespeare, Adaptation and Authorship, 1660–1769*. Oxford: Clarendon Press.

Dollimore, Jonathan and Sinfield, Alan 1985: *Political Shakespeare: New Essays in Cultural Materialism*. Ithaca, NY: Cornell University Press.

DuBois, W. E. B. 1986: *The Souls of Black Folks*. New York: Library of America.

Emerson, Ralph Waldo 1968: *Representative Men: Seven Lectures*, In vol. 4 of *The Complete Works of Ralph Waldo Emerson: Centenary Edition*, 12 vols, New York: AMS Press.

Felperin, Howard 1990: *The Uses of the Canon: Elizabethan Literature and Contemporary Theory*. Oxford: Clarendon Press.

Halpern, Richard 1997: *Shakespeare among the Moderns*. Ithaca, NY: Cornell University Press.

Holderness, Graham (ed.) 1988: *The Shakespeare Myth*. Manchester: Manchester University Press.

Johnson, Samuel 1968: *Johnson on Shakespeare*, ed. Arthur Sherbo. In *The Yale Edition of the Works of Samuel Johnson*, New Haven: Yale University Press, vols 7 and 8.

Marsden, Jean (ed.) 1991: *The Appropriations of Shakespeare: Post-Renaissance Reconstructions of the Works and the Myth*. New York: St Martin's Press.

Neely, Carol Thomas 1985: *Broken Nuptials in Shakespeare's Plays*. New Haven: Yale University Press.

Paster, Gail Kern 1993: *The Body Embarrassed: Drama and the Disciplines of Shame in Early Modern England*. Ithaca, NY: Cornell University Press.

Shakespeare, William 1974: *The Riverside Shakespeare*, ed. G. Blakemore Evans et al. Boston: Houghton Mifflin.

—— 1997: *The Norton Shakespeare*, ed. Stephen Greenblatt et al. New York: W. W. Norton.

Taylor, Gary 1989: *Re-Inventing Shakespeare: A Cultural History from the Restoration to the Present*. New York: Weidenfeld and Nicholson.

Traub, Valerie 1992: *Desire and Anxiety: Circulations of Sexuality in Shakespearean Drama*. London: Routledge.

Woolf, Virginia 1929: *A Room of One's Own*. London: Hogarth Press.

Index

absolutism, 114, 307, 384, 470
Ab urbe condita (Livy), 112–13
Academica (Cicero), 286
Actes and Monuments (Foxe), 169, 195–6, 202
"Acte to restrain the Abuses of Players," 384–5
acting companies, 227, 228, 313–314, 328, 363, 473
  bankruptcy of, 323
  children's, 226, 303, 352, 354, 375–376, 380
  as extended families, 334–5
  joint-stock shareholding, 14, 15, 320, 321, 325, 326
  licencing of 380, 383, 384
  operating costs for, 320–1
  political influence of, 338, 339
  relations with playhouse owners, 315, 325–6
  rehearsals of 16
  repertories of, 226, 303, 362, 367, 374; *see also* Admiral's Men, repertory of; Chamberlain's–King's Men's repertory touring, 330, 334, 336–7, 347, 355, 362, 363, 365, 366, 367, 383, 429
  see also Chamberlain's–King's Men *and other specific companies*
actio, 283, 285
Act of Six Articles (1540), 26
Act of Supremacy (1559), 466
actors, 313–14
  acting styles of, 230–1, 342–3
  boys, 226, 229, 317, 334, 343, 352, 354, 367, 369, 375–6, 429

doubling, 229–30, 231
  education and training of, 233, 334, 335–6, 343
  gender transgressions of, 226, 317
  as *homo rhetoricus*, 279
  incomes of, 315, 320, 334
  as servants, 328, 329, 330, 338, 339–40, 380, 404
  social status of, 334, 379, 380, 389
  playwriting by, 226, 230, 232–3
  political influence of, 338, 339
Adagia (Erasmus), 101
Adelman, Janet, 17–18, 299, 498
Admiral's Men, 227, 229, 231, 321, 334, 365, 367, 380, 383
  marketing strategies of, 353
  repertory of, 347, 351, 352, 354, 355, 357
  run with Chamberlain's Men, 346, 347
Admonition Controversy, 61
Admonition to the Parliament, 469
adulthood, 86
Advancement of Learning (Bacon), 40, 109
Adventures of Master F. J. (Gascoigne), 209
advertising, 434–5, 445, 458
advice books, 98
aesthetic of abundance, 229
Africanus, Leo, 454
agnosticism, 40
Alchemist, The (Jonson), 341, 372, 358, 359
aldermen, 44, 46, 52, 54
  Court of, 379
alehouse, Warwick, 130–2

Aleyn, Charles, 197
Alford, Francis, 29
aliens, 51, 212
allegoria, 289
Allen, Giles, 367, 369
Allen, William, 57, 59, 469
Alleyn, Edward, 54, 314, 321, 326, 365
  as Faustus, 375
  partnership with Henslowe, 323
Alleyn, Joan, 54
alliteration, 257
All's Well That Ends Well (Shakespeare), 17, 30, 354, 356
  genre of, 298, 306
  verse in, 270
almanacs, 208, 457, 458
Altman, Joel, 286
Amandis de Gaul, 216, 217
Amandis of England, 216
Ames, William, 40
amphibrachs, 263, 264
amphitheaters, 362, 365, 366, 368, 369
anagnorisis, 183, 184
analogical thinking, 174, 180, 184; *see also* typology
anapests, 265
Andria (Terence), 175–6
Anglica historia (Vergil), 194, 197
Anglicanism, *see* Church of England
Annales (Camden), 195, 199
Annales (Stow), 198, 199, 451, 454
Antidosis (Isocrates), 294
antiquarianism, 3, 188, 191, 192, 193, 195, 200
Antonio and Mellida (Marston), 354

Antonio's Revenge (Marston), 354
Antony and Cleopatra (Shakespeare),
　　4, 16, 18–19, 160, 171, 355,
　　359
　　classical sources for, 176
　　as problem play, 306
　　staging for, 374
　　verse in, 264, 265, 269
Aphorismes Civill and Militarie
　　(Dallington), 190
Apologie (Essex), 458
Apology for Actors, An (Heywood),
　　378–9, 384, 446
Apologie for Poetrie (Sidney), 194,
　　195, 281–2, 283–4, 300
Apologie of the Church of Englande, The
　　(Jewell), 454
Apology of the City (Dalton), 48
Apophthegmata (Erasmus), 101
Appel a toutes les nations de l'Europe
　　(Voltaire), 493
apprentices, apprenticeships, 44, 46,
　　48, 49–50, 52–3, 85, 87,
　　92–3, 94, 169
　　actors, 334, 335–6, 343, 344
　　gentleman, 93, 219
　　literacy and reading habits of,
　　　169, 208
　　as literary heroes, 54, 218, 219
　　printers', 436, 437, 448, 459
　　rioting of, 36, 51, 97, 228
Arcadia (Sidney), 209, 217
Arcadian Rhetoricke, The (Fraunce),
　　280
Archbishop Controversy, 32
architecture, 35, 147
Arden of Faversham, 349, 351
Aristotle, aristotelianism, 39, 40,
　　41, 121, 163, 184, 194–5, 212
　　political ideals, 107, 119, 125
　　on rhetoric, 277, 278, 280–1
Arithmeticke (Record), 457
Armin, Robert, 15, 320, 331, 333,
　　334, 335, 341, 343
Arraignment of Lewd, Idle, Froward,
　　and Unconstant Women, The
　　(Swetnam), 87–8
Arte of English Poesie, The
　　(Puttenham), 280, 289, 291,
　　300
Arte of Rhetorique (Wilson), 280,
　　283–4
Arte or Crafte of Rethoryke, The,
　　(Coxes), 280
artes historicae, 193

Artes of Logicke and Retoricke, The
　　(Fenner), 280
Arthur of Little Britain (Berners),
　　216
artisans, 161, 232, 308, 326
　　literacy and reading practices of,
　　　141, 148, 200
　　wages of, 314–15, 320
Aspley, William, 397, 408
Astrophil and Stella (Sidney), 209
　inventio in, 283
　meter in, 259
As You Like It (Shakespeare), 16,
　　183, 184, 209, 215, 353, 356
　commonplace in, 283
　verse in, 263
atheism, 40, 41, 64
Atley, John, 380, 385, 387
authorial revision, 474
authority:
　literary, 207, 220
　papal, 25
　political, 130–2
　textual, 395–6, 408–9, 412
authorization of texts, 465–6,
　　467–8, 471, 473, 479, 480
authorship, 206, 216, 398, 409
Aylmer, John, 480

Bacon, Francis, 25, 40, 41, 97, 101,
　　102, 103, 109, 113, 114, 115,
　　125, 189, 190
　as historiographer, 191, 193, 197,
　　199
Babington, Anthony, 30, 54
Bad Beginning Makes a Good Ending,
　　A, 358, 359
Baker, Richard, 199
Baldwin, T.W., 172
Bale, John, 170, 196
Ball, The (Shirley), 386
ballads, 212, 216, 457, 458
　biblical, 215
　as low culture, 209, 211
　popularity of, 208, 210–11
Barber, C.L., 498
Barclays his Argenis, 149
Barkan, Leonard, 178
Barnes, Barnabe, 374
Barnfield, Richard, 209
Barret, William, 396
Barroll, Leeds, 357
Barrow, Henry, 468
Bartholomew Fair (Jonson), 10,
　　144–5, 149, 152, 305

Basilikon Doron (James I), 33
Bate, Jonathan, 180
bawdy-houses, *see* brothels
Baynes, Thomas Spencer, 496, 498
bearbaiting, 363, 365
Bear Garden, 323
Beaumont, Francis, 152, 235, 237,
　　302, 304, 374
Beckerman, Bernard, 343
Bedlam, 305, 307
Beeston, Christopher, 322, 323,
　　324, 326, 335
Believe as You List (Massinger), 381,
　　386, 429–30
Bell inn, 379
Bell, Jane, 402
Bellum Papale (James), 453
Bel-man of London, The (Dekker), 212
Bel Savage inn, 379
benefit of clergy, 143
Benfield, Robert, 331, 333, 335,
　　341
Benn, Anthony, 47
Benson, John, 409–10
Bentley, G.E., 325
Bess of Hardwick, 35, 45
Bevis of Hampton, 216, 218
Beza, Theodore, 165
Bible(s), 150, 158–66, 168–71,
　　180, 495
　ballads, 215
　Bishops', 160, 165
　Geneva, 165, 166, 170
　as history, 187, 195, 201
　King James, 28, 159–60, 165,
　　168
　New Testament, 161–2, 163,
　　164, 165, 166, 168, 169
　Old Testament, 158, 159, 164,
　　168, 169, 170
　printing of, 169, 453, 458
　Rheims New Testament, 165
　translations of, 161–4, 168
　Tyndale's, 26, 163–4, 165, 168,
　　169
　Vulgate, 161, 162, 163, 166
　Wyclif's, 162, 164
Bill, John, 453
Bilson, Thomas, 480
biographical criticism, 16, 17,
　　18–19, 20
Bird, Theophilus, 321
Bishop's Ban, 477, 478, 480
Blacke Dogge of Newgate, The
　　(Hutton), 213

Blackfriars playhouse, 54, 337, 340, 341, 360, 366, 367–8, 374, 429
  ban on use of, 369
  boy companies at, 352, 354, 367, 369, 372, 384
  clientele for, 367, 371
  description of, 367, 368–9
  joint-stock in, 321, 322, 334
  location of, 335
  repertory, 354, 356, 357, 358, 369, 371, 372, 384, 423
  revenues of, 325
  seasonal use of, 358, 371
black letter typeface, 142, 437, 456
Blagrave, William, 431, 432
blank verse, 233–4, 236, 257, 264
  breaks within line of, 269–70
  imitating conversation, 271
Blayney, Peter, 444, 478
blockbooks, 437
Blount, Edward, 406, 408
Blundeville, Thomas, 193, 195
Boar's Head playhouse, 322, 352, 383
Boas, F. S., 306
Bodies that Matter (Butler), 301
Bodin, Jean, 193, 199
Boke Named the Governour, The (Elyot), 101, 208
Boleyn, Anne, 26, 57, 164
Bonduca (Beaumont and Fletcher), 343, 358, 360
Bonian, Richard, 403
bookbinding, 434, 440, 447, 459, 461
book buyers, 434, 447, 455
book closets, 147, 149
Booke of Marten Curtes of the Art of Navigation, The (Eden), 435
bookkeepers, 415, 416, 418–32
Book of Common Prayer, 26, 27, 165
Book of the Courtier (Castiglione), 125, 126, 208, 288–9
book ownership, 139, 145, 148, 149, 151
books:
  cutting up of, 200
  formats of, 456
  histories, 31, 452, 454
  Latin, 450, 453, 467
  news-, 454, 457
  political, 107, 454, 465
  religious, 107, 208, 214–15, 451, 452, 453, 454, 455, 456, 458

school, 121, 140, 452, 453, 456, 457, 458, 467
booksellers, 139, 140, 145, 434, 435, 436, 459, 481
book trade, 5, 107, 313, 434, 435, 450–62
  commercial aspects, 140, 461, 462
  economic importance of, 461
  English vernacular literature, 452–3
  international, 450, 452, 453
  manuscript vs print, 450, 457, 460–1, 462
  prices, 455
  print runs, 458
  regulation of, 451, 461, *see also* Stationers' Company
  size of, 457–60
Booth, Randall, 461
Borne, William, 334
Bradbrook, M. C., 329
Bradshaw, William, 75
Branagh, Kenneth, 198
Brayne, John, 323, 366
Brazen Age, The (Heywood), 360
Breton, Nicholas, 141, 151, 461
Brian, George, 15
Bridewell Hospital, 49, 51, 53, 305, 307
Bridges, John, 480
Brief Discourse (Parsons), 64
Briefe and Learned Commentary (du Jon), 170
Briefe Description of the Whole World, A (Abbott), 455
Briefe Replie, A (Sutcliffe), 454
Britannia (Camden), 192, 200, 453
broadsides, 148, 150, 213, 452, 457, 458, *see also* ballads
Brome, Richard, 439
Brooke, Arthur, 206, 236
Brooke, Ralph, 446–7
brothels, 47, 49, 50, 51, 226
Brownists, 469
Bryan, George, 331, 333, 334, 336, 340
Buc, George, 380, 381, 384–5, 387, 425, 426, 431, 467
Bufton, Joseph, 200
bullbaiting, 363, 365
Bull inn, 379
Bulmer, Bevis, 458
Bulwer, John, 343
Burbage, Cuthbert, 316, 321, 330, 335, 339–40, 341

Burbage, James, 316, 322, 323, 337, 339, 365, 366–8, 369
  as actor, 330
Burbage, Richard, 14, 16, 314, 316, 320, 321, 325, 330, 331, 334, 341, 369
  as actor, 333, 342–3, 349
  as painter, 336, 369
  social connections of, 338–9, 340
  will of 335
Burbage, Winifred, 334
Burt, Nicholas, 334
Busby, John, 478–9
Bussy D'Ambois (Chapman), 357
Butler, Judith, 301, 303
Butler, Samuel, 344
Butter, Nathaniel, 436, 471
Bynneman, Henry, 465

Caesar and Pompey, 351, 354, 373
Caesar's Fall, 354
Caesar's Tragedy, 358, 360
Calvin, Jean, 27
Calvinism, 28, 159, 165
Cambridge Bibliography of English Literature, 232
Camden, William, 15, 45, 173, 191–2, 195, 199, 200, 453, 455
Campbell, O.J., 480,
Canterbury Tales, The (Chaucer), 256–7
Capp, Bernard, 50
Captain, The (Fletcher), 343, 358
Captives, The (Heywood), 421, 424, 427, 428
Carcel de Amor (de San Pedro), 217
Cardenio (Shakespeare), 374, 359
Cardinal Wolsey, 354
Care of Christian Conscience, The (Curteys), 455
Carew, Richard, 241–2, 248
Carey, Henry, 330, 340, 341
Carlell, Lodowick, 387
Cartwright, Thomas, 78
Casaubon, Isaac, 191
cases, 438, 445, 447
Castiglione, Baldessare, 125, 126, 208, 288–9
casting off copy, 440, 442
Catalogue and Succession (Brooke), 446
catechisms, 98, 467, 468
Cater, Henry, 130, 131
Cathecism (Nowell), 214, 457

Catherine of Aragon, 25, 26, 188
catholics, catholicism, 26, 28–9, 32,
    39, 41, 54, 58, 59, 64, 67, 122
    conformity to Church of England,
    65–6
    continuity thesis, 72, 73, 74, 76,
    80
    drama associated with, 378
    gentry, 75, 76, 77
    of Henrietta Maria, 387
    in Ireland, 31
    late medieval, 72–3, 77
    as open denomination, 60, 73–4
    prosecution of, 78
    Protestant definitions of, 70–1,
    72
    and reign of Mary Tudor, 26, 68
    satires against, 212
Catiline (Jonson), 357, 358, 360
Cavell, Stanley, 498
Caxton, William, 175, 187–8
"Caxton's Chronicle," 187
Cecil, Robert, 25, 32, 33, 47, 109,
    339–40, 467, 472
Cecil, William, 27,
censorship, 464–81
    of histories, 189
    of news, 220
    of print, 382, 384, 451, 456, 462,
    465, 466, 468, 472, 473, 474,
    476–7, 478, 479, 480, 481
    by royal proclamation, 469–70
    of theater, 229, 373, 378, 380,
    381–3, 385, 425, 426–7, 430,
    472, 473, 474, 476, 477
    see also authorization of texts;
    licensing
Certaine Satyres (Marston), 215
Certamen Elegiacum (Leius), 455
Chaderton, Lawrence, 40
chain of being, 129
Chamberlain's–King's Men, 14–15,
    33, 36, 226, 235, 320,
    328–44, 365, 367, 383, 388,
    404, 429
    court performances by, 235, 237,
    332, 333, 338, 356, 358, 359
    Essex uprising and, 332, 339, 353
    generationality, 331, 333, 334
    operating costs for, 320–1
    patents for, 340, 341
    playing suspension, 386
    political allegiances of, 339
    profits of, 337, 338
    roles within, 331, 333, 334

run with Admiral's Men, 346–7
shareholding in, 14, 15, 320,
    322, 325, 326, 330, 331,
    340–2
    success of, 323, 348, 358
    ties among, 334–5
    touring of, 334, 336–7, 348
    see also acting companies
Chamberlain's–King's Men's
    repertory, 331, 339, 343,
    348–61, 405
    1594–1599: 348–52
    1599–1603: 352–5
    1603–1608: 355–7
    1608–1613: 357–60
    Blackfriars vs. Globe, 358, 371–2
    marketing of, 348, 350–2, 353,
    354, 360
    scheduling of, 347, 360, 374
    sequels and serials, 347, 351, 354,
    360
    size of, 346, 350–1, 374
Chambers, E.K., 325
Changeling, The (Middleton and
    Rowley), 301
chapbooks, 210, 211, 216, 218
Chapel Children, 367, 380
Chapman, George, 172, 173, 174,
    175, 176, 177, 209, 210
    income from playwriting, 227–8
    prison stay of, 384
charity, 52, 53, *see also* poor relief
Charlemagne (anonymous), 423,
    424–5
Charles I (King of England), 386,
    387, 431, 470
Charles II (King of England), 412
Charron, Pierre, 40
Chartier, Roger, 147
chases, 436, 442, 444
Chaste Maid in Cheapside, A
    (Middleton), 305
chastity, 17, 18, 19, 87, 88, 90, 97
Chaucer, Geoffrey, 160, 162
    meter used by, 256–7
Chettle, Henry, 211, 213, 226, 439
    collaborations of, 228, 229, 230
    income from playwriting, 227,
    228
children, 90–5
Children of the Chapel Royal, 334,
    383
Children of the Queen's Revels, 354,
    356, 384, 423
Chirologia (Bulwer), 343

Cholmley, John, 323
chorus, 229
Christian Dictionary, A (Wilson), 444
chronicle, 173, 187–8, 193, 236,
    467
    decline of, 191, 192, 196–9
    use of term, 196
Chronicle (Froissart), 167, 187
Chronicle at Large (Grafton), 196
Chronicles (Holinshed), 188, 469,
    471, 480
Church of England, 28, 29, 61, 62,
    63, 70, 73, 75, 79, 129
    conformity to, 63, 64–5, 69, 74
    skepticism and, 40
Church Papists, 58, 65–7, 71–2, 74,
    76, 80
Churchyard, Thomas, 211
Cicero, 110, 121, 122, 125, 151,
    172, 173, 190, 191, 457
    on rhetoric, 277, 278, 280, 282,
    284, 286, 294
    on truth, 286
Ciceronianus (Harvey), 280
citizens:
    as playhouse clientele, 371, 372
    in plays, 308, *see also* comedies,
    city
citizenship, 48, 52
City of God, The (Augustine), 119
Civil Warres (Daniel), 192
Civil Wars of France, 354
Clapham, John, 199
Clarke, Samuel, 74, 75
class:
    in city plays, 308
    divisions, 53, 55
    nostalgia in romances, 218
    valences of genre, 302
classical literature, 172–84
    christianizing of, 175, 182
    influence on drama, 236
    politicization of, 175
    translations of, 174–5, 176, 225
    verse form, 267
Clavell, John, 429, 430, 431
Cleaver, Robert, 86, 454
Clement, Francis, 216
clergy, 67, 70, 75, 76, 77, 121
    incomes of, 228
    literacy among, 141, 143, 208
Clifford, Anne, 149
Cloth Breeches and Velvet Hose, 353,
    354

clowns, 331, 332, 333
Cockpit playhouse, 322, 427, 428
Coke, Edward, 192, 452
Coleman, Joyce, 148
Colet, John, 279
collaboration, 5, 206, 228, 229,
    230, 398, 400, 409, 415, 419,
    421, 425–6, 439, 472, 481,
    495
Collection of the Historie of England
    (Daniel), 192, 195
Collinson, Patrick, 74, 75, 212
Colloquia (Erasmus), 457
Comedia (Terence), 457
comedies, 17, 302, 351, 354, 356
    city, 42, 301, 302, 303, 304, 305
    classical, 173, 175, 176, 181,
        182–3
    humors, 354, 356, 359
    male friendship in, 351
    marriage in, 17, 18, 303, 308,
        356, 357
    mistaken identity in, 351
    New, 181, 183
    romantic, 297
    "rules" for, 10
    Shakespeare as greatest writer of,
        11, 298
    satirical social, 10, 354
Comedy of Errors (Shakespeare), 15,
    338, 348, 351, 356
    classical influence on, 176, 183
    verse in, 266
Comenius, Joannes, 436, 442
Commentaries (Caesar), 103, 143
commerce, 45–6
Common Council of London, 379
Common Hall, 379
commonplace books, 101, 151–2,
    174, 190, 200, 448
commonplaces, 102, 103, 104, 112,
    114, 283
Commonplaces of Scripture (Taverner),
    214
commonwealth:
    ideal of, 36–7, 114, 119
    family as, 86, 90, 119
Company of Mines Royal, 320
composing stick, 436, 438, 439,
    447
compositors, 436, 437, 438–9, 440,
    442, 445, 446, 447, 448, 458,
    459, 473
Compters Common-wealth, The
    (Fennor), 213

conclusio, 284
Condell, Henry, 15, 320, 321, 332,
    335, 341
    acting career of, 333
    as folio editor, 139, 140, 142,
        144, 145, 328, 330, 331, 343,
        406, 408, 409, 491–2
    social status of, 334
*Conference about the Next Succession to
    the Crowne of England, A*
    (Parsons), 476, 479–80
confirmatio, 284
confutatio, 284
conscience, 39, 40, 41
consumption, 46, 47, 305
containment, 105, 114
*Continuation of the Historie of France,
    A* (Danett), 455
Cooke, Alexander, 15, 331, 334,
    335, 341
Coote, Edmund, 150
copia, 183, 284–5
copyright, 396, 405, *see also*
    printing, rights for
Coriolanus (Shakespeare), 16, 55,
    298, 355, 357, 359
    classical sources for, 176, 180
    verse in, 267
Cornwallis, Thomas, 76
Cornwallis, William, 211, 450, 455,
    457, 458
corrector, *see* proofreading
costumes, 320, 321, 371, 374, 376,
    417, 419, 422
coteries, 148
Cotes, Thomas, 409, 439
counsel, 122, 123–4, 125, 127, 133
Counter-Reformation, 70
Court and the Country, The (Breton),
    141
court culture, 104, 108, 109, 110,
    125–7, 129, 169, 195, 215,
    388, 397
    literature of, 209, 397
    reading in, 148
    religion and, 169
    rhetorical self within, 289
    theatrical performances, 235,
        237, 332, 333, 338, 355, 357,
        358, 359, 367, 372, 377–9,
        383
Coverdale, Miles, 164–5
Cowell, John, 469
Cowley, Richard, 320, 331, 335,
    341

Cox, Samuel, 318
Coxes, Leonard, 280
Crane, Ralph, 335, 426
Cranmer, Thomas, 26, 167
Craven, William, 44
Creede, Thomas, 401, 478
Cressy, David, 78, 140–1, 143, 148
crime, criminals, 48–9, 212, 213–4,
    215, 379
Cromwell, Oliver, 402
Cromwell, Thomas, 46, 401
crossdressing, 317
Crosse, Henry, 216
Cross Keys Inn, 348, 379
cuckoldry, 30, 50, 88, 97
culture, as term, 117–8, 119
Curtain playhouse, 51, 322, 333,
    337, 340, 348, 362, 369, 372,
    374, 378
    location of, 335, 368
    reputation of, 368
Curteys, Richard, 455
Cymbeline (Shakespeare), 16, 19, 146,
    147, 176, 184, 358, 359
    contemporary popularity of,
        219–20
    genre of, 184, 298
    staging for, 374
    verse in, 264
Cynthia's Revels (Jonson), 372
Cyropaedia (Xenophon), 281

Danett, Thomas, 455
Daniel, Samuel, 191, 192, 193, 195,
    384, 461
Danter, John, 400, 434, 435, 436
Danvers, Samuel, 150, 151
Davenant, William, 385, 387
David's Pastoral Poem, 434
Davies, John, 336, 343
Deacon, John, 213
De augentis scientiarum (Bacon), 193
deconstruction, 193
De copia (Erasmus), 101, 103, 106,
    166, 285, 288
Dedication to Sir Philip Sidney
    (Greville), 130
Dee, John, 149, 202, 203, 452
Defence of Poetry, A (Sidney), 100
Defensio Catholicae Fiede (Suarez),
    471
Defoe, Daniel, 168
DeGrazia, Margreta, 409
Dekker, Thomas, 13, 43, 48, 208,
    215, 226, 236, 303, 304, 355

Dekker, Thomas, (*contd.*)
  collaborations of, 228, 229, 230,
    301
  income from playwriting, 227,
    228
  pamphlet writing of, 211, 212,
    213
De inventione (Cicero), 283, 294
deliberative oratory, 280–1
Deloney, Thomas, 211, 219
Demonstration of Discipline (Udall),
  468
De natura deorum (Cicero), 286
De Officiis (Cicero), 121, 282,
  457
De oratore (Cicero), 190, 277, 282,
  284, 286
De partitione oratoria (Cicero), 284
*De ratione et methodo legendi historias
  dissertatio* (Wheare), 193
De ratione studii (Erasmus), 280
Derby's Men, 355, 383
De Republica Anglorum (Smith), 114,
  123
Dering, Edward, 148, 149
*Description of a New Kind of Artificiall
  Bathes, A*, 458
De Shakespeare nostrati, 9
De Vera Christi Ecclesia (Sutcliffe),
  453
de Vere, Edward, 127, 128–9
Devereux, Robert, 47, 107, 109,
  114, 115, 189, 451, 452, 458,
  475, 477, 478; *see also* Essex
  Rebellion
Devil is an Ass, The (Jonson), 193
Devil's Charter, The (Barnes), 338,
  356, 357
devils (printing), 436, 437, 447
Dial of Daily Contemplation
  (Robinson), 228
Diana (Montemayor), 217
diaries, 200
dictionaries, 248, 467, 492
Digges, L., 142
digressio, 284
Diocletian, 373
Dionysius of Halicarnassus, 190
Discourse of Life and Death (Mornay),
  454
Discourses (Machiavelli), 107
Discourses upon Seneca the Tragedian
  (Cornwallis), 176
Discoverie of a Gaping Gulf (Stubbes),
  468, 469

*Discoverie of Errours in the First
  Edition of . . .* (Vincent), 444,
  446
Discoverie of Witchcraft (Harsnett),
  207
dispositio, 283–4
disputatio in utramque partem, 102–3,
  104, 110, 278, 286, 294
Disticha (Cato), 173, 174
distribution of type, 445
divine right of kings, 32–3, 40, *see
  also* monarchy, absolutist
divisio, 284
divorce and separation, 88–9, 97
Doctor Fautus (Marlowe), 10, 357,
  373, 375, 439
*Doctrina Et Politica Ecclesiae
  Anglicanae* (Mocket), 471
Dod, John, 75, 86
Donne, John, 100, 410, 450, 461
Don Quixote (Cervantes), 216
Dorne, John, 210
Dowden, Edward, 18
Dowland, John, 455
Drake, Francis, 25, 30, 319
drama:
  classical unities of, 10, 300
  deliberative rhetoric in, 281
  generic hybridity, 300–1
  Greek, 229
  literary influences on, 217, 236
  moral function of, 175–6
  non-Shakespearian, 304
  religious, 378
  see also playing; playhouses
dramatic speech, 233, 256, 270–1,
  272
Drayton, Michael, 227–8
dress, 46–7, 87, 212
  children's, 91
Droeshout, Martin, 397, 408
Dryden, John, 253
DuBois, W.E.B., 490
Duchess of Malfi (Webster), 333, 343
Dudley, Mary, 455
Dudley, Theodosia, 455
duels, 128
Duffy, Eamonn, 69, 72–4, 76, 77
duodecimos, 456
Dutch Courtesan, The (Marston), 305
Dutton, Richard, 472, 473, 474,
  476

East India Company, 37, 45, 320
East, Thomas, 435

Eastland Company, 320
Eastward Ho (Jonson and Chapman),
  303, 305, 324, 384
Ecclestone, William, 331, 335, 341
Ecloga Oxonio-Cantabrigiensis (James),
  453, 455
economics:
  and anti-theatricalism, 317–19
  as science, 38
  of stage playing, 229, 313–26
economy:
  book trade's importance to, 461
  English, 27, 33–5, 36–7, 38, 39,
    41, 48, 322
  family, 86, 91
  London, 322, 324
  regional, 313
  Scottish, 33
Eden, Richard, 435
Edmond Ironside (anonymous), 421,
  423–4, 427
education, 91, 92, 103, 121, 127,
  166, 187
  of elite, 93–4, 186
  grammar school, 91, 92, 121, 375
  humanist, 125, 172, 280, 281,
    282
  see also literacy
Edward II (Marlowe), 349, 351
Edward III, 349, 351
Edward IV (Heywood), 303–4, 355
Edward IV (King of England), 26,
  64, 68, 69, 168, 169–70
Egerton, Thomas, 455
Eld, George, 397
Elderton, William, 211
Elizabeth I (Queen of England), 18,
  26, 27, 165
  coronation of, 188
  cult of, 32, 106, 239, 241
  and liberty of discourse, 189, 466,
    467, 468–71
  plots to assassinate, 30, 322
  projected marriage of, 47, 123,
    124, 125, 127
  religious policies of, 27, 29, 30,
    32, 60, 64, 78, 123
  succession issues surrounding, 57,
    68, 109, 123, 451
Elizabethan Church Settlement, 466
elocutio, 283, 284–5
Elton, Edward, 471
Elton, Geoffrey, 469
Elyot, Thomas, 101, 208
emblem books, 174

Emblems (Alciati), 208
Emerson, Ralph Waldo, 495, 498
enclosures, 36
Encyclopaedia Brittanica (1886), 496
Enemie of Securitie, The (Habermann), 454
Engelsing, Rolf, 149
England:
    covenant with God, 69
    economy of, 27, 33–5, 36–7, 38, 39, 41, 48, 322
    national identity, 25, 31, 58
    population of, 34
Englands Heroicall Epistles (Drayton), 455
England's Parnassus, 112
English Dictionary (Johnson), 492
English language, 160–1, 239–55
    grammatical variations of, 243–8
    in history plays, 253, 254
    as language of Protestantism, 241
    limitations of, 240, 241
    as literary, 236
    Middle, 248, 249
    mixed vocabulary of, 239–40, 241–2, 248, 249, 250, 251, 254
    Old, 241, 249
    Plain Style, 167–8
    play in, 208
    power usages of, 246–7
    printing conventions for, 242–3, 248
    pronunciation of, *see* phonology, English
    register shifts in, 247, 249–50
    Scottish, 240, 241, 242, 251
    spelling of, 242–3, 250–1, 252
    spread through colonialism, 242
    standardization of, 243, 248, 253, 255
english roman typeface, 456
English Schoole Maister (Coote), 150
Epicene (Jonson), 372
Epicureanism, 179
epideictic oratory, 281
epistemology, *see* knowledge
epitomes, 174
Erasmus, Desiderius, 40, 163, 170, 172, 173, 191, 457
    and humanist eduation, 279–80
    and rhetoric, 101, 103, 166, 285
    on selfhood, 287, 288
eschatology, 68–9
Esplandian, 216

Essay on the Writing and Genius of Shakespeare, An (Montagu), 493–5
Essays (Bacon), 101, 109, 190
Essays (Cornwallis), 211, 450, 455
Essays (Montaigne), 108
Essex Rebellion, 31–2, 107, 189, 332, 339, 353, 382, 284, 456, 478, 480; *see also* Devereux, Robert
estates satire, 354
Estienne, Charles, 454
Euphues: An Anatomy of Wit (Lyly), 208
Evans, Thomas, 321
Every Man in his Humor (Jonson), 16, 332, 338, 349, 350, 354, 359
Every Man Out of his Humor (Jonson), 236, 332, 338, 353, 354, 356, 372, 453, 456, 462
Evil May Day (1517), 51
Exemplary Lives and Memorable Acts (Heywood), 439, 443
exordium, 284

fabula, 194
Fabulae (Aesop), 457
Fabyan, Robert, 188
Faerie Queene (Spenser), 207, 216, 217, 218
    as celebration of Elizabeth, 241
    Folger copies, 455
    meter of, 257
Fair Em (anonymous), 349, 351
Fair Maid of Bristow (anonymous), 356, 357
Fair Quarrel, A (Middleton and Rowley), 439
faith, 41
Faithorne, William, 397
false authorship theory, 16
families, 85–95
    importance to Shakespeare, 496, 498
    role of, in society, 86, 89, 98, 119
    size of, 85–6
    violence within, 88, 89
    wives' role in, 86–7
Family of Love, 58, 62, 63, 64, 75, 469
famines, *see* food shortages
Farmer, Richard, 172, 184
Fasti (Ovid), 106–7, 176, 180
Faunus and Melliflora (Weever), 462

Fawkes, Guy, 32
Fawn (Marston), 444
Fenner, Dudley, 280
Fennor, William, 213
Fenton, Geoffrey, 190, 317
Fiammetta (Boccaccio), 217
fideism, 40
Field, John, 78
Field, Nathan, 331, 334, 341
Field, Richard, 14, 107, 111, 112, 396
figures of speech, 284, 291
Firste Booke of Cattell, The (Mascall), 455
First Part of the Life and Reign of Henry IIII (Hayward), 109, 451, 471, 477, 478, 480
Fisher, William, 46
Fitzgeffrey, Henry, 140
Fleetwood, William, 48, 50
Fletcher, John, 152, 176, 235, 304, 374, 444
    folio of 1647 (with Beaumont), 237, 343
    language usage, 245, 253
Fletcher, Lawrence, 320, 341
Florio, John, 239–41, 242, 248
Florio's First Fruits (Florio), 239
Floyd, Thomas, 454
Foakes, R.A., 342
Folger Shakespeare Library, 150, 200, 455
folios, 439, 456
folklore, 186
fonts, 437, 439, 456
food:
    price controls on, 319
    shortages, 27, 34, 36, 37–8, 41
forensic oratory, 281
Forman, Simon, 207, 358, 359, 360
Form of Christian Policy gathered out of French (Fenton), 317
forms, *see* sheets
Fortescue, John, 124, 125
Fortunatus, 353
Fortune, 303, 372, 383
Fortune by Land and Sea (Heywood), 357
Fortune playhouse, 335, 352
Fortune's Tennis, 353
Four Apprentices of London, The (Heywood), 302
Four-footed Beasts (Topsell), 443
Fowre Bookes of Husbandry (Heresbach), 455

Fowre Bookes on the Institution, Use and Doctrine of the Holy Sacrament (Mornay), 454
Foxe, John, 59, 169, 195–6, 200, 202, 203
Fraunce, Abraham, 280
Frederycke of Jennen, 220
Freeman's Honor, The 353, 354
free will, 40, 60
Friar Bacon and Friar Bungay (Greene), 421
Froissart, John, 167, 187, 203
Frye, Northrop, 498
Furse, Robert, 197
Fussner, F. Smith, 187

Gaiman, Neil, 499–500
galleys, 436, 439
Game at Chess, A, (Middleton), 385, 386
Garden of Eloquence, The (Peacham), 280
Gascoigne, George, 174, 176, 209
Gaskell, Philip, 442, 448
gender theory, 285
genre(s), 18, 100, 297–309
   class valences of, 302
   classical notions of, 184
   dominant, 220
   early modern, 207
   history writing, 100, 187, 190, 193, 195
   manipulation of romance, 217
   materialization of, 302–3, 304
   mixed, 208, 209, 219, 220, 300–1, 302, 303–4, 351–2, 359
   social significance, 299, 301, 304
   "upstart," 210
   uses of, 298–300, 308
gentry class, 44, 46, 47, 103
   families of, 85, 89–90
   houses of, 35, 45, 200
   literacy and reading among, 141, 143, 187, 198–9, 208, 232
   religious affiliations of, 75, 76
   role in government of, 120
   theater venues for, 371, 372
   violence of, 50–1
Geoffrey of Monmouth, 173, 190, 194
Geographical Historie of Africa, The (Africanus), 454
George Scanderbeg, 354
Gerard, John, 29

Gilborne, Samuel, 331, 334, 335
Glapthorne, Henry, 431–2
Globe Theater, 15, 235, 316, 332, 336, 337, 358, 360, 374, 383, 429
   clientele of, 371, 372
   construction of, 352, 369
   description of, 370–1
   finances of, 325, 340
   fire of 1613, 323, 325, 331, 332, 371
   location of, 335
   seasonal use of, 358, 371
   shareholding in, 321, 322, 334, 341, 342
   sign for, 353, 369
Godly Forme of Householde Government, A (Cleaver), 454
God's Holy Minde (Elton), 471
Godwin, Francis, 197, 199
Goldberg, Jonathan, 104
Golburne, John, 455
Golden Age, The (Heywood), 360
Golden Ass, The, 357
Gombrich, E.H., 299
goods, commercial, 37, 44, 45, 46–7, 313, 316
Gorboduc (Norton), 122, 257, 333, 381
Gorgias, 277, 278, 294
Gorgias (Plato), 277–8
Gosson, Stephen, 206, 318
   acting career of, 233
Gosson, Thomas, 212
Gouge, William, 50, 86
Goughe, Alexander, 334, 336, 338
Goughe, Richard, 335
Goughe, Robert, 331, 334, 336, 341
government, 118–9, 120
   court and, 125, 126
   local, 130–2
   of London, 52
   see also monarchy; Parliament; republicanism
Gowrie, 356, 357
Grafton, Richard, 188, 196, 197, 198
grammar, English, 243–8, 251
   in *Merry Wives of Windsor*, 253
   negatives, 245–6
   pronouns, 246–7, 248
   questions, 244–5
   verbs, 244, 248, 249, 250, 258
Grammar (Lily), 457

Gray's Inn, 338
"Great Contract," 33
great vowel shift, 251
Greenblatt, Stephen, 105, 206, 291, 498
Greene, Robert, 12, 176, 208, 212, 213, 236, 313, 421, 439
   attack on Shakespeare, 14, 232–4
   income of, 227
Greene's Tu Quoque, or the City Gallant, 359
Greenwich tennis court, 125, 127–8
Greenwood, John, 468
Gresham, Thomas, 313
Greville, Fulke, 127, 128, 129, 130
Grey, Jane, 26
Grindal, Edmund, 50
Groatsworth of Wit (Greene), 439
Groome-Porters Lawes at Cards, The, 458
Guicciardini, Francesco, 190
guild plays, 354
guilds, 48, 51, 52, 54, 188
Guilpin, Everard, 215, 369
Guinea Company, 320
Gunpowder Plot, 32
Gurr, Andrew, 384, 388
Gurth, Alexander, 212
Gutenberg, Johann Gensfleisch von Hofe zum, 437
Guy of Warwick. 216, 218
Gybson, Leonard, 211
Gydonius (Greene), 217

Haigh, Christopher, 69, 73–4, 75, 76, 78, 79, 80
Hakluyt, Richard, 313, 454
Hakluyt's Voyages (Hakluyt), 313, 454
Hall, Edward, 144, 188, 196, 198, 236
Hall, Joseph, 215
Hamlet (Shakespeare), 15, 16, 110, 146, 150, 160, 216, 353, 354, 371
   Burbage in, 333
   classical influence on, 176, 182, 183
   epistemology in, 41
   in first folio, 384, 395–6, 402
   play within the play, 377, 382
   as problem play, 306
   as Protestant play, 159
   quartos, 395–6, 402, 403, 409
   references to Globe in, 369

as revenge tragedy, 297
staging for, 374
verse in, 261, 262, 264, 266, 269, 270, 273
Hamlet ("Ur"), 347, 348, 351
Hampton Court, 338
Hannibal and Scipio, 354
Hardwick Hall, 35
Harington, John, 373
Harrison, John, 396
Harrison, William, 196–7
Harsnett, Samuel, 468
Hart, Alfred, 474
Hart, Charles, 334
Hart, William, 20
harvest failure, 33, 34, 53, 63, 322
Harvey Gabriel, 15, 149, 197, 202, 203
quarrel with Nashe, 211, 213, 215
Hastings, Sara, 455
Hatton, Christopher, 227
Haughton, William, 229, 230, 303
Haviland, John, 396
Hawkins, Richard, 406
Hayward, John, 109, 114, 189, 191, 199, 386, 451–2, 468, 471, 478, 480
Heminges, John, 14–15, 320, 332, 334, 335, 340–1
acting career of, 332–3
coat of arms, 334, 339
as folio editor, 139, 140, 142, 144, 145, 328, 330, 331, 343, 406, 408, 409, 491–2
Heminges, William, 322
Henrietta Maria (Queen of England), 387, 431
Henry IV Part One (Shakespeare), 15, 168, 348, 352, 355, 358
copia in, 285
publications of, 355, 401, 403, 406, 409
verse in, 259, 267
Henry IV Part Two (Shakespeare), 15, 348, 352, 354
censorship arguments, 474–7, 480
publications of, 401, 461
verse in, 269
word usage in, 250
Henry IV (Shakespeare), 15, 208, 298
Henry V (Branagh), 198

Henry V (Shakespeare), 15, 17, 31, 109, 184, 210, 338, 339, 351, 352, 354, 357, 371
censorship arguments, 477–9
English language in, 253, 254
publications of, 404, 461, 478–9
verse in, 261, 268
Henry VI Part One (Shakespeare), 348, 353, 365, 499
Henry VI Part Two (Shakespeare), 15, 102, 103–4, 113, 143–4, 215, 348, 349, 351, 353
classical references in, 184
quartos, 15, 301, 355, 404, 406, 456
verse in, 265
Henry VI (Shakespeare), 10, 14, 15, 301–2, 354, 355
Henry VI Part Three (Shakespeare), 15, 109, 110, 348, 349, 351, 353
quartos, 15, 302, 355, 401, 404, 406
rhetorical self in, 290
Henry VIII (King of England), 13, 25, 26, 57, 69, 123, 165, 169, 188, 189, 358, 382
Henry VIII (Shakespeare), 15, 16, 19, 110, 146, 160, 297
Globe fire during, 331, 371
Henslowe, Philip, 226, 228, 323, 324, 326, 335, 365, 380, 421
Henslowe's Diary, 227, 320, 324–5, 365
repertorial data, 346, 347, 348, 349, 352, 355, 365, 373
Herbert, Edward, 381
Herbert, George, 13, 381
Herbert, Henry, 380, 381, 386, 387, 388, 423, 428, 429, 430, 431
Herbert, William, 404–5
Hercules, 351, 353
Heresbach, Conrad, 455
Hero and Leander (Marlowe), 210, 257, 258, 457
Herodotus, 193
Hester and Ahasuerus, 347, 348, 352
Heyes, Thomas, 400
Heywood, Thomas, 176, 303–4, 378–9, 384, 424, 427, 428, 439, 443
as actor, 232, 233
attack on Jaggard, 446
Hic Mulier; or The Man Woman, 87–8
hierarchy, social, 37, 40, 46, 47

within book readerships, 139–40, 142
within the court,
in dramatic genres, 302
in language usage, 246–7
literature and, 210, 219
Higden, Ranulf, 187
High Commission, 466, 470–1, 481
Historia de Grisel y Mirabella (De Flores), 217
historical criticism, 4, *see also* New Historicism
historical determinism, 4–5
Historie of Serpents (Topsell), 443
History of the Rebellion (Clarendon), 203
Historie of the Troubles of Hungarie (Fumee), 454, 455
Historie of the Uniting of the Kingdom of Portugall to the Crowne of Castill (Conestaggio), 454
History of the World (Ralegh), 195, 471,
Historie of Tithes (Selden), 192
history, 31, 186–203, 213, 236, 481
cause and effect model of, 189, 191–2
early modern knowledge of, 186, 187, 189, 190
as genre, 101, 187
narrative, 196, 198–9
political and moral uses of, 186, 188–90, 191, 192, 194, 195, 196, 198, 199, 203
quartos, 454
reader responses to, 199–203
relationship to fiction, 193–5, 201
universal, 187
see also chronicle
history plays, 17, 31, 110, 186, 187, 193, 196, 198, 356, 406, 480
audience for, 198
generic instability of, 298, 299, 302
political themes in, 214
Roman, 354, 357
Scottish, 356, 357, 360
see also specific history plays
Histriomastix (Prynne), 375
Hoffman (Chettle), 357
Holinshed, Raphael, 144, 148, 182, 197, 198, 203, 236, 469, 471, 480

Holland, Aaron, 325
Holland, Hugh, 142, 451
Holland, Philemon, 454
holy days, Protestant, 78
'Homily on Obedience' (Church of
    England), 129
homo rhetoricus, 279, 287, 290
homo seriosus, 278
homosexual practices, 97
Honest Man's Fortune, The (Fletcher),
    428–9, 430
Honest Whore, The (Dekker and
    Middleton), 305–9, 357
honor, 125, 127, 128, 129, 130,
    131, 132
Hooker, Richard, 63, 71
Hope Theater, 145, 152, 323
Hopkins, John, 214–15
Horace, 12, 457
horizons of expectation, 299, 303
Hornschuch, Hieronymus, 439,
    443, 448
Hotman, Francois, 465
Hotspurr, The, 358, 359
householders, 48, 53
households, 85–7, 89, 98, 119
    actors retained by, 329, 330
    aristocratic, 147, 148
    religion in, 76, 77
    sexual disruption of, 305
    see also family; marriage
housekeepers, 321, 322, 325, 326
*How a Man May Choose a Good Wife
    from a Bad*, 357
Howard, Frances, 375
Howard, Henry, 189, 209
Howes, Edmund, 45
Howse, Walter, 39
How to Learn of a Woman to Woo
    (anonymous), 357
Huguenots, 109
humanism, 129, 163, 174, 176,
    182–3, 184
    education program, 125, 151,
        162, 172, 280, 281, 282
    historiographic tradition of, 191,
        192, 197, 201
    moral ideals of, 107, 108–9,
        110–12, 114–15, 282
    and selfhood, 287
humanist criticism, 5
human perfectibility, 60
Humble Supplication to her Majestie, A
    (Southwell), 451
Humor out of Breath, 359

Hundreth Sundrie Flowres, A
    (Gascoigne), 209
Hunsdon's Men, 340
Hunter, G.K., 151
Huon de Bordeaux (Berners), 216
husbandry, 92
husbands, 86, 87, 89–90, 97
huswifery, 92, 94; *see also* wives,
    work of
Hutton, Luke, 213
Hyde, John, 339

iambic pentameter, 256, 257–9,
    268, 269
iconoclasm, 77
*If You Know Not Me, You Know
    Nobody* (Heywood), 357
Il Principe (Machiavelli), 189
imitatio, 176, 178
Imitation of Christ, The (Kempis),
    454
imposition, 440, 442, 445
individual, changing conceptions of,
    25, 27, 37, *see also* selfhood
industry, 37, 45
inflation, 33, 34, 35
inheritance, 95
inking, 442–3
Inns of Court, 51, 92, 93, 94, 338,
    381, *see also* law courts
In Praise of the laws of England
    (Fortescue), 124
institutions, 5, 104,
    carceral, 307, 308, *see also* prisons
    government, 118, 119, 307
    Shakespeare as, 489, 490
Institutio oratoria (Quintilian), 280,
    282, 285, 291
intentionality, 5–6
Interpreter, The (Cowell), 469, 470
invention (*inventio*), 101, 102, 104,
    183, 283
Ireland, rebellion in, 31, 109, 388
Iron Age, The (Heywood), 360
Iser, Wolfgang, 299
Islam, 68
Isle of Dogs (Nashe and Jonson), 384
Isle of Gulls (Day), 384
Islip, Adam, 456
Isocrates, 121, 172, 174
    rhetorical culture and, 278, 280,
        294
italic typeface, 437, 445
Italian script, 418, 421, 424, 427,
    430

Jack of Newbury (Deloney), 219
Jaggard, Isaac, 328, 404, 406, 408
Jaggard, William, 404, 444, 446,
    447
James I (King of England), 15, 25,
    28, 40, 41, 46, 47
    and liberty of discourse, 465, 467,
        468–72, 481
    and London disorder, 304–5
    patronage of theater, 235, 331,
        383–4, 356, 372
    political style of, 32–3, 470
    relationship with catholics, 32
    writings of, 130, 242
James, Thomas, 453
Jeronimo, 353, 354
jestbooks, 208, 215, 216
Jestes of Skogyn, The, 215
Jew of Malta, The (Marlowe), 352,
    357, 373
Jews, 38, 158, 181
jigs, 332, 333, 336
Jocasta (Gascoigne and
    Kinwelmershe), 174
John a Kent and John a Cumber
    (Munday), 418–19, 420, 421,
    422, 424
John of Bordeaux (anonymous), 421,
    424
Johnson, Gerald, 405
Johnson, Richard, 211, 219, 220
Johnson, Samuel, 178, 492–3
joint-stock ventures, 319–20, 321,
    322, 324, *see also* shareholding
Jones, Emrys, 103, 104
Jones, William, 112
Jonson, Ben, 25, 193, 219, 332,
    333, 334, 372, 374, 385
    as actor, 232
    address to audiences, 144–5, 149,
        152
    careerism of, 236–7
    cast lists in plays, 340, 341, 343
    and commerical booktrade,
        139–40, 434–5, 461, 462
    folio of, 140, 149, 237, 343, 406
    library of 450, 452
    masques and pageants of, 54, 198,
        332
    prison stay of, 384
    in *Sandman*, 500
    satire writing, 176, 215, 303, 305
    on Shakespeare, 9–11, 14, 16,
        142, 172, 184, 408, 490–1,
        492

social and educational
background, 12, 13
and War of the Theaters, 354
Joseph, Bertram, 343
Jowett, John, 473–7
Joye, George, 170
Jugge, Richard, 435
Julis Caesar (Shakespeare), 17, 102,
103, 109, 110, 147, 159, 353,
354, 357, 358, 360
classicals influences in, 176,
178–9
epideixis in, 281
as problem play, 306
verse in, 265
Julius, Philip, 353
justice, 130, 131, 132
justice system, 34
Juvenal, 12, 457

Kastan, David, 105
Kempe, Philip, 332
Kempe, William, 14, 321, 331–2,
333, 334, 340, 349
Kempe's Nine Daies Wonder, 332
Kennedy, George, 278
King and No King, A (Beaumont and
Fletcher), 358, 359
King and the Subject, The (Massinger),
387, 388
King James Bible, 28
King Johan (Bale), 196
King John (Shakespeare), 15, 31, 196,
348, 352, 359
catechism in, 214
genre of, 298
publication of, 359
verse in, 272
King Lear (Shakespeare), 16, 19, 160,
170–1, 187, 207, 209, 218,
338, 355, 357
Burbage in, 333
censorship arguments, 474, 480
classical influence on, 176, 183
genre of, 298
quartos, 402, 404, 436
verse in, 261, 262, 264, 266, 270,
272
King's New School, 12
King's Revels, 359
Kinwelmershe, Francis, 174
Kipling, Rudyard, 160
Klein, Todd, 500
Knack to Know a Knave, A
(anonymous), 349, 352, 360

Knack to Know an Honest Man, A
(anonymous), 352, 360, 373
Knell, William, 334
Knight, Edward, 429, 430
Knight of the Burning Pestle, The
(Beaumont), 302
Knot of Fools, The, 358, 359
knowledge, 41, 291
contingency of, 286
rhetoric and, 278, 279, 282, 286
transmission of, 450, 451
Knyvett, Thomas, 455
Kott, Jan, 9
Kyd, Thomas, 12, 176, 234

labor, laborers, 34, 37, 48, 52, 91,
148, 161
agricultural, 35, 92
coerced, 49, 307
in *Shoemaker's Holiday*, 305
Labors of Hercules, The, 353
Lady Elizabeth's players, 335, 360,
427, 428
Lady Mother, The (Glapthorne), 427,
431–2
Lambarde, William, 192
"Lamentation of Beccles" (Deloney),
211
landed classes, 35–6, 93–4, 103,
121
Lane, John, 462
Laneman, Henry, 322
Langland, William, 160
Langley, Francis, 322, 323, 324, 325
Lanham, Richard, 278–9, 280
Lanquet, Thomas, 188
Larum for London, A (anonymous),
353, 354
Latimer, Hugh, 26
Latin, 160, 167, 168
English borrowings from, 249,
252, 253
as language of writing, 241, 248
Shakespeare's lack of, 10, 11, 172
Laudianism, 75
Launching of the Mary, The
(Mountfort), 423, 430–1
La Vita Nuova (Dante), 209
Law, Matthew, 406, 408
law, 78, 92, 118, 143
law books, 150, 455, 467, 469
law courts, 45, 131, 470
in city comedies, 305, 307
classical, 280
language of, 241, 248

see also Inns of Court
*Lawes and Statutes of the Stannaries of
Devon, The*, 455
Lawier's Logike, A (Fraunce), 280
lawyers, 121, 191, 192, 193, 208,
371
Leake, William, 396
legend, 187, 190–1, 194, 213
Legend of Humphrey Duke of Glocester
(Middleton), 462
Leicester's Commonwealth, 469
Leicester's Men, 330
Leius, Mathias, 455
Leland, John, 194
Leslie, John, 469
LeStrange, Nicholas, 94
Letter to Sir Henry Savile, A (Bacon),
103
Letting of Humours Blood in the Vaine,
451
Levant Company, 37, 320, 324
Levin, Harry, 498
Lewis, Richard, 455
liberty, 122, 123, 125, 127, 129,
133
licensing of print, 452, 453, 462,
465, 471, 473, 481
fees, 465
violation of regulations, 465
see also authorization of texts;
censorship
licensing of theater, 377–88
fees, 380
flouting of regulations, 384, 386
of playing places, 379
see also censorship of theater;
Revels, Master of; Revels,
Office of
*Life and Death of Gamaliell Ratsey,
The*, 215
*Life and Pranks of Long Meg of
Westminster, The*, 215
linguistic purity, 240, 248
Lipsius, Justus, 107, 108, 109, 111,
114
literacy, 47, 53, 91, 139, 202, 227
anxieties about spread of, 140, 169
book trade and, 457
multi-lingual, 453
partial, 141, 142
rates of, 140–1, 169
reading vs writing, 141
representations of, 139
as site of social conflict, 143–4,
146

Literacy and the Social Order (Cressy), 140–1
literature:
domestic, 454–5
pocket, 164, 454, 456, 458
literature, English vernacular, 206–20, 241, 300
bestsellers, 208
book trade in, 452–3
cheap forms of, 210, 211
continental influences on, 216–17
didacticism of, 212, 213, 218
erotic, 210, 212
mixed genres of, 208, 209, 219, 220
religious, 208, 214–215, *see also* books, religious
see also specific genres
livery companies, *see* guilds
Lives (Clarke), 74
Lives (Plutarch), 176, 180
Livy, 180, 197, 202, 203, 454, 457
Loades, David, 328
Locrine (Shakespeare apocrypha), 400–1, 412
Lodge, Thomas, 208, 232, 233, 234
Lollards, 162
London Prodigal, The (Shakespeare apocrypha), 356, 357, 401, 412
lord mayor of London, 44, 45, 51, 188, 219, 379
Love's Labor's Lost (Shakespeare), 10, 15, 106, 142, 167, 209, 348, 351
classical influence on, 183
language usage in, 248, 250
publication of, 236, 401, 409
Love's Labor's Won (Shakespeare), 15, 348, 351
Lowin, John, 15, 331, 334, 335, 336, 341
Lucian of Samosata, 190
Lumley, Jane, 174
Luther, Martin, 40, 163
Lutheranism, 28, 163, 165
Lyly, John, 176, 208, 209

Macbeth (Shakespeare), 14, 16, 17, 33, 160, 171, 174, 187, 339, 355, 357, 358, 359, 360
classical influences on, 174, 176, 181–2
collaboration in writing of, 235
linguistic doubleness in, 293
selfhood in, 287

verse in, 256, 261, 266, 270, 272
Machiavelli, Machiavellianism, 107, 109, 189, 195, 199, 203, 287, 289–90
Maid's Tragedy, The (Beaumont and Fletcher), 358, 360
Maire of Bristowe is Calendar, The, (Ricart), 188
Maison Rustique or the Countrie Farme, (Estienne and Thibault), 454–5
Malcolm King of Scots, 357
Malcontent, The (Marston), 353, 356, 357, 444
Mamillia (Greene), 217
Manningham, John, 338, 349
manuscripts, 243, 395, 406, 414, 444, 450
commercial trade in, 457, 460, 461, 462
see also playbooks, manuscript
Manwood, John, 455
Manwood, Peter, 455
marginalia, 149–51
market, 131, 215, 313
money, 316
Marlowe, Christopher, 25, 105, 176, 210, 226, 233, 373, 457
death of, 234
meter used by, 256, 257
university career of, 12, 13, 232
marriage, 17, 18, 97, 98
age at first, 86
bigamous, 89
breakdowns of, 88–9
laws on, 96
parental role in, 85, 94–5
in stage plays, 17, 18, 303, 308, 356, 357
of stage players, 334
of widows, 50
Marston, John, 145, 172, 174, 215, 304, 356, 443–4
Martin, Gregory, 468
Martin, Roger "The Recusant," 29
Martin Marprelate conflict, 211, 215, 468, 469, 472
Mary Stuart (Queen of Scotland), 30, 57, 63, 68, 322, 469
Mary Tudor (Queen of England), 26, 64, 165, 169, 186, 195
Mascall, Leonard, 455
Masque of Christmas (Jonson), 332
Massacre at Paris (Marlowe), 354
Massinger, Philip, 381, 386, 387, 388, 421, 427, 428, 429–30

masterless men, *see* vagrants, vagrancy
matrix, 437
Maxims of State, The (Ralegh), 118
McDonald, Russ, 207
McKellen, Ian, 198
McKenzie, D.F., 457, 458, 459
Measure for Measure (Shakespeare), 17, 38, 54, 158–9, 338, 355, 357
as city play, 304, 305–6, 307–9
elision of middling sort, 308
imprisonment in, 214
as problem play, 298, 306
sexual bodies in, 305
verse in, 262, 265, 266, 267, 273
Mechanick Exercises on the Whole Art of Printing (Moxon), 436
memoria, 283, 285
"Men of Good Fortune," (Gaiman), 499
Merchant Adventurers, 320
Merchant of Venice, The (Shakespeare), 15, 17, 55, 158, 338, 348, 351, 352, 356
quartos, 398–400, 401, 404, 461
rhetoric explored in, 291–4
romance elements in, 219, 220
verse in, 272
merchants, 46, 91, 148, 208, 219, 232, 313
Meres, Francis, 298, 455
Merrie conceited jests (Peele), 215
Merry Devil of Edmonton (anonymous), 349, 353, 354, 356, 358, 359
Merry Wives of Windsor, The (Shakespeare), 12, 15, 88, 147, 338, 348, 351, 356, 358, 359
classical influence on, 176, 183
English language in, 253–5
publications of, 404, 406, 409
Metamorphoses (Ovid), 146, 176, 177–8, 180
metaphor, 291, 293
metatheatricality, 374, 375–6
meter, 245, 256–75
amphibrachs, 263, 264
anapests, 265
broken-backed lines, 266, 273
caesuras, 267, 268
contrary stress, 263, 274
double ending, 264
epic caesuras, 264, 265, 273
feminine endings, 263

headless lines, 266, 273
heavy ending, 263
iambic pentameter, 256, 257–9,
    268, 269
iambic variations, 258–9, 260–3,
    273
midline breaks, 268–9
mimetic, 257
pyrrhics, 259, 260–2
spondees, 259, 260–2
squinting lines, 273
syllabic variations, 263–7, 273
trochees, 259, 260–2, 263, 269
see also verse
Methodus (Bodin), 193
metonymy, 284
Meyrick, Gelly, 456, 475
Microcosmos (Davies), 336
Midas (Lyly), 208
Middle English, 248, 249
Middle Temple, 338, 349
Middleton Christopher, 462
Middleton, Thomas, 46, 54, 301,
    305, 372, 375, 425, 444
    contributions to *Macbeth*, 235
    prison stay of, 386
midlife crisis, 18
"Midsummer Night's Dream, A"
    (Gaiman), 499
Midsummer Night's Dream, A
    (Shakespeare), 15, 150, 159,
    207, 348, 351, 377–8
    classical influence on, 176, 178,
        183
    publications of, 401, 404, 461
    verse in, 256, 258, 261, 268
Mildmay, Grace, 197
Millenary Petition (1603), 28
Millington, Thomas, 400, 434, 479
Milton, John, 100, 106, 278
Mineral and Battery Works, 320
Minte of Deformities, The (C.G.), 462
Mirror for Magistrates, A, 219
miscellanies, 208
Miscellany (Tottel), 146, 209, 257
Miseries of Enforced Marriage, The
    (Wilkins), 356, 357, 359
misogyny, 18
Mocket, Richard, 471
monarchy, 114
    absolutist, 307, 384, 470, *see also*
        divine right of kings
    court's relationship to, 126, 129,
        130
    and republicanism, 120, 125, 130

subject's relationship to, 129–30
monasteries, 25, 26, 53
monopolies, 37, 467, 481
Montagu, Elizabeth, 493–5
Montaigne, Michel de, 40, 107–8,
    109–10, 114, 207, 453
Montemayor, 236, 453
More, Thomas, 123–4, 160, 167,
    169, 196, 236
Morgante (Pulci), 217
Morte d'Arthur (Malory), 216
mothers, suffocating, 17–18
Mountfort, Walter, 423, 430–1
Moxon, Joseph, 436–40, 442–8
Mucedorus, 349, 356, 359
Much Ado About Nothing
    (Shakespeare), 15, 17, 159,
        208, 331, 348, 358, 359, 461
    language usage in, 248
    publications of, 401, 406
Mulcaster, Richard, 241, 242, 248
Munday, Anthony, 211, 216, 217,
    232, 233, 317, 418–19, 420,
    422
Muscovy Company, 320, 324
music, 368, 369, 418, 424–5, 430,
    431
mystery plays, 182, 378

Nashe, Thomas, 12, 48, 176, 197,
    208, 209, 219, 233, 234, 313,
    436
    quarrel with Gabriel Harvey, 211,
        213, 215
nationalism, 25, 31, 58, 80, 103,
    198
*Natural and Artificial Directions for
    Health* (Vaughan), 455–6
Neavoll, George, 497
Neely, Carol, 498
neighborhood, notions of, 79
New Bibliography, 444
New Historicism, 104–6, 207, 304
Newman, Karen, 47
New Organon, The (Bacon), 40
news, 212, 213, 214, 220
*News from the New World Discovered in
    the Moon* (Jonson), 198
Nice Valour, The (Middleton and
    Fletcher), 444
Nine Worthies of London (Johnson),
    219, 220
nobility:
    education of, 93–4
    families of, 85, 89–90

role in government, 120
Nobleman, The, 358
Norden, John, 214
North, Thomas, 175, 176, 178,
    179, 180
Northbrooke, John, 317
Northern Rebellion (1569), 29, 30,
    76, 122, 322
Northward Ho (Dekker and
    Webster), 303, 305
Norton, John, 453
Norton, Thomas, 122–3
"Now Chrect me save, Poor Irish
    Knave" (Shank), 336
Nowell, Alexander, 214

octavos, 439, 440, 456
Office of the Chamber, 358, 360
Of the Colours of Good and Evil
    (Bacon), 101
Oglander, John, 87
Okes, Nicholas, 436, 446
Olander, P. J., 468
Oldcastle, John, 162
Old English, 241, 249
Olney, Henry, 455
O'Neill, Hugh, 31
On Types of Style (Hermogenes), 284
oral culture, 144, 186, 199
Oration on the Dignity of Man
    (Mirandola), 287–8
Organon (Aristotle), 41
Orlando Furioso (Ariosto), 216, 217
Orlando Innamorato (Boiardo), 217
Orlin, Lena Cowen, 147
ornament, 291–4
Orthotypographia (Hornschuch), 443
Ostler, Beaumont, 335
Ostler, William, 331, 333, 334,
    335, 341, 342
Othello (Shakespeare), 10, 16, 18, 19,
    152, 160, 355, 358, 360
    Burbage in, 333
    classical sources for, 176
    publications of, 385, 405, 406,
        409
    verse in, 261, 262, 267, 270, 272
Overbury, Thomas, 336, 344
Ovid, 12, 15, 106–7, 146, 172, 176,
    177–8, 180, 183–4, 278
Oxford English Dictionary, 249
Oxford's Men, 354
Oxford University Press, 447–8
Oxinden, Henry, 151
oxymoron, 284

pageants, 45, 46, 54
Palladis Tamia (Meres), 298
Palmerin de Oliva, 216–17
Palmerin of England, 216, 217
pamphlets, 208, 210, 211, 212–14,
219, 220, 452, 457, 458, 472
anti-theatrical, 212, 225, 226
Pandosto (Greene), 217
Paradise of Daintie Devices, The, 209
paradox, 284
Paraeus, Daniel, 471
parishes, 52, 53, 54, 77
Parismus (Forde), 217
Parker, John, 396
Parker, Patricia, 291
Parliament, 93, 470
and censorship, 468–9, 481
functions of, 123–4
House of Commons, 120–1, 122,
124, 125, 388
language of, 241, 248
poor laws of, 34
in *Richard II*, 480
and taxation, 33, 123, 387
and theater, 379, 383, 384–5,
388, 389
usury laws of, 38, 39
Parliament of Love, The (Massinger),
421, 427
Parsons, Robert, 57, 59–60, 61, 64,
66, 71, 75, 469, 476, 479
Partridge, John, 455
Passionate Pilgrim. The, 410
Paster, Gail, 498
pastorals, 351, 356, 359
Patient Grissell (Chettle, Dekker,
Haughton), 229, 230, 236,
357
patriarchy, 49, 496
family as, 86, 87, 89
patronage, 336, 338, 461
of literature, 227
of theatre, 235, 315, 320, 328–9,
331, 338–40, 363, 367, 379,
383, 388
Patterson, Annabel, 382, 477–9
Paul's playhouse:
boy companies at, 303, 352, 372,
380, 383
performances at, 357
Pavier, Thomas, 403–5, 478
Peacham, Henry, 280
peasants, 44, 129
Peasants' Revolt (1381), 144
Peele, George, 215, 233, 234

Pembroke's Men, 349
Penry, John, 468
Pensive Mans Practice (Norden), 214,
454
Pepys, Samuel, 147
Perambulation of Kent, A (Lambarde),
192
Perfite platforme of a Hoppe Garden, A
(Scot), 444
performance, *see* playing
performance copyright, 381
performance theory, 285
and stage genres, 302, 303, 304
Pericles (Shakespeare), 16, 19, 176,
298, 355, 358, 374
contemporary popularity of,
219–20, 358
publications of, 358, 401–2, 403,
404, 406, 412
verse in, 265
Perkins, William, 25, 40
Perne, Andrew, 63, 64
peroratio, 284
personification, 284, 293
Petie Schole, The (Clement), 216
Petite Palace of Pettie his Pleasure
(Pettie), 208
Petrarch, 209, 278
philanthropy, 25
Philaster (Beaumont and Fletcher),
358, 359
Phillip II (King of Spain), 26, 30
Phillips, Augustine, 15, 320, 321,
325, 331, 332, 334, 341
testimony in Essex affair, 339,
353
will of, 335
Phillips, Margery, 334
Philotas (Daniel), 384
Phoenix playhouse, 322, 323, 357,
427, 428
phonology, English, 250–2
great vowel shift, 251
spelling and, 250–1
stress patterns, 252
variations in pronunciation, 251,
258
pica roman typeface, 456
Picture of a Perfit Common Wealth, A
(Floyd), 454
piracy, 319
plague, 36, 48, 54, 63, 69, 305, 323
theater closures, 228, 234, 324,
325, 337, 347, 355, 356,
357–8, 359, 369, 396, 432

Plaine Man's Pathway to Heaven, 214
Plan of True Theology (Erasmus), 288
Plato, 278, 286, 289, 292
Platter, Thomas, 87
Plautus, 12, 15, 172, 173, 176,
182–3
playbooks, manuscript, 414–33,
472, 473
physical construction of, 415–16,
430, 432
relationship to performance, 417,
418, 419, 425, 428
speech headings, 416, 418, 420,
421, 424, 426, 428, 430, 432
theatrical alterations, 416–17,
418–19, 421, 422, 423, 424,
426, 427, 428, 429, 430, 431,
432
see also playwrights, advisory
directions of; promptbooks
playhouses:
admission costs to, 144–5, 326,
365, 366, 368
boxes, 368
building of, 315, 316, 322, 324,
330, 337
clientele of, 368, 371–2
closures of, 228, 234, 324, 325,
326, 331, 337, 347, 355, 356,
357–8, 359, 369, 378, 388,
389, 396, 432
financing for, 321, 322, 325, 326,
334, 340, 342
galleries, 326, 363, 364, 365,
366, 367, 368, 370, 371
indoor stages, 363, 367, 368, 372
lighting of, 374, 376
licensing of, 380
locations of, 335–6, 379
open-air, 363, 365, 369, 372
"private" vs. "public," 369, 375
spectators of, 139, 149, 152, 317,
338, 359, 371
stages, 362, 363, 364, 366,
368–9, 371
tiring houses, 326, 363, 368
yards, 363, 364, 366, 371
playing:
anti-realistic, 375, 376
as collaborative enterprise, 5, 206,
228, 229, 230, 235, 301, 398,
400, 409, 415, 425–6, 472, 481
criticism of, 145, 226, 231, 235,
300–1, 316, 317–19, 374,
375, 376

economics of, 229, 313–26,
340–2, *see also* shareholding
genre materialization through,
302, 303, 304
in hall and inns, 330, 338, 362,
363, 381
in households, 148, 338, 381
moneylending and history of,
315–17, 319
see also drama
plays:
lost, 372–3, 374
printing rights for, 228, 396,
404, 405, 406, 408
plays, published, 5, 144, 150, 152,
417
playwrights' names on, 236,
396–7, 401–3, 404, 405, 412
readership of, 145, 418
relationship between performance
and, 145, 396, 403
see also playbooks, manuscript;
promptbooks
Plays Confuted in Five Actions
(Gosson), 206, 318
"play within the play," 374
playwrights, 315
advisory directions of, 417,
418–19, 420, 421, 422, 425,
427, 428, 429, 431
class backgrounds of, 232
courtier, 387
rivalries among, 230, 232–4
university educated, 13, 230,
232–4, 236
playwriting, 225–32
as collaborative activity, 228, 229,
230, 235, 301, 419, 421, 439,
472, 481
demand for, 226–7, 320
forms of dramatic speech in, 233
payment for, 226, 227–8, 320
process of, 229, 230
reputation of, 225, 232, 237
for specific companies and stages,
372–3, 374
see also playbooks, manuscript
Plutarch, 18, 172, 176, 178–9,
180
*Poems, By J.D. With Elegies on the
Authors Death*, 410
Poems: Written by Wil. Shake-speare
(Benson), 409–10
Poetaster (Jonson), 354
Poetics (Aristotle), 194–5

poetry, vernacular, 209–10, *see also*
verse
polemic, 150, 175
policy, 102, 107, 108, 111, 112,
113, 114, 115
Politics (Aristotle), 107, 119, 121–2
Pollard, Thomas, 334
Polychronicon (Higden), 187–8
Ponsonby, William, 461
poor, 34–5, 48, 305
families of, 85
laws concerning, 34, 305
relief, 52, 53, 54, 339, 379, *see
also* charity
Pope, Alexander, 493
Pope Clement VIII, 32
Pope, Thomas, 14, 321, 331, 332,
334, 340, 341
popery, 27, 60, 61, 63, 65, 66, 67,
68, 70, 76, 78, 80, 169
popular culture, 67, 68, 187, 220
boundaries between elite and,
209–10, 211, 216, 219, 236
literature, 207, 217, 219
population:
of England, 34
of London, 43–4, 305
of London suburbs, 48, 305
Portland Press Herald, 497
Posies, The (Gascoigne), 209
postmodernism, 193, 195
Prayer Book Religion, 27, 76, *see also*
Church of England
prayer books, 26, 27, 77, 165, 458,
467, *see also* books, religious
Presbyterians, Presbyterianism, 27,
61, 62, 78
pressmen, 436, 437, 442–3, 445,
447, 448, 459
Pretious Booke of Heavenly Meditations
(Augustine), 454
Primaleon, 216, 217
Prince Charles II's company, 321, 424
Prince Charles's company, 321, 335,
360
Prince Henry's company, 355, 359,
383
Prince of Bohemia (Forde), 217
Prince, The (Machiavelli), 107, 287,
289–90
print culture, 107, 395, 434
attitudes towards, 143–4, 146
cultural significance of, 456–7
see also book trade; printers;
printing

printers, 14, 107, 436–7, 438, 462
infractions of 448
numbers of in London, 435, 451
printing errors and, 443, 444,
445–7
profits made by, 227, 313, 448,
457
see also individual printers
printing, 143, 434–48
of bibles, 169, 453, 458
censorship of, 382, 384, 451,
456, 462, 465, 466, 468, 472,
473, 474, 476–7, 478, 479,
480, 481
collaborative, 456
edition sizes, 458
genre materialiation through,
301, 304
houses, 438, 443, 445, 447–8,
450, 459, 460–1
of plays, 373, 436, 440, 445, 451,
456, 458, 472, 473
press, 144, 436, 437, 443, 447,
459
process, 436, 437–48
rights for, 228, 396, 404, 405,
406, 408
under royal patent, 467, 471, 481
and standardization of English,
242–3, 248
print, liberty of, 464, 465
prisons, 305, 307
privacy, 147, 149
problem plays, 297, 298, 306
*Proceeding in the Harmony of King
David's Harp, A* (Robinson),
227
prodigal plays, 354
production:
craft, 52
in the household, 85, 86
promptbooks, 230, 414, 415, 417,
419, 432, 472, *see also*
playbooks, manuscript
proofreading, 439, 443–5, 456, 459,
461
"Proofs of Holy Writ" (Kipling),
160
properties, 320, 321, 362, 417,
422–3, 426, 430, 431
bar, 426
bed, 422, 426
scaffold, 426
scenery, 362, 376
table, 426, 430

prostitutes, prostitution, 49, 55, 97, 305
Protestants, Protestantism, 25–6, 27, 28, 50, 58, 59–64, 66–8, 122
  anti-theatricality of, 226
  and book trade, 454
  as term, 58, 72
  as word-centered, 77
  English as language of, 241
  French, 109, 465
  interiors of churches, 76
  popular culture and, 67, 68
  popular potential of, 53–4, 71, 79
  and press censorship, 468, 469
  and Puritanism, 59–60, 61–2, 71, 75, 76
  reformist, 68–70, 469
  ritual practices of, 77–8
  skepticism and, 40
  under Mary Tudor, 26, 69
Proud Maid's Tragedy, The, 360
providentialism, 54, 68–9, 72, 78, 79, 182, 189, 195
Prynne, William, 375, 386
psalters, 208
public space, 76, 77
publishers, 436, 437, 447, 460–1, 462
  numbers of, 459
  infractions of, 448
  vs. printers, 435
Pudsey, Edward, 152
Pueriles Sententiae (Culmann), 457
punch, 437
puns, 254, 285
purgatory, 25, 26, 76
Puritans, Puritanism, 27, 28, 39, 40, 58, 62–3, 64, 70, 388, 453
  anti-theatricality of, 226
  as term of abuse, 58, 62
  Church Papists viewed by, 66–7
  and clothing laws, 37
  complaint literature of, 60, 72, 78, 80
  gentry, 75
  historiography of, 74
  James I relationship with, 32, 33
  political power of, 75–6
  popular culture and, 67, 68
  prosecutions of, 78
  as reformist, 27, 28, 59–60, 70, 80
  relationship to Church of England, 63, 65, 71, 75, 76

  relationship to Protestantism, 58, 61–2, 75, 76
Puritan, The (Shakespeare apocrypha), 412
Puttenham, George, 280, 289, 291, 294, 300
Pym, John, 388
pyrrhics, 259, 260–2

quartos:
  cost of, 326
  histories, 454
  Pavier, 402, 403–5
  playtext, 15, 145, 152, 184, 408, 409, 456, 472
  production of, 439, 440, 441, 445, 452
  title pages, 347, 349, 355, 398–400, 401, 402–3, 404
Queen Anne's company, 321, 349, 357, 359, 360, 383, 384
Queen of Corinth, The (Fletcher), 343
Queen's Men, 330, 333, 352, 362, 365, 379, 380
Quiney, Thomas, 13, 19, 20
Quintilian, 121, 172, 173
  on rhetoric, 282, 284–5, 291, 292

Rackin, Phyllis, 198
Ralegh, Walter, 25, 100, 118, 195, 385
Ram Alley (Barry), 359
Ramus, Peter, 40, 212
Rape of Lucrece, The (Heywood), 360
Rape of Lucrece, The (Shakespeare), 12, 14, 15, 106, 107, 111–13
  classical sources for, 176
  language use in, 245, 250
  meter of, 257, 263, 269
  publications of, 396–7, 402, 461, 468
Rasmussen, Eric, 439
reading, 141
  of the Bible, 168–9
  'extensive,' 203
  practices of, 147–52, 202, 203
  represented in plays, 145–7
  see also literacy
reason, 40, 41
reason of state theory, *see* policy
rebellion, 36, 474–6, 479, *see also* Northern Rebellion; riots
Rebhorn, Wayne, 294
reception criticism, 299

Red Bull playhouse, 303, 322, 323, 325, 372, 427
Red Lion playhouse, 366, 378
Reformation, 25, 26, 27, 29, 31, 39, 67, 73, 80, 164, 165, 169, 170
  dissolution of religious houses, 25, 26, 53, 201
  revisionist reinterpretations of, 59, 72
Reformation of Manners, 27–8
Refutation of the Apology for Actors, A (I.G.), 318
Reges, Reginae, Nobiles, & alij Ecclesia Collegiata . . . (Camden), 455
regime of consent, 124, 125
Regnans in excelsis, 29
religion, 26–30, 41, 57–80
  definitions of, 60, 61, 72–3, 75
  popular, 72, 75
  voluntary, 74, 75, 77, 78
religious change, 25–7, 39, 57, 58, 59
religious literature, 107, 208, 214–15, 451, 452, 453, 454, 455, 458, 464, *see also* Bible(s); sermons
religious pluralism, 27, 29, 57–8, 60, 64
Remains (Camden), 192
Repentance (Greene), 212
reproduction, 305, *see also* wet nursing
republicanism, 114
  monarchical, 120, 125, 130
Resolved Christian, The (Powell), 454
Return from Parnassus, 435, 443
Revels, Master of, 336, 367, 372, 375, 377, 381, 387, 419–20, 425, 428, 480
  matter censored by, 381–3, 385, 387, 388, 426–7, 430, 473
  role of, 378, 379, 380, 382–3, 386, 388, 425–6, 431
  see also censorship of plays
Revels, Office of, 358, 360, 378, 385–6, 425, 431, 473, 474, 481
Revels, Yeoman of, 336
Revenger's Tragedy, The (Tourneur), 303, 356, 357
rhetoric, 101–4, 110, 114, 121, 166, 173, 175, 183, 184, 277–94
  audience of, 280–1, 282
  criticism of, 278, 289, 292

defenses of, 278, 282–3, 289, 294
deliberative, 280–1
epideictic, 281
five stages of, 283–5
forensic, 281
as persuasion, 277, 278, 282
relationship to action, 282
Renaissance, 281, 283, 285
truth and, 278, 286, 294
Rhetoric (Aristotle), 277, 278, 283
Rhetorica (Talaeus), 457
Ricart, Robert, 188
Rice, John, 331, 334, 336
Rich, Barnaby, 213
Richard Crookback (Jonson), 355
Richard II (King of England), 188, 189
Richard II (Shakespeare), 15, 109, 159, 187, 189, 208, 214, 348, 351, 353, 356
  abdication scene, 382–3, 473, 479, 480
  censorship arguments, 479–80
  English language in, 253
  Essex Rebellion and, 31–2, 332, 339, 353, 382
  genre of, 298
  publications of, 382, 403, 406, 409, 472–3
  verse in, 266
Richard III (McKellen), 198
Richard III (Shakespeare), 10, 14, 15, 17, 348, 351, 353, 354
  Burbage in, 333
  classical sources for, 176
  genre of, 298, 299
  publications of, 355, 406, 408
  verse in, 263
rime royal, 257, 269, 271
riots, 49, 382, 419, 479
  apprentice, 36, 51, 97, 228
  food, 36, 41, 51
  playhouse, 323, 324
Rise of the Common Player, The (Bradbrook), 329–30
Risley, Susan, 455
Roaring Girl, The (Middleton), 359
Robert King of Scots, 357
Robin Goodfellow, 356
Robinson, Richard, 227, 228, 331, 333, 334, 335, 341
Roe, John, 455
Roman plays, 354, 357, 359–60
romances, 208, 211, 216–20, 456
  as corrupting, 210, 216

influence on plays, 217, 236
  Shakespeare's, 297, 298, 358
roman typeface, 142, 456
Romeo and Juliet (Shakespeare), 10, 15, 142–3, 209, 298, 331, 348, 351, 352, 353, 354
  Burbage, 333
  classical influence on, 183
  publications of, 359, 406
  source for, 206, 236
  staging for, 374
  verse in, 261, 270
Room of One's Own, A (Woolf), 495–6
Rosalynde (Lodge), 217
Rose playhouse, 226, 320, 362, 367, 371, 374
  construction of, 322
  cost of, 323, 365
  description of, 363–5
  location of, 363, 367
  plays performed at, 349, 352, 357, 373, 421
  records of, 324–5, 346, 347, 365
Rosseter, Philip, 322
Rowe, Nicholas, 12, 178
Rowlands, Samuel, 375
Rowley, William, 301

Sackville, Thomas, 13
Salisbury Court, 431, 432, 439
salvation, models of, 25, 28, 40
Samwell, Richard, 322
Sanctuaries of a Troubled Soule, The (Hayward), 451–2
Sanders, Nicholas, 29
Sandman, The (Gaiman), 499–500
Sands, James, 334
Sandys, George, 175
Santa Claus, 489, 490
satire, 210, 212
  censorship of, 215, 471
Satiromastix (Dekker), 353, 354
Satyres and Satyrical Epigrams (Jonson), 139–40
Savage, Jerome, 322
Savile, Henry, 109, 114, 197
Scaliger, Joseph Justus, 191
Scoloker, Anthony, 15
Scot, Reginald, 444
Scourge of Villanie, The (Marston), 215
scribes, 416, 421, 424, 427, 429, 431, 434
scriveners, 425–6, 460, 461
Seaven Sermons (Thomas), 458

Second and Third Blast of Retrait from Plays and Theatres, 317–18
Second Maiden's Tragedy, The (anonymous), 358, 360, 385, 425–6
secretary hand, 418, 421, 424, 427
Sejanus (Jonson), 332, 333, 356, 357, 372
Selden, John, 173, 192, 193, 452
self-fashioning, 64, 126, 287, 288–90, 291
selfhood, 147, 149
  rhetoric and, 278, 279, 287–90, 293
Seneca, 12, 15, 104, 108, 122, 173, 176, 178, 180, 181, 182
sententiae, 151
Separatists, 58, 62, 63
Sermon of Repentance, A (Dent), 454
sermons, 98, 187, 190, 208, 214
servants, service, 46, 52, 85, 87, 88, 92, 93, 94
  sexual exploitation of, 96–7
Sextus Empiricus, 40
sexual actvity:
  of apprentices, 50, 97
  in city comedies, 305, 306
  and consumer goods, 47, 97
  illicit, 88, 96–8, 307, 379
Shakespeare, Anne Hathaway, 13, 20, 489
Shakespeare, Edmund, 19
Shakespeare, Hamnet, 14, 18
Shakespeare, John, 11–12, 18, 25, 27
Shakespeare, Judith, 14, 19
Shakespeare, Mary Arden, 12
Shakespeare, Susanna, 13, 19
Shakespeare, William:
  as actor, 11, 14, 15, 16, 225, 226, 232, 331, 398
  as author, 396, 400–3, 404, 405, 409, 412, 490
  character of, 9, 14, 491
  cultural prestige of, 3, 497, 498–9, 501
  education of, 172, 180, 184
  as genius, 5, 206, 235, 490, 491, 497, 499, 500
  idolatry of, 9, 498
  intellectual thought of, 109–10, 114
  as landowner, 35–6, 41, 235
  last will and testament of, 13, 335
  marketing of, 395, 397, 412

Shakespeare, William: (*contd.*)
  marriage and family of, 13, 14,
    19–20, 489, 496
  as moral philosopher, 494–5
  political thought of, 100–1,
    104–6, 109, 112, 114–15
  religious sympathies of, 54, 114
  as shareholder, 234–5, 320, 321,
    325, 340, 341
  social background of, 11–12, 13,
    496
  as social institution, 489, 490
  as 'upstart crow,' 14, 234
  wealth of, 235
Shakespeare, William–work of:
  apocrypha, 401
  biblical references in, 158–9,
    170–1
  classical influence in, 176–84
  deceit as theme in, 110–14
  eighteenth-century responses to,
    4, 492–5, 498
  family life and, 496, 498
  illiteracy represented in, 142–4
  language in, 249–50, 253, 255,
    492–3, 495
  meter in, 256–75
  Norton edition, 498
  plays of, *see specific plays*
  poems of, 396–8, 409–10, *see also
    specific poems*
  popular voice embodied in, 492,
    493, 494, 495, 496, 497
  reading represented in, 139,
    145–7
  rhetoric explored in, 290–4
  Riverside edition, 498
  as universal, 4, 11, 17, 18, 490,
    491, 495, 496
  value to book trade, 461–2
  vernacular sources for, 206–7,
    216, 220, 494, 495
Shakespeare folio (1623), 10, 237,
    328, 374, 384, 405–9, 410,
    472, 491–2
  actors' list, 328, 329, 333, 343–4
  commendatory poems of, 142,
    408, 490
  genre categories of, 184, 297–8,
    301–2, 304, 306, 308
  ownership of, 149, 150
  and Pavier collection, 405–6
  price of, 408
  readers of, 139, 140, 142, 144,
    150

Shakespeare folio (1632), 409, 410,
    412
Shakespeare folio (1663/4), 401,
    402, 410, 412
Shakespeare folio (1684/5), 401,
    410, 412
Shakespeare and the Classical Tradition
    (Velz), 172–3
Shakespeare Our Contemporary (Kott),
    9
Shakespeare's History Plays (Tillyard),
    106
"Shakespeare's Metrical Art"
    (Wright), 260
shaming rituals, 87
Shank, John, 322, 331, 334, 335,
    336, 341
Shank's Ordinary (Shank), 336
shareholding:
  in acting companies, 14, 15, 320,
    321, 325, 326, 340–2
  in playhouses, 321, 322, 325,
    326, 334, 340, 341, 342
  sheets, 436, 439–40, 442, 447
Shelburye, John, 455
Shepheardes Calender, The (Spenser),
    241
Sherry, Richard, 280
Shirley, James, 386
Shoemaker's Holiday, The (Dekker),
    305, 354
Shore's Wife, 355
Short, Peter, 456
Short-Title Catalogue, 173, 214, 457
Shrove Tuesday, 97
Sidney, Philip, 13, 25, 100, 133,
    175, 195, 209, 322
  continental influences on work of,
    217
  on genre, 300–1
  at the Greenwich tennis court,
    125, 127–30
  and historiography, 190, 194–5,
    197
  Kempe's relationship with, 332
  literary tastes of, 210, 211,
    218
  poetic meter used by, 259
Sidney, Robert, 353
signatures, 439–40
silent reading, 148, 152
Silver Age, The (Heywood), 360
Simmes, Valentine, 456
Sincler, John, 349
Sir John Falstaff, 358

Sir John Old-castle (Shakespeare
    apocrypha), 353, 354, 355,
    404, 406, 412
Sir John Van Olden Barnavelt
    (Fletcher and Massinger), 385,
    426–7, 431
Sir Thomas More, 51, 395
  licensing of, 382, 419–20, 425,
    426, 476, 477, 480
  manuscript, 395, 419–21, 422,
    424, 425, 426, 431, 432
Sir Thomas Wyatt (Heywood), 357
*Six Bookes of Politickes or Civil
    Doctrine* (Lipsius), 107, 108,
    111, 112
skepticism, 40, 108, 109, 110, 114,
    194
Skialetheia (Guilpin), 215
Skinner, John, 373
Skinner, Quentin, 118, 119
Sloane, Thomas, 285
Sly, William, 320, 321, 331, 333,
    335, 341
Smethwick, John, 408
Smith, Thomas, 87, 114, 123
Smythson, Robert, 25, 35
Soddered Citizen, The (Clavell), 429,
    430
social mobility, 37, 39, 46, 93, 219
Society of Antiquaries, 191 *see also*
    antiquarianism
Socrates, 286
soldiers, 35
Songs and Sonnets (Tottel), 209
sonnets, 209, 211, 216, 256, 257
Sonnets (Shakespeare), 17, 18, 239
  biographical readings of, 14, 16
  classical sources for, 176
  as epideictic oratory, 281
  metrics of, 262, 268
  publications of, 15, 397–8,
    409–10, 468
Sorelius, Gunnar, 151
sources:
  classical, 176–84
  study of, 206–7, 216
  vernacular, 206–7, 216, 220
Southwell, Robert, 451
Spanish Armada, 30–1
Spanish Maze, The, 356
Spanish Tragedy, The (Kyd), 176, 333
  Jonson's revisions, 354
Spanish Viceroy, The, 386
speech:
  dramatic, *see* dramatic speech

freedom of, 120–1, 122, 123–4
as moral act, 122, *see also* counsel
Spelman, Henry, 192
Spenser, Edmund, 13, 100, 207, 216, 218
continental influences on work of, 217
generic experimentation of, 209, 300
meter used by, 257–8
translations of, 173, 175
use of 'pure' English by, 241, 248
Spiritual Physicke (Downame), 454
spondees, 259, 260–2
sprezzatura, 126, 127, 128, 288–9
Stafford, Dorothea, 455
Stafford, Simon, 455
stage directions, 416, 417, 418–9, 420, 421, 422, 424, 426, 427, 428, 429, 430, 433, 445
staging, 372, 374, 414, 423
metatheatrical, 374–6
Stanley, William, 451
Stansby, John, 461
Stansby, William, 446, 461
state:
control of discourse, *see* authorization of texts; censorship; licensing; treason statues
meanings of term, 118–9, 120–1
monarchical responsibility for, 124
reasons of, *see* policy
stationers, 435, 459, 471, *see also* booksellers; printers; publishers
Stationers' Company, 213, 405, 448, 451, 452, 459, 465, 466, 467, 473, 481
Stationers' Hall, 461, 471
Stationers' Register, 184, 212, 213, 332, 349–50, 396, 403, 404, 465, 466, 468, 471, 478
Sternhold, Thomas, 214–15
stichomythia, 269
Stoicism, 108, 109, 114, 184
Stonley, Richard, 200
storia, 194
Stow, John, 45, 46, 48, 188, 192, 197, 198, 199, 200, 203, 220, 227, 451, 454
Strange's Men, 365, 380
Stratford Great Shakespeare Jubilee of 1769, 9

Stubbes, John, 386, 468
Stuhlweissenburg, 354
Suarez, Francis, 471
Substance of the Christian Religion, The (Polanus), 454
suburbs of London, 48, 54, 226, 305, 335, 363
subversion, 104, 105, 106, 114
Suffocating Mothers (Adelman), 299
Summaries (Stow), 198
Supposes (Gascoigne), 176
Survey of London (Stow), 188, 192, 220
author payment for, 227
Sussex's Men, 349, 365
Sutcliffe, Matthew, 453, 454
Sutton, Thomas, 373
Swan playhouse, 322, 323, 325, 352
Swetnam, Joseph, 87–8
synecdoche, 284, 293
Synopsis Papismi (Willet), 454

Tabula Cebetis (Cebes of Thebes), 172, 173
Tacitism, 108, 111, 197
Tacitus, 108, 109, 114, 189, 191, 194, 197, 199
Tamar Cham, 351, 352
Tamberlaine (Marlowe), 351, 352, 373
Tamer Tamed (Fletcher), 387
Taming of the Shrew, The (Shakespeare), 15, 54, 87, 150, 151, 176, 183, 184, 207, 269, 347, 348, 351
Tarleton, Richard, 215, 232, 233, 234, 333, 447
Tarletons newes out of purgatorie, 215
Tartarian Cripple, The, 349, 350, 352
Tate, Francis, 191
Taverner, Richard, 214
taverns, 148, 215, 226, 307
taxes, taxation, 31, 33, 37, 123, 192, 387
Taylor, Gary, 473–7, 479
Taylor, Joseph, 331, 334, 335, 336
'Tempest,' (Gaiman), 499–500
Tempest, The (Shakespeare), 10, 16, 20, 146, 147, 150, 159, 160, 358, 359
classical influence on, 176, 177–8, 182, 183
culture and nature in, 294
genre of, 297, 298

pronoun usage in, 247
staging from 374
verse in, 263, 274
Terence, 175–6, 182
textual scholarship, 395, 412, 479
'theater of enchantment,' 375
"theater of estrangement," 375
Theatre playhouse, 15, 226, 337, 340, 348, 362, 363, 365, 368, 374, 378
construction of, 330, 339
description of, 366
dismantling of, 352, 369, 370
financing of, 316, 323
lease expiry of, 367, 368, 369
location of, 335, 367
Thibault, Jean, 454
Thomas, Keith, 72–3, 141
Thomas, Lewis, 458
Thomas Lord Cromwell (Shakespeare apocrypha), 353, 354, 410, 412
Thomas of Woodstock, 421–3, 424, 426, 431
Thorpe, Thomas, 397
Three Partes of Commentaries, The (Tymme), 444–5
Thucydides, 191, 193, 203
Tillyard, E.M.W., 104, 106
Tilney, Edmund, 51, 378–9, 380, 381, 382, 383, 384, 387, 419–20, 425, 426, 472, 473, 476, 480
Timber, or Discoveries (Jonson), 9
Timons of Athens (Shakespeare), 16, 216, 355, 357, 359, 374
classical sources for, 176
genre of, 184
title pages, 145, 347, 349, 355, 398–400, 401, 402–3, 404, 409, 434, 438, 445
Titus Andronicus (Shakespeare), 150–1, 347, 348, 351, 359, 360, 365
classical influence in, 176, 180
genre of, 297, 298, 434
publications of, 15, 400, 403, 434, 461
reading in, 146, 147, 148–9
staging for, 374
tobacco, 213
Tom Tel-Troths Message (Lane), 462
Tooley, Nicholas, 331, 334, 335, 341
topoi, 293
Townsend, John, 130, 131, 132

Tractatus (Vorstius), 471
trade, 36, 44–5, 91, 92, 322
    cloth, 44, 46, 93, 313
tradesmen, 131, 141, 218, 232
tragedy, 174, 302, 351, 356, 357
    classical, 173, 175, 176, 182,
        183
    domestic, 303, 304, 357
    as genre, 297, 298, 302
    revenge, 297, 301, 303, 351, 354,
        356, 357
    'rules' for, 10
translations:
    of Bible, 161–4, 168
    in book trade, 453
    of classical literature, 174–5, 176,
        225
Traub, Valerie, 498
travel books, 208, 236, 313
treason statutes, 468–9, 481
Treasurie of Commodious Conceits, The
    (Partridge), 455
Treatise of Schism (Martin), 468
Treatise of Treasons against Q.
    Elizabeth, A, 469
Treatise on Schemes and Tropes, A
    (Sherry), 280
Treatise wherein Dicing, Dancing, vain
    Plays or Interludes ... are reproved
    (Northbrooke), 317
Trimpi, Wesley, 286
Triumph of Old Drapery, The
    (Munday), 46
trochees, 259, 260–2, 263, 269
Troia Britanica (Heywood), 446
Troilus and Cressida (Shakespeare),
    17, 110, 113–4, 129, 145,
    176, 196, 216, 353, 359
    genre categorization of, 184
    publications of, 403, 405, 406
    suppression arguments, 480
    verse in, 272
Troilus and Criseyde (Chaucer), 257
true and plaine report of the Furious
    outrages of Fraunce, A (Hotman),
    465
True Law of Free Monarchies, The
    (James I), 32
True Order and Methode of Wryting and
    Reading Hystories (Blundeville),
    193, 195
True, Sincere and Modest Defence of
    English Catholiques, A (Allen),
    476
Tunstall, Cuthbert, 163

Turner, Ann, 375
Twelfth Night (Shakespeare), 297,
    338, 353, 354
    verse in, 261, 262, 265
Twins Tragedy, A, 358
Two Bookes of Constancie (Lipsius),
    108, 109
Two Gentlemen of Verona
    (Shakespeare), 15, 208, 209,
    348, 351
Two Noble Kinsmen, The
    (Shakespeare), 16, 19, 176,
    358, 359, 406, 409
Two Noble Ladies, The (anonymous),
    421, 424, 427, 431
Twyne, Thomas, 213
Tymme, Thomas, 444–5
Tyndale, William, 26, 162–4, 165,
    166, 168, 170
type, movable, 437–8, 444
typesetting, 438, 442, 443
typology, 170, 189–90, *see also*
    analogical thinking

Udall, John, 468
Underwood, John, 331, 334, 335,
    341
unemployment, 34, 35, 36
Unfortunate Traveller (Nashe), 208,
    219
'University Wits,' 12–13, 233
usury, 34, 38–9, 40, 46
    1571 statute, 315, 317
    theater history and, 315–17, 319,
        324
Utopia (More), 160

vagrants, vagrancy, 34, 48, 49, 305,
    379, 380, 383
Valentinian (Fletcher), 343, 358
Valla, Lorenzo, 191
Varieties of British Political Thought,
    1500–1800 (Pocock) 100
Vaughan, Margaret, 456
Vaughan, William, 455–6
Venus and Adonis (Shakespeare), 12,
    14, 15, 106, 112, 176, 397
    meter in, 257, 262, 269
    moral condemnation of, 210
    publications of, 396, 401, 461,
        468
Vergil, Polydore, 194, 195, 196,
    197,
Verreyken, Louis, 353
verse, 256–75

blank, 233–4, 236, 257, 264,
    269–70, 271
    couplets, 269, 271
    dramatic vs nondramatic, 271
    end-stopped, 270
    enjambment, 270, 274
    printing of, 440, 442, 452, 458
    rhymed, 251–2, 263
    scanning, 260–3
    see also meter
Vess, Charles, 500
Vickers, Brian, 281
Vincent, Augustine, 444, 446
violence:
    domestic, 88
    of gentry, 50–1
    institutional, 307
Virgidemiarum (Hall), 215
Virgil, 12, 172, 173, 175, 176, 180,
    278
Virginia Company, 320
Volpone (Jonson), 219, 305, 333,
    356, 372, 385
Voltaire (Francois-Marie Arouet),
    493
Vorstius, Conrad, 471
Voyages and Travels of Sir John
    Mandeville, 208

wages, 34, 35
    of artisans, 314–15, 320, 326
    statutory controls on, 319
Walkley, Thomas, 405, 406
Wallace, C.W., 323
Walley, Henry, 403, 406
Walsham, A., 65, 66, 70, 71
Ward, John, 200–2
Warner, Elizabeth, 455
Warning for Fair Women
    (anonymous), 349, 351
War of the Theaters, 354
wars, 27, 41, 69, 212
    Continental, 36
    effect on economy of, 33–4, 35
    fifteenth-century English civil,
        10, 17
    Nine Years', 31
    in romance fictions, 218
    with Spain, 31, 32, 109, 386
Warwick, 130–2, 133
Wasp, The, 427, 432
Waterhouse, Edward, 93
'Watkins Ale,' 212
Watt, Tessa, 80
Webbe, William, 209

Webster, John, 13, 145, 301, 356
Weever, John, 15, 462
Wells, Stanley, 472
Welsh Embassador, The (Dekker), 421, 427, 428, 432
Wentworth, Peter, 120–1, 122, 123, 124–5, 130, 133
Wentworth, William, 93
Westward Ho (Dekker and Webster), 301, 303, 304, 305
wetnursing, 90, *see also* reproduction
Wheare, Degory, 193
Wheeler, Richard, 498
Wherrat, Jeffrey, 130, 131
Whigham, Frank, 280, 289
Whipping of Satyre, The (W.I.), 215
Whitaker, William, 62
Whitechapel, 366
White Devil, The (Webster), 360
White, Edward, 400, 434
Whitefriars, 323
Whitehall, 338, 402
White, Thomas, 47
Whitgift, John, 61, 63, 64, 65, 71, 467, 471, 481
Whittington, Dick, 44, 302
Whole Journey, The (Barber and Wheeler), 498
Whyte, Rowland, 353
widows, 50, 87, 88
Wilbraham, Roger, 448
Wilkins, George, 356, 357, 359
Wilkins, Nicholas, 130–1, 132

William of Malmesbury, 191
Williams, Raymond, 232
Wilson, John Dover, 442
Wilson, Robert, 232, 233
Wilson, Thomas, 175, 280, 283–4, 294, 444
Wingfield, Mary, 455
Winter's Tale, The (Shakespeare), 10, 16, 19, 147, 151, 160, 211, 213, 358, 359
genre of, 297, 298
verse in, 271, 274, 275
Wise Woman of Hogsdon, A (Heywood), 357
witchcraft, 79, 496
Wits, The (Davenant), 385, 387
Witter, John, 325
wives, 86–7, 88, 89–90, 97
in plays, 308
work of, 86–7, 90, 304
Wolfe, John, 436
Woman Hater, The (Beaumont and Fletcher), 152
Woman Killed with Kindness (Heywood), 304, 357
Woman's Prize, The (Fletcher), 387
women, 19, 169
books dedicated to, 455–6
chastity of, 17, 18, 19, 87, 88, 90
in history plays, 17
independent, 50, 54, 87
literacy and reading habits, 139, 141, 149, 150, 196–7, 208, 461

in urban areas, 49–50, 90
unmarried, 86–7, 88
unruly, 17, 87–8
Wonderfull Yeares, The (Dekker), 144
Woodcliffe, Oliver, 322
woodcuts, 195
Woolf, Virginia, 495–6, 498
Worcester's Men, 355, 357, 383
Work for Chimny-Sweepers (I.H.), 213
workhouses, 34
Works (Daniel), 461
Works (Jonson), 140, 149, 406
Wright, John, 396, 397
Wriothesley, Henry, 396
writers, commercial, 226, 227–8, 313, *see also* playwriting
writing, 141, *see also* literacy
Wyatt, Thomas, 26, 209, 257
Wyclif, John, 162

yeomanry, 44, 93
families of, 85
literacy and reading habits, 141, 197, 208, 218
role in government, 120
Yet More Work for a Mass Priest, 448
Yorkshire Tragedy, A (Shakespeare apocrypha), 356, 357, 401, 404, 406, 412
youth, 49–50, 94, *see also* apprentices, apprenticeships; children